THE COMP
D. H. LAWRENCE

BY D. H. LAWRENCE

Published by The Viking Press

NOVELS

*Sons and Lovers
*The Rainbow
*Women in Love
*The Lost Girl
*Aaron's Rod
*Kangaroo
*The Boy in the Bush (with M. L. Skinner)
*Four Short Novels
(*Love Among the Haystacks, The Ladybird,
The Fox, The Captain's Doll*)
* John Thomas and Lady Jane

NONFICTION

*Psychoanalysis and the Unconscious *and* Fantasia of the Unconscious
*Studies in Classic American Literature
*Apocalypse
*Sex, Literature and Censorship

COLLECTIONS

*Phoenix
The Portable D. H. Lawrence
*Selected Poems
*The Complete Short Stories of D. H. Lawrence
*Selected Literary Criticism
The Collected Letters of D. H. Lawrence
*The Complete Poems of D. H. Lawrence
The Complete Plays of D. H. Lawrence
*Phoenix II
*D. H. Lawrence and Italy:
Twilight in Italy, Sea and Sardinia, Etruscan Places

VIKING CRITICAL EDITION

Sons and Lovers (*edited by Julian Moynahan*)

*Available in Viking Compass edition.

THE COMPLETE POEMS OF
D. H. LAWRENCE

Collected and Edited with an
Introduction and Notes by

Vivian de Sola Pinto
and
Warren Roberts

NEW YORK   THE VIKING PRESS

Copyright © 1964, 1971 by Angelo Ravagli and C. M. Weekley, Executors
of The Estate of Frieda Lawrence Ravagli

Introduction and notes Copyright © 1964 by William Heinemann Ltd.

All rights reserved

Viking Compass Edition
Issued with corrections in 1971 by The Viking Press, Inc.
625 Madison Avenue, New York, N.Y. 10022

Distributed in Canada by
The Macmillan Company of Canada Limited

SBN 670-23472-9 (hardbound)
670-00281-x (paperbound)
Library of Congress catalog card number: 64-11226

Printed in U.S.A.

All verse and prose by D. H. Lawrence in these volumes are published by ar-
rangement with The Estate of D. H. Lawrence. Copyrights in the original
publication of previously published material were registered in various years
1914 through 1964, and renewed in various years 1942 through 1964. They may
not be reproduced without written permission from The Viking Press, Inc.
or, in the case of poems from *The Plumed Serpent,* without permission from
Alfred A. Knopf, Inc.

Fifth printing August 1975

CONTENTS

ACKNOWLEDGEMENTS

ALL VERSE and prose by D. H. Lawrence in this edition is printed by permission of the Estate of D. H. Lawrence. The work was supported in part by a grant from the Penrose Fund of the American Philosophical Society, of which the editors make grateful acknowledgement. They also acknowledge the courtesy of the following libraries, which have allowed them to make use of manuscript material in their possession: the Library of the University of California at Berkeley; the Library of the University of California at Los Angeles; the Library of the University of Chicago (Harriet Monroe Modern Poetry Collection); the New York Public Library (Henry W. and Albert A. Berg Collection); the Library of the University of Nottingham (D. H. Lawrence Collection); the Library of Princeton University; the Library of the University of Texas (Humanities Research Center). They are grateful to Mr George Lazarus for permission to make use of the "Author's Revised Typescript" of *Pansies* in the Lazarus Collection.

The Introduction "D. H. Lawrence: Poet without a Mask" is a considerably revised and enlarged version of the article "Poet without a Mask" by V. de S. Pinto published in *The Critical Quarterly*, vol. 3, No. 1, Spring 1961.

The editors acknowledge with thanks the courtesy and kindness shown to them by William Heinemann Ltd, and they are especially grateful for the valuable expert guidance, advice and assistance which they have received from Mr James Michie and Mr George Robinson in the preparation of the text of the edition for the press.

Finally, their thanks are due to Mrs V. de S. Pinto for the very useful help which she gave in the preparation of the Indexes.

INTRODUCTION
D. H. Lawrence: Poet without a mask

By V. de S. Pinto

SAMUEL PALMER in a well-known passage called William Blake "a man without a mask".* D. H. Lawrence might well be described as a poet without a mask. Nearly all the famous poets of the past have worn a mask of some sort. It may be a very grand and dignified one like Milton's, a gentlemanly one like Tennyson's, one with an ironic smile like the mask of Pope or grotesque like that of Burns or Skelton. Of course, all these poets drop the mask occasionally, for a line or two, or perhaps for a whole poem. Shakespeare dropped it altogether in the best of his sonnets and gave us a glimpse of the most enigmatic personality in the whole of literature.

R. P. Blackmur in his essay on "Lawrence and Expressive Form" makes a carefully reasoned attack on Lawrence's poetry exactly because it is poetry without a mask. Although he does not use this image, his argument is in effect that the use of the mask is necessary for the production of good poetry. He quotes the following passage from Lawrence's Note prefixed to the two-volume edition of his *Collected Poems* (1928): "A young man is afraid of his demon and puts his hand over the demon's mouth sometimes. . . . And the things the young man says are very rarely poetry." Commenting on this passage, Blackmur writes: "I take the young man in the quotation to be just what Lawrence thought he was not, the poet as craftsman, and the demon exactly that outburst of personal feeling which needed the discipline of craft to become a poem." [1] This seems to me to be a travesty of Lawrence's meaning. By the "demon", Lawrence certainly did not mean a mere "outburst of personal feel-

*A. Gilchrist, *Life of William Blake*, Everyman Library (London, Dent 1942), p. 301

I

ing". He meant what he calls in the Foreword to *Fantasia of the Unconscious* "pure passionate experience",[2] or experience at a deeper level than the personal. In the original Introduction to the *Collected Poems* (1928) he tells us that "the demon is timeless". "The demon" is what Blake calls the fourfold vision and what the Greeks called the Muse. The interpretation of "the young man" as "the poet as craftsman" is equally misleading. By "the young man", Lawrence means the immature writer who wants to make himself a mask to appear before the public by means of the imitation of fashionable verse-forms.

Blackmur's essay, however, is an important piece of criticism; like Johnson's criticism of Milton, it is one of those important wrong-headed pieces of criticism that contain valuable elements of truth. Blackmur's main contention is that Lawrence's poetry, in spite of certain great qualities which he admits that it possesses, is vitiated by what he calls "the fallacy of the faith in expressive form", which he defines as the belief "that if a thing is only intensely enough felt its mere expression in words will give it satisfactory form, the dogma, in short, that once material becomes words it is its own best form".[3] No English writer of note ever held this dogma in the crude form as stated by Blackmur, though Wordsworth, in some passages in his Preface of 1800, came dangerously near to it, and was rightly castigated for those passages by Coleridge in the seventeenth chapter of *Biographia Literaria*. Some of Lawrence's own statements about his poetry, which Blackmur does not quote, are relevant here. In an early letter (18 August 1913) to Edward Marsh, who had objected to the rhythms of some of his poems, he wrote:

> ". . . I think, don't you know, that my rhythms fit my mood pretty well, in the verse. And if the mood is out of joint, the rhythm often is. I have always tried to get an emotion out in its own course, without altering it. It needs the finest instinct imaginable; much finer than the skill of craftsmen. That Japanese Yone Noguchi [4] tried it. He doesn't quite bring it off. Often I don't – sometimes I do. Sometimes Whitman is perfect. Remember skilled verse is dead in fifty years. . . ." [5]

It is a pity that Lawrence used the word "craftsman" in this passage. What he is really pleading for is not a rejection of craftsmanship but a different kind of craftsmanship from that of the user of traditional forms. This is not, to use Blackmur's phrase, a matter of "mere expression in words". Lawrence realizes it is something very difficult, which "needs the finest instinct imaginable, much finer than the skill of craftsmen". He means "finer than the skill of craftsmen in traditional forms". Of course, his sweeping statement that "skilled verse is dead in fifty years" needs a great deal of qualification. If he meant "carefully wrought verse in traditional forms", hundreds of examples from Horace to Pope give him the lie. What he probably meant was skilled mechanical imitations of traditional verse-forms.

Lawrence's Introduction to the American edition of his *New Poems* ("Poetry of the Present", see below, pp. 181–6) though written in a rather florid style, is a much clearer and more mature statement of his poetic theory than the rather crudely phrased letter to Marsh. In this important essay he distinguishes between two kinds of poetry. One kind he describes as "the poetry of the beginning and the poetry of the end". "It is," he writes,

> "of the nature of all that is complete and consummate. This completeness, this consummateness, the finality and the perfection are conveyed in exquisite form: the perfect symmetry, the rhythm which returns upon itself like a dance where the hands link and loosen and link for the supreme moment of the end. Perfected bygone moments, perfected moments in the glimmering futurity, these are the treasured gem-like lyrics of Shelley and Keats."

Here Lawrence is recognizing the validity of the best sort of "skilled verse", all of which he had too hastily condemned in his letter to Marsh. His second kind of poetry he calls "poetry of that which is at hand: the immediate present. In the immediate present there is no perfection, no consummation, nothing finished. The strands are all flying, quivering, intermingling into the web, the waters are shaking the moon. There is no round, consummate moon on the face of running water, nor on the face of the unfinished tide. There are no gems of the living plasm. The living plasm vibrates unspeakably, it inhales the future, it exhales the past, it is the quick of both, and yet it is neither." Lawrence is here distinguishing between traditional form on the one hand an expressive or organic form on the

3

other. "Expressive form" is what Coleridge called "organic form". He contrasted "organic form" with "mechanical regularity" and wrote that it "is innate; it shapes, as it developes itself from within, and the fulness of its development is one and the same with the perfection of its outward form".[6] To use Lawrence's image, it attempts to reproduce "the unspeakable vibrations of the living plasm". Blackmur is surely wrong in his wholesale condemnation of organic or "expressive form". It is true that there are great dangers in this kind of writing, and, as Lawrence wrote, it needs the finest instinct imaginable, or it can easily lapse into empty rhetoric or mere disorder. It is, however, the kind of poetic form which is likely to have the most vitality in the modern world. The real contrast is not, as Coleridge said, with mechanical form but with what I would call traditional form. When traditional form is alive, it expresses the poetic sensibility which the poet shares with his audience – in the great ages of poetry with the whole of his nation or linguistic group. In such periods traditional form is a mask which fits the poet's face perfectly; indeed, like the mask of Lord George Hell in Max Beerbohm's parable, it may be said to become identical with the face. Ever since the Renaissance it has been increasingly difficult to use traditional poetic forms successfully. The mask tends no longer to fit the face. Hence in all European languages in the last three hundred years we can trace the progressive loosening of poetic rhythms, the mingling or abandonment of the traditional "kinds" of poetry, the movements towards free verse, the production of epic dramas and dramatic lyrics and forms that fall under none of the ancient classifications. In the twentieth century the poet is more isolated, perhaps, than he has ever been in the whole of human history. The mask, that invaluable means of communication in other ages, is now often felt to be a hindrance rather than a help to the poet. "Masked" poetry in traditional forms of real value indeed can and will be produced by skilled and sensitive craftsmen on suitable occasions; but there is always a danger today that the use of the mask may degenerate into a kind of game based on the pretence that there is a society which shares the sensibility embodied in traditional forms when no such society actually exists. The game may be a learned and esoteric one, as in much of the poetry of the Franco-American school of Ezra Pound, or a popular one, as in the writings of Mr Betjeman. A major prophetic poet like Blake or

4

Lawrence solves the problem by abandoning the mask altogether. He has to create an organic or expressive form to express his naked, passionate experience in a world where no one shares his poetic sensibility, and this is a task of enormous difficulty, requiring both heroic self-confidence and technical skill of the highest order.

It may be argued that the only possible form for great poetry in this age of science and realism is the novel or prose story, and there can be no question that Lawrence's poetic genius finds its fullest expression in prose works like *The Rainbow*, *Women in Love*, *St Mawr* and *The Man Who Died*. Nevertheless, his work in verse is a very important part of his literary achievement. He said something in his verse that he could never have said in prose, and his best poems are among the most valuable and significant in the English language written in the twentieth century. Indeed they may be described as examples of the only kind of great poetry that can be written in the world in which we live. The Blake of *Songs of Experience* and the Wordsworth of "Resolution and Independence" are the prophets of this kind of poetry, which Lawrence has well described as "poetry of this immediate present, instant poetry . . . the unrestful, ungraspable poetry of the sheer present, poetry whose permanency lies in its windlike transit".

Lawrence's early poems are mostly autobiographical, and are written in the form that was fashionable in the England of the second decade of the twentieth century, the short "nature poem" in rhyming verse, which the Georgians inherited from Hardy and Wordsworth. Lawrence uses this form clumsily enough, and much of the experience that lies behind these early poems is expressed more successfully in the early novels and stories. He himself was quite aware of the inadequacy of his early verse. In the Introduction to his *Collected Poems*, he writes, with a modesty that recalls that of the young Keats, that these poems were "struggling to say something which it takes a man twenty years to be able to say". This, by the way, is not the kind of remark that is made by a young man who, in the words of Blackmur, was "wilfully careless of craftsmanship". Nevertheless, in spite of their shortcomings, these early poems are full of interest to the student of English poetry. They show us a young poet of genius, struggling with an inadequate mode of exression, like the Blake of *Poetical Sketches* and the Wordsworth of "The Evening Walk". In them, however, we can already see the notable qualities which Blackmur admits that Lawrence's poetry possesses, and which he describes admirably. The first is "a kind of furious underlying honesty of observation",[7] and the second a religious quality, for, as Blackmur rightly argues, Lawrence is a religious poet and his poetry is an attempt "to declare and rehearse symbolically his pious recognition of the substance of life". To these should be added a third quality, a mixture of tenderness and reverence, a sort of cosmic piety.

The first two qualities are well illustrated in the poem called "Love on the Farm". This might be described as a "nature poem" and it certainly arises out of a keen-sighted observation of the "life of nature" on a Midland farm. Nature here is not the quiet landscape vision which found elegant expression in numerous Georgian poems. It is compounded of terror, beauty and cruelty, full of contradictions, something at once disturbing and mysterious, lying behind the commonplace facts of English country life. The middle of the poem shows us a man going to kill a rabbit caught in a snare:

> Oh, water-hen, beside the rushes
> Hide your quaintly scarlet blushes,
> Still your quick tail, lie still as dead,
> Till the distance folds over his ominous tread!

> The rabbit presses back her ears,
> Turns back her liquid, anguished eyes
> And crouches low; then with wild spring
> Spurts from the terror of *his* oncoming . . .

When the rabbit is killed, the man with "fingers that still smell grim of the rabbit's fur" goes into the house to embrace a woman. We are made to feel the terror of the rabbit, the large, kindly presence of the man and the woman's identification of herself with the trapped animal:

> God, I am caught in a snare!
> I know not what fine wire is round my throat;
> I only know I let him finger there
> My pulse of life, and let him nose like a stoat
> Who sniffs with joy before he drinks the blood.

Lawrence does not tell us in this poem that sex and death are close together in nature, but he makes us feel the numinous quality of their closeness, its terror and mystery. It cannot be said, however, that the commonplace rhythms, the awkward rhymes and crudely melodramatic language help Lawrence in this poem. Already he is making us feel, to use his own phrase, "the living plasm vibrate unspeakably".

The best expression of the qualities of tenderness and reverence in Lawrence's early poetry is, perhaps, the poem called "Piano":

Softly, in the dusk, a woman is singing to me;
Taking me back down the vista of years, till I see
A child sitting under the piano, in the boom of the tingling strings
And pressing the small, poised feet of a mother who smiles as
    she sings.

In spite of myself, the insidious mastery of song
Betrays me back, till the heart of me weeps to belong
To the old Sunday evenings at home, with winter outside
And hymns in the cosy parlour, the tinkling piano our guide.

So now it is vain for the singer to burst into clamour
With the great black piano appassionato. The glamour
Of childish days is upon me, my manhood is cast
Down in the flood of remembrance, I weep like a child for the past.

This poem has found its way into a number of anthologies, probably because the compilers think it an expression of sentimental nostalgia. It is nothing of the kind; it is an honest record of emotion, which, it is important to note, is *controlled* emotion. The feelings awakened by the song that brings back the scenes of his childhood to the poet are recognized as "insidious", and, although he yields to them, he is aware that in some sense they are a betrayal. "Piano" provides a complete refutation of Blackmur's charge that Lawrence was careless of craftsmanship in his poetry. The original draft of the poem, called "The Piano", survives in a manuscript now in Nottingham University Library.[8] This early version is diffuse, nostalgic and overcrowded with detail. The words "insidious" and "betray" do not occur in it. It contains five stanzas, as opposed to the three of the printed version, and it describes the concert singer whose song brought back to Lawrence the memory of his childhood as a "full throated woman . . . singing . . . a wild Hungarian air" with "her arms, and her bosom, and the whole of her soul . . . bare". All this is suppressed in the final version and the impression rendered in the concentrated phrase,

> . . . to burst into clamour
> With the great black piano appassionato. . . .

The poem in its final form is an early example of Lawrence's use of the controlled imagination which Blackmur denies to him. It is something rare in modern poetry, a successful rendering of unsentimental tenderness, worthy to be placed by Cowper's lines on his mother's picture and Wordsworth's "Poor Susan".

Lawrence wrote that many of his poems were "so personal that, in their fragmentary fashion, they make up a biography of an emotional and inner life". Actually, like Byron, he was a poet who could only reach his full maturity when he had got rid of the autobiographical preoccupation. The last phase of his autobiographical poetry, the conclusion of the saga of the young Lawrence, is to be found in the famous sequence *Look! We Have Come Through!*, which is at once a kind of poetical record of his early married life and something far more ambitious. It is an attempt to give expression to the drama of the psychological relationship between a newly-married husband and wife, a kind of duel of sex, where, in Lawrence's own words, "the conflict of love and hate goes on . . . till it reaches some sort of conclusion, they transcend into some condition of blessedness". This is a great subject and, whatever else it may be, the sequence is certainly a psychological and autobiographical record of the highest interest. Amy Lowell is said to have thought that the sequence "made up a great novel, greater even than *Sons and Lovers*". This, of course, is an exaggeration, but there is a grain of truth in it. The sequence contains the material for a notable novel or autobiographical work, and I believe Lawrence would have been well-advised to take a hint from Dante's *Vita Nuova* and cast it into the form of a prose narrative with interspersed lyrics.

At this stage of his development, Lawrence was seeking an escape from the conventional rhythms of early twentieth-century English poetry, which, he rightly felt, were hampering his poetic expression.

The logical outcome of the search for expressive form, as far as metre is concerned, was some kind of free verse, but the difficulty was to find the right kind. He was looking for a sort of verse in which he could make the individual quality of his voice heard, and which would enable him to express in appropriate form that "pure relationship with the living universe", the eternal flux of life, which he believed to be the supremely valuable human experience. His immediate guides in the period 1914–16 were the Italian Futuristi, the Anglo-American Imagist group of Ezra Pound and Amy Lowell, and Walt Whitman, whose *Leaves of Grass* had been "one of his great books" since the Eastwood days.[9] When he was living at Lerici in the early summer of 1914, he read with interest and admiration, the anthology called *I Poeti Futuristi* published at Milan in 1912.[10] In the *proclama* or manifesto of F. T. Marinetti prefixed to this volume (first published in February 1909), he would find the following sentences,[11] in which, perhaps, we can see the germ of Lawrence's conception of "poetry of this immediate present, instant poetry":

> "Il verso libero futurista, perpetuo dinamismo del pensiero, corrente ininterotta d' immagini e di suoni, è il solo mezzo per esprimere l'effimero, instabile e sinfonico universa che si fucina in noi e con noi. Il verso libero futurista è il dinamismo della nostra coscienza malleabile, interamente realizzato; *l'io* integrale cantato, dipinto, scolpito indefinitamente nel suo perpetuo divenire aggressivo."*

Lawrence read in the same volume Paolo Buzzi's essay on free verse, and, in Buzzi's poems and others in the anthology, he would find a kind of free verse which combined, with some success, lyricism with conversational ease, tough-minded directness of speech and freedom from traditional poeticism. With his usual shrewdness he saw the weakness of the Futuristi, their brashness and their childish worship of the machine, but he praised them for

*Translation: "Futurist free verse, a perpetual dynamism of thought, an uninterrupted stream of images and sounds, is the only medium to express the ephemeral, unstable and symphonic universe which is being created in us and with us. Futurist free verse is the dynamism of our malleable consciousness fully realised: the integral ego, sung, painted, sculptured indefinitely in its perpetual aggressive evolution."

9

their honesty, their vitality and their "revolt against beastly senti-
ment and slavish adherence to tradition and the dead mind".[12] With
the Imagists he had a temporary connection and contributed several
poems to their anthologies.[13] Together with the Futuristi they helped
him to escape from the vague romanticism, the excessively literary
diction, the saccharine rhythms of the Georgians. At the back of his
mind there was certainly a deeper and more vital influence in his
memories of the majestic rhythms of the poetic prose or near-verse
of the King James Bible, in which he had been steeped in his child-
hood and which he never ceased to study. Lawrence was far too big
a man to be absorbed by the Futuristi, the Imagists or any other
literary clique. Whitman was another matter. Lawrence was both
attracted and repelled by him. In his *Studies in Classic American
Literature*, he shows that he was well aware of Whitman's weak-
nesses: ". . . this awful Whitman," he calls him, "this post-mortem
poet. This poet with the private soul leaking out of him all the time."
Yet he hails him as a master and a liberator: "Whitman, the great
poet, has meant so much to me. Whitman, the one man breaking a
way ahead." [14] And in "Poetry of the Present" he praises him because
". . . his heart beats with the urgent, insurgent Now . . . He is so
near the quick." [15] He was right; Whitman was a great liberating
influence for Lawrence, but he had to absorb and digest that in-
fluence before he could derive real benefit from it. Whitman showed
him how to use large, free rhythms based on those of common
speech yet filled with a music which is not to be found in common
speech; but he also encouraged Lawrence's tendency to preach and
orate, to *talk* about experience rather than express experience. The
famous culminating poems in *Look! We Have Come Through!* –
"New Heaven and New Earth", "Elysium" and "Manifesto"– contain
many examples of the bad, undigested influence of Whitman on
Lawrence. No one can doubt that these poems record intense and
moving experiences with complete honesty and integrity, but they
fail to turn those experiences into aesthetic experience for the
reader. As Sir Herbert Read has written, in these poems "Lawrence is
expressing a wish for a wonder to happen, a wonder that is not
intrinsically present in the verse itself".[16]

The best poetry in *Look! We Have Come Through!* is certainly in
the lyrics. Such a poem as "A Doe at Evening" shows how the
Imagists helped him to "strip off the tinsel":

As I went through the marshes
a doe sprang out of the corn
and flashed up the hill-side
leaving her fawn.

On the sky-line
she moved round to watch,
she pricked a fine black blotch
on the sky.

I looked at her
And felt her watching;
I became a strange being.
Still, I had my right to be there with her.

Her nimble shadow trotting
Along the sky-line, she
put back her fine, level-balanced head.
And I knew her.

Ah yes, being male, is not my head hard-balanced,
                                        antlered?
Are not my haunches light?
Has she not fled on the same wind with me?
Does not my fear cover her fear?

Here, surely, the wonder is intrinsically present in the verse. The
lightness and delicacy of the vision of the doe find perfect expression
in the lightness and delicacy of the texture and movement of the
language, and the changes in rhythm in the last two stanzas convey
the elusive suggestion of sex in the relationship of the man to the
animal, and the dream or myth of his transformation into a stag.
Jessie Chambers in her memoir wrote that "a living vibration passed
between" Lawrence and "wild things".[17] Here, at last, Lawrence has
found a sort of verse that makes us feel that vibration.

This poem points the way to Lawrence's mature poetic achieve-
ments of his middle years in Birds, Beasts and Flowers. Here he
found a new theme which freed him from the trammels of auto-
biography. It was a subject-matter that he was particularly well-

qualified to treat: the immediate apprehension of the flux of life, especially of sexual life, in non-human organisms. In Lawrence, as Blackmur rightly stresses, this was a religious apprehension: "The love of God for him was in the declaration of life in the flux of sex." [18] In his Preface to *The Grand Inquisitor*, Lawrence wrote that ". . . *life** is the great reality . . . true living fills us with vivid life, the 'heavenly bread' ".[19] In the best of the poems he conveys the experience of immediate contact with this "vivid life", the actual taste of the "heavenly bread". Here he is carrying forward the work of the great Romantics, especially that of Wordsworth, in the exploration of what may be called the divine otherness of non-human life. The Romantics neglected the animal world and the sexual element in nature, and tended to confuse the apprehension of the life of nature with the quiet contemplation of landscape. Lawrence aims at a more complete nature poetry which will include birds, beasts, fishes and even insects as well as vegetable life. Blackmur complains that Lawrence's "pious recognition of the substance of life" is "tortured", and that he lacks "the ultimate vision" and "orderly insight" of "the great mystics".[20] Surely there is a confusion of thought here. Lawrence was not a mystic but a poet, and a poet's business is not necessarily to convey "an orderly insight", but to give artistic (i.e. orderly) expression to his own experience and the sensibility of his age. Sometimes Lawrence's apprehension of the mystery of life was tortured, and his complete honesty as an artist compelled him to exhibit this tortured apprehension as part of his own sensibility and that of his age. But the word "tortured" has been used far too freely with reference to Lawrence's poetry. *Birds, Beasts and Flowers* is an extremely varied and uneven collection. There are poems in it that may fairly be described as representing tortured states of mind, and passages that, perhaps, deserve the epithet "hysterical" that Blackmur has applied far too glibly to the whole of Lawrence's poetry.[21] Too often Lawrence succumbs to the worst part of Whitman's influence and mistakes strident statement for poetic expression. The best poetry in the collection, however, is neither tortured nor hysterical nor strident. It is an affirmation of the grandeur and mystery of the life of nature which perhaps Wordsworth alone has equalled among English poets, and it is expressed in an entirely original and un-Wordsworthian

*Lawrence's italics

idiom. Such an affirmation is to be found in the famous poem "Snake". This poem is based on that complete truthfulness to the facts of common experience that Lawrence shares with Wordsworth and Hardy, but here the common experience is transformed and invested with mythical grandeur. This is a rare and memorable achievement. Wordsworth did something similar in "Resolution and Independence", where the commonplace meeting with the old leech-gatherer is transmuted into a myth of overwhelming majesty. The old man, while remaining a poor leech-gatherer, is seen at the same time as a gigantic natural force and the embodiment of trans-cendental strength and majesty. Similarly, the snake which Lawrence saw one hot morning drinking in his water-trough at Taormina remains, in the poem, an ordinary "earth-brown, earth-golden" Sicilian snake, but at the same time becomes a mythical, godlike lord of the underworld, an embodiment of all those dark mysterious forces of nature which man ignobly fears and neglects:

> Was it cowardice, that I dared not kill him?
> Was it perversity, that I longed to talk to him?
> Was it humility, to feel so honoured?
> I felt so honoured.
>
> And yet those voices:
> *If you were not afraid, you would kill him!*
>
> And truly I was afraid, I was most afraid,
> But even so, honoured still more
> That he should seek my hospitality
> From out the dark door of the secret earth.
>
> He drank enough
> And lifted his head, dreamily, as one who has drunken,
> And flickered his tongue like a forked night on the air, so black;
> Seeming to lick his lips,
> And looked around like a god, unseeing, into the air,
> And slowly turned his head,
> And slowly, very slowly, as if thrice adream,
> Proceeded to draw his slow length curving round
> And climb again the broken bank of my wall-face. . . .

This poem surely provides the answer to Blackmur's argument that

Lawrence's use of expressive form excludes craftsmanship and the control of the rational imagination. There is no empty rhetoric or fake poetic language here. The style is very simple, the diction mostly colloquial, and the word order that of common speech, and yet the effect is one of grandeur and dignity. The verse, though free and rhymeless, moves easily from the rhythms of common speech to formal iambics and back again, but, nevertheless, has a subtle pattern expressing with curious felicity in its alternation of short and long lines the relationship between the poet's nagging thoughts and the sinuous majesty of the snake's movements. "Snake" is a triumph of style and idiom, one of the very few English poems in free verse where perception is embodied in rhythms that are an essential part of the poem's meaning.

There are other triumphs of a different kind in *Birds, Beasts and Flowers*. Blackmur speaks about a condition of "ritual frenzy" in some of the poems that "carries them beyond the confines of poetry".[22] This may be true of some passages in the collection, but, if by "ritual frenzy" he means an ecstasy of praise and adoration, there are poems in which this ecstasy controlled by the rational imagination produces memorable poetry. Such a poem is "Almond Blossom", a hymn to the miracle of renewed life as revealed in the blossoming of the almond tree:

. . . the Gethsemane blood at the iron pores unfolds, unfolds,
Pearls itself into tenderness of bud
And in a great and sacred forthcoming steps forth, steps out in one
    stride
A naked tree of blossom, like a bridegroom bathing in dew, divested
    of cover,
Frail-naked, utterly uncovered
To the green night-baying of the dog-star, Etna's snow-edged wind
And January's loud-seeming sun.

Think of it, from the iron fastness
Suddenly to dare to come out naked, in perfection of blossom,
    beyond the sword-rust.
Think, to stand there in full-unfolded nudity, smiling,
With all the snow-wind, and the sun-glare, and the dog-star baying
    epithalamion. . . .

Here the poet is not using images as illustration or decoration but is thinking in images, "recreating thought into feeling", to use T. S. Eliot's phrase. There is wit here, too, as well as magnificence. The image of the "dog-star baying epithalamion" is a conceit at once witty and imaginative, worthy of the seventeenth-century masters, Donne and Marvell. As Mr Alvarez has written in his admirable study of Lawrence's poetry, this kind of wit is "not a sparkle on top of intelligence; it is a manifestation of intelligence".[23]

The poems that Lawrence wrote at the end of his life have a peculiar quality of freshness and directness. The Whitmanesque rhetoric and the "ritual frenzy" that Blackmur condemns have now disappeared. We hear in these poems the voice of a very wise man who is also humorous, completely disillusioned yet never cynical, a man who loves life, but is saddened and embittered at the way in which it is being fouled and violated by mass "civilization". It is also, as Richard Hoggart has aptly described it in a notable broadcast, "the voice of a down-to-earth, tight, bright, witty Midlander . . . slangy, quick, flat and direct, lively, laconic, sceptical, nonconforming, nicely bloody-minded". In some of the poems, especially those written in the last months of his life, the voice is that of a seer with a majestic vision of God and life and earth. The two voices, to quote Professor Hoggart again:

"at bottom are . . . one voice . . . each reinforces and makes valid the other. We trust the visionary more because it's rooted in the solid and down-to-earth. We know that the down-to-earth is a genuine rootedness, not a cynicism, because the visionary can grow out of it".[24]

In all these later poems of Lawrence one gets the impression of a man who, like the Byron of *Don Juan*, is able to speak out his whole mind in verse with complete ease and without any sort of inhibition. Of the satiric poems in this last group Richard Aldington wrote that "nearly all these Pansies and Nettles came out of Lawrence's nerves, not out of his real self". This seems to me a gross exaggeration. Some of the pansies and nettles are written in a mood of exasperation, but many of them are brilliant and incisive satiric commentaries on Western civilization, like the poem called "Wages":

The wages of work is cash.
The wages of cash is want more cash.
The wages of want more cash is vicious competition.
The wages of vicious competition is – the world we live in.

The work-cash-want circle is the viciousest circle
that ever turned men into fiends.

Earning a wage is a prison occupation
and a wage-earner is a sort of gaol-bird.
Earning a salary is a prison overseer's job,
a gaoler instead of a gaol-bird.

Living on your income is strolling grandly outside the prison
in terror lest you have to go in. And since the work-prison covers
almost every scrap of the living earth, you stroll up and down
on a narrow beat, about the same as a prisoner taking his exercise.

This is called universal freedom.

This poem has the quality of great satire: it is at once witty and
humorous and profoundly serious. The image of the gaol is the per-
fect symbol for industrial society, and that of the man with the
private income strolling grandly outside "in terror lest you have
to go in" is, like all the best satire, at once very funny and rather
terrible. Some of the pansies and nettles are in rhyming doggerel,
very like the doggerel that Blake used to send in his letters to his
friends, with a similar mixture of mocking humour and penetrating
insight. Blake would have delighted in "Modern Prayer", surely a
prophecy of the affluent society of the nineteen-sixties:

> Almighty Mammon, make me rich!
> Make me rich quickly, with never a hitch
> in my fine prosperity! Kick those in the ditch
> who hinder me, Mammon, great son of a bitch!

In the poems that Lawrence wrote in the last months of his life
his preoccupation is no longer with the flux of life but with God and
death. In a recent memorable lecture[25] the late Christopher Hassall
drew attention to the close connection between these *Last Poems*
of Lawrence and his study of the remains of ancient Etruscan

civilization which produced the last, and perhaps the most beautiful, of his travel books, *Etruscan Places*, well described by Mr Hassall as "a prose poem on a theme of literary criticism". Indeed, as Mr Hassall has pointed out, what Lawrence writes concerning the Etruscan paintings can be applied to his own poetic art in its final development: "The subtlety of Etruscan painting, as of Chinese and Hindu, lies in the wonderfully suggestive *edge* of the figures. It is not outlined. It is not what we call 'drawing'. It is the flowing contour where the body suddenly leaves off, upon the atmosphere." With admirable insight, Mr Hassall has written that, in Lawrence's mature poems, "It is this 'suggestive *edge*' of his own verse, which at first gives the appearance of a rough sketch, and instead of exhibiting formal shape suggests a state of flux, a flowing contour, where the body 'suddenly leaves off, upon the atmosphere'". The *Last Poems* are religious poems and the religion which lies behind them is that primitive religion of wonder which Lawrence ascribed to the Etruscans:

> "The natural flowering of life! It is not so easy for human beings as it sounds. Behind all the Etruscan liveliness was a religion of life, which the chief men were seriously responsible for. Behind all the dancing was a vision, and even a science of life, a conception of the universe and man's place in the universe which made men live to the depth of their capacity.
>
> "To the Etruscan all was alive; the whole universe lived; and the business of man was himself to live amid it all. He had to draw life into himself, out of the wandering huge vitalities of the world. The cosmos was alive, like a vast creature. . . . The whole thing was alive, and had a great soul, or *anima*: and in spite of one great soul, there were myriad roving, lesser souls; every man, every creature and tree and lake and mountain and stream, was animate, and had its own peculiar consciousness."

For Lawrence, as for the Etruscan and the early pre-Socratic Greek of whom he read in two of his favourite books, John Burnet's *Early Greek Philosophy* and Gilbert Murray's *Five Stages of Greek Religion*, there was no contradiction between belief in God and belief in the gods. In the *Last Poems* God is sometimes the creative urge in nature:

God is the great urge that has not yet found a body
but urges towards incarnation with the great creative urge.

And becomes at last a clove carnation: lo! that is god!
and becomes at last Helen, or Ninon: any lovely and generous woman
at her best and her most beautiful, being god, made manifest,
any clear and fearless man being god, very god.

At other times, as in the following lines from *More Pansies*, he feels
the presence of the gods in the colours and shapes of the visible
world:

But all the time I see the gods:
the man who is mowing the tall white corn,
suddenly, as it curves, as it yields, the white wheat
and sinks down with a swift rustle, and a strange, falling flatness,
ah! the gods, the swaying body of god!
ah! the fallen stillness of god, autumnus, and it is only July
the pale-gold flesh of Priapus dropping asleep.

Lawrence is a mythological poet here, but his mythology is no
elegant fiction or learned reconstruction. The gods are realities to
him as they were to a Greek poet, and as they have been, perhaps,
to no other English poet since Keats.

The greatest of his mythological poems is certainly "Bavarian
Gentians". The immediate suggestion for this poem seems to have
come from some gentians which he saw at Rottach in Bavaria, where
he was staying in September 1929, just before he left for the South
of France, where he died in the following March. The sight of the
dark blue flowers seems to have evoked the memory of his explora-
tion of the Etruscan tombs in April 1927, as described by his friend
Earl Brewster who accompanied him on that occasion:

> "From the jewelled splendour of these dark tombs we came
> forth into the brightness of an April day and a blue sky broken
> by hurrying clouds: the fields through which we walked were
> gay with red poppies: our guide unlocked the door leading to
> another tomb and we would descend again to behold the joyous
> scenes with which the Etruscans, of such a distant world, chose
> to adorn the homes of their dead." [26]

As Mr Hassall has written: "Even the physical act of entering these tombs . . . had become for Lawrence a symbol of death with that noble lack of bitterness or protest which is so lovely an element in his last poems".[27]

Reach me a gentian, give me a torch!
let me guide myself with the blue, forked torch of this flower
down the darker and darker stairs, where blue is darkened on blueness
even where Persephone goes, just now, from the frosted September
to the sightless realm where darkness is awake upon the dark
and Persephone herself is but a voice
or a darkness invisible enfolded in the deeper dark
of the arms Plutonic, and pierced with the passion of dense gloom,
among the splendour of torches of darkness, shedding darkness on
    the lost bride and her groom.

Here Lawrence does not, as in his early poems, try to give the reader an immediate apprehension of the life of the flowers; he uses them mythologically, turning them into miraculous torches from the halls of Dis, lighting us down stairs that lead to the underworld, where the spring goddess goes to the embrace of Hades, the "arms Plutonic", and we are made to feel that she is the *anima*, the soul of man going to the embrace of death, which is not terrible but august and godlike. This is a use of mythology not as decoration or allegory, but, like that of Keats in *The Fall of Hyperion*, as a means to lead the reader to "a world of wonder and reverence".[28]

In the tomb of an Etruscan lucumo or prince, Lawrence tells us in *Etruscan Places*, he saw "the sacred treasures of the dead, the little bronze ship of death that should bear him over to the other world, the vases of jewels for his arraying, the vases of small dishes, the little bronze statuettes and tools, the armour . . .".[29] This "little bronze ship of death" became the central image of the longest and most ambitious of the last poems, "The Ship of Death", on which he was working as he lay dying in the opening months of 1930 in the South of France. The poem exists in three drafts; it is fragmentary and unfinished, and critics have pointed out that there is some confusion in the imagery, but, nevertheless, it is the final triumph of Lawrence's poetic art, combining a wonderful grandeur and tranquillity with that "free-breasted naturalness and spontaneity" which he found in Etruscan art:

> O build your ship of death, your little ark
> and furnish it with food, with little cakes, and wine
> for the dark flight down oblivion.
>
>   *   *   *   *
>
> We are dying, we are dying, so all we can do
> is now to be willing to die, and to build the ship
> of death to carry the soul on the longest journey.
>
> A little ship, with oars and food
> and little dishes, and all accoutrements
> fitting and ready for the departing soul.

Nothing, perhaps, that Lawrence ever wrote in verse or prose is more moving than the vision of resurrection at the end of the poem:

> Wait, wait, the little ship
> drifting, beneath the deathly ashy grey
> of a flood-dawn.
>
> Wait, wait! even so, a flush of yellow
> and strangely, O chilled wan soul, a flush of rose.
>
> A flush of rose, and the whole thing starts again.
>
>   *   *   *   *
>
> The flood subsides, and the body, like a worn sea-shell
> emerges strange and lovely.
> And the little ship wings home, faltering and lapsing
> on the pink flood,
> and the frail soul steps out, into her house again
> filling the heart with peace.

Blackmur calls Lawrence's poems "ruins", though he admits that they are ruins which we may admire and contemplate.[30] The word "ruin" implies that Lawrence aimed at great constructions in verse and failed. This is, surely, a misconception. To aim at "great constructions" would have meant assuming the mask of a master-builder in verse and Lawrence saw that the age of masks (i.e. traditional form) in poetry was over. In his poetry we must look for "the insurgent naked throb of the instant moment", a poetry that is "neither star nor pearl but instantaneous like plasm". To convey this sort of experience with the greatest delicacy, the finest intelligence and the most complete honesty was his aim, and, after many unsuccessful and partly successful efforts, he achieved it in such poems as "Snake", "Almond Blossom", "Bavarian Gentians" and "The Ship of Death". Like Wordsworth he wrote a good deal of bad poetry, but, like Wordsworth's, even his bad poems are important, because they are the experiments of a major poet groping his way towards the discovery of a new kind of poetic art.

EDITORS' NOTE ON THE TEXT

THIS EDITION is an attempt to provide a reliable text of the whole of Lawrence's extant writings in verse. The main body of the edition is based on the following collections:

(i) *The Collected Poems of D. H. Lawrence:* published in two volumes by Heinemann in 1928 and in a single-volume edition in 1929. This consists of two sections, called by the author respectively "Rhyming Poems" and "Unrhyming Poems". The classification is not strictly correct as there are unrhymed poems in the first section and rhymed poems in the second, but, as these were Lawrence's own headings, they have been retained. At the end of the "Rhyming Poems" we have printed three poems which were not included by Lawrence in the editions of 1928 and 1929 but were reprinted from earlier collections in Vol. I of the Phoenix Edition of *The Complete Poems of D. H. Lawrence* published by Heinemann in 1957. Lawrence's preface, entitled "Note", has been printed in its original position at the head of the collection. His important Introduction to the American edition of his *New Poems* (1918), one of the earlier collections included in the 1928 edition, has been printed at the head of the "Unrhyming Poems" immediately before the sequence entitled *Look! We Have Come Through!* There is justification for placing this Introduction here, as Lawrence himself wrote that it "should have come as a preface to *Look! We Have Come Through!*". We have restored to the Introduction its original title, "Poetry of the Present", under which it first appeared in 1919 in a periodical called *The Playboy* (see Roberts p. 38). The texts of the "Foreword" and "Argument" of *Look! We Have Come Through!* have been printed as they appeared in the original edition of 1917, and the poem "Meeting Among the Mountains", included in the 1917 edition but omitted from *The Collected Poems*, has been restored to its original position in the sequence. For the collection called *Birds, Beasts and Flowers* we have printed at the head of the different sections the short prose prefaces which Lawrence placed in these positions in the 1930 Cresset Press edition.

(ii) *Pansies*: This is the text of the privately printed "definitive edition" of 1929 (Roberts A47C) containing fourteen poems not included in the "trade edition" published by Martin Secker in the same year. The "definitive" edition contained a six-page Introduction (reprinted in *Phoenix*). Secker's "trade" edition was prefaced by a much shorter Foreword. As the Introduction and the Note are both important and revealing pieces of criticism, they have both been reprinted in this edition at the head of *Pansies*.

(iii) *Nettles*: This is the text of the edition published by Faber and Faber in 1930 (No. 11 of the "Criterion Miscellany"). Two poems have been added from the original typescript, now in the Library of the University of California.

(iv) *More Pansies* and *Last Poems*: These collections have been printed from photostats of Lawrence's manuscripts contained in two notebooks ("A" and "B") now in the Library of the University of Texas. They were published by Richard Aldington and Guiseppe Orioli at Florence in 1932 under the title *Last Poems* and by Heinemann in London. An Introduction by the late Mr Aldington was included in the volume and has been reprinted at the head of these collections in the present edition.

In the 1932 edition *Last Poems* were printed immediately after this Introduction and were followed by *More Pansies*. We have thought it more appropriate to reverse this order. Our text is based on photostats of Lawrence's manuscripts, as a collation of the text of Aldington and Orioli's edition with the manuscripts has shown that their transcription was very inaccurate and that some whole poems and a number of lines were omitted from the printed text of the 1932 edition, and there were other minor errors.

(v) The last section of the main body of our edition consists of hitherto uncollected poems from printed and manuscript sources. These include poems contributed to periodicals and anthologies not reprinted in any edition published by Lawrence, the poems in *The Plumed Serpent* and in the collection called *Fire and Other Poems* printed by the Book Club of California in 1940, and a number of poems from a notebook now in the Library of the University of Texas containing what is obviously an early draft in Lawrence's handwriting of the poems printed as *Pansies*. Some of these poems were not printed in *Pansies*; these we have thought fit to include in the section of Uncollected Poems under the title of "Additional Pansies", together with a couple of trifles: a limerick from a manuscript in the University of Texas and a curious self-parody from a manuscript in the Princeton University library.

There are four appendices. The first consists of the original draft of the Introduction to the *Collected Poems* of 1928. This was printed on pp. 251-4 of *Phoenix* (1932). Our text is based on Lawrence's manuscript, now in the Library of the University of California at Los Angeles (see Roberts, E73). The second Appendix contains juvenilia. These early manuscript poems, which Lawrence never published, are taken partly from a notebook now in the Library of the University of Nottingham (Nott. MS. 1479) and partly from a set of fair copies of early verses in Lawrence's holograph now in the Berg Collection in the New York Public Library. The third Appendix contains a selection of variants and early drafts of published poems. Like W. B. Yeats, D. H. Lawrence constantly revised and re-wrote his poems. Some of the variants and early drafts are taken from early editions and others from manuscript sources. The present work does not aim at being a "Variorum Edition" recording all extant variants of poems. The editors have, however, thought it appropriate to publish a certain number of variants and early drafts which have a particular interest for students of Lawrence's poetic development and craftsmanship. The fourth Appendix consists of the Notes and Glossary. The notes are partly textual and partly explanatory. Lawrence's own punctuation has been retained, even though it is sometimes ungrammatical, in all poems printed from texts which he himself prepared for the press. In poems printed from manuscript the editors have considered themselves at liberty to impose light grammatical punctuation where it seems necessary for the convenience of the reader. The spelling throughout is that of the original texts. Obvious typographical errors in printed texts have been silently corrected.

The editors acknowledge the help which they have received in compiling them from the useful notes of Professor Piero Nardi in his edition of Lawrence's poems in *Tutte Le Poesie di D. H. Lawrence*, published by A. Mondadori at Milan (2 vols, 1959). A glossary has been added to help the reader with the dialect and foreign words which occur in the poems.

V. de S. P.

W. R.

PREFATORY NOTE TO THE THIRD EDITION

For this edition, the editors have taken the opportunity to correct a number of errors by comparing the text with the most authoritative sources. With a few exceptions indicated in the notes, the text for "Rhyming Poems" and "Unrhyming Poems" is derived from the 1928 *Collected Poems* for which Lawrence himself was responsible.

The text for "More Pansies" and "Last Poems" is derived from manuscript sources.

"Pansies" exists in two published texts, both presumably proof-read by Lawrence; however, the text of the privately printed edition appears more reliable in minor differences of punctuation, etc., in addition to its claim to be the "definitive" version of "Pansies"; hence, this edition supplies the present text.

The editors acknowledge with thanks the valuable help received from various correspondents, especially Mr. T. A. Smailes of the University of Port Elizabeth, South Africa; Herr Otmarr Ollendorf of the University of Köln, Germany; Mr. Egon Tiedje of the University of Hamburg, Germany; and Mrs. Carole Ferrier of Auckland, New Zealand.

V. DE S.P.

W.R.

NOTE

(Preface to *Collected Poems* [1928])

THE volume of *Rhyming Poems* is collected from four little books, *Love Poems and Others, Amores, New Poems,* and *Bay.* Of these *Love Poems and Others* was the first, and was published in 1913.

I have now tried to arrange the poems, as far as possible, in chronological order, the order in which they were written. The first poems I ever wrote, if poems they were, was when I was nineteen: now twenty-three years ago. I remember perfectly the Sunday afternoon when I perpetrated those first two pieces: "To Guelder-Roses" and "To Campions"; in springtime, of course, and, as I say, in my twentieth year. Any young lady might have written them and been pleased with them; as I was pleased with them. But it was after that, when I was twenty, that my real demon would now and then get hold of me and shake more real poems out of me, making me uneasy. I never "liked" my real poems as I liked "To Guelder-Roses".

I have tried to establish a chronological order, because many of the poems are so personal that, in their fragmentary fashion, they make up a biography of an emotional and inner life. Many of the poems, again, are what one might call fictional, poems like "Love on the Farm", "Wedding Morn", "Two Wives", and the dialect poems. They have no necessary chronological sequence. But the poems to Miriam, and to my Mother, and to Helen, and to the other woman, the woman of "Kisses in the Train" and "Hands of the Betrothed", they need the order of time, as that is the order of experience. So, perhaps, do the subjective poems like "Virgin Youth".

The first change in scene comes when for the first time I left Nottinghamshire, at the age of twenty-three, to go to teach in a new school on the fringes of South London. From the playground we could look north at the blue bubble of the Crystal Palace, fairy-like to me. Then the poems to Helen begin, and the school poems, and London.

Some of the earliest poems, like "The Wild Common" and "Virgin Youth", are a good deal rewritten. They were struggling to say something which it takes a man twenty years to be able to say. Some of the fictional poems are changed, to make the "fiction" more complete. A young man is afraid of his demon and puts his hand over the demon's mouth sometimes and speaks for him. And the things the young man says are very rarely poetry. So I have tried to let the demon say his say, and to remove the passages where the young man intruded. So that, in the first volume, many poems are changed, some entirely rewritten, recast. But usually this is only because the poem started out to be something which it didn't quite achieve, because the young man interfered with his demon.

The crisis of Volume I is the death of the mother, with the long haunting of death in life, which continues to the end, through all the last poems, which come from *Bay*, and which belong to the war. *Bay* appeared in 1919, but the poems were written mostly in 1917 and 1918, after I left Cornwall perforce.

A big break in scene, however, had happened before then, in 1912, when I left England for the first time. In 1912 begins the new cycle of *Look! We Have Come Through!* Of this volume the first few poems belong to England and the end of the death-experience, but "Bei Hennef", written in May 1912, by a river in the Rhineland, starts the new cycle, which ends with "Frost Flowers", written in Cornwall at the end of the bitter winter of 1916-17. It seems to me that no poetry, not even the best, should be judged as if it existed in the absolute, in the vacuum of the absolute. Even the best poetry, when it is at all personal, needs the penumbra of its own time and place and circumstance to make it full and whole. If we knew a little more of Shakespeare's self and circumstance how much more complete the Sonnets would be to us, how their strange, torn edges would be softened and merged into a whole body! So one would like to ask the reader of *Look! We Have Come Through!* to fill in the background of the poems, as far as possible, with the place, the time, the circumstance. What was uttered in the cruel spring of 1917 should not be dislocated and heard as if sounding out of the void.

The poems of *Birds, Beasts and Flowers* were begun in Tuscany, in the autumn of 1920, and finished in New Mexico in 1923, in my thirty-eighth year. So that from first to last these poems cover all but twenty years.

D. H. L.

SCANDICCI,
12 May 1928

RHYMING POEMS

THE WILD COMMON

The quick sparks on the gorse-bushes are leaping
Little jets of sunlight texture imitating flame;
Above them, exultant, the peewits are sweeping:
They have triumphed again o'er the ages, their screamings proclaim.

Rabbits, handfuls of brown earth, lie
Low-rounded on the mournful turf they have bitten down to the
    quick.
Are they asleep?—are they living?—Now see, when I
Lift my arms, the hill bursts and heaves under their spurting kick!

The common flaunts bravely; but below, from the rushes
Crowds of glittering king-cups surge to challenge the blossoming
    bushes;
There the lazy streamlet pushes
His bent course mildly; here wakes again, leaps, laughs, and gushes

Into a deep pond, an old sheep-dip,
Dark, overgrown with willows, cool, with the brook ebbing through
    so slow;
Naked on the steep, soft lip
Of the turf I stand watching my own white shadow quivering to
    and fro.

What if the gorse-flowers shrivelled, and I were gone?
What if the waters ceased, where were the marigolds then, and the
    gudgeon?
What is this thing that I look down upon?
White on the water wimples my shadow, strains like a dog on a
    string, to run on.

33

How it looks back, like a white dog to its master!
I on the bank all substance, my shadow all shadow looking up to
    me, looking back!
And the water runs, and runs faster, runs faster,
And the white dog dances and quivers, I am holding his cord quite
    slack.

But how splendid it is to be substance, here!
My shadow is neither here nor there; but I, I am royally here!
I am here! I am here! screams the peewit; the may-blobs burst out
    in a laugh as they hear!
Here! flick the rabbits. Here! pants the gorse. Here! say the insects
    far and near.

Over my skin in the sunshine, the warm, clinging air
Flushed with the songs of seven larks singing at once, goes kissing
    me glad.
You are here! You are here! We have found you! Everywhere
We sought you substantial, you touchstone of caresses, you naked
    lad!

Oh but the water loves me and folds me,
Plays with me, sways me, lifts me and sinks me, murmurs: Oh
    marvellous stuff!
No longer shadow!—and it holds me
Close, and it rolls me, enfolds me, touches me, as if never it could
    touch me enough.

Sun, but in substance, yellow water-blobs!
Wings and feathers on the crying, mysterious ages, peewits wheeling!
All that is right, all that is good, all that is God takes substance! a
    rabbit lobs
In confirmation, I hear sevenfold lark-songs pealing.

DOG-TIRED

If she would come to me here
    Now the sunken swaths
    Are glittering paths
To the sun, and the swallows cut clear
Into the setting sun! if she came to me here!

If she would come to me now,
Before the last-mown harebells are dead;
While that vetch-clump still burns red!
Before all the bats have dropped from the bough
To cool in the night; if she came to me now!

The horses are untackled, the chattering machine
Is still at last. If she would come
We could gather up the dry hay from
The hill-brow, and lie quite still, till the green
Sky ceased to quiver, and lost its active sheen.

I should like to drop
On the hay, with my head on her knee,
And lie dead still, while she
Breathed quiet above me; and the crop
Of stars grew silently.

I should like to lie still
As if I was dead; but feeling
Her hand go stealing
Over my face and my head, until
This ache was shed.

FROM A COLLEGE WINDOW

The glimmer of the limes, sun-heavy, sleeping,
    Goes trembling past me up the College wall.
Below, the lawn, in soft blue shade is keeping
    The daisy-froth quiescent, softly in thrall.

Beyond the leaves that overhang the street,
    Along the flagged, clean pavement summer-white,
Passes the world with shadows at their feet
    Going left and right.

Remote, although I hear the beggar's cough,
    See the woman's twinkling fingers tend him a coin,
I sit absolved, assured I am better off
    Beyond a world I never want to join.

DISCORD IN CHILDHOOD

Outside the house an ash-tree hung its terrible whips,
And at night when the wind rose, the lash of the tree
Shrieked and slashed the wind, as a ship's
Weird rigging in a storm shrieks hideously.

Within the house two voices arose, a slender lash
Whistling she-delirious rage, and the dreadful sound
Of a male thong booming and bruising, until it had
    drowned
The other voice in a silence of blood, 'neath the noise
    of the ash.

CHERRY ROBBERS

Under the long dark boughs, like jewels red
        In the hair of an Eastern girl
Hang strings of crimson cherries, as if had bled
        Blood-drops beneath each curl.

Under the glistening cherries, with folded wings
        Three dead birds lie:
Pale-breasted throstles and a blackbird, robberlings
        Stained with red dye.

Against the haystack a girl stands laughing at me,
  Cherries hung round her ears.
Offers me her scarlet fruit: I will see
  If she has any tears.

DREAM-CONFUSED

  Is that the moon
At the window so big and red?
No-one in the room?
No-one near the bed?

  Listen, her shoon
Palpitating down the stair!
—Or a beat of wings at the window there?

  A moment ago
She kissed me warm on the mouth;
The very moon in the south
Is warm with a ruddy glow;
The moon, from far abysses
Signalling those two kisses.

  And now the moon
Goes clouded, having misunderstood.
And slowly back in my blood
My kisses are sinking, soon
  To be under the flood.

  We misunderstood!

RENASCENCE

We have bit no forbidden apple,
  Eve and I,
Yet the splashes of day and night
Falling round us, no longer dapple
The same valley with purple and white.

This is our own still valley,
    Our Eden, our home;
But day shows it vivid with feeling,
And the pallor of night does not tally
With dark sleep that once covered the ceiling.

The little red heifer: to-night I looked in her eyes;
    She will calve to-morrow.
Last night, when I went with the lantern, the sow was grabbing her
    litter
With snarling red jaws; and I heard the cries
Of the new-born, and then, the old owl, then the bats that flitter.

And I woke to the sound of the wood-pigeon, and lay and listened
    Till I could borrow
A few quick beats from a wood-pigeon's heart; and when I did
    rise
Saw where morning sun on the shaken iris glistened.
And I knew that home, this valley, was wider than Paradise.

I learned it all from my Eve,
    The warm, dumb wisdom;
She's a quicker instructress than years;
She has quickened my pulse to receive
Strange throbs, beyond laughter and tears.

So now I know the valley
    Fleshed all like me
With feelings that change and quiver
And clash, and yet seem to tally,
Like all the clash of a river
    Moves on to the sea.

VIRGIN YOUTH

    Now and again
    The life that looks through my eyes
    And quivers in words through my mouth,
    And behaves like the rest of men,
    Slips away, so I gasp in surprise.

And then
My unknown breasts begin
To wake, and down the thin
Ripples below the breast an urgent
Rhythm starts, and my silent and slumberous belly
In one moment rouses insurgent.

My soft, slumbering belly,
Quivering awake with one impulse and one will,
Then willy nilly
A lower me gets up and greets me;
Homunculus stirs from his roots, and strives until,
Risen up, he beats me.

He stands, and I tremble before him.
—Who then art thou?—
He is wordless, but sultry and vast,
And I can't deplore him.
—Who art thou? What hast
Thou to do with me, thou lustrous one, iconoclast?—

How beautiful he is! without sound,
Without eyes, without hands;
Yet, flame of the living ground
He stands, the column of fire by night.
And he knows from the depths; he quite
Alone understands.

Quite alone, he alone
Understands and knows.
Lustrously sure, unknown
Out of nowhere he rose.

I tremble in his shadow, as he burns
For the dark goal.
He stands like a lighthouse, night churns
Round his base, his dark light rolls
Into darkness, and darkly returns.

Is he calling, the lone one? Is his deep
Silence full of summons?
Is he moving invisibly? Does his steep
Curve sweep towards a woman's?

Traveller, column of fire,
It is vain.
The glow of thy full desire
Becomes pain.

Dark, ruddy pillar, forgive me! I
Am helplessly bound
To the rock of virginity. Thy
Strange voice has no sound.

We cry in the wilderness. Forgive me, I
Would so gladly lie
In the womanly valley, and ply
Thy twofold dance.

Thou dark one, thou proud, curved beauty! I
Would worship thee, letting my buttocks prance.
But the hosts of men with one voice deny
Me the chance.

They have taken the gates from the hinges
And built up the way. I salute thee
But to deflower thee. Thy tower impinges
On nothingness. Pardon me!

STUDY

Somewhere the long mellow note of the blackbird
Quickens the unclasping hands of hazel.
Somewhere the wind-flowers fling their heads back
Stirred by an impetuous wind. Some ways'll
All be sweet with white and blue violet—
    (Hush now, hush! Where am I?—Biuret—)

On the green wood's edge a shy girl hovers
From out of the hazel-screen on to the grass,
Where wheeling and screaming the petulant plovers
Wave frighted.—Who comes?—A labourer, alas!
    (*Work, work, you fool—*)

Somewhere the lamp hanging low from the ceiling
Lights the soft hair of a girl as she reads,
And the red firelight steadily reeling
Puts the hard hands of my friend to sleep.
And the white dog snuffs the warmth, appealing
For the man to heed lest the girl shall weep.

    Tears and dreams for them; for me
    Bitter science—the exams are near.
    I wish I did it more willingly!
    I wish you did not wait, my dear,
    For me to come; since work I must.
    Though it's all the same when we are dead—
        I wish I was only a bust,
           All head—!

TWILIGHT

Darkness comes out of the earth
    And swallows dip into the pallor of the west;
From the hay comes the clamour of children's mirth;
    Wanes the old palimpsest.

The night-stock oozes scent,
    And a moon-blue moth goes flittering by:
All that the worldly day has meant
    Wastes like a lie.

The children have forsaken their play;
    A single star in a veil of light
Glimmers: litter of day
    Is gone from sight.

LOVE ON THE FARM

What large, dark hands are those at the window
Grasping in the golden light
Which weaves its way through the evening wind
    At my heart's delight?

Ah, only the leaves! But in the west
I see a redness suddenly come
Into the evening's anxious breast—
    'Tis the wound of love goes home!

The woodbine creeps abroad
Calling low to her lover:
    The sun-lit flirt who all the day
    Has poised above her lips in play
    And stolen kisses, shallow and gay
    Of pollen, now has gone away—
    She woos the moth with her sweet, low word:
And when above her his moth-wings hover
Then her bright breast she will uncover
And yield her honey-drop to her lover.

Into the yellow, evening glow
Saunters a man from the farm below;
Leans, and looks in at the low-built shed
Where the swallow has hung her marriage bed.
    The bird lies warm against the wall.
    She glances quick her startled eyes
    Towards him, then she turns away
    Her small head, making warm display
    Of red upon the throat. Her terrors sway
    Her out of the nest's warm, busy ball,
    Whose plaintive cry is heard as she flies
    In one blue stoop from out the sties
    Into the twilight's empty hall.

Oh, water-hen, beside the rushes
Hide your quaintly scarlet blushes,
Still your quick tail, lie still as dead,
Till the distance folds over his ominous tread!

The rabbit presses back her ears,
Turns back her liquid, anguished eyes
And crouches low; then with wild spring
Spurts from the terror of *his* oncoming;
To be choked back, the wire ring
Her frantic effort throttling:
   Piteous brown ball of quivering fears!
Ah, soon in his large, hard hands she dies,
And swings all loose from the swing of his walk!
Yet calm and kindly are his eyes
And ready to open in brown surprise
Should I not answer to his talk
Or should he my tears surmise.

I hear his hand on the latch, and rise from my chair
Watching the door open; he flashes bare
His strong teeth in a smile, and flashes his eyes
In a smile like triumph upon me; then careless-wise
He flings the rabbit soft on the table board
And comes towards me: ah! the uplifted sword
Of his hand against my bosom! and oh, the broad
Blade of his glance that asks me to applaud
His coming! With his hand he turns my face to him
And caresses me with his fingers that still smell grim
Of the rabbit's fur! God, I am caught in a snare!
I know not what fine wire is round my throat;
I only know I let him finger there
My pulse of life, and let him nose like a stoat
Who sniffs with joy before he drinks the blood.

And down his mouth comes to my mouth! and down
His bright dark eyes come over me, like a hood
Upon my mind! his lips meet mine, and a flood
Of sweet fire sweeps across me, so I drown
Against him, die, and find death good.

GIPSY

I, the man with the red scarf,
  Will give thee what I have, this last week's
    earnings.
Take them and buy thee a silver ring
  And wed me, to ease my yearnings.

For the rest, when thou art wedded
  I'll wet my brow for thee
With sweat, I'll enter a house for thy sake,
  Thou shalt shut doors on me.

THE COLLIER'S WIFE

Somebody's knockin' at th' door
  Mother, come down an' see!
—I's think it's nobbut a beggar;
  Say I'm busy.

It's not a beggar, mother; hark
  How 'ard 'e knocks!
—Eh, tha'rt a mard-arsed kid,
  'E'll gie thee socks!

Shout an' ax what 'e wants,
  I canna come down.
—'E says, is it Arthur Holliday's?
  —Say Yes, tha clown.

'E says: Tell your mother as 'er mester's
  Got hurt i' th' pit——
What? Oh my Sirs, 'e never says that,
  That's not it!

Come out o' th' way an' let me see!
  Eh, there's no peace!
An' stop thy scraightin', childt,
  Do shut thy face!

"Your mester's 'ad a accident
    An' they ta'ein' 'im i' th' ambulance
Ter Nottingham."—Eh dear o' me,
    If 'e's not a man for mischance!

Wheer's 'e hurt this time, lad?
    —I dunna know,
They on'y towd me it wor bad—
    It would be so!

Out o' my way, childt! dear o' me, wheer
    'Ave I put 'is clean stockin's an' shirt?
Goodness knows if they'll be able
    To take off 'is pit-dirt!

An' what a moan 'e'll make! there niver
    Was such a man for a fuss
If anything ailed 'im; at any rate
    I shan't 'ave 'im to nuss.

I do 'ope as it's not so very bad!
    Eh, what a shame it seems
As some should ha'e hardly a smite o' trouble
    An' others 'as reams!

It's a shame as 'e should be knocked about
    Like this, I'm sure it is!
'E's 'ad twenty accidents, if 'e's 'ad one;
    Owt bad, an' it's his!

There's one thing, we s'll 'ave a peaceful 'ouse
        f'r a bit,
    Thank heaven for a peaceful house!
An' there's compensation, sin' it's accident,
    An' club-money—I won't growse.

An' a fork an' a spoon 'e'll want—an' what else?
 I s'll never catch that train!
What a traipse it is, if a man gets hurt!
 I sh'd think 'e'll get right again.

FLAPPER

Love has crept out of her sealèd heart
 As a field-bee, black and amber,
 Breaks from the winter-cell, to clamber
Up the warm grass where the sunbeams start.

Mischief has come in her dawning eyes,
 And a glint of coloured iris brings
 Such as lies along the folded wings
Of the bee before he flies.

Who, with a ruffling, careful breath,
 Has opened the wings of the wild young sprite?
 Has fluttered her spirit to stumbling flight
In her eyes, as a young bee stumbleth?

Love makes the burden of her voice.
 The hum of his heavy, staggering wings
 Sets quivering with wisdom the common things
That she says, and her words rejoice.

THIEF IN THE NIGHT

 Last night a thief came to me
  And struck at me with something dark.
 I cried, but no one heard me,
  I lay dumb and stark.

 When I awoke this morning
  I could find no trace;
 Perhaps 'twas a dream of warning,
  For I've lost my peace.

46

MONOLOGUE OF A MOTHER

This is the last of all, then, this is the last!
I must fold my hands, and turn my face to the fire,
And watch my dead days fusing together in dross,
Shape after shape, and scene after scene of my past
Clotting to one dead mass in the sinking fire
Where ash on the dying coals grows swiftly, like heavy
    moss.

Strange he is, my son, for whom I have waited like a lover;
Strange to me, like a captive in a foreign country, haunting
The confines, gazing out beyond, where the winds go free;
White and gaunt, with wistful eyes that hover
Always on the distance, as if his soul were chaunting
A monotonous weird of departure away from me.

Like a thin white bird blown out of the northern seas,
Like a bird from the far north blown with a broken wing
Into our sooty garden, he drags and beats
Along the fence perpetually, seeking release
From me, from the hand of my love which creeps up,
    needing
His happiness, whilst he in displeasure retreats.

I must look away from him, for my faded eyes
Like a cringing dog at his heels offend him now,
Like a toothless hound pursuing him with my will;
Till he chafes at my crouching persistence, and a sharp
    spark flies
In my soul from under the sudden frown of his brow
As he blenches and turns away, and my heart stands still.

This is the last, it will not be any more.
All my life I have borne the burden of myself,
All the long years of sitting in my husband's house;
Never have I said to myself as he closed the door:
"Now I am caught! You are hopelessly lost, O Self!
You are frightened with joy, my heart, like a frightened
    mouse."

Three times have I offered myself, three times rejected.
It will not be any more. No more, my son, my son!—
Never to know the glad freedom of obedience, since long
　　ago
The angel of childhood kissed me and went! I expected
This last one to claim me;—and now, my son, O my son,
I must sit alone and wait, and never know
The loss of myself, till death comes, who cannot fail.

Death, in whose service is nothing of gladness, takes me;
For the lips and the eyes of God are behind a veil.
And the thought of the lipless voice of the Father shakes me
With dread, and fills my heart with the tears of desire,
And my heart rebels with anguish, as night draws nigher.

THE LITTLE TOWN AT EVENING

The chime of the bells, and the church clock striking eight
Solemnly and distinctly cries down the babel of children
　　still playing in the hay.
The church draws nearer upon us, gentle and great
In shadow, covering us up with her grey.

Like drowsy creatures the houses fall asleep
Under the fleece of shadow, as in between
Tall and dark the church moves, anxious to keep
Their sleeping, cover them soft unseen.

Hardly a murmur comes from the sleeping brood;
I wish the church had covered me up with the rest
In the home-place. Why is it she should exclude
Me so distinctly from sleeping the sleep I'd love best?

IN A BOAT

See the stars, love,
In the water much clearer and brighter
Than those above us, and whiter,
Like nenuphars!

48

Star-shadows shine, love:
How many stars in your bowl?
How many shadows in your soul?
Only mine, love, mine?

When I move the oars, see
How the stars are tossed,
Distorted, even lost!
Even yours, do you see?

The poor waters spill
The stars, waters troubled, forsaken!—
The heavens are not shaken, you say, love;
Its stars stand still.

There! did you see
That spark fly up at us? even
Stars are not safe in heaven!
What of me then, love, me?

What then, love, if soon
Your star be tossed over a wave?
Would the darkness look like a grave?
Would you swoon, love, swoon?

LAST HOURS

The cool of an oak's unchequered shade
Falls on me as I lie in deep grass
Which rushes upward, blade beyond blade,
While higher the darting grass-flowers pass
Piercing the blue with their crocketed spires
And waving flags, and the ragged fires
Of the sorrel's cresset—a green, brave town
Vegetable, new in renown.

Over the tree's edge, as over a mountain
Surges the white of the moon,
A cloud comes up like the surge of a fountain,
Pressing round and low at first, but soon
Heaving and piling a round white dome.
How lovely it is to be at home
Like an insect in the grass
Letting life pass!

There's a scent of clover crept through my hair
From the full resource of some purple dome
Where that lumbering bee, who can hardly bear
His burden above me, never has clomb.
But not even the scent of insouciant flowers
Makes pause the hours.

Down the valley roars a townward train.
I hear it through the grass
Dragging the links of my shortening chain
Southwards, alas!

FLAT SUBURBS, S. W., IN THE MORNING

The new red houses spring like plants
    In level rows
Of reddish herbage that bristles and slants
    Its square shadows.

The pink young houses show one side bright
    Flatly assuming the sun,
And one side shadow, half in sight,
    Half-hiding the pavement-run;

Where hastening creatures pass intent
    On their level way,
Threading like ants that can never relent
    And have nothing to say.

Bare stems of street lamps stiffly stand
    At random, desolate twigs,
To testify to a blight on the land
    That has stripped their sprigs.

THE BEST OF SCHOOL

The blinds are drawn because of the sun,
And the boys and the room in a colourless gloom
Of underwater float: bright ripples run
Across the walls as the blinds are blown
To let the sunlight in; and I,
As I sit on the shores of the class, alone,
Watch the boys in their summer blouses
As they write, their round heads busily bowed:
And one after another rouses
His face to look at me,
To ponder very quietly,
As seeing, he does not see.

And then he turns again, with a little, glad
Thrill of his work he turns again from me,
Having found what he wanted, having got what was
        to be had.

And very sweet it is, while the sunlight waves
In the ripening morning, to sit alone with the class
And feel the stream of awakening ripple and pass
From me to the boys, whose brightening souls it laves
For this little hour.

            This morning, sweet it is
To feel the lads' looks light on me,
Then back in a swift, bright flutter to work;
Each one darting away with his
Discovery, like birds that steal and flee.

Touch after touch I feel on me
As their eyes glance at me for the grain
Of rigour they taste delightedly.

As tendrils reach out yearningly,
Slowly rotate till they touch the tree
That they cleave unto, and up which they climb
Up to their lives – so they to me.

I feel them cling and cleave to me
As vines going eagerly up; they twine
My life with other leaves, my time
Is hidden in theirs, their thrills are mine.

DREAMS OLD AND NASCENT

OLD
I have opened the windows to warm my hands on the sill
Where the sunlight soaks in the stone: the afternoon
Is full of dreams, my love; the boys are all still
In a wistful dream of Lorna Doone.

The clink of the shunting engines is sharp and fine
Like savage music striking far off; and there
On the great blue palace at Sydenham, lights stir and shine
Where the glass is domed on the silent air.

There lies the world, my darling, full of wonder and wist-
    fulness, and strange
Recognitions and greetings of half-acquaint things, as I
    greet the cloud
Of glass palace aloft there, among misty, indefinite things
    that range
At the back of my life's experience, where dreams from
    the old lives crowd.

Over the nearness of Norwood Hill, through the mellow
    veil
Of the afternoon glows still the old romance of David and
    Dora,
With the old, sweet, soothing tears, and laughter that
    shakes the sail
Of the ship of the soul over seas where dreamed dreams
    lure the unoceaned explorer.

All the bygone, hushèd years
Streaming back where the mists distil
To forgetfulness: soft-sailing waters where fears
No longer hurt, where the silk sails fill
With that unfelt breeze that ebbs over the seas where the
    storm
Of living has passed, ebbing on
Through the stirred iridescence that swims in the warm
Wake of a tumult now spent and gone,
Drifts my boat, wistfully lapsing after
The silence of vanishing tears, and the echoes of laughter.

SUBURBS ON A HAZY DAY

O stiffly shapen houses that change not,
    What conjurer's cloth was thrown across you, and raised
To show you thus transfigured, changed,
    Your stuff all gone, your menace almost rased?

Such resolute shapes so harshly set
    In hollow blocks and cubes deformed, and heaped
In void and null profusion, how is this?
    In what strong aqua regia now are you steeped?

That you lose the brick-stuff out of you
    And hover like a presentment, fading faint
And vanquished, evaporate away
    To leave but only the merest possible taint!

WEEKNIGHT SERVICE

The five old bells
Are hurrying and stridently calling,
Insisting,.protesting
They are right, yet clamorously falling
Into gabbling confusion, without resting,
Like spattering shouts of an orator endlessly dropping
From the tower on the town, but endlessly, never stopping.

The silver moon
That somebody has spun so high
To settle the question, heads or tails? has caught
In the net of the night's balloon,
And sits with a smooth, bland smile up there in the sky
Serenely smiling at naught,
Unless the little star that keeps her company
Makes tittering jests at the bells' obscenity;
As if *he* knew aught!

While patient Night
Sits indifferent, hugged in her rags;
She neither knows nor cares
Why the old church bellows and brags;
The noise distresses her ears, and tears
At her tattered silence, as she crouches and covers her face,
Bent, if we did but know it, on a weary and bitter grimace.

The wise old trees
Drop their leaves with a faint, sharp hiss of contempt;
A car at the end of the street goes by with a laugh.
As by degrees
The damned bells cease, and we are exempt,
And the stars can chaff
The cool high moon at their ease; while the droning church
Is peopled with shadows and wailing, and last ghosts lurch
Towards its cenotaph.

A MAN WHO DIED

Ah, stern, cold man,
How can you lie so relentless hard
While I wash you with weeping water!
Do you set your face against the daughter
Of life? Can you never discard
Your curt pride's ban?

You masquerader!
How can you shame to act this part
Of unswerving indifference to me?
You want at last, ah me!
To break my heart,
Evader!

You know your mouth
Was always sooner to soften
Even than your eyes.
Now shut it lies
Relentless, however often
I kiss it in drouth.

It has no breath
Nor any relaxing. Where,
Where are you, what have you done?
What is this mouth of stone?
How did you dare
Take cover in death!

Once you could see,
The white moon show like a breast revealed
By the slipping shawl of stars.
Could see the small stars tremble
As the heart beneath did wield
Systole, diastole.

All the lovely macrocosm
Was woman once to you,
Bride to your groom.
No tree in bloom
But it leaned you a new
White bosom.

And always and ever
Soft as a summering tree
Unfolds from the sky, for your good,
Unfolded womanhood:
Shedding you down as a tree
Sheds its flowers on a river.

I saw your brows
Set like rocks beside a sea of gloom,
And I shed my very soul down into your
     thought;
Like flowers I fell, to be caught
On the comforted pool, like bloom
That leaves the boughs.

Oh, masquerader,
With a hard face white-enamelled,
What are you now?
Do you care no longer how
My heart is trammelled,
Evader?

Is this you, after all,
Metallic, obdurate,
With bowels of steel?
Did you *never* feel?—
Cold, insensate,
Mechanical!

Ah, no!—you multiform,
You that I loved, you wonderful,
You who darkened and shone,

You were many men in one;
But never this null
This never-warm!

Is this the sum of you?
Is it all naught?
Cold, metal-cold?
Are you all told
Here, iron-wrought?
Is this what's become of you?

LETTER FROM TOWN: ON A GREY
MORNING IN MARCH

The clouds are pushing in grey reluctance slowly northward to you,
  While north of them all, at the farthest ends, stands one bright-
    bosomed, aglance
With fire as it guards the wild north-coasts, red-fire seas running
    through
    The rocks where ravens flying to windward melt as a well-shot
    lance.

You should be out by the orchard, where violets secretly darken
    the earth,
    Or there in the woods of the twilight, with northern wind-flowers
    shaken astir.
Think of me here in the library, trying and trying a song that is
    worth
    Tears and swords to my heart, arrows no armour will turn or
    deter.

You tell me the lambs have come, they lie like daisies white in
    the grass
    Of the dark-green hills; new calves in shed; peewits turn after
    the plough—
It is well for you. For me the navvies work in the road where I pass
    And I want to smite in anger the barren rock of each waterless
    brow.

Like the sough of a wind that is caught up high in the mesh of
    the budding trees,
  A sudden car goes sweeping past, and I strain my soul to hear
The voice of the furtive triumphant engine as it rushes past like
    a breeze,
    To hear on its mocking triumphance unwitting the after-echo
    of fear.

LETTER FROM TOWN: THE
ALMOND-TREE

You promised to send me some violets. Did you forget?
  White ones and blue ones from under the orchard hedge?
  Sweet dark purple, and white ones mixed for a pledge
Of our early love that hardly has opened yet.

Here there's an almond-tree—you have never seen
  Such a one in the north—it flowers on the street, and I stand
  Every day by the fence to look up at the flowers that expand
At rest in the blue, and wonder at what they mean.

Under the almond-tree, the happy lands
  Provence, Japan, and Italy repose;
  And passing feet are chatter and clapping of those
Who play around us, country girls clapping their hands.

You, my love, the foremost, in a flowered gown,
  All your unbearable tenderness, you with the laughter
  Startled upon your eyes now so wide with hereafter,
You with loose hands of abandonment hanging down.

WEDDING MORN

The morning breaks like a pomegranate
  In a shining crack of red;
Ah, when to-morrow the dawn comes late
  Whitening across the bed
It will find me watching at the marriage gate
  And waiting while light is shed
On him who is sleeping satiate
  With a sunk, unconscious head.

And when the dawn comes creeping in,
    Cautiously I shall raise
Myself to watch the daylight win
    On my first of days,
As it shows him sleeping a sleep he got
    With me, as under my gaze
He grows distinct, and I see his hot
    Face freed of the wavering blaze.

Then I shall know which image of God
    My man is made toward;
And I shall see my sleeping rod
    Or my life's reward;
And I shall count the stamp and worth
    Of the man I've accepted as mine,
Shall see an image of heaven or of earth
    On his minted metal shine.

Oh, and I long to see him sleep
    In my power utterly;
So I shall know what I have to keep. . . .
    I long to see
My love, that spinning coin, laid still
    And plain at the side of me
For me to reckon—for surely he will
    Be wealth of life to me.

And then he will be mine, he will lie
    Revealed to me;
Patent and open beneath my eye
    He will sleep of me;
He will lie negligent, resign
    His truth to me, and I
Shall watch the dawn light up for me
    This fate of mine.

And as I watch the wan light shine
    On his sleep that is filled of me,
On his brow where the curved wisps clot and twine
    Carelessly,
On his lips where the light breaths come and go
    Unconsciously,
On his limbs in sleep at last laid low
    Helplessly,
I shall weep, oh, I shall weep, I know
    For joy or for misery.

VIOLETS

Sister, tha knows while we was on th' planks
    Aside o' t' grave, an' th' coffin set
On th' yaller clay, wi' th' white flowers top of it
    Waitin' ter be buried out o' th' wet?

An' t' parson makin' haste, an' a' t' black
    Huddlin' up i' t' rain,
Did t' 'appen ter notice a bit of a lass way back
    Hoverin', lookin' poor an' plain?

    —How should I be lookin' round!
      An' me standin' there on th' plank,
      An' our Ted's coffin set on th' ground,
        Waitin' to be sank!

      I'd as much as I could do, to think
        Of 'im bein' gone
      That young, an' a' the fault of drink
        An' carryin's on!—

Let that be; 'appen it worna th' drink, neither,
Nor th' carryin' on as killed 'im.
                —No, 'appen not,
My sirs! But I say 'twas! For a blither
Lad never stepped, till 'e got in with your lot.—

All right, all right, it's my fault! But let
Me tell about that lass. When you'd all gone
Ah stopped behind on t' pad, i' t' pourin' wet
An' watched what 'er 'ad on.

Tha should ha' seed 'er slive up when yer'd gone!
Tha should ha' seed 'er kneel an' look in
At th' sloppy grave! an' 'er little neck shone
That white, an' 'er cried that much, I'd like to begin

Scraightin' mysen as well. 'Er undid 'er black
Jacket at th' bosom, an' took out
Over a double 'andful o' violets, a' in a pack
An' white an' blue in a ravel, like a clout.

An' warm, for th' smell come waftin' to me. 'Er put 'er face
Right in 'em, an' scraighted a bit again,
Then after a bit 'er dropped 'em down that place,
An' I come away, acause o' th' teemin' rain.

But I thowt ter mysen, as that wor th' only bit
O' warmth as 'e got down theer; th' rest wor stone cold.
From that bit of a wench's bosom; 'e'd be glad of it,
Gladder nor of thy lilies, if tha maun be told.

LIGHTNING

I felt the lurch and halt of her heart
   Next my breast, where my own heart was beating;
And I laughed to feel it plunge and bound,
And strange in my blood-swept ears was the sound
   Of the words I kept repeating,
Repeating with tightened arms, and the hot blood's blind-
 fold art.

Her breath flew warm against my neck,
   Warm as a flame in the close night air;

And the sense of her clinging flesh was sweet
Where her arms and my neck's thick pulse could meet.
   Holding her thus, could I care
That the black night hid her from me, blotted out every
 speck?

I leaned in the darkness to find her lips
   And claim her utterly in a kiss,
When the lightning flew across her face
And I saw her for the flaring space
   Of a second, like snow that slips
From a roof, inert with death, weeping "Not this! Not
 this!"

A moment there, like snow in the dark
   Her face lay pale against my breast,
Pale love lost in a thaw of fear
And melted in an icy tear,
   And open lips, distressed;
A moment; then darkness shut the lid of the sacred ark.

And I heard the thunder, and felt the rain,
   And my arms fell loose, and I was dumb.
Almost I hated her, sacrificed;
Hated myself, and the place, and the iced
   Rain that burnt on my rage; saying: Come
Home, come home, the lightning has made it too plain!

END OF ANOTHER HOME HOLIDAY

When shall I see the half-moon sink again
Behind the black sycamore at the end of the garden?
When will the scent of the dim white phlox
Creep up the wall to me, and in at my open window?

Why is it, the long, slow stroke of the midnight bell
    (Will it never finish the twelve?)
Falls again and again on my heart with a heavy reproach?

The moon-mist is over the village, out of the mist speaks the bell,
And all the little roofs of the village bow low, pitiful, beseeching,
    resigned.
—Speak, you my home! what is it I don't do well?

Ah home, suddenly I love you
As I hear the sharp clean trot of a pony down the road,
Succeeding sharp little sounds dropping into silence
Clear upon the long-drawn hoarseness of a train across the valley.

    .   .   .   .   .   .

The light has gone out, from under my mother's door.
    That she should love me so!—
    She, so lonely, greying now!
    And I leaving her,
    Bent on my pursuits!

      Love is the great Asker.
      The sun and the rain do not ask the secret
      Of the time when the grain struggles down in the dark.
      The moon walks her lonely way without anguish,
      Because no-one grieves over her departure.

Forever, ever by my shoulder pitiful love will linger,
Crouching as little houses crouch under the mist when I turn.
Forever, out of the mist, the church lifts up a reproachful finger,
Pointing my eyes in wretched defiance where love hides her face
    to mourn.

      Oh! but the rain creeps down to wet the grain
      That struggles alone in the dark,
      And asking nothing, patiently steals back again!
      The moon sets forth o' nights
      To walk the lonely, dusky heights
      Serenely, with steps unswerving;
      Pursued by no sigh of bereavement,

No tears of love unnerving
Her constant tread:
While ever at my side,
Frail and sad, with grey, bowed head,
The beggar-woman, the yearning-eyed
Inexorable love goes lagging.

The wild young heifer, glancing distraught,
With a strange new knocking of life at her side
    Runs seeking a loneliness.
The little grain draws down the earth, to hide.
Nay, even the slumberous egg, as it labours under the shell
    Patiently to divide and self-divide,
Asks to be hidden, and wishes nothing to tell.

But when I draw the scanty cloak of silence over my eyes
Piteous love comes peering under the hood;
Touches the clasp with trembling fingers, and tries
To put her ear to the painful sob of my blood;
While her tears soak through to my breast,
    Where they burn and cauterise.

.   .   .   .   .   .

The moon lies back and reddens.
In the valley a corncrake calls
    Monotonously,
With a plaintive, unalterable voice, that deadens
    My confident activity;
With a hoarse, insistent request that falls
    Unweariedly, unweariedly,
        Asking something more of me,
            Yet more of me.

BABY RUNNING BAREFOOT

When the white feet of the baby beat across the grass
The little white feet nod like white flowers in a wind,
They poise and run like puffs of wind that pass
Over water where the weeds are thinned.

And the sight of their white playing in the grass
Is winsome as a robin's song, so fluttering;
Or like two butterflies that settle on a glass
Cup for a moment, soft little wing-beats uttering.

And I wish that the baby would tack across here to me
Like a wind-shadow running on a pond, so she could stand
With two little bare white feet upon my knee
And I could feel her feet in either hand

Cool as syringa buds in morning hours,
Or firm and silken as young peony flowers.

SIGH NO MORE

The cuckoo and the coo-dove's ceaseless calling,
        Calling,
Of a meaningless monotony is palling
All my morning's pleasure in the sun-fleck-scattered wood.

May-blossom and blue bird's-eye flowers falling,
        Falling
In a litter through the elm-tree shade are scrawling
Messages of true-love down the dust of the highroad.

I do not like to hear the gentle grieving,
        Grieving
Of the she-dove in the blossom, still believing
Love will yet again return to her and make all good.

When I know that there must ever be deceiving,
        Deceiving
Of the mournful constant heart, that while she's weaving
Her woes, her lover woos and sings within another wood.

Oh, boisterous the cuckoo shouts, forestalling,
        Stalling
A progress down the intricate enthralling
By-paths where the wanton-headed flowers doff their hood.

And like a laughter leads me onward, heaving,
    Heaving
A sigh among the shadows, thus retrieving
A decent short regret for that which once was very good.

GUARDS

A REVIEW IN HYDE PARK, 1910: THE CROWD WATCHES

Where the trees rise like cliffs, proud and blue-tinted in the distance,
Between the cliffs of the trees, on the grey-green park
Rests a still line of soldiers, red, motionless range of guards
Smouldering with darkened busbies beneath the bayonets' slant rain.

Colossal in nearness a blue police sits still on his horse
Guarding the path; his hand relaxed at his thigh,
And skywards his face is immobile, eyelids aslant
In tedium, and mouth relaxed as if smiling—ineffable tedium!

So! So! Gaily a general canters across the space,
With white plumes blinking under the evening grey sky.
And suddenly, as if the ground moved,
The red range heaves in slow, magnetic reply.

EVOLUTIONS OF SOLDIERS

The red range heaves and compulsory sways, ah see! in the flush
    of a march.
Softly-impulsive advancing as water towards a weir from the arch
Of shadow emerging as blood emerges from inward shades of our
    night
Encroaching towards a crisis, a meeting, a spasm and throb of delight.

The wave of soldiers, the coming wave, the throbbing red breast of
    approach
Upon us; dark eyes as here beneath the busbies glittering, dark
    threats that broach
Our beached vessel; darkened rencontre inhuman, and closed warm
    lips, and dark
Mouth-hair of soldiers passing above us, over the wreck of our bark.

And so, it is ebb-time, they turn, the eyes beneath the busbies are
    gone.
But the blood has suspended its timbre, the heart from out of oblivion
Knows but the retreat of the burning shoulders, the red-swift waves
    of the sweet
Fire horizontal declining and ebbing, the twilit ebb of retreat.

AWARE

Slowly the moon is rising out of the ruddy haze,
Divesting herself of her golden shift, and so
Emerging white and exquisite; and I in amaze
See in the sky before me, a woman I did not know
I loved, but there she goes, and her beauty hurts my heart;
I follow her down the night, begging her not to depart.

A PANG OF REMINISCENCE

High and smaller goes the moon, she is small and very far from me,
Wistful and candid, watching me wistfully from her distance, and
    I see
Trembling blue in her pallor a tear that surely I have seen before,
A tear which I had hoped that even hell held not again in store.

A WHITE BLOSSOM

A tiny moon as small and white as a single jasmine flower
Leans all alone above my window, on night's wintry bower,
Liquid as lime-tree blossom, soft as brilliant water or rain
She shines, the first white love of my youth, passionless and in vain.

COROT

The trees rise taller and taller, lifted
On a subtle rush of cool grey flame
That issuing out of the east has sifted
    The spirit from each leaf's frame.

For the trailing, leisurely rapture of life
Drifts dimly forward, easily hidden
By bright leaves uttered aloud; and strife
    Of shapes by a hard wind ridden.

The grey, plasm-limpid, pellucid advance
Of the luminous purpose of Life shines out
Where lofty trees athwart-stream chance
    To shake flakes of its shadow about.

The subtle, steady rush of the whole
Grey foam-mist of advancing Time
As it silently sweeps to its somewhere, its goal,
    Is seen in the gossamer's rime.

Is heard in the windless whisper of leaves,
In the silent labours of men in the field,
In the downward-dropping of flimsy sheaves
    Of cloud the rain-skies yield.

In the tapping haste of a fallen leaf,
In the flapping of red-roof smoke, and the small
Footstepping tap of men beneath
    Dim trees so huge and tall.

For what can all sharp-rimmed substance but catch
In a backward ripple, the wave-length, reveal
For a moment the mighty direction, snatch
    A spark beneath the wheel!

Since Life sweeps whirling, dim and vast,
Creating the channelled vein of man
And leaf for its passage; a shadow cast
    And gone before we can scan.

Ah listen, for silence is not lonely!
Imitate the magnificent trees
That speak no word of their rapture, but only
    Breathe largely the luminous breeze.

MICHAEL ANGELO

Who shook thy roundness in his finger's cup?
Who sunk his hands in firmness down thy sides
And drew the circle of his grasp, O man,
Along thy limbs delighted as a bride's?

How wert thou so strange-shapen? What warm finger
Curved thy mouth for thee? and what strong shoulder
Planted thee upright? art proud to see
In the curves of thy form the trace of the unknown
    moulder?

Who took a handful of light and rolled a ball,
Compressed it till its beam grew wondrous dark,
Then gave thee thy dark eyes, O man! that all
The rest had doorway to thee through that spark?

Who, crouching, put his mouth down in a kiss
And kissed thee to a passion of life, and left
Life in thy mouth, and dim breath's hastening hiss?
Whence cometh this, that thou must guard from theft?

Whence cometh, whither goeth? still the same
Old question without answer! Strange and fain
Life comes to thee, on which thou hast no claim;
Then leaves thee, and thou canst not but complain!

HYDE PARK AT NIGHT, BEFORE
THE WAR

CLERKS

We have shut the doors behind us, and the velvet flowers of night
Lean about us scattering their pollen grains of golden light.

Now at last we lift our faces, and our faces come aflower
To the night that takes us willing, liberates us to the hour.

Now at last the ink and dudgeon passes from our fervent eyes
And out of the chambered wilderness wanders a spirit abroad on its
    enterprise.

       Not too near and not too far
       Out of the stress of the crowd
       Music screams as elephants scream
       When they lift their trunks and scream aloud
       For joy of the night when masters are
          Asleep and adream.

       So here I hide in the Shalimar
       With a wanton princess slender and proud,
       And we swoon with kisses, swoon till we seem
       Two streaming peacocks gone in a cloud
       Of golden dust, with star after star
          On our stream.

PICCADILLY CIRCUS AT NIGHT

STREET-WALKERS

When into the night the yellow light is roused like dust
    above the towns,
Or like a mist the moon has kissed from off a pool in the
    midst of the downs,

Our faces flower for a little hour pale and uncertain along
    the street,
Daisies that waken all mistaken white-spread in expectancy
    to meet

The luminous mist which the poor things wist was dawn
    arriving across the sky,
When dawn is far behind the star the dust-lit town has
    driven so high.

All the birds are folded in a silent ball of sleep,
    All the flowers are faded from the asphalt isle in the sea,
Only we hard-faced creatures go round and round, and keep
    The shores of this innermost ocean alive and illusory.

Wanton sparrows that twittered when morning looked in
    at their eyes
    And the Cyprian's pavement-roses are gone, and now
    it is we
Flowers of illusion who shine in our gauds, make a Paradise
    On the shores of this ceaseless ocean, gay birds of the
    town-dark sea.

AFTER THE OPERA

Down the stone stairs
Girls with their large eyes wide with tragedy
Lift looks of shocked and momentous emotion up at me.
And I smile.

Ladies
Stepping like birds with their bright and pointed feet
Peer anxiously forth, as if for a boat to carry them out of
    the wreckage;
And among the wreck of the theatre crowd
I stand and smile.
They take tragedy so becomingly;
Which pleases me.

71

But when I meet the weary eyes
The reddened, aching eyes of the bar-man with thin arms,
I am glad to go back to where I came from.

MORNING WORK

A gang of labourers on the piled wet timber
That shines blood-red beside the railway siding
Seem to be making out of the blue of the morning
Something faery and fine, the shuttles sliding,

The red-gold spools of their hands and their faces swinging
Hither and thither across the high crystalline frame
Of day: trolls at the cave of ringing cerulean mining
And laughing with labour, living their work like a game.

TRANSFORMATIONS

I *THE TOWN*

Oh you stiff shapes, swift transformation seethes
About you; only last night you were
A Sodom smouldering in the dense, soiled air:
To-day a thicket of sunshine with blue smoke-wreaths.

To-morrow swimming in evening's vague, dim vapour
Like a weeded city in shadow under the sea,
Below the ocean of shimmering light you will be:
Then a group of toadstools waiting the moon's white taper.

And when I awake in the morning, after rain,
To find the new houses a cluster of lilies glittering
In scarlet, alive with the birds' bright twittering,
I'll say your bond of ugliness is vain.

II THE EARTH

Oh Earth, you spinning clod of earth.
And then you lamp, you lemon-coloured beauty!
Oh Earth, you rotten apple rolling downward;
Then brilliant Earth, from the burr of night in beauty
As a jewel-brown horse-chestnut newly issued!

You are all these, and on me lies the duty
To see you all, sordid or radiant-tissued.

III MEN

Oh labourers, oh shuttles across the blue frame of morning!
You feet of the rainbow balancing the sky!
Oh you who flash your arms like rockets to heaven,
Who in lassitude lean as yachts on the sea-wind lie!

Who crowd in crowds like rhododendrons in blossom,
Who stand alone in despair like a guttering light;
Who grappling down with work or hate or passion
Take writhing forms of all beasts that sweat and that fight;
You who are twisted in grief like crumpling beech-leaves,
Who curl in sleep like kittens, who mass as a swarm
Of bees that vibrate with revolt; who fall to earth
And rot like a bean-pod; what are you, oh multiform?

A BABY ASLEEP AFTER PAIN

As a drenched, drowned bee
Hangs numb and heavy from a bending flower,
So clings to me
My baby, her brown hair brushed with wet tears
And laid against her cheek;
Her soft white legs hanging heavily over my arm
Swing to my walking movement, weak
With after-pain. My sleeping baby hangs upon my life
Like a burden she hangs on me;

She who has always seemed so light,
  Now wet with tears and pain hangs heavily,
  Even her floating hair sinks heavily
    Reaching downwards;
As the wings of a drenched, drowned bee
  Are a heaviness, and a weariness.

LAST LESSON OF THE AFTERNOON

When will the bell ring, and end this weariness?
How long have they tugged the leash, and strained apart,
My pack of unruly hounds! I cannot start
Them again on a quarry of knowledge they hate to hunt,
I can haul them and urge them no more.

No longer now can I endure the brunt
Of the books that lie out on the desks; a full threescore
Of several insults of blotted pages, and scrawl
Of slovenly work that they have offered me.
I am sick, and what on earth is the good of it all?
What good to them or me, I cannot see!

                              So, shall I take
My last dear fuel of life to heap on my soul
And kindle my will to a flame that shall consume
Their dross of indifference; and take the toll
Of their insults in punishment?—I will not!—

I will not waste my soul and my strength for this.
What do I care for all that they do amiss!
What is the point of this teaching of mine, and of this
Learning of theirs? It all goes down the same abyss.

What does it matter to me, if they can write
A description of a dog, or if they can't?
What is the point? To us both, it is all my aunt!
And yet I'm supposed to care, with all my might.

I do not, and will not; they won't and they don't;
    and that's all!
I shall keep my strength for myself; they can keep
    theirs as well.
Why should we beat our heads against the wall
Of each other? I shall sit and wait for the bell.

SCHOOL ON THE OUTSKIRTS

How different, in the midst of snow, the great school rises red!
    A red rock silent and shadowless, clung round with clusters of
      shouting lads,
Some few dark-cleaving the doorway, souls that cling as the souls
    of the dead
    In stupor persist at the gates of life, obstinate dark monads.

This new red rock in a waste of white rises against the day
    With shelter now, and with blandishment, since the winds have
      had their way
And laid the desert horrific of silence and snow on the world of
    mankind,
    School now is the rock in this weary land the winter burns and
      makes blind.

A SNOWY DAY IN SCHOOL

All the long school-hours, round the irregular hum of the class
Have pressed immeasurable spaces of hoarse silence
Muffling my mind, as snow muffles the sounds that pass
Down the soiled street. We have pattered the lessons
    ceaselessly—

But the faces of the boys, in the brooding, yellow light
Have been for me like a dazed constellation of stars,
Like half-blown flowers dimly shaking at the night,
Like half-seen froth on an ebbing shore in the moon.

Out of each face, strange, dark beams that disquiet;
In the open depths of each flower, dark, restless drops;
Twin-bubbling challenge and mystery, in the foam's
    whispering riot.
—How can I answer the challenge of so many eyes?

The thick snow is crumpled on the roof, it plunges down
Awfully!—Must I call back a hundred eyes?—A voice
Falters a statement about an abstract noun—
What was my question?—My God, must I break this
    hoarse

Silence that rustles beyond the stars?—There!—
I have startled a hundred eyes, and now I must look
Them an answer back; it is more than I can bear.

The snow descends as if the slow sky shook
In flakes of shadow down; while through the gap
Between the schools sweeps one black rook.

In the playground, a shaggy snowball stands huge and still
With fair flakes lighting down on it. Beyond, the town
Is lost in this shadowed silence the skies distil.

And all things are in silence, they can brood
Alone within the dim and hoarse silence.
Only I and the class must wrangle; this work is a bitter rood!

WHETHER OR NOT

I

Dunna thee tell me it's his'n, mother,
    Dunna thee, dunna thee!
—Oh ay, he'll come an' tell thee his-sèn,
    Wench, wunna he?

Tha doesna mean ter say ter me, mother,
    He's gone wi' that—
—My gel, owt'll do for a man i' th' dark;
    Tha's got it flat!

But 'er's old, mother, 'er's twenty year
    Older nor him—
—Ay, an' yaller as a crowflower; an' yet i' th' dark
    Er'd do for Tim.

Tha niver believes it, does ter, mother?
    It's somebody's lies.
—Ax 'im thy-sèn, wench; a widder's lodger!
    It's no surprise.

I I

A widow o' forty-five
Wi' a bitter, dirty skin,
To ha' 'ticed a lad o' twenty-five,
An' 'im to 'ave been took in!

A widow of forty-five
As 'as sludged like a horse all 'er life
Till 'er's tough as whit-leather, to slive
Atween a lad an' 'is wife!

A widow of forty-five!
A glum old otchel, wi' long
Witch teeth, an' 'er black hawk-eyes, as I've
Mistrusted all along!

An' me as 'as kep' my-sèn
Shut like a daisy bud,
Clean an' new an' nice, so's when
He wed he'd ha'e summat good!

An' 'im as nice an' fresh
As any man i' th' force,
To ha' gone an' given his clean young flesh
To a woman that coarse!

III

You're stout to brave this snow, Miss Stainwright,
    Are you makin' Brinsley way?
—I'm off up th' line to Underwood
    Wi' a dress as is wanted to-day.

Oh, are you goin' to Underwood?
    'Appen then you've 'eered!
—What's that as 'appen I've 'eered on, Missis?
    Speak up, you nedn't be feared.

Why, your young man an' Widow Naylor,
    'Er as 'e lodges wi'!
They say he's got 'er wi' childt; but there
    It's nothing to do wi' me!

Though if it's true, they'll turn 'im out
    O' th' p'lice force, without fail;
An' if it's *not* true, you may back your life
    They'll listen to *her* tale.

—Well, I'm believin' no tale, Missis,
    I'm seein' for my-sèn.
An' when I know for sure, Missis,
    I'll talk *then*.

IV

Nay, robin red-breast, tha nedna
    Sit noddin' thy head at me!
My breast's as red as thine, I reckon,
    Flayed red, if tha could but see.

Nay, yo' blessed pee-whips,
    Yo' nedna scraight at me!
I'm scraightin' my-sèn, but arena goin'
    Ter let iv'rybody see.

Tha *art* smock-ravelled, bunny,
    Larropin' neck an' crop
I' th' snow! but I's warrant thee
    I'm further ower th' top.

V

Now sithee theer at th' reelroad crossin'
Warmin' 'is-sèn at the stool o' fire
Under th' tank as fills th' ingines,
If there isn't my dearly-beloved liar!

My constable, wi' 'is buttoned breast
As stout as the truth, my Sirs! an' 'is face
As bold as a robin! It's much he cares
For this nice old shame an' disgrace.

Oh, but 'e drops 'is flag when 'e sees me!
Yi, an' 'is face goes white! Oh yes,
Tha can stare at me wi' thy fierce blue eyes;
Tha won't stare me out, I guess.

VI

Whativer brings thee out so far
    In a' this depth o' snow?
—I'm takin' 'ome a weddin'-dress,
    If yer mun know.

Why, is there a weddin' at Underwood
    As tha ne'd trudge up 'ere?
—It's Widder Naylor's weddin'-dress,
    'Er'll be wantin' it, I 'ear.

'Er doesna want no weddin'-dress—
    Why—? but what dost mean?
—Doesn't ter know what I mean, Timmy?
    Yi, tha must ha' bin 'ard ter wean!

Tha'rt a good-un at suckin'-in yet, Timmy!
    But tell me, isn't it true
As 'er'll be wantin' my weddin'-dress
    In a wik or two?

—Tha's no 'casions ter ha'e me on,
    Lizzie; what's done is done.
—Done, I should think so! An' might I ask
    When tha begun?

It's thee as 'as done it, as much as me,
    So there, an' I tell thee flat.
—Me gotten a childt ter thy landlady?
    —Tha's gotten thy answer pat.

As tha allus 'ast; but let me tell thee
    Hasna ter sent me whoam, when I
Was a'most burstin' mad o' my-sèn,
    An' walkin' in agony?

After I'd kissed thee at night, Lizzie,
    An' tha's laid against me, an' melted
Into me, melted right into me, Lizzie,
    Till I was verily swelted.

An' if my landlady seed me like it,
    An' if 'er clawkin' eyes
Went through me as the light went out,
    Is it any cause for surprise?

—No cause for surprise at all, my lad;
    After kissin' an' cuddlin' wi' me, tha could
Turn thy mouth on a woman like that!
    I hope it did thee good.

—Ay, it did; but afterwards
    I could ha' killed 'er.
—Afterwards! how many times afterwards
    Could ter ha' killed 'er?

Say no more, Liz, dunna thee;
    'Er's as good as thee.
—Then I'll say good-bye to thee, Timothy;
    Take 'er i'stead o' me.

I'll ta'e thy word good-bye, Liz,
    Though I shonna marry 'er.
Nor 'er nor nub'dy.—It is
    Very brave of you, Sir!

—T' childt maun ta'e its luck, it mun,
    An' 'er maun ta'e 'er luck.
F'r I tell yer I h'arena marryin' none
    On yer; yo'n got what yer took!

—That's spoken like a man, Timmy,
    That's spoken like a man!
" 'E up an' fired 'is pistol,
    An' then away 'e ran!"

—I damn well shanna marry 'er,
    Nor yo', so chew it no more!
I'll chuck the flamin' lot o' you—
    —Yer nedn't 'ave swore!

VII

There's 'is collar round th' candlestick,
An' there's the dark-blue tie I bought 'im!
An' these is the woman's kids 'e's so fond on,
An' 'ere comes the cat as caught 'im!

I dunno wheer 'is eyes was—a gret
Round-shouldered hag! My Sirs, to think
Of 'im stoopin' to 'er! You'd wonder 'e could
Throw 'imself down *that* sink!

I expect yer know who I am, Mrs. Naylor?
    —Who y'are? yis, you're Lizzie Stainwright.
An' 'appen you'd guess then what I've come for?
    —'Appen I mightn't, 'appen I might.

Yer knowed as I was courtin' Tim Merfin?
    —Yis, I knowed 'e wor courtin' thee.
An' yet yer've bin carryin' on wi' 'im!
    —Ay, an' 'im wi' me.

Well, now yer've got ter pay for it.
    —If I han, what's that ter thee?
'E isn't goin' ter marry yer.
    —Tha wants 'im thy-sèn, I see.

It 'asn't nothin' to do with me.
 —Then what art colleyfoglin' for?
I'm not 'avin' your orts an' slarts.
 —Which on us said you wor?

But I want you to know 'e's not *marryin'* you.
 —Tha wants 'im thy-sèn too bad.
Though I'll see as 'e pays you, an' does what's rig]
 —Tha'rt for doin' a lot wi' t' lad!

VIII

To think I should 'ave ter 'affle an' caffle
 Wi' a woman, an' name 'er a price
For lettin' me marry the lad as I thought
 Ter marry wi' cabs an' rice!

But we'll go unbeknown ter th' registrar,
 An' give *'er* the money there is;
For I won't be beholden to such as 'er,
 I won't, or my name's not Liz.

IX

Ta'e off thy duty stripes, Tim,
 An' come in 'ere wi' me;
Ta'e off thy p'liceman's helmet
 An' look at me.

I wish tha hadna done it, Tim,
 I do, an' that I do!
For whenever I look thee i' th' face, I s'll see
 Her face too.

I wish I could wesh 'er off'n thee;
 'Appen I can, if I try.
But tha'll ha'e ter promise ter be true ter me
 Till I die. . . .

X

Twenty pound o' thy own tha hast, an' fifty pound ha'e I;
Thine shall go ter pay the woman, an' wi' my bit we'll buy
All as we s'll want for furniture when tha leaves this place;
An' we'll be married at th' registrar—now lift thy face!

Lift thy face an' look at me, man! canna ter look at me?
Sorry I am for this business, an' sorry if ever I've driven thee
To do such a thing; though it's a poor tale, it is, that I'm bound to say,
Afore I can ta'e thee I've got a widder o' forty-five ter pay!

Dunnat thee think but what I've loved thee; I've loved thee too well.
An' 'deed an' I wish as this tale o' thine wor niver my tale to tell!
Deed an' I wish I c'd 'a' stood at th' altar wi' thee an' bin proud o'
    thee!
That I could 'a' bin first woman ter thee, as tha'rt first man ter me!

But we maun ma'e the best on't. So now rouse up an' look at me.
Look up an' say tha'rt sorry tha did it; say tha'rt sorry for me.
They'll turn thee out o' th' force, I doubt me; if they do, we can see
If my father can get thee a job on t' bank. Say tha'rt sorry, Timmy!

X I

Ay, I'm sorry, I'm sorry,
    But what o' that!
Ay, I'm sorry! Tha nedna worry
    Nor fret thy fat.

I'm sorry for thee, I'm sorry f'r 'er,
    I'm sorry f'r us a'.
But what then? Tha wants me, does ter
    After a'?

Ah'n put my-sèn i' th' wrong, Liz,
    An' 'er as well.
An' tha'rt that right, tha knows; 'tis
    Other folks in hell.

Tha *art* so sure tha'rt right, Liz!
 That damned sure!
But 'ark thee 'ere, that widder woman
 's less graspin', if 'er's poor.

What 'er gen, 'er gen me
 Beout a thought.
'Er gen me summat; I shanna
 Say it wor nought.

I'm sorry for th' trouble, ay
 As comes on us a'.
But sorry for what I had? why
 I'm not, that's a'.

As for marryin', I shanna marry
 Neither on yer.
Ah've 'ad a' as I can carry
 From you an' from 'er.

So I s'll go an' leave yer,
 Both on yer.
I don't like yer, Liz, I want ter
 Get away from yer.

An' I really like 'er neither,
 Even though I've 'ad
More from 'er than from you; but either
 Of yer's too much for this lad.

Let me go! what's good o' talkin'?
 Let's a' ha' done.
Talk about love o' women!
 Ter me it's no fun.

What bit o' cunt I had wi' 'er
 's all I got out of it.
An' 's not good enough, it isn't
 For a permanent fit.

I'll say good-bye, Liz, to yer,
     Yer too much i' th' right for me.
An' wi' 'er somehow it isn't right.
     So good-bye, an' let's let be!

A WINTER'S TALE

Yesterday the fields were only grey with scattered snow,
And now the longest grass-leaves hardly emerge;
Yet her deep footsteps mark the snow, and go
On towards the pines at the hill's white verge.

I cannot see her, since the mist's pale scarf
Obscures the dark wood and the dull orange sky;
But she's waiting, I know, impatient and cold, half
Sobs struggling into her frosty sigh.

Why does she come so promptly, when she must know
She's only the nearer to the inevitable farewell?
The hill is steep, on the snow my steps are slow—
Why does she come, when she knows what I have to tell?

RETURN

Now I am come again, to you who have so desired
My coming, why do you look away from me?
Why burns your cheek against me? how have I inspired
Such anger as sets your mouth unwontedly?

Now here I sit while you break the music beneath
Your bow; for broken it is, and hurting to hear.
Cease then from music! Does anguish of absence bequeath
But barbed aloofness when I would draw near?

THE APPEAL

You, Helen, who see the stars
As mistletoe berries burning in a black tree,
You surely, seeing I am a bowl of kisses
Should put your mouth to mine and drink of me.

Helen, you let my kisses steam
Wasteful into the night's black nostrils; drink
Me up, I pray; oh you, who are Night's bacchante,
How can you from my bowl of kisses shrink?

LILIES IN THE FIRE

I

Ah, you stack of white lilies, all white and gold!
I am adrift as a moonbeam, and without form
Or substance, save I light on you to warm
Your pallor into radiance, flush your cold

White petals incandescent: so that you
Are not a stack of white lilies now, but a white
And clustered star called down to me to-night,
Lighting these autumn leaves like a star dropped through

The slender bare arms of the branches, your tire-maidens
Who lift swart arms to fend me off; but I come
Upon you as an autumn wind on some
Stray whitebeam, and her white fire all unladens.

So now you're a glistening toadstool shining here
Among the crumpled beech-leaves, phosphorescent,
My stack of lilies once white incandescent,
My fallen star among the leaves, my dear!

II

Is it with pain, my dear, that you shudder so?
Is it because I hurt you with pain, my dear?

> Did I shiver? Nay, truly I do not know.
> Some dewdrop maybe splashed my face down here.

Why even now you speak through close-shut teeth.
Was this too much for you?

> Nay, dear, be still!
> The earth perhaps is chilly underneath
> The leaves—and, dear, you have had your will.

You hold yourself all hard, as if my kisses
Hurt as I gave them; you put me away—

> Nay, never, I put you away: yet each kiss hisses
> Like soft hot ashes on my helpless clay.

III

I am ashamed, you wanted me not to-night.
And it is always so, you sigh against me.
Your brightness dims when I draw too near, and my free
Fire enters you like frost, like a cruel blight.

And now I know, so I must be ashamed;
You love me while I hover tenderly
Like moonbeams kissing you; but the body of me
Closing upon you in the lightning-flamed

Moment, destroys you, you are just destroyed.
Humiliation deep to me, that all my best
Soul's naked lightning, which should sure attest
God stepping through our loins in one bright stride

Means but to you a burden of dead flesh
Heavy to bear, even heavy to uprear
Again from earth, like lilies flagged and sere
Upon the floor, that erst stood up so fresh.

RED MOON-RISE

The train, in running across the weald, has fallen into a steadier
    stroke,
So even, it beats like silence, and sky and earth in one unbroke
Embrace of darkness lie around, and crushed between them, all the
    loose
And littered lettering of trees and hills and houses closed, and we
    can use
The open book of landscape no more, for the covers of darkness have
    shut upon
Its figured pages, and sky and earth and all between are closed in
    one.

And we are crushed between the covers, we close our eyes and say
    "Hush!" We try
To escape in sleep the terror of this great bivalve darkness, and we
    lie
Rounded like pearls, for sleep.—And then, from between shut lips of
    the darkness, red
As if from the womb the slow moon rises, as if the twin-walled dark-
    ness had bled
In a new night-spasm of birth, and given us this new red moon-rise
Which lies on the knees of the night-time ruddy, and makes us hide
    our eyes.

The train beats frantic in haste, and struggles away
From this rosy terror of birth that has slid down
From out of the loins of night, to glow in our way
Like a portent; but, Lord, I am glad, so glad, I drown
My fear in accepting the portent. The train can now
Not pass the red moon risen, and I am glad,
Glad as the Magi were when they saw the brow
Of the hot-born infant bless the folly which had
Led them thither to peace;
                    for now I know
The world within worlds is a womb, whence issues all
The shapeliness that decks us here-below:

And the same fire that boils within this ball
Of earth, and quickens all herself with flowers,
Is womb-fire in the stiffened clay of us:

And every flash of thought that we and ours
Send suddenly out, and every gesture, does
Fly like a spark into the womb of passion,
To start a birth, from joy of the begetting.

World within worlds a womb, that gives and takes;
Gives us all forth, that we may give again
The seed of life incarnate, that falls and wakes
Within the womb, new shapes, and then, new men.

And pangs of birth, and joy of the begetting,
And sweat of labour, and the meanest fashion
Of fretting or of gladness, shows the jetting
Of a trail of our small fire on the darkened sky
Where we can see it, our fire to the innermost fire
Leaping like spray, in the return of passion.

And even in the watery shells that lie
Alive within the oozy under-mire,
A grain of this same fire we can descry
Spurting to soothe the womb's unslaked desire.

And so, from out the screaming birds that fly
Across the heavens when the storm leaps higher,
And from the swirling, angry folk that try
To come at last to that which they require,
And from the men that dance, and the girls that laugh,
And the flower that puts its tongue out, and fern that puffs
Dust as the puff-ball does, and birds that chaff
And chitter, and wind that shakes and cuffs
The branches, invisible seed of experience blows
Into the womb of the worlds, that nothing knows.

And though it be love's wet blue eyes that cry
To the other love, to relinquish his desire,
Even there I see a blue spark that will fly
Into the womb, to kindle an unknown fire.

SCENT OF IRISES

A faint, sickening scent of irises
Persists all morning. Here in a jar on the table
A fine proud spike of purple irises
Rising up in the class-room litter, makes me unable
To see the class's lifted and bended faces
Save in a broken pattern, amid purple and gold and sable.

I can smell the bog-end, gorgeous in its breathless
Dazzle of may-blobs, where the marigold glare overcast you
With fire on your cheeks and your brow and your chin as you dipped
Your face in the marigold bunch, to touch and contrast you,
Your own dark mouth with the bridal faint lady-smocks,
And the kingcups' glisten, that shall long outlast you.

You amid the bog-end's yellow incantation,
You sitting in the cowslips of the meadow above,
Me, your shadow on the bog-flame flowery may-blobs,
Me full length in the cowslips, muttering you love;
You, your soul like a lady-smock, lost, evanescent,
You with your face all rich, like the sheen on a dove!

You are always asking, do I remember, remember
The buttercup bog-end where the flowers rose up
And glazed you over with a sheen of gold?
You ask me, do the healing days close up
The gulf that came between us, and drew us in?
Do they wipe away the gloom the gulf throws up?

You upon the dry, dead beech-leaves, once more, only once
Taken like a sacrifice, in the night invisible;
Only the darkness, and the scent of you!—
And yes, thank God, it still is possible
The healing days shall close the dark gulf up
Wherein we fainted like a smoke or dew!

Like vapour, dew, or poison! Now, thank God
The last year's fire is gone, and your face is ash;
And the gulf that came between you, woman, and me, man,
That day, is half grown over, it need not abash
Either of us any more; henceforth we can
Forget each other and the bruise of our bodies' clash.

FORECAST

Patience, little Heart!
One day a heavy-breasted, June-hot woman
Will enter and shut the door, to stay.

And when your stifling soul would summon
Cool, lonely night, her breasts will keep the night at bay,
Leaning in your room like two tiger-lilies, curving
Their pale-gold petals back with steady will,
Killing the blue dusk with harsh scent, unnerving
Your body with their nipple-thrust, until
You thirst for coolness with a husky thirst.

And then you will remember, for the first
Time with true longing, what I was to you.
Like a wild daffodil down-dreaming,
And waiting through the blue
Chill dusk for you, and gladly gleaming
Like a little light at your feet.

Patience, little Heart! I shall be sweet
In after years, in memory, to you.

PROPHET

Ah, my darling, when over the purple horizon shall loom
The shrouded mother of a new idea, men hide their faces,
Cry out and fend her off, as she seeks her procreant groom,
Wounding themselves against her, denying her fecund
    embraces.

DISCIPLINE

It is stormy, and raindrops cling like silver bees to the panes,
The thin sycamore in the playground is swinging with flattened
    leaves;
The heads of the boys move dimly through a yellow gloom that
    stains
The class; over them all the dark net of my discipline weaves.

It is no good, dear, gentleness and forbearance; I endured too long.
I have pushed my hands in the dark soil, under the flower of my
    soul
And the gentle leaves, and have felt where the roots are strong
Fixed in the darkness, grappling for the deep soil's crowded control.

And there in the dark, my darling, where the roots are entangled
    and fight
Each one for its hold on the concrete darkness, I know that there
In the night where we first have being, before we rise on the light,
We are not lovers, my darling, we fight and we do not spare.

And in the original dark the roots cannot keep, cannot know
Any communion whatever, but they bind themselves on to the dark,
And drawing the darkness together, crush from it a twilight, a slow
Dim self that rises slowly to leaves and the flower's gay spark.

I came to the boys with love, dear, and only they turned on me;
With gentleness came I, with my heart 'twixt my hands like a bowl,
Like a loving-cup, like a grail, but they spilt it triumphantly
And tried to break the vessel, and violate my soul.

And perhaps they were right, for the young are busy deep down at
    the roots,
And love would only weaken their under-earth grip, make shallow
Their hold on reality, enfeeble their rising shoots
With too much tincture of me, instead of the dark's deep fallow.

I thought that love would do all things, but now I know I am wrong.
There are depths below depths, my darling, where love does not
    belong.
Where the fight that is fight for being is fought throughout the long
Young years, and the old must not win, not even if they love and
    are strong.

I must not win their souls, no never, I only must win
The brief material control of the hour, leave them free of me.
Learn they must to obey, for all harmony is discipline,
And only in harmony with others the single soul can be free.

Let them live, the boys, and learn not to trespass; I had to learn
Not to trespass on them with love, they must learn not to trespass in
    the young
Cruel self; the fight is not for existence, the fight is to burn
At last into blossom of being, each one his own flower outflung.

They are here to learn but one lesson, that they shall not thwart
    each other
Nor be thwarted, in life's slow struggle to unfold the flower of the
    self.
They draw their sap from the Godhead, not from me, but they must
    not smother
The sun from their neighbour either, nor be smothered in turn by
    pelf.

I will teach them the beginning of the lesson at the roots, and then
    no more.
I throw from out of the darkness myself like a flower into sight
Of the day, but it's nothing to do with the boys, so let them ignore
What's beyond them, and fight with me in discipline's little fight.

But whoever would pluck apart my flowering will burn their hands,
For flowers are tender folk, and roots can only hide.
But sometimes the opening petals are fire, and the scarlet brands
Of the blossom are roses to look at, but flames when they're
    tried.

But now I am trodden to earth, and my fires are low;
Now I am broken down like a plant in winter, and all
Myself but a knowledge of roots, of roots in the dark, that throw
A net on the undersoil, that lies passive, and quickened with gall.

Yet wait awhile, for henceforth I will love when a blossom calls
To my blossom in perfume and seed-dust, and only then; I will give
My love where it is wanted. Yet wait awhile! My fall
Is complete for the moment, yet wait, and you'll see that my flower
    will live.

THE PUNISHER

I have fetched the tears up out of the little wells,
Scooped them up with small, iron words,
        Dripping over the runnels.

The harsh, cold wind of my words drove on, and still
I watched the tears on the guilty cheeks of the boys
        Glitter and spill.

Cringing Pity, and Love, white-handed, came
Hovering about the Judgment that stood in my eyes
        Whirling a flame.

.   .   .   .   .   .

The tears are dry, and the cheek's young fruits are fresh
With laughter, and clear the exonerated eyes, since pain
        Beat through the flesh.

The Angel of Judgment has departed again to the Nearness.
Desolate I am as a church whose lights are put out
        And doubt enters in drearness.

The fire rose up in the bush and blazed apace,
The thorn-leaves crackled and twisted and sweated in anguish;
        Then God left the place.

Like a flower that the frost has hugged and let go, my head
Is heavy, and my heart beats slowly, laboriously,
    My spirit is dead.

TEASE

I will give you all my keys,
    You shall be my châtelaine,
You shall enter as you please,
    As you please shall go again.

When I hear you jingling through
    All the chambers of my soul,
How I sit and laugh at you
    In your close housekeeping rôle!

Jealous of the smallest cover,
    Angry at the simplest door;
Well, you anxious, inquisitive lover,
    Are you pleased with what's in store?

You have fingered all my treasures,
    Have you not, most curiously,
Handled all my tools and measures
    And masculine machinery?

Over every single beauty
    You have had your little rapture;
You have slain, as was your duty,
    Every sin-mouse you could capture.

Still you are not satisfied!
    Still you tremble faint reproach!
Challenge me I keep aside
    Secrets that you may not broach.

Maybe yes, and maybe no;
    Maybe there *are* secret places,
Altars barbarous below,
    Elsewhere halls of high disgraces.

Maybe yes, and maybe no,
 You may have it as you please;
Since you are so keen to know
 Everything, Miss Ill-at-ease!

MYSTERY

Now I am all
One bowl of kisses,
Such as the tall
Slim votaresses
Of Egypt filled
For divine excesses.

I lift to you
My bowl of kisses,
And through the temple's
Blue recesses
Cry out to you
In wild caresses.

As to my lips'
Bright crimson rim
The passion slips;
And down my slim
White body drips
The moving hymn.

And still before
The altar, I
Exalt the bowl
Brimful, and cry
To you to stoop
And drink, Most High.

Ah, drink me up
That I may be
Within your cup
Like a mystery,
Like wine that is still
In ecstasy.

Glimmering still
In ecstasy
Commingled wines
Of you and me
In one fulfil
The mystery.

REPULSED

The last silk-floating thought has gone from the dandelion stem,
And the flesh of the stalk holds up for nothing a blank diadem.

So night's flood-winds have lifted my last desire from me,
And my hollow flesh stands up in the night like vanity.

As I stand on this hill, with the whitening cave of the city in front
And this Helen beside me, I am blank; being nothing, I bear the
    brunt

Of the nightly heavens overhead, like an immense, open eye,
Like a cat's distended pupil, that sparkles with little stars
As with thoughts that flash and crackle in far-off malignancy,
So distant, they cannot touch me, whom now nothing mars.

In front of me, yes, up the darkness, goes the gush of the lights of
    two towns,
As the breath which rushes upwards from the nostrils of an immense
Beast crouched across the globe, ready, if need be, to pounce
Across the space on the cat in heaven's hostile eminence.

All round me, above and below, the night's twin consciousness roars
With sounds that endlessly swell and sink like the storm of thought
    in the brain,
Lifting and falling, long gasps through the sluices, like silence that
    pours
Through invisible pulses, slowly, filling the night's dark vein.

The night is immense and awful, yet to me it is nothing at all.
Or rather 'tis I am nothing, here in the fur of the heather
Like an empty dandelion stalk, bereft of connection, small
And nakedly nothing 'twixt world and heaven, two creatures hostile
    together.

I in the fur of the world, alone; but this Helen close by!
How we hate one another to-night, hate, she and I
To numbness and nothingness; I dead, she refusing to die.
The female whose venom can more than kill, can numb and then
    nullify.

COLDNESS IN LOVE

And you remember, in the afternoon
The sea and the sky went grey, as if there had sunk
A flocculent dust on the floor of the world: the festoon
Of the sky sagged dusty as spider cloth,
And coldness clogged the sea, till it ceased to croon.

A dank, sickening scent came up from the grime
Of weed that blackened the shore, so that I recoiled
Feeling the raw cold dun me: and all the time
You leapt about on the slippery rocks, and threw
Me words that rang with a brassy, shallow chime.

And all day long, that raw and ancient cold
Deadened me through, till the grey downs dulled to sleep.
Then I longed for you with your mantle of love to fold
Me over, and drive from out of my body the deep
Cold that had sunk to my soul, and there kept hold.

But still to me all evening long you were cold,
And I was numb with a bitter, deathly ache;
Till old days drew me back into their fold,
And dim hopes crowded me warm with companionship,
And memories clustered me close, and sleep was cajoled.

And I slept till dawn at the window blew in like dust,
Like a linty, raw-cold dust disturbed from the floor
Of the unswept sea; a grey pale light like must
That settled upon my face and hands till it seemed
To flourish there, as pale mould blooms on a crust.

And I rose in fear, needing you fearfully.
For I thought you were warm as a sudden jet of blood.
I thought I could plunge in your living hotness, and be
Clean of the cold and the must. With my hand on the latch
I heard you in your sleep speak strangely to me.

And I dared not enter, feeling suddenly dismayed.
So I went and washed my deadened flesh in the sea
And came back tingling clean, but worn and frayed
With cold, like the shell of the moon; and strange it seems
That my love can dawn in warmth again, unafraid.

SUSPENSE

The wind comes from the north
Blowing little flocks of birds
Like spray across the town,
And a train roaring forth
Rushes stampeding down
South, with flying curds
Of steam, from the darkening north.

Whither I turn and set
Like a needle steadfastly,
Waiting ever to get
The news that she is free;
But ever fixed, as yet,
To the lode of her agony.

ENDLESS ANXIETY

The hoar-frost crumbles in the sun,
  The crisping steam of a train
Melts in the air, while two black birds
  Sweep past the window again.

Along the vacant road a red
  Telegram-bicycle approaches; I wait
In a thaw of anxiety, for the boy
  To leap down at our gate.

He has passed us by; but is it
  Relief that starts in my breast?
Or a deeper bruise of knowing that still
  She has no rest.

THE END

If I could have put you in my heart,
If but I could have wrapped you in myself
How glad I should have been!
And now the chart
Of memory unrolls again to me
The course of our journey here, here where we part.

And oh, that you had never, never been
Some of your selves, my love; that some
Of your several faces I had never seen!
And still they come before me, and they go;
And I cry aloud in the moments that intervene.

And oh, my love, as I rock for you to-night
And have not any longer any hope
To heal the suffering, or to make requite
For all your life of asking and despair,
I own that some of me is dead to-night.

THE BRIDE

My love looks like a girl to-night,
     But she is old.
The plaits that lie along her pillow
     Are not gold,
But threaded with filigree silver,
     And uncanny cold.

She looks like a young maiden, since her brow
     Is smooth and fair;
Her cheeks are very smooth, her eyes are closed,
     She sleeps a rare,
Still, winsome sleep, so still, and so composed.

Nay, but she sleeps like a bride, and dreams her dreams
     Of perfect things.
She lies at last, the darling, in the shape of her dream;
     And her dead mouth sings
By its shape, like thrushes in clear evenings.

THE VIRGIN MOTHER

My little love, my darling,
You were a doorway to me;
You let me out of the confines
Into this strange countrie
Where people are crowded like thistles,
Yet are shapely and comely to see.

My little love, my dearest,
Twice you have issued me,
Once from your womb, sweet mother,
Once from your soul, to be
Free of all hearts, my darling,
Of each heart's entrance free.

And so, my love, my mother,
I shall always be true to you.
Twice I am born, my dearest:
To life, and to death, in you;
And this is the life hereafter
Wherein I am true.

I kiss you good-bye, my darling,
Our ways are different now;
You are a seed in the night-time,
I am a man, to plough
The difficult glebe of the future
For seed to endow.

I kiss you good-bye, my dearest,
It is finished between us here.
Oh, if I were calm as you are,
Sweet and still on your bier!
Oh God, if I had not to leave you
Alone, my dear!

Is the last word now uttered?
Is the farewell said?
Spare me the strength to leave you
Now you are dead.
I must go, but my soul lies helpless
Beside your bed.

AT THE WINDOW

The pine-trees bend to listen to the autumn wind as it mutters
Something which sets the black poplars ashake with hysterical
      laughter;
As slowly the house of day is closing its eastern shutters.

Farther down the valley the clustered tombstones recede,
Winding about their dimness the mist's grey cerements, after
The street-lamps in the twilight have suddenly started to bleed.

The leaves fly over the window, and utter a word as they pass
To the face that gazes outwards, watching for night to waft a
Meaning or a message over the window glass.

REMINDER

Do you remember
How night after night swept level and low
Overhead, at home, and had not one star
Nor one narrow gate for the moon to go
    Forth to her fields, that November?

And you remember
How towards the north a red blotch on the sky
Burns like a blot of anxiety
Over the forges, and small flames ply
    Like ghosts on the glowing of the ember?

Those were the days
When it was awful autumn to me;
When only there glowed on the dark of the sky
The red reflection of her agony,
    My beloved, smelting down in the blaze

Of death; my dearest
Love who had borne, and now was leaving me.
And I at the foot of her cross did suffer
    My own gethsemane.

So I came to you;
And twice, after wild kisses, I saw
The rim of the moon divinely rise
And strive to detach herself from the raw
    Blackened edge of the skies.

Strive to escape;
With her whiteness revealing my sunken world
Tall and loftily shadowed. But the moon
Never magnolia-like unfurled
    Her white, her lamp-like shape.

For you told me no.
Begged me to ask not for the dour
Communion, offering "a better thing."
So I lay on your breast for an obscure hour
    Feeling your fingers go

    Like a rhythmic breeze
Over my hair, and tracing my brows,
Till I knew you not from a little wind.
—I wonder if God allows
    Us only one moment his keys!

    If only then
You could have unlocked the moon on the night?
And I baptized myself in the well
Of your love? we both have entered then the right
    Rare passion, and never again?

    I wonder if only
You had taken me then, how different
Life would have been? should I have spent
Myself in anger, and you have bent
    Your head, through being lonely?

DRUNK

    Too far away, O love, I know,
    To save me from this haunted road
    Whose lofty roses break and blow
    On a night-sky bent with a load

    Of lights; each solitary rose,
    Each arc-lamp golden does expose
    Ghost beyond ghost of blossom, shows
    Night blenched with a thousand snows

    Of hawthorn and of lilac trees,
    White lilac; shows discoloured night
    Dripping with all the golden lees
    Laburnum gives back to light.

And shows the red of hawthorn set
On high to the fuming sky of night
Like flags in pale blood newly wet,
Blood shed in the silent fight

Of life with love and love with life,
Of battling for a little food
Of kisses, long seeking for a wife
Long ago, long ago wooed.

Too far away you are, my love,
To steady my brain in this phantom show
That passes the nightly road above
And returns again below.

. . . . . .

The enormous cliff of horse-chestnut trees
  Has poised on each of its ledges
An erect small girl looking down at me;
White-nightgowned little chits I see
  And they peep at me over the edges
Of the leaves as though they would leap, should I call
  Them down to my arms:
—But, child, you're too small for me; too small
  Your little charms!—

White little sheaves of nightgowned maids
  Some other will thresh you out!—
But I see leaning from the shades
A lilac there, like a lady who braids
  Her white mantilla about
Her face, and forward leans to catch the sight
  Of a lover's face;
Gracefully sighing through the white
  Flowery mantilla of lace.

And another lilac in purple veiled
  Discreetly, yet recklessly calls
In a low, shocking perfume, to know who has hailed

Her forth from the dark: my strength has failed
    In her voice, and a weak tear falls—
Oh, and see the laburnum shimmering
      Her draperies down
As if she would slip the gold, and glimmering
      White stand naked of gown.

   .   .   .   .   .   .

The pageant of flowery trees above
    The street pale-passionate goes.
And down below on the pavement, love
    In a meaner pageant flows.

Two and two are the folk that walk,
    They pass in a half embrace
Of linking elbows, and they talk
    With dull face leaning to face.

But I am alone, and wavering home
    Along this haunted road;
And never a blossoming woman will roam
    To my arms with her welcome load.

And never a girl like a chestnut flower
    Will tiptoe into my room.
I shall get no answer in any hour.
    To live alone is my doom.

SORROW

Why does the thin grey strand
Floating up from the forgotten
Cigarette between my fingers,
Why does it trouble me?

Ah, you will understand;
When I carried my mother downstairs,
A few times only, at the beginning
Of her soft-foot malady,

I should find, for a reprimand
To my gaiety, a few long grey hairs
On the breast of my coat; and one by one
I watched them float up the dark chimney.

DOLOUR OF AUTUMN

The acrid scents of autumn,
Reminiscent of slinking beasts, make me fear
Everything, tear-trembling stars of autumn
And the snore of the night in my ear.

For suddenly, flush-fallen,
All my life, in a rush
Of shedding away, has left me
Naked exposed on the bush.

I on the bush of the globe
Like a newly-naked berry shrink
Disclosed; but 'tis I who am prowling
As well in the scents that slink

Abroad: I in this naked berry
Of flesh that stands dismayed on the bush!
And I in the stealthy, brindled odours
Prowling about the lush

And acrid night of autumn!
My soul, along with the rout
Rank and treacherous, prowling
Disseminated out.

For the night, with a great breath taken
Has drawn my spirit outside
Me, till I reel with disseminated consciousness
Like a man who has died.

At the same time stand exposed
Here on the bush of the globe,
A newly-naked berry of flesh
For the stars to probe.

THE INHERITANCE

Since you did depart
Out of my reach, my darling,
Into the hidden,
I see each shadow start
With recognition, and I
Am wonder-ridden.

I am dazed with the farewell
But I scarcely feel your loss.
You left me a gift
Of tongues, so the shadows tell
Me things, and the silences toss
Me their drift.

You sent me a cloven fire
Out of death, and it burns in the draught
Of the breathing hosts,
Kindles the darkening pyre
Of the mournful, till people waft
Like candid ghosts.

Form after form, in the streets
Waves like a ghost along
Kindled to me;
The star above the house-tops greets
Me every eve with a long
Song fierily.

And all day long, the town
Glimmers with subtle ghosts
Going up and down
In the common, prison-like dress,
Yet their daunted looking flickers
To me, that I answer Yes!

So I am not lonely nor sad
Although bereaved of you,
My love.
I move among a townfolk clad
With words, but the night shows through
Their words as they move.

SILENCE

Since I lost you, I am silence-haunted;
    Sounds wave their little wings
A moment, then in weariness settle
    On the flood that soundless swings.

Whether the people in the street
    Like pattering ripples go by,
Or whether the theatre sighs and sighs
    With a loud, hoarse sigh:

Or the wind shakes a ravel of light
    Over the dead-black river,
Or last night's echoings
    Make the daybreak shiver:

I feel the silence waiting
    To sip them all up again,
In its last completeness drinking
    Down the noise of men.

LISTENING

I listen to the stillness of you,
　　My dear, among it all;
I feel your silence touch my words as I talk
　　And hold them in thrall.

My words fly off a forge
　　The length of a spark;
I see the silence easily sip them
　　Up in the dark.

The lark sings loud and glad,
　　Yet I am not loth
That silence should take the song and the bird
　　And lose them both.

A train goes roaring south,
　　The steam-flag flowing;
I see the stealthy shadow of silence
　　Alongside going.

And off the forge of the world
　　Whirling in the draught of life
Go myriad sparks of people, filling
　　The night with strife.

Yet they never change the darkness
　　Nor blench it with noise;
Alone on the perfect silence
　　The stars are buoys.

BROODING GRIEF

A yellow leaf, from the darkness
Hops like a frog before me;
Why should I start and stand still?

I was watching the woman that bore me
Stretched in the brindled darkness
Of the sick-room, rigid with will
To die: and the quick leaf tore me
Back to this rainy swill
Of leaves and lamps and the city street mingled
    before me.

LAST WORDS TO MIRIAM

Yours is the sullen sorrow,
    The disgrace is also mine;
Your love was intense and thorough,
Mine was the love of a growing flower
    For the sunshine.

You had the power to explore me,
    Blossom me stalk by stalk;
You woke my spirit, you bore me
To consciousness, you gave me the dour
    Awareness—then I suffered a balk.

Body to body I could not
    Love you, although I would.
We kissed, we kissed though we should not.
You yielded, we threw the last cast,
    And it was no good.

You only endured, and it broke
    My craftsman's nerve.
No flesh responded to my stroke;
So I failed to give you the last
    Fine torture you did deserve.

You are shapely, you are adorned
    But opaque and null in the flesh;
Who, had I but pierced with the thorned
Full anguish, perhaps had been cast
    In a lovely illumined mesh

Like a painted window; the best
    Fire passed through your flesh,
Undrossed it, and left it blest
In clean new awareness. But now
    Who shall take you afresh?

Now who will burn you free
    From your body's deadness and dross?
Since the fire has failed in me,
What man will stoop in your flesh to plough
    The shrieking cross?

A mute, nearly beautiful thing
    Is your face, that fills me with shame
As I see it hardening;
I should have been cruel enough to bring
    You through the flame.

MALADE

The sick grapes on the chair by the bed lie prone; at the window
The tassel of the blind swings constantly, tapping the pane
As the air moves in.

The room is the hollow rind of a fruit, a gourd
Scooped out and bare, where a spider,
Folded in its legs as in a bed,
Lies on the dust, watching where there is nothing to see but dusky
    walls.

And if the day outside were mine! What is the day
But a grey cave, with great grey spider-cloths hanging
Low from the roof, and the wet dust falling softly from them
Over the wet dark rocks, the houses, and over
The spiders with white faces, that scuttle on the floor of the cave!

Ah, but I am ill, and it is still raining, coldly raining!

LOTUS AND FROST

How many times, like lotus lilies risen
 Upon the surface of the waters, there
 Have risen floating on my blood the rare
Soft glimmers of desire escaped from prison!

So I am clothed all over with the light
 And sensitive, bud-like blossoming of passion;
 Till, naked for her in the finest fashion,
The flowers of all my mud swim into sight.

And then I offer all myself unto
 This woman who likes to love me; but she turns
 A look of hatred on the flower that burns
To break and pour her out its precious dew.

And slowly all the blossom shuts in pain,
 And all the lotus buds of love sink over
 To die unopened; when this moon-faced lover
Kind on the weight of suffering smiles again.

THE YEW-TREE ON THE DOWNS

A gibbous moon hangs out of the twilight,
 Star-spiders, spinning their thread,
Drop a little lower, withouten respite
 Watching us overhead.

Come then under this tree, where the tent-cloths
 Curtain us in so dark
That here we're safe from even the ermine moth's
 Twitching remark.

Here in this swarthy, secret tent,
 Whose black boughs flap the ground,
Come, draw the thorn from my discontent,
 And bless the wound.

This rare, ancient night! For in here
    Under the yew-tree tent
The darkness is secret, and I could sear
    You like frankincense into scent.

Here not even the stars can spy us,
    Not even the moths can alight
On our mystery; nought can descry us
    Nor put us to flight.

Put trust then now in the black-boughed tree,
    Lie down, and open to me
The inner dark of the mystery,
    Be penetrate, like the tree.

Waste not the yew-tree's waiting, waste
    Not this inner night!
Open the core of gloaming, taste
    The last dark delight.

TROTH WITH THE DEAD

The moon is broken in twain, and half a moon
Beyond me lies on the low, still floor of the sky;
The other half of the broken coin of troth
Is buried away in the dark, where the dead all lie.

They buried her half in the grave when they laid her away;
Pushed gently away and hidden in the thick of her hair
Where it gathered towards the plait, on that very last day;
And like a moon unshowing it must still shine there.

So half lies on the sky, for a general sign
Of the troth with the dead that we are pledged to keep;
Turning its broken edge to the dark, its shine
Ends like a broken love, that turns to the dark of sleep.

And half lies there in the dark where the dead all lie
Lost and yet still connected; and between the two
Strange beams must travel still, for I feel that I
Am lit beneath my heart with a half-moon, weird and blue.

AT A LOOSE END

Many years have I still to burn, detained
Like a candle-flame on this body; but I enclose
Blue shadow within me, a presence which lives contained
In my flame of living, the invisible heart of the rose.

So through these days, while I burn on the fuel of life,
What matter the stuff I lick up in my daily flame;
Seeing the core is a shadow inviolate,
A darkness that dreams my dream for me, ever the same.

SUBMERGENCE

When along the pavement,
Palpitating flames of life,
People flicker round me,
I forget my bereavement,
The gap in my life's constellation,
The place where a star used to be.

Nay, though the pole-star
Is blown out like a candle,
And all the heavens are wandering in disarray,
Yet when pleiads of people are
Deployed around me, and I see
The street's long, outstretched milky-way!

When people flicker down the pavement
I forget my bereavement.

THE ENKINDLED SPRING

This spring as it comes bursts up in bonfires green,
Wild puffing of green-fire trees, and flame-green bushes,
Thorn-blossom lifting in wreaths of smoke between
Where the wood fumes up, and the flickering, watery
    rushes.

I am amazed at this spring, this conflagration
Of green fires lit on the soil of earth, this blaze
Of growing, these smoke-puffs that puff in wild gyration,
Faces of people blowing across my gaze!

And I, what sort of fire am I among
This conflagration of spring? the gap in it all—!
Not even palish smoke like the rest of the throng.
Less than the wind that runs to the flamy call!

EXCURSION TRAIN

I wonder, can the night go by,
Can this shot arrow of travel fly
Shaft-golden with light, sheer into the sky
    Of a dawned to-morrow,
Without ever sleep delivering us
From each other, or loosing the dolorous
    And turgid sorrow!

What is it then that you can see,
That at the window endlessly
You watch the red sparks whirl and flee
    And the night look through?
Your presence peering lonelily there
Oppresses me so, I can hardly bear
    To share the night with you.

You hurt my heart-beat's privacy;
I wish I could put you away from me;
I suffocate in this intimacy
    In which I half love you;

How I have longed for this night in the train!
Yet now every fibre of me cries in pain
    To God to remove you!

Though surely my soul's best dream is still
That a new night pouring down shall swill
Us away in an utter sleep, until
    We are one, smooth-rounded!
Yet closely bitten in to me
Is this armour of stiff reluctancy,
    And my dream is ill-founded.

So, Helen, when another night
Comes on us, lift your fingers white
And strip me naked, touch me light
    Light, light all over.
For I ache most earnestly for your touch,
Yet I cannot move, however much
    I would be your lover.

Night after night with a blemish of day
Unblown and unblossomed has withered away;
Come another night, come a new night, say
    Will you pluck it apart?
Will you open the amorous, aching bud
Of my body, and loose the essential flood
    That would pour to you from my heart?

RELEASE

Helen, had I known yesterday
That you could discharge the ache
    Out of the wound,
Had I known yesterday you could take
The turgid electric ache away,
    Drink it up in the ground
Of your soft white body, as lightning
Is drunk from an agonised sky by the earth,
    I should have hated you, Helen.

But since my limbs gushed full of fire,
Since from out of my blood and bone
    Poured a heavy flame
To you, earth of my atmosphere, stone
Of my steel, lovely white flint of desire,
    You have no name.
Earth of my swaying atmosphere,
Substance of my inconstant breath,
    I cannot but cleave to you, Helen.

Since you have drunken up the drear
Death-darkened storm, and death
    Is washed from the blue
Of my eyes, I see you beautiful, and dear.
Beautiful, passive and strong, as the breath
    Of my yearning blows over you.
I see myself as the winds that hover
Half substanceless, and without grave worth.
    But you
    Are the earth I hover over.

THESE CLEVER WOMEN

Close your eyes, my love, let me make you blind!
    They have taught you to see
Only problems writ on the face of things,
And algebra in the eyes of desirous men,
    And God like geometry
Tangling his circles, to baffle you and me.

I would kiss you over the eyes till I kissed you blind;
    If I could—if anyone could!
Then perhaps in the dark you'd get what you want to find:
The solution that ever is much too deep for the mind;
    Dissolved in the blood. . . .
That I am the hart, and you are the gentle hind.

Now stop carping at me! Do you want me to hate you?
    Am I a kaleidoscope
For you to shake and shake, and it won't come right?
Am I doomed in a long coition of words to mate you?
    Unsatisfied! Is there no hope
Between your thighs, far, far from your peering sight?

BALLAD OF ANOTHER OPHELIA

O the green glimmer of apples in the orchard,
Lamps in a wash of rain!
O the wet walk of my brown hen through the stackyard!
O tears on the window-pane!

Nothing now will ripen the bright green apples
Full of disappointment and of rain;
Brackish they will taste, of tears, when the yellow dapples
Of autumn tell the withered tale again.

All round the yard it is cluck! my brown hen.
Cluck! and the rain-wet wings;
Cluck! my marigold bird, and again
Cluck! for your yellow darlings.

For a grey rat found the gold thirteen
Huddled away in the dark.
Flutter for a moment, oh, the beast is quick and keen,
Extinct one yellow-fluffy spark!

Once I had a lover bright like running water,
Once his face was open like the sky,
Open like the sky looking down in all its laughter
On the buttercups, and the buttercups was I.

What then is there hidden in the skirts of all the blossom?
What is peeping from your skirts, O mother hen?
'Tis the sun that asks the question, in a lovely haste for
    wisdom;
What a lovely haste for wisdom is in men!

Yea, but it is cruel when undressed is all the blossom
And her shift is lying white upon the floor,
That a grey one, like a shadow, like a rat, a thief, a rain-
    storm
Creeps upon her then and ravishes her store!

O the grey garner that is full of half-grown apples!
O the golden sparkles laid extinct!
And O, behind the cloud-leaves, like yellow autumn
    dapples,
Did you see the wicked sun that winked?

KISSES IN THE TRAIN

I saw the midlands
    Revolve through her hair;
The fields of autumn
    Stretching bare,
And sheep on the pasture
    Tossed back in a scare.

And still as ever
    The world went round,
My mouth on her pulsing
    Throat was found,
And my breast to her beating
    Breast was bound.

But my heart at the centre
    Of all, in a swound
Was still as a pivot,
    As all the ground
On its prowling orbit
    Shifted round.

And still in my nostrils
    The scent of her flesh;
And still my blind face
    Sought her afresh;
And still one pulse
    Through the world did thresh.

And the world all whirling
  Round in joy
Like the dance of a dervish
  Did destroy
My sense—and reason
  Spun like a toy.

But firm at the centre
  My heart was found;
My own to her perfect
  Heartbeat bound,
Like a magnet's keeper
  Closing the round.

TURNED DOWN

Hollow rang the house when I knocked at the door,
And I lingered on the threshold with my hand
Upraised to knock and knock once more;
Listening for the sound of her feet across the floor
Hollow re-echoed my heart.

The low-hung lamps stretched down the street
With people passing underneath,
With a rhythm of tapping, coming feet
To quicken my hope as I hastened to greet
The waking smile of her eyes.

The tired lights down the street went out,
The last car trailed the night behind;
And I in the darkness wandered about
With a flutter of hope and a quenching doubt
In the dying lamp of my love.

Two brown ponies trotting slowly
Stopped at a dim-lit trough to drink;
The dark van drummed down the distance lowly;
And city stars, so dim and holy,
Came nearer, to search through the streets.

A hastening car swept shameful past,
I saw her hid in the shadow;
I saw her step to the kerb, and fast
Run to the silent door, where last
I had stood with my hand uplifted.
She clung to the door in her haste to enter,
Entered, and quickly cast
It shut behind her, leaving the street aghast.

AFTER MANY DAYS

I wonder if with you, as it is with me,
If under your slipping words, that easily flow
About you as a garment, easily,
    Your violent heart beats to and fro!

Long have I waited, never once confessed,
Even to myself, how bitter the separation;
Now, being come again, how make the best
    Reparation?

If I could cast this clothing off from me,
If I could lift my naked self to you,
Or if only you would repulse me, a wound would be
    Good, it would let the ache come through.

But that you hold me still so kindly cold
Aloof, my flaming heart will not allow;
Yea, but I loathe you that you should withhold
    Your greeting now!

SNAP-DRAGON

She bade me follow to her garden, where
The mellow sunlight stood as in a cup
Between the old grey walls; I did not dare
To raise my face, I did not dare look up,
Lest her bright eyes like sparrows should fly in
My windows of discovery, and shrill "Sin!"

So with a downcast mien and laughing voice
I followed, followed the swing of her white dress
That rocked in a lilt along; I watched the poise
Of her feet as they flew for a space, then paused to press
The grass deep down with the royal burden of her;
And gladly I'd offered my breast to the tread of her.

"I like to see," she said, and she crouched her down,
She sunk into my sight like a settling bird;
And her bosom couched in the confines of her gown
Like heavy birds at rest there, softly stirred
By her measured breaths: "I like to see," said she,
"The snap-dragon put out his tongue at me."

She laughed, she reached her hand out to the flower,
Closing its crimson throat. My own throat in her power
Strangled, my heart swelled up so full
As if it would burst its wine-skin in my throat,
Choke me in my own crimson. I watched her pull
The gorge of the gaping flower, till the blood did float

Over my eyes, and I was blind—
Her large brown hand stretched over
The windows of my mind;
And there in the dark I did discover
Things I was out to find:

My Grail, a brown bowl twined
With swollen veins that met in the wrist,
Under whose brown the amethyst
I longed to taste! I longed to turn
My heart's red measure in her cup;
I longed to feel my hot blood burn
With the amethyst in her cup.

Then suddenly she looked up,
And I was blind in a tawny-gold day,
Till she took her eyes away.

So she came down from above
And emptied my heart of love.
So I held my heart aloft
To the cuckoo that hung like a dove,
And she settled soft.

It seemed that I and the morning world
Were pressed cup-shape to take this reiver
Bird who was weary to have furled
Her wings in us,
As we were weary to receive her.

> *This bird, this rich,*
> *Sumptuous central grain;*
> *This mutable witch,*
> *This one refrain,*
> *This laugh in the fight,*
> *This clot of night,*
> *This field of delight.*

She spoke, and I closed my eyes
To shut hallucinations out.
I echoed with surprise
Hearing my mere lips shout
The answer they did devise.

> Again I saw a brown bird hover
> Over the flowers at my feet;
> I felt a brown bird hover
> Over my heart, and sweet
> Its shadow lay on my heart.
> I thought I saw on the clover
> A brown bee pulling apart
> The closed flesh of the clover
> And burrowing in its heart.

> She moved her hand, and again
> I felt the brown bird cover
> My heart; and then
> The bird came down on my heart,

As on a nest the rover
Cuckoo comes, and shoves over
The brim each careful part
Of love, takes possession, and settles her down,
With her wings and her feathers to drown
The nest in a heat of love.

She turned her flushed face to me for the glint
Of a moment.—"See," she laughed, "if you also
Can make them yawn!"—I put my hand to the dint
In the flower's throat, and the flower gaped wide with woe.
She watched, she went of a sudden intensely still,
She watched my hand, to see what it would fulfil.

I pressed the wretched, throttled flower between
My fingers, till its head lay back, its fangs
Poised at her. Like a weapon my hand was white and keen,
And I held the choked flower-serpent in its pangs
Of mordant anguish, till she ceased to laugh,
Until her pride's flag, smitten, cleaved down to the staff.

She hid her face, she murmured between her lips
The low word "Don't!"—I let the flower fall,
But held my hand afloat towards the slips
Of blossom she fingered, and my fingers all
Put forth to her: she did not move, nor I,
For my hand like a snake watched hers, that could not fly.

Then I laughed in the dark of my heart, I did exult
Like a sudden chuckling of music. I bade her eyes
Meet mine, I opened her helpless eyes to consult
Their fear, their shame, their joy that underlies
Defeat in such a battle. In the dark of her eyes
My heart was fierce to make her laughter rise.

Till her dark deeps shook with convulsive thrills, and the dark
Of her spirit wavered like water thrilled with light;
And my heart leaped up in longing to plunge its stark
Fervour within the pool of her twilight,
Within her spacious soul, to find delight.

And I do not care, though the large hands of revenge
Shall get my throat at last, shall get it soon,
If the joy that they are lifted to avenge
Have risen red on my night as a harvest moon,
Which even death can only put out for me;
And death, I know, is better than not-to-be.

COME SPRING, COME SORROW

Round clouds roll in the arms of the wind,
The round earth rolls like a germ in the sky,
And see, where the budding hazels are thinned
  The wild anemones lie
In undulating shivers beneath the wind!

Over the blue of the duck-pond ply
White ducks, a quacking flotilla of cloud;
And look you, floating just thereby
  The blue-gleamed drake stems proud
As Abraham, whose seed shall multiply.

In the lustrous gleam of the water, there
Scramble seven toads, across silk, obscure leaves,
Seven toads that move in the dusk to share
  Dim spring that interweaves
The hidden bodies mating everywhere.

Look now, through the woods where the beech-green
 spurts
Like a storm of emerald snow, now see!
A great bay stallion dances, skirts
  The bushes sumptuously,
Going out in spring to the round of his tame deserts.

And you, my lass, with your rich warm face aglow,
What sudden expectation opens you
So wide as you watch the catkins blow
  Their dust from the birch on the blue
Lift of the pulsing wind? ah, say that you know!

Yes, say it! For, sure from the golden sun
A quickening, masculine gleam floats in to all
Us creatures, people and flowers undone
        And opened under his thrall
As he plants his new germ in us. What is there to shun?

Why, I should think that from the earth there fly
Fine thrills to the neighbour stars, fine hidden beams
Thrown lustily off from our full-sappy, high
        And fecund globe of dreams,
To quicken the spheres spring-virgin again in the sky.

Do you not hear each morsel thrill
With joy at travelling to plant itself within
The expectant one, and therein to instil
        Newness, new shape to win,
From the drowse of life wake up another will?

Surely, ah not in words alone I'd spill
The vivid, ah, the fiery surplus of life
From off my measure, to touch you deep, and fill
        You flush and rife
With this year's newness!—And is that evil?

THE HANDS OF THE BETROTHED

Her tawny eyes are onyx of thoughtlessness,
Hardened they are like gems in time-long prudery;
Yea, and her mouth's prudent and crude caress
Means even less than her many words to me.

Except her kiss betrays me this, this only
Consolation, that in her lips her blood at climax clips
Two hard, crude paws in hunger on the lonely
Flesh of my heart, ere down, rebuked, it slips.

I know from her hardened lips that still her heart is
Hungry for love, yet if I lay my hand in her breast
She puts me away, like a saleswoman whose mart is
Endangered by the pilferer on his quest.

Though her hands are still the woman, her large, strong
    hands
Heavier than mine, yet like leverets caught in steel
When I hold them; my spent soul understands
Their dumb confession of what her blood must feel.

For never her hands come nigh me but they lift
Like heavy birds from the morning stubble, to settle
Upon me like sleeping birds, like birds that shift
Uneasily in their sleep, disturbing my mettle.

How caressingly she lays her hand on my knee!
How strangely she tries to disown it, as it sinks
In my flesh and my bone, and forages into me!
How it stirs like a subtle stoat, whatever she thinks!

And often I see her clench her fingers tight
And thrust her fists suppressed in the folds of her skirt;
And sometimes, how she grasps her arms with her
    bright
Big hands, as if surely her arms did hurt.

And I have seen her stand all unaware
Pressing her spread hands over her breasts, as she
Would crush their mounds on her heart, to kill in there
The pain that is her simple ache for me.

She makes her hands take my part, the part of the man
To her; she crushes them into her bosom deep
Where I should be, and with her own strong span
Closes her arms, that should fold on me in sleep.

Ah, and she puts her hands upon the wall,
Presses them there, and kisses her big dark hands,
Then lets her black hair loose, the darkness fall
About her from her maiden-folded bands.

And sits in her own dark night of her bitter hair
Dreaming—God knows of what, for to me she's the
    same
Betrothed young lady who loves me, and takes good
    care
Of her maidenly virtue and of my good name.

A LOVE SONG

Reject me not if I should say to you
I do forget the sounding of your voice,
I do forget your eyes, that searching through
The days perceive our marriage, and rejoice.

But, when the apple-blossom opens wide
Under the pallid moonlight's fingering,
I see your blanched face at my breast, and hide
My eyes from duteous work, malingering.

Ah, then upon the bedroom I do draw
The blind to hide the garden, where the moon
Enjoys the open blossoms as they straw
Their beauty for his taking, boon for boon.

And I do lift my aching arms to you,
And I do lift my anguished, avid breast,
And I do weep for very pain of you,
And fling myself at the doors of sleep, for rest.

And I do toss through the troubled night for you,
Dreaming your yielded mouth is given to mine,
Feeling your strong breast carry me on into
The sleep no dream nor doubt can undermine.

TWOFOLD

How gorgeous that shock of red lilies, and larkspur cleaving
All with a flash of blue!—when will she be leaving
Her room, where the night still hangs like a half-folded bat,
And passion unbearable seethes in the darkness, like must
    in a vat.

TARANTELLA

Sad as he sits on the white sea-stone
And the suave sea chuckles, and turns to the moon,
And the moon significant smiles at the cliffs and the
    boulders.
He sits like a shade by the flood alone
While I dance a tarantella on the rocks, and the croon
Of my mockery mocks at him over the waves' bright
    shoulders.

What can I do but dance alone,
Dance to the sliding sea and the moon,
For the moon on my breast and the air on my limbs
    and the foam on my feet?
For surely this earnest man has none
Of the night in his soul, and none of the tune
Of the waters within him; only the world's old wisdom
    to bleat.

I wish a wild sea-fellow would come down the glitter-
    ing shingle,
A soulless neckar, with winking seas in his eyes
And falling waves in his arms, and the lost soul's kiss
On his lips: I long to be soulless, I tingle
To touch the sea in the last surprise
Of fiery coldness, to be gone in a lost soul's bliss.

UNDER THE OAK

You, if you were sensible,
When I tell you the stars flash signals, each one
    dreadful,
You would not turn and answer me
"The night is wonderful."

Even you, if you knew
How this darkness soaks me through and through,
    and infuses
Unholy fear in my essence, you would pause to
    distinguish
What hurts from what amuses.

For I tell you
Beneath this powerful tree, my whole soul's fluid
Oozes away from me as a sacrifice steam
At the knife of a Druid.

Again I tell you, I bleed, I am bound with withies,
My life runs out.
I tell you my blood runs out on the floor of this oak,
Gout upon gout.

Above me springs the blood-born mistletoe
In the shady smoke.
But who are you, twittering to and fro
Beneath the oak?

What thing better are you, what worse?
What have you to do with the mysteries
Of this ancient place, of my ancient curse?
What place have you in my histories?

BROTHER AND SISTER

The shorn moon trembling indistinct on her path,
Frail as a scar upon the pale blue sky,
Draws towards the downward slope; some sorrow hath
Worn her away to the quick, so she faintly fares
Along her foot-searched way without knowing why
She creeps persistent down the sky's long stairs.

Some say they see, though I have never seen,
The dead moon heaped within the new moon's arms;
For surely the fragile, fine young thing had been
Too heavily burdened to mount the heavens so!
But my heart stands still, as a new, strong dread alarms
Me; might a young girl be heaped with such shadow of
    woe?

Since Death from the mother moon has pared us down to
    the quick,
And cast us forth like thin, shorn moons, to travel
An uncharted way among the myriad thick
Strewn stars of unknown people, and luminous litter
Of lives which sorrows like mischievous dark mice chavel
To nought, diminishing each star's glitter;

Since Death has delivered us utterly, stripped and white,
Since the month of childhood is over, and we stand alone,
Since the beloved, faded mother that set us alight
Is delivered out and pays no heed though we moan
In sorrow; since we stand in bewilderment, strange
And fearful to sally forth down the sky's long range:

Let us not cry to her still to sustain us here,
Let us not hold her shadow back from the dark!
Oh, let us here forget, let us take the sheer
Unknown that lies before us, bearing the ark
Of the covenant onwards where she cannot go!
Let us rise and leave her now, she will never know.

THE SHADOW OF DEATH

The earth again like a ship steams out of the dark sea over
The edge of the blue, and the sun stands up to see us glide
Slowly into another day; slowly the rover
Vessel of darkness takes the rising tide.

I, on the deck, am startled by this dawn confronting
Me who am issued amazed from the darkness, stripped
And quailing here in the sunshine, betrayed from haunting
The soundless night whereon our days are shipped.

Feeling myself undawning, the day's light playing upon me,
I who am substance of shadow, I all compact
Of the stuff of the night, finding myself all wrongly
Among crowds of things in the sunshine jostled and racked.

I with the night on my lips, I sigh with the silence of death;
And what do I care though the very stones should cry me
        unreal, though the clouds
Shine in conceit of substance upon me, who am less than
        the rain!
Do I not know the darkness within them? What are they
        but shrouds?

The clouds go down the sky with a wealthy ease,
Casting a shadow of scorn upon me for my share in death;
        but I
Hold my own in the midst of them, darkling defy
The whole of the day to extinguish the shadow I lift on the
        breeze.

Yea, though the very clouds have vantage over me
Enjoying their glancing flight, though love is dead,
I still am not homeless here, I've a tent by day
Of darkness whereon she sleeps on her perfect bed.

BIRDCAGE WALK

> When the wind blows her veil
>   And uncovers her laughter
> I cease, I turn pale.
> When the wind blows her veil
> From the woes I bewail
>   Of love and hereafter:
> When the wind blows her veil
> I cease, I turn pale.

IN TROUBLE AND SHAME

I look at the swaling sunset
And wish I could go also
Through the red doors beyond the black-purple bar.

I wish that I could go
Through the red doors where I could put off
My shame like shoes in the porch,
My pain like garments,
And leave my flesh discarded lying
Like luggage of some departed traveller
Gone one knows not whither.

Then I would turn round,
And seeing my cast-off body lying like lumber,
I would laugh with joy.

CALL INTO DEATH

Since I lost you, my darling, the sky has come near,
And I am of it, the small sharp stars are quite near,
The white moon going among them like a white bird
among snow-berries,
And the sound of her gently rustling in heaven like a
bird I hear.

And I am willing to come to you now, my dear,
As a pigeon lets itself off from a cathedral dome
To be lost in the haze of the sky; I would like to come
And be lost out of sight with you, like a melting foam.

For I am tired, my dear, and if I could lift my feet,
My tenacious feet, from off the dome of the earth
To fall like a breath within the breathing wind
Where you are lost, what rest, my love, what rest!

GREY EVENING

When you went, how was it you carried with you
My missal book of fine, flamboyant Hours?
My book of turrets and of red-thorn bowers,
And skies of gold, and ladies in bright tissue?

Now underneath a blue-grey twilight, heaped
Beyond the withering snow of the shorn fields
Stands rubble of stunted houses; all is reaped
And trodden that the happy summer yields.

Now lamps like yellow echoes glimmer among
The shadowy stubble of the under-dusk;
As farther off the scythe of night is swung
Ripe little stars come rolling from their husk.

And all the earth is gone into a dust
Of greyness mingled with a fume of gold,
Timeless as branching lichens, pale as must,
Since all the sky has withered and gone cold.

And so I sit and scan the book of grey,
Feeling the shadows like a blind man reading,
All fearful lest I find the last words bleeding:
Nay, take this weary Book of Hours away.

FIRELIGHT AND NIGHTFALL

The darkness steals the forms of all the queens,
But oh, the palms of his two black hands are red
Inflamed with binding up the sheaves of the dead
Hours that were once all glory and all queens.

And I remember still the sunny hours
Of queens in hyacinth and skies of gold,
And morning singing where the woods are scrolled
And diapered above the chaunting flowers.

Here lamps are white like snowdrops in the grass;
The town is like a churchyard, all so still
And grey now night is here; nor will
Another torn red sunset come to pass.

BLUENESS

Out of the darkness, fretted sometimes in its sleeping,
Jets of sparks in fountains of blue come leaping
To sight, revealing a secret, numberless secrets keeping.

Sometimes the darkness trapped within a wheel
Runs into speed like a dream, the blue of the steel
Showing the rocking darkness now a-reel.

And out of the invisible, streams of bright blue drops
Rain from the showery heavens, and bright blue crops
Of flowers surge from below to their ladder-tops.

And all the manifold blue, amazing eyes,
The rainbow arching over in the skies,
New sparks of wonder opening in surprise:

All these pure things come foam and spray of the sea
Of Darkness abundant, which shaken mysteriously
Breaks into dazzle of living, as dolphins leap from the sea
Of midnight and shake it to fire, till the flame of the
    shadow we see.

A PASSING-BELL

Mournfully to and fro, to and fro the trees are waving,
    What did you say, my dear?
The rain-bruised leaves are suddenly shaken, as a child
Asleep still shakes in the clutch of a sob—
    Yes, my love, I hear.

One lonely bell, one only, the storm-tossed afternoon is
    braving,
        Why not let it ring?
The roses lean down when they hear it, the tender, mild
Flowers of the bleeding-heart fall to the throb—
        'Tis a little thing!

A wet bird walks on the lawn, call to the boy to come
    and look,
        Yes, it is over now.
Call to him out of the silence, call him to see
The starling shaking its head as it walks in the grass——
        Ah, who knows how?

He cannot see it, I can never show it him, how it shook
        Don't disturb it, darling!—
Its head as it walked: I can never call him to me,
Never, he *is* not, whatever shall come to pass.
        No, look at the wet starling!

THE DRAINED CUP

T' snow is witherin' off'n th' gress—
    Lad, should I tell thee summat?
T' snow is witherin' off'n th' gress
An' mist is suckin' at th' spots o' snow,
An' ower a' the thaw an' mess
There's a moon, full blow.
    Lad, but I'm tellin' thee summat!

Tha's bin snowed up i' this cottage wi' me—
    'Ark, tha'rt for hearin' summat!
Tha's bin snowed up i' this cottage wi' me
While t' clocks 'as a' run down an' stopped,
An' t' short days goin' unknown ter thee
Unbeknown has dropped.
    Yi, but I'm tellin' thee summat.

How many days dost think has gone?
  Now, lad, I'm axin' thee summat.
How many days dost think has gone?
How many times has t' candle-light shone
On thy face as tha got more white an' wan?
 —Seven days, my lad, or none!
  Aren't ter hearin' summat?

Tha come ter say good-bye ter me,
  Tha wert frit o' summat.
Tha come ter ha' finished an' done wi' me
An' off to a gel as wor younger than me,
An' fresh an' more nicer for marryin' wi'—
  Yi, but tha'rt frit o' summat.

Ah wunna kiss thee, tha trembles so!
  Tha'rt daunted, or summat.
Tha arena very flig ter go.
Dost want me ter want thee again? Nay though,
There's hardly owt left o' thee; get up an' go!
  Or dear o' me, say summat.

Tha wanted ter leave me that bad, tha knows!
  Doesn't ter know it?
But tha wanted me more ter want thee, so's
Tha could let thy very soul out. A man
Like thee can't rest till his last spunk goes
Out of 'im into a woman as can
  Draw it out of 'im. Did ter know it?

Tha thought tha wanted a little wench,
  Ay, lad, I'll tell thee thy mind.
Tha thought tha wanted a little wench
As 'ud make thee a wife an' look up ter thee.
As 'ud wince when tha touched 'er close, an'
  blench
An' lie frightened ter death under thee.
  She worn't hard ter find.

Tha thought tha wanted ter be rid o' me.
    'Appen tha did, an' a'.
Tha thought tha wanted ter marry an' see
If ter couldna be master an' th' woman's boss.
Tha'd need a woman different from me,
An' tha knowed it; ay, yet tha comes across
    Ter say good-bye! an' a'.

I tell thee tha won't be satisfied,
    Tha might as well listen, tha knows.
I tell thee tha won't be satisfied
Till a woman has drawn the last last drop
O' thy spunk, an' tha'rt empty an' mortified.
Empty an' empty from bottom to top.
    It's true, tha knows.

Tha'rt one o' th' men as has got to drain
    —An' I've loved thee for it,
Their blood in a woman, to the very last vein.
Tha *must*, though tha tries ter get away.
Tha wants it, and everything else is in vain.
    An' a woman like me loves thee for it.

Maun tha cling to the wa' as tha stan's?
    Ay, an' tha maun.
An' tha looks at me, an' tha understan's.
Yi, tha can go. Tha hates me now.
But tha'lt come again. Because when a man's
Not finished, he hasn't, no matter how.
    Go then, sin' tha maun.

Tha come ter say good-bye ter me.
    Now go then, now then go.
It's ta'en thee seven days ter say it ter me.
Now go an' marry that wench, an' see
How long it'll be afore tha'lt be
Weary an' sick o' the likes o' she,
    An' hankerin' for me. But go!

A woman's man tha art, ma lad,
    But it's my sort o' woman.
Go then, tha'lt ha'e no peace till ter's had
A go at t'other, for I'm a bad
Sort o' woman for any lad.
    —Ay, it's a rum un!

LATE AT NIGHT

Rigid sleeps the house in darkness, I alone
Like a thing unwarrantable cross the hall
And climb the stairs to find the group of doors
Standing angel-stern and tall.

I want my own room's shelter. But what is this
Throng of startled beings suddenly thrown
In confusion against my entry? Is it only the trees'
Large shadows from the outside street-lamp blown?

Phantom to phantom leaning; strange women weep
Aloud, suddenly on my mind
Startling a fear unspeakable, as the shuddering wind
Breaks and sobs in the blind.

So like to women, tall strange women weeping!
Why continually do they cross the bed?
Why does my soul contract with unnatural fear?
I am listening! Is anything said?

Ever the long black figures swoop by the bed;
They seem to be beckoning, rushing away, and
    beckoning.
Whither then, whither? what is it? say
What is the reckoning?

Tall black Bacchae of midnight, why then, why
Do you rush to assail me?
Do I intrude on your rites nocturnal?
What should it avail me?

Is there some great Iacchos of these slopes
Suburban dismal?
Have I profaned some female mystery, orgies
Black and phantasmal?

NEXT MORNING

How have I wandered here to this vaulted room
In the house of life?—the floor was ruffled with gold
Last evening, and she who was softly in bloom
Glimmered as flowers that in perfume at twilight unfold

For the flush of the night; whereas now the gloom
Of every dirty, must-besprinkled mould
And damp old web of misery's heirloom
Deadens this day's grey-dropping arras-fold.

And what is this that floats on the undermist
Of the mirror towards the dusty grate, as if feeling
Unsightly its way to the warmth?—this thing with a list
To the left?—this ghost like a candle swealing?

Pale-blurred, with two round black drops, as if it missed
Itself among everything else, here hungrily stealing
Upon me!—my own reflection! explicit gist
Of my presence there in the mirror that leans from the
    ceiling!

Then will somebody square this shade with the being I
    know
I was last night, when my soul rang clear as a bell
And happy as rain in summer? Why should it be so?
What is there gone against me, why am I in hell?

WINTER IN THE BOULEVARD

The frost has settled down upon the trees
And ruthlessly strangled off the fantasies
Of leaves that have gone unnoticed, swept like old
Romantic stories now no more to be told.

The trees down the boulevard stand naked in thought,
Their abundant summery wordage silenced, caught
In the grim undertow; naked the trees confront
Implacable winter's long,. cross-questioning brunt.

Has some hand balanced more leaves in the depths of the
    twigs?
Some dim little efforts placed in the threads of the
    birch?—
It is only the sparrows, like dead black leaves on the
    sprigs,
Sitting huddled against the cerulean, one flesh with their
    perch.

The clear, cold sky coldly bethinks itself.
Like vivid thought the air spins bright, and all
Trees, birds, and earth, arrested in the after-thought,
Awaiting the sentence out from the welkin brought.

PARLIAMENT HILL IN THE EVENING

The houses fade in a melt of mist
    Blotching the thick, soiled air
With reddish places that still resist
    The Night's slow care.

The hopeless, wintry twilight fades,
    The city corrodes out of sight
As the body corrodes when death invades
    That citadel of delight.

Now verdigris smoulderings softly spread
    Through the shroud of the town, as slow
Night-lights hither and thither shed
    Their ghastly glow.

EMBANKMENT AT NIGHT,
BEFORE THE WAR

CHARITY

By the river
In the black wet night as the furtive rain slinks down,
Dropping and starting from sleep
Alone on a seat
A woman crouches.

I must go back to her.

I want to give her
Some money. Her hand slips out of the breast of her
        gown
Asleep. My fingers creep
Carefully over the sweet
Thumb-mound, into the palm's deep pouches.

So the gift!

God, how she starts!
And looks at me, and looks in the palm of her hand
And again at me!—
I turn and run
Down the Embankment, run for my life.

But why?—why?

Because of my heart's
Beating like sobs, I come to myself, and stand
In the street spilled over splendidly
With wet, flat lights. What I've done
I know not, my soul is in strife.

The touch was on the quick. I want to forget.

EMBANKMENT AT NIGHT,
BEFORE THE WAR

OUTCASTS

The night rain, dripping unseen,
Comes endlessly kissing my face and my hands.

The river slipping between
Lamps, is rayed with golden bands
Half way down its heaving sides;
Revealed where it hides.

Under the bridge
Great electric cars
Sing through, and each with a floor-light racing along
    at its side.
Far off, oh, midge after midge
Drifts over the gulf that bars
The night with silence, crossing the lamp-touched tide.

At Charing Cross, here, beneath the bridge
Sleep in a row the outcasts,
Packed in a line with their heads against the wall.
Their feet in a broken ridge
Stretched out on the way, and a lout casts
A look as he stands on the edge of this naked stall.

Beasts that sleep will cover
Their face in their flank; so these
Have huddled rags or limbs on the naked sleep.
Save, as the tram-cars hover
Past with the noise of a breeze
And gleam as of sunshine crossing the low black heap,

Two naked faces are seen
Bare and asleep,
Two pale clots swept by the light of the cars.

Foam-clots showing between
The long, low tidal-heap,
The mud-weed opening two pale, shadowless stars.

Over the pallor of only two faces
Passes the gallivant beam of the trams;
Shows in only two sad places
The white bare bone of our shams.

A little, bearded man, peaked in sleeping,
With a face like a chickweed flower.
And a heavy woman, sleeping still keeping
Callous and dour.

Over the pallor of only two places
Tossed on the low, black, ruffled heap
Passes the light of the tram as it races
Out of the deep.

Eloquent limbs
In disarray,
Sleep-suave limbs of a youth with long, smooth thighs
Hutched up for warmth; the muddy rims
Of trousers fray
On the thin bare shins of a man who uneasily lies.

The balls of five red toes
As red and dirty, bare
Young birds forsaken and left in a nest of mud—
Newspaper sheets enclose
Some limbs like parcels, and tear
When the sleeper stirs or turns on the ebb of the flood—

One heaped mound
Of a woman's knees
As she thrusts them upward under the ruffled skirt—
And a curious dearth of sound
In the presence of these
Wastrels that sleep on the flagstones without any hurt.

Over two shadowless, shameless faces
Stark on the heap
Travels the light as it tilts in its paces
Gone in one leap.

At the feet of the sleepers, watching,
Stand those that wait
For a place to lie down; and still as they stand, they sleep;
Wearily catching
The flood's slow gait
Like men who are drowned, but float erect in the deep.

Oh, the singing mansions,
Golden-lighted tall
Trams that pass, blown ruddily down the night!
The bridge on its stanchions
Stoops like a pall
To this human blight.

On the outer pavement, slowly,
Theatre people pass,
Holding aloft their umbrellas that flash and are bright
Like flowers of infernal moly
Over nocturnal grass
Wetly bobbing and drifting away on our sight.

And still by the rotten row of shattered feet,
Outcasts keep guard.
Forgotten,
Forgetting, till fate shall delete
One from the ward.

The factories on the Surrey side
Are beautifully laid in black on a gold-grey sky.
The river's invisible tide
Threads and thrills like ore that is wealth to the eye.

And great gold midges
Cross the chasm
At the bridges
Above intertwined plasm.

SICKNESS

Waving slowly before me, pushed into the dark,
Unseen my hands explore the silence, drawing the bark
Of my body slowly behind.

Nothing to meet my fingers but the fleece of night
Invisible blinding my face and my eyes! What if in
    their flight
My hands should touch the door!

What if I suddenly stumble, and push the door
Open, and a great grey dawn swirls over my feet, before
I can draw back!

What if unwitting I set the door of eternity wide
And am swept away in the horrible dawn, am gone
    down the tide
Of eternal hereafter!

Catch my hands, my darling, between your breasts.
Take them away from their venture, before fate wrests
The meaning out of them.

IN CHURCH

In the choir the boys are singing the hymn.
    The morning light on their lips
Moves in silver-moist flashes, in musical trim.

Sudden outside the high window, one crow
    Hangs in the air
And lights on a withered oak-tree's top of woe.

One bird, one blot, folded and still at the top
    Of the withered tree!—in the grail
Of crystal heaven falls one full black drop.

Like a soft full drop of darkness it seems to sway
    In the tender wine
Of our Sabbath, suffusing our sacred day.

PIANO

Softly, in the dusk, a woman is singing to me;
Taking me back down the vista of years, till I see
A child sitting under the piano, in the boom of the tingling
    strings
And pressing the small, poised feet of a mother who smiles
    as she sings.

In spite of myself, the insidious mastery of song
Betrays me back, till the heart of me weeps to belong
To the old Sunday evenings at home, with winter outside
And hymns in the cosy parlour, the tinkling piano our
    guide.

So now it is vain for the singer to burst into clamour
With the great black piano appassionato. The glamour
Of childish days is upon me, my manhood is cast
Down in the flood of remembrance, I weep like a child for
    the past.

THE NORTH COUNTRY

In another country, black poplars shake themselves over a
    pond,
And rooks and the rising smoke-waves scatter and wheel
    from the works beyond:
The air is dark with north and with sulphur, the grass is
    a darker green,
And people darkly invested with purple move palpable
    through the scene.

Soundlessly down across the counties, out of the resonant
gloom
That wraps the north in stupor and purple travels the deep,
slow boom
Of the man-life north imprisoned, shut in the hum of the
purpled steel
As it spins to sleep on its motion, drugged dense in the
sleep of the wheel.

Out of the sleep, from the gloom of motion, soundlessly,
somnambule
Moans and booms the soul of a people imprisoned, asleep
in the rule
Of the strong machine that runs mesmeric, booming the
spell of its word
Upon them and moving them helpless, mechanic, their will
to its will deferred.

Yet all the while comes the droning inaudible, out of the
violet air,
The moaning of sleep-bound beings in travail that toil and
are will-less there
In the spellbound north, convulsive now with a dream near
morning, strong
With violent achings heaving to burst the sleep that is now
not long.

LOVE STORM

Many roses in the wind
Are tapping at the window-sash.
A hawk is in the sky; his wings
Slowly begin to plash.

The roses with the west wind rapping
Are torn away, and a splash
Of red goes down the billowing air.

Still hangs the hawk, with the whole sky moving
Past him—only a wing-beat proving
The will that holds him there.

The daisies in the grass are bending,
The hawk has dropped, the wind is spending
All the roses, and unending
Rustle of leaves washes out the rending
Cry of a bird.

A red rose goes on the wind.—Ascending
The hawk his windswept way is wending
Easily down the sky. The daisies, sending
Strange white signals, seem intending
To show the place whence the scream was heard.

But, oh, my heart, what birds are piping!
A silver wind is hastily wiping
The face of the youngest rose.

And oh, my heart, cease apprehending!
The hawk is gone, a rose is tapping
The window-sash as the west wind blows.

Knock, knock, 'tis no more than a red rose rapping,
And fear is a plash of wings.
What, then, if a scarlet rose goes flapping
Down the bright-grey ruin of things!

PASSING VISIT TO HELEN

Returning, I find her just the same,
At just the same old delicate game.

Still she says: "Nay, loose no flame
To lick me up and do me harm!

Be all yourself!—for oh, the charm
Of your heart of fire in which I look!
Oh, better there than in any book
Glow and enact the dramas and dreams
I love for ever!—there it seems
You are lovelier than life itself, till desire
Comes licking through the bars of your lips,
And over my face the stray fire slips,
Leaving a burn and an ugly smart
That will have the oil of illusion. Oh, heart
Of fire and beauty, loose no more
Your reptile flames of lust; ah, store
Your passion in the basket of your soul,
Be all yourself, one bonny, burning coal
That stays with steady joy of its own fire!
For in the firing all my porcelain
Of flesh does crackle and shiver and break in pain,
My ivory and marble black with stain,
My veil of sensitive mystery rent in twain,
My altars sullied, I bereft, remain
A priestess execrable, taken in vain——"

So the refrain
Sings itself over, and so the game
Restarts itself wherein I am kept
Like a glowing brazier faintly blue of flame,
So that the delicate love-adept
Can warm her hands and invite her soul,
Sprinkling incense and salt of words
And kisses pale, and sipping the toll
Of incense-smoke that rises like birds.

Yet I've forgotten in playing this game,
Things I have known that shall have no name;
Forgetting the place from which I came
I watch her ward away the flame
Yet warm herself at the fire—then blame
Me that I flicker in the basket;

Me that I glow not with content
To have my substance so subtly spent;
Me that I interrupt her game . . .
I ought to be proud that she should ask it
Of me to be her fire-opal. . . .

                    It is well
Since I am here for so short a spell
Not to interrupt her?—Why should I
Break in by making any reply!

TWENTY YEARS AGO

Round the house were lilacs and strawberries
    And foal-foots spangling the paths,
And far away on the sand-hills, dewberries
    Caught dust from the sea's long swaths.

Up the wolds the woods were walking,
    And nuts fell out of their hair.
At the gate the nets hung, balking
    The star-lit rush of a hare.

In the autumn fields, the stubble
    Tinkled the music of gleaning.
At a mother's knees, the trouble
    Lost all its meaning.

Yea, what good beginnings
    To this sad end!
Have we had our innings?
    God forfend!

READING A LETTER

She sits on the recreation ground
    Under an oak whose yellow buds dot the pale blue sky.
The young grass twinkles in the wind, and the sound
    Of the wind in the knotted buds makes a canopy.

So sitting under the knotted canopy
    Of the wind, she is lifted and carried away as in a balloon
Across the insensible void, till she stoops to see
    The sandy desert beneath her, the dreary platoon.

She knows the waste all dry beneath her, in one place
    Stirring with earth-coloured life, ever turning and stirring.
But never the motion has a human face
    Nor sound, only intermittent machinery whirring.

And so again, on the recreation ground
    She alights a stranger, wondering, unused to the scene;
Suffering at sight of the children playing around,
    Hurt at the chalk-coloured tulips, and the evening-green.

SEVEN SEALS

Since this is the last night I keep you home,
Come, I will consecrate you for the journey.

Rather I had you would not go. Nay come,
I will not again reproach you. Lie back
And let me love you a long time ere you go.
For you are sullen-hearted still, and lack
The will to love me. But even so
I will set a seal upon you from my lip,
Will set a guard of honour at each door,
Seal up each channel out of which might slip
Your love for me.

                    I kiss your mouth. Ah, love,
Could I but seal its ruddy, shining spring
Of passion, parch it up, destroy, remove
Its softly-stirring crimson welling-up
Of kisses! Oh, help me, God! Here at the source
I'd lie for ever drinking and drawing in
Your fountains, as heaven drinks from out their course
The floods.

I close your ears with kisses
And seal your nostrils; and round your neck you'll
    wear—
Nay, let me work—a delicate chain of kisses.
Like beads they go around, and not one misses
To touch its fellow on either side.

                                          And there
Full mid-between the champaign of your breast
I place a great and burning seal of love
Like a dark rose, a mystery of rest
On the slow bubbling of your rhythmic heart.
Nay, I persist, and very faith shall keep
You integral to me. Each door, each mystic port
Of egress from you I will seal and steep
In perfect chrism.
                        Now it is done. The mort
Will sound in heaven before it is undone.
But let me finish what I have begun
And shirt you now invulnerable in the mail
Of iron kisses, kisses linked like steel.
Put greaves upon your thighs and knees, and frail
Webbing of steel on your feet. So you shall feel
Ensheathed invulnerable with me, with seven
Great seals upon your outgoings, and woven
Chain of my mystic will wrapped perfectly
Upon you, wrapped in indomitable me.

TWO WIVES

I

Into the shadow-white chamber silts the white
Flux of another dawn. The wind that all night
Long has waited restless, suddenly wafts
A whirl like snow from the plum-trees and the pear,
Till petals heaped between the window-shafts
        In a drift die there.

154

A nurse in white, at the dawning, flower-foamed pane
Draws down the blinds, whose shadows scarcely stain
The white rugs on the floor, nor the silent bed
That rides the room like a frozen berg, its crest
Finally ridged with the austere line of the dead
      Stretched out at rest.

Less than a year the fourfold feet had pressed
The peaceful floor, when fell the sword on their rest.
Yet soon, too soon, she had him home again
With wounds between them, and suffering like a guest
That will not go. Now suddenly going, the pain
      Leaves an empty breast.

II

A tall woman, with her long white gown aflow
As she strode her limbs amongst it, once more
She hastened towards the room. Did she know
As she listened in silence outside the silent door?
Entering, she saw him in outline, raised on a pyre
      Awaiting the fire.

Upraised on the bed, with feet erect as a bow,
Like the prow of a boat, his head laid back like the stern
Of a ship that stands in a shadowy sea of snow
With frozen rigging, she saw him; she drooped like a fern
Refolding, she slipped to the floor as a ghost-white peony
    slips
      When the thread clips.

Soft she lay as a shed flower fallen, nor heard
The ominous entry, nor saw the other love,
The dark, the grave-eyed mistress who thus dared
At such an hour to lay her claim, above
A stricken wife, so sunk in oblivion, bowed
      With misery, no more proud.

I I I

The stranger's hair was shorn like a lad's dark poll
And pale her ivory face: her eyes would fail
In silence when she looked: for all the whole
Darkness of failure was in them, without avail.
Dark in indomitable failure, she who had lost
      Now claimed the host.

She softly passed the sorrowful flower shed
In blonde and white on the floor, nor even turned
Her head aside, but straight towards the bed
Moved with slow feet, and her eyes' flame steadily burned.
She looked at him as he lay with banded cheek,
      And she started to speak

Softly: "I knew it would come to this," she said,
"I knew that some day, soon, I should find you thus.
So I did not fight you. You went your way instead
Of coming mine—and of the two of us
I died the first, I, in the after-life
      Am now your wife."

I V

" 'Twas I whose fingers did draw up the young
Plant of your body: to me you looked ere sprung
The secret of the moon within your eyes!
My mouth you met before your fine red mouth
Was set to song—and never your song denies
      My love, till you went south."

" 'Twas I who placed the bloom of manhood on
Your youthful smoothness: I fleeced where fleece was none
Your fervent limbs with flickers and tendrils of new
Knowledge; I set your heart to its stronger beat;
I put my strength upon you, and I threw
      My life at your feet."

"But I whom the years had reared to be your bride,
Who for years was sun for your shivering, shade for your
    sweat,
Who for one strange year was as a bride to you—you set me
    aside
With the old, sweet things of our youth;—and never yet
Have I ceased to grieve that I was not great enough
        To defeat your baser stuff."

V

"But you are given back again to me
Who have kept intact for you your virginity.
Who for the rest of life walk out of care,
Indifferent here of myself, since I am gone
Where you are gone, and you and I out there
        Walk now as one."

"Your widow am I, and only I. I dream
God bows His head and grants me this supreme
Pure look of your last dead face, whence now is gone
The mobility, the panther's gambolling,
And all your being is given to me, so none
        Can mock my struggling."

"And now at last I kiss your perfect face,
Perfecting now our unfinished, first embrace.
Your young hushed look that then saw God ablaze
In every bush, is given you back, and we
Are met at length to finish our rest of days
        In a unity."

V I

The other woman rose, and swiftly said:
"So! you have come to get him now he's dead!
Now you can triumph, now he is no more
Than a dream of yours! 'twas all you ever could
See in him, your self's dream in his sore
        Heart's blood."

"How did you love him, you who only roused
His mind until it burnt his heart away!
'Twas you who killed him, when you both caroused
In words and things well said. But the other way
He never loved you, never with desire
        Touched you to fire."

"Take what you've got, your memory of words
Between you, but his touch you never knew.
Caresses never flew to you like birds.
You never bore his children, never drew
His body down in weight to rest in you
        The night through."

VII

"Take then eternity, for what is that
But another word, conceit and vanity!
But do not touch this man who never yet
Took pleasure in touching you. Mortality
Is not for you, and he is mortal still
        Against his will."

"Even dead, he still is mortal, and his hair
Is soft though it is cold. Do not dare
To touch him while he still is lying there!
Stand a way off, and if you like commune
With his wan spirit somewhere in the air
        Like a lost tune."

"But do not touch him, for he hated you
To touch him, and he said so, and you knew.
Why are you here? What is his corpse to you?
Stand you far off and triumph like a Jew
That he is dead and you are not. But stand
        Back, you understand!"

NOISE OF BATTLE

And all hours long, the town
   Roars like a beast in a cave
That is wounded there
And like to drown;
   While days rush, wave after wave
On its lair.

An invisible woe unseals
   The flood, so it passes beyond
All bounds: the great old city
Recumbent roars as it feels
   The foamy paw of the pond
Reach from immensity.

But all that it can do
   Now, as the tide rises,
Is to listen and hear the grim
Waves crash like thunder through
   The splintered streets, hear noises
Roll hollow in the interim.

AT THE FRONT

Far-off the lily-statues stand white-ranked in the garden
   at home.
Would God they were shattered quickly, the cattle would
   tread them out in the loam.
I wish the elder-trees in flower could suddenly heave, and
   burst
The walls of the house, and nettles puff out from the hearth
   at which I was nursed.

It stands so still in the hush composed of trees and inviolate
   peace,
The home of my fathers, the place that is mine, my fate and
   my old increase.

And now that the skies are falling, the world is spouting in
    fountains of dirt,
I would give my soul for the homestead to fall with me, go
    with me, both in one hurt.

REALITY OF PEACE, 1916

The trees in trouble because of autumn,
    And scarlet berries falling from the bush,
And all the myriad houseless seeds
    Loosing hold in the wind's insistent push

Moan softly with autumnal parturition,
    Poor, obscure fruits extruded out of light
Into the world of shadow, carried down
    Between the bitter knees of the after-night.

Bushed in an uncouth ardour, coiled at core
    With a knot of life that only bliss can unravel,
Fall all the fruits most bitterly into earth,
    Bitterly into corrosion bitterly travel.

What is it internecine that is locked
    By very fierceness into a quiescence
Within the rage? We shall not know till it burst
    Out of corrosion into new florescence.

Nay, but how tortured is the frightful seed,
    The spark intense within it, all without
Mordant corrosion gnashing and champing hard
    For ruin on the naked small redoubt.

Bitter to fold the issue, and make no sally!
    To have the mystery, but not go forth!
To bear, but retaliate nothing, given to save
    The spark from storms of corrosion, as seeds
        from the north.

The sharper, more horrid the pressure, the harder
    the heart
  That saves the blue grain of eternal fire
Within its quick, committed to hold and wait
    And suffer unheeding, only forbidden to expire.

NARCISSUS

Where the minnows trace
A glinting web quick hid in the gloom of the brook,
When I think of the place
And remember the small lad lying intent to look
Through the shadowy face
At the little fish thread-threading the watery nook—

It seems to me
The woman you are should be nixie, there is a pool
Where we ought to be.
You undine-clear and pearly, soullessly cool
And waterly,
The pool for my limbs to fathom, my soul's last school.

Narcissus
Ventured so long ago in the deeps of reflection.
Illyssus
Broke the bounds and beyond!—Dim recollection
Of fishes
Soundlessly moving in heaven's other direction!

Be
Undine towards the waters, moving back;
For me
A pool! Put off the soul you've got, oh, lack
Your human self immortal; take the watery track!

TOMMIES IN THE TRAIN

The sun shines,
The coltsfoot flowers along the railway banks
Shine like flat coin which Jove in thanks
Strews each side the lines.

A steeple
In purple elms, daffodils
Sparkle beneath; luminous hills
Beyond—and no people.

England, O Danaë
To this spring of cosmic gold
That falls on your lap of mould!—
What then are we?

What are we
Clay-coloured, who roll in fatigue
As the train falls league after league
From our destiny?

A hand is over my face,
A cold hand.—I peep between the fingers
To watch the world that lingers
Behind, yet keeps pace.

Always there, as I peep
Between the fingers that cover my face!
Which then is it that falls from its place
And rolls down the steep?

Is it the train
That falls like a meteorite
Backward into space, to alight
Never again?

Or is it the illusory world
That falls from reality
As we look? Or are we
Like a thunderbolt hurled?

One or another
Is lost, since we fall apart
Endlessly, in one motion depart
From each other.

ON THE MARCH

We are out on the open road.
Through the low west window a cold light flows
On the floor where never my numb feet trode
Before; onward the strange road goes.

Soon the spaces of the western sky
With shutters of sombre cloud will close.
But we'll still be together, this road and I,
Together, wherever the long road goes.

The wind chases by us, and over the corn
Pale shadows flee from us as if from their foes.
Like a snake we thresh on the long, forlorn
Land, as onward the long road goes.

From the sky, the low, tired moon fades out;
Through the poplars the night-wind blows;
Pale, sleepy phantoms are tossed about
As the wind asks whither the wan road goes.

Away in the distance wakes a lamp.
Inscrutable small lights glitter in rows.
They come no nearer, and still we tramp
Onwards, wherever the strange road goes.

Beat after beat falls sombre and dull.
The wind is unchanging, not one of us knows
What will be in the final lull
When we find the place where this dead road goes.

For something must come, since we pass and pass
Along in the coiled, convulsive throes
Of this marching, along with the invisible grass
That goes wherever this old road goes.

Perhaps we shall come to oblivion.
Perhaps we shall march till our tired toes
Tread over the edge of the pit, and we're gone
Down the endless slope where the last road goes.

If so, let us forge ahead, straight on,
If we're going to sleep the sleep with those
That fall for ever, knowing none
Of this land whereon the wrong road goes.

RUINATION

The sun is bleeding its fires upon the mist
That huddles in grey heaps coiling and holding back.
Like cliffs abutting in shadow a dead grey sea
Some street-ends thrust forward their stack.

On the misty waste lands, away from the flushing grey
Of the morning, the elms are loftily dimmed, and tall
As if moving in air towards us, tall angels
Of darkness advancing steadily over us all.

THE ATTACK

When we came out of the wood
Was a great light!
The night uprisen stood
In white.

164

I wondered, I looked around
It was so fair. The bright
Stubble upon the ground
Shone white

Like any field of snow;
Yet warm the chase
Of faint night-breaths did go
Across my face!

White-bodied and warm the night was,
Sweet-scented to hold in the throat;
White and alight the night was;
A pale stroke smote

The pulse through the whole bland being
Which was This and me;
A pulse that still went fleeing,
Yet did not flee.

In front of the terrible rage, the death,
This wonder stood glistening!
All shapes of wonder, with suspended breath,
Arrested listening

In ecstatic reverie;
The whole, white Night!—
With wonder, every black tree
Blossomed outright.

I saw the transfiguration
And the present Host.
Transubstantiation
Of the Luminous Ghost.

WINTER-LULL

Because of the silent snow, we are all hushed
    Into awe.
No sound of guns nor overhead no rushed
    Vibration to draw
Our attention out of the void wherein we are crushed.

A crow floats past on level wings
    Noiselessly.
Uninterrupted silence swings
    Invisibly, inaudibly
To and fro in our misgivings.

We do not look at each other, we hide
    Our daunted eyes.
White earth, and ruins, ourselves, and nothing beside . . .
    It all belies
Our existence; we wait, and are still denied.

We are folded together, men and the snowy ground
    Into nullity.
There is silence, only the silence, never a sound
    Nor a verity
To assist us; disastrously silence-bound!

BOMBARDMENT

The Town has opened to the sun.
Like a flat red lily with a million petals
She unfolds, she comes undone.

A sharp sky brushes upon
The myriad glittering chimney-tips
As she gently exhales to the sun.

Hurrying creatures run
Down the labyrinth of the sinister flower.
What is it they shun?

A dark bird falls from the sun.
It curves in a rush to the heart of the vast
Flower: the day has begun.

RONDEAU OF A CONSCIENTIOUS OBJECTOR

The hours have tumbled their leaden, monotonous sands
And piled them up in a dull grey heap in the west.
I carry my patience sullenly through the waste lands;
To-morrow will pour them all back, the dull hours I detest.

I force my cart through the sodden filth that is pressed
Into ooze, and the sombre dirt spouts up at my hands
As I make my way in twilight now to rest.
The hours have tumbled their leaden, monotonous sands.

A twisted thorn-tree still in the evening stands
Defending the memory of leaves and the happy round nest.
But mud has flooded the homes of these weary lands
And piled them up in a dull grey heap in the west.

All day has the clank of iron on iron distressed
The nerve-bare place. Now a little silence expands
And a gasp of relief. But the soul is still compressed;
I carry my patience sullenly through the waste lands.

The hours have ceased to fall, and a star commands
Shadows to cover our stricken manhood, and blest
Sleep to make us forget: but he understands:
To-morrow will pour them all back, the dull hours I detest.

OBSEQUIAL ODE

Surely you've trodden straight
        To the very door!
Surely you took your fate
Faultlessly! Now it's too late
        To say more.

It is evident you were right,
    That man has a course to go,
A voyage to sail beyond the charted seas.
You have passed from out of sight
    And my questions blow
Back from the straight horizon that ends all one sees.

    Now like a vessel in port
    You unlade your riches into death;
And glad are the eager dead to receive you there.
    Let the dead sort
Your cargo out, breath from breath
Let them disencumber your bounty, let them all share.

    I imagine dead hands are brighter,
    Their fingers in sunset shine
With jewels of passion once broken through you as a
      prism
Breaks light into gems; and dead breasts whiter
    For your wrath; and yes, I opine
They anoint their brows with your pain, as a perfect
      chrism.

    On your body, the beaten anvil,
    Was hammered out
That moon-like sword the ascendant dead unsheathe
Against us; sword that no man will
    Put to rout;
Sword that severs the question from us who breathe.

Surely you've trodden straight
    To the very door!
You have surely achieved your fate;
And the perfect dead are elate
    To have won once more.

Now to the dead you are giving
    Your last allegiance.
But what of us who are living,
And fearful yet of believing
    In your pitiless legions?

GOING BACK

The night turns slowly round,
Swift trains go by in a rush of light;
Slow trains steal past.
This train beats anxiously, outward bound.

But I am not here.
I am away, beyond the scope of this turning;
There, where the pivot is, the axis
Of all this gear.

I, who sit in tears,
I, whose heart is torn with parting;
Who cannot bear to think back to the departure
    platform;—
My spirit hears

Voices of men,
Sound of artillery, aeroplanes, presences,
And more than all, the dead-sure silence,
The pivot again. . . .

There, at the axis
Pain, or love, or grief
Sleep on speed; in dead certainty;
Pure relief.

There, at the pivot
Time sleeps again.
No has-been, no hereafter; only the perfected
Presence of men.

SHADES

Shall I tell you, then, how it is?—
There came a cloven gleam
Like a tongue of darkened flame
To flicker in me.

And so I seem
To have you still the same
In one world with me.

In the flicker of a flower,
In a worm that is blind, yet strives,
In a mouse that pauses to listen

Glimmers our
Shadow; yet it deprives
Them none of the glisten.

In every shaken morsel
I see our shadow tremble
As if it rippled from out of us hand in hand.

As if it were part and parcel,
One shadow, and we need not dissemble
Our darkness: do you understand?

For I have told you plainly how it is.

TOWN IN 1917

London
Used to wear her lights splendidly,
Flinging her shawl-fringe over the River,
Tassels in abandon.

And up in the sky
A two-eyed clock, like an owl
Solemnly used to approve, chime, chiming
Approval, goggle-eyed fowl!

There are no gleams on the River,
No goggling clock;
No sound from St Stephen's;
No lamp-fringed frock.

Instead
Darkness, and skin-wrapped
Fleet, hurrying limbs,
Soft-footed dead.

London
Original, wolf-wrapped
In pelts of wolves, all her luminous
Garments gone.

London, with hair
Like a forest darkness, like a marsh
Of rushes, ere the Romans
Broke in her lair.

It is well
That London, lair of sudden
Male and female darknesses,
Has broken her spell.

BREAD UPON THE WATERS

So you are lost to me!
Ah you, you ear of corn straight lying,
What food is this for the darkly flying
Fowls of the Afterwards!

White bread afloat on the waters,
Cast out by the hand that scatters
Food untowards;

Will you come back when the tide turns?
After many days? My heart yearns
To know!

Will you return after many days
To say your say as a traveller says,
More marvel than woe?—

Drift then, for the sightless birds
And the fish in shadow-waved herds
⠀⠀⠀To approach you!

For you are lost to me.

WAR-BABY

The child like mustard seed
Rolls out of the husk of death
⠀⠀⠀Into the woman's fertile, fathomless lap.

Look, it has taken root!
See how it flourisheth!
⠀⠀⠀See how it rises with magical, rosy sap!

As for our faith, it was there
When we did not know, did not care;
⠀⠀⠀It fell from our husk in a little hasty seed.

Say, is it all we need?
Is it true that the little weed
⠀⠀⠀Will flourish its branches in heaven when we
⠀⠀⠀⠀slumber beneath?

NOSTALGIA

The waning moon looks upward; this grey night
Slopes round the heavens in one smooth curve
Of easy sailing; odd red wicks serve
To show where the ships at sea move out of sight.

The place is palpable me, for here I was born
Of this self-same darkness. Yet the shadowy house below
Is out of bounds, and only the old ghosts know
I have come, I feel them whimper in welcome, and mourn.

My father suddenly died in the harvesting corn
And the place is no longer ours. Watching, I hear
No sound from the strangers, the place is dark, and fear
Opens my eyes till the roots of my vision seem torn.

Can I go no nearer, never towards the door?
The ghosts and I we mourn together, and shrink
In the shadow of the cart-shed. Must we hover on the brink
For ever, and never enter the homestead any more?

Is it irrevocable? Can I really not go
Through the open yard-way? Can I not go past the sheds
And through to the mowie?—Only the dead in their beds
Can know the fearful anguish that this is so.

I kiss the stones, I kiss the moss on the wall,
And wish I could pass impregnate into the place.
I wish I could take it all in a last embrace.
I wish with my breast I here could annihilate it all.

DREAMS OLD AND NASCENT

NASCENT
The world is a painted memory, where coloured shapes
Of old, spent lives linger blurred and warm;
An endless tapestry the past has woven, drapes
The halls of my mind, compelling my life to conform.

I have lived delighted in the halls of the past
Where dead men's lives glow gently, and iron hurts
No more, and money stinks not, and death at last
Is only sad men taking off their shirts.

But now I think I have seen it all, and now
I feel thick walls of stone behind the arras.
I am shut in, a prisoner, I know not how.
And past lives hamper me, clog and embarrass.

They have no hands, they have no bodies, all
These shapes that now are dreams and once were men.
And so my heart begins to cry and call
But to get out from this dim, dreadful den.

.   .   .   .   .   .

The surface of dreams is broken, the arras is torn,
There's a breach in the walls of the past, lets the daylight through.
Fluent figures of men go down the upborne
Track of the railway, alive, and with something to do.

Along the railway, active figures of men!
Each with a secret which stirs in his limbs, as they move
Out of the distance nearer, coming to prove
With a touch the dead and the living, while time counts ten.

In the subtle lift of the thighs as they come unmarching
Beats the new fresh air of life. They come for strife,
For the ripping of arras, and smashing of walls, and the fight for life;
With axe in hand, and the hammer, and the pick-axe over-arching.

Oh come, and break this prison, this house of yesterday!
The arras is all illusion, oh come and tear it away!
The walls are thick, and the inner rooms are such, they dismay
The heart, all crowded with slaves, most working, some few at play.

.   .   .   .   .   .

The old dreams are beautiful, beloved, soft-toned and sure,
But worn out, they hide no more the walls they stand before.
Walled in, walled in, the whole world is a vast impure
Interior, a house of dreams where the dreamers writhe and snore.

Oh come, and wake us up from the ghastly dream of to-day.
We asphyxiate in a sleep of dreams, rebreathing the impure air.
For the house is shut and sealed, and the breath of the hosts is grey
As they dream corrupted dreams, all poisoned with care.

The ghastly dream of labour, and the stench of steel and of oil.
The writhing of myriads of workmen, all dreaming they are going
    to be rich
And giving off dreadful effluvia in a ghastly effort of toil
Unfinished for ever, but gasping for money, as they dream and they
    itch.

The ghastly dream of riches, of masses of money to spend,
Of walking over the faces of men, like cobble-stones!
Of riding, and being envied, such envy as has no end!
Of making a triumph of envy, the rich and successful ones.

.   .   .   .   .   .

The whole wide world is interior now, and we're all shut up.
The air is all close and poisonous, it has drugged our souls, so we
    sleep
A sleep that is writhing stupor, weighed down, so we can't wake up.
The rich and the poor alike dreaming and writhing, all in one heap.

Oh come, oh, men along the railway! Oh come as men
And break the walls of possession of all the wide world!
Give us air, we cry. Oh, let us but breathe again!
Let us breathe fresh air and wake from foul dreams in which we
    are furled.

To feel fresh air in our throats, to have fresh breath in our breasts,
To make new words with our lips, to escape the foul dream
Of having and getting and owning, the struggle which wrests
Money from out of the earth or the beast or the man, as they labour
    in steam.

.   .   .   .   .   .

Oh, men with the axe and the pick-axe, break the walls of the filthy
    dream
And release us, poor ones and rich ones, let us breathe and touch
One another in wonder of wakening, let us wake to the gleam
Of real daylight upon us, released from the foul dream's hutch.

For the proper dream-stuff is molten, and moving mysteriously,
And the bodies of men and women are molten matter of dreams
That stirs with a stir which is cosmic, as ever, invisibly
The heart of the live world pulses, and the blood of the live world
    teems.

And what is life, but the swelling and shaping the dream in the flesh!
And our bodies molten drops of dream-blood that swirl and swell
In a tissue, as all the molten cells in the living mesh
Of a rose-tree move to roses and thorns and a delicate smell.

ON THAT DAY

    On that day
I shall put roses on roses, and cover your grave
With multitude of white roses: and, since you were brave,
    One bright red ray.

    So people, passing under
The ash-trees of the valley-road, will raise
Their eyes and look at the grave on the hill, in wonder,
    Wondering mount, and put the flowers asunder:

    To see whose praise
Is blazoned here so white and so bloodily red.
Then they will say: " 'Tis long since she is dead,
    Who has remembered her after many days?"

    And standing there
They will consider how you went your ways
Unnoticed among them, a still queen lost in the maze
    Of this earthly affair.

    A queen, they'll say,
Has slept unnoticed on a forgotten hill.
Sleeps on unknown, unnoticed there, until
    Dawns my insurgent day.

AUTUMN SUNSHINE

The sun sets out the autumn crocuses
    And fills them up a pouring measure
    Of death-producing wine, till treasure
Runs waste down their chalices.

All, all Persephone's pale cups of mould
    Are on the board, are over-filled;
    The portion to the gods is spilled;
Now, mortals all, take hold!

The time is now, the wine-cup full and full
    Of lambent heaven, a pledging-cup;
    Let now all mortal men take up
The drink, and a long, strong pull!

Out of the hell-queen's cup, the heaven's pale wine!
    Drink then, invisible heroes, drink!
    Lips to the vessels, never shrink,
Throats to the heavens incline.

And take within the wine the god's great oath
    By heaven and earth and hellish stream,
    To break this sick and nauseous dream
We writhe and lust in, both.

Swear, in the pale wine poured from the cups of the queen
    Of hell, to wake and be free
    From this nightmare we writhe in,
Break out of this foul has-been.

SONG-DAY IN AUTUMN

When the autumn roses
    Are heavy with dew,
Before the mist discloses
    The leaf's brown hue,
You would, among the laughing hills
    Of yesterday
Walk innocent in the daffodils,
Coiffing up your auburn hair
In a puritan fillet, a chaste white snare
To catch and keep me with you there
    So far away.

When from the autumn roses
    Trickles the dew,
When the blue mist uncloses
    And the sun looks through,
You from those startled hills
    Come away,
Out of the withering daffodils;
Thoughtful, and half afraid,
Plaiting a heavy, auburn braid
And coiling it round the wise brows of a maid
    Who was scared in her play.

When in the autumn roses
    Creeps a bee,
And a trembling flower encloses
    His ecstasy,
You from your lonely walk
    Turn away,
And leaning to me like a flower on its stalk,
Wait among the beeches
For your late bee who beseeches
To creep through your loosened hair till he reaches,
    Your heart of dismay.

DISAGREEABLE ADVICE

Always, sweetheart,
Carry into your room the blossoming boughs of cherry,
Almond and apple and pear diffuse with light, that very
Soon strews itself on the floor; and keep the radiance of spring
Fresh quivering; keep the sunny-swift March-days waiting
In a little throng at your door, and admit the one who is
    plaiting
Her hair for womanhood, and play awhile with her, then
    bid her depart.

    A come and go of March-day loves
    Through the flower-vine, trailing screen;
      A fluttering in of doves.
    Then a launch abroad of shrinking doves
    Over the waste where no hope is seen
    Of open hands:
              Dance in and out
    Small-bosomed girls of the spring of love,
    With a bubble of laughter, and shrilly shout
    Of mirth; then the dripping of tears on your glove.

RESTLESSNESS

At the open door of the room I stand and look at the night,
Hold my hand to catch the raindrops, that slant into sight,
Arriving grey from the darkness above suddenly into the light of
    the room.
I will escape from the hollow room, the box of light,
And be out in the bewildering darkness, which is always fecund,
    which might
Mate my hungry soul with a germ of its womb.

I will go out to the night, as a man goes down to the shore
To draw his net through the surf's thin line, at the dawn before
The sun warms the sea, little, lonely and sad, sifting the sobbing tide.
I will sift the surf that edges the night, with my net, the four
Strands of my eyes and my lips and my hands and my feet, sifting
    the store
Of flotsam until my soul is tired or satisfied.

I will catch in my eyes' quick net
The faces of all the women as they go past,
Bend over them with my soul, to cherish the wet
Cheeks and wet hair a moment, saying: "Is it you?"
Looking earnestly under the dark umbrellas, held fast
Against the wind; and if, where the lamplight blew
Its rainy swill about us, she answered me
With a laugh and a merry wildness that it was she
Who was seeking me, and had found me at last to free
Me now from the stunting bonds of my chastity,
How glad I should be!

Moving along in the mysterious ebb of the night
Pass the men whose eyes are shut like anemones in a dark pool;
Why don't they open with vision and speak to me? what have they
    in sight?
Why do I wander aimless among them, desirous fool?

I can always linger over the huddled books on the stalls,
Always gladden my amorous fingers with the touch of their leaves,
Always kneel in courtship to the shelves in the doorways, where falls
The shadow, always offer myself to one mistress, who always
    receives.

But oh, it is not enough, it is all no good.
There is something I want to feel in my running blood,
Something I want to touch; I must hold my face to the rain,
I must hold my face to the wind, and let it explain
Me its life as it hurries in secret.
I will trail my hands again through the drenched, cold leaves
Till my hands are full of the chillness and touch of leaves,
Till at length they induce me to sleep, and to forget.

POETRY OF THE PRESENT

(Introduction to the American Edition of *New Poems* [1918])

I T S E E M S when we hear a skylark singing as if sound were running forward into the future, running so fast and utterly without consideration, straight on into futurity. And when we hear a nightingale, we hear the pause and the rich, piercing rhythm of recollection, the perfected past. The lark may sound sad, but with the lovely lapsing sadness that is almost a swoon of hope. The nightingale's triumph is a pæan, but a death-pæan.

So it is with poetry. Poetry is, as a rule, either the voice of the far future, exquisite and ethereal, or it is the voice of the past, rich, magnificent. When the Greeks heard the *Iliad* and the *Odyssey*, they heard their own past calling in their hearts, as men far inland sometimes hear the sea and fall weak with powerful, wonderful regret, nostalgia; or else their own future rippled its time-beats through their blood, as they followed the painful, glamorous progress of the Ithacan. This was Homer to the Greeks: their Past, splendid with battles won and death achieved, and their Future, the magic wandering of Ulysses through the unknown.

With us it is the same. Our birds sing on the horizons. They sing out of the blue, beyond us, or out of the quenched night. They sing at dawn and sunset. Only the poor, shrill, tame canaries whistle while we talk. The wild birds begin before we are awake, or as we drop into dimness out of waking. Our poets sit by the gateways, some by the east, some by the west. As we arrive and as we go out our hearts surge with response. But whilst we are in the midst of life, we do not hear them.

The poetry of the beginning and the poetry of the end must have that exquisite finality, perfection which belongs to all that is far off. It is in the realm of all that is perfect. It is of the nature of all that is complete and consummate. This completeness, this consummateness, the finality and the perfection are conveyed in exquisite form: the perfect symmetry, the rhythm which returns upon itself like a dance where the hands link and loosen and link for the supreme moment of the end. Perfected bygone moments, perfected moments in the glimmering futurity, these are the treasured gem-like lyrics of Shelley and Keats.

But there is another kind of poetry: the poetry of that which is at hand: the immediate present. In the immediate present there is no perfection, no consummation, nothing finished. The strands are all flying, quivering, intermingling into the web, the waters are shaking the moon. There is no round, consummate moon on the face of running water, nor on the face of the unfinished tide. There are no gems of the living plasm. The living plasm vibrates unspeakably, it inhales the future, it exhales the past, it is the quick of both, and yet it is neither. There is no plasmic finality, nothing crystal, permanent. If we try to fix the living tissue, as the biologists fix it with formalin, we have only a hardened bit of the past, the bygone life under our observation.

Life, the ever-present, knows no finality, no finished crystallisation. The perfect rose is only a running flame, emerging and flowing off, and never in any sense at rest, static, finished. Herein lies its transcendent loveliness. The whole tide of all life and all time suddenly heaves, and appears before us as an apparition, a revelation. We look at the very white quick of nascent creation. A water-lily heaves herself from the flood, looks round, gleams, and is gone. We have seen the incarnation, the quick of the ever-swirling flood. We have seen the invisible. We have seen, we have touched, we have partaken of the very substance of creative change, creative mutation. If you tell me about the lotus, tell me of nothing changeless or eternal. Tell me of the mystery of the inexhaustible, forever-unfolding creative spark. Tell me of the incarnate disclosure of the flux, mutation in blossom, laughter and decay perfectly open in their transit, nude in their movement before us.

Let me feel the mud and the heavens in my lotus. Let me feel the heavy, silting, sucking mud, the spinning of sky winds. Let me feel them both in purest contact, the nakedness of sucking weight, nakedly passing radiance. Give me nothing fixed, set, static. Don't give me the infinite or the eternal: nothing of infinity, nothing of eternity. Give me the still, white seething, the incandescence and the coldness of the incarnate moment: the moment, the quick of all change and haste and opposition: the moment, the immediate present, the Now. The immediate moment is not a drop of water running downstream. It is the source and issue, the bubbling up of the stream. Here, in this very instant moment, up bubbles the stream of time, out of the wells of futurity, flowing on to the oceans of the past. The source, the issue, the creative quick.

There is poetry of this immediate present, instant poetry, as well as poetry of the infinite past and the infinite future. The seething poetry of the incarnate Now is supreme, beyond even the everlasting gems of the before and after. In its quivering momentaneity it surpasses the crystalline, pearl-hard jewels, the poems of the eternities. Do not ask for the qualities of the unfading timeless gems. Ask for the whiteness which is the seethe of mud, ask for that incipient putrescence which is the skies falling, ask for the never-pausing, never-ceasing life itself. There must be mutation, swifter than iridescence, haste, not rest, come-and-go, not fixity, inconclusiveness, immediacy, the quality of life itself, without dénouement or close. There must be the rapid momentaneous association of things which meet and pass on the forever incalculable journey of creation: everything left in its own rapid, fluid relationship with the rest of things.

This is the unrestful, ungraspable poetry of the sheer present, poetry whose very permanency lies in its wind-like transit. Whitman's is the best poetry of this kind. Without beginning and without end, without any base and pediment, it sweeps past forever, like a wind that is forever in passage, and unchainable. Whitman truly looked before and after. But he did not sigh for what is not. The clue to all his utterance lies in the sheer appreciation of the instant moment, life surging itself into utterance at its very well-head. Eternity is only an abstraction from the actual present. Infinity is only a great reservoir of recollection, or a reservoir of aspiration: man-made. The quivering nimble hour of the present, this is the quick of Time. This is the immanence. The quick of the universe is the *pulsating, carnal self*, mysterious and palpable. So it is always.

Because Whitman put this into his poetry, we fear him and

respect him so profoundly. We should not fear him if he sang only of the "old unhappy far-off things", or of the "wings of the morning". It is because his heart beats with the urgent, insurgent Now, which is even upon us all, that we dread him. He is so near the quick.

From the foregoing it is obvious that the poetry of the instant present cannot have the same body or the same motion as the poetry of the before and after. It can never submit to the same conditions. It is never finished. There is no rhythm which returns upon itself, no serpent of eternity with its tail in its own mouth. There is no static perfection, none of that finality which we find so satisfying because we are so frightened.

Much has been written about free verse. But all that can be said, first and last, is that free verse is, or should be, direct utterance from the instant, whole man. It is the soul and the mind and body surging at once, nothing left out. They speak all together. There is some confusion, some discord. But the confusion and the discord only belong to the reality as noise belongs to the plunge of water. It is no use inventing fancy laws for free verse, no use drawing a melodic line which all the feet must toe. Free verse toes no melodic line, no matter what drill-sergeant. Whitman pruned away his clichés—perhaps his clichés of rhythm as well as of phrase. And this is about all we can do, deliberately, with free verse. We can get rid of the stereotyped movements and the old hackneyed associations of sound or sense. We can break down those artificial conduits and canals through which we do so love to force our utterance. We can break the stiff neck of habit. We can be in ourselves spontaneous and flexible as flame, we can see that utterance rushes out without artificial foam or artificial smoothness. But we cannot positively prescribe any motion, any rhythm. All the laws we invent or discover—it amounts to pretty much the same—will fail to apply to free verse. They will only apply to some form of restricted, limited unfree verse.

All we can say is that free verse does *not* have the same nature as restricted verse. It is not of the nature of reminiscence. It is not the past which we treasure in its perfection between our hands. Neither is it the crystal of the perfect future, into which we gaze. Its tide is neither the full, yearning flow of aspiration, nor the sweet, poignant ebb of remembrance and regret. The past and the future are the two great bournes of human emotion, the two great homes of the human days, the two eternities. They are both conclusive, final. Their beauty is the beauty of the goal, finished, perfected. Finished beauty and measured symmetry belong to the stable, unchanging eternities.

But in free verse we look for the insurgent naked throb of the instant moment. To break the lovely form of metrical verse, and to dish up the fragments as a new substance, called *vers libre*, this is what most of the free-versifiers accomplish. They do not know that free verse has its own *nature*, that it is neither star nor pearl, but instantaneous like plasm. It has no goal in either eternity. It has no finish. It has no satisfying stability, satisfying to those who like the immutable. None of this. It is the instant; the quick; the very jetting source of all will-be and has-been. The utterance is like a spasm, naked contact with all influences at once. It does not want to get anywhere. It just takes place.

For such utterance any externally-applied law would be mere shackles and death. The law must come new each time from within. The bird is on the wing in the winds, flexible to every breath, a living spark in the storm, its very flickering depending upon its supreme mutability and power of change. Whence such a bird came: whither it goes: from what solid earth it rose up, and upon what solid earth it will close its wings and settle, this is not the question. This is a question of before and after. Now, *now*, the bird is on the wing in the winds.

Such is the rare new poetry. One realm we have never conquered: the pure present. One great mystery of time is terra incognita to us: the instant. The most superb mystery we have hardly recognised: the immediate, instant self. The quick of all time is the instant. The quick of all the universe, of all creation, is the incarnate, carnal self. Poetry gave us the clue: free verse: Whitman. Now we know.

The ideal—what is the ideal? A figment. An abstraction. A static abstraction, abstracted from life. It is a fragment of the before or the after. It is a crystallised aspiration, or a crystallised remembrance: crystallised, set, finished. It is a thing set apart, in the great storehouse of eternity, the storehouse of finished things.

We do not speak of things crystallised and set apart. We speak of the instant, the immediate self, the very plasm of the self. We speak also of free verse.

All this should have come as a preface to *Look! We Have Come Through!* But is it not better to publish a preface long after the book it belongs to has appeared? For then the reader will have had his fair chance with the book, alone.

D. H. L.

Pangbourne, 1919.

UNRHYMING POEMS

LOOK! WE HAVE COME THROUGH!

FOREWORD

These poems should not be considered separately, as so many single pieces. They are intended as an essential story, or history, or confession, unfolding one from the other in organic development, the whole revealing the intrinsic experience of a man during the crisis of manhood, when he marries and comes into himself. The period covered is, roughly, the sixth lustre of a man's life.

ARGUMENT

After much struggling and loss in love and in the world of man, the protagonist throws in his lot with a woman who is already married. Together they go into another country, she perforce leaving her children behind. The conflict of love and hate goes on between the man and the woman, and between these two and the world around them, till it reaches some sort of conclusion, they transcend into some condition of blessedness.

MOONRISE

And who has seen the moon, who has not seen
Her rise from out the chamber of the deep,
Flushed and grand and naked, as from the chamber
Of finished bridegroom, seen her rise and throw
Confession of delight upon the wave,
Littering the waves with her own superscription
Of bliss, till all her lambent beauty shakes towards us
Spread out and known at last, and we are sure
That beauty is a thing beyond the grave,
That perfect, bright experience never falls
To nothingness, and time will dim the moon
Sooner than our full consummation here
In this odd life will tarnish or pass away.

ELEGY

The sun immense and rosy
Must have sunk and become extinct
The night you closed your eyes for ever against me.

Grey days, and wan, dree dawnings
Since then, with fritter of flowers—
Day wearies me with its ostentation and fawnings.

Still, you left me the nights,
The great dark glittery window,
The bubble hemming this empty existence with lights.

Still in the vast hollow
Like a breath in a bubble spinning
Brushing the stars, goes my soul, that skims the bounds
    like a swallow!

I can look through
The film of the bubble night, to where you are.
Through the film I can almost touch you.

Eastwood.

NONENTITY

The stars that open and shut
Fall on my shallow breast
Like stars on a pool.

The soft wind, blowing cool,
Laps little crest after crest
Of ripples across my breast.

And dark grass under my feet
Seems to dabble in me
Like grass in a brook.

Oh, and it is sweet
To be all these things, not to be
Any more myself.

For look,
I am weary of myself!

MARTYR À LA MODE

Ah God, life, law, so many names you keep,
You great, you patient Effort, and you Sleep
That does inform this various dream of living,
You sleep stretched out for ever, ever giving
Us out as dreams, you august Sleep
Coursed round by rhythmic movement of all time,
The constellations, your great heart, the sun
Fierily pulsing, unable to refrain;
Since you, vast, outstretched, wordless Sleep
Permit of no beyond, ah you, whose dreams
We are, and body of sleep, let it never be said
I quailed at my appointed function, turned poltroon.

For when at night, from out the full surcharge
Of a day's experience, sleep does slowly draw
The harvest, the spent action to itself;
Leaves me unburdened to begin again;
At night, I say, when I am gone in sleep,
Does my slow heart rebel, do my dead hands
Complain of what the day has had them do?

Never let it be said I was poltroon
At this my task of living, this my dream,
This me which rises from the dark of sleep
In white flesh robed to drape another dream,
As lightning comes all white and trembling
From out the cloud of sleep, looks round about
One moment, sees, and swift its dream is over,
In one rich drip it sinks to another sleep,
And sleep thereby is one more dream enrichened.

If so the Vast, the God, the Sleep that still grows richer
Have said that I, this mote in the body of sleep,
Must in my transiency pass all through pain,
Must be a dream of grief, must like a crude
Dull meteorite flash only into light
When tearing through the anguish of this life,
Still in full flight extinct, shall I then turn
Poltroon, and beg the silent, outspread God
To alter my one speck of doom, when round me burns
The whole great conflagration of all life,
Lapped like a body close upon a sleep,
Hiding and covering in the eternal Sleep
Within the immense and toilsome life-time, heaved
With ache of dreams that body forth the Sleep?

Shall I, less than the least red grain of flesh
Within my body, cry out to the dreaming soul
That slowly labours in a vast travail,
To halt the heart, divert the streaming flow
That carries moons along, and spare the stress
That crushes me to an unseen atom of fire?

When pain and all
And grief are but the same last wonder, Sleep
Rising to dream in me a small keen dream
Of sudden anguish, sudden over and spent——
                                              Croydon.

DON JUAN

It is Isis the mystery
Must be in love with me.

Here this round ball of earth
Where all the mountains sit
Solemn in groups,
And the bright rivers flit
Round them for girth.

Here the trees and troops
Darken the shining grass,
And many people pass
Plundered from heaven,
Many bright people pass,
Plunder from heaven.

What of the mistresses,
What the beloved seven?
—They were but witnesses,
I was just driven.

Where is there peace for me?
Isis the mystery
Must be in love with me.

THE SEA

You, you are all unloving, loveless, you;
Restless and lonely, shaken by your own moods,
You are celibate and single, scorning a comrade even,
Threshing your own passions with no woman for the
    threshing-floor,
Finishing your dreams for your own sake only,
Playing your great game around the world, alone,
Without playmate, or helpmate, having no one to cherish,
No one to comfort, and refusing any comforter.

Not like the earth, the spouse all full of increase
Moiled over with the rearing of her many-mouthed young;
You are single, you are fruitless, phosphorescent, cold and
    callous,
Naked of worship, of love or of adornment,
Scorning the panacea even of labour,
Sworn to a high and splendid purposelessness
Of brooding and delighting in the secret of life's goings,
Sea, only you are free, sophisticated.

You who toil not, you who spin not,
Surely but for you and your like, toiling
Were not worth while, nor spinning worth the effort!

You who take the moon as in a sieve, and sift
Her flake by flake and spread her meaning out;
You who roll the stars like jewels in your palm,
So that they seem to utter themselves aloud;
You who steep from out the days their colour,
Reveal the universal tint that dyes
Their web; who shadow the sun's great gestures and
    expressions
So that he seems a stranger in his passing;
Who voice the dumb night fittingly;
Sea, you shadow of all things, now mock us to death with
    your shadowing.

Bournemouth.

HYMN TO PRIAPUS

My love lies underground
With her face upturned to mine,
And her mouth unclosed in a last long kiss
That ended her life and mine.

I dance at the Christmas party
Under the mistletoe
Along with a ripe, slack country lass
Jostling to and fro.

The big, soft country lass,
Like a loose sheaf of wheat
Slipped through my arms on the threshing floor
At my feet.

The warm, soft country lass,
Sweet as an armful of wheat
At threshing-time broken, was broken
For me, and ah, it was sweet!

Now I am going home
Fulfilled and alone,
I see the great Orion standing
Looking down.

He's the star of my first beloved
Love-making.
The witness of all that bitter-sweet
Heart-aching.

Now he sees this as well,
This last commission.
Nor do I get any look
Of admonition.

He can add the reckoning up
I suppose, between now and then,
Having walked himself in the thorny, difficult
Ways of men.

He has done as I have done
No doubt:
Remembered and forgotten
Turn and about.

My love lies underground
With her face upturned to mine,
And her mouth unclosed in the last long kiss
That ended her life and mine.

She fares in the stark immortal
Fields of death;
I in these goodly, frozen
Fields beneath.

Something in me remembers
And will not forget.
The stream of my life in the darkness
Deathward set!

And something in me has forgotten,
Has ceased to care.
Desire comes up, and contentment
Is debonair.

I, who am worn and careful,
How much do I care?
How is it I grin then, and chuckle
Over despair?

Grief, grief, I suppose and sufficient
Grief makes us free
To be faithless and faithful together
As we have to be.

BALLAD OF A WILFUL WOMAN

FIRST PART

Upon her plodding palfrey
With a heavy child at her breast
And Joseph holding the bridle
They mount to the last hill-crest.

Dissatisfied and weary
She sees the blade of the sea
Dividing earth and heaven
In a glitter of ecstasy.

Sudden a dark-faced stranger,
With his back to the sun, holds out
His arms; so she lights from her palfrey
And turns her round about.

She has given the child to Joseph,
Gone down to the flashing shore;
And Joseph, shading his eyes with his hand,
Stands watching evermore.

SECOND PART

The sea in the stones is singing,
A woman binds her hair
With yellow, frail sea-poppies,
That shine as her fingers stir.

While a naked man comes swiftly
Like a spurt of white foam rent
From the crest of a falling breaker,
Over the poppies sent.

200

He puts his surf-wet fingers
Over her startled eyes,
And asks if she sees the land, the land,
The land of her glad surmise.

THIRD PART

Again in her blue, blue mantle
Riding at Joseph's side,
She says, "I went to Cythera,
And woe betide!"

Her heart is a swinging cradle
That holds the perfect child,
But the shade on her forehead ill becomes
A mother mild.

So on with the slow, mean journey
In the pride of humility;
Till they halt at a cliff on the edge of the land
Over a sullen sea.

While Joseph pitches the sleep-tent
She goes far down to the shore
To where a man in a heaving boat
Waits with a lifted oar.

FOURTH PART

They dwelt in a huge, hoarse sea-cave
And looked far down the dark
Where an archway torn and glittering
Shone like a huge sea-spark.

He said: "Do you see the spirits
Crowding the bright doorway?"
He said: "Do you hear them whispering?"
He said: "Do you catch what they say?"

FIFTH PART

Then Joseph, grey with waiting,
His dark eyes full of pain,
Heard: "I have been to Patmos;
Give me the child again."

Now on with the hopeless journey
Looking bleak ahead she rode,
And the man and the child of no more account
Than the earth the palfrey trode.

Till a beggar spoke to Joseph,
But looked into her eyes;
So she turned, and said to her husband:
"I give, whoever denies."

SIXTH PART

She gave on the open heather
Beneath bare judgment stars,
And she dreamed of her children and Joseph,
And the isles, and her men, and her scars.

And she woke to distil the berries
The beggar had gathered at night,
Whence he drew the curious liquors
He held in delight.

He gave her no crown of flowers,
No child and no palfrey slow,
Only led her through harsh, hard places
Where strange winds blow.

She follows his restless wanderings
Till night when, by the fire's red stain,
Her face is bent in the bitter steam
That comes from the flowers of pain.

Then merciless and ruthless
He takes the flame-wild drops
To the town, and tries to sell them
With the market-crops.

So she follows the cruel journey
That ends not anywhere,
And dreams, as she stirs the mixing-pot,
She is brewing hope from despair.

Trier.

BEI HENNEF

The little river twittering in the twilight,
The wan, wondering look of the pale sky,
    This is almost bliss.

And everything shut up and gone to sleep,
All the troubles and anxieties and pain
    Gone under the twilight.

Only the twilight now, and the soft "Sh!" of the river
    That will last for ever.

And at last I know my love for you is here;
I can see it all, it is whole like the twilight,
It is large, so large, I could not see it before,
Because of the little lights and flickers and interruptions,
    Troubles, anxieties and pains.

You are the call and I am the answer,
You are the wish, and I the fulfilment,
You are the night, and I the day.
    What else? it is perfect enough.
    It is perfectly complete,
    You and I,
    What more——?

Strange, how we suffer in spite of this!

Hennef am Rhein.

FIRST MORNING

The night was a failure
    but why not——?

In the darkness
    with the pale dawn seething at the window
    through the black frame
    I could not be free,
    not free myself from the past, those others—
    and our love was a confusion,
    there was a horror,
    you recoiled away from me.

Now, in the morning
As we sit in the sunshine on the seat by the little shrine,
And look at the mountain-walls,
Walls of blue shadow,
And see so near at our feet in the meadow
Myriads of dandelion pappus
Bubbles ravelled in the dark green grass
Held still beneath the sunshine—
It is enough, you are near—
The mountains are balanced,
The dandelion seeds stay half-submerged in the grass;
You and I together
We hold them proud and blithe
On our love.
They stand upright on our love,
Everything starts from us,
We are the source.

                               Beuerberg.

''AND OH——
THAT THE MAN I AM
MIGHT CEASE TO BE——''

No, now I wish the sunshine would stop,
and the white shining houses, and the gay red flowers on
    the balconies
and the bluish mountains beyond, would be crushed out
between two valves of darkness;
the darkness falling, the darkness rising, with muffled
    sound
obliterating everything.

I wish that whatever props up the walls of light
would fall, and darkness would come hurling heavily down,
and it would be thick black dark for ever.
Not sleep, which is grey with dreams,
nor death, which quivers with birth,
but heavy, sealing darkness, silence, all immovable.

What is sleep?
It goes over me, like a shadow over a hill,
but it does not alter me, nor help me.
And death would ache still, I am sure;
it would be lambent, uneasy.
I wish it would be completely dark everywhere,
inside me, and out, heavily dark
utterly.

                                   Wolfratshausen.

SHE LOOKS BACK

The pale bubbles,
The lovely pale-gold bubbles of the globe-flowers,
In a great swarm clotted and single
Went rolling in the dusk towards the river
To where the sunset hung its wan gold cloths;

And you stood alone, watching them go,
And that mother-love like a demon drew you from me
Towards England.

Along the road, after nightfall,
Along the glamorous birch-tree avenue
Across the river levels
We went in silence, and you staring to England.

So then there shone within the jungle darkness
Of the long, lush under-grass, a glow-worm's sudden
Green lantern of pure light, a little, intense, fusing triumph,
White and haloed with fire-mist, down in the tangled
    darkness.
Then you put your hand in mine again, kissed me, and we
    struggled to be together.
And the little electric flashes went with us, in the grass,
Tiny lighthouses, little souls of lanterns, courage burst into
    an explosion of green light
Everywhere down in the grass, where darkness was ravelled
    in darkness.

Still, the kiss was a touch of bitterness on my mouth
Like salt, burning in.
And my hand withered in your hand.
For you were straining with a wild heart, back, back again,
Back to those children you had left behind, to all the æons
    of the past.
And I was here in the under-dusk of the Isar.

At home, we leaned in the bedroom window
Of the old Bavarian Gasthaus,
And the frogs in the pool beyond thrilled with exuberance,
Like a boiling pot the pond crackled with happiness,
Like a rattle a child spins round for joy, the night rattled
With the extravagance of the frogs,
And you leaned your cheek on mine,
And I suffered it, wanting to sympathise.

At last, as you stood, your white gown falling from your
    breasts,
You looked into my eyes, and said: "But this is joy!"
I acquiesced again.
But the shadow of lying was in your eyes,
The mother in you, fierce as a murderess, glaring to
    England,
Yearning towards England, towards your young children,
Insisting upon your motherhood, devastating.

Still, the joy was there also, you spoke truly,
The joy was not to be driven off so easily;
Stronger than fear or destructive mother-love, it stood
    flickering;
The frogs helped also, whirring away.
Yet how I have learned to know that look in your eyes
Of horrid sorrow!
How I know that glitter of salt,—dry, sterile, sharp, corrosive
    salt!
Not tears, but white sharp brine
Making hideous your eyes.

I have seen it, felt it in my mouth, my throat, my chest, my
    belly,
Burning of powerful salt, burning, eating through my
    defenceless nakedness.
I have been thrust into white, sharp crystals,
Writhing, twisting, superpenetrated.
Ah, Lot's Wife, Lot's Wife!
The pillar of salt, the whirling, horrible column of salt, like
    a waterspout
That has enveloped me!
Snow of salt, white, burning, eating salt
In which I have writhed.

Lot's Wife!—Not Wife, but Mother.
I have learned to curse your motherhood,
You pillar of salt accursed.
I have cursed motherhood because of you,
Accursed, base motherhood!

I long for the time to come, when the curse against you will
    have gone out of my heart.
But it has not gone yet.
Nevertheless, once, the frogs, the globe-flowers of Bavaria,
    the glow-worms
Gave me sweet lymph against the salt-burns,
There is a kindness in the very rain.

Therefore, even in the hour of my deepest, passionate
    malediction
I try to remember it is also well between us.
That you are with me in the end.
That you never look quite back; nine-tenths, ah, more
You look round over your shoulder;
But never quite back.

Nevertheless the curse against you is still in my heart
Like a deep, deep burn.
The curse against all mothers.
All mothers who fortify themselves in motherhood, devastat-
    ing the vision.
They are accursed, and the curse is not taken off;
It burns within me like a deep, old burn,
And oh, I wish it was better.

Beuerberg.

ON THE BALCONY

In front of the sombre mountains, a faint, lost ribbon of
    rainbow;
And between us and it, the thunder;
And down below in the green wheat, the labourers
Stand like dark stumps, still in the green wheat.

You are near to me, and your naked feet in their sandals,
And through the scent of the balcony's naked timber
I distinguish the scent of your hair: so now the limber
Lightning falls from heaven.

Adown the pale-green glacier river floats
A dark boat through the gloom—and whither?
The thunder roars. But still we have each other!
The naked lightnings in the heavens dither
And disappear—what have we but each other?
The boat has gone.

Icking.

FROHNLEICHNAM

You have come your way, I have come my way;
You have stepped across your people, carelessly, hurting
    them all;
I have stepped across my people, and hurt them in spite
    of my care.

But steadily, surely, and notwithstanding
We have come our ways and met at last
Here in this upper room.

Here the balcony
Overhangs the street where the bullock-wagons slowly
Go by with their loads of green and silver birch-trees
For the feast of Corpus Christi.

Here from the balcony
We look over the growing wheat, where the jade-green
    river
Goes between the pine-woods,
Over and beyond to where the many mountains
Stand in their blueness, flashing with snow and the
    morning.

I have done; a quiver of exultation goes through me, like
    the first
Breeze of the morning through a narrow white birch.
You glow at last like the mountain tops when they catch
Day and make magic in heaven.

At last I can throw away world without end, and meet you
Unsheathed and naked and narrow and white;
At last you can throw immortality off, and I see you
Glistening with all the moment and all your beauty.

Shameless and callous I love you;
Out of indifference I love you;
Out of mockery we dance together,
Out of the sunshine into the shadow,
Passing across the shadow into the sunlight,
Out of sunlight to shadow.

As we dance
Your eyes take all of me in as a communication;
As we dance
I see you, ah, in full!
Only to dance together in triumph of being together
Two white ones, sharp, vindicated,
Shining and touching,
Is heaven of our own, sheer with repudiation.

IN THE DARK

A blotch of pallor stirs beneath the high
Square picture-dusk, the window of dark sky.

A sound subdued in the darkness: tears!
As if a bird in difficulty up the valley steers.

"Why have you gone to the window? Why don't you
    sleep?
How you have wakened me!—But why, why do you
    weep?"

*"I am afraid of you, I am afraid, afraid!
There is something in you destroys me——!"*

"You have dreamed and are not awake, come here to me."
"No, I have wakened. It is you, you are cruel to me!"

"My dear!"—*"Yes, yes, you are cruel to me. You cast*
A shadow over my breasts that will kill me at last."

"Come!"—*"No, I'm a thing of life. I give*
You armfuls of sunshine, and you won't let me live."

"Nay, I'm too sleepy!"—*"Ah, you are horrible;*
You stand before me like ghosts, like a darkness upright."

"I!"—*"How can you treat me so, and love me?*
My feet have no hold, you take the sky from above me."

"My dear, the night is soft and eternal, no doubt
You love it!"—*"It is dark, it kills me, I am put out."*

"My dear, when you cross the street in the sunshine, surely
Your own small night goes with you. Why treat it so
    poorly?"

"No, no, I dance in the sun, I'm a thing of life——"
"Even then it is dark behind you. Turn round, my wife."

"No, how cruel you are, you people the sunshine
With shadows!"—"With yours I people the sunshine,
    yours and mine——

"In the darkness we all are gone, we are gone with the trees
And the restless river;—we are lost and gone with all
    these."

"But I am myself, I have nothing to do with these."
"Come back to bed, let us sleep on our mysteries.

"Come to me here, and lay your body by mine,
And I will be all the shadow, you the shine.

"Come, you are cold, the night has frightened you.
Hark at the river! It pants as it hurries through

"The pine-woods. How I love them so, in their mystery of
      not-to-be."
"—But let me be myself, not a river or a tree."

"Kiss me! How cold you are!—Your little breasts
Are bubbles of ice. Kiss me!—You know how it rests

"One to be quenched, to be given up, to be gone in the dark;
To be blown out, to let night dowse the spark.

"But never mind, my love. Nothing matters, save sleep;
Save you, and me, and sleep; all the rest will keep."

MUTILATION

A thick mist-sheet lies over the broken wheat.
I walk up to my neck in mist, holding my mouth up.
Across there, a discoloured moon burns itself out.

I hold the night in horror;
I dare not turn round.

To-night I have left her alone.
They would have it I have left her for ever.

Oh my God, how it aches
Where she is cut off from me!

Perhaps she will go back to England.
Perhaps she will go back,
Perhaps we are parted for ever.

If I go on walking through the whole breadth of Germany
I come to the North Sea, or the Baltic.

Over there is Russia—Austria, Switzerland, France, in a
    circle!
I here in the undermist on the Bavarian road.

It aches in me.
What is England or France, far off,
But a name she might take?
I don't mind this continent stretching, the sea far away;
It aches in me for her
Like the agony of limbs cut off and aching;
Not even longing,
It is only agony.

A cripple!
Oh God, to be mutilated!
To be a cripple!

And if I never see her again?

I think, if they told me so
I could convulse the heavens with my horror.
I think I could alter the frame of things in my agony.
I think I could break the System with my heart.
I think, in my convulsion, the skies would break.

She too suffers.
But who could compel her, if she chose me against them
    all?
She has not chosen me finally, she suspends her choice.
Night folk, Tuatha De Danaan, dark Gods, govern her sleep,
Magnificent ghosts of the darkness, carry off her decision
    in sleep,
Leave her no choice, make her lapse me-ward, make her,
Oh Gods of the living Darkness, powers of Night.

                                        Wolfratshausen.

HUMILIATION

I have been so innerly proud, and so long alone,
Do not leave me, or I shall break.
Do not leave me.

What should I do if you were gone again
So soon?
What should I look for?
Where should I go?
What should I be, I myself,
"I"?
What would it mean, this
I?

Do not leave me.

What should I think of death?
If I died, it would not be you:
It would be simply the same
Lack of you.
The same want, life or death,
Unfulfilment,
The same insanity of space,
You not there for me.

Think, I daren't die
For fear of the lack in death.
And I daren't live.

Unless there were a morphine or a drug.

I would bear the pain.
But always, strong, unremitting
It would make me not me.
The thing with my body that would go on living
Would not be me.
Neither life nor death could help.

Think, I couldn't look towards death
Nor towards the future:
Only not look.
Only myself
Stand still and bind and blind myself.

God, that I have no choice!
That my own fulfilment is up against me
Timelessly!
The burden of self-accomplishment!
The charge of fulfilment!
And God, that she is *necessary*!
Necessary, and I have no choice!

Do not leave me.

A YOUNG WIFE

The pain of loving you
Is almost more than I can bear.

I walk in fear of you.
The darkness starts up where
You stand, and the night comes through
Your eyes when you look at me.

Ah never before did I see
The shadows that live in the sun!

Now every tall glad tree
Turns round its back to the sun
And looks down on the ground, to see
The shadow it used to shun.

At the foot of each glowing thing
A night lies looking up.

Oh, and I want to sing
And dance, but I can't lift up
My eyes from the shadows: dark
They lie spilt round the cup.

What is it?—Hark
The faint fine seethe in the air!

Like the seething sound in a shell!
It is death still seething where
The wild-flower shakes its bell
And the skylark twinkles blue—

The pain of loving you
Is almost more than I can bear.

GREEN

The dawn was apple-green,
   The sky was green wine held up in the sun,
The moon was a golden petal between.

She opened her eyes, and green
   They shone, clear like flowers undone
For the first time, now for the first time seen.
                    Icking.

RIVER ROSES

By the Isar, in the twilight
We were wandering and singing,
By the Isar, in the evening
We climbed the huntsman's ladder and sat swinging
In the fir-tree overlooking the marshes,
While river met with river, and the ringing
Of their pale-green glacier water filled the evening.

By the Isar, in the twilight
We found the dark wild roses
Hanging red at the river; and simmering
Frogs were singing, and over the river closes
Was savour of ice and of roses; and glimmering
Fear was abroad. We whispered: "No one knows us.
Let it be as the snake disposes
Here in this simmering marsh."

Kloster Schaeftlarn.

GLOIRE DE DIJON

When she rises in the morning
I linger to watch her;
She spreads the bath-cloth underneath the window
And the sunbeams catch her
Glistening white on the shoulders,
While down her sides the mellow
Golden shadow glows as
She stoops to the sponge, and her swung breasts
Sway like full-blown yellow
Gloire de Dijon roses.

She drips herself with water, and her shoulders
Glisten as silver, they crumple up
Like wet and falling roses, and I listen
For the sluicing of their rain-dishevelled petals.
In the window full of sunlight
Concentrates her golden shadow
Fold on fold, until it glows as
Mellow as the glory roses.

Icking.

ROSES ON THE BREAKFAST TABLE

Just a few of the roses we gathered from the Isar
Are fallen, and their mauve-red petals on the cloth
Float like boats on a river, while other
Roses are ready to fall, reluctant and loth.

She laughs at me across the table, saying
I am beautiful. I look at the rumpled young roses
And suddenly realize, in them as in me,
How lovely is the self this day discloses.

I AM LIKE A ROSE

I am myself at last; now I achieve
My very self. I, with the wonder mellow,
Full of fine warmth, I issue forth in clear
And single me, perfected from my fellow.

Here I am all myself. No rose-bush heaving
Its limpid sap to culmination has brought
Itself more sheer and naked out of the green
In stark-clear roses, than I to myself am brought.

ROSE OF ALL THE WORLD

I am here myself; as though this heave of effort
At starting other life, fulfilled my own:
Rose-leaves that whirl in colour round a core
Of seed-specks kindled lately and softly blown

By all the blood of the rose-bush into being—
Strange, that the urgent will in me, to set
My mouth on hers in kisses, and so softly
To bring together two strange sparks, beget

Another life from our lives, so should send
The innermost fire of my own dim soul out-spinning
And whirling in blossom of flame and being upon me!
That my completion of manhood should be the beginning

Another life from mine! For so it looks.
The seed is purpose, blossom accident.
The seed is all in all, the blossom lent
To crown the triumph of this new descent.

Is that it, woman? Does it strike you so?
The Great Breath blowing a tiny seed of fire
Fans out your petals for excess of flame,
Till all your being smokes with fine desire?

Or are we kindled, you and I, to be
One rose of wonderment upon the tree
Of perfect life, and is our possible seed
But the residuum of the ecstasy?

How will you have it?—the rose is all in all,
Or the ripe rose-fruits of the luscious fall?
The sharp begetting, or the child begot?
Our consummation matters, or does it not?

To me it seems the seed is just left over
From the red rose-flowers' fiery transience;
Just orts and slarts; berries that smoulder in the bush
Which burnt just now with marvellous immanence.

Blossom, my darling, blossom, be a rose
Of roses unchidden and purposeless; a rose
For rosiness only, without an ulterior motive;
For me it is more than enough if the flower unclose.

A YOUTH MOWING

There are four men mowing down by the Isar;
I can hear the swish of the scythe-strokes, four
Sharp breaths taken: yea, and I
Am sorry for what's in store.

The first man out of the four that's mowing
Is mine, I claim him once and for all;
Though it's sorry I am, on his young feet, knowing
None of the trouble he's led to stall.

As he sees me bringing the dinner, he lifts
His head as proud as a deer that looks
Shoulder-deep out of the corn; and wipes
His scythe-blade bright, unhooks

The scythe-stone and over the stubble to me.
Lad, thou hast gotten a child in me,
Laddie, a man thou'lt ha'e to be,
Yea, though I'm sorry for thee.

QUITE FORSAKEN

What pain, to wake and miss you!
    To wake with a tightened heart,
And mouth reaching forward to kiss you!

This then at last is the dawn, and the bell
    Clanging at the farm! Such bewilderment
Comes with the sight of the room, I cannot tell.

It is raining. Down the half-obscure road
    Four labourers pass with their scythes
Dejectedly;—a huntsman goes by with his load:

A gun, and a bunched-up deer, its four little feet
    Clustered dead.—And this is the dawn
For which I wanted the night to retreat!

FORSAKEN AND FORLORN

The house is silent, it is late at night, I am alone.
            From the balcony
            I can hear the Isar moan
            Can see the white
Rift of the river eerily, between the pines, under a
    sky of stone.

Some fireflies drift through the middle air
        Tinily.
        I wonder where
Ends this darkness that annihilates me.

FIREFLIES IN THE CORN

She speaks.

Look at the little darlings in the corn!
    The rye is taller than you, who think yourself
So high and mighty: look how the heads are borne
    Dark and proud on the sky, like a number of knights
Passing with spears and pennants and manly scorn.

Knights indeed!—much knight I know will ride
    With his head held high-serene against the sky!
Limping and following rather at my side
    Moaning for me to love him!—O darling rye
How I adore you for your simple pride!

And the dear, dear fireflies wafting in between
    And over the swaying corn-stalks, just above
All the dark-feathered helmets, like little green
    Stars come low and wandering here for love
Of these dark knights, shedding their delicate sheen!

I thank you I do, you happy creatures, you dears,
    Riding the air, and carrying all the time
Your little lanterns behind you! Ah, it cheers
    My soul to see you settling and trying to climb
The corn-stalks, tipping with fire the spears.

All over the dim corn's motion, against the blue
    Dark sky of night, a wandering glitter, a swarm
Of questing brilliant souls going out with their true
    Proud knights to battle! Sweet, how I warm
My poor, my perished soul with the sight of you!

A DOE AT EVENING

As I went through the marshes
a doe sprang out of the corn
and flashed up the hill-side
leaving her fawn.

On the sky-line
she moved round to watch,
she pricked a fine black blotch
on the sky.

I looked at her
and felt her watching;
I became a strange being.
Still, I had my right to be there with her.

Her nimble shadow trotting
along the sky-line, she
put back her fine, level-balanced head.
And I knew her.

Ah yes, being male, is not my head hard-
    balanced, antlered?
Are not my haunches light?
Has she not fled on the same wind with me?
Does not my fear cover her fear?

Irschenhausen.

SONG OF A MAN WHO IS NOT LOVED

The space of the world is immense, before me and around me;
If I turn quickly, I am terrified, feeling space surround me;
Like a man in a boat on very clear, deep water, space frightens
    and confounds me.

I see myself isolated in the universe, and wonder
What effect I can have. My hands wave under
The heavens like specks of dust that are floating asunder.

I hold myself up, and feel a big wind blowing
Me like a gadfly into the dusk, without my knowing
Whither or why or even how I am going.

So much there is outside me, so infinitely
Small am I, what matter if minutely
I beat my way, to be lost immediately?

How shall I flatter myself that I can do
Anything in such immensity? I am too
Little to count in the wind that drifts me through.

                                        Glashütte.

SINNERS

The big mountains sit still in the afternoon light,
        Shadows in their lap;
The bees roll round in the wild-thyme with delight.

We sitting here among the cranberries
        So still in the gap
Of rock, distilling our memories,

Are sinners! Strange! The bee that blunders
        Against me goes off with a laugh.
A squirrel cocks his head on the fence, and wonders

What about sin?—For, it seems
        The mountains have
No shadow of us on their snowy forehead of dreams

As they ought to have. They rise above us
        Dreaming
For ever. One even might think that they love us.

Little red cranberries cheek to cheek,
Two great dragon-flies wrestling;
You, with your forehead nestling
Against me, and bright peak shining to peak—

There's a love-song for you!—Ah, if only
    There were no teeming
Swarms of mankind in the world, and we were less lonely!
                             Mayrhofen.

MISERY

Out of this oubliette between the mountains
five valleys go, five passes like gates;
three of them black in shadow, two of them bright
with distant sunshine;
and sunshine fills one high valley bed,
green grass shining, and little white houses
like quartz crystals,
little, but distinct a way off.

Why don't I go?
Why do I crawl about this pot, this oubliette,
stupidly?
Why don't I go?

But where?
If I come to a pine-wood, I can't say:
Now I am arrived!
What are so many straight trees to me!
                             Sterzing.

MEETING AMONG THE MOUNTAINS

The little pansies by the road have turned
Away their purple faces and their gold,
And evening has taken all the bees from the thyme,
And all the scent is shed away by the cold.

Against the hard and pale blue evening sky
The mountain's new-dropped summer snow is clear
Glistening in steadfast stillness: like transcendent
Clean pain sending on us a chill down here.

Christ on the Cross!—his beautiful young man's body
Has fallen dead upon the nails, and hangs
White and loose at last, with all the pain
Drawn on his mouth, eyes broken at last by his pangs.

And slowly down the mountain road, belated,
A bullock wagon comes; so I am ashamed
To gaze any more at the Christ, whom the mountain snows
Whitely confront; I wait on the grass, am lamed.

The breath of the bullock stains the hard, chill air,
The band is across its brow, and it scarcely seems
To draw the load, so still and slow it moves,
While the driver on the shaft sits crouched in dreams.

Surely about his sunburnt face is something
That vexes me with wonder. He sits so still
Here among all this silence, crouching forward,
Dreaming and letting the bullock take its will.

I stand aside on the grass to let them go;
—And Christ, I have met his accusing eyes again,
The brown eyes black with misery and hate, that look
Full in my own, and the torment starts again.

One moment the hate leaps at me standing there,
One moment I see the stillness of agony,
Something frozen in the silence that dare not be
Loosed, one moment the darkness frightens me.

Then among the averted pansies, beneath the high
White peaks of snow, at the foot of the sunken Christ
I stand in a chill of anguish, trying to say
The joy I bought was not too highly priced.

But he has gone, motionless, hating me,
Living as the mountains do, because they are strong,
With a pale, dead Christ on the crucifix of his heart,
And breathing the frozen memory of his wrong.

Still in his nostrils the frozen breath of despair,
And heart like a cross that bears dead agony
Of naked love, clenched in his fists the shame,
And in his belly the smouldering hate of me.

And I, as I stand in the cold, averted flowers,
Feel the shame-wounds in his hands pierce through my own,
And breathe despair that turns my lungs to stone
And know the dead Christ weighing on my bone.

EVERLASTING FLOWERS

FOR A DEAD MOTHER

Who do you think stands watching
        The snow-tops shining rosy
In heaven, now that the darkness
        Takes all but the tallest posy?

Who then sees the two-winged
        Boat down there, all alone
And asleep on the snow's last shadow,
        Like a moth on a stone?

The olive-leaves, light as gad-flies,
        Have all gone dark, gone black.
And now in the dark my soul to you
        Turns back.

To you, my little darling,
        To you, out of Italy.
For what is loveliness, my love,
        Save you have it with me!

So, there's an oxen wagon
        Comes darkly into sight:
A man with a lantern, swinging
        A little light.

What does he see, my darling,
        Here by the darkened lake?
Here, in the sloping shadow
        The mountains make?

He says not a word, but passes,
        Staring at what he sees.
What ghost of us both do you think he saw
        Under the olive-trees?

All the things that are lovely—
        The things you never knew—
I wanted to gather them one by one
        And bring them to you.

But never now, my darling,
        Can I gather the mountain-tips
From the twilight like half-shut lilies
        To hold to your lips.

And never the two-winged vessel
        That sleeps below on the lake
Can I catch like a moth between my hands
        For you to take.

But hush, I am not regretting:
        It is far more perfect now.
I'll whisper the ghostly truth to you
        And tell you how

I know you here in the darkness,
        How you sit in the throne of my eyes
At peace, and look out of the windows
        In glad surprise.

                                Lago di Garda.

227

SUNDAY AFTERNOON IN ITALY

The man and the maid go side by side
With an interval of space between;
And his hands are awkward and want to hide,
She braves it out since she must be seen.

When some one passes he drops his head,
Shading his face in his black felt hat,
While the hard girl hardens; nothing is said,
There is nothing to wonder or cavil at.

Alone on the open road again,
With the mountain snows across the lake
Flushing the afternoon, they are uncomfortable,
The loneliness daunts them, their stiff throats ache.

And he sighs with relief when she parts from him;
Her proud head held in its black silk scarf
Gone under the archway, home, he can join
The men that lounge in a group on the wharf.

His evening is a flame of wine
Among the eager, cordial men.
And she with her women hot and hard
Moves at her ease again.

> *She is marked, she is singled out*
> > *For the fire:*
> *The brand is upon him, look you!*
> > *Of desire.*

> *They are chosen, ah, they are fated*
> > *For the fight!*
> *Champion her, all you women! Men, menfolk,*
> > *Hold him your light!*

> *Nourish her, train her, harden her,*
> > *Women all!*
> *Fold him, be good to him, cherish him,*
> > *Men, ere he fall.*

Women, another champion!
This, men, is yours!
Wreathe and enlap and anoint them
Behind separate doors.

Gargnano.

WINTER DAWN

Green star Sirius
Dribbling over the lake;
The stars have gone so far on their road,
Yet we're awake!

Without a sound
The new young year comes in
And is half-way over the lake.
We must begin

Again. This love so full
Of hate has hurt us so,
We lie side by side
Moored—but no,

Let me get up
And wash quite clean
Of this hate.—
So green

The great star goes!
I am washed quite clean,
Quite clean of it all.
But e'en

So cold, so cold and clean
Now the hate is gone!
It is all no good,
I am chilled to the bone

Now the hate is gone;
There is nothing left;
I am pure like bone,
Of all feeling bereft.

A BAD BEGINNING

The yellow sun steps over the mountain-top
And falters a few short steps across the lake—
Are you awake?

See, glittering on the milk-blue, morning lake
They are laying the golden racing-track of the sun;
The day has begun.

The sun is in my eyes, I must get up.
I want to go, there's a gold road blazes before
My breast—which is so sore.

What?—your throat is bruised, bruised with my kisses?
Ah, but if I am cruel what then are you?
I am bruised right through.

What if I love you!—This misery
Of your dissatisfaction and misprision
Stupefies me.

Ah yes, your open arms! Ah yes, ah yes,
You would take me to your breast!—But no,
You should come to mine,
It were better so.

Here I am—get up and come to me!
Not as a visitor either, nor a sweet
And winsome child of innocence; nor
As an insolent mistress telling my pulse's beat.

Come to me like a woman coming home
To the man who is her husband, all the rest
Subordinate to this, that he and she
Are joined together for ever, as is best.

Behind me on the lake I hear the steamer drumming
From Austria. There lies the world, and here
Am I. Which way are you coming?

WHY DOES SHE WEEP?

Hush then
why do you cry?
It's you and me
the same as before.

If you hear a rustle
it's only a rabbit
gone back to his hole
in a bustle.

If something stirs in the branches
overhead, it will be a squirrel moving
uneasily, disturbed by the stress
of our loving.

Why should you cry then?
Are you afraid of God
in the dark?

I'm not afraid of God.
Let him come forth.
If he is hiding in the cover
let him come forth.

Now in the cool of the day
it is we who walk in the trees
and call to God "Where art thou?"
And it is he who hides.

Why do you cry?
My heart is bitter.
Let God come forth to justify
himself now.

Why do you cry?
Is it Wehmut, ist dir weh?
Weep then, yea
for the abomination of our old righteousness.

We have done wrong
many times;
but this time we begin to do right.

Weep then, weep
for the abomination of our past righteousness.
God will keep
hidden, he won't come forth.

GIORNO DEI MORTI

Along the avenue of cypresses,
All in their scarlet cloaks and surplices
Of linen, go the chanting choristers,
The priests in gold and black, the villagers. . . .

And all along the path to the cemetery
The round dark heads of men crowd silently,
And black-scarved faces of womenfolk, wistfully
Watch at the banner of death, and the mystery.

And at the foot of a grave a father stands
With sunken head, and forgotten, folded hands;
And at the foot of a grave a mother kneels
With pale shut face, nor either hears nor feels

The coming of the chanting choristers
Between the avenue of cypresses,
The silence of the many villagers,
The candle-flames beside the surplices.

ALL SOULS

They are chanting now the service of All the Dead
And the village folk outside in the burying-ground
Listen—except those who strive with their dead,
Reaching out in anguish, yet unable quite to touch them:
Those villagers isolated at the grave
Where the candles burn in the daylight, and the painted
    wreaths
Are propped on end, there, where the mystery starts.

The naked candles burn on every grave.
On your grave, in England, the weeds grow.

But I am your naked candle burning,
And that is not your grave, in England,
The world is your grave.
And my naked body standing on your grave
Upright towards heaven is burning off to you
Its flame of life, now and always, till the end.

It is my offering to you; every day is All Souls' Day.

I forget you, have forgotten you.
I am busy only at my burning,
I am busy only at my life.
But my feet are on your grave, planted.
And when I lift my face, it is a flame that goes up
To the other world, where you are now.
But I am not concerned with you.
      I have forgotten you.

I am a naked candle burning on your grave.

LADY WIFE

Ah yes, I know you well, a sojourner
    At the hearth;
I know right well the marriage ring you wear,
    And what it's worth.

The angels came to Abraham, and they stayed
    In his house awhile;
So you to mine, I imagine; yes, happily
    Condescend to be vile.

I see you all the time, you bird-blithe, lovely
    Angel in disguise.
I see right well how I ought to be grateful,
    Smitten with reverent surprise.

Listen, I have no use
    For so rare a visit;
Mine is a common devil's
    Requisite.

Rise up and go, I have no use for you
    And your blithe, glad mien.
No angels here, for me no goddesses,
    Nor any Queen.

Put ashes on your head, put sackcloth on
    And learn to serve.
You have fed me with your sweetness, now I am sick,
    As I deserve.

Queens, ladies, angels, women rare,
    I have had enough.
Put sackcloth on, be crowned with powdery ash,
    Be common stuff.

And serve now, woman, serve, as a woman should,
    Implicitly.
Since I must serve and struggle with the imminent
    Mystery.

Serve then, I tell you, add your strength to mine,
    Take on this doom.
What are you by yourself, do you think, and what
    The mere fruit of your womb?

What is the fruit of your womb then, you mother, you queen,
    When it falls to the ground?
Is it more than the apples of Sodom you scorn so, the men
    Who abound?

Bring forth the sons of your womb then, and put them
    Into the fire
Of Sodom that covers the earth; bring them forth
    From the womb of your precious desire.

You woman most holy, you mother, you being beyond
    Question or diminution,
Add yourself up, and your seed, to the nought
    Of your last solution.

BOTH SIDES OF THE MEDAL

And because you love me,
think you you do not hate me?
Ha, since you love me
to ecstasy
it follows you hate me to ecstasy.

Because when you hear me
go down the road outside the house
you must come to the window to watch me go,
do you think it is pure worship?

Because, when I sit in the room,
here, in my own house,
and you want to enlarge yourself with this friend of mine,
such a friend as he is,
yet you cannot get beyond your awareness of me,
you are held back by my being in the same world with you,
do you think it is bliss alone?
sheer harmony?

No doubt if I were dead, you must
reach into death after me,
but would not your hate reach even more madly than your
    love?
your impassioned, unfinished hate?

Since you have a passion for me,
as I for you,
does not that passion stand in your way like a Balaam's ass?
and am I not Balaam's ass
golden-mouthed occasionally?
But mostly, do you not detest my bray?

Since you are confined in the orbit of me
do you not loathe the confinement?
Is not even the beauty and peace of an orbit
an intolerable prison to you,
as it is to everybody?

But we will learn to submit
each of us to the balanced, eternal orbit
wherein we circle on our fate
in strange conjunction.

What is chaos, my love?
It is not freedom.
A disarray of falling stars coming to nought.

LOGGERHEADS

Please yourself how you have it.
Take my words, and fling
Them down on the counter roundly;
See if they ring.

Sift my looks and expressions,
And see what proportion there is
Of sand in my doubtful sugar
Of verities.

Have a real stock-taking
Of my manly breast;
Find out if I'm sound or bankrupt,
Or a poor thing at best.

For I am quite indifferent
To your dubious state,
As to whether you've found a fortune
In me, or a flea-bitten fate.

Make a good investigation
Of all that is there,
And then, if it's worth it, be grateful—
If not, then despair.

If despair is our portion
Then let us despair.
Let us make for the weeping willow.
I don't care.

DECEMBER NIGHT

Take off your cloak and your hat
And your shoes, and draw up at my hearth
Where never woman sat.

I have made the fire up bright;
Let us leave the rest in the dark
And sit by firelight.

The wine is warm in the hearth;
The flickers come and go.
I will warm your limbs with kisses
Until they glow.

NEW YEAR'S EVE

There are only two things now,
The great black night scooped out
And this fireglow.

This fireglow, the core,
And we the two ripe pips
That are held in store.

Listen, the darkness rings
As it circulates round our fire.
Take off your things.

Your shoulders, your bruised throat!
Your breasts, your nakedness!
This fiery coat!

As the darkness flickers and dips,
As the firelight falls and leaps
From your feet to your lips!

NEW YEAR'S NIGHT

Now you are mine, to-night at last I say it;
You're a dove I have bought for sacrifice,
And to-night I slay it.

Here in my arms my naked sacrifice!
Death, do you hear, in my arms I am bringing
My offering, bought at great price.

She's a silvery dove worth more than all I've got.
Now I offer her up to the ancient, inexorable God,
Who knows me not.

Look, she's a wonderful dove, without blemish or spot!
I sacrifice all in her, my last of the world,
Pride, strength, all the lot.

All, all on the altar! And death swooping down
Like a falcon. 'Tis God has taken the victim;
I have won my renown.

VALENTINE'S NIGHT

You shadow and flame,
You interchange,
You death in the game!

Now I gather you up,
Now I put you back
Like a poppy in its cup.

And so, you are a maid
Again, my darling, but new,
Unafraid.

My love, my blossom, a child
Almost! The flower in the bud
Again, undefiled.

And yet, a woman, knowing
All, good, evil, both
In one blossom blowing.

BIRTH NIGHT

This fireglow is a red womb
In the night, where you're folded up
On your doom.

239

And the ugly, brutal years
Are dissolving out of you,
And the stagnant tears.

I the great vein that leads
From the night to the source of you
Which the sweet blood feeds.

New phase in the germ of you;
New sunny streams of blood
Washing you through.

You are born again of me.
I, Adam, from the veins of me
The Eve that is to be.

What has been long ago
Grows dimmer, we both forget,
We no longer know.

You are lovely, your face is soft
Like a flower in bud
On a mountain croft.

This is Noël for me.
To-night is a woman born
Of the man in me.

RABBIT SNARED IN THE NIGHT

Why do you spurt and sprottle
like that, bunny?
Why should I want to throttle
you, bunny?

Yes, bunch yourself between
my knees and lie still.
Lie on me with a hot, plumb, live weight,
heavy as a stone, passive,
yet hot, waiting.

What are you waiting for?
What are you waiting for?
What is the hot, plumb weight of your desire on me?
You have a hot, unthinkable desire of me, bunny.

What is that spark
glittering at me on the unutterable darkness
of your eye, bunny?
The finest splinter of a spark
that you throw off, straight on the tinder of my nerves!

It sets up a strange fire,
a soft, most unwarrantable burning,
a bale-fire mounting, mounting up in me.

'Tis not of me, bunny.
It was you engendered it,
with that fine, demoniacal spark
you jetted off your eye at me.

I did not want it,
this furnace, this draught-maddened fire
which mounts up my arms
making them swell with turgid, ungovernable strength.

'Twas not *I* that wished it,
that my fingers should turn into these flames
avid and terrible
that they are at this moment.

It must have been *your* inbreathing, gaping desire
that drew this red gush in me;
I must be reciprocating *your* vacuous, hideous passion.

It must be the want in you
that has drawn this terrible draught of white fire
up my veins as up a chimney.

241

It must be you who desire
this intermingling of the black and monstrous fingers of
    Moloch
in the blood-jets of your throat.

Come, you shall have your desire,
since already I am implicated with you
in your strange lust.

PARADISE RE-ENTERED

Through the strait gate of passion,
Between the bickering fire
Where flames of fierce love tremble
On the body of fierce desire:

To the intoxication,
The mind, fused down like a bead,
Flees in its agitation
The flames' stiff speed:

At last to calm incandescence,
Burned clean by remorseless hate,
Now, at the day's renascence
We approach the gate.

Now, from the darkened spaces
Of fear, and of frightened faces,
Death, in our awed embraces
Approached and passed by;

We near the flame-burnt porches
Where the brands of the angels, like torches,
Whirl,—in these perilous marches
Pausing to sigh;

We look back on the withering roses,
The stars, in their sun-dimmed closes,
Where 'twas given us to repose us
Sure on our sanctity;

Beautiful, candid lovers,
Burnt out of our earthly covers,
We might have nestled like plovers
In the fields of eternity.

There, sure in sinless being,
All-seen, and then all-seeing,
In us life unto death agreeing,
We might have lain.

But we storm the angel-guarded
Gates of the long-discarded
Garden, which God has hoarded
Against our pain.

The Lord of Hosts and the Devil
Are left on Eternity's level
Field, and as victors we travel
To Eden home.

Back beyond good and evil
Return we. Eve dishevel
Your hair for the bliss-drenched revel
On our primal loam.

COMING AWAKE

When I woke, the lake-lights were quivering on the wall,
    The sunshine swam in a shoal across and across,
And a hairy, big bee hung over the primulas
    In the window, his body black fur, and the sound of
    him cross.

There was something I ought to remember: and yet
    I did not remember. Why should I? The running lights
And the airy primulas, oblivious
    Of the impending bee—they were fair enough sights.

243

SPRING MORNING

Ah, through the open door
Is there an almond-tree
Aflame with blossom!
    —Let us fight no more.

Among the pink and blue
Of the sky and the almond flowers
A sparrow flutters.
    —We have come through,

It is really spring!—See,
When he thinks himself alone
How he bullies the flowers.
    —Ah, you and me

How happy we'll be!—See him?
He clouts the tufts of flowers
In his impudence.
    —But, did you dream

It would be so bitter? Never mind,
It is finished, the spring is here.
And we're going to be summer-happy
    And summer-kind.

We have died, we have slain and been slain,
We are not our old selves any more.
I feel new and eager
    To start again.

It is gorgeous to live and forget.
And to feel quite new.
See the bird in the flowers?—he's making
    A rare to-do!

He thinks the whole blue sky
Is much less than the bit of blue egg
He's got in his nest—we'll be happy,
    You and I, I and you.

With nothing to fight any more—
In each other, at least.
See, how gorgeous the world is
    Outside the door!
             San Gaudenzio.

WEDLOCK

I

Come, my little one, closer up against me,
Creep right up, with your round head pushed in my breast.

How I love all of you! Do you feel me wrap you
Up with myself and my warmth, like a flame round the
    wick?

And how I am not at all, except a flame that mounts off
    you.
Where I touch you, I flame into being;—but is it me, or
    you?

That round head pushed in my chest, like a nut in its
    socket,
And I the swift bracts that sheathe it: those breasts, those
    thighs and knees,

Those shoulders so warm and smooth: I feel that I
Am a sunlight upon them, that shines them into being.

But how lovely to be you! Creep closer in, that I am more.
I spread over you! How lovely, your round head, your
    arms,

Your breasts, your knees and feet! I feel that we
Are a bonfire of oneness, me flame flung leaping round you,
You the core of the fire, crept into me.

I I

And oh, my little one, you whom I enfold,
How quaveringly I depend on you, to keep me alive
Like a flame on a wick!

I, the man who enfolds you and holds you close,
How my soul cleaves to your bosom as I clasp you,
The very quick of my being!

Suppose you didn't want me! I should sink down
Like a light that has no sustenance
And sinks low.

Cherish me, my tiny one, cherish me who enfold you.
Nourish me, and endue me, I am only of you,
I am your issue.

How full and big like a robust, happy flame
When I enfold you, and you creep into me,
And my life is fierce at its quick
Where it comes off you!

I I I

My little one, my big one,
My bird, my brown sparrow in my breast.
My squirrel clutching in to me;
My pigeon, my little one, so warm,
So close, breathing so still.

My little one, my big one,
I, who am so fierce and strong, enfolding you,
If you start away from my breast, and leave me,
How suddenly I shall go down into nothing
Like a flame that falls of a sudden.

And you will be before me, tall and towering,
And I shall be wavering uncertain
Like a sunken flame that grasps for support.

I V

But now I am full and strong and certain
With you there firm at the core of me
Keeping me.

How sure I feel, how warm and strong and happy
For the future! How sure the future is within me
I am like a seed with a perfect flower enclosed.

I wonder what it will be,
What will come forth of us.
What flower, my love?

No matter, I am so happy,
I feel like a firm, rich, healthy root,
Rejoicing in what is to come.

How I depend on you utterly,
My little one, my big one!
How everything that will be, will not be of me,
Nor of either of us,
But of both of us.

V

And think, there will something come forth from us,
We two, folded so small together,
There will something come forth from us.
Children, acts, utterance,
Perhaps only happiness.

Perhaps only happiness will come forth from us.
Old sorrow, and new happiness.
Only that one newness.

But that is all I want.
And I am sure of that.
We are sure of that.

VI

And yet all the while you are you, you are not me.
And I am I, I am never you.
How awfully distinct and far off from each other's being
     we are!

Yet I am glad.
I am so glad there is always you beyond my scope,
Something that stands over,
Something I shall never be,
That I shall always wonder over, and wait for,
Look for like the breath of life as long as I live,
Still waiting for you, however old you are, and I am,
I shall always wonder over you, and look for you.

And you will always be with me.
I shall never cease to be filled with newness,
Having you near me.

HISTORY

The listless beauty of the hour
When snow fell on the apple-trees
And the wood-ash gathered in the fire
And we faced our first miseries.

Then the sweeping sunshine of noon
When the mountains like chariot cars
Were ranked to blue battle—and you and I
Counted our scars.

And then in a strange, grey hour
We lay mouth to mouth, with your face
Under mine like a star on the lake,
And I covered the earth, and all space.

The silent, drifting hours
Of morn after morn
And night drifting up to the night
Yet no pathway worn.

Your life, and mine, my love
Passing on and on, the hate
Fusing closer and closer with love
Till at length they mate.

The Cearne.

SONG OF A MAN WHO IS LOVED

Between her breasts is my home, between her breasts.
Three sides set on me space and fear, but the fourth side
    rests
Sure and a tower of strength, 'twixt the walls of her breasts.

Having known the world so long, I have never confessed
How it impresses me, how hard and compressed
Rocks seem, and earth, and air uneasy, and waters still
    ebbing west.

All things on the move, going their own little ways, and all
Jostling, people touching and talking and making small
Contacts and bouncing off again, bounce! bounce like a
    ball!

My flesh is weary with bounce and gone again!—
My ears are weary with words that bounce on them, and
    then
Bounce off again, meaning nothing. Assertions! Asser-
    tions! stones, women and men!

Between her breasts is my home, between her breasts.
Three sides set on me chaos and bounce, but the fourth
    side rests
Sure on a haven of peace, between the mounds of her
    breasts.

I am that I am, and no more than that: but so much
I am, nor will I be bounced out of it. So at last I touch
All that I am-not in softness, sweet softness, for she is such.

And the chaos that bounces and rattles like shrapnel, at
    least
Has for me a door into peace, warm dawn in the east
Where her bosom softens towards me, and the turmoil has
    ceased.

So I hope I shall spend eternity
With my face down buried between her breasts;
And my still heart full of security,
And my still hands full of her breasts.

SONG OF A MAN WHO HAS COME THROUGH

Not I, not I, but the wind that blows through me!
A fine wind is blowing the new direction of Time.
If only I let it bear me, carry me, if only it carry me!
If only I am sensitive, subtle, oh, delicate, a winged gift!
If only, most lovely of all, I yield myself and am borrowed
By the fine, fine wind that takes its course through the
    chaos of the world
Like a fine, an exquisite chisel, a wedge-blade inserted;
If only I am keen and hard like the sheer tip of a wedge
Driven by invisible blows,
The rock will split, we shall come at the wonder, we shall
    find the Hesperides.

Oh, for the wonder that bubbles into my soul,
I would be a good fountain, a good well-head,
Would blur no whisper, spoil no expression.

What is the knocking?
What is the knocking at the door in the night?
It is somebody wants to do us harm.

No, no, it is the three strange angels.
Admit them, admit them.

ONE WOMAN TO ALL WOMEN

I don't care whether I am beautiful to you,
        You other women.
Nothing of me that you see is my own;
A man balances, bone unto bone
Balances, everything thrown
        In the scale, you other women.

You may look and say to yourselves, I do
        Not show like the rest.
My face may not please you, nor my stature; yet if you
    knew
How happy I am, how my heart in the wind rings true
Like a bell that is chiming, each stroke as a stroke falls due,
        You other women:

You would draw your mirror towards you, you would wish
        To be different.
There's the beauty you cannot see, myself and him
Balanced in glorious equilibrium,
The swinging beauty of equilibrium,
        You other women.

There's this other beauty, the way of the stars,
        You straggling women.
If you knew how I swerve in peace, in the equipoise
With the man, if you knew how my flesh enjoys
The swinging bliss no shattering ever destroys,
        You other women:

You would envy me, you would think me wonderful
        Beyond compare;
You would weep to be lapsing on such harmony
As carries me, you would wonder aloud that he
Who is so strange should correspond with me
        Everywhere.

You see he is different, he is dangerous,
      Without pity or love.
And yet how his separate being liberates me
And gives me peace! You cannot see
How the stars are moving in surety
      Exquisite, high above.

We move without knowing, we sleep, and we travel on,
      You other women.
And this is beauty to me, to be lifted and gone
In a motion human inhuman, two and one
Encompassed, and many reduced to none,
      You other women.

                        Kensington.

PEOPLE

The great gold apples of night
Hang from the street's long bough
      Dripping their light
On the faces that drift below,
On the faces that drift and blow
Down the night-time, out of sight
      In the wind's sad sough.

The ripeness of these apples of night
Distilling over me
      Makes sickening the white
Ghost-flux of faces that hie
Them endlessly, endlessly by
Without meaning or reason why
      They ever should be.

STREET LAMPS

Gold, with an innermost speck
Of silver, singing afloat
    Beneath the night,
Like balls of thistledown
Wandering up and down
Over the whispering town
    Seeking where to alight!

Slowly, above the street,
Above the ebb of feet
    Drifting in flight;
Still, in the purple distance
The gold of their strange persistence
As they cross and part and meet
    And pass out of sight!

The seed-ball of the sun
Is broken at last, and done
    Is the orb of day.
Now to their separate ends
Seed after day-seed wends
    A separate way.

No sun will ever rise
Again on the wonted skies
    In the midst of the spheres.
The globe of the day, over-ripe,
Is shattered at last beneath the stripe
Of the wind, and its oneness veers
    Out myriad-wise.

Seed after seed after seed
Drifts over the town, in its need
    To sink and have done;
To settle at last in the dark,
To bury its weary spark
    Where the end is begun.

Darkness, and depth of sleep,
Nothing to know or to weep
   Where the seed sinks in
To the earth of the under-night
Where all is silent, quite
Still, and the darknesses steep
   Out all the sin.

"SHE SAID AS WELL TO ME"

She said as well to me: "Why are you ashamed?
That little bit of your chest that shows between
the gap of your shirt, why cover it up?
Why shouldn't your legs and your good strong thighs
be rough and hairy?—I'm glad they are like that.
You are shy, you silly, you silly shy thing.
Men are the shyest creatures, they never will come
out of their covers. Like any snake
slipping into its bed of dead leaves, you hurry into your
  clothes.
And I love you so! Straight and clean and all of a piece is
  the body of a man,
such an instrument, a spade, like a spear, or an oar,
such a joy to me—"
So she laid her hands and pressed them down my sides,
so that I began to wonder over myself, and what I was.

She said to me: "What an instrument, your body!
single and perfectly distinct from everything else!
What a tool in the hands of the Lord!
Only God could have brought it to its shape.
It feels as if his handgrasp, wearing you
had polished you and hollowed you,
hollowed this groove in your sides, grasped you under the
  breasts
and brought you to the very quick of your form,
subtler than an old, soft-worn fiddle-bow.

"When I was a child, I loved my father's riding-whip
that he used so often.
I loved to handle it, it seemed like a near part of him.
So I did his pens, and the jasper seal on his desk.
Something seemed to surge through me when I touched
       them.
"So it is with you, but here
The joy I feel!
God knows what I feel, but it is joy!
Look, you are clean and fine and singled out!
I admire you so, you are beautiful: this clean sweep of
       your sides, this firmness, this hard mould!
I would die rather than have it injured with one scar.
I wish I could grip you like the fist of the Lord,
and have you—"

So she said, and I wondered,
feeling trammelled and hurt.
It did not make me free.

Now I say to her: "No tool, no instrument, no God!
Don't touch me and appreciate me.
It is an infamy.
You would think twice before you touched a weasel on a
       fence
as it lifts its straight white throat.
Your hand would not be so flig and easy.
Nor the adder we saw asleep with her head on her shoulder,
curled up in the sunshine like a princess;
when she lifted her head in delicate, startled wonder
you did not stretch forward to caress her
though she looked rarely beautiful
and a miracle as she glided delicately away, with such
       dignity.
And the young bull in the field, with his wrinkled, sad face,
you are afraid if he rises to his feet,
though he is all wistful and pathetic, like a monolith,
       arrested, static.

"Is there nothing in me to make you hesitate?
I tell you there is all these.
And why should you overlook them in me?—"

NEW HEAVEN AND EARTH

I

And so I cross into another world
shyly and in homage linger for an invitation
from this unknown that I would trespass on.

I am very glad, and all alone in the world,
all alone, and very glad, in a new world
where I am disembarked at last.

I could cry with joy, because I am in the new world, just
    ventured in.
I could cry with joy, and quite freely, there is nobody to
    know.

And whosoever the unknown people of this unknown
    world may be
they will never understand my weeping for joy to be
    adventuring among them
because it will still be a gesture of the old world I am
    making
which they will not understand, because it is quite, quite
    foreign to them.

I I

I was so weary of the world,
I was so sick of it,
everything was tainted with myself,
skies, trees, flowers, birds, water,
people, houses, streets, vehicles, machines,
nations, armies, war, peace-talking,
work, recreation, governing, anarchy,
it was all tainted with myself, I knew it all to start with
because it was all myself.

When I gathered flowers, I knew it was myself plucking my
    own flowering.
When I went in a train, I knew it was myself travelling by
    my own invention.
When I heard the cannon of the war, I listened with my
    own ears to my own destruction.
When I saw the torn dead, I knew it was my own torn dead
    body.
It was all me, I had done it all in my own flesh.

III

I shall never forget the maniacal horror of it all in the end
when everything was me, I knew it all already, I antici-
    pated it all in my soul
because I was the author and the result
I was the God and the creation at once;
creator, I looked at my creation;
created, I looked at myself, the creator:
it was a maniacal horror in the end.

I was a lover, I kissed the woman I loved,
and God of horror, I was kissing also myself.
I was a father and a begetter of children,
and oh, oh horror, I was begetting and conceiving in my
    own body.

IV

At last came death, sufficiency of death,
and that at last relieved me, I died.
I buried my beloved; it was good, I buried myself and was
    gone.
War came, and every hand raised to murder;
very good, very good, every hand raised to murder!
Very good, very good, I am a murderer!
It is good, I can murder and murder, and see them fall,

the mutilated, horror-struck youths, a multitude
one on another, and then in clusters together
smashed, all oozing with blood, and burned in heaps
going up in a fœtid smoke to get rid of them,
the murdered bodies of youths and men in heaps
and heaps and heaps and horrible reeking heaps
till it is almost enough, till I am reduced perhaps;
thousands and thousands of gaping, hideous foul dead
that are youths and men and me
being burned with oil, and consumed in corrupt thick
    smoke, that rolls
and taints and blackens the sky, till at last it is dark, dark as
    night, or death, or hell
and I am dead, and trodden to nought in the smoke-sodden
    tomb;
dead and trodden to nought in the sour black earth
of the tomb; dead and trodden to nought, trodden to nought.

V

God, but it is good to have died and been trodden out,
trodden to nought in sour, dead earth,
quite to nought,
absolutely to nothing
nothing
nothing
nothing.

For when it is quite, quite nothing, then it is everything.
When I am trodden quite out, quite, quite out,
every vestige gone, then I am here
risen and setting my foot on another world
risen, accomplishing a resurrection
risen, not born again, but risen, body the same as before,
new beyond knowledge of newness, alive beyond life,
proud beyond inkling or furthest conception of pride,
living where life was never yet dreamed of, nor hinted at,
here, in the other world, still terrestrial
myself, the same as before, yet unaccountably new.

V I

I, in the sour black tomb, trodden to absolute death
I put out my hand in the night, one night, and my hand
touched that which was verily not me,
verily it was not me.
Where I had been was a sudden blaze,
a sudden flaring blaze!
So I put my hand out further, a little further
and I felt that which was not I,
it verily was not I,
it was the unknown.

Ha, I was a blaze leaping up!
I was a tiger bursting into sunlight.
I was greedy, I was mad for the unknown.
I, new-risen, resurrected, starved from the tomb,
starved from a life of devouring always myself,
now here was I, new-awakened, with my hand stretching
    out
and touching the unknown, the real unknown, the un-
    known unknown.

My God, but I can only say
I touch, I feel the unknown!
I am the first comer!
Cortes, Pisarro, Columbus, Cabot, they are nothing,
    nothing!
I am the first comer!
I am the discoverer!
I have found the other world!

The unknown, the unknown!
I am thrown upon the shore.
I am covering myself with the sand.
I am filling my mouth with the earth.
I am burrowing my body into the soil.
The unknown, the new world!

VII

It was the flank of my wife
I touched with my hand, I clutched with my hand,
rising, new-awakened from the tomb!
It was the flank of my wife
whom I married years ago
at whose side I have lain for over a thousand nights
and all that previous while, she was I, she was I;
I touched her, it was I who touched and I who was touched.

Yet rising from the tomb, from the black oblivion
stretching out my hand, my hand flung like a drowned
    man's hand on a rock,
I touched her flank and knew I was carried by the current
    in death
over to the new world, and was climbing out on the shore,
risen, not to the old world, the old, changeless I, the old life,
wakened not to the old knowledge
but to a new earth, a new I, a new knowledge, a new world
    of time.

Ah no, I cannot tell you what it is, the new world.
I cannot tell you the mad, astounded rapture of its dis-
    covery.
I shall be mad with delight before I have done,
and whosoever comes after will find me in the new world
a madman in rapture.

VIII

Green streams that flow from the innermost continent of
    the new world,
what are they?
Green and illumined and travelling for ever
dissolved with the mystery of the innermost heart of the
    continent,
mystery beyond knowledge or endurance, so sumptuous
out of the well-heads of the new world.—

The other, she too has strange green eyes!
White sands and fruits unknown and perfumes that never
can blow across the dark seas to our usual world!
And land that beats with a pulse!
And valleys that draw close in love!
And strange ways where I fall into oblivion of uttermost
     living!—
Also she who is the other has strange-mounded breasts and
     strange sheer slopes, and white levels.

Sightless and strong oblivion in utter life takes possession
     of me!
The unknown, strong current of life supreme
drowns me and sweeps me away and holds me down
to the sources of mystery, in the depths,
extinguishes there my risen resurrected life
and kindles it further at the core of utter mystery.

Greatham.

ELYSIUM

I have found a place of loneliness
Lonelier than Lyonesse,
Lovelier than Paradise;

Full of sweet stillness
That no noise can transgress,
Never a lamp distress.

The full moon sank in state.
I saw her stand and wait
For her watchers to shut the gate.

Then I found myself in a wonderland
All of shadow and of bland
Silence hard to understand.

I waited therefore; then I knew
The presence of the flowers that grew
Noiseless, their wonder noiseless blew.

And flashing kingfishers that flew
In sightless beauty, and the few
Shadows the passing wild-beast threw.

And Eve approaching over the ground
Unheard and subtle, never a sound
To let me know that I was found.

Invisible the hands of Eve
Upon me travelling to reeve
Me from the matrix, to relieve

Me from the rest! Ah, terribly
Between the body of life and me
Her hands slid in and set me free.

Ah, with a fearful, strange detection
She found the source of my subjection
To the All, and severed the connection.

Delivered helpless and amazed
From the womb of the All, I am waiting, dazed
For memory to be erased.

Then I shall know the Elysium
That lies outside the monstrous womb
Of time from out of which I come.

MANIFESTO

I

A woman has given me strength and affluence.
Admitted!

All the rocking wheat of Canada, ripening now,
has not so much of strength as the body of one woman
sweet in ear, nor so much to give
though it feed nations.

Hunger is the very Satan.
The fear of hunger is Moloch, Belial, the horrible God.
It is a fearful thing to be dominated by the fear of hunger.

Not bread alone, not the belly nor the thirsty throat.
I have never yet been smitten through the belly, with the
    lack of bread,
no, nor even milk and honey.

The fear of the want of these things seems to be quite left
    out of me.
For so much, I thank the good generations of mankind.

II

And the sweet, constant, balanced heat
of the suave sensitive body, the hunger for this
has never seized me and terrified me.
Here again, man has been good in his legacy to us, in these
    two primary instances.

III

Then the dumb, aching, bitter, helpless need,
the pining to be initiated,
to have access to the knowledge that the great dead
have opened up for us, to know, to satisfy
the great and dominant hunger of the mind;
man's sweetest harvest of the centuries, sweet, printed
    books,
bright, glancing, exquisite corn of many a stubborn
glebe in the upturned darkness;
I thank mankind with passionate heart
that I just escaped the hunger for these,
that they were given when I needed them,
because I am the son of man.

I have eaten, and drunk, and warmed and clothed my body,
I have been taught the language of understanding,
I have chosen among the bright and marvellous books,
like any prince, such stores of the world's supply
were open to me, in the wisdom and goodness of man.
So far, so good.
Wise, good provision that makes the heart swell with love!

IV

But then came another hunger
very deep, and ravening;
the very body's body crying out
with a hunger more frightening, more profound
than stomach or throat or even the mind;
redder than death, more clamorous.

The hunger for the woman. Alas,
it is so deep a Moloch, ruthless and strong,
'tis like the unutterable name of the dread Lord,
not to be spoken aloud.
Yet there it is, the hunger which comes upon us,
which we must learn to satisfy with pure, real satisfaction;
or perish, there is no alternative.

I thought it was woman, indiscriminate woman,
mere female adjunct of what I was.
Ah, that was torment hard enough
and a thing to be afraid of,
a threatening, torturing, phallic Moloch.

A woman fed that hunger in me at last.
What many women cannot give, one woman can;
so I have known it.

She stood before me like riches that were mine.
Even then, in the dark, I was tortured, ravening, unfree,
Ashamed, and shameful, and vicious.
A man is so terrified of strong hunger;
and this terror is the root of all cruelty.
She loved me, and stood before me, looking to me.
How could I look, when I was mad? I looked sideways, furtively,
being mad with voracious desire.

V

This comes right at last.
When a man is rich, he loses at last the hunger fear.
I lost at last the fierceness that fears it will starve.
I could put my face at last between her breasts
and know that they were given for ever
that I should never starve,
never perish;
I had eaten of the bread that satisfies
and my body's body was appeased,
there was peace and richness,
fulfilment.

Let them praise desire who will,
but only fulfilment will do,
real fulfilment, nothing short.
It is our ratification,
our heaven, as a matter of fact.
Immortality, the heaven, is only a projection of this strange
    but actual fulfilment,
here in the flesh.

So, another hunger was supplied,
and for this I have to thank one woman,
not mankind, for mankind would have prevented me;
but one woman,
and these are my red-letter thanksgivings.

V I

To be, or not to be, is still the question.
This ache for being is the ultimate hunger.
And for myself, I can say "almost, almost, oh, very nearly."
Yet something remains.
Something shall not always remain.
For the main already is fulfilment.

What remains in me, is to be known even as I know.
I know her now : or perhaps, I know my own limitation against
    her.

Plunging as I have done, over, over the brink
I have dropped at last headlong into nought, plunging upon
    sheer hard extinction;
I have come, as it were, not to know,
died, as it were; ceased from knowing; surpassed myself.
What can I say more, except that I know what it is to surpass
    myself?

It is a kind of death which is not death.
It is going a little beyond the bounds.
How can one speak, where there is a dumbness on one's mouth?
I suppose, ultimately she is all beyond me,
she is all not-me, ultimately.

It is that that one comes to.
A curious agony, and a relief, when I touch that which is not
    me in any sense,
it wounds me to death with my own not-being; definite, inviol-
    able limitation,
and something beyond, quite beyond, if you understand what
    that means.
It is the major part of being, this having surpassed oneself,
this having touched the edge of the beyond, and perished, yet
    not perished.

VII

I want her though, to take the same from me.
She touches me as if I were herself, her own.
She has not realised yet, that fearful thing, that I am the other,
she thinks we are all of one piece.
It is painfully untrue.

I want her to touch me at last, ah, on the root and quick of
    my darkness
and perish on me, as I have perished on her.

Then, we shall be two and distinct, we shall have each our
    separate being.
And that will be pure existence, real liberty.

266

Till then, we are confused, a mixture, unresolved, unextricated
    one from the other.
It is in pure, unutterable resolvedness, distinction of being,
    that one is free,
not in mixing, merging, not in similarity.
When she has put her hand on my secret, darkest sources, the
    darkest outgoings,
when it has struck home to her, like a death, "this is *him*!"
she has no part in it, no part whatever,
it is the terrible *other*,
when she knows the fearful *other flesh*, ah, darkness unfathom-
    able and fearful, contiguous and concrete,
when she is slain against me, and lies in a heap like one outside
    the house,
when she passes away as I have passed away,
being pressed up against the *other*,
then I shall be glad, I shall not be confused with her,
I shall be cleared, distinct, single as if burnished in silver,
having no adherence, no adhesion anywhere,
one clear, burnished, isolated being, unique,
and she also, pure, isolated, complete,
two of us, unutterably distinguished, and in unutterable con-
    junction.

Then we shall be free, freer than angels, ah, perfect.

VIII

After that, there will only remain that all men detach themselves
    and become unique,
that we are all detached, moving in freedom more than the
    angels,
conditioned only by our own pure single being,
having no laws but the laws of our own being.

Every human being will then be like a flower, untrammelled.
Every movement will be direct.
Only to be will be such delight, we cover our faces when we
    think of it
lest our faces betray us to some untimely fiend.

Every man himself, and therefore, a surpassing singleness of
    mankind.
The blazing tiger will spring upon the deer, undimmed,
the hen will nestle over her chickens,
we shall love, we shall hate,
but it will be like music, sheer utterance,
issuing straight out of the unknown,
the lightning and the rainbow appearing in us unbidden, un-
    checked,
like ambassadors.

We shall not look before and after.
We shall *be, now.*
We shall know in full.
We, the mystic NOW.

Zennor.

AUTUMN RAIN

The plane leaves
fall black and wet
on the lawn;

the cloud sheaves
in heaven's fields set
droop and are drawn

in falling seeds of rain;
the seed of heaven
on my face

falling—I hear again
like echoes even
that softly pace

heaven's muffled floor,
the winds that tread
out all the grain

of tears, the store
harvested
in the sheaves of pain

caught up aloft:
the sheaves of dead
men that are slain

now winnowed soft
on the floor of heaven;
manna invisible

of all the pain
here to us given;
finely divisible
falling as rain.

FROST FLOWERS

It is not long since, here among all these folk
in London, I should have held myself
of no account whatever,
but should have stood aside and made them way
thinking that they, perhaps,
had more right than I—for who was I?

Now I see them just the same, and watch them.
But of what account do I hold them?

Especially the young women. I look at them
as they dart and flash
before the shops, like wagtails on the edge of a pool.

If I pass them close, or any man,
like sharp, slim wagtails they flash a little aside
pretending to avoid us; yet all the time
calculating.

269

They think that we adore them—alas, would it were true!
Probably they think all men adore them,
howsoever they pass by.

What is it, that, from their faces fresh as spring,
such fair, fresh, alert, first-flower faces,
like lavender crocuses, snowdrops, like Roman hyacinths,
scyllas and yellow-haired hellebore, jonquils, dim anemones,
even the sulphur auriculas,
flowers that come first from the darkness, and feel cold to the
      touch,
flowers scentless or pungent, ammoniacal almost;
what is it, that, from the faces of the fair young women
comes like a pungent scent, a vibration beneath
that startles me, alarms me, stirs up a repulsion?

They are the issue of acrid winter, these first-flower young
      women;
their scent is lacerating and repellent,
it smells of burning snow, of hot-ache,
of earth, winter-pressed, strangled in corruption;
it is the scent of the fiery-cold dregs of corruption,
when destruction soaks through the mortified, decomposing
      earth,
and the last fires of dissolution burn in the bosom of the ground.

They are the flowers of ice-vivid mortification,
thaw-cold, ice-corrupt blossoms,
with a loveliness I loathe;
for what kind of ice-rotten, hot-aching heart must they need
      to root in!

CRAVING FOR SPRING

I wish it were spring in the world.

Let it be spring!
Come, bubbling, surging tide of sap!

Come, rush of creation!
Come, life! surge through this mass of mortification!
Come, sweep away these exquisite, ghastly first-flowers,
which are rather last-flowers!
Come, thaw down their cool portentousness, dissolve them:
snowdrops, straight, death-veined exhalations of white and
     purple crocuses,
flowers of the penumbra, issue of corruption, nourished in
     mortification,
jets of exquisite finality;
Come, spring, make havoc of them!

I trample on the snowdrops, it gives me pleasure to tread down
     the jonquils,
to destroy the chill Lent lilies;
for I am sick of them, their faint-bloodedness,
slow-blooded, icy-fleshed, portentous.

I want the fine, kindling wine-sap of spring,
gold, and of inconceivably fine, quintessential brightness,
rare almost as beams, yet overwhelmingly potent,
strong like the greatest force of world-balancing.

This is the same that picks up the harvest of wheat
and rocks it, tons of grain, on the ripening wind;
the same that dangles the globe-shaped pleiads of fruit
temptingly in mid-air, between a playful thumb and finger;
oh, and suddenly, from out of nowhere, whirls the pear-bloom,
upon us, and apple- and almond- and apricot- and quince-
     blossom,
storms and cumulus clouds of all imaginable blossom
about our bewildered faces,
though we do not worship.

I wish it were spring
cunningly blowing on the fallen sparks, odds and ends of the
     old, scattered fire,
and kindling shapely little conflagrations
curious long-legged foals, and wide-eared calves, and naked
     sparrow-bubs.

I wish that spring
would start the thundering traffic of feet
new feet on the earth, beating with impatience.

I wish it were spring, thundering
delicate, tender spring.
I wish these brittle, frost-lovely flowers of passionate, myster-
ious corruption
were not yet to come still more from the still-flickering dis-
content.

Oh, in the spring, the bluebell bows him down for very
exuberance,
exulting with secret warm excess,
bowed down with his inner magnificence!

Oh, yes, the gush of spring is strong enough
to toss the globe of earth like a ball on a water-jet
dancing sportfully;
as you see a tiny celluloid ball tossing on a squirt of water
for men to shoot at, penny-a-time, in a booth at a fair.

The gush of spring is strong enough
to play with the globe of earth like a ball on a fountain;
At the same time it opens the tiny hands of the hazel
with such infinite patience.
The power of the rising, golden, all-creative sap could take the
earth
and heave it off among the stars, into the invisible;
the same sets the throstle at sunset on a bough
singing against the blackbird;
comes out in the hesitating tremor of the primrose,
and betrays its candour in the round white strawberry flower,
is dignified in the foxglove, like a Red-Indian brave.

Ah come, come quickly, spring!
Come and lift us towards our culmination, we myriads;
we who have never flowered, like patient cactuses.
Come and lift us to our end, to blossom, bring us to our summer,
we who are winter-weary in the winter of the world.

Come making the chaffinch nests hollow and cosy,
come and soften the willow buds till they are puffed and furred,
then blow them over with gold.
Come and cajole the gawky colt's-foot flowers.

Come quickly, and vindicate us
against too much death.
Come quickly, and stir the rotten globe of the world from
    within,
burst it with germination, with world anew.
Come now, to us, your adherents, who cannot flower from
    the ice.
All the world gleams with the lilies of Death the Unconquerable,
but come, give us our turn.
Enough of the virgins and lilies, of passionate, suffocating
    perfume of corruption,
no more narcissus perfume, lily harlots, the blades of sensation
piercing the flesh to blossom of death.
Have done, have done with this shuddering, delicious business
of thrilling ruin in the flesh, of pungent passion, of rare, death-
    edged ecstasy.
Give us our turn, give us a chance, let our hour strike,
O soon, soon!
Let the darkness turn violet with rich dawn.
Let the darkness be warmed, warmed through to a ruddy violet,
incipient purpling towards summer in the world of the heart
    of man.

Are the violets already here!
Show me! I tremble so much to hear it, that even now
on the threshold of spring, I fear I shall die.
Show me the violets that are out.

Oh, if it be true, and the living darkness of the blood of man
    is purpling with violets,
if the violets are coming out from under the rack of men,
    winter-rotten and fallen,
we shall have spring.
Pray not to die on this Pisgah blossoming with violets.
Pray to live through.

If you catch a whiff of violets from the darkness of the shadow
    of man
it will be spring in the world,
it will be spring in the world of the living;
wonderment organising itself, heralding itself with the violets,
stirring of new seasons.

Ah, do not let me die on the brink of such anticipation!
Worse, let me not deceive myself.

Zennor.

BIRDS, BEASTS AND FLOWERS

FRUITS

"F o r fruits are all of them female, in them lies the seed. And so when they break and show the seed, then we look into the womb and see its secrets. So it is that the pomegranate is the apple of love to the Arab, and the fig has been a catch-word for the female fissure for ages. I don't care a fig for it! men say. But why a fig? The apple of Eden, even, was Eve's fruit. To her it belonged, and she offered it to the man. Even the apples of knowledge are Eve's fruit, the woman's. But the apples of life the dragon guards, and no woman gives them. . . ."

"No sin is it to drink as much as a man can take and get home without a servant's help, so he be not stricken in years."

POMEGRANATE

You tell me I am wrong.
Who are you, who is anybody to tell me I am wrong?
I am not wrong.

In Syracuse, rock left bare by the viciousness of Greek
women,
No doubt you have forgotten the pomegranate-trees in
flower,
Oh so red, and such a lot of them.

Whereas at Venice,
Abhorrent, green, slippery city
Whose Doges were old, and had ancient eyes,
In the dense foliage of the inner garden
Pomegranates like bright green stone,
And barbed, barbed with a crown.
Oh, crown of spiked green metal
Actually growing!

Now in Tuscany,
Pomegranates to warm your hands at;
And crowns, kingly, generous, tilting crowns
Over the left eyebrow.

And, if you dare, the fissure!

Do you mean to tell me you will see no fissure?
Do you prefer to look on the plain side?

For all that, the setting suns are open.
The end cracks open with the beginning:
Rosy, tender, glittering within the fissure.

Do you mean to tell me there should be no fissure?
No glittering, compact drops of dawn?
Do you mean it is wrong, the gold-filmed skin, integument,
shown ruptured?

For my part, I prefer my heart to be broken.
It is so lovely, dawn-kaleidoscopic within the crack.
                                        San Gervasio in Tuscany.

PEACH

Would you like to throw a stone at me?
Here, take all that's left of my peach.

Blood-red, deep;
Heaven knows how it came to pass.
Somebody's pound of flesh rendered up.

Wrinkled with secrets
And hard with the intention to keep them.

Why, from silvery peach-bloom,
From that shallow-silvery wine-glass on a short stem
This rolling, dropping, heavy globule?

I am thinking, of course, of the peach before I ate it.

Why so velvety, why so voluptuous heavy?
Why hanging with such inordinate weight?
Why so indented?

Why the groove?
Why the lovely, bivalve roundnesses?
Why the ripple down the sphere?
Why the suggestion of incision?

Why was not my peach round and finished like a billiard
      ball?
It would have been if man had made it.
Though I've eaten it now.

But it wasn't round and finished like a billiard ball.
And because I say so, you would like to throw something
      at me.

Here, you can have my peach stone.
                                        San Gervasio.

MEDLARS AND SORB-APPLES

I love you, rotten,
Delicious rottenness.

I love to suck you out from your skins
So brown and soft and coming suave,
So morbid, as the Italians say.

What a rare, powerful, reminiscent flavour
Comes out of your falling through the stages of decay:
Stream within stream.

Something of the same flavour as Syracusan muscat wine
Or vulgar Marsala.

Though even the word Marsala will smack of preciosity
Soon in the pussyfoot West.

What is it?
What is it, in the grape turning raisin,
In the medlar, in the sorb-apple,
Wineskins of brown morbidity,
Autumnal excrementa;
What is it that reminds us of white gods?

Gods nude as blanched nut-kernels,
Strangely, half-sinisterly flesh-fragrant
As if with sweat,
And drenched with mystery.

Sorb-apples, medlars with dead crowns.
I say, wonderful are the hellish experiences,
Orphic, delicate
Dionysos of the Underworld.

A kiss, and a spasm of farewell, a moment's orgasm of
    rupture,
Then along the damp road alone, till the next turning.
And there, a new partner, a new parting, a new unfusing
    into twain,

A new gasp of further isolation,
A new intoxication of loneliness, among decaying, frost-cold
  leaves.

Going down the strange lanes of hell, more and more
  intensely alone,
The fibres of the heart parting one after the other
And yet the soul continuing, naked-footed, ever more vividly
  embodied
Like a flame blown whiter and whiter
In a deeper and deeper darkness
Ever more exquisite, distilled in separation.

So, in the strange retorts of medlars and sorb-apples
The distilled essence of hell.
The exquisite odour of leave-taking.
      Jamque vale!
Orpheus, and the winding, leaf-clogged, silent lanes of hell.

Each soul departing with its own isolation,
Strangest of all strange companions,
And best.

Medlars, sorb-apples,
More than sweet
Flux of autumn
Sucked out of your empty bladders

And sipped down, perhaps, with a sip of Marsala
So that the rambling, sky-dropped grape can add its savour
  to yours,
Orphic farewell, and farewell, and farewell
And the *ego sum* of Dionysos
The *sono io* of perfect drunkenness
Intoxication of final loneliness.

                              San Gervasio.

FIGS

The proper way to eat a fig, in society,
Is to split it in four, holding it by the stump,
And open it, so that it is a glittering, rosy, moist, honied, heavy-
    petalled four-petalled flower.

Then you throw away the skin
Which is just like a four-sepalled calyx,
After you have taken off the blossom with your lips.

But the vulgar way
Is just to put your mouth to the crack, and take out the flesh
    in one bite.

Every fruit has its secret.

The fig is a very secretive fruit.
As you see it standing growing, you feel at once it is symbolic:
And it seems male.
But when you come to know it better, you agree with the
    Romans, it is female.

The Italians vulgarly say, it stands for the female part; the
    fig-fruit:
The fissure, the yoni,
The wonderful moist conductivity towards the centre.

Involved,
Inturned,
The flowering all inward and womb-fibrilled;
And but one orifice.

The fig, the horse-shoe, the squash-blossom.
Symbols.

There was a flower that flowered inward, womb-ward;
Now there is a fruit like a ripe womb.

It was always a secret.
That's how it should be, the female should always be secret.

There never was any standing aloft and unfolded on a bough
Like other flowers, in a revelation of petals;
Silver-pink peach, venetian green glass of medlars and sorb-
apples,
Shallow wine-cups on short, bulging stems
Openly pledging heaven:
Here's to the thorn in flower! Here is to Utterance!
The brave, adventurous rosaceæ.

Folded upon itself, and secret unutterable,
And milky-sapped, sap that curdles milk and makes *ricotta*,
Sap that smells strange on your fingers, that even goats won't
taste it;
Folded upon itself, enclosed like any Mohammedan woman,
Its nakedness all within-walls, its flowering forever unseen,
One small way of access only, and this close-curtained from
the light;
Fig, fruit of the female mystery, covert and inward,
Mediterranean fruit, with your covert nakedness,
Where everything happens invisible, flowering and fertilisation,
and fruiting
In the inwardness of your you, that eye will never see
Till it's finished, and you're over-ripe, and you burst to give
up your ghost.

Till the drop of ripeness exudes,
And the year is over.

And then the fig has kept her secret long enough.
So it explodes, and you see through the fissure the scarlet.
And the fig is finished, the year is over.

That's how the fig dies, showing her crimson through the
purple slit
Like a wound, the exposure of her secret, on the open day.
Like a prostitute, the bursten fig, making a show of her secret.

That's how women die too.

The year is fallen over-ripe,
The year of our women.
The year of our women is fallen over-ripe.
The secret is laid bare.
And rottenness soon sets in.
The year of our women is fallen over-ripe.

When Eve once knew *in her mind* that she was naked
She quickly sewed fig-leaves, and sewed the same for the man.
She'd been naked all her days before,
But till then, till that apple of knowledge, she hadn't had the
    fact on her mind.

She got the fact on her mind, and quickly sewed fig-leaves.
And women have been sewing ever since.
But now they stitch to adorn the bursten fig, not to cover it.
They have their nakedness more than ever on their mind,
And they won't let us forget it.

Now, the secret
Becomes an affirmation through moist, scarlet lips
That laugh at the Lord's indignation.

What then, good Lord! cry the women.
We have kept our secret long enough.
We are a ripe fig.
Let us burst into affirmation.

They forget, ripe figs won't keep.
Ripe figs won't keep.

Honey-white figs of the north, black figs with scarlet inside, of
    the south.
Ripe figs won't keep, won't keep in any clime.
What then, when women the world over have all bursten into
    self-assertion?
And bursten figs won't keep?

                                        San Gervasio.

GRAPES

So many fruits come from roses,
From the rose of all roses,
From the unfolded rose,
Rose of all the world.

Admit that apples and strawberries and peaches and pears and
    blackberries
Are all Rosaceæ,
Issue of the explicit rose,
The open-countenanced, skyward-smiling rose.

What then of the vine?
Oh, what of the tendrilled vine?

Ours is the universe of the unfolded rose,
The explicit
The candid revelation.

But long ago, oh, long ago
Before the rose began to simper supreme,
Before the rose of all roses, rose of all the world, was even in
    bud,
Before the glaciers were gathered up in a bunch out of the
    unsettled seas and winds,
Or else before they had been let down again, in Noah's flood,
There was another world, a dusky, flowerless, tendrilled world
And creatures webbed and marshy,
And on the margin, men soft-footed and pristine,
Still, and sensitive, and active,
Audile, tactile sensitiveness as of a tendril which orientates and
    reaches out,
Reaching out and grasping by an instinct more delicate than
    the moon's as she feels for the tides.

Of which world, the vine was the invisible rose,
Before petals spread, before colour made its disturbance,
    before eyes saw too much.

In a green, muddy, web-foot, unutterably songless world
The vine was rose of all roses.

There were no poppies or carnations,
Hardly a greenish lily, watery faint.
Green, dim, invisible flourishing of vines
Royally gesticulate.

Look now even now, how it keeps its power of invisibility!
Look how black, how blue-black, how globed in Egyptian
      darkness
Dropping among his leaves, hangs the dark grape!
See him there, the swart, so palpably invisible:
Whom shall we ask about him?

The negro might know a little.
When the vine was rose, Gods were dark-skinned.
Bacchus is a dream's dream.
Once God was all negroid, as now he is fair.
But it's so long ago, the ancient Bushman has forgotten
      more utterly than we, who have never known.

For we are on the brink of re-remembrance.
Which, I suppose, is why America has gone dry.
Our pale day is sinking into twilight,
And if we sip the wine, we find dreams coming upon us
Out of the imminent night.
Nay, we find ourselves crossing the fern-scented frontiers
Of the world before the floods, where man was dark and
      evasive
And the tiny vine-flower rose of all roses, perfumed,
And all in naked communion communicating as now our
      clothed vision can never communicate.
Vistas, down dark avenues,
As we sip the wine.
The grape is swart, the avenues dusky and tendrilled, subtly
      prehensile,
But we, as we start awake, clutch at our vistas democratic,
      boulevards, tram-cars, policemen.
Give us our own back,
Let us go to the soda-fountain, to get sober.

Soberness, sobriety.
It is like the agonised perverseness of a child heavy with
    sleep, yet fighting, fighting to keep awake;
Soberness, sobriety, with heavy eyes propped open.

Dusky are the avenues of wine,
And we must cross the frontiers, though we will not,
Of the lost, fern-scented world:
Take the fern-seed on our lips,
Close the eyes, and go
Down the tendrilled avenues of wine and the otherworld.

                                                    San Gervasio.

THE REVOLUTIONARY

Look at them standing there in authority,
The pale-faces,
As if it could have any effect any more.

Pale-face authority,
Caryatids,
Pillars of white bronze standing rigid, lest the skies fall.

What a job they've got to keep it up.
Their poor, idealist foreheads naked capitals
To the entablature of clouded heaven.

When the skies are going to fall, fall they will
In a great chute and rush of débâcle downwards.

Oh and I wish the high and super-gothic heavens would
    come down now,
The heavens above, that we yearn to and aspire to.

I do not yearn, nor aspire, for I am a blind Samson.
And what is daylight to me that I should look skyward?
Only I grope among you, pale-faces, caryatids, as among a
    forest of pillars that hold up the dome of high ideal
    heaven
Which is my prison,

287

And all these human pillars of loftiness, going stiff, metallic-
    stunned with the weight of their responsibility
I stumble against them.
Stumbling-blocks, painful ones.

To keep on holding up this ideal civilisation
Must be excruciating: unless you stiffen into metal, when
    it is easier to stand stock rigid than to move.

This is why I tug at them, individually, with my arm round
    their waist,
The human pillars.
They are not stronger than I am, blind Samson.
The house sways.

I shall be so glad when it comes down.
I am so tired of the limitations of their Infinite.
I am so sick of the pretensions of the Spirit.
I am so weary of pale-face importance.

Am I not blind, at the round-turning mill?
Then why should I fear their pale faces?
Or love the effulgence of their holy light,
The sun of their righteousness?

To me, all faces are dark,
All lips are dusky and valved.

Save your lips, O pale-faces,
Which are slips of metal,
Like slits in an automatic-machine, you columns of give-
    and-take.

To me, the earth rolls ponderously, superbly
Coming my way without forethought or afterthought.
To me, men's footfalls fall with a dull, soft rumble,
    ominous and lovely,
Coming my way.

But not your foot-falls, pale-faces,
They are a clicketing of bits of disjointed metal
Working in motion.

To me, men are palpable, invisible nearnesses in the dark
Sending out magnetic vibrations of warning, pitch-dark
    throbs of invitation.
But you, pale-faces,
You are painful, harsh-surfaced pillars that give off nothing
    except rigidity,
And I jut against you if I try to move, for you are every-
    where, and I am blind,
Sightless among all your visuality,
You staring caryatids.

See if I don't bring you down, and all your high opinion
And all your ponderous roofed-in erection of right and
    wrong,
Your particular heavens,
With a smash.

See if your skies aren't falling!
And my head, at least, is thick enough to stand it, the
    smash.

See if I don't move under a dark and nude, vast heaven
When your world is in ruins, under your fallen skies.
Caryatids, pale-faces.
See if I am not Lord of the dark and moving hosts
Before I die.

Florence.

THE EVENING LAND

Oh, America,
The sun sets in you.
Are you the grave of our day?

Shall I come to you, the open tomb of my race?

I would come, if I felt my hour had struck.
I would rather you came to me.

For that matter
Mahomet never went to any mountain
Save it had first approached him and cajoled his soul.

You have cajoled the souls of millions of us,
America,
Why won't you cajole my soul?
I wish you would.

I confess I am afraid of you.

The catastrophe of your exaggerate love,
You who never find yourself in love
But only lose yourself further, decomposing.

You who never recover from out of the orgasm of loving
Your pristine, isolate integrity, lost æons ago.
Your singleness within the universe.

You who in loving break down
And break further and further down
Your bounds of isolation,
But who never rise, resurrected, from this grave of
    mingling,
In a new proud singleness, America.

Your more-than-European idealism,
Like a be-aureoled bleached skeleton hovering
Its cage-ribs in the social heaven, beneficent.

And then your single resurrection
Into machine-uprisen perfect man.

Even the winged skeleton of your bleached ideal
Is not só frightening as that clean smooth
Automaton of your uprisen self,
Machine American.

Do you wonder that I am afraid to come
And answer the first machine-cut question from the lips of
    your iron men?
Put the first cents into metallic fingers of your officers
And sit beside the steel-straight arms of your fair women,
American?

This may be a withering tree, this Europe,
But here, even a customs-official is still vulnerable.

I am so terrified, America,
Of the iron click of your human contact.
And after this
The winding-sheet of your self-less ideal love.
Boundless love
Like a poison gas.

Does no one realise that love should be intense, individual,
Not boundless.
This boundless love is like the bad smell
Of something gone wrong in the middle.
All this philanthropy and benevolence on other people's
    behalf
Just a bad smell.

Yet, America,
Your elvishness,
Your New England uncanniness,
Your western brutal faery quality.

My soul is half-cajoled, half-cajoled.

Something in you which carries me beyond,
Yankee, Yankee,
What we call human.
Carries me where I want to be carried . . .
Or don't I?

What does it matter
What we call human, and what we don't call human?
The rose would smell as sweet.
And to be limited by a mere word is to be less than a hop-
    ping flea, which hops over such an obstruction at first
    jump.

Your horrible, skeleton, aureoled ideal,
Your weird bright motor-productive mechanism,
Two spectres.

But moreover
A dark, unfathomed will, that is not un-Jewish;
A set, stoic endurance, non-European;
An ultimate desperateness, un-African;
A deliberate generosity, non-Oriental.

The strange, unaccustomed geste of your demonish New
    World nature
Glimpsed now and then.

Nobody knows you.
You don't know yourself.
And I, who am half in love with you,
What am I in love with?
My own imaginings?
Say it is not so.

Say, through the branches
America, America
Of all your machines,
Say, in the deep sockets of your idealistic skull,
Dark, aboriginal eyes
Stoic, able to wait through ages
Glancing.

Say, in the sound of all your machines
And white words, white-wash American,
Deep pulsing of a strange heart
New throb, like a stirring under the false dawn that pre-
    cedes the real.

Nascent American
Demonish, lurking among the undergrowth
Of many-stemmed machines and chimneys that smoke like
    pine-trees.

Dark, elvish,
Modern, unissued, uncanny America,
Your nascent demon people
Lurking among the deeps of your industrial thicket
Allure me till I am beside myself,
A nympholepht,

"These States!" as Whitman said,
Whatever he meant.

Baden-Baden.

PEACE

Peace is written on the doorstep
In lava.

Peace, black peace congealed.
My heart will know no peace
Till the hill bursts.

Brilliant, intolerable lava,
Brilliant as a powerful burning-glass,
Walking like a royal snake down the mountain
    towards the sea.

Forests, cities, bridges
Gone again in the bright trail of lava.
Naxos thousands of feet below the olive-roots,
And now the olive leaves thousands of feet below
    the lava fire.

Peace congealed in black lava on the doorstep.
Within, white-hot lava, never at peace
Till it burst forth blinding, withering the earth;
To set again into rock,
Grey-black rock.

Call it Peace?

Taormina.

TREES

"IT IS SAID, a disease has attacked the cypress trees of Italy, and they are all dying.
Now even the shadow of the lost secret is vanishing from earth."
"Empedokles says trees were the first living creatures to grow up out of the earth, before the sun was spread out and before day and night were distinguished; from the symmetry of their mixture of fire and water, they contain the proportion of male and female; they grow, rising up owing to the heat which is in the earth, so that they are parts of the earth just as embryos are parts of the uterus. Fruits are excretions of the water and fire in plants."

CYPRESSES

Tuscan cypresses,
What is it?

Folded in like a dark thought
For which the language is lost,
Tuscan cypresses,
Is there a great secret?
Are our words no good?

The undeliverable secret,
Dead with a dead race and a dead speech, and yet
Darkly monumental in you,
Etruscan cypresses.

Ah, how I admire your fidelity,
Dark cypresses!

Is it the secret of the long-nosed Etruscans?
The long-nosed, sensitive-footed, subtly-smiling Etruscans,
Who made so little noise outside the cypress groves?

Among the sinuous, flame-tall cypresses
That swayed their length of darkness all around
Etruscan-dusky, wavering men of old Etruria:
Naked except for fanciful long shoes,
Going with insidious, half-smiling quietness
And some of Africa's imperturbable sang-froid
About a forgotten business.

What business, then?
Nay, tongues are dead, and words are hollow as hollow
seed-pods,
Having shed their sound and finished all their echoing
Etruscan syllables,
That had the telling.

Yet more I see you darkly concentrate,
Tuscan cypresses,
On one old thought:
On one old slim imperishable thought, while you remain
Etruscan cypresses;
Dusky, slim marrow-thought of slender, flickering men of
    Etruria,
Whom Rome called vicious.

Vicious, dark cypresses:
Vicious, you supple, brooding, softly-swaying pillars of
    dark flame.
Monumental to a dead, dead race
Embowered in you!

Were they then vicious, the slender, tender-footed
Long-nosed men of Etruria?
Or was their way only evasive and different, dark, like
    cypress-trees in a wind?

They are dead, with all their vices,
And all that is left
Is the shadowy monomania of some cypresses
And tombs.

The smile, the subtle Etruscan smile still lurking
Within the tombs,
Etruscan cypresses.
He laughs longest who laughs last;
Nay, Leonardo only bungled the pure Etruscan smile.

What would I not give
To bring back the rare and orchid-like
Evil-yclept Etruscan?
For as to the evil
We have only Roman word for it,
Which I, being a little weary of Roman virtue,
Don't hang much weight on.

For oh, I know, in the dust where we have buried
The silenced races and all their abominations,
We have buried so much of the delicate magic of life.

There in the deeps
That churn the frankincense and ooze the myrrh,
Cypress shadowy,
Such an aroma of lost human life!

They say the fit survive,
But I invoke the spirits of the lost.
Those that have not survived, the darkly lost,
To bring their meaning back into life again,
Which they have taken away
And wrapt inviolable in soft cypress-trees,
Etruscan cypresses.

Evil, what is evil?
There is only one evil, to deny life
As Rome denied Etruria
And mechanical America Montezuma still.

Fiesole.

BARE FIG-TREES

Fig-trees, weird fig-trees
Made of thick smooth silver,
Made of sweet, untarnished silver in the sea-southern air—
I say untarnished, but I mean opaque—
Thick, smooth-fleshed silver, dull only as human limbs are
     dull
With the life-lustre,
Nude with the dim light of full, healthy life
That is always half-dark,
And suave like passion-flower petals,
Like passion-flowers,

With the half-secret gleam of a passion-flower hanging
    from the rock,
Great, complicated, nude fig-tree, stemless flower-mesh,
Flowerily naked in flesh, and giving off hues of life.

Rather like an octopus, but strange and sweet-myriad-
    limbed octopus;
Like a nude, like a rock-living, sweet-fleshed sea-anemone,
Flourishing from the rock in a mysterious arrogance.

Let me sit down beneath the many-branching candelabrum
That lives upon this rock
And laugh at Time, and laugh at dull Eternity,
And make a joke of stale Infinity,
Within the flesh-scent of this wicked tree,
That has kept so many secrets up its sleeve,
And has been laughing through so many ages
At man and his uncomfortablenesses,
And his attempt to assure himself that what is so is not so,
Up its sleeve.

Let me sit down beneath this many-branching candela-
    brum,
The Jewish seven-branched, tallow-stinking candlestick
    kicked over the cliff
And all its tallow righteousness got rid of,
And let me notice it behave itself.

And watch it putting forth each time to heaven,
Each time straight to heaven,
With marvellous naked assurance each single twig,
Each one setting off straight to the sky
As if it were the leader, the main-stem, the forerunner,
Intent to hold the candle of the sun upon its socket-tip,
It alone.

Every young twig
No sooner issued sideways from the thigh of his predecessor
Than off he starts without a qualm
To hold the one and only lighted candle of the sun in his
    socket-tip.

He casually gives birth to another young bud from his
    thigh,
Which at once sets off to be the one and only,
And hold the lighted candle of the sun.

Oh many-branching candelabrum, oh strange up-starting
    fig-tree,
Oh weird Demos, where every twig is the arch twig,
Each imperiously over-equal to each, equality over-reach-
    ing itself
Like the snakes on Medusa's head,
Oh naked fig-tree!

Still, no doubt every one of you can be the sun-socket as
    well as every other of you.
Demos, Demos, Demos!
Demon, too,
Wicked fig-tree, equality puzzle, with your self-conscious
    secret fruits.

Taormina.

BARE ALMOND-TREES

Wet almond-trees, in the rain,
Like iron sticking grimly out of earth;
Black almond trunks, in the rain,
Like iron implements twisted, hideous, out of the earth,
Out of the deep, soft fledge of Sicilian winter-green,
Earth-grass uneatable,
Almond trunks curving blackly, iron-dark, climbing the
    slopes.

Almond-tree, beneath the terrace rail,
Black, rusted, iron trunk,
You have welded your thin stems finer,
Like steel, like sensitive steel in the air,
Grey, lavender, sensitive steel, curving thinly and brittly
    up in a parabola.

What are you doing in the December rain?
Have you a strange electric sensitiveness in your steel tips?
Do you feel the air for electric influences
Like some strange magnetic apparatus?
Do you take in messages, in some strange code,
From heaven's wolfish, wandering electricity, that prowls
    so constantly round Etna?
Do you take the whisper of sulphur from the air?
Do you hear the chemical accents of the sun?
Do you telephone the roar of the waters over the earth?
And from all this, do you make calculations?

Sicily, December's Sicily in a mass of rain
With iron branching blackly, rusted like old, twisted
    implements
And brandishing and stooping over earth's wintry fledge,
    climbing the slopes
Of uneatable soft green!

Taormina.

TROPIC

Sun, dark sun,
Sun of black void heat,
Sun of the torrid mid-day's horrific darkness:

Behold my hair twisting and going black.
Behold my eyes turn tawny yellow
Negroid;
See the milk of northern spume
Coagulating and going black in my veins
Aromatic as frankincense.

Columns dark and soft,
Sunblack men,
Soft shafts, sunbreathing mouths,
Eyes of yellow, golden sand
As frictional, as perilous, explosive as brimstone.

Rock, waves of dark heat;
Waves of dark heat, rock, sway upwards,
Waver perpendicular.

What is the horizontal rolling of water
Compared to the flood of black heat that rolls up-
     wards past my eyes?

Taormina.

SOUTHERN NIGHT

Come up, thou red thing.
Come up, and be called a moon.

The mosquitoes are biting to-night
Like memories.

Memories, northern memories,
Bitter-stinging white world that bore us
Subsiding into this night.

Call it moonrise
This red anathema?

Rise, thou red thing,
Unfold slowly upwards, blood-dark;
Burst the night's membrane of tranquil stars
Finally.

Maculate
The red Macula.

Taormina.

FLOWERS

"A N D L O N G A G O, the almond was the symbol of resurrection.
But tell me, tell me, why should the almond be the symbol of
resurrection?

Have you not seen, in the wild winter sun of the southern Mediter-
ranean, in January and in February, the re-birth of the almond tree,
all standing in clouds of glory?

Ah yes! ah yes! would I might see it again!

Yet even this is not the secret of the secret. Do you know what was
called the almond bone, in the body, the last bone of the spine? This
was the seed of the body, and from the grave it could grow into a
new body again, like almond blossom in January.

No, no, I know nothing of that."

"Oh Persephone, Persephone, bring back to me from Hades the life
of a dead man."

"Wretches, utter wretches, keep your hands from beans!" saith
Empedokles.

For according to some, the beans were the beans of votes, and votes
were politics. But others say it was a food-taboo. Others also say the
bean was one of the oldest symbols of the male organ, for the peas-
cod is later than the beans-cod."

"But blood is red, and blood is life. Red was the colour of kings. Kings,
far-off kings, painted their faces vermilion, and were almost gods."

ALMOND BLOSSOM

Even iron can put forth,
Even iron.

This is the iron age,
But let us take heart
Seeing iron break and bud,
Seeing rusty iron puff with clouds of blossom.

The almond-tree,
December's bare iron hooks sticking out of earth.

The almond-tree,
That knows the deadliest poison, like a snake
In supreme bitterness.

Upon the iron, and upon the steel,
Odd flakes as if of snow, odd bits of snow,
Odd crumbs of melting snow.

But you mistake, it is not from the sky;
From out the iron, and from out the steel,
Flying not down from heaven, but storming up,
Strange storming up from the dense under-earth
Along the iron, to the living steel
In rose-hot tips, and flakes of rose-pale snow
Setting supreme annunciation to the world.

Nay, what a heart of delicate super-faith,
Iron-breaking,
The rusty swords of almond-trees.

Trees suffer, like races, down the long ages.
They wander and are exiled, they live in exile through
    long ages
Like drawn blades never sheathed, hacked and gone black,

The alien trees in alien lands: and yet
The heart of blossom,
The unquenchable heart of blossom!

Look at the many-cicatrised frail vine, none more scarred
    and frail,
Yet see him fling himself abroad in fresh abandon
From the small wound-stump.

Even the wilful, obstinate, gummy fig-tree
Can be kept down, but he'll burst like a polyp into
    prolixity.

And the almond-tree, in exile, in the iron age!

This is the ancient southern earth whence the vases were
    baked, amphoras, craters, cantharus, œnochœ, and
    open-hearted cylix,
Bristling now with the iron of almond-trees

Iron, but unforgotten.
Iron, dawn-hearted,
Ever-beating dawn-heart, enveloped in iron against the
    exile, against the ages.

See it come forth in blossom
From the snow-remembering heart
In long-nighted January,
In the long dark nights of the evening star, and Sirius, and
    the Etna snow-wind through the long night.

Sweating his drops of blood through the long-nighted
    Gethsemane
Into blossom, into pride, into honey-triumph, into most
    exquisite splendour.
Oh, give me the tree of life in blossom
And the Cross sprouting its superb and fearless flowers!

Something must be reassuring to the almond, in the evening
    star, and the snow-wind, and the long, long nights,
Some memory of far, sun-gentler lands,

So that the faith in his heart smiles again
And his blood ripples with that untellable delight of once-
     more-vindicated faith,
And the Gethsemane blood at the iron pores unfolds, un-
     folds,
Pearls itself into tenderness of bud
And in a great and sacred forthcoming steps forth, steps
     out in one stride
A naked tree of blossom, like a bridegroom bathing in dew,
     divested of cover,
Frail-naked, utterly uncovered
To the green night-baying of the dog-star, Etna's snow-
     edged wind
And January's loud-seeming sun.

Think of it, from the iron fastness
Suddenly to dare to come out naked, in perfection of
     blossom, beyond the sword-rust.
Think, to stand there in full-unfolded nudity, smiling,
With all the snow-wind, and the sun-glare, and the dog-
     star baying epithalamion.

Oh, honey-bodied beautiful one
Come forth from iron,
Red your heart is.
Fragile-tender, fragile-tender life-body,
More fearless than iron all the time,
And so much prouder, so disdainful of reluctances.

In the distance like hoar-frost, like silvery ghosts commun-
     ing on a green hill,
Hoar-frost-like and mysterious.
In the garden raying out
With a body like spray, dawn-tender, and looking about
With such insuperable, subtly-smiling assurance,
Sword-blade-born.

Unpromised,
No bounds being set.
Flaked out and come unpromised,

The tree being life-divine,
Fearing nothing, life-blissful at the core
Within iron and earth.

Knots of pink, fish-silvery
In heaven, in blue, blue heaven,
Soundless, bliss-full, wide-rayed, honey-bodied,
Red at the core,
Red at the core,
Knotted in heaven upon the fine light.

Open,
Open,
Five times wide open,
Six times wide open,
And given, and perfect;
And red at the core with the last sore-heartedness,
Sore-hearted-looking.

Fontana Vecchia.

PURPLE ANEMONES

Who gave us flowers?
Heaven? The white God?

Nonsense!
Up out of hell,
From Hades;
Infernal Dis!

Jesus the god of flowers——?
Not he.
Or sun-bright Apollo, him so musical?
Him neither.

Who then?
Say who.
Say it—and it is Pluto,

307

Dis,
The dark one.
Proserpine's master.

Who contradicts——?

When she broke forth from below,
Flowers came, hell-hounds on her heels.
Dis, the dark, the jealous god, the husband,
Flower-sumptuous-blooded.

Go then, he said.
And in Sicily, on the meadows of Enna,
She thought she had left him;
But opened around her purple anemones,

Caverns,
Little hells of colour, caves of darkness,
Hell, risen in pursuit of her; royal, sumptuous
Pit-falls.

All at her feet
Hell opening;
At her white ankles
Hell rearing its husband-splendid, serpent heads,
Hell-purple, to get at her—
Why did he let her go?
So he could track her down again, white victim.

Ah mastery!
Hell's husband-blossoms
Out on earth again.

Look out, Persephone!
You, Madame Ceres, mind yourself, the enemy is upon
        you.
About your feet spontaneous aconite,
Hell-glamorous, and purple husband-tyranny
Enveloping your late-enfranchised plains.

You thought your daughter had escaped?
No more stockings to darn for the flower-roots, down
    in hell?
But ah, my dear!
Aha, the stripe-cheeked whelps, whippet-slim crocuses,
At 'em, boys, at 'em!
Ho, golden-spaniel, sweet alert narcissus,
Smell 'em, smell 'em out!

Those two enfranchised women.

Somebody is coming!
Oho there!
Dark blue anemones!
Hell is up!
Hell on earth, and Dis within the depths!

Run, Persephone, he is after you already.

Why did he let her go?
To track her down;
All the sport of summer and spring, and flowers snap-
    ping at her ankles and catching her by the hair!
Poor Persephone and her rights for women.

Husband-snared hell-queen,
It is spring.

It is spring,
And pomp of husband-strategy on earth.

Ceres, kiss your girl, you think you've got her back.
The bit of husband-tilth she is,
Persephone!

Poor mothers-in-law!
They are always sold.

It is spring.

                                  Taormina.

SICILIAN CYCLAMENS

When he pushed his bush of black hair off his brow:
When she lifted her mop from her eyes, and screwed it in
    a knob behind
      —O act of fearful temerity!
When they felt their foreheads bare, naked to heaven, their
    eyes revealed:
When they felt the light of heaven brandished like a knife
    at their defenceless eyes,
And the sea like a blade at their face,
Mediterranean savages:
When they came out, face-revealed, under heaven, from
    the shaggy undergrowth of their own hair
For the first time,
They saw tiny rose cyclamens between their toes, growing
Where the slow toads sat brooding on the past.

Slow toads, and cyclamen leaves
Stickily glistening with eternal shadow
Keeping to earth.
Cyclamen leaves
Toad-filmy, earth-iridescent
Beautiful
Frost-filigreed
Spumed with mud
Snail-nacreous
Low down.

The shaking aspect of the sea
And man's defenceless bare face
And cyclamens putting their ears back.
Long, pensive, slim-muzzled greyhound buds
Dreamy, not yet present,
Drawn out of earth
At his toes.

Dawn-rose
Sub-delighted, stone-engendered
Cyclamens, young cyclamens
Arching
Waking, pricking their ears
Like delicate very-young greyhound bitches
Half-yawning at the open, inexperienced
Vista of day,
Folding back their soundless petalled ears.

Greyhound bitches
Bending their rosy muzzles pensive down,
And breathing soft, unwilling to wake to the new day
Yet sub-delighted.

Ah Mediterranean morning, when our world began!
Far-off Mediterranean mornings,
Pelasgic faces uncovered,
And unbudding cyclamens.

The hare suddenly goes uphill
Laying back her long ears with unwinking bliss.

And up the pallid, sea-blenched Mediterranean stone-slopes
Rose cyclamen, ecstatic fore-runner!
Cyclamens, ruddy-muzzled cyclamens
In little bunches like bunches of wild hares
Muzzles together, ears-aprick,
Whispering witchcraft
Like women at a well, the dawn-fountain.

Greece, and the world's morning
Where all the Parthenon marbles still fostered the roots of
    the cyclamen.
Violets
Pagan, rosy-muzzled violets
Autumnal
Dawn-pink,

Dawn-pale
Among squat toad-leaves sprinkling the unborn
Erechtheion marbles.

Taormina.

HIBISCUS AND SALVIA FLOWERS

Hark! Hark!
The dogs do bark!
It's the socialists come to town,
None in rags and none in tags,
Swaggering up and down.

Sunday morning,
And from the Sicilian townlets skirting Etna
The socialists have gathered upon us, to look at us.

How shall we know them when we see them?
How shall we know them now they've come?

Not by their rags and not by their tags,
Nor by any distinctive gown;
The same unremarkable Sunday suit
And hats cocked up and down.

Yet there they are, youths, loutishly
Strolling in gangs and staring along the Corso
With the gang-stare
And a half-threatening envy
At every *forestière*,
Every lordly tuppenny foreigner from the hotels, fattening
 on the exchange.

Hark! Hark!
The dogs do bark!
It's the socialists in the town.

Sans rags, sans tags,
Sans beards, sans bags,
Sans any distinction at all except loutish commonness.

How do we know then, that they are they?
Bolshevists.
Leninists.
Communists.
Socialists.
-Ists! -Ists!

Alas, salvia and hibiscus flowers.
Salvia and hibiscus flowers.

Listen again.
Salvia and hibiscus flowers.
Is it not so?
Salvia and hibiscus flowers.

Hark! Hark!
The dogs do bark!
Salvia and hibiscus flowers.

Who smeared their doors with blood?
Who on their breasts
Put salvias and hibiscus?

Rosy, rosy scarlet,
And flame-rage, golden-throated
Bloom along the Corso on the living, perambulating bush.

Who said they might assume these blossoms?
What god did they consult?

Rose-red, princess hibiscus, rolling her pointed Chinese petals!
Azalea and camellia, single peony
And pomegranate bloom and scarlet mallow-flower
And all the eastern, exquisite royal plants
That noble blood has brought us down the ages!
Gently nurtured, frail and splendid
Hibiscus flower—
Alas, the Sunday coats of Sicilian bolshevists!

Pure blood, and noble blood, in the fine and rose-red veins;
Small, interspersed with jewels of white gold
Frail-filigreed among the rest;
Rose of the oldest races of princesses, Polynesian
Hibiscus.

Eve, in her happy moments,
Put hibiscus in her hair,
Before she humbled herself, and knocked her knees with
    repentance.

Sicilian bolshevists,
With hibiscus flowers in the buttonholes of your Sunday suits,
Come now, speaking of rights, what right have you to this
    flower?

The exquisite and ageless aristocracy
Of a peerless soul,
Blessed are the pure in heart and the fathomless in bright pride;
The loveliness that knows *noblesse oblige*;
The native royalty of red hibiscus flowers;
The exquisite assertion of new delicate life
Risen from the roots:
Is this how you'll have it, red-decked socialists,
Hibiscus-breasted?

If it be so, I fly to join you,
And if it be not so, brutes to pull down hibiscus flowers!

Or salvia!
Or dragon-mouthed salvia with gold throat of wrath!
Flame-flushed, enraged, splendid salvia,
Cock-crested, crowing your orange scarlet like a tocsin
Along the Corso all this Sunday morning.

Is your wrath red as salvias,
You socialists?
You with your grudging, envious, furtive rage,
In Sunday suits and yellow boots along the Corso.
You look well with your salvia flowers, I must say.

Warrior-like, dawn-cock's-comb flaring flower
Shouting forth flame to set the world on fire,
The dust-heap of man's filthy world on fire,
And burn it down, the glutted, stuffy world,
And feed the young new fields of life with ash,
With ash I say,
Bolshevists,
Your ashes even, my friends,
Among much other ash.

If there were salvia-savage bolshevists
To burn the world back to manure-good ash,
Wouldn't I stick the salvia in my coat!
But these themselves must burn, these louts!

The dragon-faced,
The anger-reddened, golden-throated salvia
With its long antennæ of rage put out
Upon the frightened air.
Ugh, how I love its fangs of perfect rage
That gnash the air;
The molten gold of its intolerable rage
Hot in the throat.

I long to be a bolshevist
And set the stinking rubbish-heap of this foul world
Afire at a myriad scarlet points,
A bolshevist, a salvia-face
To lick the world with flame that licks it clean.
I long to see its chock-full crowdedness
And glutted squirming populousness on fire
Like a field of filthy weeds
Burnt back to ash,
And then to see the new, real souls sprout up.

Not this vast rotting cabbage patch we call the world;
But from the ash-scarred fallow
New wild souls.

Nettles, and a rose sprout,
Hibiscus, and mere grass,
Salvia still in a rage
And almond honey-still,
And fig-wort stinking for the carrion wasp;
All the lot of them, and let them fight it out.

But not a trace of foul equality,
Nor sound of still more foul human perfection.
You need not clear the world like a cabbage patch for me;
Leave me my nettles,
Let me fight the wicked, obstreperous weeds myself, and put
      them in their place,
Severely in their place.
I don't at all want to annihilate them,
I like a row with them,
But I won't be put on a cabbage-idealistic level of equality
      with them.

What rot, to see the cabbage and hibiscus-tree
As equals!
What rot, to say the louts along the Corso
In Sunday suits and yellow shoes
Are my equals!
I am their superior, saluting the hibiscus flower, not them.
The same I say to the profiteers from the hotels, the money-
      fat-ones,
Profiteers here being called dog-fish, stinking dog-fish, sharks.
The same I say to the pale and elegant persons,
Pale-face authorities loitering tepidly:
That I salute the red hibiscus flowers
And send mankind to its inferior blazes.
Mankind's inferior blazes,
And these along with it, all the inferior lot—
These bolshevists,
These dog-fish,
These precious and ideal ones,
All rubbish ready for fire.

And I salute hibiscus and the salvia flower
Upon the breasts of loutish bolshevists,
Damned loutish bolshevists,
Who perhaps will do the business after all,
In the long run, in spite of themselves.

Meanwhile, alas
For me no fellow-men,
No salvia-frenzied comrades, antennæ
Of yellow-red, outreaching, living wrath
Upon the smouldering air,
And throat of brimstone-molten angry gold.
Red, angry men are a race extinct, alas!

Never
To be a bolshevist
With a hibiscus flower behind my ear
In sign of life, of lovely, dangerous life
And passionate disquality of men;
In sign of dauntless, silent violets,
And impudent nettles grabbing the under-earth,
And cabbages born to be cut and eat,
And salvia fierce to crow and shout for fight,
And rosy-red hibiscus wincingly
Unfolding all her coiled and lovely self
In a doubtful world.

Never, bolshevistically
To be able to stand for all these!
Alas, alas, I have got to leave it all
To the youths in Sunday suits and yellow shoes
Who have pulled down the salvia flowers
And rosy delicate hibiscus flowers
And everything else to their disgusting level,
Never, of course, to put anything up again.

But yet
If they pull all the world down,
The process will amount to the same in the end.

Instead of flame and flame-clean ash,
Slow watery rotting back to level muck
And final humus,
Whence the re-start.

And still I cannot bear it
That they take hibiscus and the salvia flower.

Taormina.

THE EVANGELISTIC BEASTS

"OH PUT them back, put them back in the four corners of the
heavens, where they belong, the Apocalyptic beasts. For with their
wings full of stars they rule the night, and man that watches through
the night lives four lives, and man that sleeps through the night
sleeps four sleeps, the sleep of the lion, the sleep of the bull, the
sleep of the man, and the eagle's sleep. After which the lion wakes,
and it is day. Then from the four quarters the four winds blow, and
life has its changes. But when the heavens are empty, empty of the
four great Beasts, the four Natures, the four Winds, the four
Quarters, then sleep is empty too, man sleeps no more like the lion
and the bull, nor wakes from the light-eyed eagle sleep."

ST MATTHEW

They are not all beasts.
One is a man, for example, and one is a bird.

I, Matthew, am a man.

"And I, if I be lifted up, will draw all men unto me"—

That is Jesus.
But then Jesus was not quite a man.
He was the Son of Man
Filius Meus, O remorseless logic
Out of His own mouth.

I, Matthew, being a man
Cannot be lifted up, the Paraclete
To draw all men unto me,
Seeing I am on a par with all men.

I, on the other hand,
Am drawn to the Uplifted, as all men are drawn,
To the Son of Man
Filius Meus.

Wilt thou lift me up, Son of Man?
How my heart beats!
I am man.

I am man, and therefore my heart beats, and throws the dark
    blood from side to side
All the time I am lifted up.
Yes, even during my uplifting.

And if it ceased?
If it ceased, I should be no longer man
As I am, if my heart in uplifting ceased to beat, to toss the dark
    blood from side to side, causing my myriad secret streams.

After the cessation
I might be a soul in bliss, an angel, approximating to the
    Uplifted;
But that is another matter;
I am Matthew, the man,
And I am not that other angelic matter.

So I will be lifted up, Saviour,
But put me down again in time, Master,
Before my heart stops beating, and I become what I am not.
Put me down again on the earth, Jesus, on the brown soil
Where flowers sprout in the acrid humus, and fade into humus
    again.
Where beasts drop their unlicked young, and pasture, and drop
    their droppings among the turf.
Where the adder darts horizontal.
Down on the damp, unceasing ground, where my feet belong
And even my heart, Lord, forever, after all uplifting:
The crumbling, damp, fresh land, life horizontal and ceaseless.

Matthew I am, the man.
And I take the wings of the morning, to Thee, Crucified,
    Glorified.
But while flowers club their petals at evening
And rabbits make pills among the short grass
And long snakes quickly glide into the dark hole in the wall,
    hearing man approach,
I must be put down, Lord, in the afternoon,
And at evening I must leave off my wings of the spirit
As I leave off my braces,
And I must resume my nakedness like a fish, sinking down the
    dark reversion of night
Like a fish seeking the bottom, Jesus,
ΙΧΘΥΣ
Face downwards
Veering slowly
Down between the steep slopes of darkness, fucus-dark, seaweed-
    fringed valleys of the waters under the sea,

Over the edge of the soundless cataract
Into the fathomless, bottomless pit
Where my soul falls in the last throes of bottomless convulsion,
    and is fallen
Utterly beyond Thee, Dove of the Spirit;
Beyond everything, except itself.

Nay, Son of Man, I have been lifted up.
To Thee I rose like a rocket ending in mid-heaven.
But even thou, Son of Man, canst not quaff out the dregs of
    terrestrial manhood!
They fall back from Thee.

They fall back, and like a dripping of quicksilver taking the
    downward track,
Break into drops, burn into drops of blood, and dropping,
    dropping take wing
Membraned, blood-veined wings.
On fans of unsuspected tissue, like bats
They thread and thrill and flicker ever downward
To the dark zenith of Thine antipodes
Jesus Uplifted.

Bat-winged heart of man,
Reversed flame
Shuddering a strange way down the bottomless pit
To the great depths of its reversèd zenith.

Afterwards, afterwards
Morning comes, and I shake the dews of night from the wings
    of my spirit
And mount like a lark, Beloved.

But remember, Saviour,
That my heart which like a lark at heaven's gate singing, hovers
    morning-bright to Thee,
Throws still the dark blood back and forth
In the avenues where the bat hangs sleeping, upside-down
And to me undeniable, Jesus.

Listen, Paraclete.
I can no more deny the bat-wings of my fathom-flickering spirit
    of darkness
Than the wings of the Morning and Thee, Thou Glorified.

I am Matthew, the Man:
It is understood.
And Thou art Jesus, Son of Man
Drawing all men unto Thee, but bound to release them when
    the hour strikes.

I have been, and I have returned.
I have mounted up on the wings of the morning, and I have
    dredged down to the zenith's reversal.
Which is my way, being man.
Gods may stay in mid-heaven, the Son of Man has climbed to
    the Whitsun zenith,
But I, Matthew, being a man
Am a traveller back and forth.

So be it.

ST MARK

There was a lion in Judah
Which whelped, and was Mark.

But winged.
A lion with wings.
At least at Venice.
Even as late as Daniele Manin.

Why should he have wings?
Is he to be a bird also?
Or a spirit?
Or a winged thought?
Or a soaring consciousness?

Evidently he is all that,
The lion of the spirit.

Ah, Lamb of God,
Would a wingless lion lie down before Thee, as this winged
    lion lies?

The lion of the spirit.

Once he lay in the mouth of a cave
And sunned his whiskers,
And lashed his tail slowly, slowly
Thinking of voluptuousness
Even of blood.

But later, in the sun of the afternoon,
Having tasted all there was to taste, and having slept his fill
He fell to frowning, as he lay with his head on his paws
And the sun coming in through the narrowest fibril of a slit in
    his eyes.

So, nine-tenths asleep, motionless, bored, and statically angry,
He saw in a shaft of light a lamb on a pinnacle, balancing a flag
    on its paw,
And he was thoroughly startled.

Going out to investigate
He found the lamb beyond him, on the inaccessible pinnacle
    of light.
So he put his paw to his nose, and pondered.

"Guard my sheep," came the silvery voice from the pinnacle,
"And I will give thee the wings of the morning."
So the lion of the senses thought it was worth it.

Hence he became a curly sheep-dog with dangerous propensities,
As Carpaccio will tell you:
Ramping round, guarding the flock of mankind,
Sharpening his teeth on the wolves,
Ramping up through the air like a kestrel
And lashing his tail above the world
And enjoying the sensation of heaven and righteousness and
    voluptuous wrath.

There is a new sweetness in his voluptuously licking his paw
Now that it is a weapon of heaven.
There is a new ecstasy in his roar of desirous love
Now that it sounds self-conscious through the unlimited sky.
He is well aware of himself
And he cherishes voluptuous delights, and thinks about them
And ceases to be a blood-thirsty king of beasts
And becomes the faithful sheep-dog of the Shepherd, thinking
 of his voluptuous pleasures of chasing the sheep to the fold
And increasing the flock, and perhaps giving a real nip here
 and there, a real pinch, but always well meant.

And somewhere there is a lioness,
The she-mate.
Whelps play between the paws of the lion,
The she-mate purrs,
Their castle is impregnable, their cave,
The sun comes in their lair, they are well-off,
A well-to-do family.

Then the proud lion stalks abroad alone,
And roars to announce himself to the wolves
And also to encourage the red-cross Lamb
And also to ensure a goodly increase in the world.

Look at him, with his paw on the world
At Venice and elsewhere.
Going blind at last.

ST LUKE

A wall, a bastion,
A living forehead with its slow whorl of hair
And a bull's large, sombre, glancing eye
And glistening, adhesive muzzle
With cavernous nostrils where the winds run hot
Snorting defiance
Or greedily snuffling behind the cows.

Horns,
The golden horns of power,
Power to kill, power to create
Such as Moses had, and God,
Head-power.

Shall great wings flame from his shoulder sockets
Assyrian-wise?
It would be no wonder.

Knowing the thunder of his heart,
The massive thunder of his dew-lapped chest
Deep and reverberating,
It would be no wonder if great wings, like flame, fanned out
     from the furnace-cracks of his shoulder-sockets.

Thud! Thud! Thud!
And the roar of black bull's blood in the mighty passages of
     his chest.
Ah, the dewlap swings pendulous with excess.
The great, roaring weight above
Like a furnace dripping a molten drip
The urge, the massive, burning ache
Of the bull's breast.
The open furnace-doors of his nostrils.

For what does he ache, and groan?

Is his breast a wall?

Nay, once it was also a fortress wall, and the weight of a vast
     battery.
But now it is a burning hearthstone only,
Massive old altar of his own burnt offering.

It was always an altar of burnt offering
His own black blood poured out like a sheet of flame over his
     fecundating herd
As he gave himself forth.

But also it was a fiery fortress frowning shaggily on the world
And announcing battle ready.

Since the Lamb bewitched him with that red-struck flag
His fortress is dismantled
His fires of wrath are banked down
His horns turn away from the enemy.

He serves the Son of Man.

And hear him bellow, after many years, the bull that serves
    the Son of Man.
Moaning, booing, roaring hollow
Constrained to pour forth all his fire down the narrow sluice
    of procreation
Through such narrow loins, too narrow
Is he not over-charged by the dammed-up pressure of his own
    massive black blood
Luke, the Bull, the father of substance, the Providence Bull,
    after two thousand years?
Is he not over-full of offering, a vast, vast offer of himself
Which must be poured through so small a vent?

Too small a vent.

Let him remember his horns, then.
Seal up his forehead once more to a bastion,
Let it know nothing.
Let him charge like a mighty catapult on the red-cross flag,
    let him roar out challenge on the world
And throwing himself upon it, throw off the madness of his
    blood.
Let it be war.

And so it is war.
The bull of the proletariat has got his head down.

ST JOHN

John, oh John,
Thou honourable bird,
Sun-peering eagle.

Taking a bird's-eye view
Even of Calvary and Resurrection
Not to speak of Babylon's whoredom.

High over the mild effulgence of the dove
Hung all the time, did we but know it, the all-knowing shadow
Of John's great gold-barred eagle.

John knew all about it.
Even the very beginning.

"In the beginning was the Word
And the Word was God
And the Word was with God."

Having been to school
John knew the whole proposition.
As for innocent Jesus
He was one of Nature's phenomena, no doubt.

Oh that mind-soaring eagle of an Evangelist
Staring creation out of countenance
And telling it off
As an eagle staring down on the Sun!

The Logos, the Logos!
"In the beginning was the Word."

Is there not a great Mind pre-ordaining?
Does not a supreme Intellect ideally procreate the Universe?
Is not each soul a vivid thought in the great consciousness stream
    of God?

Put salt on his tail
The sly bird of John.

Proud intellect, high-soaring Mind
Like a king eagle, bird of the most High, sweeping the round
 of heaven
And casting the cycles of creation
On two wings, like a pair of compasses;
Jesus' pale and lambent dove, cooing in the lower boughs
On sufferance.

In the beginning was the Word, of course.
And the word was the first offspring of the almighty Johannine
 mind,
Chick of the intellectual eagle.

Yet put salt on the tail of the Johannine bird
Put salt on its tail
John's eagle.

Shoo it down out of the empyrean
Of the all-seeing, all-fore-ordaining ideal.
Make it roost on bird-spattered, rocky Patmos
And let it moult there, among the stones of the bitter sea.

For the almighty eagle of the fore-ordaining Mind
Is looking rather shabby and island-bound these days:
Moulting, and rather naked about the rump, and down in the
 beak,
Rather dirty, on dung-whitened Patmos.

From which we are led to assume
That the old bird is weary, and almost willing
That a new chick should chip the extensive shell
Of the mundane egg.

The poor old golden eagle of the word-fledged spirit
Moulting and moping and waiting, willing at last
For the fire to burn it up, feathers and all,
So that a new conception of the beginning and end
Can rise from the ashes.

Ah Phœnix, Phœnix,
John's Eagle!
You are only known to us now as the badge of an in-
   surance Company.

Phœnix, Phœnix,
The nest is in flames,
Feathers are singeing,
Ash flutters flocculent, like down on a blue, wan fledgeling.
                                        San Gervasio.

CREATURES

"BUT FISHES are very fiery, and take to the water to cool themselves."

"To those things that love darkness, the light of day is cruel and a pain. Yet the light of lamps and candles has no fears for them; rather they draw near to taste it, as if saying: Now what is this? So we see that the sun is more than burning, more than the burning of fires or the shining of lamps. Because with his rays he hurts the creatures that live by night, and lamplight and firelight do them no hurt. Therefore the sun lives in his shining, and is not like fires, that die."

THE MOSQUITO

When did you start your tricks,
Monsieur?

What do you stand on such high legs for?
Why this length of shredded shank,
You exaltation?

Is it so that you shall lift your centre of gravity upwards
And weigh no more than air as you alight upon me,
Stand upon me weightless, you phantom?

I heard a woman call you the Winged Victory
In sluggish Venice.
You turn your head towards your tail, and smile.

How can you put so much devilry
Into that translucent phantom shred
Of a frail corpus?

Queer, with your thin wings and your streaming legs,
How you sail like a heron, or a dull clot of air,
A nothingness.

Yet what an aura surrounds you;
Your evil little aura, prowling, and casting a numbness on
    my mind.

That is your trick, your bit of filthy magic:
Invisibility, and the anæsthetic power
To deaden my attention in your direction.

But I know your game now, streaky sorcerer.
Queer, how you stalk and prowl the air
In circles and evasions, enveloping me,
Ghoul on wings
Winged Victory.

Settle, and stand on long thin shanks
Eyeing me sideways, and cunningly conscious that I am
     aware,
You speck.

I hate the way you lurch off sideways into air
Having read my thoughts against you.

Come then, let us play at unawares,
And see who wins in this sly game of bluff.
Man or mosquito.

You don't know that I exist, and I don't know that you
     exist.
Now then!

It is your trump,
It is your hateful little trump,
You pointed fiend,
Which shakes my sudden blood to hatred of you:
It is your small, high, hateful bugle in my ear.

Why do you do it?
Surely it is bad policy.

They say you can't help it.

If that is so, then I believe a little in Providence protect·
     ing the innocent.
But it sounds so amazingly like a slogan,
A yell of triumph as you snatch my scalp.

Blood, red blood
Super-magical
Forbidden liquor.

I behold you stand
For a second enspasmed in oblivion,
Obscenely ecstasied
Sucking live blood,
My blood.

Such silence, such suspended transport,
Such gorging,
Such obscenity of trespass.

You stagger
As well as you may.
Only your accursed hairy frailty,
Your own imponderable weightlessness
Saves you, wafts you away on the very draught my anger
        makes in its snatching.

Away with a pæan of derision,
You winged blood-drop.

Can I not overtake you?
Are you one too many for me,
Winged Victory?
Am I not mosquito enough to out-mosquito you?

Queer, what a big stain my sucked blood makes
Beside the infinitesimal faint smear of you!
Queer, what a dim dark smudge you have disappeared
        into!

                                        Siracusa.

FISH

Fish, oh Fish,
So little matters!

Whether the waters rise and cover the earth
Or whether the waters wilt in the hollow places,
All one to you.

Aqueous, subaqueous,
Submerged
And wave-thrilled.

As the waters roll
Roll you.
The waters wash,
You wash in oneness
And never emerge.

Never know,
Never grasp.

Your life a sluice of sensation along your sides,
A flush at the flails of your fins, down the whorl of your
    tail,
And water wetly on fire in the grates of your gills;
Fixed water-eyes.

Even snakes lie together.

But oh, fish, that rock in water,
You lie only with the waters;
One touch.
No fingers, no hands and feet, no lips;
No tender muzzles,
No wistful bellies,
No loins of desire,
None.

You and the naked element,
Sway-wave.
Curvetting bits of tin in the evening light.

Who is it ejects his sperm to the naked flood?
In the wave-mother?
Who swims enwombed?
Who lies with the waters of his silent passion, womb-
    element?
—Fish in the waters under the earth.

What price *his* bread upon the waters?

Himself all silvery himself
In the element,
No more.

Nothing more.

Himself,
And the element.
Food, of course!
Water-eager eyes,
Mouth-gate open
And strong spine urging, driving;
And desirous belly gulping.

Fear also!
He knows fear!
Water-eyes craning,
A rush that almost screams,
Almost fish-voice
As the pike comes. . . .
Then gay fear, that turns the tail sprightly, from a shadow.

Food, and fear, and joie de vivre,
Without love.

The other way about:
Joie de vivre, and fear, and food,
All without love.

Quelle joie de vivre
Dans l'eau!
Slowly to gape through the waters,
Alone with the element;
To sink, and rise, and go to sleep with the waters;
To speak endless inaudible wavelets into the wave;
To breathe from the flood at the gills,
Fish-blood slowly running next to the flood, extracting
    fish-fire;

To have the element under one, like a lover;
And to spring away with a curvetting click in the air,
Provocative.
Dropping back with a slap on the face of the flood.
And merging oneself!

To be a fish!

So utterly without misgiving
To be a fish
In the waters.

Loveless, and so lively!
Born before God was love,
Or life knew loving.
Beautifully beforehand with it all.

Admitted, they swarm in companies,
Fishes.
They drive in shoals.
But soundless, and out of contact.
They exchange no word, no spasm, not even anger.
Not one touch.
Many suspended together, forever apart,
Each one alone with the waters, upon one wave with the
        rest.

A magnetism in the water between them only.

I saw a water-serpent swim across the Anapo,
And I said to my heart, *look, look at him!*
With his head up, steering like a bird!
He's a rare one, but he belongs . . .

But sitting in a boat on the Zeller lake
And watching the fishes in the breathing waters
Lift and swim and go their way—

I said to my heart, *who are these?*
And my heart couldn't own them. . . .

A slim young pike, with smart fins
And grey-striped suit, a young cub of a pike
Slouching along away below, half out of sight,
Like a lout on an obscure pavement. . . .

Aha, there's somebody in the know!

But watching closer
That motionless deadly motion,
That unnatural barrel body, that long ghoul nose, . . .
I left off hailing him.

I had made a mistake, I didn't know him,
This grey, monotonous soul in the water,
This intense individual in shadow,
Fish-alive.

I didn't know his God,
I didn't know his God.

Which is perhaps the last admission that life has to wring
        out of us.

I saw, dimly,
Once a big pike rush,
And small fish fly like splinters.
And I said to my heart, *there are limits*
To you, my heart;
And to the one God.
Fish are beyond me.

Other Gods
Beyond my range . . . gods beyond my God. . . .

They are beyond me, are fishes.
I stand at the pale of my being
And look beyond, and see
Fish, in the outerwards,
As one stands on a bank and looks in.

I have waited with a long rod
And suddenly pulled a gold-and-greenish, lucent fish from
    below,
And had him fly like a halo round my head,
Lunging in the air on the line.

Unhooked his gorping, water-horny mouth,
And seen his horror-tilted eye,
His red-gold, water-precious, mirror-flat bright eye;
And felt him beat in my hand, with his mucous, leaping
    life-throb.
And my heart accused itself
Thinking: *I am not the measure of creation.*
This is beyond me, this fish.
His God stands outside my God.

And the gold-and-green pure lacquer-mucus comes off in
    my hand,
And the red-gold mirror-eye stares and dies,
And the water-suave contour dims.

But not before I have had to know
He was born in front of my sunrise,
Before my day.

He outstarts me.
And I, a many-fingered horror of daylight to him,
Have made him die.

Fishes
With their gold, red eyes, and green-pure gleam, and under-
    gold,
And their pre-world loneliness,
And more-than-lovelessness,
And white meat;
They move in other circles.

Outsiders.
Water-wayfarers.
Things of one element.
Aqueous,
Each by itself.

Cats, and the Neapolitans,
Sulphur sun-beasts,
Thirst for fish as for more-than-water;
Water-alive
To quench their over-sulphureous lusts.

But I, I only wonder
And don't know.
I don't know fishes.

In the beginning
Jesus was called The Fish. . . .
And in the end.

Zell-am-See.

BAT

At evening, sitting on this terrace,
When the sun from the west, beyond Pisa, beyond the
    mountains of Carrara
Departs, and the world is taken by surprise . . .

When the tired flower of Florence is in gloom beneath the
    glowing
Brown hills surrounding . . .

When under the arches of the Ponte Vecchio
A green light enters against stream, flush from the west,
Against the current of obscure Arno . . . .

Look up, and you see things flying
Between the day and the night;
Swallows with spools of dark thread sewing the shadows
    together.

A circle swoop, and a quick parabola under the bridge
    arches
Where light pushes through;
A sudden turning upon itself of a thing in the air.
A dip to the water.

And you think:
"The swallows are flying so late!"

Swallows?

Dark air-life looping
Yet missing the pure loop . . .
A twitch, a twitter, an elastic shudder in flight
And serrated wings against the sky,
Like a glove, a black glove thrown up at the light,
And falling back.

Never swallows!
Bats!
The swallows are gone.

At a wavering instant the swallows give way to bats
By the Ponte Vecchio . . .
Changing guard.

Bats, and an uneasy creeping in one's scalp
As the bats swoop overhead!
Flying madly.

Pipistrello!
Black piper on an infinitesimal pipe.
Little lumps that fly in air and have voices indefinite, wildly
    vindictive;

Wings like bits of umbrella.

Bats!

Creatures that hang themselves up like an old rag, to sleep;
And disgustingly upside down.
Hanging upside down like rows of disgusting old rags
And grinning in their sleep.
Bats!

In China the bat is symbol of happiness.

Not for me!

MAN AND BAT

When I went into my room, at mid-morning,
Say ten o'clock . . .
My room, a crash-box over that great stone rattle
The Via de' Bardi. . . .

When I went into my room at mid-morning,
Why? . . . a bird!

A bird
Flying round the room in insane circles.

In insane circles!
. . . A bat!

A disgusting bat
At mid-morning! . . .

Out! Go out!

Round and round and round
With a twitchy, nervous, intolerable flight,
And a neurasthenic lunge,
And an impure frenzy;
A bat, big as a swallow.

Out, out of my room!

The venetian shutters I push wide
To the free, calm upper air;
Loop back the curtains. . . .

Now out, out from my room!

So to drive him out, flicking with my white handkerchief:
    Go!
But he will not.

Round and round and round
In an impure haste,
Fumbling, a beast in air,
And stumbling, lunging and touching the walls, the bell-
    wires
About my room!

Always refusing to go out into the air
Above that crash-gulf of the Via de' Bardi,
Yet blind with frenzy, with cluttered fear.

At last he swerved into the window bay,
But blew back, as if an incoming wind blew him in again.
A strong inrushing wind.

And round and round and round!
Blundering more insane, and leaping, in throbs, to clutch at
    a corner,
At a wire, at a bell-rope:
On and on, watched relentless by me, round and round in
    my room,
Round and round and dithering with tiredness and haste
    and increasing delirium
Flicker-splashing round my room.

I would not let him rest;
Not one instant cleave, cling like a blot with his breast to
    the wall
In an obscure corner.
Not an instant!

I flicked him on,
Trying to drive him through the window.
Again he swerved into the window bay
And I ran forward, to frighten him forth.
But he rose, and from a terror worse than me he flew past
 me
Back into my room, and round, round, round in my room
Clutch, cleave, stagger,
Dropping about the air
Getting tired.

Something seemed to blow him back from the window
Every time he swerved at it;
Back on a strange parabola, then round, round, dizzy in
 my room.

He *could* not go out,
I also realised. . . .
It was the light of day which he could not enter,
Any more than I could enter the white-hot door of a blast
 furnace.

He could not plunge into the daylight that streamed at the
 window.
It was asking too much of his nature.

Worse even than the hideous terror of me with my hand-
 kerchief
Saying: *Out, go out!* . . .
Was the horror of white daylight in the window!

So I switched on the electric light, thinking: *Now*
The outside will seem brown. . . .

But no.
The outside did not seem brown.
And he did not mind the yellow electric light.

Silent!
He was having a silent rest.
But never!
Not in my room.

Round and round and round
Near the ceiling as if in a web,
Staggering;
Plunging, falling out of the web,
Broken in heaviness,
Lunging blindly,
Heavier;
And clutching, clutching for one second's pause,
Always, as if for one drop of rest,
One little drop.

And I!
Never, I say. . . .
Get out!

Flying slower,
Seeming to stumble, to fall in air.
Blind-weary.

Yet never able to pass the whiteness of light into
    freedom . . .
A bird would have dashed through, come what might.

Fall, sink, lurch, and round and round
Flicker, flicker-heavy;
Even wings heavy:
And cleave in a high corner for a second, like a clot, also
    a prayer.

But no.
Out, you beast.

Till he fell in a corner, palpitating, spent.
And there, a clot, he squatted and looked at me.
With sticking-out, bead-berry eyes, black,
And improper derisive ears,
And shut wings,
And brown, furry body.

Brown, nut-brown, fine fur!
But it might as well have been hair on a spider; thing
With long, black-paper ears.

So, a dilemma!
He squatted there like something unclean.

No, he must not squat, nor hang, obscene, in my room!

Yet nothing on earth will give him courage to pass the
     sweet fire of day.

What then?
Hit him and kill him and throw him away?

Nay,
I didn't create him.
Let the God that created him be responsible for his death . . .
Only, in the bright day, I will not have this clot in my
     room.

Let the God who is maker of bats watch with them in
     their unclean corners. . . .
I admit a God in every crevice,
But not bats in my room;
Nor the God of bats, while the sun shines.

So out, out, you brute! . . .
And he lunged, flight-heavy, away from me, sideways, *a
     sghembo!*
And round and round and round my room, a clot with
     wings,
Impure even in weariness.

Wings dark skinny and flapping the air,
Lost their flicker.
Spent.

He fell again with a little thud
Near the curtain on the floor.
And there lay.

Ah death, death
You are no solution!
Bats must be bats.

Only life has a way out.
And the human soul is fated to wide-eyed responsibility
In life.

So I picked him up in a flannel jacket,
Well covered, lest he should bite me.
For I would have had to kill him if he'd bitten me, the
    impure one. . . .
And he hardly stirred in my hand, muffled up.

Hastily, I shook him out of the window.

And away he went!
Fear craven in his tail.
Great haste, and straight, almost bird straight above the
    Via de' Bardi.
Above that crash-gulf of exploding whips,
Towards the Borgo San Jacopo.

And now, at evening, as he flickers over the river
Dipping with petty triumphant flight, and tittering over
    the sun's departure,
I believe he chirps, pipistrello, seeing me here on this
    terrace writing:
There he sits, the long loud one!
But I am greater than he . . .
I escaped him. . . .

                                        Florence.

347

REPTILES

"HOMER WAS wrong in saying, 'Would that strife might pass away from among gods and men!' He did not see that he was praying for the destruction of the universe; for, if his prayer were heard, all things would pass away—for in the tension of opposites all things have their being—"

"For when Fire in its downward path chanced to mingle with the dark breath of the earth, the serpent slid forth, lay revealed. But he was moist and cold, the sun in him darted uneasy, held down by moist earth, never could he rise on his feet. And this is what put poison in his mouth. For the sun in him would fain rise half-way, and move on feet. But moist earth weighs him down, though he dart and twist, still he must go with his belly on the ground.—The wise tortoise laid his earthy part around him, he cast it round him and found his feet. So he is the first of creatures to stand upon his toes, and the dome of his house is his heaven. Therefore it is charted out, and is the foundation of the world."

SNAKE

A snake came to my water-trough
On a hot, hot day, and I in pyjamas for the heat,
To drink there.

In the deep, strange-scented shade of the great dark carob-
      tree
I came down the steps with my pitcher
And must wait, must stand and wait, for there he was at
      the trough before me.

He reached down from a fissure in the earth-wall in the
      gloom
And trailed his yellow-brown slackness soft-bellied down,
      over the edge of the stone trough
And rested his throat upon the stone bottom,
And where the water had dripped from the tap, in a small
      clearness,
He sipped with his straight mouth,
Softly drank through his straight gums, into his slack long
      body,
Silently.

Someone was before me at my water-trough,
And I, like a second comer, waiting.

He lifted his head from his drinking, as cattle do,
And looked at me vaguely, as drinking cattle do,
And flickered his two-forked tongue from his lips, and
      mused a moment,
And stooped and drank a little more,
Being earth-brown, earth-golden from the burning bowels
      of the earth
On the day of Sicilian July, with Etna smoking.

The voice of my education said to me
He must be killed,
For in Sicily the black, black snakes are innocent, the gold
    are venomous.

And voices in me said, If you were a man
You would take a stick and break him now, and finish
    him off.

But must I confess how I liked him,
How glad I was he had come like a guest in quiet, to drink
    at my water-trough
And depart peaceful, pacified, and thankless,
Into the burning bowels of this earth?

Was it cowardice, that I dared not kill him?
Was it perversity, that I longed to talk to him?
Was it humility, to feel so honoured?
I felt so honoured.

And yet those voices:
If you were not afraid, you would kill him!

And truly I was afraid, I was most afraid,
But even so, honoured still more
That he should seek my hospitality
From out the dark door of the secret earth.

He drank enough
And lifted his head, dreamily, as one who has drunken,
And flickered his tongue like a forked night on the air, so
    black,
Seeming to lick his lips,
And looked around like a god, unseeing, into the air,
And slowly turned his head,
And slowly, very slowly, as if thrice adream,
Proceeded to draw his slow length curving round
And climb again the broken bank of my wall-face.

And as he put his head into that dreadful hole,
And as he slowly drew up, snake-easing his shoulders, and
    entered farther,
A sort of horror, a sort of protest against his withdrawing
    into that horrid black hole,
Deliberately going into the blackness, and slowly drawing
    himself after,
Overcame me now his back was turned.

I looked round, I put down my pitcher,
I picked up a clumsy log
And threw it at the water-trough with a clatter.

I think it did not hit him,
But suddenly that part of him that was left behind con-
    vulsed in undignified haste,
Writhed like lightning, and was gone
Into the black hole, the earth-lipped fissure in the wall-
    front,
At which, in the intense still noon, I stared with fascination.

And immediately I regretted it.
I thought how paltry, how vulgar, what a mean act!
I despised myself and the voices of my accursed human
    education.

And I thought of the albatross,
And I wished he would come back, my snake.

For he seemed to me again like a king,
Like a king in exile, uncrowned in the underworld,
Now due to be crowned again.

And so, I missed my chance with one of the lords
Of life.
And I have something to expiate;
A pettiness.

Taormina.

BABY TORTOISE

You know what it is to be born alone,
Baby tortoise!

The first day to heave your feet little by little from the
    shell,
Not yet awake,
And remain lapsed on earth,
Not quite alive.

A tiny, fragile, half-animate bean.

To open your tiny beak-mouth, that looks as if it would
    never open,
Like some iron door;
To lift the upper hawk-beak from the lower base
And reach your skinny little neck
And take your first bite at some dim bit of herbage,
Alone, small insect,
Tiny bright-eye,
Slow one.

To take your first solitary bite
And move on your slow, solitary hunt.
Your bright, dark little eye,
Your eye of a dark disturbed night,
Under its slow lid, tiny baby tortoise,
So indomitable.

No one ever heard you complain.

You draw your head forward, slowly, from your little
    wimple
And set forward, slow-dragging, on your four-pinned toes,
Rowing slowly forward.
Whither away, small bird?
Rather like a baby working its limbs,
Except that you make slow, ageless progress
And a baby makes none.

The touch of sun excites you,
And the long ages, and the lingering chill
Make you pause to yawn,
Opening your impervious mouth,
Suddenly beak-shaped, and very wide, like some suddenly
    gaping pincers;
Soft red tongue, and hard thin gums,
Then close the wedge of your little mountain front,
Your face, baby tortoise.

Do you wonder at the world, as slowly you turn your
    head in its wimple
And look with laconic, black eyes?
Or is sleep coming over you again,
The non-life?

You are so hard to wake.

Are you able to wonder?
Or is it just your indomitable will and pride of the first life
Looking round
And slowly pitching itself against the inertia
Which had seemed invincible?

The vast inanimate,
And the fine brilliance of your so tiny eye,
Challenger.

Nay, tiny shell-bird,
What a huge vast inanimate it is, that you must row
    against,
What an incalculable inertia.

Challenger,
Little Ulysses, fore-runner,
No bigger than my thumb-nail,
Buon viaggio.

All animate creation on your shoulder,
Set forth, little Titan, under your battle-shield.

The ponderous, preponderate,
Inanimate universe;
And you are slowly moving, pioneer, you alone.

How vivid your travelling seems now, in the troubled sun-
    shine,
Stoic, Ulyssean atom;
Suddenly hasty, reckless, on high toes.

Voiceless little bird,
Resting your head half out of your wimple
In the slow dignity of your eternal pause.
Alone, with no sense of being alone,
And hence six times more solitary;
Fulfilled of the slow passion of pitching through im-
    memorial ages
Your little round house in the midst of chaos.

Over the garden earth,
Small bird,
Over the edge of all things.

Traveller,
With your tail tucked a little on one side
Like a gentleman in a long-skirted coat.

All life carried on your shoulder,
Invincible fore-runner.

TORTOISE SHELL

The Cross, the Cross
Goes deeper in than we know,
Deeper into life;
Right into the marrow
And through the bone.

Along the back of the baby tortoise
The scales are locked in an arch like a bridge,
Scale-lapping, like a lobster's sections
Or a bee's.

Then crossways down his sides
Tiger-stripes and wasp-bands.

Five, and five again, and five again,
And round the edges twenty-five little ones,
The sections of the baby tortoise shell.

Four, and a keystone;
Four, and a keystone;
Four, and a keystone;
Then twenty-four, and a tiny little keystone.

It needed Pythagoras to see life playing with counters on
    the living back
Of the baby tortoise;
Life establishing the first eternal mathematical tablet,
Not in stone, like the Judean Lord, or bronze, but in life-
    clouded, life-rosy tortoise shell.

The first little mathematical gentleman
Stepping, wee mite, in his loose trousers
Under all the eternal dome of mathematical law.

Fives, and tens,
Threes and fours and twelves,
All the *volte face* of decimals,
The whirligig of dozens and the pinnacle of seven.

Turn him on his back,
The kicking little beetle,
And there again, on his shell-tender, earth-touching belly,
The long cleavage of division, upright of the eternal cross
And on either side count five,
On each side, two above, on each side, two below
The dark bar horizontal.

The Cross!
It goes right through him, the sprottling insect,
Through his cross-wise cloven psyche,
Through his five-fold complex-nature.

So turn him over on his toes again;
Four pin-point toes, and a problematical thumb-piece,
Four rowing limbs, and one wedge-balancing head,
Four and one makes five, which is the clue to all mathe-
matics.

The Lord wrote it all down on the little slate
Of the baby tortoise.
Outward and visible indication of the plan within,
The complex, manifold involvedness of an individual
creature
Plotted out
On this small bird, this rudiment,
This little dome, this pediment
Of all creation,
This slow one.

TORTOISE FAMILY CONNECTIONS

On he goes, the little one,
Bud of the universe,
Pediment of life.

Setting off somewhere, apparently.
Whither away, brisk egg?

His mother deposited him on the soil as if he were no more
than droppings,
And now he scuffles tinily past her as if she were an old
rusty tin.

A mere obstacle,
He veers round the slow great mound of her—
Tortoises always foresee obstacles.

It is no use my saying to him in an emotional voice:
"This is your Mother, she laid you when you were an egg."

He does not even trouble to answer: "Woman, what have
    I to do with thee?"
He wearily looks the other way,
And she even more wearily looks another way still,
Each with the utmost apathy,
Incognisant,
Unaware,
Nothing.

As for papa,
He snaps when I offer him his offspring,
Just as he snaps when I poke a bit of stick at him,
Because he is irascible this morning, an irascible tortoise
Being touched with love, and devoid of fatherliness.

Father and mother,
And three little brothers,
And all rambling aimless, like little perambulating pebbles
    scattered in the garden,
Not knowing each other from bits of earth or old tins.

Except that papa and mama are old acquaintances, of
    course,
Though family feeling there is none, not even the begin-
    nings.

Fatherless, motherless, brotherless, sisterless
Little tortoise.

Row on then, small pebble,
Over the clods of the autumn, wind-chilled sunshine,
Young gaiety.

Does he look for a companion?

No, no, don't think it.
He doesn't know he is alone;
Isolation is his birthright,
This atom.

To row forward, and reach himself tall on spiny toes,
To travel, to burrow into a little loose earth, afraid of the
    night,
To crop a little substance,
To move, and to be quite sure that he is moving:
Basta!
To be a tortoise!
Think of it, in a garden of inert clods
A brisk, brindled little tortoise, all to himself—
Adam!

In a garden of pebbles and insects
To roam, and feel the slow heart beat
Tortoise-wise, the first bell sounding
From the warm blood, in the dark-creation morning.

Moving, and being himself,
Slow, and unquestioned,
And inordinately there, O stoic!
Wandering in the slow triumph of his own existence,
Ringing the soundless bell of his presence in chaos,
And biting the frail grass arrogantly,
Decidedly arrogantly.

LUI ET ELLE

She is large and matronly
And rather dirty,
A little sardonic-looking, as if domesticity had driven her
    to it.

Though what she does, except lay four eggs at random in
    the garden once a year
And put up with her husband,
I don't know.

She likes to eat.
She hurries up, striding reared on long uncanny legs
When food is going.
Oh yes, she can make haste when she likes.

She snaps the soft bread from my hand in great mouthfuls,
Opening her rather pretty wedge of an iron, pristine face
Into an enormously wide-beaked mouth
Like sudden curved scissors,
And gulping at more than she can swallow, and working
    her thick, soft tongue,
And having the bread hanging over her chin.

'O Mistress, Mistress,
Reptile mistress,
Your eye is very dark, very bright,
And it never softens
Although you watch.

She knows,
She knows well enough to come for food,
Yet she sees me not;
Her bright eye sees, but not me, not anything,
Sightful, sightless, seeing and visionless,
Reptile mistress.

Taking bread in her curved, gaping, toothless mouth,
She has no qualm when she catches my finger in her steel
    overlapping gums,
But she hangs on, and my shout and my shrinking are
    nothing to her.
She does not even know she is nipping me with her curved
    beak.
Snake-like she draws at my finger, while I drag it in horror
    away.

Mistress, reptile mistress,
You are almost too large, I am almost frightened.

He is much smaller,
Dapper beside her,
And ridiculously small.

Her laconic eye has an earthy, materialistic look,
His, poor darling, is almost fiery.

His wimple, his blunt-prowed face,
His low forehead, his skinny neck, his long, scaled, striving
    legs,
So striving, striving,
Are all more delicate than she,
And he has a cruel scar on his shell.

Poor darling, biting at her feet,
Running beside her like a dog, biting her earthy, splay
    feet,
Nipping her ankles,
Which she drags apathetic away, though without retreat-
    ing into her shell.

Agelessly silent,
And with a grim, reptile determination,
Cold, voiceless age-after-age behind him, serpents' long
    obstinacy
Of horizontal persistence.

Little old man
Scuffling beside her, bending down, catching his oppor-
    tunity,
Parting his steel-trap face, so suddenly, and seizing her
    scaly ankle,
And hanging grimly on,
Letting go at last as she drags away,
And closing his steel-trap face.

His steel-trap, stoic, ageless, handsome face.
Alas, what a fool he looks in this scuffle.

And how he feels it!
The lonely rambler, the stoic, dignified stalker through
    chaos,
The immune, the animate,
Enveloped in isolation,
Fore-runner.
Now look at him!

Alas, the spear is through the side of his isolation.
His adolescence saw him crucified into sex,
Doomed, in the long crucifixion of desire, to seek his con-
    summation beyond himself.
Divided into passionate duality,
He, so finished and immune, now broken into desirous
    fragmentariness,
Doomed to make an intolerable fool of himself
In his effort toward completion again.

Poor little earthy house-inhabiting Osiris,
The mysterious bull tore him at adolescence into pieces,
And he must struggle after reconstruction, ignominiously.

And so behold him following the tail
Of that mud-hovel of his slowly rambling spouse,
Like some unhappy bull at the tail of a cow,
But with more than bovine, grim, earth-dank persistence.

Suddenly seizing the ugly ankle as she stretches out to
    walk,
Roaming over the sods,
Or, if it happen to show, at her pointed, heavy tail
Beneath the low-dropping back-board of her shell.

Their two shells like domed boats bumping,
Hers huge, his small;
Their splay feet rambling and rowing like paddles,
And stumbling mixed up in one another,
In the race of love—
Two tortoises,
She huge, he small.

She seems earthily apathetic,
And he has a reptile's awful persistence.

I heard a woman pitying her, pitying the Mère Tortue.
While I, I pity Monsieur.
"He pesters her and torments her," said the woman.
How much more is *he* pestered and tormented, say I.

What can he do?
He is dumb, he is visionless,
Conceptionless.
His black, sad-lidded eye sees but beholds not
As her earthen mound moves on,
But he catches the folds of vulnerable, leathery skin,
Nail-studded, that shake beneath her shell,
And drags at these with his beak,
Drags and drags and bites,
While she pulls herself free, and rows her dull mound
    along.

TORTOISE GALLANTRY

Making his advances
He does not look at her, nor sniff at her,
No, not even sniff at her, his nose is blank.

Only he senses the vulnerable folds of skin
That work beneath her while she sprawls along
In her ungainly pace,
Her folds of skin that work and row
Beneath the earth-soiled hovel in which she moves.

And so he strains beneath her housey walls
And catches her trouser-legs in his beak
Suddenly, or her skinny limb,
And strange and grimly drags at her
Like a dog,
Only agelessly silent, with a reptile's awful persistency.

Grim, gruesome gallantry, to which he is doomed.
Dragged out of an eternity of silent isolation
And doomed to partiality, partial being,
Ache, and want of being,
Want,
Self-exposure, hard humiliation, need to add himself on to
    her.

Born to walk alone,
Fore-runner,
Now suddenly distracted into this mazy side-track,
This awkward, harrowing pursuit,
This grim necessity from within.

Does she know
As she moves eternally slowly away?
Or is he driven against her with a bang, like a bird flying
    in the dark against a window,
All knowledgeless?

The awful concussion,
And the still more awful need to persist, to follow, follow,
    continue,

Driven, after æons of pristine, fore-god-like singleness and
    oneness,
At the end of some mysterious, red-hot iron,
Driven away from himself into her tracks,
Forced to crash against her.

Stiff, gallant, irascible, crook-legged reptile,
Little gentleman,
Sorry plight,
We ought to look the other way.

Save that, having come with you so far,
We will go on to the end.

TORTOISE SHOUT

I thought he was dumb,
I said he was dumb,
Yet I've heard him cry.

First faint scream,
Out of life's unfathomable dawn,
Far off, so far, like a madness, under the horizon's dawning
    rim,
Far, far off, far scream.

Tortoise *in extremis*.

Why were we crucified into sex?
Why were we not left rounded off, and finished in our-
    selves,
As we began,
As he certainly began, so perfectly alone?

A far, was-it-audible scream,
Or did it sound on the plasm direct?

Worse than the cry of the new-born,
A scream,
A yell,
A shout,
A pæan,
A death-agony,
A birth-cry,
A submission,
All tiny, tiny, far away, reptile under the first dawn.

War-cry, triumph, acute-delight, death-scream reptilian,
Why was the veil torn?
The silken shriek of the soul's torn membrane?
The male soul's membrane
Torn with a shriek half music, half horror.

Crucifixion.
Male tortoise, cleaving behind the hovel-wall of that dense
    female,
Mounted and tense, spread-eagle, out-reaching out of the
    shell
In tortoise-nakedness,

Long neck, and long vulnerable limbs extruded, spread-
   eagle over her house-roof,
And the deep, secret, all-penetrating tail curved beneath
   her walls,
Reaching and gripping tense, more reaching anguish in
   uttermost tension
Till suddenly, in the spasm of coition, tupping like a jerk-
   ing leap, and oh!
Opening its clenched face from his outstretched neck
And giving that fragile yell, that scream,
Super-audible,
From his pink, cleft, old-man's mouth,
Giving up the ghost,
Or screaming in Pentecost, receiving the ghost.

His scream, and his moment's subsidence,
The moment of eternal silence,
Yet unreleased, and after the moment, the sudden, startling
   jerk of coition, and at once
The inexpressible faint yell—
And so on, till the last plasm of my body was melted back
To the primeval rudiments of life, and the secret.

So he tups, and screams
Time after time that frail, torn scream
After each jerk, the longish interval,
The tortoise eternity,
Age-long, reptilian persistence,
Heart-throb, slow heart-throb, persistent for the next
   spasm.

I remember, when I was a boy,
I heard the scream of a frog, which was caught with his
   foot in the mouth of an up-starting snake;
I remember when I first heard bull-frogs break into sound
   in the spring;
I remember hearing a wild goose out of the throat of night
Cry loudly, beyond the lake of waters;

I remember the first time, out of a bush in the darkness, a
    nightingale's piercing cries and gurgles startled the
    depths of my soul;
I remember the scream of a rabbit as I went through a
    wood at midnight;
I remember the heifer in her heat, blorting and blorting
    through the hours, persistent and irrepressible;
I remember my first terror hearing the howl of weird,
    amorous cats;
I remember the scream of a terrified, injured horse, the
    sheet-lightning,
And running away from the sound of a woman in labour,
    something like an owl whooing,
And listening inwardly to the first bleat of a lamb,
The first wail of an infant,
And my mother singing to herself,
And the first tenor singing of the passionate throat of a
    young collier, who has long since drunk himself to
    death,
The first elements of foreign speech
On wild dark lips.

And more than all these,
And less than all these,
This last,
Strange, faint coition yell
Of the male tortoise at extremity,
Tiny from under the very edge of the farthest far-off
    horizon of life.

The cross,
The wheel on which our silence first is broken,
Sex, which breaks up our integrity, our single inviolability,
    our deep silence,
Tearing a cry from us.

Sex, which breaks us into voice, sets us calling across the
    deeps, calling, calling for the complement,
Singing, and calling, and singing again, being answered,
    having found.

Torn, to become whole again, after long seeking for what
    is lost,
The same cry from the tortoise as from Christ, the Osiris-
    cry of abandonment,
That which is whole, torn asunder,
That which is in part, finding its whole again throughout
    the universe.

BIRDS

"BIRDS are the life of the skies, and when they fly, they reveal
the thoughts of the skies. The eagle flies nearest to the sun, no other
bird flies so near.
So he brings down the life of the sun, and the power of the sun, in his
wings, and men who see him wheeling are filled with the elation of
the sun. But all creatures of the sun must dip their mouths in blood,
the sun is forever thirsty, thirsting for the brightest exhalation of
blood.
You shall know a bird by his cry, and great birds cry loud, but sing
not. The eagle screams when the sun is high, the peacock screams at
the dawn, rooks call at evening, when the nightingale sings. And all
birds have their voices, each means a different thing."

TURKEY-COCK

You ruffled black blossom,
You glossy dark wind.

Your sort of gorgeousness,
Dark and lustrous
And skinny repulsive
And poppy-glossy,
Is the gorgeousness that evokes my most puzzled admiration.

Your aboriginality
Deep, unexplained,
Like a Red Indian darkly unfinished and aloof,
Seems like the black and glossy seeds of countless centuries.

Your wattles are the colour of steel-slag which has been red-hot
And is going cold,
Cooling to a powdery, pale-oxydised sky-blue.

Why do you have wattles, and a naked, wattled head?
Why do you arch your naked-set eye with a more-than-comprehensible arrogance?

The vulture is bald, so is the condor, obscenely,
But only you have thrown this amazing mantilla of oxydised sky-blue
And hot red over you.

This queer dross shawl of blue and vermilion,
Whereas the peacock has a diadem.

I wonder why.
Perhaps it is a sort of uncanny decoration, a veil of loose skin.
Perhaps it is your assertion, in all this ostentation, of raw contradictoriness.
Your wattles drip down like a shawl to your breast
And the point of your mantilla drops across your nose, unpleasantly.

Or perhaps it is something unfinished
A bit of slag still adhering, after your firing in the furnace
    of creation.

Or perhaps there is something in your wattles of a bull's
    dew-lap
Which slips down like a pendulum to balance the throb-
    bing mass of a generous breast,

The over-drip of a great passion hanging in the balance.
Only yours would be a raw, unsmelted passion, that will
    not quite fuse from the dross.

You contract yourself,
You arch yourself as an archer's bow
Which quivers indrawn as you clench your spine
Until your veiled head almost touches backward
To the root-rising of your erected tail.
And one intense and backward-curving frisson
Seizes you as you clench yourself together
Like some fierce magnet bringing its poles together.

Burning, pale positive pole of your wattled head!
And from the darkness of that opposite one
The upstart of your round-barred, sun-round tail!

Whilst between the two, along the tense arch of your back
Blows the magnetic current in fierce blasts,
Ruffling black, shining feathers like lifted mail,
Shuddering storm wind, or a water rushing through.

Your brittle, super-sensual arrogance
Tosses the crape of red across your brow and down your
    breast
As you draw yourself upon yourself in insistence.

It is a declaration of such tension in will
As time has not dared to avouch, nor eternity been able to
    unbend
Do what it may.
A raw American will, that has never been tempered by life;
You brittle, will-tense bird with a foolish eye.

The peacock lifts his rods of bronze
And struts blue-brilliant out of the far East.
But watch a turkey prancing low on earth
Drumming his vaulted wings, as savages drum
Their rhythms on long-drawn, hollow, sinister drums.
The ponderous, sombre sound of the great drum of
    Huichilobos
In pyramid Mexico, during sacrifice.

Drum, and the turkey onrush
Sudden, demonic dauntlessness, full abreast,
All the bronze gloss of all his myriad petals
Each one apart and instant.
Delicate frail crescent of the gentle outline of white
At each feather-tip
So delicate:
Yet the bronze wind-bell suddenly clashing
And the eye overweening into madness.

Turkey-cock, turkey-cock,
Are you the bird of the next dawn?

Has the peacock had his day, does he call in vain, screecher,
    for the sun to rise?
The eagle, the dove, and the barnyard rooster, do they call
    in vain, trying to wake the morrow?
And do you await us, wattled father, Westward?
Will your yell do it?

Take up the trail of the vanished American
Where it disappeared at the foot of the crucifix.
Take up the primordial Indian obstinacy,
The more than human, dense insistence of will,
And disdain, and blankness, and onrush, and prise open the
    new day with them?

The East a dead letter, and Europe moribund. . . . Is that so?
And those sombre, dead, feather-lustrous Aztecs,
    Amerindians,
In all the sinister splendour of their red blood-sacrifices,
Do they stand under the dawn, half-godly, half-demon,
    awaiting the cry of the turkey-cock?

Or must you go through the fire once more, till you're
    smelted pure,
Slag-wattled turkey-cock,
Dross-jabot?

                                                    Fiesole.

HUMMING-BIRD

I can imagine, in some otherworld
Primeval-dumb, far back
In that most awful stillness, that only gasped and hummed,
Humming-birds raced down the avenues.

Before anything had a soul,
While life was a heave of Matter, half inanimate,
This little bit chipped off in brilliance
And went whizzing through the slow, vast, succulent
    stems.

I believe there were no flowers then,
In the world where the humming-bird flashed ahead of
    creation.
I believe he pierced the slow vegetable veins with his long
    beak.

Probably he was big
As mosses, and little lizards, they say, were once big.
Probably he was a jabbing, terrifying monster.

We look at him through the wrong end of the long tele-
    scope of Time,
Luckily for us.

                                                    Española.

EAGLE IN NEW MEXICO

Towards the sun, towards the south-west
A scorched breast.
A scorched breast, breasting the sun like an answer,
Like a retort.

An eagle at the top of a low cedar-bush
On the sage-ash desert
Reflecting the scorch of the sun from his breast;
Eagle, with the sickle dripping darkly above.

Erect, scorched-pallid out of the hair of the cedar,
Erect, with the god-thrust entering him from below,
Eagle gloved in feathers
In scorched white feathers
In burnt dark feathers
In feathers still fire-rusted;
Sickle-overswept, sickle dripping over and above.

Sun-breaster,
Staring two ways at once, to right and left;
Masked-one
Dark-visaged
Sickle-masked
With iron between your two eyes;
You feather-gloved
To the feet;
Foot-fierce;
Erect one;
The god-thrust entering you steadily from below.

You never look at the sun with your two eyes.
Only the inner eye of your scorched broad breast
Looks straight at the sun.

You are dark
Except scorch-pale-breasted;
And dark cleaves down and weapon-hard downward
    curving
At your scorched breast,
Like a sword of Damocles,
Beaked eagle.

You've dipped it in blood so many times
That dark face-weapon, to temper it well,
Blood-thirsty bird.

Why do you front the sun so obstinately,
American eagle?
As if you owed him an old, old grudge, great sun: or an old,
old allegiance.

When you pick the red smoky heart from a rabbit or a
light-blooded bird
Do you lift it to the sun, as the Aztec priests used to lift
red hearts of men?

Does the sun need steam of blood do you think
In America, still,
Old eagle?

Does the sun in New Mexico sail like a fiery bird of prey
in the sky
Hovering?

Does he shriek for blood?
Does he fan great wings above the prairie, like a hovering,
blood-thirsty bird?

And are you his priest, big eagle
Whom the Indians aspire to?
Is there a bond of bloodshed between you?

Is your continent cold from the ice-age still, that the sun
is so angry?
Is the blood of your continent somewhat reptilian still,
That the sun should be greedy for it?

I don't yield to you, big, jowl-faced eagle.
Nor you nor your blood-thirsty sun
That sucks up blood
Leaving a nervous people.

Fly off, big bird with a big black back.
Fly slowly away, with a rust of fire in your tail,
Dark as you are on your dark side, eagle of heaven.

Even the sun in heaven can be curbed and chastened at last
By the life in the hearts of men.
And you, great bird, sun-starer, heavy black beak
Can be put out of office as sacrifice bringer.

Taos.

THE BLUE JAY

The blue jay with a crest on his head
Comes round the cabin in the snow.
He runs in the snow like a bit of blue metal,
Turning his back on everything.

From the pine-tree that towers and hisses like a pillar of
      shaggy cloud
Immense above the cabin
Comes a strident laugh as we approach, this little black
      dog and I.
So halts the little black bitch on four spread paws in the
      snow
And looks up inquiringly into the pillar of cloud,
With a tinge of misgiving.
Ca-a-a! comes the scrape of ridicule out of the tree.

What voice of the Lord is that, from the tree of smoke?

Oh, Bibbles, little black bitch in the snow,
With a pinch of snow in the groove of your silly snub nose,
What do you look at *me* for?
What do you look at me for, with such misgiving?

It's the blue jay laughing at us.
It's the blue jay jeering at us, Bibs.

Every day since the snow is here
The blue jay paces round the cabin, very busy, picking up
      bits,
Turning his back on us all,
And bobbing his thick dark crest about the snow, as if
      darkly saying:
I ignore those folk who look out.

You acid-blue metallic bird,
You thick bird with a strong crest,
Who are you?
Whose boss are you, with all your bully way?
You copper-sulphate blue bird!

                                            Lobo.

375

ANIMALS

"Yes, and if oxen or lions had hands, and could paint with their hands, and produce works of art as men do, horses would paint the forms of the gods like horses, and oxen like oxen, and make their bodies in the image of their several kinds."

"Once, they say, he was passing by when a dog was being beaten, and he spoke this word: 'Stop! don't beat it! For it is the soul of a friend I recognised when I heard its voice.' "

"Swine wash in mire, and barnyard fowls in dust."

THE ASS

The long-drawn bray of the ass
In the Sicilian twilight—

All mares are dead!
All mares are dead!
Oh–h!
Oh–h–h!
Oh–h–h–h–h—h!!
I can't bear it, I can't bear it.
I can't!
Oh, I can't!
Oh—
There's one left!
There's one left!
One!
There's one . . . left. . . .

So ending on a grunt of agonised relief.

This is the authentic Arabic interpretation of the braying
of the ass.
And Arabs should know.

And yet, as his brass-resonant howling yell resounds
through the Sicilian twilight
I am not sure—

His big, furry head,
His big, regretful eyes,
His diminished, drooping hindquarters,
His small toes.

Such a dear!
Such an ass!
With such a knot inside him!
He regrets something that he remembers.
That's obvious.

The Steppes of Tartary,
And the wind in his teeth for a bit,
And *noli me tangere.*

Ah then, when he tore the wind with his teeth,
And trod wolves underfoot,
And over-rode his mares as if he were savagely leaping an
  obstacle, to set his teeth in the sun. . . .

Somehow, alas, he fell in love,
And was sold into slavery.

He fell into the rut of love,
Poor ass, like man, always in rut,
The pair of them alike in that.

All his soul in his gallant member
And his head gone heavy with the knowledge of desire
And humiliation.

The ass was the first of all animals to fall finally into love,
From obstacle-leaping pride,
Mare obstacle,
Into love, mare-goal, and the knowledge of love.

Hence Jesus rode him in the Triumphant Entry.
Hence his beautiful eyes.
Hence his ponderous head, brooding over desire, and down-
  fall, Jesus, and a pack-saddle,
Hence he uncovers his big ass-teeth and howls in that agony
  that is half insatiable desire and half unquenchable
  humiliation.
Hence the black cross on his shoulders.

The Arabs were only half right, though they hinted the
  whole;
Everlasting lament in everlasting desire.

See him standing with his head down, near the Porta
    Cappuccini,
Asinello, Ciuco,
Somaro;
With the half-veiled, beautiful eyes, and the pensive face
    not asleep,
Motionless, like a bit of rock.

Has he seen the Gorgon's head, and turned to stone?
Alas, Love did it.
Now he's a jackass, a pack-ass, a donkey, somaro, burro,
    with a boss piling loads on his back.
Tied by the nose at the Porta Cappuccini.
And tied in a knot, inside, dead-locked between two desires:
To overleap like a male all mares as obstacles
In a leap at the sun;
And to leap in one last heart-bursting leap like a male at
    the goal of a mare.
And there end.
Well, you can't have it both roads.

Hee! Hee! Ehee! Ehow! Ehaw!! Oh! Oh! Oh–h–h!!
The wave of agony bursts in the stone that he was,
Bares his long ass's teeth, flattens his long ass's ears,
    straightens his donkey neck,
And howls his pandemonium on the indignant air.

Yes, it's a quandary.
Jesus rode on him, the first burden on the first beast of
    burden.
Love on a submissive ass.
So the tale began.

But the ass never forgets.

The horse, being nothing but a nag, will forget.
And men, being mostly geldings and knacker-boned hacks,
    have almost all forgot.
But the ass is a primal creature, and never forgets.

The Steppes of Tartary,
And Jesus on a meek ass-colt: mares: Mary escaping to
    Egypt: Joseph's cudgel.

Hee! Hee! Ehee! Ehow–ow!–ow!–aw!–aw!–aw!
All mares are dead!

Or else I am dead!
One of us, or the pair of us,
I don't know–ow!–ow!
Which!
Not sure–ure–ure
Quite which!
Which!

                        Taormina.

HE-GOAT

See his black nose snubbed back, pressed over like a whale's
    blow-holes,
As if his nostrils were going to curve back to the root of
    his tail.

As he charges slow among the herd
And rows among the females like a ship pertinaciously,
Heavy with a rancid cargo, through the lesser ships—
Old father
Sniffing forever ahead of him, at the rear of the goats, that
    they lift the little door,
And rowing on, unarrived, no matter how often he enter:
Like a big ship pushing her bowsprit over the little ships
Then swerving and steering afresh
And never, never arriving at journey's end, at the rear of
    the female ships.

Yellow eyes incomprehensible with thin slits
To round-eyed us.

Yet if you had whorled horns of bronze in a frontal dark
    wall
At the end of a back-bone ridge, like a straight *sierra
    roqueña,*
And nerves urging forward to the wall, you'd have eyes
    like his,
Especially if, being given a needle's eye of egress elsewhere
You tried to look back to it, and couldn't.

Sometimes he turns with a start, to fight, to challenge, to
    suddenly butt.
And then you see the God that he is, in a cloud of black
    hair
And storm-lightning-slitted eye.
Splendidly planting his feet, one rocky foot striking the
    ground with a sudden rock-hammer announcement.

I am here!
And suddenly lowering his head, the whorls of bone and
    of horn
Slowly revolving towards unexploded explosion,
As from the stem of his bristling, lightning-conductor tail
In a rush up the shrieking duct of his vertebral way
Runs a rage drawn in from the ether divinely through him
Towards a shock and a crash and a smiting of horns ahead.

That is a grand old lust of his, to gather the great
Rage of the sullen-stagnating atmosphere of goats
And bring it hurtling to a head, with crash of horns against
    the horns
Of the opposite enemy goat,
Thus hammering the mettle of goats into proof, and smiting
    out
The godhead of goats from the shock.

Things of iron are beaten on the anvil,
And he-goat is anvil to he-goat, and hammer to he-goat
In the business of beating the mettle of goats to a godhead.

But they've taken his enemy from him
And left him only his libidinousness,
His nostrils turning back, to sniff at even himself
And his slitted eyes seeking the needle's eye,
His own, unthreaded, forever.

So it is, when they take the enemy from us,
And we can't fight.

He is not fatherly, like the bull, massive Providence of hot
    blood;
The goat is an egoist, aware of himself, devilish aware of
    himself,
And full of malice prepense, and overweening, determined
    to stand on the highest peak
Like the devil, and look on the world as his own.

And as for love:
With a needle of long red flint he stabs in the dark
At the living rock he is up against;
While she with her goaty mouth stands smiling the while
    as he strikes, since sure
He will never *quite* strike home, on the target-quick, for
    her quick
Is just beyond range of the arrow he shoots
From his leap at the zenith in her, so it falls just short of
    the mark, far enough.
It is over before it is finished.
She, smiling with goaty munch-mouth, Mona Lisa, arranges
    it so.

Orgasm after orgasm after orgasm
And he smells so rank and his nose goes back,
And never an enemy brow-metalled to thresh it out with
    in the open field;
Never a mountain peak, to be king of the castle.
Only those eternal females to overleap and surpass, and
    never succeed.

The involved voluptuousness of the soft-footed cat
Who is like a fur folding a fur,
The cat who laps blood, and knows
The soft welling of blood invincible even beyond bone or
    metal of bone.

The soft, the secret, the unfathomable blood
The cat has lapped;
And known it subtler than frisson-shaken nerves,
Stronger than multiplicity of bone on bone,
And darker than even the arrows of violentest will
Can pierce, for that is where will gives out, like a sinking
    stone that can sink no further.

But he-goat,
Black procreant male of the selfish will and libidinous
    desire,
God in black cloud with curving horns of bronze,
Find an enemy, Egoist, and clash the cymbals in face-to-
    face defiance,
And let the lightning out of your smothered dusk.

Forget the female herd for a bit,
And fight to be boss of the world.

Fight, old Satan with a selfish will, fight for your selfish
    will;
Fight to be the devil on the tip of the peak
Overlooking the world for his own.

But bah, how can he, poor domesticated beast!

Taormina.

SHE-GOAT

Goats go past the back of the house like dry leaves in the
    dawn,
And up the hill like a river, if you watch.

At dusk they patter back like a bough being dragged on
    the ground,
Raising dusk and acridity of goats, and bleating.

Our old goat we tie up at night in the shed at the back of
    the broken Greek tomb in the garden,
And when the herd goes by at dawn she begins to bleat for
    me to come down and untie her.

Merr–err–err! Merr–er–errr! Mer! Mé!
—Wait, wait a bit, I'll come when I've lit the fire.
Merrr!
—Exactly.
Mé! Mer! Merrrrrrr!!!
—Tace, tu, crapa, bestia!
Merr–ererrr–ererrrr! Merrrr!

She is such an alert listener, with her ears wide, to know
    am I coming!
Such a canny listener, from a distance, looking upwards,
    lending first one ear, then another.

There she is, perched on her manger, looking over the
    boards into the day
Like a belle at her window.
And immediately she sees me she blinks, stares, doesn't
    know me, turns her head and ignores me vulgarly with
    a wooden blank on her face.

What do I care for her, the ugly female, standing up there
    with her long tangled sides like an old rug thrown
    over a fence.
But she puts her nose down shrewdly enough when the
    knot is untied,
And jumps staccato to earth, a sharp, dry jump, still
    ignoring me,
Pretending to look round the stall.

Come on, you, crapa! I'm not your servant!

She turns her head away with an obtuse, female sort of
   deafness, bête.
And then invariably she crouches her rear and makes
   water.
That being her way of answer, if I speak to her.—Self-
   conscious!
Le bestie non parlano, poverine!

She was bought at Giardini fair, on the sands, for six
   hundred lire.

An obstinate old witch, almost jerking the rope from my
   hands to eat the acanthus, or bite at the almond buds,
   and make me wait.
Yet the moment I hate her she trips mild and smug like a
   woman going to mass.
The moment I really detest her.

Queer it is, suddenly, in the garden
To catch sight of her standing like some huge, ghoulish
   grey bird in the air, on the bough of the leaning
   almond-tree,
Straight as a board on the bough, looking down like some
   hairy horrid God the Father in a William Blake
   imagination.
Come down, crapa, out of that almond-tree!

Instead of which she strangely rears on her perch in the
   air, vast beast,
And strangely paws the air, delicate,
And reaches her black-striped face up like a snake, far up,
Subtly, to the twigs overhead, far up, vast beast,
And snaps them sharp, with a little twist of her anaconda
   head;
All her great hairy-shaggy belly open against the morning.

At seasons she curls back her tail like a green leaf in the
   fire,
Or like a lifted hand, hailing at her wrong end.

And having exposed the pink place of her nakedness,
    fixedly,
She trots on blithe toes,
And if you look at her, she looks back with a cold, sardonic
    stare.
Sardonic, sardonyx, rock of cold fire.
See me? She says, *That's me!*

That's her.

Then she leaps the rocks like a quick rock,
Her backbone sharp as a rock,
Sheer will.

Along which ridge of libidinous magnetism
Defiant, curling the leaf of her tail as if she were curling
    her lip behind her at all life,
Libidinous desire runs back and forth, asserting itself in
    that little lifted bare hand.

Yet she has such adorable spurty kids, like spurts of black
    ink.
And in a month again is as if she had never had them.

And when the billy goat mounts her
She is brittle as brimstone.
While his slitted eyes squint back to the roots of his ears.
                                            Taormina.

ELEPHANT

You go down shade to the river, where naked men sit on
    flat brown rocks, to watch the ferry, in the sun;
And you cross the ferry with the naked people, go up the
    tropical lane
Through the palm-trees and past hollow paddy-fields where
    naked men are threshing rice
And the monolithic water-buffaloes, like old, muddy stones
    with hair on them, are being idle;

And through the shadow of bread-fruit trees, with their
    dark green, glossy, fanged leaves
Very handsome, and some pure yellow fanged leaves;
Out into the open, where the path runs on the top of a
    dyke between paddy-fields:
And there, of course, you meet a huge and mud-grey
    elephant advancing his frontal bone, his trunk curled
    round a log of wood:
So you step down the bank, to make way.

Shuffle, shuffle, and his little wicked eye has seen you as
    he advances above you,
The slow beast curiously spreading his round feet for the
    dust.
And the slim naked man slips down, and the beast deposits
    the lump of wood, carefully.
The keeper hooks the vast knee, the creature salaams.

White man, you are saluted.
Pay a few cents.

But the best is the Pera-hera, at midnight, under the
    tropical stars,
With a pale little wisp of a Prince of Wales, diffident, up
    in a small pagoda on the temple side
And white people in evening dress buzzing and crowding
    the stand upon the grass below and opposite:
And at last the Pera-hera procession, flambeaux aloft in
    the tropical night, of blazing cocoa-nut,
Naked dark men beneath,
And the huge frontal of three great elephants stepping
    forth to the tom-tom's beat, in the torch-light,
Slowly sailing in gorgeous apparel through the flame-light,
    in front of a towering, grimacing white image of
    wood.

The elephant bells striking slow, tong-tong, tong-tong,
To music and queer chanting:
Enormous shadow-processions filing on in the flare of fire
In the fume of cocoa-nut oil, in the sweating tropical night,
In the noise of the tom-toms and singers:

Elephants after elephants curl their trunks, vast shadows,
  and some cry out
As they approach and salaam, under the dripping fire of
  the torches,
That pale fragment of a Prince up there, whose motto is
  Ich dien.

Pale, dispirited Prince, with his chin on his hands, his
  nerves tired out,
Watching and hardly seeing the trunk-curl approach and
  clumsy, knee-lifting salaam
Of the hugest, oldest of beasts in the night and the fire-
  flare below.
He is royalty, pale and dejected fragment up aloft.
And down below huge homage of shadowy beasts; bare-
  foot and trunk-lipped in the night.

Chieftains, three of them abreast, on foot
Strut like peg-tops, wound around with hundreds of yards
  of fine linen.
They glimmer with tissue of gold, and golden threads on
  a jacket of velvet,
And their faces are dark, and fat, and important.
They are royalty, dark-faced royalty, showing the con-
  scious whites of their eyes
And stepping in homage, stubborn, to that nervous pale
  lad up there.

More elephants, tong, tong-tong, loom up,
Huge, more tassels swinging, more dripping fire of new
  cocoa-nut cressets
High, high flambeaux, smoking of the east;
And scarlet hot embers of torches knocked out of the
  sockets among bare feet of elephants and men on the
  path in the dark.
And devil-dancers luminous with sweat, dancing on to the
  shudder of drums,
Tom-toms, weird music of the devil, voices of men from
  the jungle singing;
Endless, under the Prince.

Towards the tail of the everlasting procession
In the long hot night, more dancers from insignificant
     villages,
And smaller, more frightened elephants.

Men-peasants from jungle villages dancing and running
     with sweat and laughing,
Naked dark men with ornaments on, on their naked arms
     and their naked breasts, the grooved loins
Gleaming like metal with running sweat as they suddenly
     turn, feet apart,
And dance, and dance, forever dance, with breath half
     sobbing in dark, sweat-shining breasts,
And lustrous great tropical eyes unveiled now, gleaming
     a kind of laugh,
A naked, gleaming dark laugh, like a secret out in the dark,
And flare of a tropical energy, tireless, afire in the dark,
     slim limbs and breasts,
Perpetual, fire-laughing motion, among the slow shuffle
Of elephants,
The hot dark blood of itself a-laughing, wet, half-devilish,
     men all motion
Approaching under that small pavilion, and tropical eyes
     dilated look up
Inevitably look up
To the Prince
To that tired remnant of royalty up there
Whose motto is *Ich dien*.

As if the homage of the kindled blood of the east
Went up in wavelets to him, from the breasts and eyes
     of jungle torch-men,
And he couldn't take it.

What would they do, those jungle men running with sweat,
     with the strange dark laugh in their eyes, glancing up,
And the sparse-haired elephants slowly following,
If they knew that his motto was *Ich dien*?
And that he meant it.

389

They begin to understand.
The rickshaw boys begin to understand.
And then the devil comes into their faces,
But a different sort, a cold, rebellious, jeering devil.

In elephants and the east are two devils, in all men maybe.
The mystery of the dark mountain of blood, reeking in
  homage, in lust, in rage,
And passive with everlasting patience,
Then the little, cunning pig-devil of the elephant's lurking
  eyes, the unbeliever.

We dodged, when the Pera-hera was finished, under the
  hanging, hairy pigs' tails
And the flat, flaccid mountains of the elephants' standing
  haunches,
Vast-blooded beasts,
Myself so little dodging rather scared against the eternal
  wrinkled pillars of their legs, as they were being
  dismantled;
Then I knew they were dejected, having come to hear the
  repeated
Royal summons: *Dient Ihr!*
Serve!
*Serve, vast mountainous blood, in submission and splen-
  dour, serve royalty.*
Instead of which, the silent, fatal emission from that pale,
  shattered boy up there:
Ich dien.

That's why the night fell in frustration.
That's why, as the elephants ponderously, with unseeming
  swiftness, galloped uphill in the night, going back to
  the jungle villages,
As the elephant bells sounded tong-tong-tong, bell of the
  temple of blood in the night, swift-striking,
And the crowd like a field of rice in the dark gave way
  like liquid to the dark
Looming gallop of the beasts,

It was as if the great bulks of elephants in the obscure
    light went over the hill-brow swiftly, with their tails
    between their legs, in haste to get away,
Their bells sounding frustrate and sinister.

And all the dark-faced, cotton-wrapped people, more
    numerous and whispering than grains of rice in a
    rice-field at night,
All the dark-faced, cotton-wrapped people, a countless
    host on the shores of the lake, like thick wild rice by
    the water's edge,
Waiting for the fireworks of the after-show,
As the rockets went up, and the glare passed over countless
    faces, dark as black rice growing,
Showing a glint of teeth, and glancing tropical eyes aroused
    in the night,
There was the faintest twist of mockery in every face,
    across the hiss of wonders as the rocket burst
High, high up, in flakes, shimmering flakes of blue fire,
    above the palm-trees of the islet in the lake,
O faces upturned to the glare, O tropical wonder, wonder,
    a miracle in heaven!
And the shadow of a jeer, of underneath disappointment,
    as the rocket-coruscation died, and shadow was the
    same as before.

They were foiled, the myriad whispering dark-faced
    cotton-wrapped people.
They had come to see royalty,
To bow before royalty, in the land of elephants, bow deep,
    bow deep.
Bow deep, for it's good as a draught of cool water to bow
    very, very low to the royal.

And all there was to bow to, a weary, diffident boy whose
    motto is *Ich dien*.
I serve! I serve! in all the weary irony of his mien—*'Tis I
    who serve!*
Drudge to the public.

I wish they had given the three feathers to me;
That I had been he in the pavilion, as in a pepper-box aloft
    and alone
To stand and hold feathers, three feathers above the world,
And say to them: *Dient Ihr! Dient!*
Omnes, vos omnes, servite.
Serve me, I am meet to be served.
Being royal of the gods.

And tc the elephants:
First great beasts of the earth,
A prince has come back to you,
Blood-mountains.
Crook the knee and be glad.

                                             Kandy.

KANGAROO

In the northern hemisphere
Life seems to leap at the air, or skim under the wind
Like stags on rocky ground, or pawing horses, or springy
    scut-tailed rabbits.

Or else rush horizontal to charge at the sky's horizon,
Like bulls or bisons or wild pigs.

Or slip like water slippery towards its ends,
As foxes, stoats, and wolves, and prairie dogs.

Only mice, and moles, and rats, and badgers, and beavers,
    and perhaps bears
Seem belly-plumbed to the earth's mid-navel.
Or frogs that when they leap come flop, and flop to the
    centre of the earth.

But the yellow antipodal Kangaroo, when she sits up,
Who can unseat her, like a liquid drop that is heavy, and
    just touches earth.

The downward drip
The down-urge.
So much denser than cold-blooded frogs.

Delicate mother Kangaroo
Sitting up there rabbit-wise, but huge, plumb-weighted,
And lifting her beautiful slender face, oh! so much more
    gently and finely lined than a rabbit's, or than a hare's,
Lifting her face to nibble at a round white peppermint
    drop, which she loves, sensitive mother Kangaroo.

Her sensitive, long, pure-bred face.
Her full antipodal eyes, so dark,
So big and quiet and remote, having watched so many
    empty dawns in silent Australia.

Her little loose hands, and drooping Victorian shoulders.
And then her great weight below the waist, her vast pale
    belly
With a thin young yellow little paw hanging out, and
    straggle of a long thin ear, like ribbon,
Like a funny trimming to the middle of her belly, thin
    little dangle of an immature paw, and one thin ear.

Her belly, her big haunches
And, in addition, the great muscular python-stretch of her
    tail.

There, she shan't have any more peppermint drops.
So she wistfully, sensitively sniffs the air, and then turns,
    goes off in slow sad leaps

On the long flat skis of her legs,
Steered and propelled by that steel-strong snake of a tail.

Stops again, half turns, inquisitive to look back.
While something stirs quickly in her belly, and a lean
    little face comes out, as from a window,

Peaked and a bit dismayed,
Only to disappear again quickly away from the sight of
the world, to snuggle down in the warmth,
Leaving the trail of a different paw hanging out.

Still she watches with eternal, cocked wistfulness!
How full her eyes are, like the full, fathomless, shining eyes
of an Australian black-boy
Who has been lost so many centuries on the margins of
existence!

She watches with insatiable wistfulness.
Untold centuries of watching for something to come,
For a new signal from life, in that silent lost land of the
South.

Where nothing bites but insects and snakes and the sun,
small life.
Where no bull roared, no cow ever lowed, no stag cried,
no leopard screeched, no lion coughed, no dog barked,
But all was silent save for parrots occasionally, in the
haunted blue bush.

Wistfully watching, with wonderful liquid eyes.
And all her weight, all her blood, dripping sack-wise down
towards the earth's centre,
And the live little-one taking in its paw at the door of her
belly.

Leap then, and come down on the line that draws to the
earth's deep, heavy centre.

Sydney.

BIBBLES

Bibbles,
Little black dog in New Mexico,
Little black snub-nosed bitch with a shoved-out jaw
And a wrinkled reproachful look;

Little black female pup, sort of French bull, they say,
With bits of brindle coming through, like rust, to show
    you're not pure;
Not pure, Bibbles,
Bubsey, bat-eared dog;
Not black enough!

First live thing I've "owned" since the lop-eared rabbits
    when I was a lad,
And those over-prolific white mice, and Adolph, and Rex
    whom I didn't own.
And even now, Bibbles, little Ma'am, it's you who
    appropriated me, not I you.
As Benjamin Franklin appropriated Providence to his
    purposes.

Oh Bibbles, black little bitch,
I'd never have let you appropriate me, had I known.
I never dreamed, till now, of the awful time the Lord must
    have, "owning" humanity,
Especially democratic live-by-love humanity.

Oh Bibbles, oh Pips, oh Pipsey,
You little black love-bird!
Don't you love *everybody!*
Just everybody.
You love 'em all.
Believe in the One Identity, don't you,
You little Walt-Whitmanesque bitch?
First time I lost you in Taos plaza,
And found you after endless chasing,
Came upon you prancing round the corner in exuberant,
    bibbling affection
After the black-green skirts of a yellow-green old Mexican
    woman
Who hated you, and kept looking round at you and cursing
    you in a mutter,

While you pranced and bounced with love of her, you
    indiscriminating animal,
All your wrinkled *miserere* Chinese black little face
    beaming
And your black little body bouncing and wriggling
With indiscriminate love, Bibbles;
I had a moment's pure detestation of you.

As I rushed like an idiot round the corner after you
Yelling: *Pips! Pips! Bibbles!*

I've had moments of hatred of you since,
Loving everybody!
"To you, whoever you are, witn endless embrace!"—
That's you, Pipsey,
With your imbecile bit of a tail in a love-flutter.
You omnipip.

Not that you're merely a softy, oh dear me, no.
You know which side your bread is buttered.
You don't care a rap for anybody.
But you love lying warm between warm human thighs,
    indiscriminate,
And you love to make somebody love you, indiscriminate,
You love to lap up affection, to wallow in it,
And then turn tail to the next comer, for a new dollop.

And start prancing and licking and cuddling again,
    indiscriminate.

Oh yes, I know your little game.

Yet you're so nice,
So quick, like a little black dragon.
So fierce, when the coyotes howl, barking like a whole
    little lion, and rumbling,
And starting forward in the dusk, with your little black
    fur all bristling like plush
Against those coyotes, who would swallow you like an
    oyster.

And in the morning, when the bedroom door is opened,
Rushing in like a little black whirlwind, leaping straight as
    an arrow on the bed at the pillow
And turning the day suddenly into a black tornado of *joie
de vivre*, Chinese dragon.

So funny
Lobbing wildly through deep snow like a rabbit,
Hurtling like a black ball through the snow,
Champing it, tossing a mouthful,
Little black spot in the landscape!

So absurd
Pelting behind on the dusty trail when the horse sets off
    home at a gallop:
Left in the dust behind like a dust-ball tearing along,
Coming up on fierce little legs, tearing fast to catch up, a
    real little dust-pig, ears almost blown away,
And black eyes bulging bright in a dust-mask
Chinese-dragon-wrinkled, with a pink mouth grinning,
    under jaw shoved out
And white teeth showing in your dragon-grin as you race,
    you split-face,
Like a trundling projectile swiftly whirling up,
Cocking your eyes at me as you come alongside, to see if
    I'm I on the horse,
And panting with that split grin,
All your game little body dust-smooth like a little pig,
    poor Pips.

Plenty of game old spirit in you, Bibbles.
Plenty of game old spunk, little bitch.

How you hate being brushed with the boot-brush, to brush
    all that dust out of your wrinkled face,
Don't you?
How you hate being made to look undignified, Ma'am;
How you hate being laughed at, Miss Superb!

Blackberry face!

Plenty of conceit in you.
Unblemished belief in your own perfection
And utter lovableness, you ugly-mug;
Chinese puzzle-face,
Wrinkled underhung physiog that looks as if it had done
    with everything,
Through with everything.

Instead of which you sit there and roll your head like a
    canary
And show a tiny bunch of white teeth in your underhung
    blackness,
Self-conscious little bitch,
Aiming again at being loved.

Let the merest scallywag come to the door, and you leap
    your very dearest love at him,
As if now, at last, here was the one you *finally* loved,
Finally loved;
And even the dirtiest scallywag is taken in,
Thinking: *This dog sure has taken a fancy to me.*

You miserable little bitch of love-tricks,
I know your game.

Me or the Mexican who comes to chop wood
All the same,
All humanity is jam to you.

Everybody so dear, and yourself so ultra-beloved
That you have to run out at last and eat filth,
Gobble up filth, you horror, swallow utter abomination
    and fresh-dropped dung.

You stinker.
You worse than a carrion-crow.
Reeking dung-mouth.
You love-bird.

Reject nothing, sings Walt Whitman.
So you, you go out at last and eat the unmentionable,
In your appetite for affection.

And then you run in to vomit it in my house!
I get my love back.
And I have to clean up after you, filth which even blind
     Nature rejects
From the pit of your stomach;
But you, you snout-face, you reject nothing, you merge so
     much in love
You must eat even that.

Then when I dust you a bit with a juniper twig
You run straight away to live with somebody else,
Fawn before them, and love them as if they were the ones
     you had *really* loved all along.
And they're taken in.
They feel quite tender over you, till you play the same
     trick on them, dirty bitch.

Fidelity! Loyalty! Attachment!
Oh, these are abstractions to your nasty little belly.
You must always be a-waggle with LOVE.
Such a waggle of love you can hardly distinguish one
     human from another.

You love one after another, on one condition, that each
     one loves you most.
Democratic little bull-bitch, dirt-eating little swine.

But now, my lass, you've got Nemesis on your track,
Now you've come sex-alive, and the great ranch-dogs are
     all after you.
They're after what they can get, and don't you turn tail!
You loved 'em all so much before, didn't you, loved 'em
     indiscriminate.

You don't love 'em now.
They want something of you, so you squeak and come
     pelting indoors.

Come pelting to me, now the other folk have found you
     out, and the dogs are after you.
Oh yes, you're found out. I heard them kick you out of
     the ranch house.
Get out, you little, soft fool!!

And didn't you turn your eyes up at me then?
And didn't you cringe on the floor like any inkspot!
And crawl away like a black snail!
And doesn't everybody loathe you then!
And aren't your feelings violated, you high-bred little love-
     bitch!

For you're sensitive,
In many ways very finely bred.
But bred in conceit that the world is all for love
Of you, my bitch: till you get so far you eat filth.
Fool, in spite of your pretty ways, and quaint, know-all,
     wrinkled old aunty's face.

So now, what with great Airedale dogs,
And a kick or two,
And a few vomiting bouts,
And a juniper switch,
You look at me for discrimination, don't you?
Look up at me with misgiving in your bulging eyes,
And fear in the smoky whites of your eyes, you nigger;
And you're puzzled,
You think you'd better mind your P's and Q's for a bit,
Your sensitive love-pride being all hurt.

All right, my little bitch.
You learn loyalty rather than loving,
And I'll protect you.

                                        Lobo.

MOUNTAIN LION

Climbing through the January snow, into the Lobo canyon
Dark grow the spruce-trees, blue is the balsam, water
    sounds still unfrozen, and the trail is still evident.

Men!
Two men!
Men! The only animal in the world to fear!

They hesitate.
We hesitate.
They have a gun.
We have no gun.

Then we all advance, to meet.

Two Mexicans, strangers, emerging out of the dark and
    snow and inwardness of the Lobo valley.
What are they doing here on this vanishing trail?

What is he carrying?
Something yellow.
A deer?

Qué tiene, amigo?
León—

He smiles, foolishly, as if he were caught doing wrong.
And we smile, foolishly, as if we didn't know.
He is quite gentle and dark-faced.

It is a mountain lion,
A long, long slim cat, yellow like a lioness.
Dead.

He trapped her this morning, he says, smiling foolishly.

Lift up her face,
Her round, bright face, bright as frost.
Her round, fine-fashioned head, with two dead ears;
And stripes in the brilliant frost of her face, sharp, fine
    dark rays,
Dark, keen, fine rays in the brilliant frost of her face.
Beautiful dead eyes.

Hermoso es!

They go out towards the open;
We go on into the gloom of Lobo.
And above the trees I found her lair,
A hole in the blood-orange brilliant rocks that stick up, a
    little cave.
And bones, and twigs, and a perilous ascent.

So, she will never leap up that way again, with the yellow
    flash of a mountain lion's long shoot!
And her bright striped frost-face will never watch any
    more, out of the shadow of the cave in the blood-
    orange rock,
Above the trees of the Lobo dark valley-mouth!

Instead, I look out.
And out to the dim of the desert, like a dream, never real;
To the snow of the Sangre de Cristo mountains, the ice of
    the mountains of Picoris,
And near across at the opposite steep of snow, green trees
    motionless standing in snow, like a Christmas toy.

And I think in this empty world there was room for me
    and a mountain lion.
And I think in the world beyond, how easily we might
    spare a million or two of humans
And never miss them.
Yet what a gap in the world, the missing white frost-face
    of that slim yellow mountain lion!

                                        Lobo.

THE RED WOLF

Over the heart of the west, the Taos desert,
Circles an eagle,
And it's dark between me and him.

The sun, as he waits a moment, huge and liquid
Standing without feet on the rim of the far-off mesa
Says: *Look for a last long time then! Look! Look well!*
    I am going.
So he pauses and is beholden, and straightway is gone.

And the Indian, in a white sheet
Wrapped to the eyes, the sheet bound close on his brows,
Stands saying: *See, I'm invisible!*
Behold how you can't behold me!
The invisible in its shroud!

Now that the sun has gone, and the aspen leaves
And the cotton-wood leaves are fallen, as good as fallen,
And the ponies are in corral,
And it's night.

Why, more has gone than all these;
And something has come.
A red wolf stands on the shadow's dark red rim.

Day has gone to dust on the sage-grey desert
Like a white Christus fallen to dust from a cross;
To dust, to ash, on the twilit floor of the desert.

And a black crucifix like a dead tree spreading wings;
Maybe a black eagle with its wings out
Left lonely in the night
In a sort of worship.

And coming down upon us, out of the dark concave
Of the eagle's wings,
And the coffin-like slit where the Indian's eyes are,

And the absence of cotton-wood leaves, or of aspen,
Even the absence of dark-crossed donkeys:
Come tall old demons, smiling
The Indian smile,
Saying: *How do you do, you pale-face?*

I am very well, old demon.
How are you?

Call me Harry if you will,
Call me Old Harry, says he.
Or the abbreviation of Nicolas,
Nick, Old Nick, maybe.

Well, you're a dark old demon,
And I'm a pale-face like a homeless dog
That has followed the sun from the dawn through the east,
Trotting east and east and east till the sun himself went
     home,
And left me homeless here in the dark at your door.
How do you think we'll get on,
Old demon, you and I?

You and I, you pale-face,
Pale-face you and I
Don't get on.

Mightn't we try?

Where's your God, you white one?
Where's your white God?

He fell to dust as the twilight fell,
Was fume as I trod
The last step out of the east.

Then you're a lost white dog of a pale-face,
And the day's now dead. . . .

Touch me carefully, old father,
My beard is red.

Thin red wolf of a pale-face,
Thin red wolf, go home.

I have no home, old father,
That's why I come.

We take no hungry stray from the pale-face . . .

Father, you are not asked.
I am come. I am here. The red-dawn-wolf
Sniffs round your place.
Lifts up his voice and howls to the walls of the pueblo,
Announcing he's here.

The dogs of the dark pueblo
Have long fangs . . .

Has the red wolf trotted east and east and east
From the far, far other end of the day
To fear a few fangs?

Across the pueblo river
That dark old demon and I
Thus say a few words to each other

And wolf, he calls me, and red.
I call him no names.
He says, however, he is Star-Road.
I say, he can go back the same gait.

As for me . . .
Since I trotted at the tail of the sun as far as ever the
    creature went west,
And lost him here,
I'm going to sit down on my tail right here
And wait for him to come back with a new story.
I'm the red wolf, says the dark old father.
All right, the red-dawn-wolf I am.

Taos.

405

GHOSTS

"A N D as the dog with its nostrils tracking out the fragments of the beasts' limbs, and the breath from their feet that they leave in the soft grass, runs upon a path that is pathless to men, so does the soul follow the trail of the dead, across great spaces. For the journey is a far one, to sleep and a forgetting, and often the dead look back, and linger, for now they realise all that is lost. Then the living soul comes up with them, and great is the pain of greeting, and deadly the parting again. For oh, the dead are disconsolate, since even death can never make up for some mistakes."

MEN IN NEW MEXICO

Mountains blanket-wrapped
Round a white hearth of desert—

While the sun goes round
And round and round the desert,
The mountains never get up and walk about.
They can't, they can't wake.

They camped and went to sleep
In the last twilight
Of Indian gods;
And they can't wake.

Indians dance and run and stamp—
No good.
White men make gold-mines and the mountains unmake
    them
In their sleep.

The Indians laugh in their sleep
From fear,
Like a man when he sleeps and his sleep is over, and he
    can't wake up,
And he lies like a log and screams and his scream is silent
Because his body can't wake up;
So he laughs from fear, pure fear, in the grip of the sleep.

A dark membrane over the will, holding a man down
Even when the mind has flickered awake;
A membrane of sleep, like a black blanket.

We walk in our sleep, in this land,
Somnambulist wide-eyed afraid.

We scream for someone to wake us
And our scream is soundless in the paralysis of sleep,
And we know it.

The Penitentes lash themselves till they run with blood
In their efforts to come awake for one moment;
To tear the membrane of this sleep . . .
No good.

The Indians thought the white man would awake them . . .
And instead, the white men scramble asleep in the
    mountains,
And ride on horseback asleep forever through the desert,
And shoot one another, amazed and mad with somnam-
    bulism,
Thinking death will awaken something . . .
No good.

Born with a caul,
A black membrane over the face,
And unable to tear it,
Though the mind is awake.

Mountains blanket-wrapped
Round the ash-white hearth of the desert;
And though the sun leaps like a thing unleashed in the sky
They can't get up, they are under the blanket.

Taos.

AUTUMN AT TAOS

Over the rounded sides of the Rockies, the aspens of
    autumn,
The aspens of autumn,
Like yellow hair of a tigress brindled with pines.

Down on my hearth-rug of desert, sage of the mesa,
An ash-grey pelt
Of wolf all hairy and level, a wolf's wild pelt.

Trot-trot to the mottled foot-hills, cedar-mottled and piñon;
Did you ever see an otter?
Silvery-sided, fish-fanged, fierce-faced, whiskered, mottled.

When I trot my little pony through the aspen-trees of the
 canyon,
Behold me trotting at ease betwixt the slopes of the golden
Great and glistening-feathered legs of the hawk of Horus;
The golden hawk of Horus
Astride above me.

But under the pines
I go slowly
As under the hairy belly of a great black bear.

Glad to emerge and look back
On the yellow, pointed aspen-trees laid one on another like
 feathers,
Feather over feather on the breast of the great and golden
Hawk as I say of Horus.

Pleased to be out in the sage and the pine fish-dotted foot-
 hills,
Past the otter's whiskers,
On to the fur of the wolf-pelt that strews the plain.

And then to look back to the rounded sides of the squatting
 Rockies,
Tigress brindled with aspen,
Jaguar-splashed, puma-yellow, leopard-livid slopes of
 America.

Make big eyes, little pony,
At all these skins of wild beasts;
They won't hurt you.

Fangs and claws and talons and beaks and hawk-eyes
Are nerveless just now.
So be easy.

        Taos.

SPIRITS SUMMONED WEST

England seems full of graves to me,
Full of graves.

Women I loved and cherished, like my mother;
Yet I had to tell them to die.

England seems covered with graves to me,
Women's graves.

Women who were gentle
And who loved me
And whom I loved
And told to die.

Women with the beautiful eyes of the old days,
Belief in love, and sorrow of such belief.
"Hush, my love, then, hush.
Hush, and die, my dear!"

Women of the older generation, who knew
The full doom of loving and not being able to take back.
Who understood at last what it was to be told to die.

Now that the graves are made, and covered;
Now that in England pansies and such-like grow on the
      graves of women;
Now that in England is silence, where before was a moving
      of soft-skirted women,
Women with eyes that were gentle in olden belief in love;
Now then that all their yearning is hushed, and covered
      over with earth.

England seems like one grave to me.

And I, I sit on this high American desert
With dark-wrapped Rocky Mountains motionless squatting
      around in a ring,
Remembering I told them to die, to sink into the grave in
      England,
The gentle-kneed women.

So now I whisper: *Come away,*
Come away from the place of graves, come west,
Women,
Women whom I loved and told to die.

Come back to me now,
Now the divided yearning is over;
Now you are husbandless indeed, no more husband to
cherish like a child
And wrestle with for the prize of perfect love.
No more children to launch in a world you mistrust.
Now you need know in part
No longer, or carry the burden of a man on your heart,
Or the burden of Man writ large.

Now you are disemburdened of Man and a man
Come back to me.
Now you are free of the toils of a would-be-perfect love
Come to me and be still.

Come back then, you who were wives and mothers
And always virgins
Overlooked.

Come back then, mother, my love, whom I told to die.
It was only I who saw the virgin you
That had no home.

The overlooked virgin,
My love.

You overlooked her too.

Now that the grave is made of mother and wife,
Now that the grave is made and lidded over with turf:

Come, delicate, overlooked virgin, come back to me
And be still,
Be glad.

I didn't tell you to die, for nothing.
I wanted the virgin you to be home at last
In my heart.

Inside my innermost heart,
Where the virgin in woman comes home to a man.

The homeless virgin
Who never in all her life could find the way home
To that difficult innermost place in a man.

Now come west, come home,
Women I've loved for gentleness,
For the virginal you.
Find the way now that you never could find in life,
So I told you to die.

Virginal first and last
Is woman.
Now at this last, my love, my many a love,
You whom I loved for gentleness,
Come home to me.

They are many, and I loved them, shall always love them,
And they know it,
The virgins.
And my heart is glad to have them at last.

Now that the wife and mother and mistress is buried in
    earth,
In English earth,
Come home to me, my love, my loves, my many loves,
Come west to me.

For virgins are not exclusive of virgins
As wives are of wives;
And motherhood is jealous,
But in virginity jealousy does not enter.

Taos.

THE AMERICAN EAGLE

The dove of Liberty sat on an egg
And hatched another eagle.

But didn't disown the bird.

Down with all eagles! cooed the Dove.
And down all eagles began to flutter, reeling from their
    perches:
Eagles with two heads, eagles with one, presently eagles
    with none
Fell from the hooks and were dead.

Till the American Eagle was the only eagle left in the
    world.

Then it began to fidget, shifting from one leg to the other,
Trying to look like a pelican,
And plucking out of his plumage a few loose feathers to
    feather the nests of all
The new naked little republics come into the world.

But the feathers were, comparatively, a mere flea-bite.
And the bub-eagle that Liberty had hatched was growing a
    startling big bird
On the roof of the world;
A bit awkward, and with a funny squawk in his voice,
His mother Liberty trying always to teach him to coo
And him always ending with a yawp
Coo! Coo! Coo! Coo-ark! Coo-ark! Quark!! Quark!!
YAWP!!!

So he clears his throat, the young Cock-eagle!
Now if the lilies of France lick Solomon in all his glory;
And the leopard cannot change his spots;
Nor the British lion his appetite;
Neither can a young Cock-eagle sit simpering
With an olive-sprig in his mouth.

It's not his nature.

The big bird of the Amerindian being the eagle,
Red Men still stick themselves over with bits of his fluff,
And feel absolutely IT.

So better make up your mind, American Eagle,
Whether you're a sucking dove, *Roo—coo—ooo! Quark!
Yawp!!*
Or a pelican
Handing out a few loose golden breast-feathers, at moulting
time;
Or a sort of prosperity-gander
Fathering endless ten-dollar golden eggs.

Or whether it actually is an eagle you are,
With a Roman nose
And claws not made to shake hands with,
And a Me-Almighty eye.

The new Proud Republic
Based on the mystery of pride.
Overweening men, full of power of life, commanding a
teeming obedience.

Eagle of the Rockies, bird of men that are masters,
Lifting the rabbit-blood of the myriads up into something
splendid,
Leaving a few bones;
Opening great wings in the face of the sheep-faced ewe
Who is losing her lamb,
Drinking a little blood, and loosing another royalty unto
the world.

Is that you, American Eagle?

Or are you the goose that lays the golden egg?
Which is just a stone to anyone asking for meat.
And are you going to go on for ever
Laying that golden egg,
That addled golden egg?

Lobo.

414

PANSIES

INTRODUCTION TO *PANSIES*

T H I S little bunch of fragments is offered as a bunch of *pensées*, anglicé pansies; a handful of thoughts. Or, if you will have the other derivation of pansy, from *panser*, to dress or soothe a wound; these are my tender administrations to the mental and emotional wounds we suffer from. Or you can have heartsease if you like, since the modern heart could certainly do with it.

Each little piece is a thought; not a bare idea or an opinion or a didactic statement, but a true thought, which comes as much from the heart and the genitals as from the head. A thought, with its own blood of emotion and instinct running in it like the fire in a fire-opal, if I may be so bold. Perhaps if you hold up my pansies properly to the light, they may show a running vein of fire. At least, they do not pretend to be half-baked lyrics or melodies in American measure. They are thoughts which run through the modern mind and body, each having its own separate existence, yet each of them combining with all the others to make up a complete state of mind.

It suits the modern temper better to have its state of mind made up of apparently irrelevant thoughts that scurry in different directions, yet belong to the same nest; each thought trotting down the page like an independent creature, each with its own small head and tail, trotting its own little way, then curling up to sleep. We prefer it, at least the young seem to prefer it to those solid blocks of mental pabulum packed like bales in the pages of a proper heavy book. Even we prefer it to those slightly didactic opinions and slices of wisdom which are laid horizontally across the pages of Pascal's *Pensées* or La Bruyère's *Caractères*, separated only by *pattes de mouches*, like faint sprigs of parsley. Let every pensée trot on its own little paws, not be laid like a cutlet trimmed with a *patte de mouche*.

Live and let live, and each pansy will tip you its separate wink. The fairest thing in nature, a flower, still has its roots in earth and

417

manure; and in the perfume there hovers still the faint strange scent of earth, the under-earth in all its heavy humidity and darkness. Certainly it is so in pansy-scent, and in violet-scent; mingled with the blue of the morning the black of the corrosive humus. Else the scent would be just sickly sweet.

So it is: we all have our roots in earth. And it is our roots that now need a little attention, need the hard soil eased away from them, and softened so that a little fresh air can come to them, and they can breathe. For by pretending to have no roots, we have trodden the earth so hard over them that they are starving and stifling below the soil. We have roots, and our roots are in the sensual, instinctive and intuitive body, and it is here we need fresh air of open consciousness.

I am abused most of all for using the so-called "obscene" words. Nobody quite knows what the word "obscene" itself means, or what it is intended to mean: but gradually all the *old* words, that belong to the body below the navel, have come to be judged obscene. Obscene means today that the policeman thinks he has a right to arrest you, nothing else.

Myself, I am mystified at this horror over a mere word, a plain simple word that stands for a plain simple thing. "In the beginning was the Word, and the Word was God and the Word was with God." If that is true, then we are very far from the beginning. When did the Word "fall"? When did the Word become unclean "below the navel"? Because today, if you suggest that the word arse was in the beginning and was God and was with God, you will just be put in prison at once. Though a doctor might say the same of the word *ischial tuberosity*, and all the old ladies would piously murmur "Quite"! Now that sort of thing is idiotic and humiliating. Whoever the God was that made us, He made us complete. He didn't stop at the navel and leave the rest to the devil. It is too childish. And the same with the Word which is God. If the Word is God—which in the sense of the human mind it is—then you can't suddenly say that all the words which belong below the navel are obscene. The word arse is as much god as the word face. It must be so, otherwise you cut off your god at the waist.

What is obvious is that the words in these cases have been dirtied by the mind, by unclean mental associations. The words themselves are clean, so are the things to which they apply. But the mind drags in a filthy association, calls up some repulsive emotion. Well, then, cleanse the mind, that is the real job. It is the mind which is the Augean stables, not language. The word arse is clean enough. Even the part of the body it refers to is just as much me as my hand and my brain are me. It is not for *me* to quarrel with my own natural make-up. If I am, I am all that I am. But the impudent and dirty mind won't have it. It hates certain parts of the body, and makes the words representing these parts scapegoats. It pelts them out of the consciousness with filth, and there they hover, never dying, never dead, slipping into the consciousness again unawares, and pelted out again with filth, haunting the margins of the consciousness like jackals or hyenas. And they refer to parts of our own living bodies, and to our most essential acts. So that man turns himself into a thing of shame and horror. And his consciousness shudders with horrors that he has made for himself.

That sort of thing has got to stop. We can't have the consciousness haunted any longer by repulsive spectres which are no more than poor simple scapegoat words representing parts of man himself; words that the cowardly and unclean mind has driven out into the limbo of the unconscious, whence they return upon us looming and magnified out of all proportion, frightening us beyond all reason. We must put an end to that. It is the self divided against itself most dangerously. The simple and natural "obscene" words must be cleaned up of all their depraved fear-associations, and re-admitted into the consciousness to take their natural place. Now they are magnified out of all proportion, so is the mental fear they represent. We must accept the word arse as we accept the word face, since arses we have and always shall have. We can't start cutting off the buttocks of unfortunate mankind, like the ladies in the Voltaire story, just to fit the mental expulsion of the word.

This scapegoat business does the mind itself so much damage. There is a poem of Swift's which should make us pause. It is written to Celia, his Celia—and every verse ends with the mad, maddened refrain: "But—Celia, Celia, Celia shits!" Now that, stated baldly, is so ridiculous it is almost funny. But when one remembers the gnashing insanity to which the great mind of Swift was reduced by that and similar thoughts, the joke dies away. Such thoughts poisoned him, like some terrible constipation. They poisoned his mind. And why, in heaven's name? The *fact* cannot have troubled him, since it applied to himself and to all of us. It was not the fact that Celia shits which so deranged him, it was the *thought*. His mind couldn't bear the thought. Great wit as he was, he could not see how ridiculous his revulsions were. His arrogant mind over-bore him. He couldn't even see how much worse it would be if Celia didn't shit. His physical sympathies were too weak, his guts were too cold to sympathise with poor Celia in her natural functions. His insolent and sicklily squeamish mind just turned her into a thing of horror, because she was merely natural and went to the W.C. It is monstrous! One feels like going back across all the years to poor Celia to say to her: It's all right, don't you take any notice of that mental lunatic.

And Swift's form of madness is very common today. Men with cold guts and over-squeamish minds are always thinking those things and squirming. Wretched man is the victim of his own little revulsions, which he magnifies into great horrors and terrifying taboos. We are all savages, we all have taboos. The Australian black may have the kangaroo for his taboo. And then he will probably die of shock and terror if a kangaroo happens to touch him. Which is what I would call a purely unnecessary death. But modern men have even more dangerous taboos. To us, certain words, certain ideas are taboo, and if they come upon us and we can't drive them away, we die or go mad with a degraded sort of terror. Which is what happened to Swift. He was such a great wit. And the modern mind altogether is falling into this form of degraded taboo-insanity. I call it a waste of sane human consciousness. But it is very dangerous, dangerous to the individual and utterly dangerous to society as a whole. Nothing is so fearful in a mass-civilisation like ours as a mass-insanity.

The remedy is, of course, the same in both cases: lift off the taboo. The kangaroo is a harmless animal, the word shit is a harmless word. Make either into a taboo, and it becomes most dangerous. The result of taboo is insanity. And insanity, especially mob-insanity, mass-insanity, is the fearful danger that threatens our civilisation. There are certain persons with a sort of rabies, who live only to infect the mass. If the young do not watch out, they will find themselves, before so very many years are past, engulfed in a howling manifesta-tion of mob-insanity, truly terrifying to think of. It will be better to be dead than to live to see it. Sanity, wholeness, is everything. In the name of piety and purity, what a mass of disgusting insanity is spoken and written. We shall have to fight the mob, in order to keep sane, and to keep society sane.

D. H. L.

BANDOL,
January 1929

FOREWORD

T H E S E poems are called *Pansies* because they are rather *Pensées* than anything else. Pascal or La Bruyère wrote their *Pensées* in prose, but it has always seemed to me that a real thought, a single thought, not an argument, can only exist easily in verse, or in some poetic form. There is a didactic element about prose thoughts which makes them repellent, slightly bullying. "He who hath wife and children hath given hostages to fortune." There is a thought well put; but immediately it irritates by its assertiveness. It applies too direct to actual practical life. If it were put into poetry it wouldn't nag at us so practically. We don't want to be nagged at.

So I should wish these *Pansies* to be taken as thoughts rather than anything else; casual thoughts that are true while they are true and irrelevant when the mood and circumstance changes. I should like them to be as fleeting as pansies, which wilt so soon, and are so fascinating with their varied faces, while they last. And flowers, to my thinking, are not merely pretty-pretty. They have in their fragrance an earthiness of the humus and the corruptive earth from which they spring. And pansies, in their streaked faces, have a look of many things besides heartsease.

Some of the poems are perforce omitted—about a dozen from the bunch. When Scotland Yard seized the MS. in the post, at the order of the Home Secretary, no doubt there was a rush of detectives, postmen, and Home Office clerks and heads, to pick out the most lurid blossoms. They must have been very disappointed. When I now read down the list of the omitted poems, and recall the dozen amusing, not terribly important bits of pansies which have had to stay out of print for fear a policeman might put his foot on them, I can only grin once more to think of the nanny-goat, nanny-goat-in-a-white-petticoat silliness of it all. It is like listening to a Mrs Caudle's curtain lecture in the next house, and wondering whether Mrs Caudle is funnier, or Mr Caudle; or whether they aren't both of them merely stale and tedious.

Anyhow I offer a bunch of pansies, not a wreath of *immortelles*. I don't want everlasting flowers, and I don't want to offer them to anybody else. A flower passes, and that perhaps is the best of it. If we can take it in its transience, its breath, its maybe mephistophelian, maybe palely ophelian face, the look it gives, the gesture of its full bloom, and the way it turns upon us to depart—that was the flower, we have had it, and no *immortelle* can give us anything in comparison. The same with the pansy poems; merely the breath of the moment, and one eternal moment easily contradicting the next eternal moment. Only don't nail the pansy down. You won't keep it any better if you do.

D. H. LAWRENCE

BANDOL,
March 1929

OUR DAY IS OVER

Our day is over, night comes up
shadows steal out of the earth.
Shadows, shadows
wash over our knees and splash between our thighs,
our day is done;
we wade, we wade, we stagger, darkness rushes
    between our stones,
we shall drown.

Our day is over
night comes up.

HARK IN THE DUSK!

Hark! in the dusk
voices, gurgling like water
wreathe strong weed round the knees, as the darkness
lifts us off our feet.

As the current
thrusts warm through the loins, so the little one
wildly floats, swirls,
and the flood strikes the belly, and we are gone.

ELEPHANTS IN THE CIRCUS

Elephants in the circus
have æons of weariness round their eyes.
Yet they sit up
and show vast bellies to the children.

ELEPHANTS PLODDING

Plod! Plod!
And what ages of time
the worn arches of their spines support!

ON THE DRUM

The huge old female on the drum
shuffles gingerly round
and smiles; the vastness of her elephant antiquity
is amused.

TWO PERFORMING ELEPHANTS

He stands with his forefeet on the drum
and the other, the old one, the pallid hoary female
must creep her great bulk beneath the bridge of him.

On her knees, in utmost caution
all agog, and curling up her trunk
she edges through without upsetting him.
Triumph! the ancient, pig-tailed monster!

When her trick is to climb over him
with what shadow-like slow carefulness
she skims him, sensitive
as shadows from the ages gone and perished
in touching him, and planting her round feet.

While the wispy, modern children, half-afraid
watch silent. The looming of the hoary, far-gone ages
is too much for them.

TWILIGHT

Twilight
thick underdusk
and a hidden voice like water clucking
callously continuous.
While darkness submerges the stones
and splashes warm between the buttocks.

CUPS

Cups, let them be dark
like globules of night about to plash.
I want to drink out of dark cups that drip down on
      their feet.

BOWLS

Take away all this crystal and silver
and give me soft-skinned wood
that lives erect through long nights, physically
to put to my lips.

YOU

You, you don't know me.
When have your knees ever nipped me
like fire-tongs a live coal
for a minute?

AFTER DARK

Can you, after dark, become a darkie?
Could one, at night, run up against the standing flesh
    of you
with a shock, as against the blackness of a negro,
and catch flesh like the night in one's arms.

TO LET GO OR TO HOLD ON——?

Shall we let go,
and allow the soul to find its level
downwards, ebbing downwards, ebbing downwards to the
    flood?
till the head floats tilted like a bottle forward tilted
on the sea, with no message in it; and the body is submerged
heavy and swaying like a whale recovering
from wounds, below the deep black wave?
like a whale recovering its velocity and strength
under the cold black wave.

Or else, or else
shall a man brace himself up
and lift his face and set his breast
and go forth to change the world?
gather his will and his energy together
and fling himself in effort after effort
upon the world, to bring a change to pass?

Tell me first, O tell me,
will the dark flood of our day's annihilation
swim deeper, deeper, till it leaves no peak emerging?
Shall we be lost, all of us
and gone like weed, like weed, like eggs of fishes,
like sperm of whales, like germs of the great dead past
into which the creative future shall blow strange, unknown
    forms?

Are we nothing, already, but the lapsing of a great dead
    past?
Is the best that we are but sperm, loose sperm, like the
    sperm of fishes
that drifts upon time and chaos, till some unknown future
    takes it up
and is fecund with a new Day of new creatures? different
    from us.

Or is our shattered Argosy, our leaking ark
at this moment scraping tardy Ararat?
Have we got to get down and clear away the debris
of a swamped civilisation, and start a new world for man
that will blossom forth the whole of human nature?

Must we hold on, hold on
and go ahead with what is human nature
and make a new job of the human world?

Or can we let it go?
O, can we let it go,
and leave it to some nature that is more than human
to use the sperm of what's worth while in us
and thus eliminate us?
Is the time come for humans
now to begin to disappear,
leaving it to the vast revolutions of creative chaos
to bring forth creatures that are an improvement on
    humans,
as the horse was an improvement on the ichthyosaurus?

Must we hold on?
Or can we now let go?

Or is it even possible we must do both?

DESTINY

O destiny, destiny,
do you exist, and can a man touch your hand?

O destiny
if I could see your hand, and it were thumbs down,
I would be willing to give way, like the pterodactyl,
and accept obliteration.
I would not even ask to leave a fossil claw extant,
nor a thumb-mark like a clue,
I would be willing to vanish completely, completely.

But if it is thumbs up, and mankind must go on being man-
    kind,
then I am willing to fight, I will roll my sleeves up
and start in.

Only, O destiny
I wish you'd show your hand.

HOW BEASTLY THE BOURGEOIS IS

How beastly the bourgeois is
especially the male of the species—

Presentable, eminently presentable—
shall I make you a present of him?

Isn't he handsome? Isn't he healthy? Isn't he a fine
    specimen?
Doesn't he look the fresh clean Englishman, outside?
Isn't it God's own image? tramping his thirty miles a day
after partridges, or a little rubber ball?
wouldn't you like to be like that, well off, and quite the
    thing?

Oh, but wait!
Let him meet a new emotion, let him be faced with another
    man's need,
let him come home to a bit of moral difficulty, let life face
    him with a new demand on his understanding
and then watch him go soggy, like a wet meringue.
Watch him turn into a mess, either a fool or a bully.
Just watch the display of him, confronted with a new
    demand on his intelligence,
a new life-demand.

How beastly the bourgeois is
especially the male of the species—

Nicely groomed, like a mushroom
standing there so sleek and erect and eyeable—
and like a fungus, living on the remains of bygone life
sucking his life out of the dead leaves of greater life than
    his own.

And even so, he's stale, he's been there too long.
Touch him, and you'll find he's all gone inside
just like an old mushroom, all wormy inside, and hollow
under a smooth skin and an upright appearance.

Full of seething, wormy, hollow feelings
rather nasty—
How beastly the bourgeois is!

Standing in their thousands, these appearances, in damp
    England
what a pity they can't all be kicked over
like sickening toadstools, and left to melt back, swiftly
into the soil of England.

WORM EITHER WAY

If you live along with all the other people
and are just like them, and conform, and are nice
you're just a worm—

and if you live with all the other people
and you don't like them and won't be like them and won't
    conform
then you're just the worm that has turned,
in either case, a worm.

The conforming worm stays just inside the skin
respectably unseen, and cheerfully gnaws away at the
    heart of life,
making it all rotten inside.

The unconforming worm—that is, the worm that has
    turned—
gnaws just the same, gnawing the substance out of life,
but he insists on gnawing a little hole in the social
    epidermis
and poking his head out and waving himself
and saying: Look at me, I am *not* respectable,
I do all the things the bourgeois daren't do,
I booze and fornicate and use foul language and despise
    your honest man.—

But why should the worm that has turned protest so
    much?
The bonnie, bonnie bourgeois goes a-whoring up back
    streets
just the same.
The busy, busy bourgeois imbibes his little share
just the same
if not more.
The pretty, pretty bourgeois pinks his language just as pink
if not pinker,
and in private boasts his exploits even louder, if you ask
    me,
than the other.
While as to honesty, Oh, look where the money lies!

So I can't see where the worm that has turned puts any-
    thing over
the worm that is too cunning to turn.

On the contrary, he merely gives himself away.
The turned worm shouts: I bravely booze!
The other says: What? Cat-piss?
The turned worm boasts: I copulate!
the unturned says: You look it.
You're a d—— b—— b—— p—— bb——, says the worm
    that's turned.
Quite! says the other. Cuckoo!

NATURAL COMPLEXION

But, you see, said the handsome young man with the
    chamois gloves
to the woman rather older than himself,
if you don't use rouge and a lip-stick, in Paris
they'll take you for a woman of the people.

So spoke the British gentleman
pulling on his chamois gloves
and using his most melodious would-be-oxford voice.

And the woman said: Dear me!
how rough that would be on you, darling!
Only, if you insist on pulling on those chamois gloves
I swear I'll pull off my knickers, right in the *Rue de la Paix*.

THE OXFORD VOICE

When you hear it languishing
and hooing and cooing and sidling through the front teeth,
        the Oxford voice
            or worse still
        the would-be Oxford voice
you don't even laugh any more, you can't.

For every blooming bird is an Oxford cuckoo nowadays,
you can't sit on a bus nor in the tube
but it breathes gently and languishingly in the back of your
    neck.

And oh, so seductively superior, so seductively
        self-effacingly
        deprecatingly
           superior.—

We wouldn't insist on it for a moment
        but we are
         we are
        you admit we are
           superior.——

TRUE DEMOCRACY

I wish I was a gentleman
as full of wet as a watering-can
to pee in the eye of a police-man—

But my dear fellow, my dear fellow
can it be that you still don't know
that every man, whether high or low
is a gentleman if he thinks himself so?

He is an' all, you bet 'e is!
I bet I am.—You can 'old yer phiz
abaht it.—Yes, I'm a gent, an' Liz
'ere, she's a lidy, aren't yer, old quizz?

Of course I'm a lidy, what d'yer think?
You mind who yer sayin' isn't lidies!
All the Hinglish is gentlemen an' lidies,
like the King an' Queen, though they're
    up just a wink.

—Of course you are, but let me say
I'm American, from New Orleans,
and in my country, just over the way,
we are *all* kings and queens!

TO BE SUPERIOR

How nice it is to be superior!
Because really, it's no use pretending, one *is* superior,
    isn't one?
I mean people like you and me.

Quite! I quite agree.
The trouble is, everybody thinks they're just as superior
as we are; just as superior.

That's what's so boring! people are so boring.
But they can't really think it, do you think?
At the bottom, they must *know* we are really superior
don't you think?
Don't you think, *really*, they *know* we're their
    superiors?

I couldn't say.
I've never got to the bottom of superiority.
I should like to.

SWAN

Far-off
at the core of space
at the quick
of time
beats
and goes still
the great swan upon the waters of all endings
the swan within vast chaos, within the electron.

For us
no longer he swims calmly
nor clacks across the forces furrowing a great gay trail
of happy energy,
nor is he nesting passive upon the atoms,
nor flying north desolative icewards
to the sleep of ice,
nor feeding in the marshes,
nor honking horn-like into the twilight.

But he stoops, now
in the dark
upon us;
he is treading our women
and we men are put out
as the vast white bird
furrows our featherless women
with unknown shocks
and stamps his black marsh-feet on their white and
marshy flesh.

LEDA

Come not with kisses
not with caresses
of hands and lips and murmurings;
come with a hiss of wings
and sea-touch tip of a beak
and treading of wet, webbed, wave-working feet
into the marsh-soft belly.

GIVE US GODS

Give us gods, Oh give them us!
Give us gods.
We are so tired of men
and motor-power.—

But not gods grey-bearded and dictatorial,
nor yet that pale young man afraid of fatherhood
shelving substance on to the woman, Madonna mia!
    shabby virgin!
nor gusty Jove, with his eye on immortal tarts,
nor even the musical, suave young fellow
wooing boys and beauty.

Give us gods
give us something else—

Beyond the great bull that bellowed through space, and
    got his throat cut.
Beyond even that eagle, that phœnix, hanging over the
    gold egg of all things,
further still, before the curled horns of the ram stepped
    forth
or the stout swart beetle rolled the globe of dung in which
    man should hatch,
or even the sly gold serpent fatherly lifted his head off
    the earth to think—

Give us gods before these—
Thou shalt have other gods before these.

Where the waters end in marshes
swims the wild swan
sweeps the high goose above the mists
honking in the gloom the honk of procreation from such
    throats.

Mists
where the electron behaves and misbehaves as it will,
where the forces tie themselves up into knots of atoms
and come untied;

Mists
of mistiness complicated into knots and clots that barge
    about
and bump on one another and explode into more mist,
    or don't,

mist of energy most scientific—
But give us gods!

Look then
where the father of all things swims in a mist of atoms
electrons and energies, quantums and relativities
mists, wreathing mists,
like a wild swan, or a goose, whose honk goes through my
    bladder.

And in the dark unscientific I feel the drum-winds of his
    wings
and the drip of his cold, webbed feet, mud-black
brush over my face as he goes
to seek the women in the dark, our women, our weird
    women whom he treads
with dreams and thrusts that make them cry in their sleep.

Gods, do you ask for gods?
Where there is woman there is swan.

Do you think, scientific man, you'll be father of your own
    babies?
Don't imagine it.
There'll be babies born that are cygnets, O my soul!
young wild swans!
And babies of women will come out young wild geese,
    O my heart!
the geese that saved Rome, and will lose London.

WON'T IT BE STRANGE——?

Won't it be strange, when the nurse brings the new-born
    infant
to the proud father, and shows its little, webbed greenish
    feet
made to smite the waters behind it?
or the round, wild vivid eye of a wild-goose staring
out of fathomless skies and seas?

or when it utters that undaunted little bird-cry
of one who will settle on ice-bergs, and honk across the
    Nile?

And when the father says: This is none of mine!
Woman, where got you this little beast?
will there be a whistle of wings in the air, and an icy
    draught?
will the singing of swans, high up, high up, invisible
break the drums of his ears
and leave him forever listening for the answer?

SPIRAL FLAME

There have been so many gods
that now there are none.
When the One God made a monopoly of it
He wore us out, so now we are godless and unbelieving.

Yet, O my young men, there is a vivifier.
There is that which makes us eager.
While we are eager, we think nothing of it.
Sum, ergo non cogito.
But when our eagerness leaves us, we are godless and full
    of thought.

We have worn out the gods, and they us.
That pale one, filled with renunciation and pain and white
    love
has worn us weary of renunciation and love and even pain.
That strong one, ruling the universe with a rod of iron
has sickened us thoroughly with rods of iron and rulers
    and strong men.
The All-wise has tired us of wisdom.
The weeping mother of god, inconsolable over her son
makes us prefer to be womanless, rather than be wept over.
And that poor late makeshift, Aphrodite emerging in a
    bathing-suit from our modern sea-side foam
has successfully killed all desire in us whatsoever.

Yet, O my young men, there is a vivifier.
There is a swan-like flame that curls round the centre of
    space
and flutters at the core of the atom,
there is a spiral flame-tip that can lick our little atoms into
    fusion
so we roar up like bonfires of vitality
and fuse in a broad hard flame of many men in a oneness.

O pillars of flame by night, O my young men
spinning and dancing like flamey fire-spouts in the dark
    ahead of the multitude!
O ruddy god in our veins, O fiery god in our genitals!
O rippling hard fire of courage, O fusing of hot trust
when the fire reaches us, O my young men!

And the same flame that fills us with life, it will dance and
    burn the house down,
all the fittings and elaborate furnishings
and all the people that go with the fittings and the
    furnishings,
the upholstered dead that sit in deep arm-chairs.

LET THE DEAD BURY THEIR DEAD

Let the dead go bury their dead
don't help them.
Let the dead look after the dead
leave them to one another,
don't serve them.

The dead in their nasty dead hands
have heaps of money,
don't take it.

The dead in their seething minds
have phosphorescent teeming white words
of putrescent wisdom and sapience that subtly stinks;
don't ever believe them.

The dead are in myriads, they seem mighty.
They make trains chuff, motor-cars titter, ships lurch,
mills grind on and on,
and keep you in millions at the mills, sightless pale slaves,
pretending these are the mills of God.

It is the great lie of the dead.
The mills of industry are not the mills of God.
And the mills of God grind otherwise, with the winds of
    life for the mill-stones.
Trust the mills of God, though they grind exceeding small.
But as for the mills of men
don't be harnessed to them.

The dead give ships and engines, cinema, radio and gramo-
    phone,
they send aeroplanes across the sky,
and they say: Now, behold, you are living the great life!
While you listen in, while you watch the film, while you
    drive the car,
while you read about the air-ship crossing the wild Atlantic
behold, you are living the great life, the stupendous life!

As you know, it is a complete lie.
You are all going dead and corpse-pale
listening in to the lie.
Spit it out.

O cease to listen to the living dead.
They are only greedy for your life!
O cease to labour for the gold-toothed dead,
they are so greedy, yet so helpless if not worked for.
Don't ever be kind to the smiling, tooth-mouthed dead
don't ever be kind to the dead
it is pandering to corpses,
the repulsive, living fat dead.

Bury a man gently if he has lain down and died.
But with the walking and talking and conventionally per-
   suasive dead
with bank accounts and insurance policies
don't sympathise, or you taint the unborn babies.

WHEN WILT THOU TEACH
THE PEOPLE——?

When wilt thou teach the people,
God of justice, to save themselves——?
They have been saved so often
and sold.

O God of justice, send no more saviours
of the people!

When a saviour has saved a people
they find he has sold them to his father.
They say: We are saved, but we are starving.
He says: The sooner will you eat imaginary cake in the
   mansions of my father.
They say: Can't we have a loaf of common bread?
He says: No, you must go to heaven, and eat the most
   marvellous cake.

Or Napoleon says: Since I have saved you from the ci-
   devants,
you are my property, be prepared to die for me, and to
   work for me.

Or later republicans say: You are saved,
therefore you are our savings, our capital
with which we shall do big business.

Or Lenin says: You are saved, but you are saved wholesale.
You are no longer men, that is bourgeois;
you are items in the soviet state,
and each item will get its ration,
but it is the soviet state alone which counts
the items are of small importance,
the state having saved them all.

And so it goes on, with the saving of the people.
God of justice, when wilt thou teach them to save them-
     selves?

A LIVING

A man should never earn his living,
if he earns his life he'll be lovely.

A bird
picks up its seeds or little snails
between heedless earth and heaven
in heedlessness.

But, the plucky little sport, it gives to life
 song, and chirruping, gay feathers, fluff-shadowed
     warmth
and all the unspeakable charm of birds hopping
     and fluttering and being birds.
—And we, we get it all from them for nothing.

WHEN I WENT TO THE FILM

When I went to the film, and saw all the black-and-white
     feelings that nobody felt,
and heard the audience sighing and sobbing with all the
     emotions they none of them felt,
and saw them cuddling with rising passions they none of
     them for a moment felt,

and caught them moaning from close-up kisses, black-and-
    white kisses that could not be felt,
It was like being in heaven, which I am sure has a white
    atmosphere
upon which shadows of people, pure personalities
are cast in black and white, and move
in flat ecstasy, supremely unfelt,
and heavenly.

WHEN I WENT TO THE CIRCUS

When I went to the circus that had pitched on the waste
    lot
it was full of uneasy people
frightened of the bare earth and the temporary canvas
and the smell of horses and other beasts
instead of merely the smell of man.

Monkeys rode rather grey and wizened
on curly plump piebald ponies
and the children uttered a little cry—
and dogs jumped through hoops and turned somersaults
and then the geese scuttled in in a little flock
and round the ring they went to the sound of the whip
then doubled, and back, with a funny up-flutter of wings—
and the children suddenly shouted out.

Then came the hush again, like a hush of fear.

The tight-rope lady, pink and blonde and nude-looking,
    with a few gold spangles
footed cautiously out on the rope, turned prettily, spun
    round
bowed, and lifted her foot in her hand, smiled, swung her
    parasol
to another balance, tripped round, poised, and slowly sank
her handsome thighs down, down, till she slept her
    splendid body on the rope.

When she rose, tilting her parasol, and smiled at the
        cautious people
they cheered, but nervously.

The trapeze man, slim and beautiful and like a fish in the
        air
swung great curves through the upper space, and came
        down like a star
—And the people applauded, with hollow, frightened
        applause.

The elephants, huge and grey, loomed their curved bulk
        through the dusk
and sat up, taking strange postures, showing the pink soles
        of their feet
and curling their precious live trunks like ammonites
and moving always with soft slow precision
as when a great ship moves to anchor.
The people watched and wondered, and seemed to resent
        the mystery that lies in beasts.

Horses, gay horses, swirling round and plaiting
in a long line, their heads laid over each other's necks;
they were happy, they enjoyed it;
all the creatures seemed to enjoy the game
in the circus, with their circus people.

But the audience, compelled to wonder
compelled to admire the bright rhythms of moving bodies
compelled to see the delicate skill of flickering human
        bodies
flesh flamey and a little heroic, even in a tumbling clown,
they were not really happy.
There was no gushing response, as there is at the film.

When modern people see the carnal body dauntless and
        flickering gay
playing among the elements neatly, beyond competition
and displaying no personality,
modern people are depressed.

Modern people feel themselves at a disadvantage.
They know they have no bodies that could play among the
    elements.
They have only their personalities, that are best seen flat,
    on the film,
flat personalities in two dimensions, imponderable and
    touchless.

And they grudge the circus people the swooping gay
    weight of limbs
that flower in mere movement,
and they grudge them the immediate, physical understand-
    ing they have with their circus beasts,
and they grudge them their circus-life altogether.

Yet the strange, almost frightened shout of delight that
    comes now and then from the children
shows that the children vaguely know how cheated they
    are of their birthright
in the bright wild circus flesh.

THE NOBLE ENGLISHMAN

I know a noble Englishman
who is sure he is a gentleman,
that sort—

This moderately young gentleman
is very normal, as becomes an Englishman,
rather proud of being a bit of a Don Juan
you know—

But one of his beloveds, looking a little peaked
towards the end of her particular affair with him
said: Ronald, you know, is like most Englishmen,
by instinct he's a sodomist
but he's frightened to know it
so he takes it out on women.

Oh come! said I. That Don Juan of a Ronald!
Exactly, she said. Don Juan was another of them, in love
    with himself
and taking it out on women.

Even that isn't sodomitical, said I
But if a man is in love with himself, isn't that the meanest
    form of homosexuality? she said.

You've no idea, when men are in love with themselves,
    how they wreak all their spite on women,
pretending to love them.
Ronald, she resumed, doesn't like women, just acutely
    dislikes them.
He might possibly like men, if he weren't too frightened
    and egoistic.
So he very cleverly tortures women, with his sort of love.
He's instinctively frightfully clever.
He can be so gentle, so gentle
so delicate in his love-making.
Even now, the thought of it bewilders me: such gentleness!
Yet I know he does it deliberately, as cautiously and
    deliberately as when he shaves himself.
Then more than that, he makes a woman feel he is *serving*
    her
really living in her service, and serving her
as no man ever served before.

And then, suddenly, when she's feeling all lovely about it
suddenly the ground goes from under her feet, and she
    clutches in mid-air,
but horrible, as if your heart would wrench out;
while he stands aside watching with a superior little grin
like some malicious indecent little boy.
—No, don't talk to me about the love of Englishmen!

THINGS MEN HAVE MADE

Things men have made with wakened hands, and put soft
    life into
are awake through years with transferred touch, and go
    on glowing
for long years.
And for this reason, some old things are lovely
warm still with the life of forgotten men who made them.

THINGS MADE BY IRON

Things made by iron and handled by steel
are born dead, they are shrouds, they soak life out of us.
Till after a long time, when they are old and have steeped
    in our life
they begin to be soothed and soothing; then we throw
    them away.

NEW HOUSES, NEW CLOTHES

New houses, new furniture, new streets, new clothes, new
    sheets
everything new and machine-made sucks life out of us
and makes us cold, makes us lifeless
the more we have.

WHATEVER MAN MAKES

Whatever man makes and makes it live
lives because of the life put into it.
A yard of India muslin is alive with Hindu life.
And a Navajo woman, weaving her rug in the pattern of
    her dream
must run the pattern out in a little break at the end
so that her soul can come out, back to her.

But in the odd pattern, like snake-marks on the sand
it leaves its trail.

WE ARE TRANSMITTERS

As we live, we are transmitters of life.
And when we fail to transmit life, life fails to flow
through us.

That is part of the mystery of sex, it is a flow onwards.
Sexless people transmit nothing.

And if, as we work, we can transmit life into our work,
life, still more life, rushes into us to compensate, to be
ready
and we ripple with life through the days.

Even if it is a woman making an apple dumpling, or a man
a stool,
if life goes into the pudding, good is the pudding
good is the stool,
content is the woman, with fresh life rippling in to her,
content is the man.

Give, and it shall be given unto you
is still the truth about life.
But giving life is not so easy.
It doesn't mean handing it out to some mean fool, or
letting the living dead eat you up.
It means kindling the life-quality where it was not,
even if it's only in the whiteness of a washed pocket-
handkerchief.

ALL THAT WE HAVE IS LIFE

All that we have, while we live, is life;
and if you don't live during your life, you are a piece of
dung.

And work is life, and life is lived in work
unless you're a wage-slave.
While a wage-slave works, he leaves life aside
and stands there a piece of dung.

Men should refuse to be lifelessly at work.
Men should refuse to be heaps of wage-earning dung.
Men should refuse to work at all, as wage-slaves.
Men should demand to work for themselves, of themselves,
    and put their life in it.
For if a man has no life in his work, he is mostly a heap
    of dung.

LET US BE MEN

For God's sake, let us be men
not monkeys minding machines
or sitting with our tails curled
while the machine amuses us, the radio or film or
    gramophone.

Monkeys with a bland grin on our faces.

WORK

There is no point in work
unless it absorbs you
like an absorbing game.

If it doesn't absorb you
if it's never any fun,
don't do it.

When a man goes out into his work
he is alive like a tree in spring,
he is living, not merely working.

450

When the Hindus weave thin wool into long, long lengths
of stuff
with their thin dark hands and their wide dark eyes and
their still souls absorbed
they are like slender trees putting forth leaves, a long white
web of living leaf,
the tissue they weave,
and they clothe themselves in white as a tree clothes itself
in its own foliage.

As with cloth, so with houses, ships, shoes, wagons or cups
or loaves
men might put them forth as a snail its shell, as a bird that
leans
its breast against its nest, to make it round,
as the turnip models his round root, as the bush makes
flowers and gooseberries,
putting them forth, not manufacturing them,
and cities might be as once they were, bowers grown out
from the busy bodies of people.

And so it will be again, men will smash the machines.

At last, for the sake of clothing himself in his own leaf-
like cloth
tissued from his life,
and dwelling in his own bowery house, like a beaver's
nibbled mansion
and drinking from cups that came off his fingers like
flowers off their five-fold stem,
he will cancel the machines we have got.

W H Y ——?

Why have money?
why have a financial system to strangle us all in its
octopus arms?
why have industry?

why have the industrial system?
why have machines, that we only have to serve?
why have a soviet, that only wants to screw us all in as
    parts of the machine?
why have working classes at all, as if men were only
    embodied jobs?
why not have men as men, and the work as merely part
    of the game of life?

True, we've got all these things
industrial and financial systems, machines and soviets,
    working classes.
But why go on having them, if they belittle us?
Why should we be belittled any longer?

WHAT IS HE?

What is he?
—A man, of course.
Yes, but what does he do?
—He lives and is a man.
Oh quite! but he must work. He must have a job of some
    sort.
—Why?
Because obviously he's not one of the leisured classes.
—I don't know. He has lots of leisure. And he makes
    quite beautiful chairs.—
There you are then! He's a cabinet maker.
—No no!
Anyhow a carpenter and joiner.
—Not at all.
But you said so.
—What did I say?
That he made chairs, and was a joiner and carpenter.
—I said he made chairs, but I did not say he was a
    carpenter.
All right then, he's just an amateur.

—Perhaps! Would you say a thrush was a professional
    flautist, or just an amateur?—
I'd say it was just a bird.
—And I say he is just a man.
All right! You always did quibble.

O! START A REVOLUTION

O! start a revolution, somebody!
not to get the money
but to lose it all for ever.

O! start a revolution, somebody!
not to install the working classes
but to abolish the working classes for ever
and have a world of men.

MOON MEMORY

When the moon falls on a man's blood
white and slippery, as on the black water in a port
shaking asunder, and flicking at his ribs—

then the noisy, dirty day-world
exists no more, nor ever truly existed;
but instead
this wet white gleam
twitches, and ebbs hitting, washing inwardly, silverily
    against his ribs
on his soul that is dark ocean within him.

And under the flicking of the white whip-lash of the
    moon
sea-beasts immersed lean sideways and flash bright
in pure brilliance of anger, sea-immersed anger
at the trashy, motor-driven transit of dirty day
that has left scum on the sea, even in the night.

THERE IS RAIN IN ME

There is rain in me
running down, running down, trickling
away from memory.

There is ocean in me
swaying, swaying O, so deep
so fathomlessly black
and spurting suddenly up, snow-white, like snow-leopards
    rearing
high and clawing with rage at the cliffs of the soul
then disappearing back with a hiss
of eternal salt rage; angry is old ocean within a man.

DESIRE GOES DOWN INTO THE SEA

I have no desire any more
towards woman or man, bird, beast or creature or thing.

All day long I feel the tide rocking, rocking
though it strikes no shore
in me.

Only mid-ocean.—

THE SEA, THE SEA

The sea dissolves so much
and the moon makes away with so much
    more than we know—

Once the moon comes down
and the sea gets hold of us
cities dissolve like rock-salt
and the sugar melts out of life
iron washes away like an old blood-stain
gold goes out into a green shadow
money makes even no sediment
and only the heart
glitters in salty triumph
over all it has known, that has gone now
    into salty nothingness.

NOVEMBER BY THE SEA

Now in November nearer comes the sun
down the abandoned heaven.

As the dark closes round him, he draws nearer
as if for our company.

At the base of the lower brain
the sun in me declines to his winter solstice
and darts a few gold rays
back to the old year's sun across the sea.

A few gold rays thickening down to red
as the sun of my soul is setting
setting fierce and undaunted, wintry
but setting, setting behind the sounding sea between
    my ribs.

The wide sea wins, and the dark
winter, and the great day-sun, and the sun in my soul
sinks, sinks to setting and the winter solstice
downward, they race in decline
my sun, and the great gold sun.

OLD SONG

The day is ending, the night descending,
the heart is frozen, the spirit dead;
but the moon is wending her way, attending
to other things that are left unsaid.

GOOD HUSBANDS MAKE
UNHAPPY WIVES

Good husbands make unhappy wives
so do bad husbands, just as often;
but the unhappiness of a wife with a good husband
is much more devastating
than the unhappiness of a wife with a bad husband.

FIGHT! O MY YOUNG MEN

Fight! don't you feel you're fading
into slow death?
Fight then, poor duffers degrading
your very breath.

Open your half-dead eyes
you half-alive young,
look round and realise
the muck from which you've sprung.

The money-muck, you simple flowers
of your forefathers' muck-heap;
and the money-muck-worms, the extant powers
that have got you in keep.

Old money-worms, young money-worms
money-worm professors
spinning a glamour round money, and clergymen
lifting a bank-book to bless us!

In the odour of lucrative sanctity
stand they—and god, how they stink!
Rise then, my young men, rise at them!
Or if you can't rise, just think—

Think of the world that you're stifling in,
think what a world it might be!
Think of the rubbish you're trifling in
with enfeebled vitality!

And then, if you amount to a hill o' beans
start in and bust it all;
money, hypocrisy, greed, machines
that have ground you so small.

WOMEN WANT FIGHTERS FOR THEIR LOVERS

Women don't want wistful
mushy, pathetic young men
struggling in doubtful embraces
then trying again.

Mushy and treacherous, tiny
Peterlets, Georgelets, Hamlets,
Tomlets, Dicklets, Harrylets, whiney
Jimlets and self-sorry Samlets.

Women are sick of consoling
inconsolable youth, dead-beat;
pouring comfort and condoling
down the sink of the male conceit.

Women want fighters, fighters
and the fighting cock.
Can't you give it them, blighters!

The fighting cock, the fighting cock—
have you got one, little blighters?
Let it crow then, like one o'clock!

457

IT'S EITHER YOU FIGHT OR YOU DIE

It's either you fight or you die,
young gents, you've got no option.
No good asking the reason why
it's either you fight or you die,
die, die, lily-liveredly die
or fight and make the splinters fly
bust up the holy apple-pie
you've got no option.

Don't say you can't, start in and try;
give great hypocrisy the lie
and tackle the blowsy big blow-fly
of money; do it or die!
you've got no option.

DON'TS

Fight your little fight, my boy,
fight and be a man.
Don't be a good little, good little boy
being as good as you can
and agreeing with all the mealy-mouthed, mealy-mouthed
truths that the sly trot out
to protect themselves and their greedy-mouthed, greedy-
    mouthed
cowardice, every old lout.

Don't live up to the dear little girl who costs
you your manhood, and makes you pay.
Nor the dear old mater who so proudly boasts
that you'll make your way.

Don't earn golden opinions, opinions golden,
or at least worth Treasury notes,
from all sorts of men; don't be beholden
to the herd inside the pen.

Don't long to have dear little, dear little boys
whom you'll have to educate
to earn their livings; nor yet girls, sweet joys
who will find it so hard to mate.

Nor a dear little home, with its cost, its cost
that you have to pay,
earning your living while your life is lost
and dull death comes in a day.

Don't be sucked in by the su-superior,
don't swallow the culture bait,
don't drink, don't drink and get beerier and beerier,
do learn to discriminate.

Do hold yourself together, and fight
with a hit-hit here and a hit-hit there,
and a comfortable feeling at night
that you've let in a little air.

A little fresh air in the money sty,
knocked a little hole in the holy prison,
done your own little bit, made your own little try
that the risen Christ should *be* risen.

THE RISEN LORD

The risen lord, the risen lord
has risen in the flesh,
and treads the earth to feel the soil
though his feet are still nesh.

The risen lord, the risen lord
has opened his eyes afresh,
and sees strange looks on the faces of men
all held in leash.

And he says: I never have seen them before,
these people of flesh;
these are no spirits caught and sore
in the physical mesh.

They are substance itself, that flows in thick
flame of flesh forever travelling
like the flame of a candle, slow and quick
fluttering and softly unravelling.

It moves, it ripples, and all the time
it changes, and with it change
moods, thoughts, desires, and deeds that chime
with the rippling fleshly change.

I never saw them, how they must soften
themselves with oil, and lard
their guts with a certain fat, and often
laugh, and laugh hard.

If they didn't, if they did not soften
themselves with oil, and lard
their guts with a certain fat, and often
laugh, and laugh hard

they would not be men, and they must be men,
they are their own flesh.—I lay
in the tomb and was not; I have risen again
to look the other way.

Lo! I am flesh, and the blood that races
is me in the narrows of my wrists.
Lo, I see fear in the twisted faces
of men, they clench fear in their fists!

Lo! on the other side the grave
I have conquered the fear of death,
but the fear of life is still here; I am brave
yet I fear my own breath.

Now I must conquer the fear of life,
the knock of the blood in my wrists,
the breath that rushes through my nose, the strife
of desires in the loins' dark twists.

What do you want, wild loins? and what
do you want, warm heart? and what
wide eyes and wondering spirit?—not
death, no not death for your lot!

They ask, and they must be answered; they
are, and they shall, to the end.
Lo! there is woman, and her way is a strange way,
I must follow also her trend.

I died, and death is neuter; it speaks not, it gives
no answer; man rises again
with mouth and loins and needs, he lives
again man among men.

So it is, so it will be, for ever and ever.
And still the great needs of men
will clamour forth from the flesh, and never
can denial deny them again.

THE SECRET WATERS

What was lost is found
what was wounded is sound,
The key of life on the bodies of men
unlocks the fountains of peace again.

The fountains of peace, the fountains of peace
well softly up for a new increase,
but they bubble under the heavy wall
of this house of life that encloses us all.

They bubble under the heavy wall
that was once a house, and is now a prison,
and never a one among us all
knows that the waters have risen.

None of us knows, O none of us knows
the welling of peace when it rises and flows
in secret under the sickening wall
of the prison house that encloses us all.

And we shall not know, we shall not know
till the secret waters overflow
and loosen the brick and the hard cement
of the walls within which our lives are spent.

Till the walls begin to loosen and crack,
to gape, and our house is going to wrack
and ruin above us, and the crash of release
is death to us all, in the marshes of peace.

BEWARE, O MY DEAR YOUNG MEN

Beware, O my dear young men, of going rotten.
        It's so easy to follow suit;
people in their thirties, and the older ones, have gotten
        bad inside, like fruit
that nobody eats and nobody wants, so it rots, but is not
        forgotten.

Rotten inside, they are, and seething
        with small obscenities;
and they whisper it out, and they titter it out, breathing
        among soft amenities,
a vapour of rottenness out of their mouths, like sewer-
        stench wreathing.

And it's funny, my dear young men, that you in your
        twenties
        should love the sewer scent
of obscenity, and lift your noses where the vent is
        and run towards it, bent
on smelling it all, before your bit of vitality spent is.

For obscenity, after all, my dear young men
        is only mental dirt,
the dirty mind like a urinal again
        or a dung squirt;
and I thought you wanted life and experience, dear young
        men!

All this obscenity is just mental, mental, mental,
        it's the village-idiot mind
playing with muck; and I thought you young gents
        experimental
        were out to find
new life for yourselves and your women, complemental.

But if obscene village idiots you want to be, then be it.
        But don't imagine you'll get
satisfactory experience from it; can't you see it?
        the idiot with his chin all wet
goggling obscenities! If that's you and your fate, why then,
        dree it.

OBSCENITY

The body of itself is clean, but the caged mind
is a sewer inside, it pollutes, O it pollutes
the guts and the stones and the womb, rots them down,
    leaves a rind
of maquillage and pose and malice to shame the brutes.

SEX ISN'T SIN

Sex isn't sin, ah no! sex isn't sin,
nor is it dirty, not until the dirty mind pokes in.

We shall do as we like, sin is obsolete, the young assert.
Sin is obsolete, sin is obsolete, but not so dirt.

And sex, alas, gets dirtier and dirtier, worked from the
    mind.
Sex gets dirtier and dirtier, the more it is fooled with, we
    find.

And dirt, if it isn't sin, is worse, especially dirt inside.
If you're dirty inside you go rotten, and once rotten, woe
    betide!

Sex isn't sin, but dirty sex is worse, so there you are!
Why don't you know what's what, young people? Seems
    to me you're far

duller than your grandmothers. But leave that aside.
Let's be honest at last about sex, or show at least that we've
    tried.

Sex isn't sin, it's a delicate flow between women and men,
and the sin is to damage the flow, force it or dirty it or
    suppress it again.

Sex isn't something you've got to play with; sex is *you*.
It's the flow of your life, it's your moving self, and you
    are due
to be true to the nature of it, its reserve, its sensitive pride
that it always has to begin with, and by which you ought
    to abide.

Know yourself, O know yourself, that you are mortal; and
    know
the sensitive delicacy of your sex, in its ebbing to and fro,
and the mortal reserve of your sex, as it stays in your
    depths below.

And don't, with the nasty, prying mind, drag it out from
    its deeps
and finger it and force it, and shatter the rhythm it keeps
when it's left alone, as it stirs and rouses and sleeps.

O know yourself, O know your sex! You must know, there
    is no escape.
You must know sex in order to save it, your deepest self,
    from the rape
of the itching mind and the mental self, with its pruriency
    always agape.

THE ELEPHANT IS SLOW TO MATE

The elephant, the huge old beast,
        is slow to mate;
he finds a female, they show no haste
        they wait

for the sympathy in their vast shy hearts
        slowly, slowly to rouse
as they loiter along the river-beds
        and drink and browse

and dash in panic through the brake
        of forest with the herd,
and sleep in massive silence, and wake
        together, without a word.

So slowly the great hot elephant hearts
        grow full of desire,
and the great beasts mate in secret at last,
        hiding their fire.

Oldest they are and the wisest of beasts
        so they know at last
how to wait for the loneliest of feasts
        for the full repast.

They do not snatch, they do not tear;
        their massive blood
moves as the moon-tides, near, more near,
        till they touch in flood.

SEX AND TRUST

If you want to have sex, you've got to trust
at the core of your heart, the other creature.
The other creature, the other creature
not merely the personal upstart;
but the creature there, that has come to meet you;
trust it you must, you must
or the experience amounts to nothing,
mere evacuation-lust.

THE GAZELLE CALF

The gazelle calf, O my children,
goes behind its mother across the desert,
goes behind its mother on blithe bare foot
requiring no shoes, O my children!

LITTLE FISH

The tiny fish enjoy themselves
in the sea.
Quick little splinters of life,
their little lives are fun to them
in the sea.

THE MOSQUITO KNOWS

The mosquito knows full well, small as he is
he's a beast of prey.
But after all
he only takes his bellyful,
he doesn't put my blood in the bank.

SELF-PITY

I never saw a wild thing
sorry for itself.
A small bird will drop frozen dead from a bough
without ever having felt sorry for itself.

NEW MOON

The new moon, of no importance
lingers behind as the yellow sun glares and is gone beyond
    the sea's edge;
earth smokes blue;
the new moon, in cool height above the blushes,
brings a fresh fragrance of heaven to our senses.

SPRAY

It is a wonder foam is so beautiful.
A wave bursts in anger on a rock, broken up
in wild white sibilant spray
and falls back, drawing in its breath with rage,
with frustration how beautiful!

SEA-WEED

Sea-weed sways and sways and swirls
as if swaying were its form of stillness;
and if it flushes against fierce rock
it slips over it as shadows do, without hurting itself.

MY ENEMY

If it is a question of him or me
then down with him!

If he is not with me but against me,
if his presence and his breath are poison to me,
then, if he comes near me
down with him.

Down with him
to the pit of annihilation.

But if he stays far from me, and does not touch me,
he is no longer my concern, he ceases to be
my enemy.

TOUCH

Since we have become so cerebral
we can't bear to touch or be touched.

Since we are so cerebral
we are humanly out of touch.

And so we must remain.
For if, cerebrally, we force ourselves into touch,
      into contact
physical and fleshly,
we violate ourselves,
we become vicious.

NOLI ME TANGERE

Noli me tangere, touch me not!
O you creatures of mind, don't touch me!
O you with mental fingers, O never put your hand on me!
O you with mental bodies, stay a little distance from me!

And let us, if you will, talk and mingle
in mental contact, gay and sad.
But only that.
O don't confuse
the body into it, let us stay apart.

Great is my need to be chaste
and apart, in this cerebral age.
Great is my need to be untouched,
untouched.
Noli me tangere!

CHASTITY

Chastity, beloved chastity,
O beloved chastity,
how infinitely dear to me
chastity, beloved chastity!

That my body need not be
fingered by the mind,
or prostituted by the dree
contact of cerebral flesh—

O leave me clean from mental fingering
from the cold copulation of the will,
from all the white, self-conscious lechery
the modern mind calls love!

From all the mental poetry
of deliberate love-making,
from all the false felicity
of deliberately taking

the body of another unto mine,
O God deliver me!
leave me alone, let me be!

Chastity, dearer far to me
than any contact that can be
in this mind-mischievous age!

LET US TALK, LET US LAUGH

Let us talk, let us laugh, let us tell
all kinds of things to one another;
men and women, let us be
gay and amusing together, and free
from airs and from false modesty.

But at the same time, don't let's think
that this quite real intimacy
of talk and thought and me-and-thee
means anything further and physical.

Nay, on the very contrary,
all this talking intimacy
is only real and right if we
keep ourselves separate physically
and quite apart.

To proceed from mental intimacy
to physical is just messy,
and really, a nasty violation,
and the ruin of any decent relation
between us.

TOUCH COMES

Touch comes when the white mind sleeps
and only then.
Touch comes slowly, if ever; it seeps
slowly up in the blood of men
and women.

Soft slow sympathy
of the blood in me, of the blood in thee
rises and flushes insidiously
over the conscious personality
of each of us, and covers us
with a soft one warmth, and a generous
kindled togetherness, so we go
into each other as tides flow
under a moon they do not know.

Personalities exist apart;
and personal intimacy has no heart.
Touch is of the blood
uncontaminated, the unmental flood.

When again in us
the soft blood softly flows together
towards touch, then this delirious
day of the mental welter and blether
will be passing away, we shall cease to fuss.

LEAVE SEX ALONE

Leave sex alone, leave sex alone, let it die right away,
let it die right away, till it rises of itself again.

Meanwhile, if we must, let us think about it, and talk
    about it
straight, to the very end,
since the need is on us.

But while we think of it, and talk of it
let us leave it alone, physically, keep apart.
For while we have sex in the mind, we truly have none in
    the body.

Sex is a state of grace
and you'll have to wait.
You'll even have to repent.
And in some strange and silent way
you'll have to pray to the far-off gods
to grant it you.

At present, sex is the mind's preoccupation,
and in the body we can only mentally fornicate.
To-day, we've got no sex.
We have only cerebral excitations.

The mind will have to glut itself,
and the ego will have to burst like the swollen frog,
and then perhaps we shall know true sex, in ourselves.

THE MESS OF LOVE

We've made a great mess of love
since we made an ideal of it.

The moment I swear to love a woman, a certain woman,
    all my life
that moment I begin to hate her.

The moment I even say to a woman: I love you!—
my love dies down considerably.

The moment love is an understood thing between us, we
    are sure of it,
it's a cold egg, it isn't love any more.

Love is like a flower, it must flower and fade;
if it doesn't fade, it is not a flower,
it's either an artificial rag blossom, or an immortelle, for
    the cemetery.

The moment the mind interferes with love, or the will
    fixes on it,
or the personality assumes it as an attribute, or the ego
    takes possession of it,
it is not love any more, it's just a mess.
And we've made a great mess of love, mind-perverted, will-
    perverted, ego-perverted love.

CLIMB DOWN, O LORDLY MIND

Climb down, O lordly mind!
O eagle of the mind, alas, you are more like a buzzard.

Come down now, from your pre-eminence, O mind, O
    lofty spirit!
Your hour has struck
your unique day is over.
Absolutism is finished, in the human consciousness too.

A man is many things, he is not only a mind.
But in his consciousness, he is two-fold at least:
he is cerebral, intellectual, mental, spiritual,
but also he is instinctive, intuitive, and in touch.

The mind, that needs to know all things
must needs at last come to know its own limits,
even its own nullity, beyond a certain point.

Know thyself, and that thou art mortal,
and therefore, that thou art forever unknowable;
the mind can never reach thee.

Thou art like the moon,
and the white mind shines on one side of thee
but the other side is dark forever,
and the dark moon draws the tides also.

Thou art like the day
but thou art also like the night,
and thy darkness is forever invisible,
for the strongest light throws also the darkest shadow.

The blood knows in darkness, and forever dark,
in touch, by intuition, instinctively.
The blood also knows religiously,
and of this, the mind is incapable.
The mind is non-religious.

To my dark heart, gods *are*.
In my dark heart, love is and is not.
But to my white mind
gods and love alike are but an idea,
a kind of fiction.

Man is an alternating consciousness.
Man is an alternating consciousness.

Only that exists which exists in my own consciousness.
Cogito, ergo sum.
Only that exists which exists dynamically and un-
    mentalised, in my blood.

Non cogito, ergo sum.
I am, I do not think I am.

EGO-BOUND

As a plant becomes pot-bound
man becomes ego-bound
enclosed in his own limited mental consciousness.

Then he can't feel any more
or love, or rejoice or even grieve any more,
he is ego-bound,
pot-bound
in the pot of his own conceit,
and he can only slowly die.

Unless he is a sturdy plant.
Then he can burst the pot,
shell off his ego
and get his roots in earth again,
raw earth.

JEALOUSY

The jealousy of an ego-bound woman
is hideous and fearful,
it is so much stronger than her love could ever be.

The jealousy of an ego-bound woman
is a fearful thing to behold.
The ego revealed in all its monstrous inhumanity.

EGO-BOUND WOMEN

Ego-bound women are often lesbian,
perhaps always.

Perhaps the ego-bound can only love their own
        kind,
if they can love at all.

And of all passions
the lesbian passion is the most appalling,
a frenzy of tortured possession
and a million frenzies of tortured jealousy.

Possessive, possessive, possessive!
gentle woman gone mad
with possessive vindictiveness.

But the real fault lies in the ego-bound condition of
        mankind
Individuals must go mad.

FIDELITY

Fidelity and love are two different things, like a flower
     and a gem.
And love, like a flower, will fade, will change into some-
     thing else
or it would not be flowery.

O flowers they fade because they are moving swiftly; a
     little torrent of life
leaps up to the summit of the stem, gleams, turns over
     round the bend
of the parabola of curved flight,
sinks, and is gone, like a comet curving into the invisible.

O flowers they are all the time travelling
like comets, and they come into our ken
for a day, for two days, and withdraw, slowly vanish again.

And we, we must take them on the wing, and let them go.
Embalmed flowers are not flowers, immortelles are not
     flowers;
flowers are just a motion, a swift motion, a coloured
     gesture;
that is their loveliness. And that is love.

But a gem is different. It lasts so much longer than we do
so much much much longer
that it seems to last forever.
Yet we know it is flowing away
as flowers are, and we are, only slower.
The wonderful slow flowing of the sapphire!

All flows, and every flow is related to every other flow.
Flowers and sapphires and us, diversely streaming.

In the old days, when sapphires were breathed upon and
    brought forth
during the wild orgasms of chaos
time was much slower, when the rocks came forth.
It took æons to make a sapphire, æons for it to pass away.

And a flower it takes a summer.

And man and woman are like the earth, that brings forth
    flowers
in summer, and love, but underneath is rock.
Older than flowers, older than ferns, older than fora-
    miniferæ
older than plasm altogether is the soul of a man under-
    neath.

And when, throughout all the wild orgasms of love
slowly a gem forms, in the ancient, once-more-molten
    rocks
of two human hearts, two ancient rocks, a man's heart
    and a woman's,
that is the crystal of peace, the slow hard jewel of trust,
the sapphire of fidelity.
The gem of mutual peace emerging from the wild chaos
    of love.

KNOW DEEPLY, KNOW THYSELF
MORE DEEPLY

Go deeper than love, for the soul has greater depths,
love is like the grass, but the heart is deep wild rock
molten, yet dense and permanent.

Go down to your deep old heart, woman, and lose sight of
    yourself.
And lose sight of me, the me whom you turbulently loved.

Let us lose sight of ourselves, and break the mirrors.

For the fierce curve of our lives is moving again to the
    depths
out of sight, in the deep dark living heart.

But say, in the dark wild metal of your heart
is there a gem, which came into being between us?
is there a sapphire of mutual trust, a blue spark?
Is there a ruby of fused being, mine and yours, an inward
    glint?

If there is not, O then leave me, go away.
For I cannot be bullied back into the appearances of love,
any more than August can be bullied to look like March.

Love out of season, especially at the end of the season
is merely ridiculous.
If you insist on it, I insist on departure.

Have you no deep old heart of wild womanhood
self-forgetful, and gemmed with experience,
and swinging in a strange unison of power
with the heart of the man you are supposed to have loved?

If you have not, go away.
If you can only sit with a mirror in your hand, an ageing
    woman
posing on and on as a lover,
in love with a self that now is shallow and withered,
your own self—that has passed like a last summer's
    flower—
then go away—

I do not want a woman whom age cannot wither.
She is a made-up lie, a dyed immortelle
of infinite staleness.

ALL I ASK

All I ask of a woman is that she shall feel gently towards
    me
when my heart feels kindly towards her,
and there shall be the soft, soft tremor as of unheard bells
    between us.
It is all I ask.
I am so tired of violent women lashing out and insisting
on being loved, when there is no love in them.

THE UNIVERSE FLOWS

The universe flows in infinite wild streams, related
in rhythms too big and too small for us to know,
since man is just middling, and his comprehension just
    middling.

If once, for a second, the universe ceased to flow
of course it would cease to exist.
The thought is unthinkable, anyhow.

Only man tries not to flow,
repeats himself over and over in mechanical monotony of
    conceit
and hence is a mess.

If only Cleopatra had left off being so Cleopatra-ish
—she was it too long—
if only she had gone down to a deeper self in herself
as time went on,
Anthony might have made a splendid thing of the East,
she might have saved herself the asp
and him from sticking himself like a pig
and us from the dreary inheritance of Roman stupidity.

UNDERNEATH

Below what we think we are
we are something else,
we are almost anything.

Below the grass and trees
and streets and houses and even seas
is rock; and below the rock, the rock
is we know not what,
the hot wild core of the earth, heavier than we can even
     imagine.

Pivotal core of the soul, heavier than iron
so ponderously central;
heavier and hotter than anything known;
and also alone.—
And yet
reeling with connection
spinning with the heaviness of balance
and flowing invisibly, gasping
towards the breathing stars and the central of all sunni-
     nesses.

The earth leans its weight on the sun, and the sun on the
     sun of suns.
Back and forth goes the balance and the electric breath.

The soul of man also leans in the unconscious inclination
     we call religion
towards the sun of suns, and back and forth goes the breath
of incipient energetic life.

Out of the soul's middle to the middle-most sun, way-off,
     or in every atom.

THE PRIMAL PASSIONS

If you will go down into yourself, under your surface
    personality
you will find you have a great desire to drink life direct
from the source, not out of bottles and bottled personal
    vessels.

What the old people call immediate contact with God.
That strange essential communication of life
not bottled in human bottles.

What even the wild witchcraft of the past was seeking
before it degenerated.

Life from the source, unadulterated
with the human taint.

Contact with the sun of suns
that shines somewhere in the atom, somewhere pivots the
    curved space,
and cares not a straw for the put-up human figments.

Communion with the Godhead, they used to say in the
    past.
But even that is human-tainted now,
tainted with the ego and the personality.

To feel a fine, fine breeze blowing through the navel and
    the knees
and have a cool sense of truth, inhuman truth at last
softly fluttering the senses, in the exquisite orgasm of
    coition
with the Godhead of energy that cannot tell lies.

The cool, cool truth of pure vitality
pouring into the veins from the direct contact with the
    source.
Uncontaminated by even the beginnings of a lie.

The soul's first passion is for sheer life
entering in shocks of truth, unfouled by lies.

And the soul's next passion is to reflect
and then turn round and embrace the extant body of life
with the thrusting embrace of new justice, new justice
between men and men, men and women, and earth and
    stars, and suns.
The passion of justice being profound and subtle
and changing in a flow as all passions change.

But the passion of justice is a primal embrace
between man and all his known universe.

And the passion of truth is the embrace between man and
    his god
in the sheer coition of the life-flow, stark and unlying.

ESCAPE

When we get out of the glass bottles of our own ego,
and when we escape like squirrels from turning in the
    cages of our personality
and get into the forest again,
we shall shiver with cold and fright
but things will happen to us
so that we don't know ourselves.

Cool, unlying life will rush in,
and passion will make our bodies taut with power,
we shall stamp our feet with new power
and old things will fall down,
we shall laugh, and institutions will curl up like burnt
    paper.

THE ROOT OF OUR EVIL

The root of our present evil is that we buy and sell.
Ultimately, we are all busy buying and selling one another.

It began with Judas, and goes on in the wage-system.
Men sell themselves for a wage, and employers look out
    for a bargain.
And employers are bought by financiers, and financiers are
    sold to the devil.

—Get thou behind me, Satan!—
That was just what Satan wanted to do,
for then nobody would have their eye on him.

And Jesus never looked round.
That is the great reproach we have against *him*.
He was frightened to look round
and see Satan bargaining the world away
and men, and the bread of men
behind his back
with satanically inspired financiers.

If Jesus had kept a sharp eye on Satan,
and refused to let so many things happen behind his back
we shouldn't be where we are now.

Come, Satan, don't go dodging behind my back any longer.
If you've got the goods, come forward, boy, and let's see
    'em.
I'm perfectly willing to strike a decent bargain.
But I'm not having any dodging going on behind my
    back.

What we want is some sort of communism
not based on wages, nor profits, nor any sort of buying and
    selling
but on a religion of life.

THE IGNOBLE PROCESSION

When I see the ignoble procession
streaming forth from little doorways
citywards, in little rivers that swell to a great stream,
of men in bowler hats, hurrying
and a mingling of wallet-carrying women
hurrying, hurrying, legs going quick quick quick
in ignoble haste, for fear of being late—
I am filled with humiliation.

Their haste
is so
humiliating.

NO JOY IN LIFE

Never, my young men,
you who complain you know no joy in your lives,
never will you know any joy in your lives
till you ask for lightning instead of love
till you pray to the right gods, for the thunder-bolt instead
        of pity
till you look to the right man, to put you into touch.

Then you will hit the Flat-iron Building and flatten it out.
Then you will shatter the Bank.
Then you will settle the hash of Business finally.

WILD THINGS IN CAPTIVITY

Wild things in captivity
while they keep their own wild purity
won't breed, they mope, they die.

All men are in captivity,
active with captive activity,
and the best won't breed, though they don't know why.

The great cage of our domesticity
kills sex in a man, the simplicity
of desire is distorted and twisted awry.

And so, with bitter perversity,
gritting against the great adversity,
the young ones copulate, hate it, and want to cry.

Sex is a state of grace.
In a cage it can't take place.
Break the cage then, start in and try.

MOURNFUL YOUNG MAN——

Mournful young man in your twenties
who think the only way out of your mournfulness is
    through a woman,
yet you fail to find the woman, when there are so many
    women about—

Why don't you realise
that you're not desirable?
that no woman will ever desire you, as you are,
except, of course, for secondary motives.

The women are in the cage as much as you are.
They look at you, they see a cagéd monkey.
How do you expect them ever to desire you?
Anyhow they never will, except for secondary motives,
or except you change.

THERE IS NO WAY OUT

There is no way out, we are all caged monkeys
blue-arsed with the money-bruise
and wearing our seats out sitting on money.

There is no way out, the cage has no door, it's rusted
    solid.

If you copulate with the finest woman on earth
there's no relief, only a moment's sullen respite.

You're a caged monkey again in five minutes.
Therefore be prepared to tackle the cage.

MONEY-MADNESS

Money is our madness, our vast collective madness.

And of course, if the multitude is mad
the individual carries his own grain of insanity around with
    him.

I doubt if any man living hands out a pound note without
    a pang;
and a real tremor, if he hands out a ten-pound note.

We quail, money makes us quail.
It has got us down, we grovel before it in strange terror.
And no wonder, for money has a fearful cruel power
    among men.

But it is not money we are so terrified of,
it is the collective money-madness of mankind.
For mankind says with one voice: How much is he worth?
Has he no money? Then let him eat dirt, and go cold.—

And if I have no money, they will give me a little bread
so I do not die,
but they will make me eat dirt with it.
I shall have to eat dirt, I shall have to eat dirt
if I have no money.

It is that that I am frightened of.
And that fear can become a delirium.
It is fear of my money-mad fellow-men.

We must have some money
to save us from eating dirt.

And this is all wrong.

Bread should be free,
shelter should be free,
fire should be free
to all and anybody, all and anybody, all over the world.

We must regain our sanity about money
before we start killing one another about it.
It's one thing or the other.

KILL MONEY

Kill money, put money out of existence.
It is a perverted instinct, a hidden thought
which rots the brain, the blood, the bones, the stones, the
    soul.

Make up your mind about it:
that society must establish itself upon a different principle
from the one we've got now.

We must have the courage of mutual trust.
We must have the modesty of simple living.
And the individual must have his house, food and fire all
    free like a bird.

MEN ARE NOT BAD

Men are not bad, when they are free.
Prison makes men bad, and the money compulsion makes
　　men bad.
If men were free from the terror of earning a living
there would be abundance in the world
and men would work gaily.

NOTTINGHAM'S NEW UNIVERSITY

In Nottingham, that dismal town
where I went to school and college,
they've built a new university
for a new dispensation of knowledge.

Built it most grand and cakeily
out of the noble loot
derived from shrewd cash-chemistry
by good Sir Jesse Boot.

Little I thought, when I was a lad
and turned my modest penny
over on Boot's Cash Chemist's counter,
that Jesse, by turning many

millions of similar honest pence
over, would make a pile
that would rise at last and blossom out
in grand and cakey style

into a university
where smart men would dispense
doses of smart cash-chemistry
in language of common-sense!

That future Nottingham lads would be
cash-chemically B.Sc.
that Nottingham lights would rise and say:
—By Boots I am M.A.

From this I learn, though I knew it before
that culture has her roots
in the deep dung of cash, and lore
is a last offshoot of Boots.

I AM IN A NOVEL

I read a novel by a friend of mine
in which one of the characters was me,
the novel it sure was mighty fine
but the funniest thing that could be

was me, or what was supposed for me,
for I had to recognise
a few of the touches, like a low-born jake,
but the rest was a real surprise.

Well damn my eyes! I said to myself.
Well damn my little eyes!
If this is what Archibald thinks I am
he sure thinks a lot of lies.

Well think o' that now, think o' that!
That's what he sees in me!
I'm about as much like a Persian cat,
or a dog with a harrowing flea.

My Lord! a man's friends' ideas of him
would stock a menagerie
with a marvellous outfit! How did Archie see
such a funny pup in me?

NO! MR LAWRENCE!

No, Mr. Lawrence, it's not like that!
I don't mind telling you
I know a thing or two about love,
perhaps more than you do.

And what I know is that you make it
too nice, too beautiful.
It's not like that, you know; you fake it.
It's really rather dull.

RED-HERRING

My father was a working man
    and a collier was he,
at six in the morning they turned him down
    and they turned him up for tea.

My mother was a superior soul
    a superior soul was she,
cut out to play a superior rôle
    in the god-damn bourgeoisie.

We children were the in-betweens
    little non-descripts were we,
indoors we called each other *you*,
    outside, it was *tha* and *thee*.

But time has fled, our parents are dead
    we've risen in the world all three;
but still we are in-betweens, we tread
    between the devil and the deep cold sea.

O I am a member of the bourgeoisie
    and a servant-maid brings me my tea—
But I'm always longing for someone to say:
    'ark 'ere, lad! atween thee an' me

they're a' a b—d — lot o' ——s,
 an' I reckon it's nowt but right
we should start an' kick their ——ses for 'em
 an' tell 'em to ——.

OUR MORAL AGE

Of course, if you make naughtiness nasty,
  spicily nasty, of course,
then it's quite all right; we understand
  life's voice, even when she's hoarse.

But if you go and make naughtiness nice
  there's no excuse;
if such things were nice, and we needn't think twice,
  what would be the use——?

MY NAUGHTY BOOK

They say I wrote a naughty book
With perfectly awful things in it,
putting in all the impossible words
like b—— and f—— and sh——.

Most of my friends were deeply hurt
and haven't forgiven me yet;
I'd loaded the camel's back before
with dirt they couldn't forget.

And now, no really, the final straw
was words like sh—— and f——!
I heard the camel's back go crack
beneath the weight of muck.

Then out of nowhere rushed John Bull,
that mildewed pup, good doggie!

squeakily bellowing for all he was worth,
and slavering wet and soggy.

He couldn't bite 'em he was much too old,
but he made a pool of dribblings;
so while the other one heaved her sides
with moans and hollow bibblings.

He did his best, the good old dog
to support her, the hysterical camel,
and everyone listened and loved it, the
ridiculous bimmel-bammel.

But still, one has no right to take
the old dog's greenest bones
that he's buried now for centuries
beneath England's garden stones.

And, of course, one has no right to lay
such words to the camel's charge,
when she prefers to have them left
in the W.C. writ large.

Poor homely words. I must give you back
to the camel and the dog,
for her to mumble and him to crack
in secret, great golliwog!

And hereby I apologise
to all my foes and friends
for using words they privately keep
for their own immortal ends.

And henceforth I will never use
more than the chaste, short dash;
so do forgive me! I sprinkle my hair
with grey, repentant ash.

THE LITTLE WOWSER

There is a little wowser
  John Thomas by name,
and for every bloomin', mortal thing
  that little blighter's to blame.

It was 'im as made the first mistake
  of putting us in the world,
forcin' us out of the unawake,
  an' makin' us come uncurled.

And then when you're gettin' nicely on
  an' life seems to begin,
that little bleeder comes bustin' in
  with: Hello boy! what about sin?

An' then he leads you by the nose
  after a lot o' women
as strips you stark as a monkey nut
  an' leaves you never a trimmin'.

An' then somebody has ter marry you
  to put him through 'is paces;
then when John Thomas don't worry you,
  it's your wife, wi' her airs an' graces.

I think of all the little brutes
  as ever was invented
that little cod's the holy worst.
  I've chucked him, I've repented.

THE YOUNG AND THEIR
MORAL GUARDIANS

O the stale old dogs who pretend to guard
the morals of the masses,
how smelly they make the great back-yard,
wetting after everyone that passes.

If a man goes by who doesn't give
a damn for their dirty kennels,
how they rush out and want to rive
him to pieces, the good-hearted spaniels!

And the young, the modern and jaunty young
how scared they all are, even now
of the yellow dogs, how they slink away
in silence from the great bow-wow!

When a low bull-mongrel starts declaiming,
there's not a young man in the whole
of England with the guts to turn round on him, aiming
a good kick at his dirty old hole.

WHEN I READ SHAKESPEARE

When I read Shakespeare I am struck with wonder
that such trivial people should muse and thunder
in such lovely language.

Lear, the old buffer, you wonder his daughters
didn't treat him rougher,
the old chough, the old chuffer!

And Hamlet, how boring, how boring to live with,
so mean and self-conscious, blowing and snoring
his wonderful speeches, full of other folks' whoring!

And Macbeth and his Lady, who should have been choring,
such suburban ambition, so messily goring
old Duncan with daggers!

How boring, how small Shakespeare's people are!
Yet the language so lovely! like the dyes from gas-tar.

SALT OF THE EARTH

Slowly the salt of the earth becomes salt of the sea.
Slowly the raindrops of appreciation
carry the salt of the earth, the wisdom of wise men,
    the gifts of the great
down to the ocean of the afterwards, where it remains
    as brine
in which to pickle the younger generations
who would be so much better without pickling.

Slowly the salt of the earth becomes salt of the sea.

FRESH WATER

They say it is very difficult
to distil sea-water into sweet.

Perhaps that's why it is so difficult
to get a refreshing drink out of old wisdom
old truth, old teaching of any sort.

PEACE AND WAR

People always make war when they say they love peace.
The loud love of peace makes one quiver more than any
    battlecry.
Why should one love peace? it is so obviously vile to make
    war.

Loud peace propaganda makes war seem imminent.
It is a form of war, even, self-assertion and being wise for
    other people.
Let people be wise for themselves. And anyhow
nobody can be wise except on rare occasions, like getting
    married or dying.

It's bad taste to be wise all the time, like being at a perpet-
ual funeral.
For everyday use, give me somebody whimsical, with not
too much purpose in life,
then we shan't have war, and we needn't talk about peace.

MANY MANSIONS

When a bird flips his tail in getting his balance on a tree
he feels much gayer than if somebody had left him a fortune
or than if he'd just built himself a nest with a bathroom—
Why can't people be gay like that?

GLORY

Glory is of the sun, too, and the sun of suns,
and down the shafts of his splendid pinions
run tiny rivers of peace.

Most of his time, the tiger pads and slouches in a burning peace.
And the small hawk high up turns round on the slow pivot of peace.
Peace comes from behind the sun, with the peregrine falcon, and
the owl.
Yet all of these drink blood.

WOE

Woe, woe to the world!
For we're all self-consciously aware of ourselves
yet not sufficiently conscious to be able to forget ourselves
and be whimsically at home in ourselves.

So everybody makes an assertion of himself,
and every self-assertion clashes on every other.

ATTILA

I would call Attila on his little horse
a man of peace.

For after all, he helped to smash a lot of old Roman lies,
the lies, the treachery, the slippery cultured squalor of that
     sneaking court of Ravenna.

And after all, lying and base hypocrisy and treachery
are much more hellishly peaceless than a little straight-
     forward bloodshed
which may occasionally be a preliminary to the peace that
     passes understanding.

So that I would call Attila on his little horse
a man of peace.

WHAT WOULD YOU FIGHT FOR?

I am not sure I would always fight for my life.
Life might not be worth fighting for.

I am not sure I would always fight for my wife.
A wife isn't always worth fighting for.

Nor my children, nor my country, nor my fellow-men.
It all depends whether I found them worth fighting for.

The only thing men invariably fight for
is their money. But I doubt if I'd fight for mine, anyhow
     not to shed a lot of blood over it.

Yet one thing I do fight for, tooth and nail, all the time.
And that is my bit of inward peace, where I am at one
     with myself.

And I must say, I am often worsted.

CHOICE

I would rather sit still in a state of peace on a stone
than ride in the motor-car of a multimillionaire
and feel the peacelessness of the multimillionaire
poisoning me.

RICHES

When I wish I was rich, then I know I am ill.
Because, to tell the truth, I have enough as I am.
So when I catch myself thinking: Ah, if I was rich——!
I say to myself: Hello! I'm not well. My vitality is low.

POVERTY

The only people I ever heard talk about My Lady Poverty
were rich people, or people who imagined themselves rich.
Saint Francis himself was a rich and spoiled young man.

Being born among the working people
I know that poverty is a hard old hag,
and a monster, when you're pinched for actual necessities.
And whoever says she isn't, is a liar.

I don't want to be poor, it means I am pinched.
But neither do I want to be rich.
When I look at this pine-tree near the sea,
that grows out of rock, and plumes forth, plumes forth,
I see it has a natural abundance.

With its roots it has a grand grip on its daily bread,
and its plumes look like green cups held up to sun and air
and full of wine.

I want to be like that, to have a natural abundance
and plume forth, and be splendid.

NOBLE

I know I am noble with the nobility of the sun.
A certain peace, a certain grace.
I would say the same if I were a chaffinch or tree.

WEALTH

Peace I have from the core of the atom, from the core of space,
and grace, if I don't lose it, from the same place.
And I look shabby, yet my roots go beyond my knowing,
deep beyond the world of man.
And where my little leaves flutter highest
there are no people, nor ever will be.

Yet my roots are in a woman too.
and my leaves are green with the breath of human experience.

TOLERANCE

One can be tolerant with a bore
and suffer fools, though not gladly
—why should a man pretend to be glad about
    his sufferings?

But it is hard to be tolerant with the smarties,
or to put up with the clever mess-makers,
or to endure the jazzy person;
one can't stand peaceless people any more.

COMPARI

I would like a few men to be at peace with.
Not friends, necessarily, they talk so much.
Nor yet comrades, for I don't belong to any cause.
Nor yet "brothers", it's so conceited.
Nor pals, they're such a nuisance.
But men to be at peace with.

SICK

I am sick, because I have given myself away.
I have given myself to the people when they came
so cultured, even bringing little gifts,
so they pecked a shred of my life, and flew off with a
    croak
of sneaking exultance.
So now I have lost too much, and am sick.

I am trying now to learn never
to give of my life to the dead,
never, not the tiniest shred.

DEAD PEOPLE

When people are dead and peaceless
they hate life, they only like carrion.

When people are dead and peaceless
they hate happiness in others
with thin, screaming hatred,
as the vulture that screams high up, almost inaudible,
hovering to peck out the eyes of the still-living creature.

CEREBRAL EMOTIONS

I am sick of people's cerebral emotions
that are born in their minds and forced down by the will
on to their poor deranged bodies.

People feeling things they intend to feel, they mean to feel,
they *will* feel,
just because they don't feel them.

For of course, if you really feel something
you don't have to assert that you feel it.

WELLSIAN FUTURES

When men are made in bottles
and emerge as squeaky globules with no bodies to speak of,
and therefore nothing to have feelings with,

they will still squeak intensely about their feelings
and be prepared to kill you if you say they've got none.

TO WOMEN, AS FAR AS I'M
CONCERNED

The feelings I don't have I don't have.
The feelings I don't have, I won't say I have.
The feelings you say you have, you don't have.
The feelings you would like us both to have, we
        neither of us have.
The feelings people ought to have, they never have.
If people say they've got feelings, you may be pretty
        sure they haven't got them.

So if you want either of us to feel anything at all
you'd better abandon all idea of feelings altogether.

BLANK

At present I am a blank, and I admit it.
In feeling I am just a blank.
My mind is fairly nimble, and is not blank.
My body likes its dinner and the warm sun, but otherwise is blank.
My soul is almost blank, my spirit quite.
I have a certain amount of money, so my anxieties are blank.
And I can't do anything about it, even there I am blank.
So I am just going to go on being a blank, till something nudges me
        from within,
and makes me know I am not blank any longer.

ELDERLY DISCONTENTED WOMEN

Elderly discontented women ask for intimate companionship,
by which they mean more talk, talk, talk
especially about themselves and their own feelings.

Elderly discontented women are so full of themselves
they have high blood-pressure and almost burst.

It is as if modern women had all got themselves on the brain
and that sent the blood rushing to the surface of the body
and driving them around in frenzied energy
stampeding over everybody,
while their hearts become absolutely empty,
and their voices are like screw-drivers
as they try to screw everybody else down with their will.

OLD PEOPLE

Nowadays everybody wants to be young,
　so much so, that even the young are old with the
　　　effort of being young.
As for those over fifty, either they rush forward
　in self-assertion
fearful to behold,
or they bear everybody a grim and grisly grudge
because of their own fifty or sixty or seventy or
　　　eighty summers.
As if it's my fault that the old girl is seventy-seven!

THE GRUDGE OF THE OLD

The old ones want to be young, and they aren't young,
and it rankles, they ache when they see the young,
and they can't help wanting to spite it on them
venomously.

The old ones say to themselves: We are not going to be old,
we are not going to make way, we are not going to die,
we are going to stay on and on and on and on and on
and make the young look after us
till they are old. We are stronger than the young.
We have more energy, and our grip on life is harder.
Let us triumph, and let the young be listless
with their puny youth.
We are younger even now than the young, we can put their
    youth in abeyance.

And it is true.
And they do it.
And so it goes on.

BEAUTIFUL OLD AGE

It ought to be lovely to be old
to be full of the peace that comes of experience
and wrinkled ripe fulfilment.

The wrinkled smile of completeness that follows a life
lived undaunted and unsoured with accepted lies.
If people lived without accepting lies
they would ripen like apples, and be scented like pippins
in their old age.

Soothing, old people should be, like apples
when one is tired of love.
Fragrant like yellowing leaves, and dim with the soft
stillness and satisfaction of autumn.

And a girl should say:
It must be wonderful to live and grow old.
Look at my mother, how rich and still she is!

And a young man should think: By Jove
my father has faced all weathers, but it's been a life!

COURAGE

What makes people unsatisfied
is that they accept lies.

If people had courage, and refused lies
and found out what they really felt and really meant
and acted on it,

They would distil the essential oil out of every
     experience
and like hazel-nuts in autumn, at last
be sweet and sound.

And the young among the old
would be as in the hazel-woods of September
nutting, gathering nuts of ripe experience.

As it is, all that the old can offer
is sour, bitter fruits, cankered by lies.

DESIRE IS DEAD

Desire may be dead
and still a man can be
a meeting place for sun and rain,
wonder outwaiting pain
as in a wintry tree.

WHEN THE RIPE FRUIT FALLS

When the ripe fruit falls
its sweetness distils and trickles away into
    the veins of the earth.

When fulfilled people die
the essential oil of their experience enters
the veins of living space, and adds a glisten
to the atom, to the body of immortal chaos.

For space is alive
and it stirs like a swan
whose feathers glisten
silky with oil of distilled experience.

ELEMENTAL

Why don't people leave off being lovable
or thinking they are lovable, or wanting to be lovable,
and be a bit elemental instead?

Since man is made up of the elements
fire, and rain, and air, and live loam
and none of these is lovable
but elemental,
man is lop-sided on the side of the angels.

I wish men would get back their balance among the elements
and be a bit more fiery, as incapable of telling lies
as fire is.

I wish they'd be true to their own variation, as water is,
which goes through all the stages of steam and stream and ice
without losing its head.

I am sick of lovable people,
somehow they are a lie.

FIRE

Fire is dearer to us than love or food,
hot, hurrying, yet it burns if you touch it.

What we ought to do
is not to add our love together, or our good-will,
    or any of that,
for we're sure to bring in a lot of lies,
but our fire, our elemental fire
so that it rushes up in a huge blaze like a phallus
    into hollow space
and fecundates the zenith and the nadir
and sends off millions of sparks of new atoms
and singes us, and burns the house down.

I WISH I KNEW A WOMAN

I wish I knew a woman
who was like a red fire on the hearth
glowing after the day's restless draughts.

So that one could draw near her
in the red stillness of the dusk
and really take delight in her
without having to make the polite effort of loving her
or the mental effort of making her acquaintance.
Without having to take a chill, talking to her.

TALK

I wish people, when you sit near them,
wouldn't think it necessary to make conversation
and send thin draughts of words
blowing down your neck and your ears
and giving you a cold in your inside.

THE EFFORT OF LOVE

I am worn out
with the effort of trying to love people
and not succeeding.

Now I've made up my mind
I love nobody, I'm going to love nobody,
I'm not going to tell any lies about it
and it's final.

If there's a man here and there, or a woman
whom I can really like,
that's quite enough for me.

And if by a miracle a woman happened to come along
who warmed the cockles of my heart
I'd rejoice over the woman and the warmed cockles of my
    heart
so long as it didn't all fizzle out in talk.

CAN'T BE BORNE

Any woman who says to me
—Do you really love me?—
earns my undying detestation.

MAN REACHES A POINT

I cannot help but be alone
for desire has died in me, silence has grown,
and nothing now reaches out to draw
other flesh to my own.

GRASSHOPPER IS A BURDEN

Desire has failed, desire has failed
and the critical grasshopper
has come down on the heart in a burden of locusts
and stripped it bare.

BASTA!

When a man can love no more
and feel no more
and desire has failed
and the heart is numb

then all he can do
is to say: It is so!
I've got to put up with it
and wait.

This is a pause, how long a pause I know not,
in my very being.

TRAGEDY

Tragedy seems to me a loud noise
louder than is seemly.

Tragedy looks to me like man
in love with his own defeat.
Which is only a sloppy way of being in love with yourself.

I can't very much care about the woes and tragedies
of Lear and Macbeth and Hamlet and Timon:
they cared so excessively themselves.

And when I think of the great tragedy of our material-
mechanical civilisation
crushing out the natural human life
then sometimes I feel defeated; and then again I know
my shabby little defeat would do neither me any good
nor anybody else.

AFTER ALL THE TRAGEDIES ARE OVER

After all the tragedies are over and worn out
and a man can no longer feel heroic about being a Hamlet—

When love is gone, and desire is dead, and tragedy has left
    the heart
then grief and pain go too, withdrawing
from the heart and leaving strange cold stretches of sand.

So a man no longer knows his own heart;
he might say into the twilight: What is it?
I am here, yet my heart is bare and utterly empty.
I have passed from existence, I feel nothing any more.
I am a nonentity.

Yet, when the time has come to be nothing, how good it is
    to be nothing!
a waste expanse of nothing, like wide foreshores where not
    a ripple is left
and the sea is lost
in the lapse of the lowest of tides.

Ah, when I have seen myself left by life, left nothing!

Yet even waste, grey foreshores, sand, and sorry, far-out
    clay
are sea-bed still, through their hour of bare denuding.
It is the moon that turns the tides.
The beaches can do nothing about it.

NULLUS

I know I am nothing.
Life has gone away, below my low-water mark.

I am aware I feel nothing, even at dawn.
The dawn comes up with a glitter and a blueness, and I say:
    How lovely!
But I am a liar, I feel no loveliness, it is a mental remark, a
    cliché.

My whole consciousness is cliché
and I am null;
I exist as an organism
and a nullus.

But I can do nothing about it
except admit it and leave it to the moon.

There are said to be creative pauses,
pauses that are as good as death, empty and dead as death
    itself.
And in these awful pauses the evolutionary change takes
    place.
Perhaps it is so.
The tragedy is over, it has ceased to be tragic, the last pause
    is upon us.
Pause, brethren, pause!

DIES IRAE

Even the old emotions are finished,
we have worn them out.
And desire is dead.
And the end of all things is inside us.

Our epoch is over,
a cycle of evolution is finished,
our activity has lost its meaning,
we are ghosts, we are seed;
for our word is dead
and we know not how to live wordless.

We live in a vast house
full of inordinate activities,
and the noise, and the stench, and the dreariness
    and lack of meaning
madden us, but we don't know what to do.

All we can know at this moment
is the fulfilment of nothingness.
Lo, I am nothing!

It is a consummation devoutly to be wished
in this world of mechanical self-assertion.

DIES ILLA

Dies irae, dies illa
solvet saeclum in favilla—

Day of wrath, O day of warning!
Flame devours the world.

It does, even if we don't see it.
For there are all sorts of flame:
slow, creeping cold ones
that burn inwardly
like flickering cancers.

And the slow cold flames
may burn for long years
before they've eaten through the joists and
the girders
and the house comes down, with a subsiding
crash.

STOP IT

The one thing the old will never understand
is that you can't prevent change.
All flows, and even the old are rapidly flowing away.
And the young are flowing in the throes of a great
alteration.

THE DEATH OF OUR ERA

Our era is dying
yet who has killed it?
Have we, who are it?

In the middle of voluted space
its knell has struck.
And in the middle of every atom, which is the same thing,
a tiny bell of conclusion has sounded.

The curfew of our great day
the passing-bell of our way of knowing
the knell of our bald-headed consciousness
the tocsin of this our civilisation.

Who struck the bell?
Who rang the knell?
Not I, not you,
yet all of us.

At the core of space the final knell
of our era has struck, and it chimes
in terrible rippling circles between the stars
till it reaches us, and its vibrations shatter us
each time they touch us.

And they keep on coming, with greater force
striking us, the vibrations of our finish.

And all that we can do
is to die the amazing death
with every stroke, and go on
till we are blank.

And yet, as we die, why should not our vast mechanised
    day die with us,
so that when we are re-born, we can be born into a fresh
    world.

For the new word is Resurrection.

THE NEW WORD

Shall I tell you again the new word,
the new word of the unborn day?
It is Resurrection.
The resurrection of the flesh.

For our flesh is dead
only egoistically we assert ourselves.

And the new word means nothing to us,
it is such an old word,
till we admit how dead we are,
till we actually feel as blank as we really are.

SUN IN ME

A sun will rise in me,
I shall slowly resurrect,
already the whiteness of false dawn is on my inner ocean.

A sun in me.
And a sun in heaven.
And beyond that, the immense sun behind the sun,
the sun of immense distances, that fold themselves together
within the genitals of living space.
And further, the sun within the atom
which is god in the atom.

BE STILL !

The only thing to be done, now,
now that the waves of our undoing have begun to strike
       on us,
is to contain ourselves.

To keep still, and let the wreckage of ourselves go,
let everything go, as the wave smashes us,
yet keep still, and hold
the tiny grain of something that no wave can wash away,
not even the most massive wave of destiny.

Among all the smashed debris of myself
keep quiet, and wait.
For the word is Resurrection.
And even the sea of seas will have to give up its dead.

AT LAST

When things get very bad, they pass beyond tragedy.
And then the only thing we can do is to keep quite still
and guard the last treasure of the soul, our sanity.

Since, poor individuals that we are,
if we lose our sanity
we lose that which keeps us individual
distinct from chaos.

In death, the atom takes us up
and the suns.
But if we lose our sanity
nothing and nobody in the whole vast realm of space
wants us, or can have anything to do with us.
We can but howl the lugubrious howl of idiots,
the howl of the utterly lost
howling their nowhereness.

NEMESIS

The Nemesis that awaits our civilisation
is social insanity
which in the end is always homicidal.

Sanity means the wholeness of the consciousness.
And our society is only part conscious, like an idiot.

If we do not rapidly open all the doors of consciousness
and freshen the putrid little space in which we are cribbed
the sky-blue walls of our unventilated heaven
will be bright red with blood.

THE OPTIMIST

The optimist builds himself safe inside a cell
and paints the inside walls sky-blue
and blocks up the door
and says he's in heaven.

THE THIRD THING

Water is H_2O, hydrogen two parts, oxygen one,
but there is also a third thing, that makes it water
and nobody knows what that is.

The atom locks up two energies
but it is a third thing present which makes it an atom.

THE SANE UNIVERSE

One might talk of the sanity of the atom,
the sanity of space,
the sanity of the electron,
the sanity of water—
For it is all alive
and has something comparable to that which
        we call sanity in ourselves.
The only oneness is the oneness of sanity.

FEAR OF SOCIETY IS THE ROOT OF ALL EVIL

To-day, the social consciousness is mutilated
so everything is insane:
success is insane, and failure is insane,
chastity is insane, and debauchery is insane,
money is insane, and poverty is insane.

A fearful thing is the mutilated social consciousness.

GOD

Where sanity is
there God is.
And the sane can still recognise sanity
so they can still recognise God.

SANE AND INSANE

The puritan is insane
and the profligate is insane
and they divide the world.

The wealthy are insane
and the poverty-stricken are insane
and the world is going to pieces between them.

The puritan is afraid
and the profligate is afraid.

The wealthy are afraid
and the poverty-stricken are afraid.

They are afraid with horrible and opposing fears
which threaten to tear the world in two, between
    them.

A SANE REVOLUTION

If you make a revolution, make it for fun,
don't make it in ghastly seriousness,
don't do it in deadly earnest,
do it for fun.

Don't do it because you hate people,
do it just to spit in their eye.

Don't do it for the money,
do it and be damned to the money.

Don't do it for equality,
do it because we've got too much equality
and it would be fun to upset the apple-cart
and see which way the apples would go a-rolling.

Don't do it for the working classes.
Do it so that we can all of us be little aristocracies on our
    own
and kick our heels like jolly escaped asses.

Don't do it, anyhow, for international Labour.
Labour is the one thing a man has had too much of.
Let's abolish labour, let's have done with labouring!
Work can be fun, and men can enjoy it; then it's not
    labour.
Let's have it so! Let's make a revolution for fun!

ALWAYS THIS PAYING

Nothing is really any fun, to-day,
because you've always got to pay for everything.
And whatever costs you money, money, money, is really
    no fun.
That's why women aren't much fun. You're always having
    to pay for them.

Or else, poor things, they're having to pay for themselves,
which is perhaps worse.
Why isn't anything free, why is it always pay, pay, pay?

A man can't get any fun out of wife, sweetheart or tart
because of the beastly expense.

Why don't we do something about the money system?

POOR YOUNG THINGS

The young to-day are born prisoners,
poor things, and they know it.
Born in a universal workhouse,
and they feel it.
Inheriting a sort of confinement,
work, and prisoners' routine
and prisoners' flat, ineffectual pastime.

A PLAYED-OUT GAME

Success is a played-out game, success, success!
because what have you got when you've got it?

The young aren't vitally interested in it any more.
Only third-rate swabs are pushing to get on, nowadays.

Getting the better of other people! Who cares?
Getting the better of them! Which better, what better,
    anyhow?

Our poor old daddies *got on*,
and then could never get off again.

If only we could make life a bit more just
so that we could all get along gaily
instead of getting on and not being able to get off again.

TRIUMPH

It seems to me that for five thousand years at least
men have been wanting to triumph, triumph, triumph,
triumph over their fellow-men, triumph over obstacles,
    triumph over evil,
till now the very word is nauseating, we can't hear it any
    more.

If we looked in our hearts we should see
we loathe the thought of any sort of triumph,
we are sick of it.

THE COMBATIVE SPIRIT

As a matter of fact, we are better than we know.
We trail behind us an endless tradition, of combat,
    triumph, conquest,
and we feel we've got to keep it up, keep on combating,
    triumphing, conquering.
When as a matter of fact, the thought of this endless,
    imbecile struggle of combat
kills us, we are sick of it to die.
We are fed up with combat,
we feel that if the whole combative, competitive system
    doesn't soon go bust
we shall.
We want a new world of wild peace, where living is free.

Not this hyena tame peace where no man dare tell another
    he's a thief
and yet every man is driven into robbing every other man;
this pretty peace where every man has to fight, and fight
    foul,
to get a living, in the dastardly mean combat
we call free competition and individual enterprise and
    equal opportunity.

Why should we have to fight for a living?
Living should be as free to a man as to a bird,
though most birds have to pay, with their lives, where men
    are.

Why should we brace ourselves up with mean emulation?
If we brace ourselves up, it should be for something we
    want to do
and we feel is worth doing.
The efforts of men, like the efforts of birds in spring,
would be lovely if they rose from the man himself, spon-
    taneous
pure impulse to make something, to put something forth.
Even if it was only a tin pan.

I see the tin-man, the tinker, sitting day after day on the
    beach
mending and tinning the pans of all the village
and happy as a wagtail by a pool,
the same with the fishermen sitting darning their nets,
happy as perhaps kings used to be, but certainly aren't.
Work is the clue to a man's life.
But it must be free work, not done just for money, but for
    fun.

Why should we compete with one another?
As a matter of fact, when the tinker looks so happy
    tinkering
I immediately want to go and do something jolly too.
One free, cheerful activity stimulates another.
Men are not really mean.
Men are made mean, by fear, and a system of grab.

The young know these things quite well.
Why don't they prepare to act on them?
Then they'd be happy. For we are all so much better than
    the system allows us to be.

WAGES

The wages of work is cash.
The wages of cash is want more cash.
The wages of want more cash is vicious competition.
The wages of vicious competition is—the world we live in.

The work-cash-want circle is the viciousest circle
that ever turned men into fiends.

Earning a wage is a prison occupation
and a wage-earner is a sort of gaol-bird.
Earning a salary is a prison overseer's job,
a gaoler instead of a gaol-bird.

Living on your income is strolling grandly outside the
        prison
in terror lest you have to go in. And since the work-prison
        covers
almost every scrap of the living earth, you stroll up and
        down
on a narrow beat, about the same as a prisoner taking his
        exercise.

This is called universal freedom.

YOUNG FATHERS

Young men, having no real joy in life and no hope in the
        future
how can they commit the indecency of begetting children
without first begetting a new hope for the children to
        grow up to?

But then, you need only look at the modern perambulator
to see that a child, as soon as it is born,
is put by its parents into its coffin.

A TALE TOLD BY AN IDIOT

Modern life is a tale told by an idiot;
flat-chested, crop-headed, chemicalised women, of indeter-
minate sex,
and wimbly-wambly young men, of sex still more in-
determinate,
and hygienic babies in huge hulks of coffin-like perambu-
lators—
The great social idiot, it must be confessed,
tells dull, meaningless, disgusting tales,
and repeats himself like the flushing of a W.C.

BEING ALIVE

The only reason for living is being fully alive;
and you can't be fully alive if you are crushed by secret
fear,
and bullied with the threat: Get money, or eat dirt!—
and forced to do a thousand mean things meaner than
your nature,
and forced to clutch on to possessions in the hope they'll
make you feel safe,
and forced to watch everyone that comes near you, lest
they've come to do you down.

Without a bit of common trust in one another, we can't
live.
In the end, we go insane.
It is the penalty of fear and meanness, being meaner than
our natures are.

To be alive, you've got to feel a generous flow,
and under a competitive system that is impossible, really.
The world is waiting for a new great movement of
generosity,
or for a great wave of death.
We must change the system, and make living free to all
men,
or we must see men die, and then die ourselves.

SELF-PROTECTION

When science starts to be interpretive
it is more unscientific even than mysticism.

To make self-preservation and self-protection the first law
of existence
is about as scientific as making suicide the first law of
existence,
and amounts to very much the same thing.

A nightingale singing at the top of his voice
is neither hiding himself nor preserving himself nor propa-
gating his species;
he is giving himself away in every sense of the word;
and obviously, it is the culminating point of his existence.

A tiger is striped and golden for his own glory.
He would certainly be much more invisible if he were
grey-green.

And I don't suppose the ichthyosaurus sparkled like the
humming-bird,
no doubt he was khaki-coloured with muddy protective
coloration,
so why didn't he survive?

As a matter of fact, the only creatures that seem to survive
are those that give themselves away in flash and sparkle
and gay flicker of joyful life;
those that go glittering abroad
with a bit of splendour.

Even mice play quite beautifully at shadows,
and some of them are brilliantly piebald.

I expect the dodo looked like a clod,
a drab and dingy bird.

A MAN

All I care about in a man
is that unbroken spark in him
where he is himself
undauntedly.

And all I want is to see the spark flicker
vivid and clean.

But our civilisation, alas,
with lust crushes out the spark
and leaves men living clay.

Because when the spark is crushed in a man
he can't help being a slave, a wage-slave,
a money-slave.

LIZARD

A lizard ran out on a rock and looked up, listening
no doubt to the sounding of the spheres.
And what a dandy fellow! the right toss of a chin for you
and swirl of a tail!

If men were as much men as lizards are lizards
they'd be worth looking at.

RELATIVITY

I like relativity and quantum theories
because I don't understand them
and they make me feel as if space shifted
        about like a swan that can't settle,
refusing to sit still and be measured;
and as if the atom were an impulsive thing
always changing its mind.

SPACE

Space, of course, is alive
that's why it moves about;
and that's what makes it eternally spacious and unstuffy.

And somewhere it has a wild heart
that sends pulses even through me;
and I call it the sun;
and I feel aristocratic, noble, when I feel a pulse go
    through me
from the wild heart of space, that I call the sun of suns.

SUN-MEN

Men should group themselves into a new order
of sun-men.
Each one turning his breast straight to the sun of suns
in the centre of all things,
and from his own little inward sun
nodding to the great one.

And receiving from the great one
his strength and his promptings,
and refusing the pettifogging promptings of human
    weakness.

And walking each in his own sun-glory
with bright legs and uncringing buttocks.

SUN-WOMEN

How strange it would be if some women came
    forward and said:
We are sun-women!
We belong neither to men nor our children nor
    even ourselves
but to the sun.

And how delicious it is to feel sunshine upon one!
And how delicious to open like a marigold
when a man comes looking down upon one
with sun in his face, so that a woman cannot but open
like a marigold to the sun,
and thrill with glittering rays.

DEMOCRACY

I am a democrat in so far as I love the free sun in men
and an aristocrat in so far as I detest narrow-gutted,
    possessive persons.

I love the sun in any man
when I see it between his brows
clear, and fearless, even if tiny.

But when I see these grey successful men
so hideous and corpse-like, utterly sunless,
like gross successful slaves mechanically waddling,
then I am more than radical, I want to work a guillotine.

And when I see working men
pale and mean and insect-like, scuttling along
and living like lice, on poor money
and never looking up,
then I wish, like Tiberius, the multitude had only one head
so that I could lop it off.

I feel that when people have gone utterly sunless
they shouldn't exist.

ARISTOCRACY OF THE SUN

To be an aristocrat of the sun
you don't need one single social inferior to exalt you;
you draw your nobility direct from the sun
let other people be what they may.

I am that I am
from the sun,
and people are not my measure.

Perhaps, if we started right, all the children could grow up
        sunny
and sun-aristocrats.
We need have no dead people, money-slaves, and social
        worms.

CONSCIENCE

Conscience
is sun-awareness
and our deep instinct
not to go against the sun.

THE MIDDLE CLASSES

The middle classes
are sunless.
They have only two measures:
mankind and money,
they have utterly no reference to the sun.

As soon as you let *people* be your measure
you are middle-class and essentially non-existent.

Because, if the middle classes had no poorer people to be
        superior to
they would themselves at once collapse into nullity.
And if they had no upper classes either, to be inferior to,
they wouldn't suddenly become themselves aristocratic,
they'd become nothing.
For their middleness is only an unreality separating two
        realities.

No sun, no earth,
nothing that transcends the bourgeois middlingness,
the middle classes are more meaningless
than paper money when the bank is broke.

IMMORALITY

It is only immoral
to be dead-alive,
sun-extinct
and busy putting out the sun
in other people.

CENSORS

Censors are dead men
set up to judge between life and death.
For no live, sunny man would be a censor,
he'd just laugh.

But censors, being dead men,
have a stern eye on life.
—That thing's alive! It's dangerous. Make away
     with it!—
And when the execution is performed
you hear the stertorous, self-righteous heavy
     breathing of the dead men,
the censors, breathing with relief.

MAN'S IMAGE

What a pity, when a man looks at himself in a glass
he doesn't bark at himself, like a dog does,
or fluff up in indignant fury, like a cat!

What a pity he sees himself so wonderful,
a little lower than the angels!
and so interesting!

IMMORAL MAN

Man is immoral because he has got a mind
and can't get used to the fact.

The deep instincts, when left alone, are quite moral,
and clear intuition is more than moral,
it really makes us men.

Why don't we learn to tame the mind
instead of killing the passions and the instincts and
        feelings?
It is the mind which is uncouth and overweening
and ruins our complex harmony.

COWARDS

In all creation, only man cowers and is afraid of life.
Only man is terrified of his own possible splendour and
        delight.
Only is man agonised in front of the necessity to be some-
        thing better than he is,
poor mental worm.

Though maybe the mammoth got too big in tusk and teeth,
and the extinct giant elk too big in antlers,
out of fear of the unknown enemy;
so perhaps they too died out from fear,
as man is likely to do.

THINK——!

Imagine what it must have been to have existence
in the wild days when life was sliding whirlwinds, blue-hot
        weights,
in the days called chaos, which left us rocks, and gems!

Think that the sapphire is only alumina, like kitchen pans
crushed utterly, and breathed through and through
with fiery weight and wild life, and coming out
clear and flowery blue!

PEACOCK

Think how a peacock in a forest of high trees
shimmers in a stream of blueness and long-
    tressed magnificence!
And women even cut their shimmery hair!

PALTRY-LOOKING PEOPLE

And think how the nightingale, who is so shy,
makes of himself a belfry of throbbing sound!
While people mince mean words through their teeth.

And think how wild animals trot with splendour
till man destroys them!
how vividly they make their assertion of life!

But how paltry, mingy and dingy and squalid people look
in their rag garments scuttling through the streets,
or sitting stuck like automata in automobiles!

TARTS

I suppose tarts are called tarts because they're tart,
meaning sour, make you pull a face after.
And I suppose most girls are a bit tarty to-day,
so that's why so many young men have long faces.
The father eats the pear, and the son's teeth are set on edge.

LATTER-DAY SINNERS

The worst of the younger generation, those Latter-Day
    sinners,
is that they calmly assert: We only thrill to perversity,
    murder, suicide, rape——
bragging a little, really,
and at the same time expect to go on calmly eating good
    dinners for the next fifty years.

They say: *Après moi le déluge!* and calmly expect
that the deluge will never be turned on them, only *after*
    them.

Post me, nihil!—But perhaps, my dears,
nihil will come along and hit you on the head.

Why should the deluge wait while these young gentry go
    on eating
good dinners for fifty more long years?
Why should our Latter-Day sinners expect such a long
    smooth run
for their very paltry little bit of money?

If you are expecting a Second Advent in the shape of a
    deluge
you mustn't expect it also to wait for your convenience.

WHAT MATTERS

As one of our brightest young intellectuals said to me:
It's not so much what we think,
or even what we like or dislike, or approve or disapprove
that matters so very much.

What matters is what we thrill to.
We are ultimately determined by what we thrill to.
And, of course, thrilling is like loving, you have no choice
    about it.

Pondering this new truth of the sensational young, I said:
But what do you thrill to? Do you know?
I suppose, as a matter of fact, it's getting a little difficult,
he replied, to thrill to anything.

A thrill rather easily exhausts itself—take even the war,
and look at the sodomitical and lesbian stuff—wearing
    rather thin.
Beauty, of course! Beauty is still a delicious escape.

And the pure intellect gives one a last, masturbating sense
    of excited freedom!
But, of course, one knows that both beauty and pure
    intellect are only escapes,
mild forms of cocaine; they're not life, exactly.

No, when it comes to thrills, there are really very few.
Judging from the fiction it is possible to read, I should say
    rape was rather thrilling
or being raped, either way, so long as it was consciously
    done, and slightly subtle.

Yes, if it's a keen match, rape is rather thrilling.
And then perhaps murder. That is to say
quite cold-blooded, intellectual murder, with a sufficient
    cool motive
and a complete absence of consequence to the murderer.

I should say that was rather thrilling,
rather thrilling to contemplate.

After that, of course, there's suicide—certain aspects,
    perhaps,
Yes, I should say the contemplation of clever suicide *is*
    rather thrilling,
so long as the thing is done neatly, and the world is left
    looking very fooled.

Quite thrilling, I should say, at least to contemplate.
For the rest—no! I should say life held very few
further thrilling possibilities.
So one of the brightest young intellectuals put it to me.
And I had to give him credit for his rather exhibitionist
    honesty.

And in the intervals of their thrills, I suppose
they must go on
they must go on scratching the eczema of their mental itch
with finger-nails of septic criticising.

FATE AND THE YOUNGER
GENERATION

It is strange to think of the Annas, the Vronskys, the
    Pierres, all the Tolstoyan lot
wiped out.

And the Alyoshas and Dmitris and Myshkins and Stavro-
    gins, the Dostoevsky lot
all wiped out.

And the Tchekov wimbly-wambly wet-legs all wiped out.

Gone! Dead, or wandering in exile with their feathers
    plucked,
anyhow, gone from what they were, entirely.

Will the Proustian lot go next?
And then our English imitation intelligentsia?
Is it the *Quos vult perdere Deus* business?

Anyhow the Tolstoyan lot simply asked for extinction:
Eat me up, dear peasant!—So the peasant ate him.
And the Dostoevsky lot wallowed in the thought:
Let me sin my way to Jesus!—So they sinned themselves
    off the face of the earth.

And the Tchekov lot: I'm too weak and lovable to live!
    So they went.
Now the Proustian lot: Dear darling death, let me wriggle
    my way towards you
like the worm I am!—So he wriggled and got there.

Finally our little lot: I don't want to die, but by Jingo if
    I do!
—Well, it won't matter so very much, either.

AS FOR ME, I'M A PATRIOT

> Whatever else they say of me
> they'll never be able to say
> I was one of the little blighters
> who so brilliantly betray
> the tough old England that made us
> and in them is rotting away.
>
> I'd betray the middle classes
> and money and industry
> and the intellectual asses
> and cash christianity,
>
> but not the England that made me
> the stuff of a man,
> the old England that doesn't upbraid me,
> nor put me under a ban.

THE ROSE OF ENGLAND

Oh the rose of England is a single rose
and damasked red and white!

But roses, if they're fed too much,
change from being single and become gradually double,
and that's what's happened to the English rose.

The wild rose in a sheltered garden
when it need struggle no more
softly blows out its thin little male stamens
into broad sweet petals,
and through the centuries goes on and on
puffing its little male stamens out into sterile petal flames
till at last it's a full, full rose, and has no male dust any
     more,
it propagates no more.

So it is with Englishmen.
They are all double roses
and their true maleness is gone.

Oh the rose of England is a single rose
and needs to be raised from seed.

ENGLAND IN 1929

England was always a country of men
and had a brave destiny, even when she went wrong.

Now it's a country of frightened old mongrels
snapping out of fear,
and young wash-outs pretending to be in love with death
yet living on the fat of the land;

so of course the nation is swollen with insoluble problems
and like to become incurably diseased inside.

LIBERTY'S OLD OLD STORY

Men fight for liberty, and win it with hard knocks.
Their children, brought up easy, let it slip away again,
     poor fools.
And their grandchildren are once more slaves.

NEW BROOMS

New brooms sweep clean
but they often raise such a dust in the sweeping
that they choke the sweeper.

POLICE SPIES

Start a system of official spying
and you've introduced anarchy into your country.

NOW IT'S HAPPENED

One cannot now help thinking
how much better it would have been
if Vronsky and Anna Karenin
had stood up for themselves, and seen
Russia across her crisis,
instead of leaving it to Lenin.

The big, flamboyant Russia
might have been saved, if a pair
of rebels like Anna and Vronsky
had blasted the sickly air
of Dostoevsky and Tchekov,
and spy-government everywhere.

But Tolstoi was a traitor
to the Russia that needed him most,
the clumsy, bewildered Russia
so worried by the Holy Ghost.
He shifted his job on to the peasants
and landed them all on toast.

Dostoevsky, the Judas,
with his sham christianity
epileptically ruined
the last bit of sanity
left in the hefty bodies
of the Russian nobility.

So our goody-good men betray us
and our sainty-saints let us down,
and a sickly people will slay us
if we touch the sob-stuff crown
of such martyrs; while Marxian tenets
naturally take hold of the town.

Too much of the humble Willy wet-leg
and the holy can't-help-it touch,
till you've ruined a nation's fibre
and they loathe all feeling as such,
and want to be cold and devilish hard
like machines—and you can't wonder much.

ENERGETIC WOMEN

Why are women so energetic?
prancing their knees under their tiny skirts
like war-horses; or war-ponies at least!

Why are they so centrifugal?
Why are they so bursting, flinging themselves about?
Why, as they grow older, do they suffer from blood-pressure?

Why are they never happy to be still?
Why did they cut off their long hair
which they could comb by the hour in luxurious quiet?

I suppose when the men all started being Willy wet-legs
women felt it was no longer any use being a linger-longer-
    Lucy.

FILM PASSION

If all those females who so passionately loved
the film face of Rudolf Valentino
had had to take him for one night only, in the flesh,
how they'd have hated him!

Hated him just because he was a man
and flesh of a man.
For the luscious filmy imagination loathes the male
    substance
with deadly loathing.

All the women who adored the shadow of the man on
    the screen
helped to kill him in the flesh.
Such adoration pierces the loins and perishes the man
worse than the evil eye.

FEMALE COERCION

If men only fought outwards into the world
women might be devoted and gentle.
The fight's got to go in some direction.

But when men turn Willy wet-legs
women start in to make changes;
only instead of changing things that might be changed
they want to change the man himself
and turn the poor silk glove into a lusty sow's ear.

And the poor Willy wet-legs, the soft silk gloves,
how they hate the women's efforts to turn them
into sow's ears!

The modern Circe-dom!

VOLCANIC VENUS

What has happened in the world?
the women are like little volcanoes
all more or less in eruption.

It is very unnerving, moving in a world of smouldering
    volcanoes.
It is rather agitating, sleeping with a little Vesuvius.

And exhausting, penetrating the lava-crater of a tiny
    Ixtaccihuatl
and never knowing when you'll provoke an earthquake.

WHAT DOES SHE WANT?

What does she want, volcanic Venus, as she goes fuming
    round?
What does she want?
She says she wants a lover, but don't you believe her.
She's seething like a volcano, and volcanos don't want
    lovers.

Besides, she's had twenty lovers, only to find she didn't
    really want them.

So why should I, or you, be the twenty-first?
How are we going to appease her, maiden and mother
now a volcano of rage?
I tell you, the penis won't do it.

She bites him in the neck and passes on.

WONDERFUL SPIRITUAL WOMEN

The wonderful thoughtful women who make such good
    companions to a man
are only sitting tight on the craters of their volcano
and spreading their skirts.

Or like the woman who sat down on a sleeping mastodon
thinking he was a little hill, and she murmured such
    beautiful things
the men stood around like crocuses agape in the sun.

Then suddenly the mastodon rose with the wonderful lady
and trampled all the listeners to a smush.

POOR BIT OF A WENCH!

Will no one say hush! to thee,
poor lass, poor' bit of a wench?
Will never a man say: Come, my pigeon,
come an' be still wi' me, my own bit of a wench!

And would you peck out his eyes if he did?

WHAT AILS THEE?

What ails thee then, woman, what ails thee?
doesn't ter know?
If tha canna say't, come then an' scraight it out on my
    bosom!
Eh?—Men doesna ha'e bosoms? 'appen not, on'y tha knows
    what I mean.
Come then, tha can scraight it out on my shirt-front
an' tha'lt feel better.

    —In the first place, I don't scraight.
    And if I did, I certainly couldn't *scraight it out.*
    And if I could, the last place I should choose
    would be your shirt-front
    or your manly bosom either.
    So leave off trying to put the Robbie Burns touch
        over me
    and kindly hand me the cigarettes
    if you haven't smoked them all,
    which you're much more likely to do
    than to shelter anybody from the cau-auld blast.—

IT'S NO GOOD!

It's no good, the women are in eruption,
and those that have been good so far
now begin to steam ominously,
and if they're over forty-five, hurl great stones into the air
which are very like to hit you on the head as you sit
on the very slopes of the matrimonial mountain
where you've sat peacefully all these years.

Vengeance is mine, saith the Lord,
but the women are my favourite vessels of wrath.

DON'T LOOK AT ME

My dears, don't look at me, I am merely terrified of you.
I don't know what you want, but I certainly haven't got
    it to give you.

No, my poor little penis would be of no use to you
dear ladies, none whatsoever.

It's something else you are after, if you could but
    formulate it.

As for bearing my children—why there
I wouldn't insult you with the suggestion.

The son of man goes forth to war
no more, he sends his daughter
collecting foreskins.

But I consider I was sufficiently circumcised long ago.

My dears, if you want the skies to fall
they are established on the many pillars of the phallus,
so perhaps you'll do it.

SHIPS IN BOTTLES

O ship in a bottle
with masts erect and spars all set and sails spread
how you remind me of my London friends,
O ships in bottles!

Little fleets
that put to sea on certain evenings,
frigates, barks and pinnaces, yawls
all beautifully rigged and bottled up
that put to sea and boldly sink Armadas
in a pub parlour, in literary London, on certain evenings.

O small flotilla of sorry souls
sail on, over perilous seas of thought,
cast your little anchors in ports of eternity,
then weigh, and out to the infinities,
skirting the poles of being and of not-being.

Ah, in that parlour of the London pub
what dangers, ah what dangers!
Caught between great icebergs of doubt
they are all but crushed
little ships.

Nipped upon the frozen floods of philosophic despair
they lie high and dry,
high and dry.
Reeling in the black end of all beliefs
they sink.

Yet there they are, there they are,
little ships
safe inside their bottles!

Whelmed in profundities of profound conversation,
lost between great waves of ultimate ideas
they are—why there they are,
safe inside their bottles!

Safer than in the arms of Jesus!
Oh safer than anything else is a well-corked, glassy ego,
and sounder than all insurance is a shiny mental conceit!

Sail, little ships in your glass bottles
safe from every contact,
safe from all experience,
safe, above all, from life!

And let the nodding tempests of verbosity
weekly or twice-weekly whistle round your bottles.
Spread your small sails immune, little ships!
The storm is words, the bottles never break.

KNOW THYSELF, AND THAT
THOU ART MORTAL

If you want to know yourself
you've got to keep up with yourself.
Your self moves on, and is not to-day what it was yesterday;
and you've got to run, to keep up with it.

But sometimes we run ahead too fast
running after a figment of ourselves.
And that's what we've done to-day.

We think we're such clever little johnnies
with our sharp little eyes and our high-power machines
which get us ahead so much faster than our feet could
ever carry us.

When alas, it's only part of our clever little self that gets
ahead!
Something is left behind, lost and howling, and we know it.

Ah, clever Odysseus who outwitted the cyclop
and blinded him in his one big eye,
put out a light of consciousness and left a blinded brute.

Clever little ants in spectacles, we are,
performing our antics.

But what we also are, and we need to know it,
is blinded brutes of cyclops, with our cyclopean eye put
    out.

And we still bleed, and we grope and roar;
for spectacles and bulging clever ant-eyes are no good to
    the cyclop,
he wants his one great wondering eye, the eye of the
    cavern and the portent.

As little social ants perhaps we function all right.
But oh, our human lives, the lunging blind cyclops we are!
hitting ourselves against unseen rock, crashing our head
    against the roof
of the ancient cave, smashing into one another,
tearing each other's feelings, trampling each other's ten-
    derest emotions to mud
and never knowing what we are doing, roaring blind with
    pain and dismay.

Ah, cyclops, the little ant-men can never enlighten you
with their bulging policeman's-lamp eyes.
You need your own great wondering eye that flashes with
    instinct in the cavern
and gleams on the world with the warm dark vision of
    intuition!

Even our brilliantest young intellectuals
are also poor blind cyclops, moaning
with all the hurt to their instinctive and emotional selves,
and grieving with puppy-like blind crying
over their mutilated cyclopean eye.

WHAT IS MAN WITHOUT
AN INCOME?

What is man without an income?
—Well, let him get on the dole!

Dole, dole, dole
hole, hole, hole
soul, soul, soul—

What is man without an income?
Answer without a rigmarole.

On the dole, dole, dole
he's a hole, hole, hole
in the nation's pocket.

—Now then, you leave a man's misfortunes alone!

He's got a soul, soul, soul
but the coal, coal, coal
on the whole, whole, whole
doesn't pay,
so the dole, dole, dole's
the only way.

And on the dole, dole, dole
a man's a hole, hole, hole
in the nation's pocket,
and his soul, soul, soul
won't stop a hole, hole, hole
though his ashes might.

*Immortal Cæsar dead and turned to clay
would stop a hole to keep the wind away.*

But a man without a job
isn't even as good as a gob
of clay.

Body and soul
he's just a hole
down which the nation's resources roll
away.

CANVASSING FOR THE ELECTION

—Excuse me, but are you a superior person?
—I beg your pardon?
—Oh, I'm sure you'll understand. We're making a census of all the
really patriotic people—the right sort of people, you know—of
course you understand what I mean—so *would* you mind giving
me your word?—and signing here, please—that you *are* a superior
person—that's all we need to know—
—Really, I don't know what you take me for!
—Yes, I know! It's too bad! Of course it's perfectly superfluous to
ask, but the League insists. Thank you so much! No, sign here,
please, and there I countersign. That's right! Yes, that's all!—
I declare I am a superior person—. Yes, exactly! and here I
countersign your declaration. It's so simple, and really, it's *all* we
need to know about anybody. And do you know, I've never been
denied a signature! We English *are* a solid people, after all. This
proves it. Quite! Thank you so much! We're getting on simply
splendidly—and it *is* a comfort, isn't it?—

ALTERCATION

Now look here,
if you were really superior,
really superior,
you'd have money, and you know it!

Well what abaht it?

What about it?
what about it?
why, isn't it obvious?
Here you are, with no money,
and here am I, paying income tax and god-knows-what
taxes
just to support you and find you money,
and you stand there and expect me to treat you like an
equal!—
Whereas, let me tell you, if you *were* my equal
you'd *have* money, you'd *have* it, enough to support your-
self, anyhow—
And there you stand with *nothing*, and expect me to hand
it you out
as if it were your dues, and I didn't count at all—

All right, guvnor! What abaht it?

Do you mean to say what about it?
My God, it takes some beating!
If you were a *man*, and up to my mark, you'd *have* money
—can't you see it?
You're my inferior, that's what you are, you're my inferior.
And do you think it's my business to be handing out money
to a lot of inferior swipe?
Eh? Answer me that!

Right ch'are, boss! An' what abaht it?

FINDING YOUR LEVEL

Down, down, down!
There must be a nadir somewhere
of superiority.

Down, and still
the superior persons, though somewhat inferior,
are still superior.

They are still superior, so there must be something they
    are superior to.
There must be a bed-rock somewhere, of people who are
    not superior,
one must come down to *terra firma* somewhere!

Or must one simply say:
All my inferiors are very superior.

There has been great progress
in superiority.

Fortunately though, some superior persons are still superior
to the quite superior persons who are not so superior as
    they are.

May I ask if you are *really* superior
or if you only look it so wonderfully?
Because we English *do* appreciate a *real* gentleman, or a
    real lady;
but appearances *are* deceptive nowadays, aren't they?

And if you only *look* so distinguished and superior
when really you are slightly inferior,
like a shop-lady or a lady-secretary,
you mustn't expect, my dear, to get away with it.
There's a list kept of the truly superior
and if you're not on the list, why there you are, my dear,
you're off it.

There are great numbers of quite superior persons who are
    not on the list,
poor things—but we can't help that, can we!
We must draw a line somewhere
or we should never know when we were crossing the
    equator.

What is man, that thou art mindful of him
or the son of man, that thou pitiest him?
for thou hast made him a little lower than the angels
who are *very* superior people,
Oh *very*!

CLIMBING UP

When you climb up to the middle classes
you leave a lot behind you,
you leave a lot, you've lost a lot
and you've nobody to remind you
of all the things they squeezed out of you
when they took you and refined you.

When they took you and refined you
they squeezed out most of your guts;
they took away your good old stones
and gave you a couple of nuts;
and they taught you to speak King's English
and butter your slippery buts.

Oh you've got to be like a monkey
if you climb up the tree!
You've no more use for the solid earth
and the lad you used to be.
You sit in the boughs and gibber
with superiority.

They all gibber and gibber and chatter,
and never a word they say
comes really out of their guts, lad,
they make it up half way;
they make it up, and it's always the same,
if it's serious or if it's play.

You think they're the same as you are
and then you find they're not,
and they never were nor would be,
not one of the whole job lot.
And you have to act up like they do
or they think you're off your dot.

There isn't a man among 'em,
not one; they all seemed to me
like monkeys or angels or something, in a limited
liability company;
like a limited liability company
they are, all limited liability.

What they're limited to or liable
to, I could never make out.
But they're all alike, an' it makes you
want to get up an' shout
an' blast 'em forever; but they'd only
think you a lower-class lout.

I tell you, something's been done to 'em,
to the pullets up above;
there's not a cock bird among 'em
though they're always on about love,
an' you could no more get 'em a move on,
no! no matter how you may shove!

TO CLARINDA

Thank you, dear Clarinda
for helping with Lady C.,
It was you who gave her her first kiss
and told her not to be
afraid of the world, but to sally forth
and trip it for all she was worth.

So out she came, and she said she was Jane,
and you clapped your hands, and said: Say it again!
And you cried: 'Ooray! Play up John Thomas!
Let's have no full stops, let's just manage with commas!—

And the white snow glistened, the white world was gay
up there at that height in the Diablerets.
And we slid, and you ski'd, and we came in to tea
and we talked and we roared and you typed Lady C.

And how jolly it was with us up in the snow
with the crest of the dirty drab world down below!

And how bitter it is to come down
to the dirty drab world,
and slowly feel yourself drown
in its mud, and its talk, slowly swirled
to the depths, to the depths
of London town!

CONUNDRUMS

Tell me a word
that you've often heard,
yet it makes you squint
if you see it in print!

Tell me a thing
that you've often seen,
yet if put in a book
it makes you turn green!

Tell me a thing
that you often do,
which described in a story
shocks you through and through!

Tell me what's wrong
with words or with you
that you don't mind the thing
yet the name is taboo.

A RISE IN THE WORLD

I rose up in the world, Ooray!
rose very high, for me.
An earl once asked me down to stay
and a duchess once came to tea.

I didn't stay very long with the earl
and the duchess has done with me.
But still, I rose quite high in the world
don't you think?—or don't you agree?

But now I am slithering down again,
down the trunk of the slippery tree;
I find I'd rather get back to earth,
where I belong, you see.

Up there I didn't like it,
chattering, though not with glee,
the whole of the time, and nothing
mattering—at least, not to me.

God, let me down to earth again
away from the upper ten
millions—for there's millions of 'em
up there—but not any men.

UP HE GOES!

Up I rose, my lads, an' I heard yer
sayin': Up he goes!

Up like a bloomin' little Excelsior
in his Sunday clothes!

Up he goes, up the bloomin' ladder
about to the giddy top!
Who'd ever have thought it of that lad, a
pasty little snot!—

Never you mind, my lads, I left you
a long long way behind.
You'll none of you rise in the world like I did;
an' if you did, you'd find

it damn well wasn't worth it,
goin' up an' bein' refined;
it was nowt but a dirty sell, that's all,
a *damn fraud*, underlined.

They're not any better than we are,
the upper classes—they're worse.
Such bloomin' fat-arsed dool-owls
they aren't even fit to curse!

There isn't a damn thing in 'em,
they're as empty as empty tins;
they haven't the spunk of a battle-twig,
an' all they can think of is sins.

No, there's nowt in the upper classes
as far as I can find;
a worse lot o' jujubey asses
than the lot I left behind.

They'll never do a thing, boys,
they can't, they're simply fused.
So if any of you's live wires, with wits
to use, they'd better be used.

If there's anything got to be done, why
get up an' do it yourselves!
Though God knows if you're any better,
sittin' there in rows on your shelves!

An' if you're not any better,
if you've none of you got more spunk
than they've got in the upper classes,
why, let's all of us do a bunk.

We're not fit for the earth we live on,
we're not fit for the air we breathe.
We'd better get out, an' make way for
the babes just beginning to teethe.

THE SADDEST DAY

"We climbed the steep ascent to heaven
      Through peril, toil and pain.
O God to us may strength be given
      To scramble back again."

O I was born low and inferior
but shining up beyond
I saw the whole superior
world shine like the promised land.

So up I started climbing
to join the folks on high,
but when at last I got there
I had to sit down and cry.

For it wasn't a bit superior,
it was only affected and mean;
though the house had a fine interior
the people were never in.

I mean, they were never entirely
there when you talked to them;
away in some private cupboard
some small voice went: *Ahem!*

Ahem! they went. *This fellow*
is a little too open for me;
with such people one has to be careful
though, of course, we won't let him see!—

And they thought you couldn't hear them
privately coughing: *Ahem!*
And they thought you couldn't see them
cautiously swallowing their phlegm!

But of course I always heard them,
and every time the same.
They all of them always kept up their sleeve
their class-superior claim.

Some narrow-gutted superiority,
and trying to make you agree,
which, for myself, I couldn't.
it was all cat-piss to me.

And so there came the saddest day
when I had to tell myself plain:
the upper classes are just a fraud,
you'd better get down again.

PRESTIGE

I never met a single
middle-class person whose
nerves didn't tighten against me
as if they'd got something to lose.

Though what it was, you can ask me:
some mysterious sort of prestige
that was nothing to me; though they always
seemed to think I was laying it siege.

It was something I never could fathom,
that mysterious prestige which they all
seemed to think they'd got, like a halo
around them, an invisible wall.

If *you* were willing to see it
they were only too eager to grant
you a similar glory, since you'd risen
to their levels, my holy aunt!

But never, no never could I see it,
and so I could never feel
the proper unction about it,
and it worried me a good deal.

For years and years it bothered me
that I couldn't feel one of them,
till at last I saw the reason:
they were just a bloody sham.

As far as any superiority
or halo or prestige went
they were just a bloody collective fraud,
that was what their *Ahem!* meant.

Their superiority was meanness,
they were cunning about the goods
and sly with a lot of after-thought,
and they put it over us, the duds!

And I'd let myself be swindled
half believing 'em, till one day
I suddenly said: I've finished!
My God, let me get away!

HAVE DONE WITH IT

Once and for all, have done with it,
all the silly bunk
of upper-class superiority; that superior
stuff is just holy skunk.

Just you walk around them
and look at the fat-arsed lot
and tell me how they can put it across,
this superior rot!

All these gracious ladies
graciously bowing down
from their pedestals! Holy Moses
they've done you brown!

And all the sacred gentry
so responsible and good,
feeling so *kind* towards you
and suckin' your blood!

My! the bloomin' pompoms!
Even as trimmings they're stale.
Still, if you don't want to bother,
I don't care myself a whale.

HENRIETTE

O Henriette
I remember yet
how cross you were
over Lady C.
how you hated her
and detested me.

Yet now you see
you don't mind a bit.
You've got used to it,
and you feel more free.

And now you know
how good we were
up there in the snow
with Lady C.
though you hated her
at the first go.

Yet now you can see
how she set us free
to laugh, and to be
more spontaneous, and we
were happy, weren't we
up there in the snow
with the world below!

So now, when you say
your prayers at night
you must sometimes pray:
Dear Lord of delight
may I be Jane
tonight, profane
but sweet in your sight,
though last night I was Mary—

You said I might
dear Lord of right
be so contrary.
So may I be *Jane*
tonight, and refrain
from being Mary?

VITALITY

Alas, my poor young men,
do you lack vitality?

Has the shell grown too heavy for the tortoise?
Does he just squirm?

Is the frame of things too heavy
for poor young wretched men?
Do they jazz and jump and wriggle
and rush about in machines
and listen to bodiless noises
and cling to their thin young women
as to the last straw

just in desperation,
because their spirit can't move?
Because their hope is pinned down by the system
and can't even flutter?

Well well, if it is so it is so;
but remember, the undaunted gods
give vitality still to the dauntless.

And sometimes they give it as love,
ah love, sweet love, not so easy!
But sometimes they give it as lightning.

And it's no good wailing for love
if they only offer you lightning.
And it's no good mooning for sloppy ease
when they're holding out the thunderbolt
for you to take.

You might as well take the lightning
for once, and feel it go through you.
You might as well accept the thunderbolt
and prepare for storms.

You'll not get vitality any other way.

WILLY WET-LEG

I can't stand Willy wet-leg,
can't stand him at any price.
He's resigned, and when you hit him
he lets you hit him twice.

MAYBE

Ah well! ah well! maybe
the young have learned some sense.
They ought at last to see through the game,
they've sat long enough on the fence.

Maybe their little bottoms
will get tired and sore at last
of sitting there on the fence, and letting
their good youth go to waste.

Maybe a sense of destiny
will rise in them one day,
maybe they'll realise it's time
they slipped into the fray.

Maybe they're getting tired
of sitting on the fence;
it dawns on them that the whole damn swindle
is played at their expense.

STAND UP!

Stand up, but not for Jesus!
It's a little late for that.
Stand up for justice and a jolly life.
I'll hold your hat.

Stand up, stand up for justice,
ye swindled little blokes!
Stand up and do some punching,
give 'em a few hard pokes.

Stand up for jolly justice
you haven't got much to lose:
a job you don't like and a scanty chance
for a dreary little booze.

Stand up for something different,
and have a little fun
fighting for something worth fighting for
before you've done.

Stand up for a new arrangement
for a chance of life all round
for freedom, and the fun of living
bust in, and hold the ground!

TRUST

Oh we've got to trust
one another again
in some essentials.

Not the narrow little
bargaining trust
that says: I'm for you
if you'll be for me.

But a bigger trust,
a trust of the sun
that does not bother
about moth and rust,
and we see it shining
in one another.

Oh don't you trust me,
don't burden me
with your life and affairs; don't thrust
    me
into your cares.

But I think you may trust
the sun in me
that glows with just
as much glow as you see
in me, and no more.

But if it warms
your heart's quick core
why then trust it, it forms
one faithfulness more.

And be, oh be
a sun to me,
not a weary, insistent
personality

but a sun that shines
and goes dark, but shines
again and entwines
with the sunshine in me

till we both of us
are more glorious
and more sunny.

DEMON JUSTICE

If you want justice
let it be demon justice
that puts salt on the tails
of the goody good.

For the sins of omission,
for leaving things out,
not even a suspicion
of John Thomas about—

not even an inkling
that Lady Jane
is quietly twinklin'
up the lane—

not even a hint
that a pretty bottom
has a gay little glint
quite apart from Sodom—

that you and I
were both begotten
when our parents felt spry
beneath the cotton—

that the face is not only
the mind's index,
but also the comely
shy flower of sex—

that a woman is always
a gate to the flood,
that a man is forever
a column of blood—

for these most vital
things omitted,
now make requittal
and get acquitted.

Now bend you down
to demon justice,
and take sixty slashes
across your rusties.

Then with a sore
arse perhaps you'll remember
not quite to ignore
the jolly little member.

BE A DEMON!

Oh be a demon
outside all class!
If you're a woman
or even an ass
still be a demon
beyond the mass.

Somewhere inside you
lives your own little fiend,
and woe betide you
if he feels demeaned,
better do him justice,
keep his path well cleaned.

When you've been being
too human, too long,
and your demon starts lashing out
going it strong,
don't get too frightened
it's you who've been wrong.

You're not altogether
such a human bird,
you're as mixed as the weather,
not just a good turd,
so shut up pie-jaw blether,
let your demon be heard.

Don't look for a saviour,
you've had some, you know!
Drop your sloppy behaviour
and start in to show
your demon rump twinkling
with a hie! hop below!

If, poor little bleeder,
you still feel you must follow
some wonderful leader
now the old ones ring hollow,
then follow your demon
and hark to his *holloa*!

THE JEUNE FILLE

Oh the innocent girl
in her maiden teens
knows perfectly well
what everything means.

If she didn't, she oughter;
it's a silly shame
to pretend that your daughter
is a blank at the game.

Anyhow she despises
your fool pretence
that she's just a sheep
and can't see through the fence.

Oh every lass
should hear all the rough words
and laugh, let them pass;
and be used to the turds

as well as the grass;
and know that she's got
in herself a small treasure
that may yet give a lot

of genuine pleasure
to a decent man;
and beware and take care
of it while she can.

If she never knows
what is her treasure,
she grows and throws
it away, and you measure

the folly of that
from her subsequent woes.
Oh the innocent maid,
when she knows what's what

from the top of her head
to the tips of her toes
is more innocent far
than the blank-it-out girl

who gets into the car
and just fills you with hell.

NETTLES

A ROSE IS NOT A CABBAGE

And still, in spite of all they do, I love the rose of England,
but the cabbages of England leave me cold.

Oh the cabbages of England leave me cold
even though they grow on genuine English mould,
with their caterpillars, and the care with which they fold
nothingness, pale nothingness in their hearts.

Now that the winter of our discontent
is settled on the land, roses are scarce in England, very
    scarce, there are none any more.
But look at the cabbages, Oh count them by the score!
Oh aren't they green. Oh haven't we, haven't we spent
a lot of money rearing them——!

Yet the cabbages of England leave me cold
no matter of what sort the cabbage be.

THE MAN IN THE STREET

I met him in the street
I said: How do you do?—
He said: And who are you
when we meet?—

I sadly went my way
feeling anything but gay,
yet once more I met a man and I had to stay——
    May I greet——?

He cut me very dead,
but then he turned and said:
I see you're off your head
thus to greet
in the street
a member of the British Public: don't you see
the policeman on his beat?
Well, he's there protecting *me*!——

But! said I,
but why——?

And they ran me in, to teach me why.

BRITANNIA'S BABY

Oh Britannia's got a baby, a baby, a baby
Britannia's got a baby, and she got it by and by.

It's called the British Public, the Public, the Public
It's called the British Public, including you and I.

It's such a bonny baby, a baby, a baby
It's such a bonny baby, we daren't let it cry.

So we've got a lot of nurses, of nurses, of nurses
to feed the bonny baby, and keep its tara dry.

Eat your pap, little man, like a man!
Drink its minky-winky, then, like a man!

Does it want to go to bye-bye! there then, take its little
      dummy,
take its dummy, go to bye-bye like a man, little man!

Drop of whiskey in its minky? well it shall, yet it shall
if it's good, if it's going to be a *good* little man.

Want to go a little tattah? so it shall, of course it shall
go a banging little tattah with its Auntie
if it's good!
If it's good today, and tomorrow-day as well
then when Sunday comes, it shall go tattah with its Auntie
in a motor, in a pap-pap pap-pap motor, little man!

Oh isn't it a lucky little man!
to have whiskey in its minky
and to go a banging tattah with its Auntie
who loves her little man,
such a dear, kind Auntie, isn't she, to a lucky little
      man——!

For Oh, the British Public, the Public, the Public
For Oh, the British Public is a lucky little man!

CHANGE OF GOVERNMENT

We've got a change of government
if you know what I mean.
Auntie Maud has come to keep house
instead of Aunt Gwendoline.

They say that Auntie Maud, you know,
is rather common; she's not
so well brought up as Aunt Gwendoline is,
so perhaps she'll be more on the spot.

That's what we hope: we hope she'll be
a better manager: for Oh dear me
Aunt Gwen was a poor one! but Aunt Maud, you see
was brought up poor, so she'll *have* to be

more careful. Though if she's not
won't it be awful! what shall we do?
Aunt Libby's really a feeble lot,
and I simply daren't think of Aunt Lou!

I've never seen her, but they say
she's a holy terror: she takes your best frock
and *all* your best things, and just gives them away
to the char, who's as good as you are, any day.

And she makes you go to work, even if
you've got money of your own.
And she shuts you in the cellar for the least little tiff,
and just loves to hear you sob and groan.

Oh I do hope Aunt Maud will manage all right!
Because they say, if she doesn't
Aunt Louie is almost bound to come
with all our horrible cousins

that we've never seen, coming stamping and swearing
and painting the wood-work red
just to show how dangerous they are!
Oh, Aunt Louie's the one *I* dread.

THE BRITISH WORKMAN AND
THE GOVERNMENT

Hold my hand, Auntie, Auntie,
Auntie, hold my hand!
I feel I'm going to be naughty, Auntie,
and you don't seem to understand.

Hold my hand and love me, Auntie,
love your little boy!
We want to be loved, especially, Auntie,
us whom you can't employ.

Idle we stand by the kerb-edge, Auntie,
dangling our useless hands.
But we don't mind so much if you love us, and we
    feel
that Auntie understands.

But wages go down, and really, Auntie,
we get a pretty thin time.
But so long as we know that Auntie loves us
we'll try to act up sublime.

Hold my hand, Auntie, Auntie,
Auntie, hold my hand!
Perhaps I'm going to be naughty, Auntie,
and you don't seem to understand.

CLYDESIDER

If Maudie doesn't love us
then why should we be good?
Why shouldn't we steal the jam in the cupboard
and all the dainty food

as we never get a taste of! really
it ought all to be Jock's and mine.
Maudie is nought but the housekeeper
and she kens it fine.

So if Maudie doesn't suit us
she's got to pack and go.
We're getting to be big lads now, an' soon
we can run our own show.

FLAPPER VOTE

We voted 'em in, and we'll vote 'em out!
We'll show 'em a thing or two, never you doubt.

Lizzie and Lucy and me and Flossie
we'll show these old uncles who's going to be bossy!

Now then, Prime Minister, hold on a bit!
Remember who voted you into your seat!

But for Lizzie and Lucy and Flossie and me
you all of you know where you'd jolly well be.

But me and Lucy and Flossie and Lizzie
we thought we'd elect you to keep you all busy.

So be a nice uncle, be good to us girls;
just vote us some pin-money, to encourage our
    curls!

    And Lizzie and me and Flossie and Lucy
    we'll back you up, uncle! We're young, and we're
       juicy!——

SONGS I LEARNT AT SCHOOL

I. NEPTUNE'S LITTLE AFFAIR
WITH FREEDOM

Father Neptune one day to Freedom did say:
If ever I lived upon dry—y land,
The spot I should hit on would be little Britain——
Said Freedom: Why that's my own I—sland!——

    "Oh what a bright little I—sland!
    A right little, tight little I—sland!
    Seek all the world round there's none can be found
    So happy as our little I—sland!"

So Father Neptune walked up the shore
bright and naked aft and fore
as he's always been, since the Flood and before.

And instantly rose a great uproar
of Freedom shrieking till her throat was sore:
Arrest him, he's indecent, he's obscene what's more!——

Policemen and the British nation
threw themselves on him in indignation
with handcuffs, and took him to the police-station.

The sea-god said, in consternation:
But I came at Freedom's invitation!——
So then they charged him with defamation.

And all the sea-nymphs out at sea
rocked on the waves and sang lustily
thinking old Neptune was off on a spree
with giddy Freedom in the land of the Free:

> *"Oh what a bright little I—sland!*
> *A right little, tight little I—sland!——"*

II. MY NATIVE LAND

First verse:
>> Of every land or east or west
>> I love my native land the best, etc. etc.

Second verse:
>> Of every tongue or east or west
>> I love my native tongue the best
>> Though not so smoothly spoken,
>> Nor woven with Italian art
>> Yet when it speaks from heart to heart
>> The spell is never broken
>> The—e spell is—s never bro—o—ken!

Oh a man may travel both east and west
and still speak his native language the best.

But don't try it on, Oh never start
this business of speaking from heart to heart
in mother English, or you're in the cart.

For our honest and healthy English tongue
is apt to prove a great deal too strong

for our dainty, our delicate English ears.
Oh touch the harp, touch the harp gently, my dears!
We English are so sensitive, much more than appears.——

Oh don't for an instant ever dream
of speaking plain English to an Englishman; you'll seem

to him worse than a bolshevist Jew, or an utter
outsider sprung up from some horrible gutter.

Oh mince your words, and mince them well
if you don't want to break the sweet English spell.

For we English are really a race apart,
superior to everyone else: so don't start

being crude and straightforward, you'll only prove
you're a rank outsider of the fifth remove.

III. THE BRITISH BOY

First verse:

    Oh I'm a British bo—oy, Sir,
    A joy to—o tell it you.
    God make me of it worthy
    Life's toilsome journey through!
    And when to man's estate I grow
    My British blood the world shall know,
    For I'm a British bo—oy, Sir,
    A joy to—o tell it you!——

And so to man's estate he grew
and his British blood the world it knew.

And the world it didn't give a hoot
if his blood was British or Timbuctoot.

But with that British blood of his
he painted some pictures, real beauties

he thought them, so he sent them home
to Britain, where his blood came from.

But Britannia turned pale, and began to faint.
—Destroy, she moaned, these horrors in paint!——

He answered: Dear Britannia, why?
I'm your British boy, and I did but try——!

If my pictures are nude, so once were you,
and you will be again, therefore why look blue!——

Britannia hid behind her shield
lest her heel of Achilles should be revealed,

and she said: Don't dare, you wretch, to be lewd!
I never was nor will be nude!——

And she jabbed her British trident clean
through the poor boy's pictures: You see what I
    mean!——

But the British boy he turned and fled
for the trident was levelled at his head.

Henceforth he'll keep clear of her toasting-fork.
Pleasing Britannia is no light work.

13,000 PEOPLE

Thirteen thousand people came to see
my pictures, eager as the honey bee

for the flowers; and I'll tell you what
all eyes sought the same old spot

in every picture, every time,
and gazed and gloated without rhyme

or reason, where the leaf should be,
the fig-leaf that was not, woe is me!

And they blushed, they giggled, they sniggered, they
    leered,
or they boiled and they fumed, in fury they sneered

and said: Oh boy! I tell you what,
look at that one there, that's pretty hot!——

And they stared and they stared, the half-witted lot
at the spot where the fig-leaf just was not!

But why, I ask you? Oh tell me why?
Aren't they made quite the same, then, as you and I?

Can it be they've been trimmed, so they've never seen
the innocent member that a fig-leaf will screen?

What's the matter with them? aren't they women and
    men?
or is something missing? or what's wrong with them
    then?

that they stared and leered at the single spot
where a fig-leaf might have been, and was not.

I thought it was a commonplace
that a man or a woman in a state of grace

in puris naturalibus, don't you see,
had normal pudenda, like you and me.

But it can't be so, for they behaved
like lunatics looking, they bubbled and raved

or gloated or peeped at the simple spot
where a fig-leaf might have been, but was not.

I tell you, there must be something wrong
with my fellow-countrymen; or else I don't belong.

INNOCENT ENGLAND

Oh what a pity, Oh! don't you agree
that figs aren't found in the land of the free!

Fig-trees don't grow in my native land;
there's never a fig-leaf near at hand

when you want one; so I did without;
and that is what the row's about.

Virginal, pure policemen came
and hid their faces for very shame,

while they carried the shameless things away
to gaol, to be hid from the light of day.

And Mr Mead, that old, old lily
said: "Gross! coarse! hideous!"—and I, like a silly,

thought he meant the faces of the police-court officials,
and how right he was, and I signed my initials

to confirm what he said; but alas, he meant
my pictures, and on the proceedings went.

The upshot was, my picture must burn
that English artists might finally learn

when they painted a nude, to put a *cache sexe* on,
a cache sexe, a cache sexe, or else begone!

A fig-leaf; or, if you cannot find it
a wreath of mist, with nothing behind it.

A wreath of mist is the usual thing
in the north, to hide where the turtles sing.

Though they never sing, they never sing,
don't you dare to suggest such a thing

or Mr Mead will be after you.
—But what a pity I never knew

A wreath of English mist would do
as a cache sexe! I'd have put a whole fog.

But once and forever barks the old dog,
so my pictures are in prison, instead of in the Zoo.

GIVE ME A SPONGE

Give me a sponge and some clear, clean water
and leave me alone awhile
with my thirteen sorry pictures that have just been rescued
from durance vile.

Leave me alone now, for my soul is burning
as it feels the slimy taint
of all those nasty police-eyes like snail-tracks smearing
the gentle souls that figure in the paint.

Ah, my nice pictures, they are fouled, they are dirtied
not by time, but by unclean breath and eyes
of all the sordid people that have stared at them uncleanly
looking dirt on them, and breathing on them lies.

Ah my nice pictures, let me sponge you very gently
to sponge away the slime
that ancient eyes have left on you, where obscene eyes
    have crawled
leaving nasty films upon you every time.

Ah the clean waters of the sky, ah! can you wash
away the evil starings and the breath
of the foul ones from my pictures? Oh purify
them now from all this touch of tainted death!

PUSS-PUSS!

—Oh, Auntie, isn't he a beauty! And is he a gentleman or
    a lady?
—Neither, my dear! I had him fixed. It saves him from so
    many undesirable associations.

LONDON MERCURY

Oh when Mercury came to London
they "had him fixed".
It saves him from so many undesirable associations.

And now all the Aunties like him so much
because, you see, he is "neither, my dear!"

MY LITTLE CRITICS

My little critics must all have been brought up by their
    Aunties
who petted them, and had them fixed
to save them from undesirable associations.

It must be so. Otherwise
the sight of an ordinary Tom wouldn't send them into
    such silly hysterics,
my little critics, dear, safe little pets.

DADDY-DO-NOTHING

Mr Gladstone was a very good man.
He used to give kind advice to the prostitutes on Piccadilly.

And the prostitutes on Piccadilly, or in the Circus
called him: Old Daddy-do-nothing.

QUESTION

Was your's a daddy
or a Daddy-do-nothing?

EDITORIAL OFFICE

Applicant for post as literary critic: Here are my
   credentials, Sir!—
Editor: Er—quite. But—er—biologically! Have you been
   fixed?—*arrangé*—you understand what I mean?
Applicant: I'm afraid I don't.
Editor (sternly): Have you been made safe for the great
   British Public? Has everything objectionable been
   removed from you?
Applicant: In what way, quite?
Editor: By surgical operation. Did your parents have you
   sterilised?
Applicant: I don't think so, Sir. I'm afraid not.
Editor: Good morning! Don't trouble to call again. We
   have the welfare of the British Public at heart.

THE GREAT NEWSPAPER EDITOR TO HIS SUBORDINATE

Mr Smith, Mr Smith
haven't I told you to take the pith
and marrow and substance out of all
the articles passing beneath your scrawl?

And now look here what you've gone and done!
You've told them that life isn't really much fun,
when you know that they've got to think that they're
    happy,

as happy as happy, Oh, so happy, you sappy.
Think of the effect on Miss Harrison
when she reads that her life isn't really much fun.
She'll take off her specs. and she'll put down the paper
as if it was giving off poison vapour.

And she'll avoid it; she'll go and order
The Morning Smile, sure that it will afford her
comfort and cheer, sure that it will tell her
she's a marv'lous, delicious, high-spirited feller.

You must chop up each article, make it pappy
and easy to swallow; always tell them they're happy,
suggest that they're spicy, yet how *pure* they are,
and what a sense of true humour they've got, ha-ha!

Mr Smith, Mr Smith,
have you still to learn that pith
and marrow and substance are sure to be
indigestible to Miss Ponsonby!

Mr Smith, Mr Smith
if you stay in my office, you've got to be kith
and kin with Miss Jupson, whose guts are narrow
and can't pass such things as substance and marrow.

Mr Smith, Mr Smith
consider Miss Wilks, or depart forthwith.
For the British Public, once more be it said,
is summed up in a nice, narrow-gutted old maid.

MODERN PRAYER

Almighty Mammon, make me rich!
Make me rich quickly, with never a hitch
in my fine prosperity! Kick those in the ditch
who hinder me, Mammon, great son of a bitch!

CRY OF THE MASSES

Give us back, Oh give us back
Our bodies before we die!

Trot, trot, trot, corpse-body, to work.
Chew, chew, chew, corpse-body, at the meal.
Sit, sit, sit, corpse-body, in the car.
Stare, stare, stare, corpse-body, at the film.
Listen, listen, listen, corpse-body, to the wireless.
Talk, talk, talk, corpse-body, newspaper talk.
Sleep, sleep, sleep, corpse-body, factory-hand sleep.
Die, die, die, corpse-body, doesn't matter!

Must we die, must we die
bodiless, as we lived?
Corpse-anatomies with ready-made sensations!
Corpse-anatomies, that can work.
Work, work, work,
rattle, rattle, rattle,
sit, sit, sit,
finished, finished, finished——

584

Ah no, Ah no! before we finally die
or see ourselves as we are, and go mad,
give us back our bodies, for a day, for a single day
to stamp the earth and feel the wind, like wakeful
    men again.

Oh, even to know the last wild wincing of despair,
aware at last that our manhood is utterly lost,
give us back our bodies for one day.

WHAT HAVE THEY DONE TO YOU——?

What have they done to you, men of the masses
creeping back and forth to work?

What have they done to you, the saviours of the people?
Oh what have they saved you from?

Alas, they have saved you from yourself,
from your own body, saved you from living your own
    life.

And given you this jig-jig-jig
tick-tick-ticking of machines,
this life which is no-man's-life.

Oh a no-man's-life in a no-man's-land
this is what they've given you
in place of your own life.

THE PEOPLE

Ah the people, the people!
surely they are flesh of my flesh!

When, in the streets of the working quarters
they stream past, stream past, going to work;

then, when I see the iron hooked in their faces,
their poor, their fearful faces

then I scream in my soul, for I know I cannot
cut the iron hook out of their faces, that makes them so
     drawn,
nor cut the invisible wires of steel that pull them

back and forth to work,
back and forth, to work

like fearful and corpse-like fishes hooked and being played
by some malignant fisherman on an unseen, safe shore
where he does not choose to land them yet, hooked fishes
     of the factory world.

THE FACTORY CITIES

Oh, over the factory cities there seems to hover a doom
so dark, so dark, the mind is lost in it.

Ah, the industrial masses, with the iron hook through their
     gills,
when the evil angler has played them long enough,
another little run for their money, a few more turns of the
     reel
fixing the hook more tightly, getting it more firmly in—

Ah, when he begins to draw the line in tight, to land his
     fish,
the industrial masses—Ah, what will happen, what will
     happen?

Hark! the strange noise of millions of fish in panic
in panic, in rebellion, slithering millions of fish
whistling and seething and pulling the angler down into
     boiling black death!

LEAVES OF GRASS, FLOWERS OF GRASS

Leaves of grass, what about leaves of grass?
Grass blossoms, grass has flowers, flowers of grass
dusty pollen of grass, tall grass in its midsummer maleness
hay-seed and tiny grain of grass, graminiferae
not far from the lily, the considerable lily;

even the blue-grass blossoms;
even the bison knew it;
even the stupidest farmer gathers his hay in bloom, in
    blossom
just before it seeds.

Only the best matters; even the cow knows it;
grass in blossom, blossoming grass, risen to its height and its
    natural pride
in its own splendour and its own feathery maleness
the grass, the grass.

Leaves of grass, what are leaves of grass, when at its best
    grass blossoms.

MAGNIFICENT DEMOCRACY

Oh, when the grass flowers, the grass
how aristocratic it is!
Cock's-foot, fox-tail, fescue and tottering-grass
see them wave, see them wave, plumes
prouder than the Black Prince,
flowers of grass, fine men.

Oh, I am a democrat
of the grass in blossom
a blooming aristocrat all round.

INTRODUCTION TO
Last Poems and *More Pansies*

By Richard Aldington
[1932]

NOTE

I

T H E S E poems are printed from two manuscripts found among Lawrence's papers after his death; and, apart from the unlikely event of other MSS. being discovered, this book contains the whole of Lawrence's posthumous poetry.

For the sake of convenience I shall call these manuscript books "A" and "B".

MS. "A" is a thickish, bound book, labelled outside: "Papeterie W. Bouvier, Genève". The inner cover has one or two literary notes in Lawrence's handwriting. At one end is the unfinished translation of a story by Lasca, whose *Doctor Manente* was translated by Lawrence. Beginning from the other end, thirty pages in Lawrence's handwriting are filled with poems, on both sides of each page, except in one case where Mrs Lawrence has made some notes. There is no general title, and the book begins with the poem: "The Greeks are Coming!"; the last poem of this MS. is the "Phoenix"—sixty-seven poems in all.

MS. "B" is a thinner book, obviously French. The inner cover is inscribed: "D. H. Lawrence, Bandol, Var, France. 23rd Nov. 1928". The book is written on both sides of the page and is completely filled, except for one blank page at the end. It is headed "Pensées", and is the draft MS. which supplied some of the later poems for *Pansies*,* nearly all for *Nettles*, and all those included in *The Imagist Anthology*, 1930. Poems taken from the MS. for publication have been lightly struck through with the pen. In most cases the MS. drafts are different from those published, sometimes very different. From "Image-making Love" down to "The White Horse" there are two hundred and three poems which we believe to be unpublished, except for the half-dozen in *The Imagist Anthology*.

---

* The MS. book which supplied most of the other material for *Pansies* has not yielded anything unpublished.

After "The White Horse" a bit of a puzzle begins. There are two rough drafts, one in ink and one in pencil, of a poem headed "Glory of Darkness"; but these were afterwards made into a poem called "Bavarian Gentians", which appears quite early in MS. "A". Then comes "Flowers and Men", and then a long draft of "The Ship of Death", part of which appears in the MS. "A" version of that poem, while other parts reappear in "The Homeless Dead" and other poems of the same group. After this MS. "B" has a version of "The Song of Death" different from that in MS. "A". The "Prayer", which concludes MS. "B", is unfinished, and written in a very uncertain hand. There is some reason for believing that this unfinished poem is actually the last thing Lawrence ever wrote.

Finally there exists Lawrence's own typescript of part of "The Ship of Death".

From merely internal evidence, I think it can be said that MS. "B" was used as a first jotting-book, mostly for "occasional pieces" of the type of *Pansies*. There are very many alterations and rewritings, and in some cases whole poems have been crossed out. The differences between these drafts and the published versions (of the poems in *Pansies* and *Nettles*) show that Lawrence either had another "final draft" book or revised drastically when typing them out. The poems in MS. "A" are of a different character, more pondered and *soignés*. In the earlier part, the poems are considerably re-worked, but afterwards page after page has scarcely a correction. This makes me think that MS. "A" must have been used first as a draft-book for more serious poems, and then for fair copies. Finally, although at the very end of MS. "B" there are early drafts of a few of the more serious poems, I believe these two MSS. represent two different books, one a continuation of *Pansies*, the other a new series leading up to the death poems, for which Lawrence had not found a general title. The two books must also have been in progress simultaneously.

There is no indication of how Lawrence wished these poems to be published. Therefore I have decided on the following principles:

(1) The text has been reproduced as exactly as possible, even to the extent of admitting errors in punctuation or spelling, though the latter are very rare.

(2) Nothing that Lawrence crossed out has been included, and no poems hitherto published, except the small "Imagist Anthology" group.

(3) Whenever, as sometimes happens, words or phrases or lines are duplicated – i.e. one version written above another without either being crossed out – I have always taken that written above as being the preferred one.

(4) Believing as I do that there are two unfinished books of poems represented in these MSS., I have kept them separate. MS. "A" comes first, as being obviously the more important, and I have supplied the title "Last Poems". I abandoned the idea of calling the book "The Ship of Death", as I once thought of doing, since I felt I had no right to give a fancy title without MS. authority.

(5) MS. "B" is also printed exactly as it stands, except that I have omitted all poems I know to have been published, all that are lightly struck through by Lawrence, and all poems or parts of poems which he had crossed out.

(6) I have used MS. "A" versions of "The Ship of Death", but I have included in an appendix the other existing versions of "The Ship of Death", "Bavarian Gentians" and "Song of Death".

(7) Finally I have ventured to give MS. "B" the title of "More Pansies", since I know that *Pansies* were originally called "Pensées" and this MS. is clearly a continuation of the same book.

Thus I have tried to treat these Lawrence MSS. with the utmost respect. I have not imposed my own ideas, but have set out to give these poems exactly as he wrote them.

I I

At two opposite poles of modern literature stand D. H. Lawrence and James Joyce. Lawrence, no doubt, is more widely read since nearly all his books circulate freely and are kept in print. Joyce has been much more the prey of the swarms of imitative writers who want to appear original, and this is because he has made numerous technical and verbal experiments which can easily be copied. The contrasts between the work of these two men can be elaborated almost indefinitely. The great difference I want to touch on now is that Joyce's writing is founded on the conception of Being, and Lawrence's on the conception of Becoming. It is not merely the difference between Catholic and Protestant (though, of course, Joyce is as essentially Catholic as Lawrence is Protestant) because this fundamental dilemma was stated long before Christianity by pre-Socratic Greeks.

Ulysses is static and solid, logically planned, smelling of the lamp, a sort of unchristmas present to the Lord in Whose sight a thousand years are as a day, a day is as a thousand years. It is a little static cosmos, like a huge rigid glass bubble blown out of the top of a head. It is, and there is nothing to be done about it. A strange, perfect, rather awful product of man's will and mind, a sort of literary Frankenstein which has devoured its creator.

Now turn to Lawrence's work – how fluid, how personal, how imperfect, a series of inconclusive adventures only related because they all happened to the same man. There is nothing static about this – everything flows. There is perpetual intercourse with the Muse, but the progeny is as surprising to the parent as to anybody else. Lawrence's writing was not something outside himself, it was part of himself, it came out of his life and in turn fed his life. He adventured into himself in order to write, and by writing discovered himself. From the first sentence in *The White Peacock* to the last broken utterance:

> Give me the moon at my feet,
> Set my feet upon the crescent like a Lord!

written by a dying hand, all this mass of writing forms one immense autobiography.

This differs completely from the *Confessions* of Rousseau, since it is not a conscious confessing, but an instinctive revealing. With Lawrence the book is not conceived as something made, something apart from the author, but as a prolongation of his own life. A creation, yes, but a kind of parthenogenesis, a begetting of children more intimately his than any child, who must always be the result of a collaboration. It is the product of an individualism so assertive, so arrogant, as to be disconcerting. In this intense fluidity where and what is the individual after all? Most people think of themselves at least as a little hard static core in the midst of the universal flux. But the individual Lawrence is as fluid as everything else. You can't bind him down to anything, because today isn't yesterday, and tomorrow will be neither. All of which goes to explain what critics deplore as "the uneven quality" of his writing. Lawrence didn't care much whether his "writing" was "good" or "bad". He didn't admit that sort of distinction, the implication of a fixed standard. Even the standard must flow.* Writing was just a part of living. Take it or leave it.

The poems printed here are a kind of diary of the last year of Lawrence's life. He followed his fluid ego to the verge of dissolution, always the adventure. In "More Pansies" especially, but even in the other poems, you will find his daily moods and thoughts, often repeated and repeated. There is the irritability of the consumptive breaking out all the time – irritations over the petty annoyances of suppression by law and the stupidities of journalists, irritations with healthy people and the people of a different class and machines and machine men, in fact with almost everybody. You will find echoes of *Apocalypse* and of his delight in his last fine days by the Mediterranean. And you will find the wonderful group of poems written as he entered into death and prepared himself for "the last, the longest voyage".

I don't know if anyone has pointed out that when he left Europe Lawrence practically ceased to write poetry. England, Germany and Italy were all favourable, but not America and the East. The best poems in *Birds, Beasts and Flowers* were written in Florence and Taormina. After he left Taormina he seems to have written only a handful of poems until he began to write *Pansies*. And that book cannot have been started before October 1928. I cannot feel that *Pansies* is anything but a decline from his earlier poems, while *Nettles* is about the worst and most trivial thing he ever published. It seems to me that nearly all these Pansies and Nettles came out of Lawrence's nerves, and not out of his real self. They are one long hammer, hammer, hammer of exasperation. Sometimes they are like the utterances of a little Whitman, but without Walt's calm *sostenuto* quality; and sometimes they are like a little Blake raving, but without the fiery vision. Yet it is always Lawrence speaking, even in the most disconcertingly trivial or spiteful, but to me at least very much the Lawrence of off days, the Lawrence one could most easily do without. I don't say this of all the Pansies, but of a good many, and certainly of all the Nettles.

So it is a relief to find the latest poems of all beginning to soar

---

* Is not Lawrence the poetic complement of men like Eddington?

upwards again, from the very first poem, on the Mediterranean, which begins so splendidly:

> This sea will never die, neither will it ever grow old
> nor cease to be blue, nor in the dawn
> cease to lift up its hills . . .

Going through these poems again, I find I like the one about geraniums and mignonette. It is very characteristic, and so too is "The Body of God". I think Lawrence rises into beauty with "The Man of Tyre", a very personal re-working of the story of Odysseus and Nausicaa, with that romantic sensuality of which Lawrence alone had the secret in our days, perhaps simply because he kept his perceptions so fresh and clear. The Whales poem is also entirely Lawrence, owing nothing to anyone else,* but it seems rather to belong to the *Birds, Beasts and Flowers* collection than to this one, where the theme is reconciliation with fate through beauty, and reconciliation with death as the last and greatest adventure. The "Invocation to the Moon" is not wholly comprehensible unless you have read *Apocalypse*. He has not yet faced death as an imminent, personal, inevitable transformation, still prays:

> . . . Set me again on moon-remembering feet
> a healed, whole man, O Moon!

In *Apocalypse* Lawrence says the moon is "the mistress and mother of our watery bodies, the pale body of our nervous consciousness and our moist flesh". And so this Invocation means that he was still desperately holding to life. Yet very close upon this Moon poem comes "Bavarian Gentians", one of his lovely flower poems, which seems a first statement of the Death theme:

> Reach me a gentian, give me a torch!

let me guide myself with the blue, forked torch of this flower down the darker and darker stairs, where blue is darkened

> on blueness
> even where Persephone goes . . .

*[But see Note, p. 1024. *Edd.*]

This, however, is immediately abandoned, and "Bavarian Gentians" is followed by a series of "mythological" poems whose inner personal meaning is clear only after one has thoroughly absorbed *Apocalypse*. Indeed I will say that nobody can really understand and judge these poems until he has made a study of *Apocalypse*. Only thus can the references to God and to the gods, to the Sunderers, to Fire and Wet and so forth be perceived as symbols, instead of vague abstractions.

Then come meditations on evil, and especially on the evil machine, a very favourite theme in these last years. In "Death is not Evil, Evil is Mechanical" there is a passage which perfectly expresses the "Becoming", the fluid ego perpetually adventuring:

> a thing of kisses and strife
> a lit-up shaft of rain
> a calling column of blood
> a rose tree bronzey with thorns
> a mixture of yea and nay
> a rainbow of love and hate
> a wind that blows back and forth
> a creature of conflict, like a cataract.*

So, in this perpetual flowing it is perfectly understandable that the sweep of his meditation should suddenly flutter down and down into a series of scoldings, which are little better than *Pansies*. And this only makes the surprise and delight more keen when we turn the page and come upon "The Ship of Death" and the grandeur of its beginning.

> Now it is autumn and the falling fruit
> and the long journey towards oblivion. . . .

> And it is time to go, to bid farewell
> to one's own self, and find an exit
> from the fallen self.

From here to the end of the MS. there is really only one poem, the poem of "The Ship of Death", and it does not matter that he split it

*[Aldington quotes his own incorrect transcription of this passage. See pp. 714, 1025. *Edd.*]

up into smaller pieces, since they all fit together and in all of them suffering and the agony of departure are turned into music and reconciliation. As the first draft shows [Appendix III], Lawrence probably meant to make this one long poem, and if this could have been done it would have been his greatest achievement as a poet. But:

> My soul has had a long, hard day
> she is tired,
> she is seeking her oblivion!

He was too weary, he could not find strength to build his ship of death and at the same time to build the full whole song of it. But after all these little snarling Pansy poems, and the nasty stinging little Nettles, how good it is to know that the great and lovely spirit had always been there, that those were only the bitter husks, the snapping of worn exasperated nerves, and that when he came to face the last reality, it was the beauty in him that found a new voice of grandeur and dignity:

> And if, as autumn deepens and darkens
> I feel the pain of falling leaves, and stems that break in
>   storms
> and trouble and dissolution and distress
> and the softness of deep shadows folding, folding
> around my soul and spirit, around my lips
> so sweet, like a swoon, or more like the drowse of a low,
>   sad song
> singing darker than the nightingale, on, on to the solstice
> and the silence of short days, the silence of the year, the
>   shadow,
> then I shall know that my life is moving still
> with the dark earth, and drenched
> with the deep oblivion of earth's lapse and renewal.

RICHARD ALDINGTON

MORE PANSIES

IMAGE-MAKING LOVE

And now
the best of all
is to be alone, to possess one's soul in silence.

Nakedly to be alone, unseen
is better than anything else in the world,
a relief like death.

Always
at the core of me
burns the small flame of anger, gnawing
from trespassed contacts, from red-hot finger
        bruises, on my inward flesh,
from hot, digging-in fingers of love.

Always
in the eyes of those who loved me
I have seen at last the image of him they loved
and took for me
mistook for me.

And always
it was a simulacrum, something
like me, and like a gibe at me.

So now I want, above all things
to preserve my nakedness
from the gibe of image-making love.

PEOPLE

I like people quite well
at a little distance.
I like to see them passing and passing
and going their own way,
especially if I see their aloneness alive in them.

Yet I don't want them to come near.
If they will only leave me alone
I can still have the illusion that there is room enough
    in the world.

DESIRE

Ah, in the past, towards rare individuals
I have felt the pull of desire:
Oh come, come nearer, come into touch!
Come physically nearer, be flesh to my flesh—

But say little, oh say little,
and afterwards, leave me alone.
Keep your aloneness, leave me my aloneness.
I used to say this, in the past—but now no more.
It has always been a failure.
They have always insisted on love
and on talking about it
and on the me-and-thee and what we meant to each
    other.

So now I have no desire any more
Except to be left, in the last resort, alone, quite alone.

TO A CERTAIN FRIEND

You are so interested in yourself
that you bore me
thoroughly, I am unable to feel any interest in
    your interesting self.

THE EMOTIONAL FRIEND

He said to me: You don't trust me!
I said: Oh yes I do!
I know you won't pick my pocket,
I know you'll be very kind to me.
But it was not enough, he looked at me almost with hate.
And I failed entirely to see what he meant—
Since there was no circumstance requiring trust between
    us.

CORRESPONDENCE IN AFTER YEARS

A man wrote to me: We missed it, you and I.
We were meant to mean a great deal to one another;
but we missed it.
And I could only reply:
A miss is as good as a mile
mister!

THE EGOISTS

The only question to ask today, about man or woman
is: Has she chipped the shell of her own ego?
Has he chipped the shell of his own ego?

They are all perambulating eggs
going: "Squeak! Squeak! I am all things unto myself,
yet I can't be alone, I want somebody to keep me warm."

CHIMAERA

Most people, today, are chimaera
chimerical:
just fantasies of self-importance
their own self-importance
and sphinxes of self-consciousness.

ULTIMATE REALITY

A young man said to me:
I am interested in the problem of reality.

I said: Really!
Then I saw him turn to glance again, surreptitiously,
in the big mirror, at his own fascinating shadow.

SPHINX

But why do I feel so strangely about you?
said the lovely young lady, half wistful, half menacing.

I took to my heels and ran
before she could set the claws of her self-conscious question-
        ing in me
or tear me with the fangs of disappointment
because I could not answer the riddle of her own self-
        importance.

INTIMATES

Don't you care for my love? she said bitterly.

I handed her the mirror, and said:
Please address these questions to the proper person!
Please make all requests to head-quarters!
In all matters of emotional importance
please approach the supreme authority direct!
So I handed her the mirror.

And she would have broken it over my head,
but she caught sight of her own reflection
and that held her spellbound for two seconds
while I fled.

TRUE LOVE AT LAST

The handsome and self-absorbed young man
looked at the lovely and self-absorbed girl
and thrilled.

The lovely and self-absorbed girl
looked back at the handsome and self-absorbed young man
and thrilled.

And in that thrill he felt:
Her self-absorption is even as strong as mine.
I must see if I can't break through it
And make her interested in me.

And in that thrill she felt:
His self-absorption is even stronger than mine!
What fun, stronger than mine!
I must see if I can't absorb this Samson of self-absorption.

So they simply adored one another
and in the end
they were both nervous wrecks, because
In self-absorption and self-interest they were equally
    matched.

ANDRAITX—POMEGRANATE FLOWERS

It is June, it is June
the pomegranates are in flower,
the peasants are bending cutting the bearded wheat.

The pomegranates are in flower
beside the high- road, past the deathly dust,
and even the sea is silent in the sun.

Short gasps of flame in the green of night, way off
the pomegranates are in flower,
small sharp red fires in the night of leaves.

And noon is suddenly dark, is lustrous, is silent and dark
men are unseen, beneath the shading hats;
only, from out the foliage of the secret loins
red flamelets here and there reveal
a man, a woman there.

I DARE DO ALL

"I dare do all that may become a man."
But tell me, oh tell me, what is becoming to a man!
Tell me first what I am,
that I may know what is unbecoming to me.

BATTLE OF LIFE

Is life strife, is it the long combat?
Yes, it is true. I fight all the time.
I am forced to.
Yet I am not interested in fight, in strife, in combat,
I am only involved.

THERE ARE TOO MANY PEOPLE

There are too many people on earth
insipid, unsalted, rabbity, endlessly hopping.
They nibble the face of the earth. to a desert.

THE HEART OF MAN

There is the other universe, of the heart of man
that we know nothing of, that we dare not explore.

A strange grey distance separates
our pale mind still from the pulsing continent
of the heart of man.

Fore-runners have barely landed on the shore
and no man knows, no woman knows
the mystery of the interior
when darker still than Congo or Amazon
flow the heart's rivers of fulness, desire and distress.

MORAL CLOTHING

When I am clothed I am a moral man,
and unclothed, the word has no meaning for me.

When I put on my coat, my coat has pockets
and in the pockets are things I require,
so I wish no man to pick my pocket,
and I will pick the pocket of no man.

A man's business is one of his pockets, his bank
    account too
his credit, his name, his wife even may be just another
    of his pockets.
And I loathe the thought of being a pilferer
a pick-pocket.
That is why business seems to me despicable,
and most love-affairs, just sneak-thief pocket-picking
of dressed-up people.

When I stand in my shirt I have no pockets
therefore no morality of pockets;
but still my nakedness is clothed with responsibility
towards those near and dear to me, my very next
    of kin.
I am not yet alone.

Only when I am stripped stark naked I am alone
and without morals, and without immorality.
The invisible gods have no moral truck with us.

And if stark naked I approach a fellow-man or fellow-
        woman
they must be naked too,
and none of us must expect morality of each other:
I am that I am, take it or leave it.
Offer me nothing but that which you are, stark and
        strange.
Let there be no accommodation at this issue.

BEHAVIOUR

It is well to be disciplined in all the social usages
and to have manners for all occasions
as we have clothes.
It is absurd for me to display my naked soul at the tea-table.

If we are properly clothed and disciplined in the dining-room or the
        street
then the private intimacy of friendship will be real and precious
and our naked contact will be rare and vivid and tremendous.

But when everybody goes round with soul half-bared, or quite
in promiscuous intimate appeal
then friendship is impossible
and naked embrace an anti-climax, humiliating and ridiculous.

THE HOSTILE SUN

Sometimes the sun turns hostile to men
when the daytime consciousness has got overweening
when thoughts are stiff, like old leaves
and ideas are hard, like acorns ready to fall.

Then the sun turns hostile to us
and bites at our throats and chests
as he bites at the stems of leaves in autumn, to make them fall.

Then we suffer, and though the sun bronzes us
we feel him strangling even more the issues of our soul
for he is hostile to all the old leafy foliage of our thoughts
and the old upward flowing of our sap, the pressure of our
      upward flow of feeling
is against him.

Then only under the moon, cool and unconcerned
calm with the calm of scimitars and brilliant reaping hooks
sweeping the curve of space and mowing the silence
we have peace.

THE CHURCH

If I was a member of the Church of Rome
I should advocate reform:
the marriage of priests
the priests to wear rose-colour or magenta in the streets
to teach the Resurrection in the flesh
to start the year on Easter Sunday
to add the mystery of Joy-in-Resurrection to the Mass
to inculcate the new conception of the Risen Man.

THE PROTESTANT CHURCHES

The Protestant Churches have had their day
and served their great purpose.
They knew the useful Godhead of Providence.
But now we have to go back to the Creative Godhead
which overshadows the other
and which we have lost.

LONELINESS

I never know what people mean when they complain of
     loneliness.
To be alone is one of life's greatest delights, thinking one's
     own thoughts,
doing one's own little jobs, seeing the world beyond
and feeling oneself uninterrupted in the rooted connection
with the centre of all things.

THE UPROOTED

People who complain of loneliness must have lost some-
     thing,
lost some living connection with the cosmos, out of them-
     selves,
lost their life-flow
like a plant whose roots are cut.
And they are crying like plants whose roots are cut.
But the presence of other people will not give them new,
     rooted connection
it will only make them forget.
The thing to do is in solitude slowly and painfully put
     forth new roots
into the unknown, and take root by oneself.

DELIGHT OF BEING ALONE

I know no greater delight than the sheer delight of being alone.
It makes me realise the delicious pleasure of the moon
that she has in travelling by herself: throughout time,
or the splendid growing of an ash-tree
alone, on a hill-side in the north, humming in the wind.

REFUSED FRIENDSHIP

He said to me: Your life will be so much the poorer
since you refuse my friendship.

But I, honestly, don't know what he means.
I can't see that I refuse anything.
I like him. What else is there?

FUTURE RELATIONSHIPS

The world is moving, moving still, towards further democracy.
But not a democracy of idea or ideal, nor of property, nor even of
    the emotion of brotherhood.
But a democracy of men, a democracy of touch.

FUTURE RELIGION

The future of religion lies in the mystery of touch.
The mind is touchless, so is the will, so is the spirit.
First comes the death, then the pure aloneness, which is permanent
then the resurrection into touch.

FUTURE STATES

Once men touch one another, then the modern industrial
    form of machine civilisation will melt away
and universalism and cosmopolitanism will cease;
the great movement of centralising into oneness will stop
and there will be a vivid recoil into separateness;
many vivid small states, like a kaleidoscope, all colours
and all the differences given expression.

FUTURE WAR

After our industrial civilisation has broken, and the civilisation of
    touch has begun
war will cease, there will be no more wars.
The heart of man, in so far as it is budding, is budding warless
and budding towards infinite variety, variegation
and where there is infinite variety, there is no interest in war.
Oneness makes war, and the obsession of· oneness.

SIGNS OF THE TIMES

If you want to get a glimpse of future possibilities
look at the young men under thirty.
Those that are fresh and alive are the same in every
    country,
a certain carelessness, a certain tenderness, a certain
    instinctive contempt
for old values and old people:
a certain warlessness even moneylessness,
a waiting for the proper touch, not for any word or deed.

INITIATION DEGREES

No man, unless he has died, and learned to be alone
will ever come into touch.

UNHAPPY SOULS

The unhappy souls are those that can't die and become silent
but must ever struggle on to assert themselves.

FULL LIFE

A man can't fully live unless he dies and ceases to care,
ceases to care.

PEOPLE WHO CARE

People who care, who care, who care
and who dare not die for fear they should be nothing at all
probably are nothing at all.

NON-EXISTENCE

We don't exist unless we are deeply and sensually in touch
with that which can be touched but not known.

ALL-KNOWING

All that we know is nothing, we are merely crammed waste-paper
baskets
unless we are in touch with that which laughs at all our knowing.

SALVATION

The only salvation is to realise that we know nothing about it
and there is nothing to save
and nothing to do
and effort is the ruin of all things.
Then, if we realise that we never were lost, we realise we couldn't
be saved.

For you can't save that which was never lost,
at the worst, you can only save it up
and once you realise that you never were lost
you realise the fatuity of saving up against possible loss.
The one thing easiest to lose is savings.

OLD ARCHANGELS

And so the official archangels
Orthodox Michael, and that whispering Gabriel
have had their term of office, they must go.
It is Lucifer's turn, the turn of the Son of the Morning
to sway the earth of men,
the Morning Star.

LUCIFER

Angels are bright still, though the brightest fell.
But tell me, tell me, how do you know
that he lost any of his brightness in falling?
He only fell out of your ken, you orthodox angels,
you dull angels, tarnished with centuries of conventionality.

THE MILLS OF GOD

Why seek to alter people, why not leave them alone?
The mills of God will grind them small, anyhow, there is no escape.
The heavens are the nether mill-stone, and our heavy earth
rolls round and round, grinding exceeding small.

MULTITUDES

The multitudes are like droppings of birds, like dung of sea-fowl that
    have flown away,
Oh they are grist for the mills of God, their bones ground down
to fertilise the roots of unknown men who are still to come
in fresh fields.

FALLEN LEAVES

There is the organic connection, like leaves that belong to a tree
and there is the mechanical connection, like leaves that are cast
    upon the earth.

Winds of heaven fan the leaves of the tree like flames and tunes,
but winds of heaven are mills of God to the fallen leaves
grinding them small to humus, on earth's nether mill-stone.

THE DIFFERENCE

People are like leaves, fluttering and gay on the bush of the globe,
or they are like leaves, rustling thick, in crowds on the floor of the
    earth.
And the thick, fallen crowds crackle and crumble under the milling
    of the winds,
the winds of change that will not be still
the breath of life.
But the living leaves in the breath of the wind are more lively
they glisten and shake.

THE BREATH OF LIFE

The breath of life and the sharp winds of change are the same thing.
But people who are fallen from the organic connection with the
    cosmos
feel the winds of change grind them down
and the breath of life never comes to nourish them.

VENGEANCE IS MINE

Vengeance is mine, saith the Lord, I will repay.
And the stiff-necked people, and the self-willed people, and self-
important ones, the self-righteous, self-absorbed
all of them who wind their energy round the idea of themselves
and so strangle off their connection with the ceaseless tree of life,
and fall into sharp, self-centred self-assertion, sharp or soft,
they fall victim at once to the vengeance of the unforgiving god
as their nerves are stretched till they twangle and snap
and irritation seethes secretly through their guts, as their tissue
disintegrates
and flames of katabolistic energy alternate
with ashes of utter boredom, ennui, and disgust.

It is the vengeance of the Lord, long and unremitting
till the soul of the stiff-necked is ground to dust, to fertilising meal
with which to manure afresh the roots of the tree of life.
And so the Lord of Vengeance pays back, repays life
for the defection of the self-centred ones.

ASTRONOMICAL CHANGES

Dawn is no longer in the house of the Fish
Pisces, oh Fish, Jesus of the watery way,
your two thousand years are up.

And the foot of the Cross no longer is planted in the place of the
birth of the Sun.
The whole great heavens have shifted over, and slowly pushed aside
the Cross, the Virgin, Pisces, the Sacred Fish
that casts its sperm upon the waters, and knows no intercourse;
pushed them all aside, discarded them, make way now for something
else.

Even the Pole itself has departed now from the Pole Star
and pivots on the invisible,
while the Pole Star lies aside, like an old axle taken from the wheel.

FATALITY

No one, not even God, can put back a leaf on to a tree
once it has fallen off.

And no one, not God nor Christ nor any other
can put back a human life into connection with the living
cosmos
once the connection has been broken
and the person has become finally self-centred.

Death alone, through the long processes of disintegration
can melt the detached life back
through the dark Hades at the roots of the tree
into the circulating sap, once more, of the tree of life.

FREE WILL

The human will is free, ultimately, to choose one of two things:
either to stay connected with the tree of life, and submit
the human will to the flush of the vaster impulsions of the tree;
or else to sever the connection, to become self-centred, self-willed,
self-motived—
and subject, really, to the draught of every motor-car or the kicking
tread of every passer-by.

IN A SPANISH TRAM-CAR

She fanned herself with a violet fan
and looked sulky, under her thick straight brows.

The wisp of modern black mantilla
made her half Madonna, half Astarte.

Suddenly her yellow-brown eyes looked with a flare into
    mine.
—We could sin together!—

The spark fell and kindled instantly on my blood,
then died out almost as swiftly.

She can keep her sin
She can sin with some thick-set Spaniard.
Sin doesn't interest me.

SPANISH PRIVILEGE

The inward cocky assertiveness of the Spaniard seems to say:
God is supreme,
but He can't stop me from sinning against Him if I want to,
and when I want to, I'm going to;
though you bloody outsiders had better not try it on.

So they go on sinning, though sin is obsolete,
and nobody but themselves is interested.

AT THE BANK IN SPAIN

Even the old priest, in his long black robe and silvery hair
came to the counter with his hat off, humble at the shrine,
and was immensely flattered when one of the fat little
    clerks of the bank
shook hands with him.

THE SPANISH WIFE

When I saw her straying a little dazed through her untidy house.
I realised the secret joy her young Spanish husband had
in frustrating her, just inwardly frustrating her,
this foreign woman of the wealthy north.

THE PAINTER'S WIFE

She was tangled up in her own self-conceit, a woman,
and her passion could only flare through the meshes
towards other women, in communion;
the presence of a man made her recoil
and burn blue and cold, like the flame in a miner's lamp
when the after-damp is around it.

Yet she seemed to know nothing about it
and devoted herself to her husband
and made him paint her nude, time after time,
and each time it came out the same, a horrible sexless, lifeless
     abstraction
of the female form, technically "beautiful", actually a white
     machine-drawing, more null than death.

And she was so pleased with it, she thought one day it would
     be recognised as "great".
And he thought so too.
Nobody else did.

MODERN PROBLEMS

The worst of it is
When a woman can only love, flamily, those of her own sex
she has a secret, almost ecstasised hatred of maleness in any man
that she exudes like pearly white poison gas,
and men often succumb like white mice in a laboratory, around her,
specimens to be anatomised.

DOMINANT WOMAN

Dominant women are as a rule so subtly and fiendishly domineering
that the young of their own sex revolt against them, at last,
and turn once more to men, to save them, Perseus, St. George
from the Dragon of the modern female.

MEN AND WOMEN

All this talk of equality between the sexes is merely an
    expression of sex-hate.
Men and women should learn tenderness to each other
and to leave one another alone.

THE SCIENTIFIC DOCTOR

When I went to the scientific doctor
I realised what a lust there was in him to wreak his so-called
    science on me
and reduce me to the level of a thing.
So I said: Good-morning! and left him.

HEALING

I am not a mechanism, an assembly of various sections.
And it is not because the mechanism is working wrongly,
    that I am ill.
I am ill because of wounds to the soul, to the deep emotional
    self
and the wounds to the soul take a long, long time, only
    time can help
and patience, and a certain difficult repentance
long, difficult repentance, realisation of life's mistake, and
    the freeing oneself
from the endless repetition of the mistake
which mankind at large has chosen to sanctify.

EN MASSE

Today, society has sanctified
the sin against the Holy Ghost,
and all are encouraged into the sin
so that all may be lost together, *en masse*, the great
    word of our civilisation.

GOD AND THE HOLY GHOST

There is no sinning against God, what does God care about sin!
But there is sinning against the Holy Ghost, since the Holy Ghost is
    with us
in the flesh, is part of our consciousness.

The Holy Ghost is the deepest part of our own consciousness
wherein we know ourselves for what we are
and know our dependence on the creative beyond.

So if we go counter to our own deepest consciousness
naturally we destroy the most essential self in us,
and once done, there is no remedy, no salvation for this,
nonentity is our portion.

HUMILITY

Nowadays, to talk of humility is a sin against the Holy Ghost.
It is a sneaking evasion of the responsibility
of our own consciousness.

PROPER PRIDE

Everything that lives has its own proper pride
as a columbine flower has, or even a starling walking and looking
    around.

And the base things like hyaenas or bed-bugs have least pride of
    being,
they are humble, with a creeping humility, being parasites or carrion
    creatures.

HUMILITY MONGERS

When I hear a man spouting about humility, today
I know he is either a bed-bug, battening on sleeping people
or a hyaena, eating corpses.

TENDER REVERENCE

To be humble before other men is degrading, I am humble before
    no man
and I want no man to be humble before me.

But when I see the life-spirit fluttering and struggling in a man
I want to show always the human tender reverence.

ABSOLUTE REVERENCE

I feel absolute reverence to nobody and to nothing human
neither to persons nor things nor ideas, ideals nor religions
    nor institutions,
to these things I feel only respect, and a tinge of reverence
when I see the fluttering of pure life in them.

But to something unseen, unknown, creative
from which I feel I am a derivative
I feel absolute reverence. Say no more!

BELIEF

Forever nameless
Forever unknown
Forever unconceived
Forever unrepresented
Yet forever felt in the soul.

BELLS

The Mohammedans say that the sound of bells
especially big ones, is obscene;

That hard clapper striking in a hard mouth
and resounding after with a long hiss of insistence
is obscene.

Yet bells call the Christians to God
especially clapper bells, hard tongues wagging in hard mouths,
metal hitting on metal, to enforce our attention . . .
and bring us to God.

The soft thudding of drums
 of fingers or fists or soft-skinned sticks upon the stretched membrane
    of sound
sends summons in the old hollows of the sun.

And the accumulated splashing of a gong
where tissue plunges into bronze with wide wild circles of sound
and leaves off,
belongs to the bamboo thickets, and the drake in the air flying past.

And the sound of a blast through the sea-curved core of a shell
when a black priest blows on a conch,
and the dawn-cry from a minaret, God is Great,
and the calling of the old Red Indian high on the pueblo roof
whose voice flies on and on, calling like a swan
singing between the sun and the marsh,
on and on, like a dark-faced bird singing alone
singing to the men below, the fellow-tribesmen
who go by without pausing, soft-foot, without listening, yet who
    hear:
there are other ways of summons, crying: Listen! Listen! Come near!

THE TRIUMPH OF THE MACHINE

They talk of the triumph of the machine,
but the machine will never triumph.

Out of the thousands and thousands of centuries of man
the unrolling of ferns, white tongues of the acanthus lapping at the
    sun,
for one sad century
machines have triumphed, rolled us hither and thither,
shaking the lark's nest till the eggs have broken.

Shaken the marshes, till the geese have gone
and the wild swans flown away singing the swan-song of us.

Hard, hard on the earth the machines are rolling,
but through some hearts they will never roll.

The lark nests in his heart
and the white swan swims in the marshes of his loins,
and through the wide prairies of his breast a young bull herds his
    cows,
lambs frisk among the daisies of his brain.

And at last
all these creatures that cannot die, driven back
into the uttermost corners of the soul,
will send up the wild cry of despair.

The trilling lark in a wild despair will trill down arrows from the sky,
the swan will beat the waters in rage, white rage of an enraged swan,
even the lambs will stretch forth their necks like serpents,
like snakes of hate, against the man in the machine:
even the shaking white poplar will dazzle like splinters of glass
    against him.

And against this inward revolt of the native creatures of the soul
mechanical man, in triumph seated upon the seat of his machine
will be powerless, for no engine can reach into the marshes and
    depths of a man.

So mechanical man in triumph seated upon the seat of his machine
will be driven mad from within himself, and sightless, and on that day
the machines will turn to run into one another
traffic will tangle up in a long-drawn-out crash of collision
and engines will rush at the solid houses, the edifice of our life
will rock in the shock of the mad machine, and the house will come
    down.

Then, far beyond the ruin, in the far, in the ultimate, remote places
the swan will lift up again his flattened, smitten head
and look round, and rise, and on the great vaults of his wings
will sweep round and up to greet the sun with a silky glitter of
    a new day
and the lark will follow trilling, angerless again,
and the lambs will bite off the heads of the daisies for very friskiness.
But over the middle of the earth will be the smoky ruin of iron
the triumph of the machine.

FORTE DEI MARMI

The evening sulks along the shore, the reddening sun
reddens still more on the blatant bodies of these all-but-naked, sea-
    bathing city people.

Let me tell you that the sun is alive, and can be angry,
and the sea is alive, and can sulk,
and the air is alive, and can deny us as a woman can.

But the blatant bathers don't know, they know nothing;
the vibration of the motor-car has bruised their insensitive bottoms
into rubber-like deadness, Dunlop inflated unconcern.

SEA-BATHERS

Oh the handsome bluey-brown bodies, they might just as well be
    gutta-percha,
and the reddened limbs red india-rubber tubing, inflated,
and the half-hidden private parts just a little brass tap, robinetto,
turned on for different purposes.

They call it health; it looks like nullity.

Only here and there a pair of eyes, haunted, stares out as if asking:
Where then is life?

TALK OF LOYALTY

I have noticed that people who talk a lot about loyalty
are always themselves by nature disloyal
and they fear the come-back.

TALK OF FAITH

And people who talk about faith
usually want to force somebody to agree with them,
as if there was safety in numbers, even for faith.

AMO SACRUM VULGUS

Oh I am of the people!
the people, the people!
Oh I am of the people
and proud of my descent.

And the people always love me,
they love me, they love me,
the people always love me,
in spite of my ascent.

You must admit I've risen
I've risen, I've risen,
you must admit I've risen
above the common run.

The middle classes hate it,
they hate it, they hate it
the middle classes hate it
and want to put me down.

But the people always love me
they love me, they love me,
the people always love me
because I've risen clear.

Therefore I know the people
the people, the people
are still in bud, and eager
to flower free of fear.

And so I sing a democracy
a democracy, a democracy
that puts forth its own aristocracy
like bearded wheat in ear.

Oh golden fields of people
of people, of people,
oh golden fields of people
all moving into flower.

No longer at the mercy
the mercy, the mercy
of middle-class mowing-machines, and
the middle-class money-power.

BOREDOM, ENNUI, DEPRESSION

And boredom, ennui, depression
are long slow vibrations of pain
that possess the whole body
and cannot be localised.

THE DEADLY VICTORIANS

We hate the Victorians so much
because we are the third and fourth generation
expiating their sins
in the excruciating torment of hopelessness, helpless-
    ness, listlessness,
because they were such base and sordid optimists
successfully castrating the body politic,
and we are the gelded third and fourth generation.

WHAT ARE THE WILD WAVES SAYING?

What are the wild waves saying
sister the whole day long?

It seems to me they are saying:
How disgusting, how infinitely sordid this humanity is
that dabbles its body in me
and daubs the sand with its flesh
in myriads, under the hot and hostile sun!
and so drearily "enjoys itself"!
What are the wild waves saying?

WELCOME DEATH

How welcome death would be
if first a man could have his full revenge
on our castrated society.

DARK SATANIC MILLS

The dark, satanic mills of Blake
how much darker and more satanic they are now!
But oh, the streams that stream white-faced, in and out,
in and out when the hooter hoots, white-faced, with a
        dreadful gush
of multitudinous ignominy,
what shall we think of these?
They are millions to my one!

They are millions to my one! But oh
what have they done to you, white-faced millions
mewed and mangled in the mills of man?
What have they done to you, what have they done to you,
what is this awful aspect of man?

Oh Jesus, didn't you see, when you talked of service
this would be the result!
When you said: Retro me, Satanas!
this is what you gave him leave to do
behind your back!

And now, the iron has entered into the soul
and the machine has entangled the brain, and got it fast,
and steel has twisted the loins of man, electricity has
    exploded the heart
and out of the lips of people jerk strange mechanical noises
    in place of speech.

What is man, that thou art no longer mindful of him?
and the son of man, that thou pitiest him not?
Are these no longer men, these millions, millions?
What are they then?

WE DIE TOGETHER

Oh, when I think of the industrial millions, when I see
    some of them,
a weight comes over me heavier than leaden linings of
    coffins
and I almost cease to exist, weighed down to extinction
and sunk into a depression that almost blots me out.

Then I say to myself: Am I also dead? is that the truth?
Then I know
that with so many dead men in mills
I too am almost dead.
I know the unliving factory-hand, living-dead millions
is unliving me, living-dead me,
I, with them, am living-dead, mechanical at the machine.

And enshrouded in the vast corpse of the industrial millions
embedded in them, I look out on the sunshine of the South.

And though the pomegranate has red flowers outside the
    window
and oleander is hot with perfume under the afternoon sun
and I am "il Signore" and they love me here,
yet I am a mill-hand in Leeds
and the death of the Black Country is upon me
and I am wrapped in the lead of a coffin-lining, the living
    death of my fellow men.

WHAT HAVE THEY DONE TO YOU?

What have they done to you, men of the masses, creeping
    back and forth to work?

What have they done to you, the saviours of the people, oh
    what have they saved you from, while they pocketed
    the money?

Alas, they have saved you from yourself, from your own
    frail dangers
and devoured you with the machine, the vast maw of iron.

They saved you from your squalid cottages and poverty of
    hand to mouth
and embedded you in workmen's dwellings, where
    your wage is the dole of work, and the dole is your
    wage of nullity.

They took away, oh they took away your man's native
    instincts and intuitions
and gave you a board-school education, newspapers, and
    the cinema.

They stole your body from you, and left you an animated
    carcass
to work with, and nothing else:
unless goggling eyes, to goggle at the film
and a board-school brain, stuffed up with the ha'penny
    press.

Your instincts gone, your intuitions gone, your passions
    dead
Oh carcass with a board-school mind and a ha'penny news-
    paper intelligence,
what have they done to you, what have they done to you,
    Oh what have they done to you?

Oh look at my fellow-men, oh look at them
the masses! Oh, what has been done to them?

WHAT IS A MAN TO DO?

Oh, when the world is hopeless
what is a man to do?

When the vast, vast masses of men have been caught by the
    machine
into the industrial dance of the living death, the jigging of
    wage-paid work,
and fed on condition they dance this dance of corpses
    driven by steam.

When year by year, year in, year out, in millions, in increas-
    ing millions
they dance, dance, dance this dry industrial jig of the
    corpses entangled in iron
and there's no escape, for the iron goes through their
    genitals, brains, and souls

then what is a single man to do?

For mankind is a single corpus, we are all one flesh
even with the industrial masses, and the greedy middle
    mass.

Is it hopeless, hopeless, hopeless?
has the iron got them fast?
are their hearts the hub of the wheel?
the millions, millions of my fellow-men!

Then must a single man die with them, in the clutch of
    iron?
Or must he try to amputate himself from the iron-
    entangled body of mankind
and risk bleeding to death, but perhaps escape into some
    unpopular place
and leave the fearful Laocoön of his fellow-man entangled
    in iron
to its fearful fate.

CITY-LIFE

When I see the great cities—

When I am in a great city, I know that I despair.
I know there is no hope for us, death waits, it is useless to
    care.

For oh the poor people, that are flesh of my flesh,
I, that am flesh of their flesh,
when I see the iron hooked into their faces
their poor, their fearful faces
I scream in my soul, for I know I cannot
take the iron hook out of their faces, that makes them so
    drawn,
nor cut the invisible wires of steel that pull them
back and forth, to work,
back and forth, to work,
like fearful and corpse-like fishes hooked and being played
by some malignant fisherman on an unseen shore
where he does not choose to land them yet, hooked fishes
    of the factory world.

13 PICTURES

O my thirteen pictures are in prison!
O somebody bail them out!
I don't know what they've done, poor things, but justice has
    arisen
in the shape of half-a-dozen stout
policemen and arrested them, and hauled them off to gaol.

O my nice Boccaccio, O how goes your pretty tale
locked up in a dungeon cell
with Eve and the Amazon, the Lizard and the frail
Renascence, all sent to hell
at the whim of six policemen and a magistrate whose stale
sensibilities hate everything that's well.

AUTO-DA-FÉ

Help! Help! they want to burn my pictures,
they want to make an *auto-da-fé*!
They want to make an *act of faith*, and burn my pretty
    pictures.
They've seized them and carried them away!

Help! Help! I am calling still in English;
is the language dead and empty of reply!
An Unholy Inquisition has arrested all my pictures,
a magistrate, and six fat smaller fry.

Six fat smaller bobbies are the inquisitors minor
who've decided that Boccaccio must burn.
But the Grand Inquisitor is a stale old magistrate
in Marlborough Road, and it is now his turn.

Oh he has put his pince-nez on, and stoutly has stepped
    down
to the police-station cell
where my darling pictures, prisoners, await his deadly
    frown
and his grand-inquisitorial knell.

Oh he knows all about it, he casts a yellow eye
on the gardener whose shirt's blown back:
Burn that!—he sees Eve running from the likes of him: I
order you, destroy the whole vile pack.

All my pretty pictures huddled in the dark awaiting
their doom at the hands of Mr. Meade.
But the day they burn my pictures they burn the rose of
England
and fertilise the weeds on every mead.

Help! Oh help! they want to burn my pictures:
we've got the Inquisition back
with a set of cankered magistrates and busy-busy bobbies.
Look out, my lad, you've got 'em on your track.

SHOWS

Today, if a man does something pretentious and deliberate
let him show it to the crowd, probably they will applaud
and anyhow they can't do any hurt.

But if he produces something beautiful, with the frail
beauty of life
let him hide it away, so it can go on blossoming.
If he shows it, the eyes and the breath of the crowd
will defile it, and spoil its beauty.

Even the very flowers, in the shops or parks
are deflowered by being looked at by so many unclean
eyes.

ROSE AND CABBAGE

And still I look for the men who will dare to be
roses of England
wild roses of England
men who are wild roses of England
with metal thorns, beware!
but still more brave and still more rare
the courage of rosiness in a cabbage world
fragrance of roses in a stale stink of lies
rose-leaves to bewilder the clever fools
and rose-briars to strangle the machine.

THE GULF

Now again and now for ever breaks the great illusion
of human oneness.

Sons of earth, sons of fire, sons of air and water
sons of the living elements, sons of the unthinking gods,
women, women the same.

And then the hordes of the spawn of the machine
the hordes of the ego-centric, the robots.

For listen! the ego-centric self is the same as the machine
the ego running in its own complex and disconnected
      motion
using all life only as power, as an engine uses steam or gas
power to repeat its own egocentric motions
this is the machine incarnate:
and the robot is the machine incarnate
and the slave is the machine incarnate
and the hopeless inferior, he is the machine incarnate
an engine of flesh, useless unless he is a tool
of other men.

The great industrialists know it.
Mr. Ford knows it.
The brain of the machine knows the limbs and trunk of
      the machine.

But oh, men, men still unmechanised,
sons of the elements and the unspeaking gods
sons of the wind and rain, sons of the fire and rock
what are you going to do, entangled among all the engines?

Behold the gulf, impassable
between machine-spawn, myriads
mechanical and intellectual,
and the sons of men, with the wind and the fire of life
in their faces, and motion never mechanical in their limbs.

THE CROSS

Behold your Cross, Christians!
With the upright division into sex
men on this side, women on that side
without any division into inferiority and superiority
only difference,
divided in the mystic, tangible and intangible difference.

And then, truth much more bitter to accept,
the horizontal division of mankind
into that which is below the level, and that which is
    above. . . .

That which is truly man, and that which is robot,
the ego-bound.

On this cross of division, division into sex
division into slave and freeman
Christ, the human consciousness
was crucified
to set all men free
to make all men noble
to wipe away the mystic barriers of sex.

In vain, in vain, in vain, oh vastly in vain
this horrific crucifixion.

Now risen Man and risen lord
risen from the dead, after this crucifixion
must learn the supreme lesson—

That sex is an eternal upright division, before which we
    must bow
and live in the acceptance of it,
it can never be wiped out;
the gods that made us are greater than our consciousness
and we, we are mostly unexplored hinterland
and our consciousness is a spot of light in a great but
    living darkness.

And then, risen, we must learn the most cruel lesson
of the horizontal division of mankind
the eternal division between the base and the beautiful.
The base, those that are below the bar of the cross
the small-ones, ego-bound, little machines running in an
     enclosed circle of self
the inferiors.

The inferiors, the inferiors, there they are, in hordes.
And they will destroy all, unless they are made to submit
and to serve that which is flamey or pure and watery or
     swift wind or sound ringing rock
that which is elemental and of the substantial gods in man.
Mankind is lost and lost forever
unless men swiftly divide again, and the base are thrust
     down
into service, like the roots of trees.

For today, the base, the robots sit on the thrones of the
     world
in all the high places, and they are masters of industry
and rulers of millions of robots, being robots themselves,
     the same
only the brainy sort:
But brainy robot, or aesthetic robot, or merely muscular or
     mechanical robot
it is all the same
less than real men, inferiors, inferiors.

How then are the few men, men of the wind and rain
men of the fire and rock, how are they going to come forth
from the robot mass of rich and poor, mechanical ego-
     bound myriads?

Life will find a way.
Life always finds a way.
Only, Oh man, stare, stare into the gulf
between you and the robot-hordes, misnamed your fellow-
     men.

FELLOW-MEN

A few are my fellow-men
a few, only a few:
the mass are not.

The mass are not my fellow-men,
I repudiate them as such.
Let them serve.

THE SIGHT OF GOD

Men are not alike in the sight of God
Oh no, oh no!
Men are anything but alike in the sight of God.

In the sight of God and the unknown gods
most men don't matter at all, any more than ants matter
    to men:
only the few, the very few, matter in the sight of God, and
    the living substantial gods.

SOULS TO SAVE

You tell me every man has a soul to save?
I tell you, not one man in a thousand has even
    a soul to lose.
The automat has no soul to lose
so it can't have one to save.

WHEN MOST MEN DIE

When most men die, today,
when most women die
it is merely a machine breaks down
and can't be mended.

HOLD BACK!

Oh men, living men, vivid men, ocean and fire
don't give any more life to the machines!
Draw it away, draw it away, for these horrible machine-
    people
can't live any more, except for a spell, when the living
    cease to accept them as brothers
and give them life.

Machines of iron must be tended by hands of flesh
and robots must have encouragement from men of the
    vivid life
or they break down.

Oh men of life and of living
withdraw, withdraw your flow
from the grinning and insatiable robots.

IMPULSE

You can count on anything, but you can't count on
    impulse.
You can't even count on the mechanical impulse for
    money and motor-cars
which rules the robot-classes and the robot-masses, now.

Once disillusion falls on living men, and they feel the
    illusion ebb away
the illusion of mankind, the illusion of a hopeful future
    for these masses and classes of men
once disillusion falls on living men, and illusion of brother-
    hood and hope bleeds right away

Then, then comes the great moment of choice.
Oh, life is nothing if not choice.
And that which is choice alone matters.

In the moment of choice, the soul rolls back
away from the robot-classes and the robot-masses
and withdraws itself, and recognises a flower, or the
    morning-star
but utterly fails to recognise any more the grey rat-hordes
    of classes and masses.

And then, when the soul of living men repudiates them
then at once the impulse of the greedy classes and masses
    breaks down
and a chaos of impulses supervenes
in which is heard the crashing splinter of machines
and the dull breaking of bones.

For the robot classes and masses are only kept sane
by the kindness of living women and men.

Now living women and men are threatened with extinction
and the time has come to cease to be kind any more
to the robot classes and masses.

Oh, if the huge tree dies
save some shoots, some lovely flowering shoots
to graft on another tree.

Trees raised from seed have wild and bitter fruits
they need grafting:
and even the loveliest flowers, you must graft them on a
    new stock.

MEN LIKE GODS

Men wanted to be like gods
so they became like machines
and now even they're not satisfied.

MAN AND MACHINE

Man invented the machine
and now the machine has invented man.

God the Father is a dynamo
and God the Son a talking radio
and God the Holy Ghost is gas that keeps it all going.

And men have perforce to be little dynamos
and little talking radios
and the human spirit is so much gas, to keep it all going.

Man invented the machine
so now the machine has invented man.

MASSES AND CLASSES

There are masses, and there are classes
but the machine it is that has invented them both.

The classes are so superior
because they are the brains of the machine.
And the masses are also so superior
because they are the arms and legs of the machine.

An old Frenchman uttered the truism:
God cannot do without me!
Certainly the god in the machine cannot!
It has all the time to be soothed and consoled by
the hands of life.

GIVE US THE THEBAÏD

Modern society is a mill
that grinds life very small.

The upper millstone of the robot-classes,
the lower millstone of the robot-masses,
and between them, the last living human beings
being ground exceeding small.

Turn away, O turn away, man of flesh!
Slip out, O slip out from between the millstones
extract and extricate yourself
and hide in your own wild Thebaïd.

Then let the millstones grind, for they can't stop
    grinding, so let them grind
without grist.
Let them grind on one another, upper-class robot
    weight upon lower-class robot weight
till they grow hot, and burst, as even stone can
    explode.

SIDE-STEP, O SONS OF MEN!

Sons of men, from the wombs of wistful women,
not piston-mechanical-begotten,
sons of men, with the wondering eyes of life
hark! hark! step aside silently and swiftly.

The machine has got you, is turning you round and round
and confusing you, and feeding itself on your life.
Softly, subtly, secretly, in soul first, then in spirit, then in
    body
slip aside, slip out
from the entanglement of the giggling machine
that sprawls across the earth in iron imbecility.

Softly, subtly, secretly, saying nothing
step aside, step out of it, it is eating you up,
O step aside, with decision, sons of men, with decision.

ON AND ON AND ON

The machine will run on and on and on—
then let it!

Oh, never fight the machine,
nor its mechanised robots, robot classes and masses!
Lift never a finger against them, that they can see,
Let them run on and on and on—
It is their heaven and their doom.

OH WONDERFUL MACHINE!

Oh wonderful machine, so self-sufficient, so sufficient unto
    yourself!
You who have no feeling of the moon as she changes her
    quarters!
You who don't hear the sea's uneasiness!
You to whom the sun is merely something that makes the
    thermometer rise!

Oh wonderful machine, you who are man's idea of godliness,
you who feel nothing, who know nothing, who run on
    absolved
from any other connection!
Oh you godly and smooth machine, spinning on in your
    own Nirvana,
turning the blue wheels of your own heaven
almighty machine
how is it you have to be looked after by some knock-kneed
    wretch
at two pounds a week?

Oh great god of the machine
what lousy archangels and angels you have to surround
    yourself with!
And you can't possibly do without them!

BUT I SAY UNTO YOU:
LOVE ONE ANOTHER

Oh I have loved my fellow-men—
and lived to learn they are neither fellows nor men
but machine-robots.

Oh I have loved the working class
where I was born,
and lived to see them spawn into machine-robots
in the hot-beds of the board-schools and the film.

Oh how I loved the thought of thoughtful people
gentle and refined,
and lived to find out
that their last thought was money
and their last refinement bluff, a hate disguised,
and one trapped one's fingers in their brassy, polished
    works!

LOVE THY NEIGHBOUR

I love my neighbour
but
are these things my neighbours?
these two-legged things that walk and talk
and eat and cachinnate, and even seem to smile
seem to smile, ye gods!

Am I told that these things are my neighbours?

All I can say then is Nay! nay! nay! nay! nay!

AS THYSELF!

Supposing I say: dogs are my neighbours
I will love dogs as myself!

Then gradually I approximate to the dog,
wriggle and wag and slaver, and get the mentality of a dog!
This I call a shocking humiliation.

The same with my robot neighbours.
If I try loving them, I fall into their robot jig-jig-jig,
their robot cachinnation comes rattling out of my throat—
and I had better even have approximated to the dog.

Who then, O Jesus, is my neighbour?
If you point me to that fat money-smelling man in a motor-
car,
or that hard-boiled young woman beside him
I shall have to refuse entirely to accept either of them.

My neighbour is not the man in the street, and never was:
he jigs along in the imbecile cruelty of the machine
and is implacable.

My neighbour, O my neighbour!
Occasionally I see him, silent, a little wondering
with his ears pricked and his body wincing
threading his way among the robot machine-people.

O my neighbour
sometimes I see her, like a flower, nodding her way and
shrinking
from the robot contact on every hand!

How can that be my neighbour
which I shrink from!

LONELY, LONESOME, LONEY—O!

When I hear somebody complain of being lonely
or, in American, lonesome
I really wonder and wonder what they mean.

Do they mean they are a great deal alone?

But what is lovelier than to be alone?
escaping the petrol fumes of human conversation
and the exhaust-smell of people
and be alone!

Be alone, and feel the trees silently growing.
Be alone, and see the moonlight outside, white and busy
    and silent.
Be quite alone, and feel the living cosmos softly rocking
soothing and restoring and healing.

Soothed, restored and healed
when I am alone with the silent great cosmos
and there is no grating of people with their presences
    gnawing
at the stillness of the air.

TREES IN THE GARDEN

Ah in the thunder air
how still the trees are!

And the lime-tree, lovely and tall, every leaf silent
hardly looses even a last breath of perfume.

And the ghostly, creamy coloured little tree of leaves
white, ivory white among the rambling greens
how evanescent, variegated elder, she hesitates on the green gras
as if, in another moment, she would disappear
with all her grace of foam!

And the larch that is only a column, it goes up too tall to see:
and the balsam-pines that are blue with the grey-blue blueness of
    things from the sea,
and the young copper beech, its leaves red-rosy at the ends
how still they are together, they stand so still
in the thunder air, all strangers to one another
as the green grass glows upwards, strangers in the silent garden.

Lichtental

STORM IN THE BLACK FOREST

Now it is almost night, from the bronzey soft sky
jugfull after jugfull of pure white liquid fire, bright white
tipples over and spills down,
and is gone
and gold-bronze flutters bent through the thick upper air.

And as the electric liquid pours out, sometimes
a still brighter white snake wriggles among it, spilled
and tumbling wriggling down the sky:
and then the heavens cackle with uncouth sounds.

And the rain won't come, the rain refuses to come!

This is the electricity that man is supposed to have mastered
chained, subjugated to his use!
supposed to!

REVOLUTIONS AS SUCH!

Curiously enough, actual revolutions are made by robots,
living people never make revolutions,
they can't, life means too much to them.

ROBOT FEELINGS

It is curious, too, that though the modern man in the street
is a robot, and incapable of love
he is capable of an endless, grinding, nihilistic hate:
that is the only strong feeling he is capable of;
and therein lies the danger of robot-democracy and all the
    men in the street,
they move in a great grind of hate, slowly but inevitably.

ROBOT-DEMOCRACY

In a robot-democracy, nobody is willing to serve
even work is unwilling, the worker is unwilling, unwilling.

The great grind of unwillingness, the slow undergrind of hate
and democracy is ground into dust
then the mill-stones burst with the internal heat of their own
    friction.

REAL DEMOCRACY

If the robot can recognise the clean flame of life
in men who have never fallen from life
then he repents, and his will breaks, and a great love of life
brings him to his knees, in homage and pure passion of service.

Then he receives the kiss of reconciliation
and ceases to be a robot, and becomes a servant of life
serving with delight and with reverence those men whose flame
of life undimmed delights him, so even he is lit up.

WORSHIP

All men are worshippers
unless they have fallen, and become robots.

All men worship the wonder of life
until they collapse into egoism, the mechanical, self-centred
    system of the robot.

But even in pristine men, there is this difference :
some men can see life clear and flickering all around,
and some can only see what they are shown.

Some men look straight into the eyes of the gods
and some men can see no gods, they only know
the gods are there because of the gleam on the faces of the
    men who see.

Most men, even unfallen, can only live
by the transmitted gleam from the faces of vivider men
who look into the eyes of the gods.

And worship is the joy of the gleam from the eyes of the gods,
and the robot is the denial of the same,
even the denial that there *is* any gleam.

CLASSES

There are two classes of men:
those that look into the eyes of the gods, and these are few,
and those that look into the eyes of the few other men
to see the gleam of the gods there, reflected in the human eye.

All other class is artificial.
There is, however, the vast third homogeneous amorphous
    class of anarchy
the robots, those who deny the gleam.

DEMOCRACY IS SERVICE

Democracy is service, but not the service of demos.
Democracy is demos serving life
and demos serves life as it gleams on the faces of the few,
and the few look into the eyes of the gods, and serve the sheer
    gods.

FALSE DEMOCRACY AND REAL

If man only looks to man, and no-one sees beyond
then all is lost, the robot supervenes.

The few must look into the eyes of the gods, and obey the look
in the eyes of the gods:
and the many must obey the few that look into the eyes of the gods;
and the stream is towards the gods, not backwards, towards man.

SERVICE

Ah yes, men must learn to serve
not for money, but for life.

Ah yes, men must learn to obey
not a boss, but the gleam of life on the face of a man
who has looked into the eyes of the gods.

Man is only perfectly human
when he looks beyond humanity.

WHAT ARE THE GODS?

What are the gods, then, what are the gods?

The gods are nameless and imageless
yet looking in a great full lime-tree of summer
I suddenly saw deep into the eyes of god:
it is enough.

THE GODS! THE GODS!

People were bathing and posturing themselves on the beach
and all was dreary, great robot limbs, robot breasts
robot voices, robot even the gay umbrellas.

But a woman, shy and alone, was washing herself under a tap
and the glimmer of the presence of the gods was like lilies,
and like water-lilies.

NAME THE GODS!

I refuse to name the gods, because they have no name.
I refuse to describe the gods, because they have no form nor
    shape nor substance.

Ah, but the simple ask for images!
Then for a time at least, they must do without.

But all the time I see the gods:
the man who is mowing the tall white corn,
suddenly, as it curves, as it yields, the white wheat
and sinks down with a swift rustle, and a strange, falling
    flatness,
ah! the gods, the swaying body of god!
ah the fallen stillness of god, autumnus, and it is only July
the pale-gold flesh of Priapus dropping asleep.

THERE ARE NO GODS

There are no gods, and you can please yourself
have a game of tennis, go out in the car, do some shopping, sit and
    talk, talk, talk
with a cigarette browning your fingers.

There are no gods, and you can please yourself—
go and please yourself—

But leave me alone, leave me alone, to myself!
and then in the room, whose is the presence
that makes the air so still and lovely to me?

Who is it that softly touches the sides of my breast
and touches me over the heart
so that my heart beats soothed, soothed, soothed and at peace?

Who is it smooths the bed-sheets like the cool
smooth ocean where the fishes rest on edge
in their own dream?

Who is it that clasps and kneads my naked feet, till they unfold,
till all is well, till all is utterly well? the lotus-lilies of the feet!

I tell you, it is no woman, it is no man, for I am alone.
And I fall asleep with the gods, the gods
that are not, or that are
according to the soul's desire,
like a pool into which we plunge, or do not plunge.

FOOD OF THE NORTH

The food of the north tastes too much of the fat
    of the pig
fat of the pig!

Take me south again, to the olive trees
and oil me with the lymph of silvery trees,
oil me with the lymph of trees
not with the fat of the pig.

RETORT TO WHITMAN

And whoever walks a mile full of false sympathy
walks to the funeral of the whole human race.

RETORT TO JESUS

And whoever forces himself to love anybody
begets a murderer in his own body.

THE DEEPEST SENSUALITY

The profoundest of all our sensualities
is the sense of truth
and the next deepest sensual experience
is the sense of justice.

SENSE OF TRUTH

You must fuse mind and wit with all the senses
before you can feel truth.
And if you can't feel truth you can't have any other
satisfactory sensual experience.

SATISFACTION

The profound sensual experience of truth: Yea, this *is*!
alone satisfies us, in the end.

VIBRATION OF JUSTICE

profound and thrilling vibration of justice, sense of ultimate
justice
es the heart suddenly quiver with love.

LIES

Lies are not a question of false fact
but of false feeling and perverted justice.

POISON

What has killed mankind—for the bulk of mankind is dead—
is lies:
the nasty lying pretence of seeming to feel what we don't feel.

COMMANDMENTS

When Jesus commanded us to love our neighbour
he forced us either to live a great lie, or to disobey:
for we can't love anybody, neighbour or no neighbour, to order,
and faked love has rotted our marrow.

EMOTIONAL LIES

You hear a woman say: I love my husband dearly—
and you look in her eyes and see it is a lie.
Even it is a trick: but she is not ashamed.

LAUGHTER

Listen to people laughing
and you will hear what liars they are
or cowards.

DRAWING-ROOM

You sit talking in all earnestness to a woman,
hearing her talk, that is:
and you know all the while
that every syllable, every accent, every intonation and every
    cadence is a lie:
yet you go on talking, in all earnestness.

CABBAGE-ROSES

You may smell the breath of the gods in the common roses,
and feel the splendour of the gods go through you, even as you see
    the green-fly on the stems,
in the summer morning:
or you may not.

If you don't, then don't pretend you do—
but if you don't, you are suffering from an amnesia
of the senses:
you are like to die of malnutrition of the senses:
and your sensual atrophy
will at last send you insane.

COLD BLOOD

In cold blood, I cannot feel goddesses in the summer evening
trafficking mysteriously through the air.

But what right has my blood to be cold
before I'm dead?
If I cut my finger, my blood is hot, not cold.

And even in cold blood I know this:
I am more alive, more aware and more wise
when my blood is kindled:
and when, in the summer evening
I feel goddesses trafficking mysteriously through the air.

SUNSET

There is a band of dull gold in the west, and say what you like
again and again some god of evening leans out of it
and shares being with me, silkily
all of twilight.

LISTEN TO THE BAND!

There is a band playing in the early night,
but it is only unhappy men making a noise
to drown their inner cacophony: and ours.

A little moon, quite still, leans and sings to herself
throughout the night
and the music of men is like a mouse gnawing,
gnawing in a wooden trap, trapped in.

THE HUMAN FACE

Hardly ever, now, has a human face
the baffling light or the strange still gleam of the gods
within it, upon it.

Even from the faces of the children, now,
that spangled glisten is gone, that at-oneness without afterthought,
and they are bridled with cunning, and bitted
with knowledge of things that shall never be admitted,
even the fact of birth: even little children.

Holbein and Titian and Tintoret could never paint faces, now:
because those faces were windows to the strange horizons, even
    Henry VIII;
whereas faces now are only human grimaces,
with eyes like the interiors of stuffy rooms, furnished.

PORTRAITS

Portraits are now supremely uninteresting
because all the faces contain sets of emotional and
    mental furniture
all more or less alike,
as all drawing-rooms are, arranged!

FURNITURE

Some women live for the idiotic furniture of their houses,
some men live for the conceited furniture of their minds,
some only live for their emotional furnishings—

and it all amounts to the same thing, furniture,
usually in "suites".

CHILDREN SINGING IN SCHOOL

Class-children are singing in school
and what an awful concatenation of sound it is!
They have no song in their souls, none in their spirits,
none in their little throats or class-room bodies
only they are made to utter these cog-wheel sounds
which are meant to be the old folk-song: Strawberry Fair!

KEEP IT UP

People go on singing when they have no song in them.
People go on talking when they have nothing to say.
People go on walking when they have nowhere to go.
People keep it up, because they daren't stop.

So here we go round the mulberry bush,
mulberry bush, mulberry bush!
Here we go round the mulberry bush—
never having seen a mulberry bush in our lives.

RACE AND BATTLE

The race is not to the swift
but to those that can sit still
and let the waves go over them.

The battle is not to the strong
but to the frail, who know best
how to efface themselves
to save the streaked pansy of the heart from
being trampled to mud.

NOTHING TO SAVE

There is nothing to save, now all is lost,
but a tiny core of stillness in the heart
like the eye of a violet.

EMASCULATION

When Mercury and Love and Death
and even the grand horse of Physical Energy
have all, by Mr. Watts and the Victorians, been carefully
emasculated—

so that all our Daddies were quite British "pure",
they never did anything—
all dear Daddy-do-nothings!
Hypocrites and eunuchs,
eunuchs and hypocrites!

What are we, O what are we
immaculately conceived
Daddyless
children of Daddy-do-nothing?

Little boy blue
come blow up your horn—

BRITISH SINCERITY

They tell me that these British moral birds
all the great Jixery up in the fixery
are "perfectly sincere".
and "perfectly honest".

If it is perfectly sincere to deny your own make-up
and perfectly honest to pretend to be unbegotten
may I ask you then, where insincerity and dishonesty begin.

The Jixery perhaps never picked a man's pocket
but my god, they sneak-thiefed his very genitals away from him:
going a bit further than his pocket, what?

And the poor man never knew he was jixed,
fixed, jixed, fixed!
He feels for his purse, and finds it there, and says
Oh my jixer, my fixer
oh he's an honest man! anyhow!

Is British hypocrisy a form of softening of the brain?
Or what is it that my nation is suffering from?

THE ENGLISH ARE SO NICE!

The English are so nice
so awfully nice
they're the nicest people in the world.

And what's more, they're very nice about being nice
about your being nice as well!
If you're not nice, they soon make you feel it.

Americans and French and Germans and so on
they're all very well
but they're not *really* nice, you know.
They're not nice in *our* sense of the word, are they now?

That's why one doesn't have to take them seriously.
We must be nice to them, of course,
of course, naturally—
But it doesn't really matter what you say to them,
they don't really understand—
you can just say anything to them:
be nice, you know, just be nice
but you must never take them seriously, they wouldn't understand.
just be nice, you know! oh, fairly nice,
not too nice of course, they take advantage—
but nice enough, just nice enough
to let them feel they're not quite as nice as they might be.

THE HILLS

I lift up mine eyes unto the hills
and there they are, but no strength comes from
    them to me.

Only from darkness
and ceasing to see
strength comes.

TOURISTS

There is nothing to look at any more,
everything has been seen to death.

SEEKERS

Oh seekers, when you leave off seeking
you will realise there was never anything to seek for.

You were only seeking to lose something,
not to find something,
when you went forth so vigorously in search.

SEARCH FOR LOVE

Those that go searching for love
only make manifest their own lovelessness,

and the loveless never find love,
only the loving find love,
and they never have to seek for it.

SEARCH FOR TRUTH

Search for nothing any more, nothing
except truth.
Be very still, and try and get at the truth.

And the first question to ask yourself is:
How great a liar am I?

LIES ABOUT LOVE

We are all liars, because
the truth of yesterday becomes a lie tomorrow,
whereas letters are fixed,
and we live by the letter of truth.

The love I feel for my friend, this year,
is different from the love I felt last year.
If it were not so, it would be a lie.
Yet we reiterate love! love! love!
as if it were coin with a fixed value
instead of a flower that dies, and opens a different bud.

TRAVEL IS OVER

I have travelled, and looked at the world, and loved it.
Now I don't want to look at the world any more,
there seems nothing there.
In not-looking, and in not-seeing
comes a new strength
and undeniable new gods share their life with us, when we
    cease to see.

OLD MEN

Whom the gods love, die young.
How the gods must hate most of the old, old men today,
the rancid old men that don't die
because the gods don't want them
won't have them
leave them to stale on earth.

Old people fixed in a rancid resistance
to life, fixed to the letter of the law.

The gods, who are life, and the fluidity of living change
leave the old ones fixed to their ugly, cogged self-will
which turns on and on, the same, and is hell on earth.

DEATH

Death is no escape, ah no! only a doorway to the inevitable.
That's why the dogged, resistant old ones dare not die
dare not die!—they daren't go through the door.

They dare not die, because they know
in death they cannot any more escape
the retribution for their obstinacy.

Old men, old obstinate men and women
dare not die, because in death
their hardened souls are washed with fire, and washed and seared
till they are softened back to life-stuff again, against which they
      hardened themselves.

BOURGEOIS AND BOLSHEVIST

The bourgeois produces the bolshevist, inevitably
as every half-truth at length produces the contradic-
    tion of itself
in the opposite half-truth.

PROPERTY AND NO-PROPERTY

The bourgeois asserts that he owns his property by divine right,
and the bolshevist asserts that by human right no man shall own
    property
and between the two blades of this pair of shears, property and no-
    property
we shall all be cut to bits.

COWARDICE AND IMPUDENCE

Bourgeois cowardice produces bolshevist impudence
in direct ratio.
As the bourgeois gets secretly more cowardly, knowing he is in the
    wrong
the bolshevist gets openly more impudent, also knowing he is in
    the wrong.
And between the cowardice and impudence of this pair who are in
    the wrong,
this pair of property mongrels
the world will be torn in two.

LORD TENNYSON AND LORD MELCHETT

"Dost tha hear my horse's feet, as he canters away?
Property! Property! Property! that's what they seem to say!"

Do you hear my Rolls Royce purr, as it glides away?
—I lick the cream off property! that's what it seems to say!

CHOICE OF EVILS

If I have to choose between the bourgeois and the bolshevist
I choose the bourgeois
he will interfere with me less.

But in choosing the bourgeois, one brings to pass
only more inevitably, the bolshevist.
Since the bourgeois is the direct cause of the bolshevist,
as a half-lie causes the immediate contradiction of the other half-lie.

HARD-BOILED CONSERVATIVES

O you hard-boiled conservatives, and you soft-boiled liberals
don't you *see* how you make bolshevism inevitable?

SOLOMON'S BABY

Property is now Solomon's baby
and whoever gets it, it'll be a dead baby
a corpse, even of property.

THE PROPERTY QUESTION

In settling the property question between them,
bourgeois and bolshevist,

they'll merely destroy all property and a great many people
like the two lions who devoured one another, and left the tail-tufts
    wagging.
Let's hope there'll be more sense in the tail-tufts
than there was in the lions.

THE WAY OUT

The only way to settle the property question
is to cease to be interested in it; to be so interested in
    something else
that the property problem solves itself by the way.

ST GEORGE AND THE DRAGON

The more you tackle the property dragon
the more deadly and dangerous it becomes.

Whereas if you ride away and become deeply concerned in some-
    thing else,
the old dragon will dwindle down to the size of a stray cat, neglected,
whom some recalcitrant old maid will adopt, as a hobby.

It is all a question of being profoundly interested in property, or not.
And quite a lot of people are not.
But they let themselves be overwhelmed by those that are.

THE HALF-BLIND

The bourgeois and the bolshevist are both quite blind
hence the ridiculous way they rush in where angels fear to tread.
They can't see it.

But among the bourgeois and the bolshevist bounders
one notices men here and there, going hesitatingly, faltering
with the pathos of those who can see, but whose sight is dim.
And these, the minority of men who can still see the light of life
give way all the time before the mechanical rushing of the ugly
    stone-blind ones.

MINORITIES IN DANGER

Now above all is the time for the minorities of men,
those who are neither bourgeois nor bolshevist, but true to life,
to gather and fortify themselves, in every class, in every country,
    in every race.

Instead of which, the minorities that still see the gleam of life
submit abjectly to the blind mechanical traffic-streams of those
    horrors
the stone-blind bourgeois, and the stone-blind bolshevist,
and pander to them.

IF YOU ARE A MAN

If you are a man, and believe in the destiny of mankind
then say to yourself: we will cease to care
about property and money and mechanical devices,
and open our consciousness to the deep, mysterious life
that we are now cut off from.

The machine shall be abolished from the earth again;
it is a mistake that mankind has made;
money shall cease to be, and property shall cease to perplex
and we will find the way to immediate contact with life
and with one another.

To know the moon as we have never known
yet she is knowable.
To know a man as we have never known
a man, as never yet a man was knowable, yet still shall be.

TERRA INCOGNITA

There are vast realms of consciousness still undreamed of
vast ranges of experience, like the humming of unseen harps,
we know nothing of, within us.

666

Oh when man has escaped from the barbed-wire entanglement
of his own ideas and his own mechanical devices
there is a marvellous rich world of contact and sheer fluid beauty
and fearless face-to-face awareness of now-naked life
and me, and you, and other men and women
and grapes, and ghouls, and ghosts and green moonlight
and ruddy-orange limbs stirring the limbo
of the unknown air, and eyes so soft
softer than the space between the stars,
and all things, and nothing, and being and not-being
alternately palpitant,
when at last we escape the barbed-wire enclosure
of *Know Thyself*, knowing we can never know,
we can but touch, and wonder, and ponder, and make our effort
and dangle in a last fastidious fine delight
as the fuchsia does, dangling her reckless drop
of purple after so much putting forth
and slow mounting marvel of a little tree.

CLIMBING DOWN

They are afraid of climbing down from this idiotic tin-pot heaven
 of ours
because they don't know what they'll find when they do get down.

They needn't bother, most of them will never get down at all,
they've got to stay up.
And those that do descend have got to suffer a sense-change
into something new and strange.

Become aware as leaves are aware
and fine as flowers are fine
and fierce as fire is fierce
and subtle, silvery, tinkling and rippling
as rain-water
and still a man,
but a man re-born from the rigidity of fixed ideas
resurrected from the death of mechanical motion and emotion.

ONLY THE BEST MATTERS

Only the best matters, in man especially.
True, you can't produce the best without attending to the whole
but that which is secondary is only important
in so far as it goes to the bringing forth of the best.

TO PINO

O Pino
What a bean-o!
when we printed Lady C.!

Little Giuntina
couldn't have been a
better little bee!

When you told him
perhaps they'd scold him
for printing those naughty words

All he could say:
"But we do it every day!
like the pigeons and the other little birds!"

And dear old lady Jean
"I don't know what you mean
by publishing such a book.

We're all in it, all my family
me and Ekkehart and Somers and Pamelie—
you're no better than a crook—!"

"Wait, dear Lady Jean, wait a minute!
What makes you think that you're all in it?
Did you ever open the book?

Is Ekke Sir Clifford? it's really funny!
And you, dear Lady Jean, are you Connie?
So open the book and look!—"

But off she went, being really rattled
and there's a battle that's still to be battled
along with the others! what luck!

BROADCASTING TO THE G. B. P.

"Hushaby baby, on a tree top
when the wind blows, the cradle shall rock,
when the bough breaks——"

                              Stop that at once!
You'll give the Great British Public a nervous shock!

"Goosey goosey gander
whither do you wander
upstairs, downstairs
in my lady's——"

                    Stop! where's your education?
Don't you know that's obscene?
Remember the British Public!

"Baa-baa black sheep
have you any wool?
yes sir! yes sir!
three bags full!
One for the master, and one for the dame,
and one for the little boy that lives down the——"

                                          No!
You'd better omit that, too communistic!
Remember the state of mind of the British Public.

"Pussy-cat pussy-cat where have you been?
I've been up to London to see the fine queen!
Pussy-cat pussy-cat what did you there?
I frightened a little mouse——"

Thank you! thank you!
There are no mice in our Royal Palaces. Omit it!

WE CAN'T BE TOO CAREFUL

We can't be too careful
about the British Public.
It gets bigger and bigger
and its perambulator has to get bigger and bigger
and its dummy-teat has to be made bigger and bigger and bigger
and the job of changing its diapers gets bigger and bigger and bigger
    and bigger
and the sound of its howling gets bigger and bigger and bigger and
    bigger and bigger
and the feed of pap that we nurses and guardian angels of the press
    have to deal out to it
gets bigger and bigger and bigger and bigger and bigger and bigger
yet its belly-ache seems to get bigger too
and soon even God won't be big enough to handle that infant.

LUCKY LITTLE BRITISHER

Oh you'd think the British Public
was a great big hydrocephalous, water-on-the-brain infant
to see the way they treat it.

THE WORKING MAN

If Auntie doesn't love me
then why should I be good?
why shouldn't I steal the jam in the cupboard
and all the dainty food

that I never get a taste of! Really
it all belongs to me.
Auntie is only my housekeeper
during my minority.

So if Auntie doesn't love me
I shall tell her the house is mine
and I'm going to do what I jolly well please
and enjoy myself fine.

GLIMPSES

What's the good of a man
unless there's the glimpse of a god in him?

And what's the good of a woman
unless she's a glimpse of a goddess of some sort?

ALL SORTS OF GODS

There's all sorts of gods, all sorts and every sort,
and every god that humanity has ever known is still a god today
the African queer ones and Scandinavian queer ones,
the Greek beautiful ones, the Phoenician ugly ones, the Aztec hideous
      ones,
goddesses of love, goddesses of dirt, excrement-eaters or lily virgins,
Jesus, Buddha, Jehovah and Ra, Egypt and Babylon,
all the gods, and you see them all if you look, alive and moving today,
ind alive and moving tomorrow, many tomorrows, as yesterdays.

Where do you see them, you say?
You see them in glimpses, in the faces and forms of people, in
      glimpses.

When men and women, when lads and girls are not thinking,
when they are pure, which means when they are quite clean from
    self-consciousness
either in anger or tenderness, or desire or sadness or wonder or mere
    stillness
you may see glimpses of the gods in them.

FOR A MOMENT

For a moment, at evening, tired, as he stepped off the tram-car,
—the young tram-conductor in a blue uniform, to himself for-
    gotten,—
and lifted his face up, with blue eyes looking at the electric rod
    which he was going to turn round,
for a moment, pure in the yellow evening light, he was Hyacinthus.

In the green garden darkened the shadow of coming rain
and a girl ran swiftly, laughing breathless, taking in her white
    washing
in rapid armfuls from the line, tossing it in the basket,
and so rapidly, and so flashing, fleeing before the rain
for a moment she was Io, Io, who fled from Zeus, or the Danaë.

When I was waiting and not thinking, sitting at a table on the hotel
    terrace
I saw suddenly coming towards me, lit up and uplifted with pleasure
advancing with the slow-swiftness of a ship backing her white sails
    into port
the woman who looks for me in the world
and for the moment she was Isis, gleaming, having found her Osiris.

For a moment, as he looked at me through his spectacles
pondering, yet eager, the broad and thick-set Italian who works
    in with me,
for a moment he was the Centaur, the wise yet horse-hoofed Centaur
in whom I can trust.

GOETHE AND POSE

When Goethe becomes an Apollo, he becomes a plaster cast.
When people pose as gods, they are Crystal Palace statues,
made of cement poured into a mould, around iron sticks.

MEN LIKE GODS

When men think they are like gods
they are usually much less than men
being conceited fools.

THOUGHT

Thought, I love thought.
But not the jiggling and twisting of already existent ideas
I despise that self-important game.
Thought is the welling up of unknown life into consciousness,
Thought is the testing of statements on the touchstone of the con-
    science,
Thought is gazing on to the face of life, and reading what can be read,
Thought is pondering over experience, and coming to a conclusion.
Thought is not a trick, or an exercise, or a set of dodges,
Thought is a man in his wholeness wholly attending.

[THE GODS]

The gods are all things, and so are we.
The gods are only ourselves, as we are in our
    moments of pure manifestation.

BE IT SO

O, if a flame is in you, be it so!
When your flame flickers up, and you flicker forth in sheer purity
for a moment pure from all conceit of yourself, and all afterthought
you are for that moment one of the gods, Jesus or Fafnir or Priapus
    or Siva.

CONCEIT

It is conceit that kills us
and makes us cowards instead of gods.

Under the great Command: Know thyself, and that thou art mortal!
we have become fatally self-conscious, fatally self-important, fatally
    entangled in the Laocoön coils of our own conceit.

Now we have to admit we *can't* know ourselves, we can only know
    about ourselves.
And I am not interested to know about myself any more,
I only entangle myself in the knowing.

Now let me be myself,
now let me be myself, and flicker forth,
now let me be myself, in the being, one of the gods.

MAN IS MORE THAN *HOMO SAPIENS*

Man is not quite a man
unless he has his pure moments, when he is surpassing.
I saw an angry Italian seize an irritating little official by the throat
and all but squeeze the life out of him:
and Jesus himself could not have denied that at that moment the
    angry man
was a god, in godliness pure as a Christ, beautiful
but perhaps Ashtaroth, perhaps Siva, perhaps Huitzilopochtli
with the dark and gleaming beauty of the messageless gods.

SELF-CONSCIOUS PEOPLE

O are you tangled up in yourself
poor little man, poor little man!

Is she tangled up in herself then
poor woman, poor woman!

But beware!
They are like cats with unclean claws, tangled up in nets,
and if you try to get them out
they will tear you terribly, and give you blood-poisoning.

TWO WAYS OF LIVING AND DYING

While people live the life
they are open to the restless skies, and streams flow in and out
darkly from the fecund cosmos, from the angry red sun, from the
    moon
up from the bounding earth, strange pregnant streams, in and out
    of the flesh,
and man is an iridescent fountain, rising up to flower
for a moment godly, like Baal or Krishna, or Adonis or Balder, or
    Lucifer.

But when people are only self-conscious and self-willed
they cannot die, their corpus still runs on,
while nothing comes from the open heaven, from earth, from the
    sun and moon
to them, nothing, nothing;
only the mechanical power of self-directed energy
drives them on and on, like machines,
on and on, with the triumphant sense of power, like machines,
on and on, and their triumph in mere motion
full of friction, full of grinding, full of danger to the gentle passengers
of growing life,

but on and on, on and on, till the friction wears them out
and the machine begins to wobble
and with hideous shrieks of steely rage and frustration
the worn-out machine at last breaks down:
it is finished, its race is over.

So self-willed, self-centred, self-conscious people die
the death of nothingness, worn-out machines, kaput!

But when living people die in the ripeness of their time
terrible and strange the god lies on the bed, wistful, coldly wonderful,
beyond us, now beyond, departing with that purity
that flickered forth in the best hours of life,
when the man was himself, so a god in his singleness,
and the woman was herself, never to be duplicated, a goddess there
gleaming her hour in life as she now gleams in death
and departing inviolate, nothing can lay hands on her,
she who at her best hours was herself, warm, flickering, herself,
    therefore a goddess,
and who now draws slowly away, cold, the wistful goddess receding.

SO LET ME LIVE

So let me live that I may die
eagerly passing over from the entanglement of life
to the adventure of death, in eagerness
turning to death as I turn to beauty
to the breath, that is, of new beauty unfolding in death.

GLADNESS OF DEATH

Oh death
about you I know nothing, nothing—
about the afterwards
as a matter of fact, we know nothing.

Yet oh death, oh death
also I know so much about you
the knowledge is within me, without being a matter of fact.

And so I know
after the painful, painful experience of dying
there comes an after-gladness, a strange joy
in a great adventure
oh the great adventure of death, where Thomas Cook cannot guide
    us.

I have always wanted to be as the flowers are
so unhampered in their living and dying,
and in death I believe I shall be as the flowers are.

I shall blossom like a dark pansy, and be delighted
there among the dark sun-rays of death.
I can feel myself unfolding in the dark sunshine of death
to something flowery and fulfilled, and with a strange sweet perfume.

Men prevent one another from being men
but in the great spaces of death
the winds of the afterwards kiss us into blossom of manhood.

HUMANITY NEEDS PRUNING

Humanity needs pruning
It is like a vast great tree with a vast great lot of sterile, dead,
    rotting wood
and an amount of fungoid and parasitic growth.
The tree of humanity needs pruning, badly,
it needs thoroughly pruning, not as in the late war, blasting
with unintelligent and evil destruction
but pruning, severely, intelligently and ruthlessly pruning.

The tree of human existence needs badly pruning
or the whole tree may fall rotten.

SELF-SACRIFICE

Self-sacrifice, after all, is a wrong and mistaken idea.
It cannot be anything but wrong to sacrifice
good, healthy, natural feelings, instincts, passions or desires,
just as it cannot be anything but wrong to cut the throats
of doves for Venus, or of steers for Hermes,
if it is merely Venus or Hermes you are thinking of.

Venus would rather have live doves than dead, if you want to make
    an offering.
If you want to make her an offering, let the doves fly from her altar.

But what we may sacrifice, if we call it sacrifice, from the self,
are all the obstructions to life, self-importance, self-conceit, egoistic
    self-will,
    or all the ugly old possessions that make up the impedimenta of life,
ugly old furniture, ugly old books, ugly old buildings, ugly old "art",
anything that belongs to us, and is ugly and an impediment to the
    free motion of life
sacrifice that to the bright gods, and satisfy the destructive instinct.

SHEDDING OF BLOOD

"Without shedding of blood there is no remission of sin."
What does it mean?
Does it mean that life which has gone ugly and unliving is sin
and the blood of it must be spilt?

O spill the blood, not of your firstling lamb, without spot or blemish,
but kill the scabbed and ugly lamb, that spreads contagion.

O slay, not the best bright proud life that is in you, that can be happy,
but the craven, the cowardly, the creeping you, that can only be
    unhappy, kill it, the unliving thing.

O sacrifice, not that which is noble and generous and spontaneous in
    humanity
but that which is mean and base and squalid and degenerate,
destroy it, shed its unclean blood, kill it, put it out of existence.
O shed the unclean, mean, cowardly, greedy, egoistic, degenerate
    blood
and let mankind make new blood, fresh and bright.

THE OLD IDEA OF SACRIFICE

The old idea of sacrifice was this:
that blood of the lower life must be shed
for the feeding and strengthening of the handsomer, fuller life.

O when the old world sacrificed a ram
it was to the gods who make us splendid
and it was for a feast, a feast of meat, for men and maids
on a day of splendour, for the further splendour of being men.

It was the eating up of little lives,
even doves, even small birds
into the dance and splendour of a bigger life.

There is no such thing as sin.
There is only life and anti-life.

And sacrifice is the law of life which enacts
that little lives must be eaten up into the dance and splendour
of bigger lives, with due reverence and acknowledgement.

SELF-SACRIFICE

Self-sacrifice is perhaps the vilest deed a man can do.
The self that we are, at its best, is all that we are
is the very individual flame of life itself
which is the man's pure self.

And to sacrifice that, to anything or anybody whatsoever
is the vilest cowardice and treachery.

Yet a woman can add her flame to a man's
or a man can add his flame to the flame of another man
as a gift of gladness, seeing the glamour of life go up
swifter and higher and brighter, for the yielding and the adding
      together.

[THOMAS EARP]

I heard a little chicken chirp:
My name is Thomas, Thomas Earp!
And I can neither paint nor write
I only can set other people right.

All people that can write or paint
do tremble under my complaint.
For I am a chicken, and I can chirp;
and my name is Thomas, Thomas Earp.

"GROSS, COARSE, HIDEOUS"

(Police description of my pictures)

Lately I saw a sight most quaint:
London's lily-like policemen faint
in virgin outrage as they viewed
the nudity of a Lawrence nude!

[MR SQUIRE]

Dearly-beloved Mr Squire
So long as you lead the gawky choir
of critical cherubs that chirrup and pipe
in the weekly press their self-satisfied swipe.

Oh London's Mercury, Sunday-School Squire
so long as you tune your turn-turn lyre
with its tinkle-winkle and tweedle-dee
to the lesser fry in the hierarchy.

So long will they lift their impertinent voices
and chirrup their almost indecent noises
almost as empty as belching or hiccup
in grand chorale to your monthly kick-up.

So now we beg you, Mr Squire,
do now, once and forever, retire
and leave the critical piggy-wiggies.

LET THERE BE LIGHT!

If ever there was a beginning
there was no god in it
there was no Verb
no Voice
no Word.

There was nothing to say:
Let there be light!
All that story of Mr God switching on day
is just conceit.

Just man's conceit!
—Who made the sun?
—My child, I cannot tell a lie,
I made it!

George Washington's Grandpapa!

All we can honestly imagine in the beginning
is the incomprehensible plasm of life, of creation
struggling
and *becoming* light.

GOD IS BORN

The history of the cosmos
is the history of the struggle of becoming.
When the dim flux of unformed life
struggled, convulsed back and forth upon itself,
and broke at last into light and dark
came into existence as light,
came into existence as cold shadow
then every atom of the cosmos trembled with delight.
Behold, God is born!
He is bright light!
He is pitch dark and cold!

And in the great struggle of intangible chaos
when, at a certain point, a drop of water began to drip downwards
and a breath of vapour began to wreathe up
Lo again the shudder of bliss through all the atoms!
Oh, God is born!
Behold, He is born wet!
Look, He hath movement upward! He spirals!

And so, in the great aeons of accomplishment and débâcle
from time to time the wild crying of every electron:
Lo! God is born!

When sapphires cooled out of molten chaos:
See, God is born! He is blue, he is deep blue, he is forever blue!
When gold lay shining threading the cooled-off rock:
God is born! God is born! bright yellow and ductile He is born.

When the little eggy amoeba emerged out of foam and nowhere
then all the electrons held their breath:
Ach! Ach! Now indeed God is born! He twinkles within.

When from a world of mosses and of ferns
at last the narcissus lifted a tuft of five-point stars
and dangled them in the atmosphere,
then every molecule of creation jumped and clapped its hands:
God is born! God is born perfumed and dangling and with a little
    cup!

Throughout the aeons, as the lizard swirls his tail finer than water,
as the peacock turns to the sun, and could not be more splendid,
as the leopard smites the small calf with a spangled paw, perfect.
the universe trembles: God is born! God is here!

And when at last man stood on two legs and wondered,
then there was a hush of suspense at the core of every electron:
Behold, now very God is born!
God Himself is born!

And so we see, God is not
until he is born.

And also we see
there is no end to the birth of God.

THE WHITE HORSE

The youth walks up to the white horse, to put its halter on
and the horse looks at him in silence.
They are so silent, they are in another world.

FLOWERS AND MEN

Flowers achieve their own floweriness and it is a miracle.
Men don't achieve their own manhood, alas, oh alas! alas!

All I want of you, men and women,
all I want of you
is that you shall achieve your own beauty
as the flowers do.

Oh leave off saying I want you to be savages.
Tell me, is the gentian savage, at the top of its coarse stem?
Oh what in you can answer to this blueness?

[I want you to be as savage] as the gentian and the daffodil.
Tell me! tell me! is there in you a beauty to compare
to the honeysuckle at evening now
pouring out his breath.

PRAYER

Give me the moon at my feet
Put my feet upon the crescent, like a Lord!
O let my ankles be bathed in moonlight, that I
    may go
sure and moon-shod, cool and bright-footed
towards my goal.

For the sun is hostile, now
his face is like the red lion.

LAST POEMS

THE GREEKS ARE COMING!

Little islands out at sea, on the horizon
keep suddenly showing a whiteness, a flash and a furl, a hail
of something coming, ships a-sail from over the rim of the sea.

And every time, it is ships, it is ships,
it is ships of Cnossos coming, out of the morning end of the sea,
it is Aegean ships, and men with archaic pointed beards
coming out of the eastern end.

But it is far-off foam.
And an ocean liner, going east, like a small beetle walking the edge
is leaving a long thread of dark smoke
like a bad smell.

THE ARGONAUTS

They are not dead, they are not dead!
Now that the sun, like a lion, licks his paws
and goes slowly down the hill:
now that the moon, who remembers, and only cares
that we should be lovely in the flesh, with bright, crescent feet,
pauses near the crest of the hill, climbing slowly, like a queen
looking down on the lion as he retreats—

Now the sea is the Argonauts' sea, and in the dawn
Odysseus calls the commands, as he steers past those foamy islands;
wait, wait, don't bring me the coffee yet, nor the *pain grillé*.
The dawn is not off the sea, and Odysseus' ships
have not yet passed the islands, I must watch them still.

MIDDLE OF THE WORLD

This sea will never die, neither will it ever grow old
nor cease to be blue, nor in the dawn
cease to lift up its hills
and let the slim black ship of Dionysos come sailing in
with grape-vines up the mast, and dolphins leaping.

What do I care if the smoking ships
of the P. & O. and the Orient Line and all the other stinkers
cross like clock-work the Minoan distance!
They only cross, the distance never changes.

And now that the moon who gives men glistening bodies
is in her exaltation, and can look down on the sun
I see descending from the ships at dawn
slim naked men from Cnossos, smiling the archaic smile
of those that will without fail come back again,
and kindling little fires upon the shores
and crouching, and speaking the music of lost languages.

And the Minoan Gods, and the Gods of Tiryns
are heard softly laughing and chatting, as ever;
and Dionysos, young and a stranger
leans listening on the gate, in all respect.

FOR THE HEROES ARE DIPPED IN SCARLET

Before Plato told the great lie of ideals
men slimly went like fishes, and didn't care.

They had long hair, like Samson,
and clean as arrows they sped at the mark
when the bow-cord twanged.

They knew it was no use knowing
their own nothingness:
for they were not nothing.

So now they come back! Hark!
Hark! the low and shattering laughter of bearded men
with the slim waists of warriors, and the long feet
of moon-lit dancers.

Oh, and their faces scarlet, like the dolphin's blood!
Lo! the loveliest is red all over, rippling vermilion
as he ripples upwards!
laughing in his black beard!

They are dancing! they return, as they went, dancing!
For the thing that is done without the glowing as of god,
    vermilion,
were best not done at all.
How glistening red they are!

DEMIURGE

They say that reality exists only in the spirit
that corporal existence is a kind of death
that pure being is bodiless
that the idea of the form precedes the form substantial.

But what nonsense it is!
as if any Mind could have imagined a lobster
dozing in the under-deeps, then reaching out a savage and iron claw!

Even the mind of God can only imagine
those things that have become themselves:
bodies and presences, here and now, creatures with a foothold in
    creation
even if it is only a lobster on tip-toe.

Religion knows better than philosophy.
Religion knows that Jesus was never Jesus
till he was born from a womb, and ate soup and bread
and grew up, and became, in the wonder of creation, Jesus,
with a body and with needs, and a lovely spirit.

THE WORK OF CREATION

The mystery of creation is the divine urge of creation,
but it is a great, strange urge, it is not a Mind.
Even an artist knows that his work was never in his mind,
he could never have *thought* it before it happened.
A strange ache possessed him, and he entered the struggle,
and out of the struggle with his material, in the spell of the urge
his work took place, it came to pass, it stood up and saluted his mind.

God is a great urge, wonderful, mysterious, magnificent
but he knows nothing before-hand.
His urge takes shape in the flesh, and lo!
it is creation! God looks himself on it in wonder, for the first time.
Lo! there is a creature, formed! How strange!
Let me think about it! Let me form an idea!

RED GERANIUM AND GODLY MIGNONETTE

Imagine that any mind ever *thought* a red geranium!
As if the redness of a red geranium could be anything but a sensual
   experience
and as if sensual experience could take place before there were any
   senses.
We know that even God could not imagine the redness of a red
   geranium
nor the smell of mignonette
when geraniums were not, and mignonette neither.
And even when they were, even God would have to have a nose
to smell at the mignonette.
You can't imagine the Holy Ghost sniffing at cherry-pie heliotrope.
Or the Most High, during the coal age, cudgelling his mighty brains
even if he had any brains: straining his mighty mind
to think, among the moss and mud of lizards and mastodons
to think out, in the abstract, when all was twilit green and muddy:
"Now there shall be tum-tiddly-um, and tum-tiddly-um,
hey-presto! scarlet geranium!"
We know it couldn't be done.

But imagine, among the mud and the mastodons
God sighing and yearning with tremendous creative yearning, in
    that dark green mess
oh, for some other beauty, some other beauty
that blossomed at last, red geranium, and mignonette.

BODILESS GOD

Everything that has beauty has a body, and is a body;
everything that has being has being in the flesh:
and dreams are only drawn from the bodies that are.

And God?
Unless God has a body, how can he have a voice
and emotions, and desires, and strength, glory or honour?
For God, even the rarest God, is supposed to love us
and wish us to be this that and the other.
And he is supposed to be mighty and glorious.

THE BODY OF GOD

God is the great urge that has not yet found a body
but urges towards incarnation with the great creative urge.

And becomes at last a clove carnation: lo! that is god!
and becomes at last Helen, or Ninon: any lovely and generous
    woman
at her best and her most beautiful, being god, made manifest,
any clear and fearless man being god, very god.

There is no god
apart from poppies and the flying fish,
men singing songs, and women brushing their hair in the sun.
The lovely things are god that has come to pass, like Jesus came.
The rest, the undiscoverable, is the demi-urge.

THE RAINBOW

Even the rainbow has a body
made of the drizzling rain
and is an architecture of glistening atoms
built up, built up
yet you can't lay your hand on it,
nay, nor even your mind.

MAXIMUS

God is older than the sun and moon
and the eye cannot behold him
nor voice describe him.

But a naked man, a stranger, leaned on the gate
with his cloak over his arm, waiting to be asked in.
So I called him: Come in, if you will!—
He came in slowly, and sat down by the hearth.
I said to him: And what is your name?—
He looked at me without answer, but such a loveliness
entered me, I smiled to myself, saying: He is God!
So he said: *Hermes!*

God is older than the sun and moon
and the eye cannot behold him
nor the voice describe him:
and still, this is the God Hermes, sitting by my hearth.

THE MAN OF TYRE

The man of Tyre went down to the sea
pondering, for he was Greek, that God is one and all alone and ever
more shall be so.

And a woman who had been washing clothes in the pool of rock
where a stream came down to the gravel of the sea and sank in,
who had spread white washing on the gravel banked above the bay,
who had lain her shift on the shore, on the shingle slope,
who had waded to the pale green sea of evening, out to a shoal,
pouring sea-water over herself
now turned, and came slowly back, with her back to the evening sky.

Oh lovely, lovely with the dark hair piled up, as she went deeper,
  deeper down the channel, then rose shallower, shallower,
with the full thighs slowly lifting of the wader wading shorewards
and the shoulders pallid with light from the silent sky behind
both breasts dim and mysterious, with the glamorous kindness of
  twilight between them
and the dim blotch of black maidenhair like an indicator,
giving a message to the man—

So in the cane-brake he clasped his hands in delight
that could only be god-given, and murmured:
Lo! God is one god! But here in the twilight
godly and lovely comes Aphrodite out of the sea
towards me!

THEY SAY THE SEA IS LOVELESS

 They say the sea is loveless, that in the sea
 love cannot live, but only bare, salt splinters
 of loveless life.

 But from the sea
 the dolphins leap round Dionysos' ship
 whose masts have purple vines,
 and up they come with the purple dark of rainbows
 and flip! they go! with the nose-dive of sheer delight:
 and the sea is making love to Dionysos
 in the bouncing of these small and happy whales.

WHALES WEEP NOT!

They say the sea is cold, but the sea contains
the hottest blood of all, and the wildest, the most urgent.

All the whales in the wider deeps, hot are they, as they urge
on and on, and dive beneath the icebergs.
The right whales, the sperm-whales, the hammer-heads, the killers
there they blow, there they blow, hot wild white breath out of the
      sea!

And they rock, and they rock, through the sensual ageless ages
on the depths of the seven seas,
and through the salt they reel with drunk delight
and in the tropics tremble they with love
and roll with massive, strong desire, like gods.
Then the great bull lies up against his bride
in the blue deep bed of the sea,
as mountain pressing on mountain, in the zest of life:
and out of the inward roaring of the inner red ocean of whale-blood
the long tip reaches strong, intense, like the maelstrom-tip, and
      comes to rest
in the clasp and the soft, wild clutch of a she-whale's fathomless
      body.

And over the bridge of the whale's strong phallus, linking the
      wonder of whales
the burning archangels under the sea keep passing, back and forth,
keep passing, archangels of bliss
from him to her, from her to him, great Cherubim
that wait on whales in mid-ocean, suspended in the waves of the
      sea
great heaven of whales in the waters, old hierarchies.

And enormous mother whales lie dreaming suckling their whale-
      tender young
and dreaming with strange whale eyes wide open in the waters of
      the beginning and the end.

And bull-whales gather their women and whale-calves in a ring
when danger threatens, on the surface of the ceaseless flood
and range themselves like great fierce Seraphim facing the threat
encircling their huddled monsters of love.
And all this happens in the sea, in the salt
where God is also love, but without words:
and Aphrodite is the wife of whales
most happy, happy she!

and Venus among the fishes skips and is a she-dolphin
she is the gay, delighted porpoise sporting with love and the sea
she is the female tunny-fish, round and happy among the males
and dense with happy blood, dark rainbow bliss in the sea.

INVOCATION TO THE MOON

You beauty, O you beauty
you glistening garmentless beauty!
great lady, great glorious lady
greatest of ladies
crownless and jewelless and garmentless
because naked you are more wonderful than anything we can
    stroke—

Be good to me, lady, great lady of the nearest
heavenly mansion, and last!
Now I am at your gate, you beauty, you lady of all nakedness!
Now I must enter your mansion, and beg your gift
Moon, O Moon, great lady of the heavenly few.

Far and forgotten is the Villa of Venus the glowing
and behind me now in the gulfs of space lies the golden house of the
    sun,
and six have given me gifts, and kissed me god-speed
kisses of four great lords, beautiful, as they held me to their bosom
    in farewell
and kiss of the far-off lingering lady who looks over the distant fence
    of the twilight,
and one warm kind kiss of the lion with golden paws—

Now, lady of the Moon, now open the gate of your silvery house
and let me come past the silver bells of your flowers, and the cockle-
    shells
into your house, garmentless lady of the last great gift:
who will give me back my lost limbs
and my lost white fearless breast
and set me again on moon-remembering feet
a healed, whole man, O Moon!

Lady, lady of the last house down the long, long street of the stars
be good to me now, as I beg you, as you've always been good to men
who begged of you and gave you homage
and watched for your glistening feet down the garden path!

BUTTERFLY

Butterfly, the wind blows sea-ward, strong beyond the garden wall!
Butterfly, why do you settle on my shoe, and sip the dirt on my shoe,
Lifting your veined wings, lifting them? big white butterfly!

Already it is October, and the wind blows strong to the sea
from the hills where snow must have fallen, the wind is polished
    with snow.
Here in the garden, with red geraniums, it is warm, it is warm
but the wind blows strong to sea-ward, white butterfly, content on
    my shoe!

Will you go, will you go from my warm house?
Will you climb on your big soft wings, black-dotted,
as up an invisible rainbow, an arch
till the wind slides you sheer from the arch-crest
and in a strange level fluttering you go out to sea-ward, white speck!

Farewell, farewell, lost soul!
you have melted in the crystalline distance,
it is enough! I saw you vanish into air.

BAVARIAN GENTIANS

Not every man has gentians in his house
in soft September, at slow, sad Michaelmas.

Bavarian gentians, big and dark, only dark
darkening the day-time, torch-like with the smoking blueness of
    Pluto's gloom,
ribbed and torch-like, with their blaze of darkness spread blue
down flattening into points, flattened under the sweep of white day
torch-flower of the blue-smoking darkness, Pluto's dark-blue daze,
black lamps from the halls of Dis, burning dark blue,
giving off darkness, blue darkness, as Demeter's pale lamps give off
    light,
lead me then, lead the way.

Reach me a gentian, give me a torch!
let me guide myself with the blue, forked torch of this flower
down the darker and darker stairs, where blue is darkened on blue-
    ness
even where Persephone goes, just now, from the frosted September
to the sightless realm where darkness is awake upon the dark
and Persephone herself is but a voice
or a darkness invisible enfolded in the deeper dark
of the arms Plutonic, and pierced with the passion of dense gloom,
among the splendour of torches of darkness, shedding darkness on
    the lost bride and her groom.

LUCIFER

Angels are bright still, though the brightest fell.
But tell me, tell me, how do you know
he lost any of his brightness in the falling?
In the dark-blue depths, under layers and layers of
    darkness,
I see him more like the ruby, a gleam from within
of his own magnificence,
coming like the ruby in the invisible dark, glowing
with his own annunciation, towards us.

697

THE BREATH OF LIFE

The breath of life is in the sharp winds of change
mingled with the breath of destruction.
But if you want to breathe deep, sumptuous life
breathe all alone, in silence, in the dark,
and see nothing.

SILENCE

Come, holy Silence, come
great bride of all creation.

Come, holy Silence! reach, reach
from the presence of God, and envelop us.

Let the sea heave no more in sound,
hold the stars still, lest we hear the heavens dimly ring with their
     commotion!
fold up all sounds.

Lo! the laugh of God!
Lo! the laugh of the creator!
Lo! the last of the seven great laughs of God!
Lo! the last of the seven great laughs of creation!

Huge, huge roll the peals of the thundrous laugh
huge, huger, huger and huger pealing
till they mound and fill and all is fulfilled of God's last and greatest
     laugh
till all is soundless and senseless, a tremendous body of Silence
enveloping even the edges of the thought-waves,
enveloping even me, who hear no more,
who am embedded in a shell of Silence,
of silence, lovely silence
of endless and living silence
of holy silence
the silence of the last of the seven great laughs of God.

Ah! the holy silence—it is meet !
It is very fitting! there is nought beside!
For now we are passing through the gate, stilly,
in the sacred silence of gates
in the silence of passing through doors,
in the great hush of going from this into that,
in the suspension of wholeness, in the moment of division within
    the whole!

Lift up your heads, O ye Gates!
for the silence of the last great thundrous laugh
screens us purely, and we can slip through.

THE HANDS OF GOD

It is a fearful thing to fall into the hands of the living God.
But it is a much more fearful thing to fall out of them.

Did Lucifer fall through knowledge?
oh then, pity him, pity him that plunge!

Save me, O God, from falling into the ungodly knowledge
of myself as I am without God.
Let me never know, O God
let me never know what I am or should be
when I have fallen out of your hands, the hands of the living God.

That awful and sickening endless sinking, sinking
through the slow, corruptive levels of disintegrative knowledge
when the self has fallen from the hands of God,
and sinks, seething and sinking, corrupt
and sinking still, in depth after depth of disintegrative consciousness
sinking in the endless undoing, the awful katabolism into the abyss!
even of the soul, fallen from the hands of God!

Save me from that, O God!
Let me never know myself apart from the living God!

699

PAX

All that matters is to be at one with the living God
to be a creature in the house of the God of Life.

Like a cat asleep on a chair
at peace, in peace
and at one with the master of the house, with the mistress,
at home, at home in the house of the living,
sleeping on the hearth, and yawning before the fire.

Sleeping on the hearth of the living world
yawning at home before the fire of life
feeling the presence of the living God
like a great reassurance
a deep calm in the heart
a presence
as of the master sitting at the board
in his own and greater being,
in the house of life.

ABYSMAL IMMORTALITY

It is not easy to fall out of the hands of the living God:
They are so large, and they cradle so much of a man.
It is a long time before a man can get himself away.
Even through the greatest blasphemies, the hands of the living God
    still continue to cradle him.

And still through knowledge and will, he can break away,
man can break away, and fall from the hands of God
into himself alone, down the godless plunge of the abyss,
a god-lost creature turning upon himself
in the long, long fall, revolving upon himself
in the endless writhe of the last, the last self-knowledge
which he can never reach till he touch the bottom of the abyss
which he can never touch, for the abyss is bottomless.

And there is nothing else, throughout time and eternity
but the abyss, which is bottomless,
and the fall to extinction, which can never come,
for the abyss is bottomless,
and the turning plunge of writhing of self-knowledge, self-
    analysis
which goes further and further, and yet never finds an end
for there is no end,
it is the abyss of the immortality
of those that have fallen from God.

ONLY MAN

Only man can fall from God
Only man.

No animal, no beast nor creeping thing
no cobra nor hyaena nor scorpion nor hideous white ant
can slip entirely through the fingers of the hands of god
into the abyss of self-knowledge,
knowledge of the self-apart-from-god.

For the knowledge of the self-apart-from-God
is an abyss down which the soul can slip
writhing and twisting in all the revolutions
of the unfinished plunge
of self-awareness, now apart from God, falling
fathomless, fathomless, self-consciousness wriggling
writhing deeper and deeper in all the minutiae of self-knowledge,
    downwards, exhaustive,
yet never, never coming to the bottom, for there is no bottom;
zigzagging down like the fizzle from a finished rocket
the frizzling falling fire that cannot go out, dropping wearily,
neither can it reach the depth
for the depth is bottomless,
so it wriggles its way even further down, further down
at last in sheer horror of not being able to leave off
knowing itself, knowing itself apart from God, falling.

RETURN OF RETURNS

Come in a week
Yes, yes, in the seven-day week!
for how can I count in your three times three
of the sea-blown week of nine.

Come then, as I say, in a week,
when the planets have given seven nods
"It shall be! It shall be!" assented seven times
by the great seven, by Helios the brightest
and by Artemis the whitest
by Hermes and Aphrodite, flashing white glittering words,
by Ares and Kronos and Zeus,
the seven great ones, who must all say yes.

When the moon from out of the darkness
has come like a thread, like a door just opening
opening, till the round white doorway of delight
is half open.

Come then!
Then, when the door is half open.
In a week!
The ancient river week, the old one.
Come then!

STOIC

Groan then, groan.
For the sun is dead, and all that is in heaven
is the pyre of blazing gas.

And the moon that went
so queenly, shaking her glistening beams
is dead too, a dead orb wheeled once a month round the park.

And the five others, the travellers
they are all dead!
In the hearse of night you see their tarnished coffins
travelling, travelling still, still travelling
to the end, for they are not yet buried.

Groan then, groan!
Groan then, for even the maiden earth
is dead, we run wheels across her corpse.

Oh groan
groan with mighty groans!

But for all that, and all that
"in the centre of your being, groan not".
In the centre of your being groan not, do not groan.
For perhaps the greatest of all illusions
is this illusion of the death of the undying.

IN THE CITIES

In the cities
there is even no more any weather
the weather in town is always benzine, or else petrol
        fumes
lubricating oil, exhaust gas.

As over some dense marsh, the fumes
thicken, miasma, the fumes of the automobile
densely thicken in the cities.

In ancient Rome, down the thronged streets
no wheels might run, no insolent chariots.
Only the footsteps, footsteps
of people
and the gentle trotting of the litter-bearers.

In Minos, in Mycenae
in all the cities with lion gates
the dead threaded the air, lingering
lingering in the earth's shadow
and leaning towards the old hearth.

In London, New York, Paris
in the bursten cities
the dead tread heavily through the muddy air
through the mire of fumes
heavily, stepping weary on our hearts.

LORD'S PRAYER

For thine is the kingdom
the power, and the glory—

Hallowed be thy name, then
Thou who art nameless—

Give me, Oh give me
besides my daily bread
my kingdom, my power, and my glory.

All things that turn to thee
have their kingdom, their power, and their glory.

Like the kingdom of the nightingale at twilight
whose power and glory I have often heard and felt.

Like the kingdom of the fox in the dark
yapping in his power and his glory
which is death to the goose.

Like the power and the glory of the goose in the mist
honking over the lake.

And I, a naked man, calling
calling to thee for my mana,
my kingdom, my power, and my glory.

MANA OF THE SEA

Do you see the sea, breaking itself to bits against the islands
yet remaining unbroken, the level great sea?

Have I caught from it
the tide in my arms
that runs down to the shallows of my wrists, and breaks
abroad in my hands, like waves among the rocks of sub-
    stance?

Do the rollers of the sea
roll down my thighs
and over the submerged islets of my knees
with power, sea-power
sea-power
to break against the ground
in the flat, recurrent breakers of my two feet?

And is my body ocean, ocean
whose power runs to the shores along my arms
and breaks in the foamy hands, whose power rolls out
to the white-treading waves of two salt feet?

I am the sea, I am the sea!

SALT

Salt is scorched water that the sun has scorched
into substance and flaky whiteness
in the eternal opposition
between the two great ones, Fire, and the Wet.

THE FOUR

To our senses, the elements are four
and have ever been, and will ever be
for they are the elements of life, of poetry, and of perception,
the four Great Ones, the Four Roots, the First Four
of Fire and the Wet, Earth and the wide Air of the world.

To find the other many elements, you must go to the laboratory
and hunt them down.
But the Four we have always with us, they are our world.
Or rather, they have us with them.

THE BOUNDARY STONE

So, salt is the boundary mark between Fire that burns, and the Wet.
It is the white stone of limits, the term, the landmark between
the two great and moving Ones, Fire and the yielding Wet.
It is set up as a boundary, and blood and sweat
are marked out with the boundary of salt, between Fire and the Wet.

SPILLING THE SALT

Don't spill the salt, for it is the landmark,
and cursed be he that removeth his neighbour's landmark.

And the watchers, the dividers, those swift ones with dark sharp
    wings
and keen eyes, they will hover, they will come between you,
between you and your purpose like a knife's edge shadow
cutting you off from your joy.

For the unseen witnesses are the angels of creation
but also the sunderers, the angels with black, sharp wing-tips.

WALK WARILY

Walk warily, walk warily, be careful what you say:
because now the Sunderers are hovering round,
the Dividers are close upon us, dogging our every breath
and watching our every step,
and beating their great wings in our panting faces.

The angels are standing back, the angels of the Kiss.
They wait, they give way now
to the Sunderers, to the swift ones
the ones with the sharp black wings
and the shudder of electric anger
and the drumming of pinions of thunder
and hands like salt
and the sudden dripping down of the knife-edge cleavage of the
    lightning
cleaving, cleaving.

Lo, we are in the midst of the Sunderers
the Cleavers, that cleave us forever apart from one another
and separate heart from heart, and cut away all caresses
with the white triumphance of lightning and electric delight,
the Dividers, the Thunderers, the Swift Ones, blind with speed
who put salt in our mouths
and currents of excitement in our limbs
and hotness, and then more crusted brine in our hearts.

It is the day of the Sunderers
and the angels are standing back.

MYSTIC

They call all experience of the senses *mystic*, when the experience
    is considered.
So an apple becomes *mystic* when I taste in it
the summer and the snows, the wild welter of earth
and the insistence of the sun.

707

All of which things I can surely taste in a good apple.
Though some apples taste preponderantly of water, wet and sour
and some of too much sun, brackish sweet
like lagoon-water, that has been too much sunned.

If I say I taste these things in an apple, I am called *mystic*, which
    means a liar.
The only way to eat an apple is to hog it down like a pig
and taste nothing
that is *real*.

But if I eat an apple, I like to eat it with all my senses awake.
Hogging it down like a pig I call the feeding of corpses.

ANAXAGORAS

When Anaxagoras says: Even snow is black!
he is taken by the scientists very seriously
because he is enunciating a "principle", a "law"
that all things are mixed, and therefore the purest white snow
has in it an element of blackness.

That they call science, and reality.
I call it mental conceit and mystification
and nonsense, for pure snow is white to us
white and white and only white
with a lovely bloom of whiteness upon white
in which the soul delights and the senses
have an experience of bliss.

And life is for delight, and for bliss
and dread, and the dark, rolling ominousness of doom.
Then the bright dawning of delight again
from off the sheer white snow, or the poised moon.

And in the shadow of the sun the snow is blue, so blue-aloof
with a hint of the frozen bells of the scylla flower
but never the ghost of a glimpse of Anaxagoras' funeral black.

KISSING AND HORRID STRIFE

I have been defeated and dragged down by pain
and worsted by the evil world-soul of today.

But still I know that life is for delight
and for bliss
as now when the tiny wavelets of the sea
tip the morning light on edge, and spill it with delight
to show how inexhaustible it is:

And life is for delight, and bliss
like now when the white sun kisses the sea
and plays with the wavelets like a panther playing with its cub:
cuffing them with soft paws,
and blows that are caresses,
kisses of the soft-balled paws, where the talons are.

And life is for dread,
for doom that darkens, and the Sunderers
that sunder us from each other,
that strip us and destroy us and break us down
as the tall foxgloves and the mulleins and mallows
are torn down by dismembering autumn
till not a vestige is left, and black winter has no trace
of any such flowers;
and yet the roots below the blackness are intact:
the Thunderers and the Sunderers have their term,
their limit, their thus far and no further.

Life is for kissing and for horrid strife.
Life is for the angels and the Sunderers.
Life is for the daimons and the demons,
those that put honey on our lips, and those that put salt.
But life is not
for the dead vanity of knowing better, nor the blank
cold comfort of superiority, nor silly
conceit of being immune,
nor puerility of contradictions
like saying snow is black, or desire is evil.

Life is for kissing and for horrid strife,
the angels and the Sunderers.
And perhaps in unknown Death we perhaps shall know
Oneness and poised immunity.
But why then should we die while we can live?
And while we live
the kissing and communing cannot cease
nor yet the striving and the horrid strife.

WHEN SATAN FELL

When Satan fell, he only fell
because the Lord Almighty rose a bit too high,
a bit beyond himself.

So Satan only fell to keep a balance.
"Are you so lofty, O my God?
Are you so pure and lofty, up aloft?
Then I will fall, and plant the paths to hell
with vines and poppies and fig-trees
so that lost souls may eat grapes
and the moist fig
and put scarlet buds in their hair on the way to hell,
on the way to dark perdition."

And hell and heaven are the scales of the balance of life
which swing against each other.

DOORS

But evil is a third thing.
No, not the ithyphallic demons
not even the double Phallus of the devil himself
with his key to the two dark doors
is evil.

Life has its palace of blue day aloft
and its halls of the great dark below,
and there are the bright doors where souls go gaily in:
and there are the dark doors where souls pass silently
holding their breath, naked and darkly alone
entering into the other communion.

There is a double sacredness of doors.
Some you may sing through, and all men hear,
but others, the dark doors, oh hush! hush!
let nobody be about! slip in! go all unseen.
But evil, evil is another thing! in another place!

EVIL IS HOMELESS

Evil has no home,
only evil has no home,
not even the home of demoniacal hell.
Hell is the home of souls lost in darkness,
even as heaven is the home of souls lost in light.
And like Persephone, or Attis
there are souls that are at home in both homes.
Not like grey Dante, colour-blind
to the scarlet and purple flowers at the doors of hell.

But evil
evil has no dwelling-place
the grey vulture, the grey hyaena, corpse-eaters
they dwell in the outskirt fringes of nowhere
where the grey twilight of evil sets in.

And men that sit in machines
among spinning wheels, in an apotheosis of wheels
sit in the grey mist of movement which moves not
and going which goes not
and doing which does not
and being which is not:

that is, they sit and are evil, in evil,
grey evil, which has no path, and shows neither light nor
    dark,
and has no home, no home anywhere.

WHAT THEN IS EVIL?

Oh, in the world of the flesh of man
iron gives the deadly wound
and the wheel starts the principle of all evil.

Oh, in the world of things
the wheel is the first principle of evil.

But in the world of the soul of man
there, and there alone lies the pivot of pure evil
only in the soul of man, when it pivots upon the ego.

When the mind makes a wheel which turns on the hub of the ego
and the will, the living dynamo, gives the motion and the speed
and the wheel of the conscious self spins on in absolution, absolute
absolute, absolved from the sun and the earth and the moon,
absolute consciousness, absolved from strife and kisses
absolute self-awareness, absolved from the meddling of creation
absolute freedom, absolved from the great necessities of being
then we see evil, pure evil
and we see it only in man
and in his machines.

THE EVIL WORLD-SOUL

Oh, there is evil, there is an evil world-soul.
But it is the soul of man only, and his machines
which has brought to pass the fearful thing called evil,
hyaenas only hint at it.

Do not think that a machine is without a soul.
Every wheel on its hub has a soul, evil,
it is part of the evil world-soul, spinning.

And every man who has become a detached and self-
    activated ego
is evil, evil, part of the evil world-soul
which wishes to blaspheme the world into greyness,
into evil neutrality, into mechanism.
The Robot is the unit of evil.
And the symbol of the Robot is the wheel revolving.

THE WANDERING COSMOS

Oh, do not tell me the heavens as well are a wheel.
For every revolution of the earth around the sun
is a footstep onwards, onwards, we know not whither
and we do not care,
but a step onwards in untravelled space,
for the earth, like the sun, is a wanderer.
Their going round each time is a step
onwards, we know not whither,
but onwards, onwards, for the heavens are wandering
the moon and the earth, the sun, Saturn and Betelgeuse,
    Vega and Sirius and Altair,
they wander their strange and different ways in heaven
past Venus and Uranus and the signs.

For life is a wandering, we know not whither, but going.

Only the wheel goes round, but it never wanders.
It stays on its hub.

DEATH IS NOT EVIL, EVIL IS MECHANICAL

Only the human being, absolved from kissing and strife
goes on and on and on, without wandering
fixed upon the hub of the ego
going, yet never wandering, fixed, yet in motion,

the kind of hell that is real, grey and awful
sinless and stainless going round and round
the kind of hell grey Dante never saw
but of which he had a bit inside him.

Know thyself, and that thou art mortal.
But know thyself, denying that thou art mortal:
a thing of kisses and strife
a lit-up shaft of rain
a calling column of blood
a rose tree bronzey with thorns
a mixture of yea and nay
a rainbow of love and hate
a wind that blows back and forth
a creature of beautiful peace, like a river
and a creature of conflict, like a cataract:
know thyself, in denial of all these things—

And thou shalt begin to spin round on the hub of the
        obscene ego
a grey void thing that goes without wandering
a machine that in itself is nothing
a centre of the evil world-soul.

STRIFE

When strife is a thing of two
each knows the other in struggle
and the conflict is a communion
a twoness.

But when strife is a thing of one
a single ego striving for its own ends
and beating down resistances
then strife is evil, because it is not strife.

THE LATE WAR

The War was not strife;
it was murder,
each side trying to murder the other side
evilly.

MURDER

Killing is not evil.
A man may be my enemy to the death,
and that is passion and communion.

But murder is always evil
being an act of one
perpetrated upon the other
without cognisance or communion.

MURDEROUS WEAPONS

So guns and strong explosives
are evil, evil
they let death upon unseen men
in sheer murder.

And most murderous of all devices
are poison gases and air-bombs,
refinements of evil.

DEPARTURE

Now some men must get up and depart
from evil, or all is lost.

The evil will in many evil men
makes an evil world-soul, which purposes
to reduce the world to grey ash.

Wheels are evil
and machines are evil
and the will to make money is evil.

All forms of abstraction are evil:
finance is a great evil abstraction
science has now become an evil abstraction
education is an evil abstraction.

Jazz and film and wireless
are all evil abstractions from life.

And politics, now, are an evil abstraction from life.

Evil is upon us and has got hold of us.
Men must depart from it, or all is lost.
We must make an isle impregnable
against evil.

THE SHIP OF DEATH

I

Now it is autumn and the falling fruit
and the long journey towards oblivion.

The apples falling like great drops of dew
to bruise themselves an exit from themselves.

And it is time to go, to bid farewell
to one's own self, and find an exit
from the fallen self.

II

Have you built your ship of death, O have you?
O build your ship of death, for you will need it.

The grim frost is at hand, when the apples will fall
thick, almost thundrous, on the hardened earth.

And death is on the air like a smell of ashes!
Ah! can't you smell it?

And in the bruised body, the frightened soul
finds itself shrinking, wincing from the cold
that blows upon it through the orifices.

III

And can a man his own quietus make
with a bare bodkin?

With daggers, bodkins, bullets, man can make
a bruise or break of exit for his life;
but is that a quietus, O tell me, is it quietus?

Surely not so! for how could murder, even self-murder
ever a quietus make?

IV

O let us talk of quiet that we know,
that we can know, the deep and lovely quiet
of a strong heart at peace!

How can we this, our own quietus, make?

V

Build then the ship of death, for you must take
the longest journey, to oblivion.

And die the death, the long and painful death
that lies between the old self and the new.

Already our bodies are fallen, bruised, badly bruised,
already our souls are oozing through the exit
of the cruel bruise.

Already the dark and endless ocean of the end
is washing in through the breaches of our wounds,
already the flood is upon us.

Oh build your ship of death, your little ark
and furnish it with food, with little cakes, and wine
for the dark flight down oblivion.

V I

Piecemeal the body dies, and the timid soul
has her footing washed away, as the dark flood rises.

We are dying, we are dying, we are all of us dying
and nothing will stay the death-flood rising within us
and soon it will rise on the world, on the outside world.

We are dying, we are dying, piecemeal our bodies are dying
and our strength leaves us,
and our soul cowers naked in the dark rain over the flood,
cowering in the last branches of the tree of our life.

V I I

We are dying, we are dying, so all we can do
is now to be willing to die, and to build the ship
of death to carry the soul on the longest journey.

A little ship, with oars and food
and little dishes, and all accoutrements
fitting and ready for the departing soul.

Now launch the small ship, now as the body dies
and life departs, launch out, the fragile soul
in the fragile ship of courage, the ark of faith
with its store of food and little cooking pans
and change of clothes,
upon the flood's black waste
upon the waters of the end
upon the sea of death, where still we sail
darkly, for we cannot steer, and have no port.

There is no port, there is nowhere to go
only the deepening black darkening still
blacker upon the soundless, ungurgling flood
darkness at one with darkness, up and down
and sideways utterly dark, so there is no direction any more.
And the little ship is there; yet she is gone.
She is not seen, for there is nothing to see her by.
She is gone! gone! and yet
somewhere she is there.
Nowhere!

VIII

And everything is gone, the body is gone
completely under, gone, entirely gone.
The upper darkness is heavy on the lower,
between them the little ship
is gone
she is gone.

It is the end, it is oblivion.

IX

And yet out of eternity, a thread
separates itself on the blackness,
a horizontal thread
that fumes a little with pallor upon the dark.

Is it illusion? or does the pallor fume
A little higher?
Ah wait, wait, for there's the dawn,
the cruel dawn of coming back to life
out of oblivion.

Wait, wait, the little ship
drifting, beneath the deathly ashy grey
of a flood-dawn.

Wait, wait! even so, a flush of yellow
and strangely, O chilled wan soul, a flush of rose.

A flush of rose, and the whole thing starts again.

X

The flood subsides, and the body, like a worn sea-shell
emerges strange and lovely.
And the little ship wings home, faltering and lapsing
on the pink flood,
and the frail soul steps out, into her house again
filling the heart with peace.

Swings the heart renewed with peace
even of oblivion.

Oh build your ship of death, oh build it!
for you will need it.
For the voyage of oblivion awaits you.

DIFFICULT DEATH

It is not easy to die, O it is not easy
to die the death.

For death comes when he will
not when we will him.

And we can be dying, dying, dying
and longing utterly to die
yet death will not come.

So build your ship of death, and let the soul drift
to dark oblivion.
Maybe life is still our portion
after the bitter passage of oblivion.

ALL SOULS' DAY

Be careful, then, and be gentle about death.
For it is hard to die, it is difficult to go through
the door, even when it opens.

And the poor dead, when they have left the walled
and silvery city of the now hopeless body
where are they to go, Oh where are they to go?

They linger in the shadow of the earth.
The earth's long conical shadow is full of souls
that cannot find the way across the sea of change.

Be kind, Oh be kind to your dead
and give them a little encouragement
and help them to build their little ship of death.

For the soul has a long, long journey after death
to the sweet home of pure oblivion.
Each needs a little ship, a little ship
and the proper store of meal for the longest journey.

Oh, from out of your heart
provide for your dead once more, equip them
like departing mariners, lovingly.

THE HOUSELESS DEAD

Oh pity the dead that are dead, but cannot take
the journey, still they moan and beat
against the silvery adamant walls of life's exclusive city.

Oh pity the dead that were ousted out of life
all unequipped to take the long, long voyage.
Gaunt, gaunt they crowd the grey mud-beaches of shadow
that intervene between the final sea
and the white shores of life.

The poor gaunt dead that cannot die
into the distance with receding oars,
but must roam like outcast dogs on the margins of life!
Oh think of them, and with the soul's deep sigh
set food for them, and encourage them to build
the bark of their deliverance from the dilemma
of non-existence to far oblivion.

BEWARE THE UNHAPPY DEAD!

Beware the unhappy dead thrust out of life
unready, unprepared, unwilling, unable
to continue on the longest journey.

Oh, now as November draws near
the grey, grey reaches of earth's shadow,
the long, mean marginal stretches of our existence
are crowded with lost souls, the uneasy dead
that cannot embark on the slinking sea beyond.

Oh, now they moan and throng in anger, and press back
through breaches in the walls of this our by-no-means impregnable
    existence
seeking their old haunts with cold, ghostly rage
old haunts, old habitats, old hearths,

old places of sweet life from which they are thrust out
and can but haunt in disembodied rage.

Oh, but beware, beware the angry dead.
Who knows, who knows how much our modern woe
is due to the angry, unappeasèd dead
that were thrust out of life, and now come back at us
malignant, malignant, for we will not succour them.

Oh, on this day of the dead, now November is here
set a place for the dead, with a cushion and soft seat
and put a plate, and put a wine-glass out
and serve the best of food, the fondest wine
for your dead, your unseen dead, and with your hearts
speak with them and give them peace and do them honour.

Or else beware their angry presence, now
within your walls, within your very heart.
Oh, they can lay you waste, the angry dead.
Perhaps even now you are suffering from the havoc they make
unknown within your breast and your deadened loins.

AFTER ALL SAINTS' DAY

Wrapped in the dark-red mantle of warm memories
the little, slender soul sits swiftly down, and takes the oars
and draws away, away, towards dark depths
wafting with warm love from still-living hearts
breathing on his small frail sail, and helping him on
to the fathomless deeps ahead, far, far from the grey shores
of marginal existence.

SONG OF DEATH

Sing the song of death, O sing it!
for without the song of death, the song of life
becomes pointless and silly.

Sing then the song of death, and the longest journey
and what the soul takes with him, and what he leaves behind,
and how he enters fold after fold of deepening darkness
for the cosmos even in death is like a dark whorled shell
whose whorls fold round to the core of soundless silence and pivotal
    oblivion
where the soul comes at last, and has utter peace.

Sing then the core of dark and absolute
oblivion where the soul at last is lost
in utter peace.
Sing the song of death, O sing it!

THE END, THE BEGINNING

If there were not an utter and absolute dark
of silence and sheer oblivion
at the core of everything,
how terrible the sun would be,
how ghastly it would be to strike a match, and make a light.

But the very sun himself is pivoted
upon a core of pure oblivion,
so is a candle, even as a match.

And if there were not an absolute, utter forgetting
and a ceasing to know, a perfect ceasing to know
and a silent, sheer cessation of all awareness
how terrible life would be!
how terrible it would be to think and know, to have consciousness!

But dipped, once dipped in dark oblivion
the soul has peace, inward and lovely peace.

SLEEP

Sleep is the shadow of death, but not only that.
Sleep is a hint of lovely oblivion.
When I am gone, completely lapsed and gone
and healed from all this ache of being.

SLEEP AND WAKING

In sleep I am not, I am gone
I am given up.
And nothing in the world is lovelier than sleep,
dark, dreamless sleep, in deep oblivion!
Nothing in life is quite so good as this.

Yet there is waking from the soundest sleep,
waking, and waking new.

Did you sleep well?
Ah yes, the sleep of God!
The world is created afresh.

FATIGUE

My soul has had a long, hard day
she is tired,
she is seeking her oblivion.

O, and in the world
there is no place for the soul to find her oblivion
the utter darkness of her peace,
for man has killed the silence of the earth
and ravished all the peaceful oblivious places
where the angels used to alight.

FORGET

To be able to forget is to be able to yield
to God who dwells in deep oblivion.
Only in sheer oblivion are we with God.
For when we know in full, we have left off
    knowing.

KNOW-ALL

Man knows nothing
till he knows how not-to-know.

And the greatest of teachers will tell you:
The end of all knowledge is oblivion
sweet, dark oblivion, when I cease
even from myself, and am consummated.

TABERNACLE

Come, let us build a temple to oblivion
with seven veils, and an innermost
Holy of Holies of sheer oblivion.

And there oblivion dwells, and the silent soul
may sink into god at last, having passed the veils.

But anyone who shall ascribe attributes to God or
    oblivion
let him be cast out, for blasphemy.
For God is a deeper forgetting far than sleep
and all description is a blasphemy.

TEMPLES

Oh, what we want on earth
is centres here and there of silence and forgetting,
where we may cease from knowing, and, as far as we know,
may cease from being
in the sweet wholeness of oblivion.

SHADOWS

And if tonight my soul may find her peace
in sleep, and sink in good oblivion,
and in the morning wake like a new-opened flower
then I have been dipped again in God, and new-created.

And if, as weeks go round, in the dark of the moon
my spirit darkens and goes out, and soft, strange gloom
pervades my movements and my thoughts and words
then I shall know that I am walking still
with God, we are close together now the moon's in shadow.

And if, as autumn deepens and darkens
I feel the pain of falling leaves, and stems that break in storms
and trouble and dissolution and distress
and then the softness of deep shadows folding, folding
around my soul and spirit, around my lips
so sweet, like a swoon, or more like the drowse of a low, sad song
singing darker than the nightingale, on, on to the solstice
and the silence of short days, the silence of the year, the shadow,
then I shall know that my life is moving still
with the dark earth, and drenched
with the deep oblivion of earth's lapse and renewal.

And if, in the changing phases of man's life
I fall in sickness and in misery
my wrists seem broken and my heart seems dead
and strength is gone, and my life
is only the leavings of a life:

and still, among it all, snatches of lovely oblivion, and snatches of
    renewal
odd, wintry flowers upon the withered stem, yet new, strange
    flowers
such as my life has not brought forth before, new blossoms of me—

then I must know that still
I am in the hands [of] the unknown God,
he is breaking me down to his own oblivion
to send me forth on a new morning, a new man.

CHANGE

Do you think it is easy to change?
Ah, it is very hard to change and be different.
It means passing through the waters of oblivion.

PHOENIX

Are you willing to be sponged out, erased, cancelled,
made nothing?
Are you willing to be made nothing?
dipped into oblivion?

If not, you will never really change.

The phoenix renews her youth
only when she is burnt, burnt alive, burnt down
to hot and flocculent ash.
Then the small stirring of a new small bub in the nest
with strands of down like floating ash
shows that she is renewing her youth like the eagle,
immortal bird.

UNCOLLECTED POEMS

REBUKED

How big and white the night is!
I stumble where the shadows lie
Fooling my feet!—does the night-moth
Mock as it flutters by?

Who is it the owl is hooting?
Is it me the dark firs mean
When they point their slanting fingers
With the white of the moon between?

The moon is high—I am little!
She leans forward her smooth pale face
And smiles at my furtive shadow
Dodging behind in disgrace.

THE WIND, THE RASCAL

The wind, the rascal, knocked at my door, and I said:
     My love is come!
But oh, wind, what a knave thou art
To make sport of me when the days of my heart
     Are drearisome,
     And wearisome.

THE YOUNG SOLDIER WITH BLOODY SPURS

A Servant Girl Speaks

The sergeant says that eight and twenty wagons
Are coming behind, and we must put out all
The water we can at the gate, for the horses.—He gallops
To the next farm, pulls up where the elder flowers fall.

The wheat on both sides of the road stands green,
And hundreds of soldiers on horseback have filed between
It, gone by our farm to the mountains that stand back blue
This morning.

        I think perhaps the man that came
To Wolfratshausen last winter's end, comes through
This place today. These soldiers wear the same
Helmets as his he lost in the wood that night,
And their uniforms are the same of white and blue——

It was cold, and he put his cloak right round me
As we walked; dark, so he held his arm close round me.
In the stillness, he took off his helmet to kiss me——
It snowed, and his helmet was lost, he forgot me, he did not miss me.

The Isar whispers again in the valley; the children
Are ducking their heads in the water tubs at the gate
As they go from school; some of the officers rally
At the door of the Gasthaus down the road: great
Threads of blue wind far, and down the road
I wait for the eight and twenty wagons to come.

At last I hear a rattle, and there away
Crawls the first load into sight—and now there are some
Drawing near, they cover the München road.

                                 Nay,
I dread him coming; I wonder how he will take it.
I can see his raging black eyes blaze at me
And feel him gripping my wrist as if he would break it.

Here comes the first of the wagons, a grey, a dreary
Shut-up coffin of a thing, with a soldier weary
In the box, and four hot horses going drearily,
And a soldier in the saddle of the left-hand draught-horse, sitting
     wearily.

One by one they go by—at last
There he sits in the saddle of this the five
And twentieth wagon.—And he will not drive past
He pulls up for our water; would he drive
On if he knew that *I* was at this farm?

And he swings his heavy thigh
Out of the saddle, and staggering
With stiffness comes for the water that I
Have poured for the horses—a dark-blue, staggering
Strong young man.—He leans sighing
With head against the shaft, and takes
His helmet off, and wipes his hair, trying
To ease himself in his clothes. It makes
Me want to cry, to see him so strong and easy,
Swarthy and strong with his damp thick hair
Pushed up on end—and the breath sighing
Between his thick lips.—I wonder where
He thinks I am—if ever he thinks at all.
But his handkerchief is white with a broad blue border,
A nice one, I like it.—He'll think it's a tall order
When I say he ought to marry me.—And small
I feel to have to tell him.

                            But why, before
He waters the horses, does he wash his heel?
Jesus!—his spurs are red with shining blood!

He splashes water from the pail upon them,
And rubs the silver clean with his thick brown fingers,
Bending backwards awkwardly,
And anxiously, like a boy afraid to be found out.

And he goes and washes the belly of the horse,
A poor roan thing: its hind leg twitches
Forwards as he rubs the wound,
And bloody water falls upon the road
Soiling the clean white dust.—He rubs the belly
Carefully again, and again, to stop the bleeding.
Jesus!—his fingers are red!

And again, rolling in his heavy high boots,
He comes to the side of the road and washes his hand,
And looks round again at his heel, the bright spur,
And bends again and looks at the belly of the horse,
And kicks dust over the red stain in the road.

And all the time his handsome, swarthy red face
With savage black eyes is sulky: and all the time
He frowns as if he were worried, as if the place
On the horse's belly hurt him, for he was rather gentle
To the thing, and rather fretted. And his thick black hair
Was wet with sweat, and his movements strong and heavy.
—I wonder, will he care!

Now I take the big stone jug of water
Down to the gate, and stand and wait
For a word. He is coming towards the gate—
His eyes meet mine as he takes the jug of water,
He knows me, but does not speak: instead
He drinks and drinks, then turns away his head.

"Do you remember me?"
—"Yes!"
"Who then?"
—"Maria, of the Gasthaus Green Hat, Wolfratshausen."
"I am with child by you——"

He looked at me, and his heavy brows came over
His eyes and he sulked.—He had another lover.

"It is true," I said.
—"And what do you want?"
"What do you think?" I said.

He looked away down the road.

Suddenly his horses began to start.
He shouted, ran heavily after them,
And jerked back their bridles, pushing their heads apart.

I waited, but he would not come back to me,
He stayed with the horses, sulkily,
Till the whistle went.—Then swiftly he

Swung strong and heavy to saddle again
And called to his horses, and his strong blue body
Had its back to me;
And away went the last of the wagons.

AH, MURIEL!

I have many prayers to say.
If I string the planets and the beady stars
Into a glistening rosary,
'Twill not be too many prayers to say.

For I have injured you;
Under the moon's sharp scimitar's
Flashing of delicate wrath,
I did you an injury.

When I come home, promise me,
Promise you will not watch the scar's
Red stroke across my lips,
When I stand in the doorway, shamefully.

WE HAVE GONE TOO FAR

We have gone too far, oh very much too far,
Only attend to the noiseless multitudes
Of ghosts that throng about our muffled hearts.

Only behold the ghosts, the ghosts of the slain,
Behold them homeless and houseless, without complaint
Of their patient waiting upon us, the throng of the ghosts.

And say, what matters any more, what matters,
Save the cold ghosts that homeless flock about
Our serried hearts, drifting without a place?

What matters any more, but only love?
There's only love that matters any more.
There's only love, the rest is all outspent.

Let us receive our ghosts and give them place,
Open the ranks, and let them in our hearts,
And lay them deep in love, lay them to sleep.

The foe can take our goods, our homes and land,
Also the lives that still he may require,
But leave us still to love, still leave us love.

Leave us to take our ghosts into our hearts,
To lap them round with love, and lay them by
To sleep at last in immemorial love.

We let the weapons slip from out our hands,
We loose our grip, and we unstrain our eyes,
We let our souls be pure and vulnerable.

We cover the houseless dead, so they sleep in peace,
We yield the enemy his last demands,
So he too may be healed, be soothed to peace.

For now the hosts of homeless ghosts do throng
To many about us, so we wander about
Blind with the gossamer of prevalent death.

But let us free our eyes, and look beyond
This serried ecstasy of prevalent death,
And pass beyond, with the foe and the homeless ghosts.

Let us rise up, and go from out this grey
Last twilight of the Gods, to find again
The lost Hesperides where love is pure.

For we have gone too far, oh much too far
Towards the darkness and the shadow of death;
Let us turn back, lest we should all be lost.

Let us go back now, though we give up all
The treasure and the vaunt we ever had,
Let us go back, the only way is love.

RESURRECTION OF THE FLESH

Oh then be nameless and be never seen!
And speak no syllable, and never be
Even thought of!—but between
Your nothing and my nothingness, touch me!

They should never have given you names, and never, never
Have lent you voice, nor spoken of the face
That shone and darkened. They were all too clever.
Now let it all be finished! leave no trace!

Reveal us nothing! roll the scripts away!
Destroy at last the heavy books of stone!
Kill off the Word, that's had so much to say!
And show us nothing! leave us quite alone!

Go, go away, and leave us not a trace
Of any Godhead, leave us in the dark!
And let the dark be soundless, without face
Or voice or any single spark

Of what was God! Be gone, be utterly gone!
Relieve us now of all rememberance even
Of what was godly! Leave us quite alone
Within the silence, void of echoes even.

Oh, it is finished! I would like to take
My garments off, but all, even memory,
And what I've understood, and the utter ache
Of everything I've known, even dreamily.

To take it off, this clothing of a man,
This content of my consciousness, this very me
Which I am still and have been all I can
And am and was, shed it all thoroughly.

To come at last to nothingness, and know
Nothing and nothing any more, and so
Not even dream, not even pass away
Nor cease to be: dark on the darkness stay.

And then within the night where nothing is,
And I am only next to nothingness,
Touch me, oh touch me, give me destinies
By touch, and a new nakedness.

I want to know no more. I want to see
Not anything, nor ever again ask: "Why?"
I let the whole thing go! Still there is me!
Touch me then, touch me, touch me, I did not die!

Upon the wincingness of next to nothingness
That I am now, Ah, lay one little touch
To start my heart afresh! Give me the soft, small stress
Of just one touch! Even so, do I ask too much?

ERINNYES

There has been so much noise,
Bleeding and shouting and dying,
Clamour of death.

There are so many dead,
Many have died unconsenting,
Their ghosts are angry, unappeased.

So many ghosts among us,
Invisible, yet strong,
Between me and thee, so many ghosts of the slain.

They come back, over the white sea, in the mist,
Invisible, trooping home, the unassuaged ghosts
Endlessly returning on the uneasy sea.

They set foot on this land to which they have the right,
They return relentlessly, in the silence one knows their tread,
Multitudinous, endless, the ghosts coming home again.

They watch us, they press on us,
They press their claim upon us,
They are angry with us.

What do they want?
We are driven mad,
Madly we rush hither and thither:
Shouting, "Revenge, Revenge,"
Crying, "Pour out the blood of the foe,"
Seeking to appease with blood the insistent ghosts.

Out of blood rise up new ghosts,
Grey, stern, angry, unsatisfied,
The more we slay and are slain, the more we raise up new
    ghosts against us.

Till we are mad with terror, seeing the slain
Victorious, grey, grisly ghosts in our streets,
Grey, unappeased ghosts seated in the music-halls.
The dead triumphant, and the quick cast down,
The dead, unassuaged and angry, silencing us,
Making us pale and bloodless, without resistance.

What do they want, the ghosts, what is it
They demand as they stand in menace over against us?
How shall we now appease whom we have raised up?

Since from blood poured out rise only ghosts again,
What shall we do, what shall we give to them?
What do they want, forever there on our threshold?

Must we open the doors, and admit them, receive them home,
And in the silence, reverently, welcome them,
And give them place and honour and service meet?

For one year's space, attend on our angry dead,
Soothe them with service and honour, and silence meet,
Strengthen, prepare them for the journey hence,
Then lead them to the gates of the unknown,
And bid farewell, oh stately travellers,
And wait till they are lost upon our sight.

Then we shall turn us home again to life
Knowing our dead are fitly housed in death,
Not roaming here disconsolate, angrily.

And we shall have new peace in this our life,
New joy to give more life, new bliss to live,
Sure of our dead in the proud halls of death.

ELOI, ELOI, LAMA SABACHTHANI?

How I hate myself, this body which is me;
How it dogs me, what a galling shadow!
How I would like to cut off my hands,
And take out my intestines to torture them!

But I can't, for it is written against me I must not,
I must preserve my life from hurt.

But then, that shadow's shadow of me,
The enemy!

God, how glad I am to hear the shells
Droning over, threatening me!
It is their threat, their loud, jeering threat,
Like screaming birds of Fate
Wheeling to lacerate and rip up this my body,
It is the loud cries of these birds of pain
That gives me peace.

For I hate this body, which is so dear to me:
My legs, my breast, my belly:
My God, what agony they are to me;
For I dote on them with tenderness, and I hate them,
I hate them bitterly.

My God, that they should always be with me!
Nay, now at last thank God for the jeopardy,
For the shells, that the question is now no more before me.

I do not die, I am not even hurt,
But I kill my shadow's shadow of me!
And God is good, yes, God is very good!
I shot my man, I saw him crumble and hang
A moment as he fell—and grovel, and die.

And God is good, for I wanted him to die,
To twist, and grovel, and become a heap of dirt
In death. This death, his death, my death—
It is the same, this death.

So when I run at length thither across
To the trenches, I see again a face with blue eyes,
A blanched face, fixed and agonized,
Waiting. And I knew he wanted it.
Like a bride he took my bayonet, wanting it,
Like a virgin the blade of my bayonet, wanting it,
And it sank to rest from me in him,
And I, the lover, am consummate,
And he is the bride, I have sown him with the seed
And planted and fertilized him.

But what are you, woman, peering through the rents
In the purple veil?
Would you peep in the empty house like a pilferer?
You are mistaken, the veil of the flesh is rent
For the Lord to come forth at large, on the scent of blood,
Not for the thieves to enter, the pilferers.

Is there no reconciliation?
Is marriage only with death?
In death the consummation?
What I beget, must I beget of blood?
Are the guns and the steel the bridegroom,
Our flesh the bride?

I had dreamed of love, oh love, I had dreamed of love,
And the veil of the temple rent at the kiss on kiss,
And God revealed through the sweat and the heat of love,
And God abroad and alight on us everywhere,
Everywhere men and women alight with God,
My body glad as the bell of a flower
And hers a flowerbell swinging
In a breeze of knowledge.

Why should we hate, then, with this hate incarnate?
Why am I bridegroom of War, war's paramour?
What is the crime, that my seed is turned to blood,

My kiss to wounds?
Who is it will have it so, who did the crime?
And why do the women follow us satisfied,
Feed on our wounds like bread, receive our blood
Like glittering seed upon them for fulfilment?

Lord, what we have done we hereby expiate,
We expiate in our bodies' rents and rags
In our sheaf of self-gathered wounds: we go to meet
Our bride among the rustling chorus of shells,
Whose birds they are,
We give up, O Lord, our bodies to deadly hate,
We take the bride, O God, and our seed of life
Runs richly from us.
We expiate it thus, the unknowable crime,
We give hate her dues, O God, we yield her up
Our bodies to the expiation, Lord.

But shall I touch hands with death in killing that other,
The enemy, my brother?
Shall I offer to him my brotherly body to kill,
Be bridegroom or best man, as the case turns out?

The odds are even, and he will have it so.
It may be I shall give the bride
And the marriage shall be my brother's—it may be so—
I walk the earth intact hereafterwards;
The crime full-expiate, the Erinnyes sunk
Like blood in the earth again; we walk the earth
Unchallenged, intact, unabridged, henceforth a host
Cleansed and in concord from the bed of death.

RESURRECTION

Now all the hosts are marching to the grave;
The hosts are leaping from the edge of life
In a cascade of souls to sorrowful death.

And I am just awakened from the tomb;
And whither they are going, I have been
In timelessness laid by, in noiseless death.

Now, like a crocus in the autumn time,
My soul comes lambent from the endless night
Of death—a cyclamen, a crocus flower
Of windy autumn when the winds all sweep
The hosts away to death, where heap on heap
The dead are burning in the funeral wind.

Now, like a strange light breaking from the ground,
I venture from the halls of shadowy death—
A frail white gleam of resurrection.

I know where they are going, all the lives
That whirl and sweep like anxious leaves away
To have no rest save in the utter night
Of noiseless death; I know it well—
The death they will attain to, where they go—
I, who have been, and now am risen again.

Now like a cyclamen, a crocus flower
In autumn, like to a messenger come back
From embassy in death, I issue forth
Amid the autumn rushing red about
The bitter world, amid the smoke
From burning fires of many smouldering lives,
All bitter and corroding to the grave.

If they would listen, I could tell them now
The secret of the noiseless, utter grave,
The secret in the blind mouth of the worm.
But on they go, like leaves within a wind,
Scarlet and crimson and a rust of blood,
Into the utter dark: they cannot hear.

So like a cyclamen, a crocus flower
I lift my inextinguishable flame
Of immortality into the world,
Of resurrection from the endless grave,
Of sweet returning from the sleep of death.

And still against the dark and violent wind,
Against the scarlet and against the red
And blood-brown flux of lives that sweep their way
In hosts towards the everlasting night,
I lift my little pure and lambent flame,
Unquenchable of wind or hosts of death
Or storms of tears, or rage, or blackening rain
Of full despair, I lift my tender flame
Of pure and lambent hostage from the dead—
Ambassador from halls of noiseless death,
He who returns again from out the tomb
Dressed in the grace of immortality,
A fragile stranger in the flux of lives
That pour cascade-like down the blackening wind
Of sheer oblivion.

Now like a cyclamen, a crocus flower
In putrid autumn issuing through the fall
Of lives, I speak to all who cannot hear;
I turn towards the bitter, blackening wind,
I speak aloud to fleeting hosts of red
And crimson and the blood-brown heaps of slain,
Just as a cyclamen or crocus flower
Calls to the autumn, *Resurrection!*
I speak with a vain mouth.

Yet is uplifted in me the pure beam
Of immortality to kindle up
Another spring of yet another year,
Folded as yet: and all the fallen leaves
Sweep on to bitter, to corrosive death
Against me, yet they cannot make extinct
The perfect lambent flame which still goes up,

A tender gleam of immortality,
To start the glory of another year,
Another epoch in another year,
Another triumph on the face of earth,
Another race, another speech among
The multitudinous people unfused,
Unborn and unproduced, yet to be born.

LABOUR BATTALION

I

The town grows fiercer with heat!
It does not shrivel like big herbage,
But it makes the sunlight beat
Backward and forward from wall to wall
And exults in its bitter usage of us all.

Our hands, our breasts rebel against us,
Our eyes darken, and impotence hurts
Our soul. Nothing but the mad monotonous
Stress of compulsion remains, and a band that girts
The heart—heart that has beat
    As free as the running of angels' feet.

II

    Oh, and I wish that I
Was at Mablethorpe,
Where the long fawn foreshores lie
Taut as a wetted warp,
And the long waves rush and ply
Like a shuttle that carries the weft,
Like a harpist that strikes his deft
    Fingers across the harp.

Oh, to see the long waves rush,
Like the woof the shuttle carries
Along the coast; to hear the hush
    Of the waves that wash
To the distance, the wave that tarries
    Way down the coast, then comes up flush.

III

The cool, the cleanness of the sea,
    The sea all wet
Would wash away this ignominy:
    And better yet,
To hear the long waves strike the coast
As a harpist running along the strings,
Would take away the sickening fret
Of nerves that grind and a soul that stings
    And shame that hurts most.

For oh, to feel the rhythm set
    In me again,
The substance tangled in the net
Of this hour's ignominy and sweat
    Set free again.
For the sound of the sea as it furls and unfurls
To sing in the shell of my heart the lull and increase;
For a rhythm to compel me back, for peace
    In the whispering whorls.

IV

But I'll never reach the long sweet shore
    Of Lincolnshire.
Only the waste night lies in store.
Already I see the shelled moon lie
Like a shed white husk on the torrid sky
    A thing of fear.

For the moon like a Fata Morgana will lean
    Out of the sky tonight.
The town will cluster her herbage then,
And sinister beings will beckon between
The thick rank streets; and a stark white light
    Envelop our den.

And we shall be sealed and stowed away
    And not like men.
We shall strip to the Fata Morgana then
    And essay to disown ourselves; and then when the light
Of morning is back, we shall change again and essay
    To disown the night.

NO NEWS

Ah heaven, send
Her letter somehow
To tell me
How she fares at her end
Of this journey
So terrible now.

Rain, and a falling world
And never a word
To my silenced heart.
Explosions have whirled,
And a silence that stirred
Saw my last hope start
In vain.

Has she sent me a letter?
The skies fall
The unseen cloud
Rains heavy: to me
Nothing again.
Nothing yet.

Were it better
To forget?
Forget all?
Is death so proud
That he dares demand
Everything from me
Thus beforehand?

Am I lost?
Has death set me apart
Beforehand?
Have I crossed
That border?
Have I nothing in this dark land,
Even no pain of heart
To afford her?

BITS

I

THE LAST MINUTE

When in the morning I rose to depart, my love came to say farewell.
She wept bitterly, hiding her face in her kerchief. I said, "Why
    then?"
She said to me, "Stay three hours, to comfort me." Such is a girl!
Do not ask me, Almighty God, to part from her again.

II

VICAR'S SON

Child dear to my eye, God's blessing is on thy service;
The praise of Jesus is my success.
Close friend in everything is our Lord, my boy.
The willow shall lift her leaves to soothe thy distress,
The cattle run anxious in quest as the time draws nigh;

And stones shall make place for thy foot, become easy to press
When thou runnest the race with the foremost. God bless thee! Bless
Me too at last ere thou goest, child dear to my eye.

III

DRILL IN THE HEAT

Go forward, sun, do not torment us
With this appearance of faltering.
We leak like a barrel that is sprung, but yet
See no hope of altering
The greed of this infamous fellow for our sweat.

IV

MOTHER'S SON IN SALONIKA

The midnight shadow sinking down has slung
Over your tent the one tent of us all, my love;
In whose close folds above you, near above,
The flame of my soul like a trembling star is hung.

That is my spirit hovering close above
You now as you turn your face towards the sky.
Oh, as you stand looking up, do you know it is I?
Do you lift your lips to kiss me good night, my love?

V

CASUALTY

As I went down the street in my rose-red pelerine
Some one stopped me and said, "Your lover is hurt."
"Oh, bring him to me," I said. "Oh, lay him between
My arms, let me cover him up in my skirt."

And you—oh, see the myriad doves that walk
Beneath the steps of St Paul's! Catch several
And kill for Aphrodite. Don't speak, do not talk!—
One of you kindle a fire to consume them withal.

VI

MAIDEN'S PRAYER

I have come to the house of God
And found grey doves in the fountain court
Feeding on pure white sugar
Curving their feet and dancing and fluttering in sport.

I wish I could have some too
Some sugar of the same white sort
And let them feed from my hand.
But alas, this is not what I came for! I have fallen short.

Lord, cherish and comfort
The man Andrew; keep him safe in the war
From falling iron and horrible shell's report.
And Lord—But hark at the pigeons, what are they chattering
for?

VII

MAN HAULING A WAGON

Hast thou determined to strangle me, O God?
Release me from this mule-drawing!
Loosen this rope!

Alas, but the rope is gnawing
The strings of my heart!
I am losing hope.

No woman takes my part,
No mother weeps for me
No sister!

What are the odds to me!
Let this old cart
Blister—!

VIII

SIGHS

Ah, my love, my dear!
But what if my love should chance to hear
As he is passing unbeknown?
What if he turned and saw me here?

I should lean and whisper in his ear,
"Love, my love, now all is known
Love me and put me out of fear—
Or leave me alone."

IX

DAUGHTER OF THE GREAT MAN

The daughter of the great man rolls her khaki wool,
And in her hands the sparkling needles fly
Swiftly. I wish I might kiss her fingers; but full
Of danger I find her, even worse than the fields where we die.

X

THE CHILD AND THE SOLDIER

Oh brother, put me in your pouch
As you would a fresh, sweet locust-pod.
For I am frail as a flask of glass,
As a fine grey egg, or a slender rod,
Oh brother, and I am the golden ring
You wear on your finger so gladly. For God
Takes everything from you tomorrow,
   and gives me everything.

XI

PIETÀ

Thou our Maiden, thou who dwellest in Heaven
We pray for thee, Mary delightful, that God may bless thee!
Do thou, O Virgin, at day when we rise from our sleeping
Speak soothingly for us to God, and when in distress we
Cry for thee out of the night wherein we are prone,
Struck down, do thou part us the darkness that we see thee.
Be near us. And God's will be done!

XII

THE GREY NURSE

The grey nurse entered a rose garden
Where roses' shadows dappled her.
Her apron was brown with blood. She prayed,
And roses wondered at her prayer.

XIII

LITANY OF GREY NURSES

Sister, oh holy Sister
Thou door into heaven, Sister!
Thou of the dark, clenched tomb!
Thou newcomer to the Angels!
Thou silver beam in the Presence!
So long as we're here in life, our Sister, we come
And deliver our lips of their praise and their bitterness,
here by thy tomb.

XIV

MESSAGE TO A PERFIDIOUS SOLDIER

If you meet my young man,
    Greet him from me.
Touch him on the shoulder,
    And tell him from me
The moon is not any warmer, the sun no
    colder.

If he understands
    You will know by his eyes.
If he only stands
    And stares in surprise
Tell him prayer is stronger than iron, faith
    makes no demands.

XV

DUST IN THE EAST

Rain, pour down, pour down
Till geese can swim in your pools;
Till my parched vision cools;
Till all my memories drown.

My brother died in the heat
And the jackal found his grave;
Nibbled his fingers, the knave;
No more would I let him eat.

XVI

THE GIRL IN CAIRO

Oh Colonel, you from Embaba
Join me to my well-beloved friend.
    And if this night my love should come to me
    My cashmere shawl I'll hang for a canopy
    And say—Be welcome, dearest friend;
    Oh, how this night has happened perfectly!

XVII

THE JEWESS AND THE V.C.

Ah, young man!—
What sort of timorous potion of love have you drunk?
 If you see my rings, how they sparkle within my ears,
You go about in a dream, with your countenance sunk,
 And children behind you taunting you to tears.

Why, if you saw my limbs, how they shine on my body,
 What then would you do? Then for sure you would go
And die like a dog in a hole. 'Tis strange what a shoddy
 Lover you make, such a hero in front of the foe!

XVIII

ZEPPELIN NIGHTS

  Now, will you play all night!
  Come in, my mother says.
 Look in the sky, at the bright
  Moon all ablaze!
 Look at the shaking, white
  Searchlight rays!

 Tonight they're coming!
  It's a full moon!
 When you hear them humming
  Very soon,
 You'll stop that blooming
  Tune—

(*Children sing on unheeding:*)

  Sally go round the sun!
  Sally go round the moon!
  Sally go round the chimney-pots
   On Sunday afternoon!

XIX

MUNITIONS

For God's sake, let us stop, oh you who stand behind us,
    Let us eat the last meal!
Must we go on till we drop, oh you who stand behind us,
    Cannot we feel
That we've had enough? The brain is stretched till it parts.
    But you, you would steal
The blood from our hearts, oh you who stand behind us.

XX

LAND-WORKER

As she goes about the homestead
    To and from the cattle-shed
She lingers in the doorways
    When the cattle are fed,
And in her left hand, gaily,
    Her kerchief flutters red.

XXI

MOURNING

Why do you go about looking for me, mother?
I and my betrothed are together in the shed
Sitting there together for a little while.
Why are you so anxious? Leave me peaceful with my dead.

756

XXII

MESOPOTAMIA

The sun is gone from mid-heaven, the soldiers are gone from hence
    Oh out-lander, weary soul!
Alas, my land is England, and I know not how nor whence
    I came hither, nor what is my goal!
How can I find my way to the river?
    How hasten? And what will console
Me now if I've lost my mess-mates, lost them forever?

XXIII

TALES

The gazelle-calf, oh my children,
Goes behind his mother where the sand is hot
Goes behind his mother with bare, blithe foot
Wearing no boot, my children.

XXIV

FOREIGN SUNSET

Oh master, let it be loose-all, it is enough!
Work has made us blind, and now the dusk
Ah master, master, you who have brought us hither,
The sun has crept like a scarlet beetle in the husk
Of the hills, and the hearts within us dither
With weariness, faint as fluff
We are, so let us have done. Ah master, we wait
For the word. Now let us go through the gate.

XXV

PRISONER AT WORK IN
A TURKISH GARDEN

Appeal from the garden:
    Over the fountains and the orange-trees
        The evening shadow has sunk,
    Bringing night once more, and the man with the keys
        That shut me up in my bunk.

    You forty ladies in the harem bower,
        Listen, for I will complain.
    Bitter to me is this evening hour;
        Each evening, bitter again.

XXVI

Response from the harem:
    Sisters, I am sorry for this foreign man
        Who labours all day in the sun.
    Sisters, the searchlight's swinging fan
        In heaven has begun.

    Stranger, soft are the tears that fall
        For pity of thee.
    Sisters, the guns are speaking; let all
        Sing soothingly.

XXVII

SWING SONG OF A GIRL AND A SOLDIER

        Brother, the scent of your clothing
        Is like biscuits baked for a feast
        Of victory, kneaded with sulphur
        Worked with clean sweat for yeast.

Brother, I like your fragrance.
It smells strange like the shouting of men
Womanless shouting in anger.
Brother, let me die down again.

XXVIII

PRISONERS AT WORK IN THE RAIN

Oh, the moist, full water-jar!
You lad, will you ask the boss
To let us have done for today: we are
Steeped enough. Tell him to come across
And take a swim with us here.
Lord God above, would it cost me dear
To make an end of the malice of this overseer?

XXIX

THE WELL IN AFRICA

Thou well of Kilossa, thy well-chords are of silver
And a draught of thee is strength to a soul in hell.
Kilossa, sweet well of my strength, thou corded with silk
Heal me, for body and soul I am not well.

XXX

NEITHER MOTH NOR RUST

God, only God is eternally.
God is forever, and only He.
Where, white maid, are the men you have loved?
They are dead, so God was between you, you see.

APOSTROPHE TO A BUDDHIST MONK

Oh my bald head
Cranium
duck-egg
how thou dost poke up among the spokes of my
umbrella.

Oh my marigold robe
how thou castest up a sickly glare
a bilious blast
a mango-fleshed aura nauseously steaming
a pawpaw effulgence
into my eyes and nostrils.

Oh my wife's brass incense-bowl
bought second-hand from Mrs Justice Ennis
for 3½ rupees,
I am inclined to heap thy coals of fire on my own
bald and prickly pate
and lick up thy ashes with a repentant tongue
and consider the lily, not the pawpaw nor the mango-
flesh
and give up the ghost incontinent
in the hope of resurrecting or rather re-incarnating
as a vendor of fried fish, once more yellow.

HIM WITH HIS TAIL IN HIS MOUTH

When the cuckoo, the cow, and the coffee-plant chipped the
Mundane Egg, at various points, they stepped out, and immediately
set off in different directions. Not different directions of space and
time, but different directions in creation: within the fourth
dimension. The cuckoo went cuckoo-wards, the cow went cow-
wise, and the coffee-plant started coffing. Three very distinct roads
across the fourth dimension.

The cow was dumb, and the cuckoo too.
They went their ways, as creatures do,
Till they chanced to meet, in the Lord's green Zoo.

The bird gave a cluck, the cow gave a coo,
At the sight of each other the pair of them flew
Into tantrums, and started their hullabaloo.

They startled creation; and when they were through
Each said to the other: till I came across you
I wasn't aware of the things I could do!

> Cuckoo!
> Moo!
> Cuckoo!

And this, I hold, is the true history of evolution.

The Greeks made equilibrium their goal. Equilibrium is hardly a goal to travel towards. Yet it's something to attain. You travel in the fourth dimension, not in yards and miles, like the eternal serpent.

[FLAT-FOOT'S SONG]

Because Flat-foot is the favourite of the white leghorn cock, and he shakes the tid-bit for her with a most wooing noise, and when she lays an egg, he bristles like a double white poppy, and rushes to meet her, as she flounders down from the chicken-house, and his echo of her *I've-laid-an-egg* cackle is rich and resonant. Every pine-tree on the mountains hears him:

> She's ⎫
> I've ⎭ *laid an egg!*
>
> She's ⎫
> I've ⎭ *laid an egg!*

And his poem would be:

> "Oh you who make me feel so good, when
>   you sit next me on the perch
>   At night! (temporarily, of course!)

Oh you who make my feathers bristle with
   the vanity of life!
Oh you whose cackle makes my throat go
   off like a rocket!
Oh you who walk so slowly, and make me
   feel swifter
Than my boss!
Oh you who bend your head down, and
   move in the under
Circle, while I prance in the upper!
Oh you, come! come! come! for here is a bit
   of fat from
The roast veal; I am shaking it for you."

TRAITORS

Traitors, oh liars, you Judas lot!
Jesus! You've not only sold Jesus
You've sold every man there was to be sold.

You liars, you dirty lot!
You've sold every great man that ever appeared
You cultured canaille!

Oh the canaille of culture, the Christian canaille
The dirty dogs of wisdom
The purveyors of education
The superior classes.

They've sold everything, but everything
And everybody.
They sold Plato to the sausage factories of universities
Where now they deal out slices of Plato-sausage to the cultured
   appetite.

And all the heroes of the bible they sold for cats-meat to the
    churches.
And the churches cry "Puss! Puss! Come and be fed!"

Napoleon they sold to Madame Tussauds and to the artificial manure
    factories,
Shakespeare they sold to Crosse and Blackwells, to be jammed into
    jam
And Beethoven they sold to certain conductors, to be conducted into
    treacle.

Everything in the world of culture and superiority
Has been successfully sold.
And whatever new comes along will be successfully sold.

I would warn anybody against a culture
Which the superior classes are making money out of.

REACH OVER

Reach over, then, reach over
across the chasm
in the dark.

I am coming down
down to the levels where you have stayed.
I am coming back.

But between us still
lies a chasm
though it narrows now,
perhaps one could step across.

But reach over, reach over
and give me a hand.
I come back to you
men dumb in the dusk
but men,

and dearer to me
than everything else
than woman or triumph, money or success
men in the dusk
dumb
but masculine as the sun,
waiting for the sun to rise on you.

Reach over, then, reach over
And let us embrace.

I have come back to you, for I never left you.
Half-way round the circle now
I feel I'm coming near.

Opposite ways round the circle
Is a sure way to meet.

It is very dark
It is a nadir.
Are you near?
Have you come round the curve, your way
Towards me?

Reach out, reach out towards me.
Are you near?

I never left you.
I went the opposite way round the circle,
Because it was the surest way of meeting you at last.

Have you travelled?

Have you travelled your downward arc?
Are you curving up to me?

For I have traversed my upward curve
And am coming down.
Are you near? have you travelled your portion?
Reach out, reach out, say not a word,
Silent, reach out, let us touch.

It is very dark, oh kindred dearer than blood,
And dearly dearer than money.
Oh men, dumb in the darkness,
Oh men, dearer than success to me
Men, dearer to me than peace
Dearer than love
Dearer than triumph.

Reach out, reach out in this dark!

SOFTLY, THEN, SOFTLY

Do they block the way?
Do they obstruct?
Tripping about with their ladylike hams
And their groomed and mushroom-like faces?

Do they stop their flow?
Do they prevent the touch?

Like india-rubber and asbestos
Do they prevent the current?

Is that all they exist for?
Mushroom-faced, heavy-bottomed
And oh so "upper"!
Are they just the deadening fungus
On the decaying effort of mankind?

So plausible, oh so plausible!
We wouldn't hurt you for the world, says the parasite,
The smooth-faced, fat-hammed, fungussy fat one
To its victim.

Ugh! down with them!
Down with them, down with them!
Kick them over, the toadstools,
Smash them up, the smooth-faced, fat-faced plausibles.

But softly, softly.
And swiftly, swiftly,
With no shouting
And no talking whatsoever.
But softly, softly and ruthlessly
Down with them!

CHANGE OF LIFE

I

The Woman Weeps her Change of Life.

Languidly month by month
Minute by minute ebbs
My brood in retreat.

Leaving me, going away from me,
Departing, departing, departing
Out of the blood
The greying nerve,
Out of the flaccid limbs
Departing.

The rosy river that sprang
In my brood-soul withering,
Leaving the riverbed
To blanch slowly.

Into the dead sea falling
My rosy river, my best,
My life, my broody self.

Warm of me fading to white!
God, what shall I do in the white days?
My years have been
Ruddy, rosy, and orange.
How can my heart keep beating in this pallor of whitish
    brine!

Heart! There is no word to say!
Except,
Where once the blood sang
Tears now fall on white sand.

God! Oh make it stop,
This change!
Don't take the blood of my body!

I I

She Weeps, and Cannot be Comforted.

Even remembrance seeps out
This way.
I cannot even remember my life that has been.
It drips slowly away
Through an inevitable, irreparable leak.

Seeping, seeping, receding
My life from the me that remains
Alive and yet drained of life.

Flutter of fear in the nerves
Where before the assurance chuckled!
Along the nerves, a low throbbing,
A slow, heavy patter of lessening vibration
Lowered to pain.

Rosy best of the blood gone out of the body!
Deserter!
Leaving this congerie behind and in danger.

Utterly gone away on another errand,
Leaving this naked, pallid, helpless, vulnerable remains.
Death! Death! Take me with you, to spare me this last!

III

Yet through the Tears steals a sense of Peace, and Greater Being.

Ah be still, be still! After all
All is not said.
It is change that is coming upon me,
Not merely loss!

Ah be still, be still and stop shuddering!
This blood that was once my own
Is my own as ever, and faithful.

Ah no, not bleeding away,
Not bleeding away, to leave me with whitened gums.
Only breaking camp, and entering
Slowly, insidiously, into new places,
River of my life.

Wandering into new valleys,
Making pools in new hollow places
Where the world is virgin and houseless,
And the singing is low and sensitive
Non-combative.

Where life looks me in the eyes
And goes his way silently, unasserting.
Where the meadow-lark wears his collar of submission
On his throat below his song.

IV

She Rejoices in her New Nakedness.

Blessed in all things,
Eve in the afterward.

The high, virgin valley
With suffused light
Smokeless, houseless, homeless
Paradisal, through the long afternoon.

Eve of the afterwards
Having been through the fire.
Having been through fire, through many fires,
Through smoke, through smokiness
With singed, hot eyes and relentlessness
Through the auto-da-fé of love.

Love's long, moiled, maddened auto-da-fé!
Flushed, frenzied, relentless me.

And to emerge at last
In another, softened springtime
As a flower above charred remains.

To be carried at last from the fire
As one dying, with the charred rags falling away,
And lifted in the long, seeping swoon
Away, away through the trees
To a higher place that is virgin.

To a virgin valley high up
Where no people are, and no fires.
No fires, no hearths, no houses
No battle, no will-to-live
No will to love.

The delicate afternoon
Where no house is needed.
Where only the women of the afterwards
Walk through the trees as virgins
Whom the leopard looks in the eyes,
And knows, departing in silence.

Whom the meadow-lark, singing, speaks to
In tones of the afterwards, paradisal,
Down the golden slopes to sunset,
Towards the silent doors of the West.

V

She Sees Men Walking towards her, under the Trees.

Tall virgins of the afterwards
Who have been through the fire,
Walking slowly westwards, houseless
In the afterglow.
But not alone nor forlorn
Nor homeless.
Home at last in the open again, and unhouseled.

With men of the afterwards walking to meet us from
　　the doors of the west,
With faces in shadow, but smiling
The smile of the leopard and the meadow-lark,
The knowing smile of the final virgin in man
As he slowly walks from the western door of the world
Back into paradise.

Past saluting swords of the angels
Acquiescence of watchful lions,
With his brow wiped bright of the toil of sweat
And his mouth wiped clean of the bitterness of reproach,
Towards the women who are virgins of the afterwards,
Sauntering down the long slope from the east.

VI

And on the Trees hang the Apples of Gold.

At last, at last, after all
Peace like a river flows
From the east to the west in the upper valley
Of stillness and afternoon.
Where the fire-burnt virgin in man and the virgin in fire-
　　scathed woman
At last, at last, after all
Look into each other's eyes with knowledge;
And peace like a river flows
Between them.

Where the leopard pausing to drink
Looks up, and knows, and is known.
Where the meadow-lark as he lifts
His throat to sing, glances down
And sees what he sees in the faces of men
That are virgins at last from the furnace, with virgin
　　women the same.

VII

And the Serpents wander their own ways, reconciled,
　　without any more envy.

The men come in by the furnace-gate of the west,
The women by the gate of the east.
The women with light on their faces,
The men with their faces in shade.
And they meet, in the glade between morning and
　　evening
Where peace like a river flows,
Saying nothing, no more to be said.

WHAT DO I CARE?

And what do I care
　　though all the crowded sunlight jostling
Its way across the dark should mock my nakedness.
What do I care though the very stones
　　should scoff me discovered
A naked nightly thing too frail and wise for the stress
Of the day that battles its journey
　　over the face of the Dark
Only to wreck on the shores of night again,
　　and again
To sink unconscious in the rocking dark,
　　what though
The day shall mock me inefficacious, what then?

What though the clouds should shine
    in conceit of substance upon me
Frailer than they,
    what though the clouds go glancing down
The sky with a wealth of ease and assurance
    and cast me scorn
For my tainted transiency as a thing unreal—
    I wear my frailty as a crown.
Yea, though the very clouds have vantage over me
I have a darkness intact within me, glowing secure,
A lovely shadow of death
    in the place of my love that was
Keeps me proud in shame, pledge of the Night dark-pure.

I have a tent of darkness by day
    that nothing can stale or profane
I have a knowledge of lovely night,
    and scarcely can refrain
From seeking the utter drowning,
    to share the rhythm of the deathless wave
Of Death; but I wait awhile in this tabernacle,
    singing my stave.

What do I care though from the day's white envelope
I tear but news of sorrow and pain;—
    I bear the hope
Of sharing the Night with God, of mingling up again
With all the unquenchable darkness
    that nothing not life can stain.

For I know the host,
    the minute sparkling of darkness which
Vibrates untouched and virile, in life unutterable, rich,
And which when day crows challenge,
    flings out its vivid black notes
Of life unborn and is fretted.

Life is dark and rippling, but fretted
Bursts like an arc lamp into light
Blue at the core; and when is whetted
A blade on the wheel, then the slumbering night
In the stone and iron leaps in fire.
And darkness runs the racing wheel,
And self-same darkness, chafed to ire
Thunders in heaven till the brave worlds reel
Which else were a silent grasp that held the skies.

ARE YOU PINING?

Are you pining to be superior?—
Then go to hell!
Do you want to rise in the world?—
Go to hell!

Rise, do you want to rise?
Dear, dear working-man,
    do you want to look like a bank-clerk?
Dear, dear bank-clerk,
    do you want to look like a bank-manager?
Dear dear! dear dear! they're all on the rise
They're all looking superior!

Oh, but a man wants to get on in the world!
Does he then? does he really?
Progress, you know, we believe in progress!
Do we really? Well I never! fancy now, fancy that!
Progress!

I want my son to be something better than his father was!
—Think of that now!
    Pa has such a poor opinion of himself!

All the little boys whose fathers were colliers or farmers
They are going to be school-teachers or bank-clerks.
And all the little boys
     whose fathers were school-teachers or bank-clerks
Are going to be
     clergymen, professors, bank-directors and stock-brokers.
Till there won't be any lower classes left.
None at all, mind you. Progress is a fact.
The lower classes shall all be made upper.

We can do without the sole of the shoe,
     since nobody sees it.
Let us walk about in uppers
Very handsome uppers
Very refined uppers
Very superior
Classy!

Aren't you pining to be classy, superior, "upper"?

Oh you mangy hound, go to hell!

O! AMERICANS

Americans!
The word stands for something,
     carries its own patent, and its own obligation.

Americans are the people of America.
The destiny of America is in their hands.
The living America is in the hearts of Americans.

What the America of the future will be, we don't know.
What we know is, that the future America
     is a germ lying in the hearts of Americans,
       there and nowhere else.
Not in dollars, nor in banks, nor in syndicates,
     nor in Washington,
But a germ in the hearts of men and women, Americans.

We can't know what the future of America will be.
But the germ of that future is inside the American people
     in their hearts.
It is their responsibility, their point of honour.
Politicians may be bad, industrial magnates may be at fault,
Scandals may destroy every man's faith in man:
And yet, there is a speck, a germ of American future
     in the heart of every intelligent American, whether
     he is politician or magnate or mere individual.
And for the sake of this nascent, unborn, as-yet-unknowable
     American future
There is, I believe, scarcely one intelligent American who
     will shirk, or fail in point of honour.

The old countries have a past, to be faithful to.
America still has only an unrevealed future.
And it is much more difficult and delicate to be true
     to an unborn future, than to an accomplished past.
Tradition, tradition, tradition, it is easy enough
     to be faithful to a tradition,
But to be faithful to something that has not yet
     come to pass, that does not yet exist, save as a subtle,
     struggling germ in individual hearts,
Not a mob thing, nor a mass thing, nor a class thing, nor
     a hundred-per-cent thing
But a subtle, struggling little germ struggling half-unrealised
     in individual hearts, and nowhere else,
That is a difficult thing to be faithful to.

Yet it is a point of honour.

And so, when the outside world calls upon America to act in
     certain ways, perform certain sacrifices,
Why should Americans immediately acquiesce?
America will have to find her own way into the future,
     the old lights won't show the way.

But if, taken at its very best, the title *American*
     is a patent of nobility,
As it must be, taken at its very best,—
Then *noblesse oblige.*

It is a point of honour.

And at the moment, there is an obligation.
It is the obligation of the citizens of this country towards
 the aborigines of their country.

The American Indian lingers here, ward of the
 American government.
Now make up your mind about him, he is not as we are.
He lingers on from an old, savage world, that still has
 its treasures of consciousness, its subtle barbaric
 forms of civilisation.
He is, basically, a savage: it is a term of reproach,
 but also, it is not a term of reproach.

The American Indian is, basically, a savage.
But be careful how you destroy him.
Because he is so *absolutely* in your power, that,
 before God, you must be careful.
Noblesse oblige!

Be careful, before you destroy him.
Be careful how you turn him into a hundred-per-cent
 American.
He is the one thing that is aboriginally American.
Don't sentimentalize about him.
Realize.

Strictly—don't forget it—he is a savage who has, for
 the most part, long ago entered the Roman Catholic
 Church.
But strictly, he is a savage.

He is a savage with his own peculiar consciousness, his own
 peculiar customs and observances.
Don't sentimentalize his savage consciousness,
 customs and observances.
But be careful how you utterly quash them.
He is so absolutely at your mercy.
He is the last of the originally American race.
You are Americans.
And *noblesse oblige*.

Turn the Poles, the Germans, the English, the Italians,
     the Russians,
Turn them into hundred-per-cent Americans.
What else have they come to this country for?

But the Indian never came.
It was you who came, Americans.
And before you put out the old savage light for ever,
     hesitate.

The Indian does no harm.
He is far too few to cause any apprehension
     in any direction.
Well then!

The Indian question has, worse luck, become a political
     question.
It has been made a cause for strife, a *casus belli*.
On your honour, Americans, what are you doing?
The Indian should never have been made a *casus belli*,
     between conflicting political parties, and
     contending interests.

Yet the clash has been started, the Indian is about to be
     finished off.
Today is Easter Sunday: Christ Risen! Two days ago was
     Good Friday: Christ Crucified!
On Good Friday the big white men of the Indian Bureau
     and big white men from Washington drove out to
     the pueblo, summoned the old Indian men, and
     held a meeting behind closed doors.

Then the big men of the White Americans
     told the old American aborigines that it would
     be well if these old fathers abandoned their foolish,
     heathen dances and ceremonies, and tilled their
     land better, instead of wasting time:
That the boys must stay at school, not be kept away
     at seasons to prepare themselves and to partake
     in these useless practices of ceremonial:

That it would be far, far better for the Indian youth
  to grow up true, hundred-per-cent American,
  than to remain a dancing savage:
That the old dark fathers should not trust these artists
  and long-haired people who pretend to espouse
  their cause, because they, the artists and long-haired
  people, want to keep the Indian back, want to
  prevent his becoming a hundred-per-cent American;
  because they live on him. Artists and
  long-haired people, painting the Indian and writing
  about the Indian, make their living off him,
  so naturally they want to keep him back, down, poor.
  If he were a hundred-per-cent American citizen,
  he would go out into the world and become
  as rich as anybody else, on the same terms
  with the white men, his brothers.

Furthermore the White big-men said to the old Indians
That the Indians complained of being poor,
  of having short crops;
That the Indians wanted the White Man's Government
  to supply them with farm-implements,
  so they could have more food.

But why so!
The White Man's Government was under no obligation
  to give the Indians one single thing, not one cent.
The Indians of the pueblos have land.
Let them lease their land to the American Government,
  as the Oklahoma Indians have done;
And in return the Government would supply them with
  excellent farm-machinery.

So, the speech in the pueblo, on Good Friday,
  behind closed doors.
And when the doors were opened,
  the White Men drove away.
And the old dark-faced men came out heavily, with a
  greater gloom than for many years,
Though their souls have been growing heavy for centuries.

What does it mean, they say?
That our boys must stay at school till they are eighteen,
    and not be allowed to absent themselves
    for ceremonies and ceremonial preparations?
Then our life is finished, our day is over completely.
Consummatum est!

Consummatum est! Oh God, and on Good Friday!
"It is finished!"

That we lease our lands and get reapers
    and binders in exchange?
So, it is finished.

Now, Americans, what about it?
The bit of land in question is a flea-bite,
    to this great nation.
Even if there were oil, copper, gold upon these
    bits of reserved land, it were a flea-bite,
    to this great nation.

To make this bit of land, and water-rights,
    or oil or copper or gold a cause for political action,
This is going beyond the bounds of present honour.

It is your test, Americans.
Can you leave the remnants of the old race
    on their own ground,
To live their own life, fulfil their own ends
    in their own way?
Can you? Can you?

Decide whether you can, because it is a test
    before the everlasting witnesses.
If you can, submit to it.
Submit to it, and let your American *noblesse* compel you
To draw a line around the Indians, beyond which line
    you abstain from further interference.
That is all.
And that is a test of you.

Solve the Indian question finally.
Make it cease to be a political question for ever.
Remove the Indians forever from the hands of
    the politicians.
Either make the Indian Bureau into a permanent office,
    endowed with a sufficient endowment,
      and controlled by men of science, competent
      anthropologists, historians, and men of letters;
Or transfer the control to the American Institute
    of Ethnology;
Do anything, but do something to draw this one
    delicate line of non-interference.

It is a test, Americans.

But if you cannot keep political, domineering hands
    off the Indians,
Then destroy them, throw them out into the cities
    among the negroes
As hundred-per-cent Americans, well-educated.
Do it.

Only know that, doing it, you fail in point of honour.
And damage once more the frail quick of the future
    America, that is in you.

EAGLE IN NEW MEXICO

On a low cedar-bush
In the flocculent ash of the sage-grey desert,
Ignoring our motor-car, black and always hurrying,
Hurrying,
Sits an eagle, erect and scorch-breasted;
From the top of a dark-haired cedar-bush
Issuing like a great cloven candle-flame
With its own alien aura.

Towards the sun, to south-west
A scorched breast, sun-turned forever.
A scorched breast breasting the blaze.
The sun-blaze of the desert.

Eagle, in the scorch forever,
Eagle, south-westward facing
Eagle, with the sickle dripping darkly above;

Can you still ignore it?
Can you ignore our passing in this machine?

Eagle, scorched-pallid out of the hair of the cedar,
Erect, with the God-thrust entering from below;
Eagle, gloved in feathers;
Oh soldier-erect big bird
In scorched white feathers
In burnt dark feathers
In feathers still fire-rusted;
Sickle-overswept, sickle dripping over and above.

Sunbreaster
Staring two ways at once, to right and left;
Masked-one,
Dark-wedged
Sickle-masked
With iron between your two eyes,
You feather-gloved
Down to the feet,
You foot-flint
Erect one,
With the God-thrust thrusting you silent from below.

You only stare at the sun with the one broad eye of your
        breast.
With your face, you face him with a rock,
A wedge,
The weapon of your face.

Oh yes, you face the sun
With a dagger of dark, live iron
That's been whetted and whetted in blood.

The dark cleaves down and weapon-hard downwards curving;
The dark drips down suspended
At the sun of your breast
Like a down-curved sword of Damocles,
Beaked eagle.

The God-thrust thrusting you silent and dark from beneath.
From where?
From the red-fibred bough of the cedar, from the cedar-roots,
     from the earth,
From the dark earth over the rock, from the dark rock over
     the fire,
          from the fire that boils in the molten heart of the world.

The heart of the world is the heart of the earth where a fire
          that is living throbs
Throb, throb, throb
And throws up strength that is living strength and regal into
     the feet;
Into the roots of the cedar, into the cedar-boughs,
And up the iron feet of the eagle in thrills of fiery power.

Lifts him fanning in the high empyrean
Where he stares at the sun.

Feather-ankles,
Fierce-foot,
Eagle, with Egyptian darkness jutting in front of your face;
Old one, erect on a bush,
Do you see the gold sun fluttering buoyantly in heaven
Like a boy in a meadow playing,
And his father watching him?

Are you the father-bird?
And is the sun your first-born, Only-begotten?

The gold sun shines in heaven only because he's allowed.
The old Father of life at the heart of the world, life-fire
    at the middle of the earth, this earth
Sent out the sun so that something should flutter in heaven;
And sent the eagle to keep an eye on him.

Erect, scorched-pallid out of the hair of the cedar,
All sickle-overswept, sickle dripping over and above,
Soldier-erect from the God-thrust, eagle
        with tearless eyes,
You who came before rock was smitten into weeping,
Dark-masked-one, day-starer, threatening the sun with your
    beak
Silent upon the American cedar-bush,
Threatener!

Will you take off your threat?
Or will you fulfil it?
Will you strike at the heart of the sun with your blood-welded
    beak?
Will you strike the sun's heart out again?
Will you? like an Aztec sacrifice reversed.

Oh vindictive eagle of America!
Oh sinister Indian eagle!
Oh eagle of kings and emperors!
What next?

FIRE

Wave them
Flap white wings and yellow pinions
From a red breast!

Fly then, fly!
Because you are ever there on the hearth,
They say you do not travel.
But you fly, you soar, you sweep away.

You flutter in a host of flames, like winter starlings risen,
You are off, you are on the wing, whither, whither?
Yet you are here, like God upon the hearth.
All the while travelling, travelling
But not across, nor up nor down, for you still are here,
But into the inwards of the unseen
Into the verity of the only one
Who breathed you out, and breathes you in again.

There is a breast of a vast and unknown body
Where flames wheel in like breath
Rush in and fill the living cavities
And in one instant's pause, are revolved round and changed,
Transmuted, the dark redness taken out
Then driven back, in a new silent rush
Of expiration turned into the world again
As fire, but soft as sunshine, soft as kisses
Soft as a kind heart's kindness tremulous
Upon the outer air.

Oh brands
Oh withered, crackling twigs of brushwood people
Myriad, myriad dead twigs of pallid and chafing people
You will never catch fire.
You will never fly on yellow, kindled wings
Into that breast,
To be revolved, and in one instant, changed
And the flame of you swept back in a new breath of life.

You will take the other way.
Slow, slow, fungoid, clammily decay
The slow way, not the swift;
But as inevitable.
Only cold, instead of quick.

POEMS FROM *THE PLUMED SERPENT*

I

[THE COMING OF QUETZALCOATL]

In the place of the west
In peace, beyond the lashing of the sun's bright tail,
In the stillness where waters are born
Slept I, Quetzalcoatl.

In the cave which is called Dark Eye,
Behind the sun, looking through him as a window
Is the place. There the waters rise,
There the winds are born.

On the waters of the after-life
I rose again, to see a star falling, and feel a breath on
    my face.
The breath said: Go! And lo!
I am coming.

The star that was falling was fading, was dying.
I heard the star singing like a dying bird;
My name is Jesus, I am Mary's Son.
I am coming home.
My mother the Moon is dark.
Oh brother, Quetzalcoatl
Hold back the dragon of the sun,
Bind him with shadow while I pass
Homewards. Let me come home.

I bound the bright fangs of the Sun
And held him while Jesus passed
Into the lidless shade,
Into the eye of the Father,
Into the womb of refreshment.

And the breath blew upon me again.
So I took the sandals of the Saviour
And started down the long slope
Past the mount of the sun.
Till I saw beneath me
White breast-tips of my Mexico
My bride.

Jesus the Crucified
Sleeps in the healing waters
The long sleep.
Sleep, sleep, my brother, sleep.
My bride between the seas
Is combing her dark hair,
Saying to herself: Quetzalcoatl.

II

[LORD OF THE MORNING STAR]

The Lord of the Morning Star
Stood between the day and the night:
As a bird that lifts its wings, and stands
With the bright wing on the right
And the wing of the dark on the left,
The Dawn Star stood into sight.

Lo! I am always here!
Far in the hollow of space
I brush the wing of the day
And put light on your face.
The other wing brushes the dark.
But I, I am always in place.

Yea, I am always here. I am Lord
In every way. And the lords among men
See me through the flashing of wings.
They see me and lose me again.
But lo! I am always here
Within ken.

The multitudes see me not.
They see only the waving of wings,
The coming and going of things.
The cold and the hot.

But ye that perceive me between
The tremors of night and the day,
I make you the Lords of the Way
Unseen.

The path between gulfs of the dark and the steeps of
the light;
The path like a snake that is gone, like the length of a
fuse to ignite
The substance of shadow, that bursts and explodes
into sight.

I am here undeparting. I sit tight
Between wings of the endless flight,
At the depths of the peace and the fight.

Deep in the moistures of peace,
And far down the muzzle of the fight
You shall find me, who am neither increase
Nor destruction, different quite.

I am far beyond
The horizons of love and strife.
Like a star, like a pond
That washes the lords of life.

III

[SOMEONE WILL ENTER BETWEEN
THE GATES]

Someone will enter between the gates,
    Now, at this moment, Ay!
See the light on the man that waits.
    Shall you? Shall I?

Someone will come to the place of fire,
Now, at this moment, Ay!
And hark to the words of their heart's desire.
Shall you? Shall I?

Someone will knock when the door is shut,
Ay! in a moment, Ay!
Hear a voice saying: I know you not!
Shall you? Shall I?

IV

[MY NAME IS JESUS]

My name is Jesus, I am Mary's son,
I am coming home,
My mother the Moon is dark.

Brother, Quetzalcoatl,
Hold back the wild hot sun.
Bind him with shadow while I pass.
Let me come home.

V

QUETZALCOATL LOOKS DOWN
ON MEXICO

Jesus had gone far up the dark slope, when he looked back.
Quetzalcoatl, my brother! he called. Send me my images,
And the images of my mother, and the images of my saints.
Send me them by the swift way, the way of the sparks,
That I may hold them like memories in my arms when I go to sleep.

And Quetzalcoatl called back: I will do it.

Then he laughed, seeing the sun dart fiercely at him.
He put up his hand, and held back the sun with his shadow.

So he passed the yellow one, who lashed like a dragon in vain.
And having passed the yellow one, he saw the earth beneath.
And he saw Mexico lying like a dark woman with white breast-tips.

Wondering he stepped nearer, and looked at her,
At her trains, at her railways and her automobiles,
At her cities of stone and her huts of straw.
And he said: Surely this looks very curious!

He sat within the hollow of a cloud, and saw the men that worked
    in the fields, with foreign overseers.
He saw the men that were blind, reeling with aguardiente.
He saw the women that were not clean.
He saw the hearts of them all, that were black, and heavy, with a
    stone of anger at the bottom.

Surely, he said, this is a curious people I have found!

So leaning forward on his cloud, he said to himself:
I will call to them.
Hola! Hola! Mexicanos! Glance away a moment towards me.
Just turn your eyes this way, Mexicanos!

They turned not at all, they glanced not one his way.

Holala! Mexicanos! Holala!

They have gone stone deaf! he said.

So he blew down on them, to blow his breath in their faces.
But in the weight of their stupefaction, none of them knew.

Holala! What a pretty people!
All gone stupefied!

A falling star was running like a white dog over a plain.
He whistled to it loudly, twice, till it fell to his hand.
In his hand it lay and went dark.
It was the Stone of Change.

This is the stone of change! he said.

So he tossed it awhile in his hand, and played with it.
Then suddenly he spied the old lake, and he threw it in.
It fell in.
And two men looked up.

Holala! he said. *Mexicanos!*
Are there two of you awake?
So he laughed, and one heard him laughing.

Why are you laughing? asked the first man of Quetzalcoatl.

I hear the voice of my First Man ask me why I am laughing?
   Holala, Mexicanos! It is funny!
To see them so glum and so lumpish!

Hey! First Man of my name! Hark here!
Here is my sign.
Get a place ready for me.

Send Jesus his images back, Mary and the saints and all.
Wash yourself, and rub oil in your skin.
On the seventh day, let every man wash himself, and put oil on his
      skin; let every woman.
Let him have no animal walk on his body, nor through the shadow
      of his hair. Say the same to the women.
Tell them they all are fools, that I'm laughing at them.

The first thing I did when I saw them, was to laugh at the sight of
      such fools.
Such lumps, such frogs with stones in their bellies.
Tell them they are like frogs with stones in their bellies, can't hop!
Tell them they must get the stones out of their bellies,

Get rid of their heaviness,
Their lumpishness,
Or I'll smother them all.

I'll shake the earth, and swallow them up, with their cities.
I'll send fire and ashes upon them, and smother them all.
I'll turn their blood like sour milk rotten with thunder,
They will bleed rotten blood, in pestilence.
Even their bones shall crumble.

Tell them so, First Man of my Name.

For the sun and the moon are alive, and watching with gleaming
    eyes.
And the earth is alive, and ready to shake off his fleas.
And the stars are ready with stones to throw in the faces of men.
And the air that blows good breath in the nostrils of people and
    beasts
Is ready to blow bad breath upon them, to perish them all.

The stars and the earth and the sun and the moon and the winds
Are about to dance the war dance round you, men!
When I say the word, they will start.
For sun and stars and earth and the very rains are weary
Of tossing and rolling the substance of life to your lips.
They are saying to one another: Let us make an end
Of those ill-smelling tribes of men, these frogs that can't jump,
These cocks that can't crow
These pigs that can't grunt
This flesh that smells
These words that are all flat
These money vermin.

These white men, and red men, and yellow men, and brown men,
    and black men
That are neither white, nor red, nor yellow, nor brown, nor black
But everyone of them dirtyish.
Let us have a spring cleaning in the world.

For men upon the body of the earth are like lice,
Devouring the earth into sores.
This is what stars and sun and earth and moon and winds and rain
Are discussing with one another; they are making ready to start.
So tell the men I am coming to,
To make themselves clean, inside and out.
To roll the grave-stone off their souls, from the cave of their bellies,
To prepare to be men.

Or else prepare for the other things.

VI

WHAT QUETZALCOATL SAW
IN MEXICO

Who are these strange faces in Mexico?
Palefaces, yellowfaces, blackfaces? These are no Mexicans!
Where do they come from, and why?

Lord of the Two Ways, these are the foreigners.
They come out of nowhere.
Sometimes they come to tell us things,
Mostly they are the greedy ones.

What then do they want?

They want gold, they want silver from the mountains,
And oil, much oil from the coast.
They take sugar from the tall tubes of the cane,
Wheat from the high lands, and maize;
Coffee from the bushes in the hot lands, even the juicy rubber.
They put up tall chimneys that smoke,
And in the biggest houses they keep their machines, that talk
And work iron elbows up and down,
And hold myriad threads from their claws!
Wonderful are the machines of the greedy ones!

And you, Mexicans and peons, what do you do?

We work with their machines, we work in their fields,
They give us pesos made of Mexican silver.
They are the clever ones.

Do you love them then?

We love them not, and never.
Their faces are ugly, yet they make wonderful things.
And their wills are like their machines of iron.
What can we do?

I see dark things rushing across the country.

Yea, Lord! Even trains and camions and automobiles.

Trains and camions, automobiles and aeroplanes.
How nice! says the peon, to go rushing in a train!
How nice, to get in the camion, and for twenty centavos, to be gone!
How nice, in the great cities, where all things rush, and huge lights
    flare bright, to wander and do nothing!
How nice to sit in the cine, where the picture of all the world
    dances before the eyes!
How nice if we could take all these things away from the foreigners,
    and possess them!
Take back our lands and silver and oil, take the trains and the
    factories and the automobiles
And play with them all the time!
How nice!

Oh, fools! Mexicans and peons!
Who are you, to be masters of machines which you cannot make?
Which you can only break!
Those that can make are masters of these machines.
Not you, poor boobs.

How have these palefaces, yellowfaces crossed the waters of the
    world?
Oh, fools! Mexicans and peons, with muddy hearts!

Did they do it by squatting on their hams?
You do nothing but squat on your hams, and stare with vacant eyes,
    and drink fire-waters, and quarrel and stab.
And then run like surly dogs at the bidding of paleface masters.

Oh, dogs and fools, Mexicans and peons!
Watery-hearted, with wishy-washy knees.
Sulky in spirit, and inert.
What are you good for, but to be slaves, and rot away?

You are not worth a god!
Lo! the universe tangles its great dragons,
The dragons in the cosmos are stirring with anger again.

The dragon of the disappointed dead, that sleeps in the snow-white
    north
Is lashing his tail in his sleep; the winds howl, the cold rocks round.
The spirits of the cold dead whistle in the ears of the world.
Prepare for doom.

For I tell you, there are no dead dead, not even your dead.
There are dead that sleep in the waves of the Morning Star, with
    freshening limbs.
There are dead that weep in bitter rains.
There are dead that cluster in the frozen north, shuddering and
    chattering among the ice
And howling with hate.
There are dead that creep through the burning bowels of the earth,
Stirring the fires to acid of bitterness.
There are dead that sit under the trees, watching with ash-grey eyes
    for their victims.
There are dead that attack the sun like swarms of black flies, to suck
    his life.
There are dead that stand upon you, when you go in to your women,
And they dart to her womb, they fight for the chance to be born,
    they struggle at the gate you have opened,
They gnash when it closes, and hate the one that got in, to be born
    again,

Child of the living dead, the dead that live and are not refreshed.
I tell you, sorrow upon you; you shall all die.
And being dead, you shall not be refreshed.
There are no dead dead.
Being dead, you shall rove like dogs with broken haunches
Seeking the offal and garbage of life, in the invisible lanes of the air.

The dead that have mastered fire live on, salamanders, in fire.
The dead of the water-lords rock and glimmer in the seas.
The dead of the steel machines go up in motion, *away*!
The dead of electric masters are electricity itself.

But the dead of those who have mastered nothing, nothing at all,
Crawl like masterless dogs in the back streets of the air,
Creeping for the garbage of life, and biting with venomous mouths.

Those that have mastered the forces of the world, die into the forces,
    they have homes in death.
But you! what have you mastered, among the dragon hosts of the
    cosmos?
There are dragons of sun and ice, dragons of the moon and the earth,
    dragons of salty waters, dragons of thunder;
There is the spangled dragon of the stars at large.
And far at the centre, with one unblinking eye, the dragon of the
    Morning Star.

Conquer! says the Morning Star. Pass the dragons, and pass on to me.
For I am sweet, I am the last and the best, the pool of new life.
But lo! you inert ones, I will set the dragons upon you.
They shall crunch your bones.
And even then they shall spit you out, as broken-haunched dogs,
You shall have nowhere to die into.

Lo! in the back streets of the air, dead ones are crawling like curs!
Lo! I release the dragons! The great white one of the north,
Him of the disappointed dead, he is lashing and turning round.
He is breathing cold corruption upon you, you shall bleed in your
    chests.

I am going to speak to the dragon of the inner fires,
He who housels the dead of the guns,
To withdraw his warmth from your feet, so your feet turn cold with
    death.

I am about to tell the dragon of the waters to turn round on you
And spue out corrosion into your streams, on your rains.

And I wait for the final day, when the dragon of thunder, waking
    under the spider-web nets
Which you've thrown upon him, shall suddenly shake with rage,
And dart his electric needles into your bones, and curdle your blood
    like milk with electric venom.

Wait! Only wait! Little by little it all shall come upon you.

VII

[SONG TO THE TUNE OF
LA CUCARACHA]

Don Ramón don't drink, don't smoke.
Doña Carlota wished he would.
He's going to wear the sky-blue cloak
That he's stolen from the Mother of God.

VIII

JESUS' FAREWELL

Farewell, Farewell, *Despedida!*
The last of my days is gone.
Tomorrow Jesus and Holy Mary
Will be bone.

797

It is a long, long way
From Mexico to the Pool of Heaven.
Look back the last time, Mary Mother.
Let us call the eleven.

James, and John, and Mark,
Felipe and San Cristobal,
All my saints, and Anna, Teresa,
Guadalupe whose face is oval.

Come then, now, it is finished for all of us.
Let us all be gone.
Follow me now up the ladders of sparks,
Every one.

Joaquin, Francis, and Anthony
And many-named Maria,
Purisima, Refugio, and Soledad
Follow here.

Ho! all my saints and my Virgins
Troop out of your shrines,
After your master, the Crucified;
Bring all your signs.

Run up the flames, and with feet on the sparks
Troop into the sky.
Once more following the Master,
Back again now, on high.

Farewell, let all be forgotten
In Mexico.

To the pool of peace and forgetting in heaven
We go.

       *   *   *

Jesus, the Son of God, bids you farewell.
Mary, the Mother of God, bids you farewell.
For the last time they bless you, as they leave you.
Answer *Adiós!*
Say *Adiós!* my children.

IX

[THE SONG OF DON RAMON]

What is God, we shall never know!
But the Sons of God come and go.
They come from beyond the Morning Star;
And thither they return from the land of men.

Mary and Jesus have left you and gone to the place of renewal.
And Quetzalcoatl has come. He is here.
He is your lord.

Those that follow me, must cross the mountains of the sky,
And shall pass the houses of the stars by night.
They shall find me only in the Morning Star.

But those that will not follow, must not peep.
Peeping, they will lose their sight, and lingering, they will fall very
    lame.

X

[SON OF THE MORNING STAR]

I am the Son of the Morning Star, and child of the deeps.
No man knows my Father, and I know Him not.
My Father is deep within the deeps, whence He sent me forth.
He sends the eagle of silence down on wide wings
To lean over my head and my neck and my breast
And fill them strong with strength of wings.
He sends the serpent of power up my feet and my loins
So that strength wells up in me like water in hot springs.
But midmost shines as the Morning Star midmost shines
Between night and day, my Soul-star in one,
Which is my Father whom I know not.
I tell you, the day should not turn into glory,
And the night should not turn deep,
Save for the morning and evening stars, upon which they turn.

Night turns upon me, and Day, who am the star between.
Between your breast and belly is a star.
If it be not there
You are empty gourd-shells filled with dust and wind.
When you walk, the star walks with you, between your breast and
    your belly.
When you sleep, it softly shines.
When you speak true and true, it is bright on your lips and your
    teeth.
When you lift your hands in courage and bravery, its glow is clear in
    your palms.
When you turn to your wives as brave men turn to their women
The Morning Star and the Evening Star shine together.
For man is the Morning Star.
And woman is the Star of Evening.
I tell you. you are not men alone.
The star of the beyond is within you.
But have you seen a dead man, how his star has gone out of him?
So the star will go out of you, even as a woman will leave a man if
    his warmth never warms her.
Should you say: *I have no star; I am no star.*
So it will leave you, and you will hang like a gourd on the vine of life
With nothing but rind:
Waiting for the rats of the dark to come and gnaw your inside.
Do you hear the rats of the darkness gnawing at your inside?
Till you are as empty as rat-gnawed pomegranates hanging hollow
    on the Tree of Life?
If the star shone, they dare not, they could not.
If you were men with the Morning Star.
If the star shone within you
No rat of the dark dared gnaw you.
But I am Quetzalcoatl, of the Morning Star.
I am the living Quetzalcoatl.
And you are men who should be men of the Morning Star.
See you be not rat-gnawed gourds.
I am Quetzalcoatl of the eagle and the snake.
The earth and air.
Of the Morning Star.
I am Lord of the Two Ways—

XI

[THE LIVING QUETZALCOATL]

I am the Living Quetzalcoatl.
Naked I come from out of the deep
From the place which I call my Father,
Naked have I travelled the long way round
From heaven, past the sleeping sons of God.

Out of the depths of the sky, I came like an eagle.
Out of the bowels of the earth like a snake.

All things that lift in the lift of living between earth and sky, know
    me.

But I am the inward star invisible.
And the star is the lamp in the hand of the Unknown Mover.
Beyond me is a Lord who is terrible, and wonderful, and dark to
    me forever.
Yet I have lain in his loins, ere he begot me in Mother space.

Now I am alone on earth, and this is mine.
The roots are mine, down the dark, moist path of the snake.
And the branches are mine, in the paths of the sky and the bird,
But the spark of me that is me is more than mine own.

And the feet of men, and the hands of the women know me.
And knees and thighs and loins, and the bowels of strength and seed
    are lit with me.
The snake of my left-hand out of the darkness is kissing your feet
    with his mouth of caressive fire,
And putting his strength in your heels and ankles, his flame in your
    knees and your legs and your loins, his circle of rest in your
    belly.
For I am Quetzalcoatl, the feathered snake.
And I am not with you till my serpent has coiled his circle of rest in
    your belly.

And I, Quetzalcoatl, the eagle of the air, am brushing your faces
    with vision.
I am fanning your breasts with my breath.
And building my nest of peace in your bones.
I am Quetzalcoatl, of the Two Ways.

XII

[WELCOME TO QUETZALCOATL]

We are not wasted. We are not left out.
Quetzalcoatl has come!
There is nothing more to ask for.
Quetzalcoatl has come!

He threw the Fish in the boat.
The cock rose, and crew over the waters.
The naked one climbed in.
Quetzalcoatl has come!

Quetzalcoatl loves the shade of trees.
Give him trees! Call back the trees!
We are like trees, tall and rustling.
Quetzalcoatl is among the trees.

Do not tell me my face is shining.
Quetzalcoatl has come!
Over my head his noiseless eagle
Fans a flame.

Tie my spotted shoes for dancing.
The snake has kissed my heel.
Like a volcano my hips are moving
With fire, and my throat is full.

Blue daylight sinks in my hair.
The star comes out between the two
Wonders, shines out of everywhere,
Saying without speech: Look you!

Ah, Quetzalcoatl!
Put sleep as black as beauty in the secret of my belly.
Put star-oil over me.
Call me a man.

XIII

[THE MID-DAY VERSE]

The sun has climbed the hill, the day is on the downward slope.
Between the morning and the afternoon, stand I here with my soul,
    and lift it up.
My soul is heavy with sunshine, and steeped with strength.
The sunbeams have filled me like a honeycomb,
It is the moment of fulness,
And the top of the morning.

XIV

[THE DAWN VERSE]

The dark is dividing, the sun is coming past the wall.
Day is at hand.
Lift your hand, say Farewell! say Welcome!
Then be silent.
Let the darkness leave you, let the light come into you,
Man in the twilight.

XV

[THE SUNSET VERSE]

Leave off! Leave off! Leave off!
Lift your hand, say Farewell! say Welcome!
Man in the twilight.
The sun is in the outer porch, cry to him: Thanks! Oh, Thanks!
Then be silent.
You belong to the night.

XVI

[METAL FOR RESISTANCE]

Metal for resistance.
Drums for the beating heart.
The heart ceases not.

XVII

[FIRST SONG OF HUITZILOPOCHTLI]

I am Huitzilopochtli,
The Red Huitzilopochtli,
The blood-red.

I am Huitzilopochtli,
Yellow of the sun,
Sun in the blood.

I am Huitzilopochtli,
White of the bone,
Bone in the blood.

I am Huitzilopochtli,
With a blade of grass between my teeth.

I am Huitzilopochtli, sitting in the dark.
With my redness staining the body of the dark.

I watch by the fire.
I wait behind men.

In the stillness of my night
The cactus sharpens his thorn.
The grass feels with his roots for the other sun.

Deeper than the roots of the mango tree
Down in the centre of the earth
Is the yellow, serpent-yellow shining of my sun.

Oh, beware of him!
Oh, beware of me!
Who runs athwart my serpent-flame
Gets bitten and must die.

I am the sleeping and waking
Of the anger of the manhood of men.
I am the leaping and quaking
Of fire bent back again.

XVIII

[SECOND SONG OF HUITZILOPOCHTLI]

He is Huitzilopochtli,
The Red Huitzilopochtli,
The blood-red.

He is Huitzilopochtli,
Yellow of the sun,
Sun in the blood.

He is Huitzilopochtli,
White of the bone,
Bone in the blood.

He is Huitzilopochtli,
With a blade of green grass between his teeth.

He is Huitzilopochtli, sitting in the dark,
With his redness staining the body of the night.

He is watching by the fire.
Waiting behind men.

In the stillness of his night
Cactuses sharpen their thorns.
Grass feels downwards with his roots.

Deeper than the roots of the mango tree
Down in the centre of the earth
Shines the yellow, serpent-yellow shining of the sun.

Oh, men, take care, take care!
Take care of him and it.
Nor run aslant his rays.·
Who is bitten, dies.

He is Huitzilopochtli, sleeping or waking
Serpent in the bellies of men.
Huitzilopochtli, leaping and quaking
Fire of the passion of men.

XIX

[THIRD SONG OF HUITZILOPOCHTLI]

Man that is man is more than a man.
No man is man till he is more than a man.
Till the power is in him
Which is not his own.

The power is in me from behind the sun,
And from middle earth.
I am Huitzilopochtli.
I am dark as the sunless under-earth,
And yellow as the fire that consumes,
And white as bone,
And red as blood.

But I touched the hand of Quetzalcoatl.
And between our fingers rose a blade of green grass.
I touched the hand of Quetzalcoatl.
Lo! I am lord of the watches of the night
And the dream of the night rises from me like a red feather.

I am the watcher, and master of the dream.
In the dream of the night I see the grey dogs prowling.
Prowling to devour the dream.

In the night the soul of a coward creeps out of him
Like a grey dog whose mouth is foul with rabies,
Creeping among the sleeping and the dreaming, who are lapped in
    my dark,
And in whom the dream sits up like a rabbit, lifting long ears tipped
    with night,
On the dream-slopes browsing like a deer in the dusk.

In the night I see the grey dogs creeping, out of the sleeping men
Who are cowards, who are liars, who are traitors, who have no
    dreams
That prick their ears like a rabbit, or browse in the dark like deer,
But whose dreams are dogs, grey dogs with yellow mouths.

From the liars, from the thieves, from the false and treacherous and
    mean
I see the grey dogs creeping out, where my deer are browsing in the
    dark.
Then I take my knife, and throw it upon the grey dog.
And lo! it sticks between the ribs of a man!
The house of the grey dog!

Beware! Beware!
Of the men and the women who walk among you.
You know not how many are houses of grey dogs.
Men that seem harmless, women with fair words,
Maybe they kennel the grey dog.

XX

THE SONG OF THE GREY DOG

When you sleep and know it not
The grey dog creeps among you.
In your sleep, you twist, your soul hurts you.
The grey dog is chewing your entrails.

Then call on Huitzilopochtli:
The grey dog caught me at the cross-roads
As I went down the road of sleep
And crossed the road of the uneasy.

The grey dog leapt at my entrails.
Huitzilopochtli, call him off.
Lo! the Great One answers. *Track him down!*
Kill him in his unclean house.

Down the road of the uneasy
You track the grey dog home
To his house in the heart of a traitor,
A thief, a murderer of dreams.

And you kill him there with one stroke,
Crying: *Huitzilopochtli, is this well done?*
That your sleep be not as a cemetery
Where dogs creep unclean.

XXI

[THE LORDS OF LIFE
ARE THE MASTERS OF DEATH]

The Lords of Life are the Masters of Death.
Blue is the breath of Quetzalcoatl.
Red is Huitzilopochtli's blood.
But the grey dog belongs to the ash of the world.
The Lords of Life are the Masters of Death.
Dead are the grey dogs.
Living are the Lords of Life.
Blue is the deep sky and the deep water.
Red is the blood and the fire.
Yellow is the flame.
The bone is white and alive.

The hair of night is dark over our faces.
But the grey dogs are among the ashes.
The Lords of Life are the Masters of Death.

XXII

[HUITZILOPOCHTLI GIVES THE BLACK
BLADE OF DEATH]

Huitzilopochtli gives the black blade of death.
Take it bravely.
Take death bravely.
Go bravely across the border, admitting your mistake.

Determine to go on and on, till you enter the Morning Star.
Quetzalcoatl will show you the way.
Malintzi of the green dress will open the door.
In the fountain you will lie down.
If you reach the fountain, and lie down
And the fountain covers your face, forever,
You will have departed forever from your mistake.

And the man that is more than a man in you
Will wake at last from the clean forgetting
And stand up, and look about him,
Ready again for the business of being a man.

But Huitzilopochtli touched the hand of Quetzalcoatl
And one green leaf sprang among the black.
The green leaf of Malintzi
Who pardons once, and no more.

XXIII

HUITZILOPOCHTLI'S WATCH

Red Huitzilopochtli
Keeps day and night apart.

Huitzilopochtli the golden
Guards life from death, and death from life.

No grey-dogs, cowards, pass him.
No spotted traitors crawl by,
False fair ones cannot slip through
Past him, from the one to the other.

Brave men have peace at nightfall,
True men look up at the dawn,
Men in their manhood walk out
Into blue day, past Huitzilopochtli.

Red Huitzilopochtli
Is the purifier

Black Huitzilopochtli
Is doom.

Huitzilopochtli golden
Is the liberating fire.

White Huitzilopochtli
Is washed bone.

Green Huitzilopochtli
Is Malintzi's blade of grass.

XXIV

[SONG OF THE DEAD]

The dead are on their journey, the way is dark.
There is only the Morning Star.
Beyond the white of whiteness,
Beyond the blackness of black.
Beyond spoken day,
Beyond the unspoken passion of night,
The light which is fed from two vessels

From the black oil and the white
Shines at the gate.

A gate to the innermost place
Where the Breath and the Fountains commingle,
Where the dead are living, and the living are dead.
The deeps that life cannot fathom,
The Source and the End, of which we know
Only that it is, and its life is our life and our death.

All men cover their eyes
Before the unseen.
All men be lost in silence,
Within the noiseless.

XXV

[LIKE THE GREEN CANDLES OF MALINTZI]

Like the green candles of Malintzi
Like a tree in new leaf.
The rain of blood is fallen, is gone into the earth.

The dead have gone the long journey
Beyond the star.
Huitzilopochtli has thrown his black mantle
To those who would sleep.
When the blue wind of Quetzalcoatl
Waves softly,
When the water of Malintzi falls
Making a greenness:

Count the red grains of the Huitzilopochtli
Fire in your hearts, Oh men.
And blow the ash away.

For the living live,
And the dead die.
But the fingers of all touch the fingers of all
In the Morning Star.

XXVI

[MY WAY IS NOT THY WAY]

My way is not thy way, and thine is not mine.
But come, before we part
Let us separately go to the Morning Star,
And meet there.

I do not point you to my road, nor yet
Call: "Oh come!"
But the Star is the same for both of us,
Winsome.

The good ghost of me goes down the distance
To the Holy Ghost.
Oh you, in the tent of the cloven flame
Meet me, you I like most.

Each man his own way forever, but towards
The hoverer between;
Who opens his flame like a tent-flap,
As we slip in unseen.

A man cannot tread like a woman,
Nor a woman step out like a man.
The ghost of each through the leaves of shadow
Moves as it can.

But the Morning Star and the Evening Star
Pitch tents of flame
Where we foregather like gypsies, none knowing
How the other came.

I ask for nothing except to slip
In the tent of the Holy Ghost
And be there in the house of the cloven flame,
Guest of the Host.

Be with me there, my woman
Be bodily there.
Then let the flame wrap round us
Like a snare.

Be there along with me, oh men!
Reach across the hearth,
And laugh with me while the woman rests
For all we are worth.

———————————————

MEDITERRANEAN IN JANUARY

The Blue anemone with a dark core
That has flowered before
Shows one bud more!

Far-off, far-off, in the hyacinth ages
It flowered, before men took to flowering for wages;
Flowers now, as we're crossing the dreary stages.

Today, when the sun is computed old
And Europe's tail-spin rolls still unrolled;
And bank-tellers tell the one tale that is told;
And bank-notes are poetry purer than gold;
When the end of the world, we are told, is scrolled;
And a man, when he isn't bought, feels sold:

Out of the winter's silky fur
Buds a blue anemone, still bluer.

Nations beside the sea are old,
Folk-flowers have faded, men have grown cold.
Nothing remains now but mould unto mould—
Ichabod! Ichabod! lo and behold!

Oh age! that is hoar as anemone buds!
Oh chew, old cows, at your ancient cuds!
Chew also, young heifers, your juicier cuds!

The wisdom of ages droops! It is folly
To laugh when we're feeling melancholy!
Tears wrinkle our faces, like rain in the holly.
The wisdom of ages droops! Ain't it jolly!

The sea has its bud-lips smilingly curled,
What! Yet another bad end of the world!
Why, 'twas only yesterday every man twirled
His moustache with an elbow lifted, and hurled
Braggadoccios around the blue rims of the world!

Now the world is ending in dust and in sorrow.
The world is ending; let's hurry to borrow
Black for the funeral! Wow! waly! and worrow!

The age is a joke! and surely, tomorrow
We'll see the joke, and how funny is sorrow!

Yesterday, yes! is a tale that is told.
Tomorrow comes stealthily out of the mould
Like a bud from winter disguised in grey,
Hidden blue with the blueness of one more day.

When I see this sea looking shoddy and dead,
And this sun cease shining overhead,
And no more anemones rise from the dead,
And never another *per Bacco!* is said:
I shall come to New York, and live on Manhattan,
And deep in Central Park I'll fatten
My griefs, and on New York newspapers batten.

Till then, I like better this sea, I must say,
Which is blue with the blueness of one more day.
The which, since it coincides with my day
And will shine if I stay or I go away
Persuades me to stay, since stay I may. . . .

BEYOND THE ROCKIES

There are people there, beyond the Rockies
As there are people here, on this side.

But the people there, beyond the Rockies
Seem always to be asking, asking something.

The new moon sets at sundown,
And there, beyond the sunset, quivers.

An Indian, walking wrapt in his winding sheet
Answers the question as he puts it, in his stride.

Mexicans, like people who have died
Ask, in the space of their eyes:
What have we lost?

What have we lost, in the west?
We who have gone west?
There is no answer.

In the land of the lost
Nothing but to make lost music.

On the rim of the desert
Round the lost man's camp-fire
Watch the new moon
Curved, cut the last threads.

It is finished: the rest is afterwards
With grey on the floor of the desert,
And more space than in life.

THE OLD ORCHARD

Now shut your eyes
all you who hate apples!
Last red light dapples
wild skies.

Hie! Hie! fruit topples
down, apples lie
rolling below
the nightfall. I

want apples
from the tree
of life, and to know
more.

Revive me with apples
to forget;
and make me know
afresh.

Pallid, poor thing! yet I
revive with apples.
Shake the bough
harder yet!

Long ago, once before
we tasted
and wasted;
now let's eat up the core.

Let us know in full!
Pull
down apples!
—Hark! how they thresh

the floor!
Eat, woman, eat more
the crisp flesh!
Yes! be rash!

Eat it all! Oh
the whole apple!
Last time we were both
too nesh.

Eat, and lie down!
Between your thighs
disclose
the soft gulf. Be wise!

Lift up your heads
O ye gates! Even lift them up
ye everlasting doors!
That the king of glory may come in.

Who is this king of glory?
Lift up your heads O ye gates!
He treads
without feet the red floors.

Lie down beneath the tree!
If God looks, let him see
we are even as he
busy.

He is wise, is he?
At last, so are we.
Let us know, you and me,
one another.

Let us in full know
one another;
and be known just so!
For the rest, don't bother!

RAINBOW

One thing that is bow-legged
and can't put its feet together
is the rainbow.

Even if the Lord God shouted
—Attention!—
it couldn't put its feet together.

Yet it's got two feet
as you know,
and two pots of gold
we are told.

What I see
when I look at the rainbow
is one foot in the lap of a woman
and one in the loins of a man.

The feet of the arch
that the Lord God rested the worlds on.

And wide, wide apart,
with nothing but desire between them.

The two feet of the rainbow
want to put themselves together.
But they can't, or there'd be the vicious circle.

So they leap up like a fountain.
He leaps up, she leaps up,
like rockets!
and they curve over.

From the heart a red ray,
from the brow a gold,
from the hips a violet
leaps.

Dark blue the whole desire leaps
brindled with rays
all of the colours
that leap

and lean over
in the arch
of the rainbow.

They will always do it.
The Lord God said so.

If there are pots of gold
they are pails
of the honey of experience
hanging from the shoulders of the rainbow.

But the one thing that is bow-legged
and can't put its feet together
is the rainbow.

Because one foot is the heart of a man
and the other is the heart of a woman.
And these two, as you know,
never meet.

Save they leap
high—
Oh hearts, leap high!
—they touch in mid-heaven like an acrobat
and make a rainbow.

ADDITIONAL PANSIES

HYMN TO NOTHINGNESS

The angels have somewhere fought and lost,
    Fought and lost.
All over the sky their wings are tossed
And tattered and red with the life that has bled
    Finally out of the host.

The angels have everywhere fought and lost,
    Fought and lost.
Their debris is flotsam, and flung on the coast
Of darkening night, and the quivering light
    Departs without counting the cost.

Never an angel will soar again
    In the world without end, amen!
Michael and Gabriel, all of them, slain,
And the glowing throne of the Absolute One
    Overset in disdain.

There is no Great God in the innermost,
    There is even no innermost.
The angels are gone, all the heavenly host
Is swept from out of the endless sky,
The vastness is empty, except that there ply
Worlds without end, without reason why
    In spaces wide with mistrust.

The vast great reaches between the suns
    Are all unpeopled of God.
Uninhabited space now runs
In curls and flaps between worlds that plod
Patiently round and round in ellipses
Avoiding each other, yet incurring eclipses
    And never yet known to nod.

There is now no why, there is now no wherefore,
You can't say: I am I, and therefore—
    Therefore nothing, and therefore nought.
The battle that the angels fought
Is lost entirely, you cannot fool us.
    It was won by the one Almighty Nullus.

Nullus, nullus, nothing and nought
Nichts and *niente, rien* and *nada*
Hail and be damned to thee, empty, most emptily,
Nothing to sell in thee, nought to be bought,
Gulping up science's smart Armada,
Sipping to nothingness even thought,
Soul and body, bone and blood
Mind and spirit, bad and good
Thou sips them up, and 'tis all the same,
Nullus, nothingness—what's in a name!
Hail and be damned to thee, winning the game!

AUGUST HOLIDAYS

Along the lake, like seals, like seals
That bask and wake, oh high and dry
High and dry
The humans lie
Naked and white, not quite, not quite
Some turning pink, some turning purple dusk
As they drink, through their husk
The light that reels
Like bees above them and feels for their weals
And soothes them quite, quite: or not quite?

As a bee waxes over a wound
The hot sun waxes and heals
These people that lie like seals
Without a sound,

Waxes them over till all is forgotten
The bitter and sweet, raw and the rotten,
Bad yesterdays, unsure tomorrows
—There is nothing between—

Forlorn enjoyments, forlorner sorrow
All that will be, all that has been
—There is nothing between—

Now is nothing!
They lie like seals
Only stark, without clothing.
And then one steals
To the water and is gone,
Calling another one.

Wet and dry, wet and dry
Like seals in sunny summer they hie
From element to element
Now wet, now dry
Without wherefore or why
Back and forth in a blind movement.

They are making the pause
Between the epochs.
The life without laws
The time without clocks
Between the epochs.
When nothing is said
And nothing is done.

And we are not dead
We feel the sun
Yet we are not living
We have not begun
Taking and giving,
We have only finished
And have still not done.

We ask more and more to be diminished
Like seals that hie
From wet to dry
Without reason why.

From element to element
Back and forth, without content
Time without end, amen, amen!
Oh, let us never begin again!
Let us only finish
Finish, finish, diminish, diminish.

Fade, and yet flourish
Pass out, and yet nourish
Our corpus with food
With sun, and with wetness
With sleekness and fatness
While we relinquish
Relax and relinquish
Everything, everything
Bad and the good
All except . . .

BATHING RESORT

Health is everything, health is all—
Money is merely
The wherewithal
To have health:—wealth! health! wealth! health!
The last two things we can still hold dearly

Here they are nearly
All of them healthy, more or less wealthy.
And clearly
They are all healthy, healthy, healthy.

They are gold, they are brown, they are purplish, they
    glisten
Like silk, they are flesh, sheer flesh;
The dark ones are curiously purplish, like fresh
Plums; the blond ones are gold, with less glisten.

They move and they plash in the water
They lie on the shore and heave
Deep panting breaths, like great beasts ready for
    slaughter.

They are so healthy, sufficiently wealthy
And sunburnt and water-washed, full-fed and sleek
Ever again lying prone, lying slack
Stretching their big, full limbs to seek
Sun and inertia, on the belly, on the back.

The upright is temporal, is effort, outreach,
Horizontal eternity, fluid or null.

Crawl out of the water and lie on the beach
Horizontal and meaningless, desirably dull.

Great thighs that lead nowhere
Yet are fleeced with soft hair.
Breasts that wink not
Heads that think not
Bellies that shrink not
In the white air.
Not flowers, nor fruit
Without mystery, mute
Well-grown like potatoes on a lifted root
They all should be underground, sifted with soot.

Health is everything, health is all.

They are all healthy
Sufficiently wealthy
To be always healthy
Full-fed in stall.

As if the butcher were biding his time.

All of them healthy
More or less wealthy
Naked presentable
Like a well-washed vegetable
Their skins all neat
With full-fed meat
Biologically admirable
They'd be good to eat.

But if nobody eats them
Or beats them, or cheats them
Or in hell overheats them
They'll melt miraculously back into slime.

THE YOUNG ARE NOT MEAN IN
MATERIAL THINGS

The good thing about the younger generations—
That is, the men of my age, and I am forty-three
And the younger ones
Is that they are not mean in material things.

They don't begrudge you a drink
Or the butter, or the apples or peaches from the basket,
Or even a little money
As the elder generations are apt to do,
The men older than me.

They don't really care vastly.
They don't even mind doing things for you, in reason.
They aren't afraid of losing something, as the older ones are.
And they aren't out on the make,

Which seems to me a great advance.

And it seems to me, that the young ones, though they grudge
    success
Do it because they dislike success in itself.

And therefore, since the people I meet of the younger
    generation
The younger intelligentsia, so to speak
Are this way
It seems to me that some sort of decent socialism, even
    communism
Lies latent in the souls of the young, a latent desire.

THE YOUNG WANT TO BE JUST

It is odd, again, about the young.
They don't mind being depraved, immoral, or anything of that sort,
But they do mind being unjust, unfair.

Which is very odd, being the exact reverse of their fathers and
    mothers.

It shows, again, how highly developed the social conscience now is,
How highly aware we are of one another, *socially*,
How decent is our desire towards one another, socially.
We want to be fair.
Even in the most immoral sets, there is still this desire to be fair.
Almost an instinct.

Which shows, once more, that our social conscience is developed
    far beyond the present social form.
For our society is based on grab, and devil take the hindmost.
And to the young, this is really immoral and distasteful.
That is the important point: really distasteful.

To grandfathers and grandmothers, it was grab
And devil take the hindmost.
But watch your sexual step, oh dear my dear
Mind the banana-skin!

To us and the young ones
It is very squalid to grab somebody else's share.
We do want to be materially fair.

As for sex, Granny hasn't got any—
Leave us alone.

In a system established on grab
The young ones, in whom the grabbing instinct has died down,
Naturally are nonplussed
And cynical;
Cynical above all things about the grabbing morale
Of grandpa and of grandma, even of Daddy and Mum.

THE GENTLEMAN

When is a man not a man?
When he's a gentleman.

The funny thing about a gentleman
—And by gentleman I mean that ubiquitous Englishman
Who considers himself a gentleman—
—He considers himself such, if you please—
Is that he doesn't seem to have any inside to him.

He has a very nice apple-of-Sodom rind
—Fresh, clean, well-groomed Englishman—
And on the surface shell of him
He has fresh, clean, well-groomed emotions
Opinions, ideas, and so forth
Quite the fresh, clean, manly fellow.

But poke him a little
And you stir up the most amazing mud.
All his emotions, his feelings that are not superficial and
        well-groomed
Are an amazing putrescent slush.

He's like a bonny, rosy sea-crab with healthy claws
Full inside of weird brown slushy crab-meat

Carrion-greedy in its sensations.
But what I would like to know
Is where does it come from, this lovely English voice
Whooing and cooing and fading away with wonderful
    genteel deprecation?
Wherever is it produced?
This manly voice?

It has neither heart nor bowels nor genitals.
Even its brain seems upside down.
But it has front-teeth
And a goo-goo sort of voice-box.

The lovely English voice.

It seems to come out of some hollow rind of a man.

ROSES

Nature responds so beautifully.
Roses are only once-wild roses, that were given an extra chance,
So they bloomed out and filled themselves with coloured fulness
Out of sheer desire to be splendid, and more splendid.

THE YOUNG ARE NOT GREEDY

Say what we like, our civilisation has learnt a great lesson:
It is sick of greed.
It is sick of people out on the make.
They are really low class, people out on the make.

But what can you do, in a system which forces you to go out on the
    make
Or practically starve?
What can you do?

Our fathers' and grandfathers' ideal
Of success, money—
Even while we admit the ghastly importance of money
Is base to us, and distasteful.

And the destiny of mankind depends at last
Not on what men think
But on what they find distasteful, repulsive, or attractive.

MIDDLE-CLASS CHILDREN

Another curious thing about the English middle classes
Is how they hate their children.
Those under fifty, and more still, those under forty
They instinctively hate their own children
Once they've got them.

At the same time, they take the greatest possible care of them
—Nurses, doctors, proper food, hygiene, schools, all that—
The greatest possible *care*—
And they hate them.

They seem to feel the children a ghastly limitation
—But for these children I should be free—
Free what for, nobody knows. But free!
—Awfully sorry, dear, but I can't come because of the children.

The children, of course, know that they are cared for
And disliked.
There is no means of really deceiving a child.

So they accept covered dislike as the normal feeling between people
And superficial attention and care and fulfilment of duty
As normal activity
They may even, one day, discover simple affection as a great
    discovery.

KNOW THYSELF

The great command will never be obsolete
Know Thyself.
New life bubbles in, we become something else,
Something we have not been, and therefore cannot yet know.

We shall go on finding out about ourselves
Forever and ever, and never come to the end.

At the same time, we learn a lot.
We have learned a lot since Jesus, from Jesus and all the rest.
We have learnt not to have slaves, not to want them.

We have learned that another man's liberty is as essential almost as
      our own.
We have learned, I think, not to be greedy
Not to want to pile up possessions
Not to want to bully those weaker than ourselves.

I speak of the younger generations
Of whom I think this is true.

But we are maimed, crippled, contorted and sick
When it comes to our emotional selves.
There we have learned nothing
And we have lost our natural spontaneity—

What we need, indeed
Is a new frame of society
Where the attention will be lifted off material things,
Money, machines, furniture—
And where we can begin to learn our great emotional lessons
Wherein we are now blind ugly boors.
The one eye of our cyclopaean instinct put out
We grope and foam and lash around
And hurt, hurt ourselves and everybody,
Roaring and doing damage.

What we need is a long, long war-less epoch
Where we can learn to fulfil our new knowledge of material fairness
Justice, human decency in material things—

And where, with the slow patience of intuition
We can uncoil the ghastly snake-tangle of our unconscious emotions.
Emotions which would come up like flowers, were they not coiled
    strangling on one another like snakes.
It will take an epoch—two thousand years and more.
Meanwhile we bite ourselves and everyone near us
With snake-bites of tangled, unconscious emotion
That we can never escape, not even in sleep
Nor in analysis.
For the analyst is tangled in an especially tangled bunch, inside him-
    self.

NIGHT

Now that the night is here
A new thing comes to pass, eyes close
And the animals curl down on the dear earth, to sleep.
But the limbs of man long to fold and close upon the living body of
    another human being
In shut-eyed touch.

LOVE

One thing is certain, we've got to take hands off love.
The moment I swear to love a woman all my life, that very moment
    I begin to hate her.
In the same way, if I swore to hate a woman all my life, I should
    instantly feel a pang of compunction
Amounting almost to love.

SO THERE!

It's no good my dear
My dear little girly-wirly

With hair that was bobbed so early—
You won't get away with it.

Just look at your mamma
And see yourself as in a glass, darkly.
What about girly-wirly at her age?

At her age? Why I'll be earning a jolly good screw!—
—A jolly good screw, when the dear little girly-wirly's over fifty
And even more wirly-burly—?—
Oh well, I suppose I shall have some knife-edged Terence or other in
     the background
To be husbandly, and give perpendicular to the landscape.

To the effulgent landscape of our immortal girly-wirly?
Darling, I see your iron-grey chevelure
Disastrously reminiscent of hammers and files and door-knobs
Or still more disastrously reminiscent of that-will-be-glory for me
In Japanese henna or whatever it is, cheap at the price.
Oh my dear little girly-wirly
In your fifties, with a short frock [showing] your fore and aft
—Madame est si bien cambrée—
Cambrée, my word, cambrée!
Dear little girly-wirly
Don't let me last beyond your thirties—
     at any price.
No my darling child
You look like the toppingest topping fifth-form Eton boy [turning]
With your tailored cut-away coat
And your shred of a skirt
And your face, your most marvellously Eton-Adonis face.

But my dearest dearest laddie-lass
You won't get away with it.

At fifty you're not going to be the Apollo Belvedere, don't imagine it,
Nor yet the gay Lord Ribblesdale,
You won't even be Lloyd George.

You've a delicious tendency to embonpoint—
And do look at your mamma,
Full fore-and-aft in good grey crêpe de chine.
Showing her shins.

My dear, you won't get away with it.
If I were you, as I passed the forties
I'd hang my hams with puckered petticoats swaying
Easy, easy and easy down to my ankles
Like the fullness of ocean round my faraglioni.

And I'd gather my hair
Back in a Grecian knot, or a jug handle, or a chignon
Anything, rather than that certain back of a neck
Shorn like the shorn lamb to every icy gaze.

Didon dina dit-on du dos d'un dodu dindon.
Probably, as she grew older, she ate her rivals.

MORALITY

Man alone is immoral
Neither beasts nor flowers are.

Because man, poor beast, can look at himself
And know himself in the glass.

He doesn't bark at himself, as a dog does
When he looks at himself in the glass.
He takes himself seriously.

It would be so much nicer if he just barked at himself
Or fluffed up rather angry, as a cat does,
Then turned away and forgot.

IMMORALITY

The real immorality, as far as I can see it
Lies in forcing yourself or somebody else
Against all your deeper instincts and your intuition.

CENSORS

The trouble about those that set up to be moral judges
Is that they are invariably immoral persons.
They are either immorally good, the word * * * * does not and
    shall not exist for them—
Or else they are immorally nasty, and the word * * * * looms
    lusciously lurid to them—
Whereas to the ordinary moral human being, the word * * * *
    exists and means just what it means,
Like any other word of four letters.

After all, it is immoral for a word to mean less than it means
Or to mean more than it means.
In all honesty, a word is neither a gap in the consciousness
Nor a dose of capsicum essence, giving an orgasm.

LIFE AND THE HUMAN CONSCIOUSNESS

I love life, I love life so dearly, I could almost die
Of chagrin at being a man.

When I see what a mess men have made of the world:
When I see what messes men have made of themselves:
When I see the messed-up chemicalised women:

I wish I had fins and gills
Or a gizzard like a turkey.
Anything that expressed life.
Instead of this mess, which expresses the impudent human
    consciousness
In all its idiocy.

I think idiots tell dull, stupid, disgusting tales
And repeat themselves like the flushing of a W.C.

THE LATENT DESIRE

The latent desire in all decent men today
Is for some more natural, more decent social arrangement
Wherein a man can live his life without being a slave to "earning
    his living" and "getting on".

But, of course, this means smashing the present system of grab and
    devil take the hindmost.

FOR ALL THAT

For all that, life will only be good again when there is a generous,
    determined effort among men
To alter the present frame of civilisation
To abolish the tyranny of money.

LOVE AS AN ESCAPE

It is time men took their thoughts off women
And love and sex and all that.
Because they only try to make women and love and sex
An escape from their horror of imprisonment in our civilisation.

And since women are inside the prison just as much as men,
The men in the end only hate them because the escape was no escape.

The thing for men to do is to start to pull down money
Pull it down, and prepare for a new fresh house of life.
Then they'd be able to love. Despair can't love, it can only violate.

WHAT'S TO BE DONE?

The only thing for a man to do now, or a woman,
Is to learn to contain himself.

Man is kept sane, not by his mind, which by nature is unstable
But by the heavy drift of his unperverted instincts
And his intuition.

This is the massive solid fly-wheel which saves man from running
    insane.

At the moment, we tend to run insane, the mind having broken the
    deep instincts
And dislocated the intuitive Conscience.

So the only thing to do, is to keep still, to hold still at any price,
To learn to contain ourselves.
So that in the long pause the instincts can reassert themselves
And our intuition can come to life and give us direction.
For at present, in the whirring insanity of the mental consciousness
We violate ourselves every moment, and violate everybody else
In a cog-wheel clatter of violation.

RALLYING-POINT

If we rally at all, today, instead of keeping
    stark asunder,
let us rally for our own sanity
and even our collective sanity.
It is so shameful to be insane
and so hideously dangerous to be at the mercy
    of collective insanity.

Let us contain ourselves,
and rally together
to keep a sane core to life.

TODAY

Today, life is a choice of insanities.
Success, failure, love, chastity, debauchery, money or soviets
It is a string of insanities.
All insane.

Why not stay out, and learn to contain oneself?

THE ELEMENTS

We don't know how lovely the elements are.
Why trouble about people?
The sun is so lovely.
If a man looked at me for one moment as the sun does
I could accept men.
If twilight came in the eyes of women
As it comes over the milk-blue sea, hinting at gold and darkness,
Oh lovely women!

GODS

There will always be a father of all things, in some shape, in our
    minds.
The vivifier exists, and therefore we know it.
Sum, ergo cogito.

But the father of all things is he who makes us eager.
He-who-makes-me-eager, who is he, oh, who is he?

He is not a pale man filled with love and compassion and pain:
love nor compassion nor pity nor dearness nor pain make me feel
    eager at all.

Nor is he a strong man ruling the earth.
Ruling the earth rouses no eagerness in me at all.
Nor a wise man knowing all things:
I only want to know some things, to know all things would be
    ridiculous.
Nor is he a woman with a bosom of sorrow and consolation.
I have no desire in the least to be sorrowed over or consoled.
Nor even a lovely woman foamy to sting me like brine
with sharp desire: I am not eager for sharp desire any more.

The vivifier exists, but for me is neither man-like nor woman-like
nor even like an animal, bull, ram, or lion, or lamb.
Yet when I think of the wild swan, or the ripple-marked black-
    headed goose
far off upon the misty waters of the depths of space
silently swimming and sleeping, and pressing the flood
with webbed fecundity, plunging the seed of life in the wet wilder-
    ness
and honking with a horn-like annunciation of life from the marshes
    of chaos
something thrills in me, and I know
the next day is the day of the goose, the wild swan's day.

LITTLE-BOY BRILLIANT

Another type that England has produced
to its sorrow
Is the little-boy brilliant.

Its mother did something to it at about the age of twelve
so it never moved on any more, except mentally, and in mere
    stature.

It has grown up often a big and often "interesting-looking" man
and "quite clever"—brilliant is the modern word.
If you hear a man called brilliant, you may be pretty sure he is
        The little-boy of thirty or forty or fifty or sixty.

His mind developed at the expense of his male self
hypertrophy of the mind, atrophy of the senses.
A keen far-reaching curious mind, cynical with little-boy cynicism
and destructive—in short brilliant.

And women fall for these little-boy minds, they feel quite humble
    before them.
The modern young woman thinks it wonderful to be so brilliant and
    destructive
She bows quite humble: such a subtle destroying mind must surely be
    great!

So she marries one of these little-boy brilliants
and finds that the subtle destructive cynicism is only a small-boy's
    compensation
for his own deficiency, most mawkish in its inverted sentimentalism
and when she has most unsatisfactorily shared his little-boy bed for
    a year or two
and born him a son or so, who at the age of seven is so infinitely the
    better man of the two,
why, the modern young wife of the little-boy brilliant begins to feel
    cynical even about cynicism
and wonders if a parrot hasn't more to it.

I HEARD HER SAY

I heard her say to her brilliant young husband
in a boat on a rough sea, when we were all nearly sea-sick:
Darling, you look so like baby!
You look so like baby, it wrings my heart!
And the brilliant young husband made a little move, pouting rather
    peevish and seasick
and nesting his chin in his hand.

Then she turned to the other man—there was usually another man—
saying: You know, I always have to say that Archie looks like baby.
I can never even *think* that it's baby who looks like Archie:
it's so much the other way round.

Baby was her little boy of seven.
And true enough, he was infinitely the more manly fellow.
Yet the husband was most brilliant and famous.

And we still have to see what baby will be like, at thirty.
Seven is still a safe-ish age.

WHAT'S WRONG

Perhaps what's wrong is simply lack of vitality.
The frame of things has grown so heavy, it's just too heavy for men
    altogether.
So, the poor male has succumbed under it.
And a boy, as he reaches the age of fourteen, when he should become
    manly and tackle the outside world,
Caves inward, knowing it is useless.
The wild gods send vitality, they put the lightning into the hand
Of those that can use it, smite with it.

MONEY

Money is the vast stinking beast
and men are the lice that creep on it
and live from its secondary sweat.

All people, like lice
creep on the vast money-beast
and feed on it.

SEX WON'T WORK

Sex won't work in captivity.
Man is one of those beasts that will breed in a cage.
He can copulate and beget children
but without desire, without joy, without release.

The cage, which does not kill the mechanism of sex
kills entirely the true experience of sex.
Which is why the young, who copulate so freely,
have no experience of sex at all, it is almost nothing to them.
They are in the cage.

DEEPER THAN LOVE

There is love, and it is a deep thing
but there are deeper things than love.

First and last, man is alone.
He is born alone, and alone he dies
and alone he is while he lives, in his deepest self.

Love, like the flowers, is life, growing.
But underneath are the deep rocks, the living rock that lives alone
and deeper still the unknown fire, unknown and heavy, heavy
and alone.

Love is a thing of twoness.
But underneath any twoness, man is alone.

And underneath the great turbulent emotions of love, the violent
      herbage,
lies the living rock of a single creature's pride,
the dark, naïf pride.
And deeper even than the bedrock of pride
lies the ponderous fire of naked life
with its strange primordial consciousness of justice
and its primordial consciousness of connection,
connection with still deeper, still more terrible life-fire
and the old, old final life-truth.

Love is of twoness, and is lovely
like the living life on the earth
but below all roots of love lies the bedrock of naked pride, subter-
      ranean,

and deeper than the bedrock of pride is the primordial fire of the
    middle
which rests in connection with the further forever unknowable fire
    of all things
and which rocks with a sense of connection, religion
and trembles with a sense of truth, primordial consciousness
and is silent with a sense of justice, the fiery primordial imperative.

All this is deeper than love
deeper than love.

[BAWDY CAN BE SANE]

Bawdy can be sane and wholesome,
in fact a little bawdy is necessary in every life
to keep it sane and wholesome.

And a little whoring can be sane and wholesome.
In fact a little whoring is necessary in every life
to keep it sane and wholesome.

Even sodomy can be sane and wholesome
granted there is an exchange of genuine feeling.

But get any of them on the brain, and they become pernicious:
bawdy on the brain becomes obscenity, vicious.
Whoring on the brain becomes really syphilitic
and sodomy on the brain becomes a mission,
all the lot of them, vice, missions, etc., insanely unhealthy.

In the same way, chastity in its hour is sweet and wholesome.
But chastity on the brain is a vice, a perversion.
And rigid suppression of all bawdy, whoring or other such commerce
is a straight way to raving insanity.
The fifth generation of puritans, when it isn't obscenely profligate,
is idiot. So you've got to choose.

[THERE WAS A GAY BIRD
NAMED CHRISTINE]

There was a gay bird named Christine
Who could horoscope fit for a queen.
Some of them were quite true—
About one or two—
But the rest were obscure or obscene.

À LA MANIERE DE D. H. LAWRENCE

They have green tram in Florence now.
O! so smart and so mechanically finished.
They have taken off the beautiful red Lilly
and put a dirty green large cabage.

The people in it are grim
Oh! dear what's happening!
I don't recognize my Tuscans
in those ugly green large cars.

They were so small and denty
like toys
The one that went to Vingone
They had red Lilly and people singing songs

But now they are like cabages
and people are sad and grim
and all so very mechanical
Oh dear! what's happening to Tuscans!

APPENDICES

*I N S T E A D of bewailing a lost youth, a man nowadays begins to wonder, when he reaches my ripe age of forty-two, if ever his past will subside and be comfortably by-gone. Doing over these poems makes me realise that my teens and my twenties are just as much me, here and now and present, as ever they were, and the pastness is only an abstraction. The actuality, the body of feeling, is essentially alive and here.

And I remember the slightly self-conscious Sunday afternoon, when I was nineteen, and I "composed" my first two "poems." One was to *Guelder-roses*, and one to *Campions*, and most young ladies would have done better: at least I hope so. But I thought the effusions very nice, and so did Miriam.

Then much more vaguely I remember subsequent half-furtive moments when I would absorbedly scribble at verse for an hour or so, and then run away from the act and the production as if it were secret sin. It seems to me that "knowing oneself" was a sin and a vice for innumerable centuries, before it became a virtue. It seems to me, it is still a sin and vice, when it comes to new knowledge.— In those early days—for I was very green and unsophisticated at twenty—I used to feel myself at times haunted by something, and a little guilty about it, as if it were an abnormality. Then the haunting would get the better of me, and the ghost would suddenly appear, in the shape of a usually rather incoherent poem. Nearly always I shunned the apparition once it had appeared. From the first, I was a little afraid of my real poems—not my "compositions," but the poems that had the ghost in them. They seemed to me to come from somewhere, I didn't quite know where, out of a me whom I didn't know and didn't want to know, and to say things I would much rather not have said: for choice. But there they were. I never read them again. Only I gave them to Miriam, and she loved them, or she seemed to. So when I was twenty-one, and went to Nottingham University as a day student, I began putting them down in a little college notebook, which was the foundation of the poetic me.

*[This Foreword is transcribed from D. H. L.'s MS. and retains his spelling, punctuation, etc. *Edd.*]

Sapientiae Urbs Conditur,* it said on the cover. Never was anything less true. The city is founded on a passionate unreason.

To this day, I still have the uneasy haunted feeling, and would rather not write most of the things I do write—including this note. Only now I know my demon better, and, after bitter years, respect him more than my other, milder and nicer self. Now I no longer like my "compositions." I once thought the poem *Flapper* a little masterpiece: when I was twenty: because the demon isn't in it. And I must have burnt many poems that had the demon fuming in them. The fragment *Discord in Childhood* was a long poem, probably was good, but I destroyed it. Save for Miriam, I perhaps should have destroyed them all. She encouraged my demon. But alas, it was me, not he whom she loved. So for her too, it was a catastrophe. My demon is not easily loved: whereas the ordinary me is. So poor Miriam was let down. Yet in a sense, she let down my demon, till he howled. And there it is. And no more *past* in me than my blood in my toes or my nose is past.

I have tried to arrange the poems in chronological order: that is, in the order in which they were written. The first are either subjective, or Miriam poems. *The Wild Common* was very early and very confused. I have re-written some of it, and added some, till it seems complete. It has taken me twenty years to say what I started to say, incoherently, when I was nineteen, in this poem. The same with *Virgin Youth*. and others of the subjective poems with the demon fuming in them smokily. To the demon, the past is not past. The wild common, the gorse, the virgin youth are here and now, the same: the same me, the same one experience. Only now perhaps I can give it more complete expression.

The poems to Miriam, at least the early ones like *Dog-Tired* and *Cherry-Robbers* and *Renascence* are not much changed. But some of the later ones had to be altered, where sometimes the hand of commonplace youth had been laid on the mouth of the demon. It is not for technique these poems are altered: it is to say the real say.

Other verses, those I call the imaginative or fictional, like *Love on the Farm* and *Wedding Morn*, I have sometimes changed, to get them into better form, and take out the dead bits. It took me many years to learn to play with the form of a poem: even if I can do it now. But it is only in the less immediate, the more fictional poems that

*[See note, p. 1034.]

the form has to be played with. The demon, when he's really there, makes his own form willy-nilly, and is unchangeable.

The poems to Miriam run into the first poems to my mother. Then when I was twenty-three, I went away from home for the first time, to the south of London. From the big new red school where I taught, we could look north and see the Crystal Palace; to me, who saw it then for the first time, in lovely autumn weather, beautiful and softly blue on its hill to the north. And past the school, on an embankment, the trains rushed south to Brighton or to Kent. And round the school the country was still only just being built over, and the elms of Surrey stood tall and noble. It was different from the Midlands.

Then begin the poems to Helen, and all that trouble of *Lilies in the Fire*: and London, and school, a whole new world. Then starts the rupture with home, with Miriam, away there in Nottinghamshire. And gradually the long illness, and then the death of my mother; and in the sick year after, the collapse for me of Miriam, of Helen, and of the other woman, the woman of *Kisses in the Train* and *The Hands of the Betrothed*.

Then, in that year, for me, everything collapsed, save the mystery of death, and the haunting of death in life. I was twenty-five, and from the death of my mother, the world began to dissolve around me, beautiful, iridescent, but passing away substanceless. Till I almost dissolved away myself, and was very ill: when I was twenty-six.

Then slowly the world came back: or I myself returned: but to another world. And in 1912, when I was still twenty-six, the other phase commenced, the phase of *Look! We Have Come Through!*— When I left teaching, and left England, and left many other things, and the demon had a new run for his money.

But back in England again during the war, there are the war poems from the little volume: *Bay*. These, beginning with *Tommies in the Train*, make up the end of the volume of Rhyming Poems. They are the end of the cycle of purely English experience, and death experience.

The first poems I had published were *Dreams Old* and *Dreams Nascent*, which Miriam herself sent to Ford Madox Hueffer, in 1910 I believe, just when the *English Review* had started so brilliantly. Myself, I had offered the little poem *Study* to the Nottingham University Magazine, but they returned it. But Hueffer accepted the *Dreams* poems for the English Review, and was very kind to me, and was the first man I ever met who had a real, and a true feeling for literature. He introduced me to Edward Garnett, who, somehow, introduced me to the world. How well I remember the evenings at Garnett's house in Kent, by the log fire. And there I wrote the best of the dialect poems. I remember Garnett disliked the old ending to *Whether or Not*. Now I see he was right, it was the voice of the commonplace me, not the demon. So I have altered it. And there again, those days of Hueffer and Garnett are not past at all, once I recall them. They were good to the demon, and the demon is time-less. But the ordinary meal-time me has yesterdays. And that is why I have altered *Dreams Nascent*, that exceedingly funny and optimistic piece of rhymeless poetry which Ford Hueffer printed in the English Review, and which introduced me to the public. The public seemed to like it. The M.P. for school-teachers said I was an ornament to the educational system, whereupon I knew it must be the ordinary me which had made itself heard, and not the demon. Anyhow, I was always uneasy about it.

There is a poem added to the second volume, which had to be left out of *Look! We Have Come Through!*, when that book was first printed, because the publishers objected to mixing love and religion, so they said, in the lines:

> "But I hope I shall spend eternity
> with my face down buried between
> her breasts. . ."

But surely there are many eternities, and one of them Adam spends with his face buried and at peace between the breasts of Eve: just as Eve spends one of her eternities with her face hidden in the breast of Adam. But the publishers coughed out that gnat, and I was left wondering, as usual.

Some of the poems in *Look!* are re-written, but not many, not as in the first volume. And *Birds, Beasts and Flowers* are practically untouched. They are what they are. They are the same me as wrote *The Wild Common*, or *Renascence*.

Perhaps it may seem bad taste to write this so personal foreword. But since the poems are so often personal themselves, and hang together in a life, it is perhaps only fair to give the demon his body of mere man, as far as possible.

Scandicci. 12 May 1928.

CAMPIONS

The unclouded seas of bluebells have ebbed and passed
And the pale stars of forget-me-nots have climbed to the last
Rung of their life-ladders' fragile heights.
Now the trees with interlocked hands and arms uplifted hold back
    the light.

Though the purple dreams of the innocent spring have gone
And the glimmering dreamlets of the morning are pallid and wan
Though the year is ripening like a woman who has conceived
And the wood, like a manly husband, spreads softness and silence,
    thick-leaved:

The Campions drift in fragile, rosy mist,
Draw nearer, redden and laugh like young girls kissed
Into a daring, short-breath'd confession
Which opens earth and Heaven to Love's fugitive, glowing
    progression

Love-fire is drifting, though the bugle is prim and demure,
Love-light is glowing, though the guelder-rose is too chaste and pure
Ever to suffer love's wild attack,
For with the redness of laughter the battle is waging in the Campions'
    rosy wrack.

GUELDER ROSES

The guelder rose-bush is hung with coronets
Gently issuing from the massèd green;
Pale dreamy chaplets; a grey nun-sister sets
Such on the virgin hair of dead sixteen.

Chaplets of cream and distant green
That impress me like the thought-drenched eyes
Of some Pre-Raphaelite mystic queen
Who haunts me—with her lies.

Such pearled zones of fair sterility
Girdling with jewels the meanness of common things
Preaching in sad-moving silence a heart-hungry purity
In a day they are lost in the nothingness purity brings.

[At the end of a sweet spring day they will vanish;
Eloquent purity voiceless in the dust;
Utterly dead; who lived but to banish
The quick, kindling spark of a generous trust.

In the autumn I'll look for immortal fruit,
Heavy nodding clusters of crimson red,
Not on the stems of virginity, lovely and mute
But of those life-loving, careless of their rank among the dead.]

At the end of the sweet spring day they are gone
Forgotten, like last year's linnet song:
They were the halo, the eloquence—now is none
Left of their light, among the mean flowers' throng.

In the garnering autumn a glow of immortal fruit
—Heavy hanging clusters of crimson red
Swings round the stems of the many, insignificant mute
Life lovers, who could hope for no rank among the pallid dead.

THE FALL OF DAY

Torn wings of flame are wafting down the sky
Pinioned like sweeping scythes now idly hanging at rest;
The soft clustered shoulder-feathers in rosy confusion lie
Helpless; another day has flown too high
And falls wingless, blood streaming through its yellow hair, headlong
    into the west.

Slowly the wings of Day are eddying lower
Their feathers lifeless, and the rose lights turning to gray.
No longer they sweep the hours, as the scythe of the mower
Hisses through the flowers; the timid night-airs blow
A cool ointment over the earth, blistered in the flight of Day.

Our overweening Days strive too far, till the heat and the sweat
Sicken us, and we are stunned by the rushings of the labouring wings.
And then all our days in a plunge of death pay the debt
Of their vain up-striving, and night remains for regret
And the ignoble prayers of the panic-stricken whom darkness
    enrings.

MARRIED IN JUNE

In the white morning, where is the enchanted room of the night
    before?
This is comfortless and unlovely, with cushions and those silk covers
    on the floor
And the strewn, tawdry trappings that last night's poetry wore.

A hat quaintly curiously woven, luxurious with big roses
With long pins leaning out, their porcelain globes wreathed with
    roses,
And beside it, on the table, her gloves and my wilted wild roses.

Sunbeams, lusty and clean from the bath of night
Sport on her littered piano, and mock at the sight
Of my wilted wild roses, pink and ivory white.

She kissed their coolness last night, breathed their clean scent
Drew her lips over the moon-pale petals softly bent
Inwards; I can see whence the thorns were rent.

THE WORM TURNS

    There is no passion in my life,
    There is no action, it is almost a sleep.
    Oh for a delirium of love or of strife
    Or Sorrow to weep!

I am quite sick of books,
Give them to the dead.
My chafed curbed blood no longer brooks
Old things thrice said.

No readings and writings
While the blood is alive,
But lovings and hatings, struggle and fightings—
I'll work and I'll wive.

ON THE ROAD

I am out alone on the road;
From the low west windows the cold light flows
Along where my slow feet never trode;
I wish I knew where this pale road goes.

Soon the western windows of the sky
With shutters of clouded night will close.
And we'll still be together, the road and I
Together, wherever the dumb road goes.

The wind chases by me, and over the corn
Pale shadows flee from us as if from their foes
And save for me the road is forlorn
For none go whither this long road goes.

In the sky the low, tired moon goes out,
Wearily, through the oaks, the night wind blows,
Pale, sleepy flowers are tossed about
As the wind asks whither the dark road goes.

Away on the hillside wakes a star,
Below, the pit-lights glitter in rows
That is my home where the lamp gleams afar
But it's the other way that my dark road now goes.

I am tired of this journey, it is stupid and chill
The road winds forever, and which of us knows
What lies over the next dark hill?
Anywhere, nowhere, the dead road goes.

When morning comes, I find me a love
And I'll lie in her lap where the world's wild rose
Blushes and flaunts in the sunshine above.
Why should I care where the old road goes?

THE DEATH OF THE BARON

The shadows of the ash-trees stride across the hay
Winrow after winrow falls under this first stroke of night,
Which treads out the glow of fugitive orange light
Leaving them shadow stripes barred on a field of grey.

Tiny black moths flutter out at the touch of the fork,
Shaken softly from the heavy-folded skirts of Night;
After them issues a dark-winged, fluttering sprite
And soon the owl winged with stillness will float out to hawk.

The last row is finished, the jingling rake is lifted;
We rest at the hedge, my horse and I, where the scent
Medicinal of the elder-flowers with meadow-sweet is blent
And along the scent and the coolness a drowse of sleep is drifted.

I start from the droop of forgetfulness as the sound of a bell
From the quiet church-tower that knows no prattle of chimes
But sleeps the long week out embosomed in murmuring limes
Sharply beats out a thrice-told funeral knell.

Startling the thick-spun twilight the bells shake out
A thrill through the listening trees, and hold the breath
Of the dying grass with a thrice-told tale of death
Startling my horse, who stirs and would turn her about.

I hold her still, and wait till the bell shall falter
The burdened age,—seventy-nine—the vicar
Is dead at last then; his poor sunk flame must flicker
And gutter to extinction like a taper on a forgotten altar.

He was a soldier once, our fierce little Baron—a Pole
Fleeing in exile to England at the end of the fight.
He was a soldier always; in church it was a sight
To see him flash and tremble with the fire of his soul.

They are tolling his failure, after all these years, to the tired birds.
He had hoped to die in the pulpit, to conquer in death.—
For his mission had cruelly failed, while his passionate foreign breath
Refused to be moulded in arrows of English words.

Sunday after Sunday they carried him trembling to his place
In the pulpit, where, shrivelled and ghastly, in unintelligible speech
He preached to the stolid farmers, till at last he could preach
No more, and he lay at home, unutterable despair in his face.

The fierce black eyes are closed, they will open no more,
Startled, and full of agony to find he had but slept,
Eyes where his hot, imprisoned soul has kept
A fiery sign of the chained power that wasted him to the core.

Slow, infirm Death has at last gathered up the waste
Of Godhead in Man despised, carelessly thrown over.
There are enough of great souls to complete an efficient Jehovah,
And behold them deplorably dead, by wrong usage defaced.

Come on, turn home, old lass. Are we wasted too—
Hey?—with this endless labour and little-souled fret?
We must keep yon lamp alight, nevertheless, Jeannette,—
Poor dream-heavy slaves at the mill, what we have to do, we must do.

Hold up, Jeannette!—Why!—poor old girl, are you sad?
Come on—let's take off your collar—and don't reproach me
With your tired eyes, Jeannette—we suffer the same—don't we?
And no more than the Baron did—eh? No, old girl, and not so bad.

LOVE COMES LATE

I did not know Love had settled down on me:
He came like a sea-gull, sinking with uplifted wings down on a
    slow-breathing sea,
And hardly disturbing wavering shimmer
Of sunset, but merging unnoticed into the rosy glimmer.

It settled so softly I was all unaware,
And the flush faded and it came dark; I slept, still ignorant love was
    there,
Till a dream came trembling through my flesh in the night
And I woke, wondering who touched me with such fear and delight.

With the first dawn I rose to look in the glass
And I started with pleasure, for in the night it had come to pass
That the time-threads spun across my face
Had been woven into a glorious mesh, like a bridal lace.

I have a charm like laughter through a veil,
Like a girl's tinkling merriment at night when the sea is pale;
My heart has a warmth like this sea where the dawn
Has strewn myriad twinkling poppy-petals down the path of a love
    late born.

All these glittering sea-birds wheel and fret
Below me, complaining that never, never yet
Has the warmth of a night kiss spread through their blood
Sending them rioting at dawn down the lane of scarlet poppy petals
    strewn across the flood.

SONG

Up in the high
  Swinging cherry-tree
Like a bird am I
  Clinging merrily.

Leaves whisper and titter
　　As the wind races south;
And the red fruits glitter
　　Cool on my mouth.

Sallies of swinging fruit
　　Cold on my cheek
Swaying I snatch, and loot
　　Beauties so sleek.

Scarlet and cherry red,
　　Insolent gold,
Down the dark bough have fled
　　Out of my hold.

Who is it singing
　　Down there below?
When Red rain goes flinging—
　　Hark—her quick "Oh!"

See her laugh up at me
　　Through wind-snatched hair
Now see her turn to flee:
　　"Oh, if you dare!"

A FAILURE

Tiny fingers outspread,
Crisped with intense desire,
And the little mouth red
And round eyes afire
To touch it, that new thing.

Stretching, reaching
Clutching, tasting, dropping:
The soul beseeching
Yet something stopping
The life-current flowing.

Stiff and despairing
Still yearning, but withered and numb,
With Age declaring
Now never can come
The

A DECISION

She is sweet and soft-throated,
Her eyes glow, as she
Tunes her voice, many noted
For me.

Her warm red lips
Are budded, as she
With a quick kiss clips
Them to me.

Her hair's live curl
Clutches for me.
Alas! Tossed back in my hearts swirl
Is she.

A TRAIN AT NIGHT

The frantic throb of the train
As we drop through the night,
The Night, a big black stain
Against my helpless sight,
Sets my heart also throbbing with pain
With the pain of this flight.

Like a lonely star dropping through space
To extinction rushing—
Towns, constellations, race
Past, and we're brushing
A brilliant station, the chase
Through ever onward night pushing.

BABY SONGS
TEN MONTHS OLD

See how she snuggles against my neck—
My wee mouse—
And her fingers move in the ruts of my ears
And my throat is wet with her tears.

I can just see the nape of her white little neck—
My pale, wet butterfly, fluffy chicken.
The rest is a cloud of thistle down.
Soft, tickling brown.

I cannot call her "Sweet Joy" now—
My wee squirrel—
She is no longer two days old:
Twas a tale soon told.

And dark now is the sky that she came through
My white bird—
Heavy with drops of the first cruel rain—
Tears for her pain.

There, press your hot, red cheek against mine
My own baby—
There, for the heat of it causes a smart
That stings down to my heart.

EVE

Eve, swinging her dusky limbs disconsolate
Strayed down the hill, crushing the silken moss,
Shaking the heath-bells down with her petulant gait.
The rosy periwinkles that clustered and leaned across
Were broken against her thighs; she shattered the hibiscus with her
    hands
And scattered with her hair clouds of pale mimosa sands.

Eve, alone, unsatisfied, among the orange and guava trees
Hungry, and discontent in the fruitful shade
Drifted, with the blood of the flowers on her feet and knees,
With her suave form dusty with spices, honey sweet, strayed
Into the gloom-woven forest, where the birds and cicalas were still,
Where the blue crabs rustled, in quest of her aimless will.

Eve, pushing the festooned vanilla trembling aside,
Looked where the red fruit hung like coals of fire,
Overhead the reddest. She lifted her long arms and tried
To pull down the bough; the leaves broke, and the fruit swung higher,
But pressing her supple body into the cool dark leaves—
Her breasts uplifted in endeaver—she touches—she reeves.

Eve, with her resistless, virgin-budded breast,
Has brought down a ripe fruit heavily to her feet
Its cool weight lay full on her bosom; now it rolls to rest
Forgotten in the grass. Eva, fearful and fleet
Runs into the shadow with her capture; a few little bites are enough;
Her fruit is unripe and her soft mouth is bitter and rough.

Eve, running with swift limbs quickened by dread
Presses her hand to her bosom where the fruit has lain.
Eve, with a heart of resentment, is quickly sped.
The mouth of the man is full of the taste of pain;
Strong, with eyes of defiance, Eve walks into Sorrows:
Out of Eden, weary with the wistfulness of her silent tomorrows.

AFTER SCHOOL

In a little, half-built street, where red and white villas
Look brightly on a confusion of mud, and sand, and mortar,
As I came home in the dusk, despoiled by school, a mere blossomless
    husk—
A light like mellow moonlight gleamed on the water
In the deep cart-ruts, gleamed through the blue of the darkening dusk,

And I looked in a room where the lamp, as a moon in mist
Shone sweetly through yellow silk: a man full in the light,
Looked up, and the words moved like a smile from his lips.
A woman came into the glow from out of the shadowy light
Leans over to read his work, and her dark head dips
Deep into the heart of the light, the centre of a star,
There in the heart of a star set far off in the night
She turned and kissed him, and his eyes were the soul of the star,
And the white nape of her neck was the beauty of the star
And I, in immeasurable night, looked on from afar,—afar!

A SNOWY DAY AT SCHOOL

Snow, and the silence of snow, heavy on the rousing day.
Surely I cannot just be going to school—
Yet—in the little new road, the young wife turns away
From her fluttered farewells at the approach of my well-remembered
    smile
And in the unfinished houses, the ring of the joiner's tool
And his singing, sound as they always do at the beginning of the mile.

How different, in the middle of snows, the great school rises red
Like a picture by Thaulow—dark clusters of shouting lads
Scatter over the whiteness. One boy alone in the classroom, his head
Bristling with animation "Oh please sir, how d'you like this? Fine
But I've had such a job! My crutches! I fairly dragged them—the pads
Slipped like anything—But don't you like it?—Ain't it Fine? an
    awful job!"

The inrush, the clatter, the stamping, eyes laughing wide with
    pleasure,
Breathless sounds of satisfaction, clamour of delight!
Lads in their warm, light slippers bound down the hall to the measure
Of their dancing blood; lads sucking the cold moisture from their
    hands
With gusto, begin again the brisk fight
In battle of heated words, hardly stilled by my reiterated commands.

Clinging to the radiators, like numbed bees to the drenched grass,
The boys from the Home, blue and inanimate,
Like sad processions of exiles you could have seen them shivering,
    pass
Down the glad streets, pinched waifs in ill-assorted clothes
—Shuffling his ragged boots, there comes one boy late
—When he lifts his foot, I see the pad of his soaked stocking under
    his toes.

"Please sir, I was sweeping snow, an' I never heard the bell
I didn't know it was so late. No Sir—I 'ad to—because
He—he's in prison my father. Yes Sir—One and six—with my sister's
    as well."
We all march out to prayers, soft slippered feet—and clattering soles
And shuffle of broken, soddened boots; yet singing goes rather
By nature than by boots, and wet feet often carry merry souls.

Coming home over the waste-lands, wide and lonely with snow,
I saw a dark figure approaching, a ragged, solitary crow—
He had a shovel and a brush on his shoulder:—his face was aglow
Till he saw me. "But please Sir, my movver said I could—an'—
We ain't got no farver—only a movver, an' she 'as ter go
Cleanin'—Yes Sir—a shilln, by myself—all right Sir."

READING IN THE EVENING

I have sat in the recreation ground
Under an oak tree whose yellow buds dotted the pale blue sky:
The young grass twinkled in the wind, and the sound
Of the wind hung round the knotted buds like a canopy.

I have travelled in Russia two hours or more,
No, a long season I have been with Dostoïevsky in the dark
Ways of St Petersburg, I have dwelled in the core
Of Russia, through the new great naïveté of Russia, her wide sad
    child eyes so clear.

Now to the Recreation Ground
I am come back a foreigner, wondering and shrinking from the scene
From the noise of children playing around
From the tulips coloured with chalk, and the dull grass' evening
    green.

How lonely in the wide world is this playground.
How lonely, under the tree; unnoticed.

A MAN AT PLAY ON THE RIVER

Where the flickering river loiters
To keep the reflected variety of the houseboats;
The glow of red in a grey-green shadow of trees;
Like a fly that weaves through the shadows,
Like a bee that plays with the reflection of flowers
Darts a man at play;
Over the surface of shadow-colour floats
His little punt, an autumn-brown beech-leaf,
Playing with the eddies
Hither and thither
Anywhere;
Playing with the soft-slipping water,
Playing with the shadow colours, and the waving, reflected trees
With the rings that the fishes have made,
A swift, dexterous man, plying the slender pole,
His body pulsing with play
His full, fine body bending and urging like the stress of a song,
Darting his light punt with the quick-shifting fancy of verse,
Among the shadows of blossoms and trees and rushes,
In-weaving the bright thread of his joy
Flashing his bright, brown arms as he leans on the pole,
His blue shirt glimmering in the water among the shadow of trees,
Threading the round joy of his white-flannelled hips full of play,
Up the river, under the trees,
Down the river, in the gleam of the sun,

Across the river, bending low
In one swift bound to the house-boat.
There, among the flowers of the boat-roof
Passes the ever-changing joy of his active body:
His round, brown head bends like a bee above a blossom
Over a girl who has strewn herself in a hammock
As a white rose strews the ground,
His ruddy arms glow across her
His full round hips supporting him above her
While the soft caress of her hidden laughter
Plays round him, as colour-ripples played
Round his bright joyful body
When he swung like the rhythm of a poem over the river,
That made shadows and shimmering ripples the soft notes of a song,
And now hangs like the fragrant close of the measure
Over her strewn, white, laughing form.

AMOUR

The sun sets wide the yellow crocuses
    To fill them up a brimful measure,
And deep in the glowing wine-filled chalices
    Sways the golden pearl of pleasure.

The breeze wakes up a music in the sallow
    Around its golden stoppèd notes:
Like grains of music crossing the fertile fallow
    Go winging glad the yellow motes.

When softly I call at her door, and enter the room
    The gold-brown flowers of her eyes unfold
And trembling somewhere deep in their sunkist gloom
    A little wild bubble is loosening hold.

She may cover her eyes, yet the aimless breeze of my words
    Carries a dim low song that stirs
Her quivering answer, and kisses like thieving birds
    Flock unseen from my lips to hers.

BEREAVEMENT

My chest gapes open sometimes
 At the wound's aching cicatrice,
And especially at nightfall,
When I see the sky's blue darken.

My mother had blue eyes,
They seemed to grow darker as she came to the edge of death
 And I could not bear her look upon me.

When the sky's blue darkens at nightfall
 My breast's aching cicatrice
 Tears open.
She glanced at me timidly—
 Do you know why I could not
 Why I cannot even now
Bear the thought of my mother's pain-darkened blue eyes.
 Looking timidly upon me.

 I always loved her—.

LOSS

What is the heavy, hot hand
That is always grasping me;
I can always feel it on my chest.

I think it is the hand of Sorrow
Pressing to grasp my heart.

I think sometimes it will crush my heart inward,
Smash it in like a frail vessel
That carries a heavy, rich liquor.

GRIEF

As I pause at the side of the bath
And forget,
As the sun comes in the bathroom
I pause, and forget.
I forget the towel and my wet limbs,
I feel the sun on me.

How am I clotted together
Out of the soft matrix
The air, and the flowing sunshine and bright dust.

What is it that clots me, holds me together out of these,
    these things—apart?
Why should I grieve that my mother is no longer clotted
    together,
No longer a large fleck, moving in the sunshine,
    But dissipated, dissolved again
    Why should it grieve me?

    Ah, but my mother had blue eyes—

[TWO FRAGMENTS ON SLEEP]

[I]

Ah life, God, Law, whatever name you have
You great Will patient [struggling], you the sleep
That does inform this various dream of living
You sleep stretched out forever, in whose body we
Are bidden up as dreams, you great grand sleep
Coursed round by rhythmic movement of the stars
The constellations with your great heart the sun
Fierily pulsing unable to refrain
Since you, vast, outstretched, silent sleep,
Permit of no beyond, ah you whose dreams

We are, and whose body, let it never be said
That at my appointed function, I turned poltroon.

For when at night, from out the charged cells
Of my past day's experience, sleep does draw
The surcharge, the spent action to itself
And leaves me lightened to begin again
At night, I say, when I am lost in sleep
Does my red heart rebel at labour, my still
Brain make complaint about herself[?]

Ah, never let it be said I was poltroon
At this my task of living, this my dream,
This me which is risen out of the spell of sleep,
In white flesh robed to drape another dream
As lightning falls all white, and trembles
Looks round, and sees, its swift dream is over
Drops swift to sleep, the dream enrichened sleep
And if the Vast, the God, the Sleep that yet grows richer
Shall say that I, this mote of the Body of Sleep, this vanishing dream
Must in my transiency pass all through pain,
Must be a dream of grief, must like a crude
Dull meteorite burst light only when torn
In burning anguish through space extinct
Still in full flight, shall I then turn poltroon
Shall I for my little hour have aught but wonder
Of what is there to complain, since pain [   ]
And grief too all of them, are but wonder
Struck out of the flint of sleep by my thin white blade
Of a body
When the Great, still God has sent me out to bring
Enrichment back into the vasty sleep
Whence all dreams spring.

[II]

Is not the wondrous sense of being flung
From out the flint of sleep for a moment again
Onto the tinder of this substantial life

And if life be blown upon, it still must burn
And since in burning all things wondrous grow
And so in burning I waste not up too soon
This substance whereon my dream is shown
What difference grief or pain or happiness
All is the same

And oh vast sleeper, still I am glad, for out
Of thee there comes such new, such rarer
Beauty of blowing dreams
Oh Sleep, how art thou enriched
Since I have seen, as never were seen before
The men who are this body lapped
In with thy darkness, move so subtle soft
And gentle, since there is more love toward
All things that be, now in the eyes of men
Than ever there before.

[TO TOSS THE TROUBLED NIGHT LONG]

To toss the troubled night long through for you
To dream the bliss of your great mouth on mine
To feel the bliss of your strong life lift through
The weight of this my body, fallen on thine.

LOVE MESSAGE

If you happen upon my love
Just greet him from me,
Catch him by the sleeve of his coat
And invite him to me.
If he will not come at your request
God spare him all sorrow of me,
—I wish him still, the best.

THE WITCH I

You, browed maiden, your eyes' bright pictures have caught me
    And I have changed into another man

—She bound her brows in a scarlet kerchief, she bound
    Her breasts in a velvet bodice's span
She slowly closed her eyes upon me, and I
Having no time to bridle my horse, ran
    Whither I know not—where am I?

THE WITCH II

Thou, strange maiden, I can see nought but the glistening
    Pictures of thine eyes—I am blind.
—The strange one put silk trash across her bosom
    And round her throat strung pearls did wind
And hid her hair with red and golden ramel
    —Nay dear friend, canst thou go and find
Her, mount thee on my swift, high, rustling camel
    Bring her to me here that I may unbind
The precious thing from out her precious trash
    That we may lie together, twined
Like corn together in the night's soft sash.

ELIXIR

Nay Cousin, Dearest
What sort of love-sorrow has come over you?
Surely, if you saw my breasts
Like pomegranates on my body, like a Jew
You would let yourself die in ignominy
Without turning your face from folks jeering "Hue!"

If I unveiled myself
And you saw my ear-rings neath my hair
Like a fool they might bedizen you
And you would not notice, you would not care.

GOOD NIGHT

Goodnight!
You came, and my sorrow faded;
Sorrow sat beside me, Sorrow had her mouth on mine,

But you looked at me with grave eyes that upbraided
My heaviness, and Sorrow rose and left me.
Goodnight!
She is heavy and jaded.
Goodnight
My love, thou hast set the stars to shine.

SYMPATHY

Midnight shadows have come over what was the green of Spring
Silence has crept upon me, I cry for folk to hear.
Over forty empty fields, from the darkened chamber I fling
My appeal. I am a foreigner in this Death space here.
Oh, how sad I am—Oh what a stranger, Sister!
How bitterly I weep within Thee, Death shadow, Encyster.

[THE TRAIN]

Train, with your smoke flag waving,
    Flashing your window-glass
Stay a moment and take me
    Up as you pass.

The train with its irons chuckling
    Laughing a laugh to itself
Waited while the boy scrambled
    Up by himself.

            that where
    The three men went from Daniel
    And where, where in the fire
        All running to?

The train rushed on, the houses bowed down
    The town spun round and was gone
And from the downs the sheep ran fast
    And horses kicked as the train went past
And the sun came out, and flowers were cast
    Over the grass like foam.

AT MIDNIGHT

The midnight shadow has drooped and drooped
    Over thy dark divan, my Lord,
And high in the Divan of Darkness, my Soul
    Shimmers o'er thy tent like a sword.

In the desert's night thou standest up-gazing
    At my soul, the brilliant of the sky,
And by the dark divan thy sword's shining silver
    Glitters me thy soul's reply.

BELOVED

As she goes about the homestead
    And to the cattle shed
She glances at the shepherd
    When the camels are fed
And in her left hand, gaily
    Her handkerchief shines red.

THE PROPHET IN THE ROSE GARDEN

The Prophet entered a rose garden
    And the roses tall did shadow him
He spread his shawl sewn with gold at the hem
    And prayed, while the roses listened to him.

MOTH AND RUST

God, only God is eternal
    God is eternal and only He.
'And where, white maid, are your African slaves?'
    They are dead, so God was their owner, you see.

IRREVERENT THOUGHTS

I have come to the house of God
    And found gray doves in the fountain court
Feeding on pure white sugar,
    Their rosy feet curved for joy in the sport.

Ah, if I might touch my tongue
    In his hand and taste sweet of that sort—!
—But alas, dear God, I have fallen short
    Of thy will, my thoughts are wrong.

TWO-FOLD

As I went down our street
In my rosy-brown jacket-sleeves
Some one said to me "your lover is sick".
I said "Oh bring him to me, you thieves
I will put ostrich featherlets
On my breast which is his bed-head.
Oh gather the pigeons of the village
I fly for the fat to roast them—bring brown bread!"

A LOVE-PASSAGE

Do not hold me, Siegmund.
Siegmund, the strong beating of your heart hurts me,
Siegmund, with your arms and your heart you are choking me,
You are crushing me, let me go, let me go!
    (Oh Siegmund, Siegmund what has happened to you?)
No, do not touch me, leave me on the grey sea-turf
    (Siegmund, only this morning you were shining for me,
    You were all the morning to me, all the sea and the morning sky,
    And what was the sound of the birds and the water but Siegmund
    Always Siegmund.—Where are you now?
    Oh what were you, what were you but the stuff of my soul!
    I breathed my dreams upon you, I laid my mouth on your mouth
    And breathed on you the picture-mist of my dreams
    And my soul's desire, and made you real—
    But you were all of me . . .
    And now the mist of my dreams has dried from you
    Has evaporated from you like steam from glass
    And you stand a stranger to me.
    —And now with the knocking of his heart against my soul
    I run awake to the house of my soul, and find it empty.

The breath of my dream is faded from off the mirror
And where he stood I see my own shadow stand
And the house is empty, and I am alone.
I am alone, alone, there is no more Siegmund for me,
No meaning in the sky, the meaning has vanished from the
    morning
Gone—and I am alone, alone.)
Poor Siegmund, take the sobs from out of your voice,
You sound so dreadful, so cruelly hurt, my dear.
There, I cannot bear to see the sobs in your throat,
Siegmund dear, kiss me, kiss me.

        (—Oh, with his heart
How he hurts me with his heart, and his throat so near to my
    eyes
Frightens me, frightens me. He is not my Siegmund at all,
His coat and his arms and his labouring heart are strange,
And terribly strange is the throat that is working with sobs,
And terribly strange are his tears that are wetting my face . . .
I dare not look at his eyes.
        Oh, my other Siegmund
That are dead, you have left me cruelly—Siegmund)

        Why, dear
Are you letting me go, and hiding your face to the ground!
Siegmund, dear, what are you doing, lying with your face on the turf,
Lying rigid and silent with your face on the short sea turf?
Siegmund, Siegmund get up and look at me—listen
Siegmund, lift up your face again off the turf.
        (God, that I should have to repudiate him!)

[AH, WITH HIS BLESSING BRIGHT ON THY MOUTH AND THY BROW]

    Ah, with his blessing bright on thy mouth and thy brow
    Travel thine avocation here, and learn
    To help Him lift the weltering darkness, turn
    Earth-clods and night to flowers that praise and burn.

Do thou, oh travelling apprentice, likewise.
Strive with the formless things, and gently touch
Some shapeless Dark to the lovely curve of Light
As thou art shown: and having done so much

Return where all in beauty stand erect,
Where shape on spirit in superb degree
Married make perfect beauty, no defect
Of form or movement or of harmony.

All matter and all spirit standing upright
In shapeliness, with happy linkèd hands
Shall sing of heaven achieved, where every bright
Shape shines, alone like a melody, and where
Shape answers shape in chorus to the sight.

Where throngs of angels hastening upon
Their several errands here and there shall make
Movement of multitudes surpassing rhythm;
And all their faces, like bright flowers awake
With beauty, shine and bow in God's great wake.

ALOOF IN GAIETY

Too much you mint me that cheating counterfeit
Of gaiety: too often pay me thus.
I know, I know you are winsome so, but you cheat
Me out of my proper dues with your chinking jests . . .
Ah coin me speech of your heart's gold furnace heat.

Mint me beautiful medals, and hand them me hot
From the fiery hammering of your heart: I cast
My all into your flux, you melting pot
Of my old, white metal of meaning, you fine
Crucible where new blossoms of shape are begot.

AND JUDE THE OBSCURE AND
HIS BELOVED

Oh my God what a bitter shame,
After all this time of patience and pain
Still to answer me just the same,
Still to say: "I want no flame
To lick me up, but only the warm
The steady glow: for oh the charm
Of your heart of fire in which I look!
Oh better there than in any book
Glow and enact the dramas and dreams
I love for ever: and it seems
Richer than life itself, till desire
Comes licking in flame through the bars of your lips,
And over my face your stray fire slips
Leaving a burn and a smart
That must have the oil of illusion: Oh heart
Of love and beauty loose no more
Your reptile flames of passion: store
Your beauty in the basket of your soul,
Be all yourself one bonny, burning coal,
That steady stays with joy of its own fire,
But do not seek to take me by desire,
Oh do not seek to thrust in me your fire.

For in the firing all my porcelain
Of flesh would crack and shiver with keen pain,
My ivory and idols split in twain,
My temples broken, then I should remain
A priestess execrated, full of stain."

But Oh my God what a bitter shame
That I, who have known her a little, am kept
Like a glowing brazier, faintly blue of flame,
Floating above my silver, so that the adept
At love should sprinkle me daily with a rare
Sweet fragrance of love, and feed me with kisses fair,

And gather my burning, beautiful dreams for her share,
And leave me torture and wrath and a drossed despair.

Oh my God what a bitter shame
After all this time it should be the same,
That she should ward away the flame,
Yet warm herself at the fire, and blame
Me that I flicker in the basket:
Me that I glow not still in content
When all my substance is being spent;
What a bitter shame that she should ask it
        Of love not to desire,
        Not to reach one tongue of fire
        Burning like Dives in Hell, to her
        Not to utter one cry to her.

A DRAMA

The Man Speaks:

Though you move with a quiet grace, like a cloud
Emerging and crossing the clear sky unperceived,
Though white you are, cool-drooping, and rich
As wild white fox gloves drooping with fulness,
Because when your eyes look up at me they startle
Me as a dark blue water between the hills
Revealing the sky through the ragged earth; and sudden
I see the strong sound earth betrayed as a floating
Flimsy husk-ball through whose rifts there looks
The naked sky:
                So, as you look up at me
From out your face's fair forgetful contours,
You startle me with reminiscence of the great
Faint-fashioned wonder wherein lost we spin,
And I am dazed:
                You always loose me adrift:
For whether I see you set the daffodils
Along the table at noon, or when you bring

The lighted lamp into my room at night,
Or softly tapping at my study door
Set down the tray before me as I work,
Always, before you go, the heavy blue
Of your eyes draws open my sheltering, flimsy doors
To the vast of space where brightness races the blue,
Where this frail shadowy husk of a day is lost,
Bewildered amid the moving immensity
Of this eternal life:
                            And though we two
Have closed in love like very death for stress,
Pleasure so heavy-intense it hurt too much,
Though we have closed together through the nights,
Still I will leave you, still forsake you too:

For you set wide the doors of my venturesome ark
And all my doves are launched abroad and lost,
And I am drifting like a shell discarded.

Yea, I would shut my eyes, I would close my windows
Upon these awful waters of Life and Death,
And in my fragile, awkward boat, between
The two immensities would float unwilling,
Still gay and laughing in my own vain strength,
Aye busy with a few hard tasks, and wrath
With a few swift passions, would I drift away
To founder at last within the dreadful flood
That I have laughed my way across with zest,
Unmindful of its terrors:
                            And so, and so
I leave you while I play my game of living,
I play my reckless game to win my point,
So tiny when you open sky-doors on me,
So big and worthy in my own small ark:
And having won I will lie down to sleep
As buoyant as a sea-bird on the sea.

And I will leave you who would make me turn
Aside to lose myself for very smallness—I

Will leave you, for I must forget myself;
I go to play my game of life within
The bonny floating ark of this fair world,
Roofed with a day's near ceiling, and a dark
Low naked ceiling of the night-sky held
Aloft by one great bending rafter, dusty
With dim light, showing the heads of the silver nails.
—So much, so rare a game, So quick a heart-beating,
I would not miss it for your ache of wonder,
Nor, Eve, for your heavy anguish of embrace
That drinks me up, as if I were a speck
Of seed to lose myself in the body of this blue,
And losing mingle in the procreant womb—
          —I leave you so—I must.

The Woman Speaks:
And shall I see him never, nor will he turn
Ever again and laughing look at me,
His reckless red mouth laughing cruelly,
Even while in his innermost eyes there burn
Blue darknesses of wonder, that hold all
The mystery I strive toward; however
I beat my wings toward it, never
To come at it, to breathe it in, this dark
Wonder I crave for that burns strong in him.

I know the sweet red hutch of his mouth, where warm
Live things caress me and entreat my fondling:
But there within the blue-sky rims that cope
The loop-holes of that innermost Night of him,
Within his eyes' sincerest pupils, there,
Ah there within that blue-coped well, ah there
I wish to drown myself.
              Yea, and he leaves
Me for another, lesser, sorrier love:
Tomorrow marries, tomorrow fetters himself
Upon a rock from whence, ah charlatan,
He strikes the gush of passion easily,
And puts his mouth down to the gushing stream

And drinks himself, like a soaked, gorged creature, dull,
Aye, suffocated with a drunk surfeit,
And all the wonder lost from out his eyes,
From out his fingers, from that supple string
His body that does shake like the wire of a harp.

He leaves me, goes down to the Southron folk,
Further, into another rank, beyond
All hope of my attainment. Thence, serene,
He will look round and note me not, no more
Than he will note the other ordinary women
Who pass along the street.
                              Yet still
This one night yet he lieth here to hand,
Here in this house where I have served so long,
And where he came to lilt my life along
His own song-measure, many months ago.
                              I served him so
In all things, to the last, like a rhapsody
Filling his single measure with music full,
Setting the flowers along the midday meal
As if for him alone of all our men
They should flutter and turn his way; and saving the fresh
Linen within my own old, fragrant chest,
As if the Southern-wood should soothe his dreams,
And stealing into his sleep, should set him longing
For me, who am cold as a Christmas rose.
And once again, as many a time before
I steal across the hushèd corridor
To his guest chamber; knowing each sinew and vein
Of this old house whose strangers I now entertain.

He sleeps, as ever, generously unlocked . . .
And well I know to open silently,
And ah!—I know the shadows that the tree
Shakes o'er his walls when the wind disturbs the night,
And the boughs of the lime tree shake and toss the light
Of the street-lamp through the unblinded window pane.

And well I know he sleeps to wake no more
After tonight;—for "See," I said to him,
"Tonight, this very last of our nights, we
Will dream into the future." Did he guess?
For he has drunk the morsels white of sleep,
Reckless about the bitterness of the draught,
And smiling curiously, with watchful eyes,
As he did sip the bitter milk of sleep
I brought for him, and waited while he drank.
I waited, and my silence challenged him:
In recklessness he drank, with a bitter mouth,
And curious, smiling eyes.
        And now he sleeps,
With head thrown back and partly opened mouth,
Whose edge of hair curves thickly to the red.
        But ah, ah me,
He draws a deep, hard breath from space to space,
From space to longer space lifts a harsh breath:
And I can see the pulse within his throat
Shake, and sink down to rest, then shake again;
And still the long, harsh breath sinks hoarsely out,
And still his life shakes at the latch of sleep,
To open ere the thief have done his work,
Have stolen the treasure of Awakening.
        —So, he will wake no more—

And ever and anon the great breaths come
Like water sucked from deep down underground
By a slow, gasping pump, that has awful intervals
Of waiting: —And the room stands still with fright
At these wide-spacèd, torn, enormous breaths,
That lift up high, then drop his strange harsh breast
In terrible rhythm like blows that are struck, till the leaves
Bristle and fly in shadows across the walls—
—And I have come to watch.

        And Oh, Oh beautiful,
Before the life shall cease to urge and stride
Through that white strait of thy thick, shaken throat,

I wish that I might dip myself within
The stream, and cloak me over with thy red,
And hands, and face, and breast with that hot cloak,
The fiery mixture of thy life, so I
Might follow swift behind thee when thou lets
Thyself slip out the leash, and hunts thy way
Through the close thickets to the clear of death;
—Might follow warm and glad, who sit here cold
Watching thy great soul tug within the leash
That holds it back—might follow soon to thee;
For watching I am frozen as in ice,
My limbs are numb and heavy, and my heart
Cleaves frozen to the walls of my cold breast.
                   And I must wait
Till off thy mouth has leapt the flame of life
Up the dark shaft to death. And what if I,
Though I shall hasten after when I see
Thy flame leap free, what if I am left behind!
Ah sure, to venture all alone in death
Were worse than being left alone in life.

But I will catch thee up at a stride of death,
And we will pass together like one red flame,
We leap like two clasped flames from off the fire
Of living, and waver in sweet extinguishment.

And who can separate us any more
Than who can separate two lithe, rich flames
That leap and meet together at the mouth
Of the dark shaft that issues to the Night
From the lit room of living.

And what is death to us but a begetting?
What are we but as seed ripened within
The loins of this our tissue of travail, our life's
Twin flesh. And what is death for me, what is it
But the utter anguished springing forth of me,
Like seed from out the ripened loins of life
Into the passive, unknown, monstrous womb,
Into the fertile darkness after death?

SEPARATED

Ah I know how you have sought me,
The books that you have touched cleave close to me,
The withering flowers that days ago you brought me
Speak in half-bitter scent your dream of me.

And ever, ere I come, you have departed,
And it must be so ever, we must not meet,
And ever I see your traces, broken-hearted
Hear re-echo your slow, reluctant feet.

ASSUMING THE BURDEN

My eyes being downcast,
I saw on the red earth
Hundreds of violet-heads, in a shower
Over the withered mosses and red earth
About her feet.

And looking at her bosom,
I saw the broken violets,
The heavy, purple, perfumed bunch
Was shattered altogether
About her feet.

And looking in her eyes
I saw the pain among the iris there,
And ruin of her innocence upon
Her naked soul of fear,
And I was hurt.

I kissed her once again upon the mouth,
With sorrowful fingers stroked her eyelids shut,
Then looked again within her eyes,
Loving her tenderly
Whom I had hurt.

Then up from out her very soul there seemed
To rise an odour of purple violets crushed

And broken by my weight: and the purple steam
Of her soul's pained perfume
Enveloped us.

So that within a pillar of purple smoke,
Dark incense, did I feel her offer up
Her soul to me, and she was very glad,
But I was afraid, henceforth
To acknowledge "Us."

THE CHIEF MYSTERY

The stinging nettles on my wrists woke me,
    Who had not slept . . .
I do not know where I had been
Nor what had become of me
    But I had not slept . . .
I only know that like a sod
In a meadow lost I lay,
And that a peewit called . . .
    But whether it called in my soul,
    Or whether it rang in the air,
    Or whether my heart was its nest,
    I do not know.
I was there, that was all . . .
And like a sod in a meadow
I was embedded in the rest of things
Along with the moon.
    For the full moon shone: but whether
    It lay on me as on water,
    Or whether I was the darkness with arched wings
    Hovering over it
    To fold in a shining concave the pale night,
    I do not know.
I awoke with the young nettles on my wrists,
    And I lifted my head:
And then I knew I had taken my mouth from her throat—
    And I raised my breast;

Knowing then I had taken my bosom from her crushed breasts.
    And I went back with my mouth to her mouth
    So glad to have been lost,
    So glad to find myself again.

Yet looking again at the night
Still I could not distinguish myself:
I said "This is grass that twinkles in the dark,
    There is something about that they call the wind,
    And that white scud of heaven
    Is a track of clouds across the moon;
    But I, where among them all am I?"

  Then the stinging nettles on my wrists
  Showed me some other lovers stealing down the other hedgerow,
  And I lay close down,
  Saying "It is she—it is I—
  That is her small ear against my eyes,
  This is I—this is I—

Perhaps the tiny young nettles have stung her ears."
And I took her ear like the leaf of a water-flower between my lips,
And I said "Love?"
For I was not sure of myself.
But she put her fingers on my neck, under my collar,
And her fingers were cool,
And I said, " 'Tis I,
I am here!"

EROTIC

  And when I see the heavy red fleece
  Of the creeper on the breast of the house opposite
  Lift and ruffle in the wind,
  I feel as if feathers were lifted and shook
  On the breast of a robin that is fluttered with pain,
  And my own breast opens in quick response
  And its beat of pain is distributed on the wind.

And when I see the trees sway close,
Lean together and lift wild arms to embrace,
I lift my breast and lean forward,
Holding down my leaping arms.

And when black leaves stream out in a trail down the wind,
I raise my face so it shall wreathe me
Like a tress of black hair,
And I open my lips to take a strand of keen hair.

And when I see the thick white body of train-smoke break
And fly fast away,
I stifle a cry of despair.

MOON NEW-RISEN

I saw the sky was lit
   Behind the sand-hills
But when I crossed the dunes
   And the moon stood opposite
    I was afraid.

For the golden moon communes
   With the darkness opposite
And small on the sand swills
   The sea, afraid
    To interrupt,
    But I, abrupt
Broke into the privacy
   Of the moon and the night:
The moon was in love, and she
Looked up at the night, and he
   Kissed her deliciously,
   And the world was alight.

RED

Then he laid down the bow of his violin
And, turning round in pain from the music he
Had made and played for me, he said in grief,

Lifting his haunted eyes to me: "I am wanting in song.
You must make my songs for me, love. I have none;
Being too mirthless to move the lilt of singing,
Meshed and tangled too much in the skein of guilt,
Caught, when my heart would leap, in a net of lives,
Lapped prisoner in the cords of love I have spun
From out of my heart and loins, choked and shackled
By my own bonds of blood, and music-less,
Who ache with an anguish of music to make for you . . ."

And I was songless as he was, and looked at him
Through a pain of rising tears, and did not reply.
But laying forever our effort at music by,
Together we trode the evening, where the sun
Streamed redness down the air, shot red on his eyes . . .
And all the sorrel spears in the lush long grass
As if withdrawn from living wounds ran red
And rank, and dripped with blood, and dripped again
As we crossed the mow-fields down the glowing hill
In showers of minute ruddy drops from their blades . . .
And moony-daisies underneath the mist
Of dusty grasses, like the stars that dawn
Under the coloured fading-off of the sky,
Frightened me with the steadfastness of their looking
Up through the veil as we passed.
                                    And now, and now
That evening evermore hangs red for me,
Red on my memory, heavy with our own blood;
And ah, with all his blood! for ere the stain
Of my breaking had died upon him, ere the stain,
The crimson sheaf of the west, the deep fetched sigh
Which yields the day to death, ere yet the light,
Had utterly gone from out of the trembling sky,
He opened the valves of life, and his life sighed out
Into the darkness sighing on dark, and I
Was unaware: but his wife cried in her dream,
And his children stirred in their sleep, and when they woke
A shadow was deep in their eyes.

SHE WAS A GOOD LITTLE WIFE

The hum of the bees in the pear-tree bloom
    Penetrated my blood.

I looked in her eyes. The gloom
    In them did me good.

I knew that she was waiting,
    Ah she,
I knew that she was baiting
Her looks, her bearing to me;

For all her shyness, baiting
    Her looks with desire.
And the bustle of bees in the pear-tree bloom,
And their subtle, eager booming,
    Like a murmur of fire
    Passed into my blood.

PEAR-BLOSSOM

The pear-blossom is a fountain of foam
At your cottage-end; it falls back again
In sprays and spurts of foam.

The flowers against your window pane
Are a "poppy-show". Peep, while you comb
Your hair, peep out on the lane!—

That year, when the pear was out, my delight
As you crawled nakèd over me,
Your small breasts clumps of white

Pear-blossom hanging! And one small knee
Dug firm in my breast as you reached out right
To the window and the white pear-tree!

And you climbed back nakèd over me
As I lay on the bed, and you sat with the flowers on your thighs,
And looked at me;

And as I lay and looked in your eyes
You wept, and the bed trembled under me.
I was faint with surprise—

I am terrified of the pear-blossom
Round and white as a small bosom
With a nipple centre of red:

My God, to think it is gone for ever,
To think that you are gone for ever,
I am terrified you are dead.

AT THE CEARNE

On the little bank, below the orchard,
Beyond the gay, pink blossom,
Under the beechen hedge,
Am I for ever making love to you.

The Weald, the enormous bed
Between the downs, grows hazy with sunshine
Slow cattle stir on the steep meadow near by.
On the little bank our two souls
Glow like blossoms astart
With gladness.

No, I am not here, I am not here.
Life twisting its crazed machinery
Has conveyed this thing that sits and writes
Hither, has taken away to that hell
In the city, something of you.
But you and I, you and I
On the little bank where bluebells droop
Sit and make love to each other.

As you sit on the trestle, I on the ground,
The glitter of the buckle of your shoe
Laughs like an eye at me. And I

Shy of your face, still bend to woo
Your feet, and touching your ankles, try
To find you and fill my soul with you.

A KISS

A red flower falls to its dim reflection
    —Hush then, never a word.
A red flower falls to its red reflection,
The shadow dances up in affection,
And two are one in sweet connection,
    —Never a sound was heard.

Something has gone down the silent river
    —What does the robin say?
Silver slow goes by the river,
Far off in gold the willows quiver,
And further still 'neath the sunset gather
    Red flowers that have floated away.

[OTHER WOMEN HAVE REARED IN ME]

Other women have reared in me
Bitter and painful flowers;
Different, yes, shall the posies be
From this love of ours!

My flesh is ready like tilled loam
To catch afire with life,
With a steady rush of living, a foam
Of flowering strife.

My heart is firm and solid, it needs
Only you like the sun
Of spring upon it, and it speeds
For the joy like a fount undone.

Happy am I, a naked sprig,
In my bursting and budding; I feel
My joy-blossoms shaping, am big
With gladness, reel
Prolific; I am a blossoming twig.

THE WILD COMMON

The quick sparks on the gorse bushes are leaping,
Little jets of sunlight-texture imitating flame;
Above them, exultant, the peewits are sweeping:
They are lords of the desolate wastes of sadness their screamings
proclaim.

Rabbits, handfuls of brown earth, lie
Low-rounded on the mournful grass they have bitten down to the
quick.
Are they asleep?—Are they alive?—Now see, when I
Move my arms the hill bursts and heaves under their spurting kick.

The common flaunts bravely; but below, from the rushes
Crowds of glittering king-cups surge to challenge the blossoming
bushes;
There the lazy streamlet pushes
Its curious course mildly; here it wakes again, leaps, laughs, and
gushes.

Into a deep pond, an old sheep-dip,
Dark, overgrown with willows, cool, witn the brook ebbing through
so slow,
Naked on the steep, soft lip
Of the bank I stand watching my own white shadow quivering to
and fro.

What if the gorse flowers shrivelled and kissing were lost?
Without the pulsing waters, where were the marigolds and the songs
of the brook?
If my veins and my breasts with love embossed
Withered, my insolent soul would be gone like flowers that the hot
wind took.

So my soul like a passionate woman turns,
Filled with remorseful terror to the man she scorned, and her love
For myself in my own eyes' laughter burns,
Runs ecstatic over the pliant folds rippling down to my belly from
the breast-lights above.

Over my sunlit skin the warm, clinging air,
Rich with the songs of seven larks singing at once, goes kissing me
glad.
And the soul of the wind and my blood compare
Their wandering happiness, and the wind, wasted in liberty, drifts
on and is sad.

Oh but the water loves me and folds me,
Plays with me, sways me, lifts me and sinks me as though it were
living blood,
Blood of a heaving woman who holds me,
Owning my supple body a rare glad thing, supremely good.

RENAISSANCE

We have bit no forbidden apple—
Eve and me—
Yet the splashes of day and night
Falling round us no longer dapple
The same Eden with purple and white.

This is our own still valley
My Eden, my home
But the day shows it vivid with feeling
And the pallor of night does not tally
With the dark sleep that once covered the ceiling.

My little red heifer—go and look at her eyes—
She will calve tomorrow—
Take the lantern, and watch the Sow, for fear she grab her new litter
With red snarling jaws; let yourself listen to the cries
Of the new-born, and the unborn; and the old owl and the bats as
they flitter
And wake to the sound of the woodpigeons, and lie and listen
Till you can borrow
A few quick beats of a woodpigeon's heart—then rise
See the morning sun on the shaken iris glisten
And say that this home, this valley, is wider than Paradise.

I have learned it all from my Eve,
This warm dumb wisdom,
She's a finer instructor than years,
She has shown me the strands that weave
Us all one in laughter and tears.

I didn't learn from her speech—
Staggering words.
I can't tell how it comes
But I think her kisses reach
Down where the live web hums.

VIRGIN YOUTH

Now and again
All my body springs alive,
And the life that is polarised in my eyes,
That quivers between my eyes and mouth,
Flies like a wild thing across my body,
Leaving my eyes half empty, and clamorous,
Filling my still breasts with a flush and a flame,
Gathering the soft ripples below my breasts
Into urgent, passionate waves,
And my soft, slumbering belly
Quivering awake with one impulse of desire,
Gathers itself fiercely together;
And my docile, fluent arms
Knotting themselves with wild strength
To clasp—what they have never clasped.
Then I tremble, and go trembling
Under the wild, strange tyranny of my body,
Till it has spent itself,
And the relentless nodality of my eyes reasserts itself,
Till the bursten flood of life ebbs back to my eyes,
Back from my beautiful, lonely body
Tired and unsatisfied.

THE SCHOOLMASTER [A]

To one of my boys

How can I teach you when your blue
   Eyes look at me so?
Your deep bewilderment filters through
   My mind, and I know
That I put to flight from out of you
   Rare birds that no
Enticing will recall: when I
   Do watch your eyes,
Wherein the timid wonders fly
   Off in surprise,
Then, oh, I do forget all my
   Enterprise,
And all the lessons let slip by:
   For you are wise.

I

Morning

Scripture Lesson
The hum and whisper of the class, like a little wind
From the surf, has arisen: the boys are muttering
The psalms, and furtively from among the texts
Forbidden things and thoughts come fluttering.

Now I am on the strand of a turbulent sea,
A tossing sea of turbulent strife, where now
I stand reluctant to enter, to dream no more, but to bow
Myself and gather the waters beneath me, and lose
Myself in the roar of life, which shall take and obliterate me.

For the sun is pouring like yellow wine outside;
The mist is a cup of wine, and the new and old
Woodstacks beside the railway glisten and glow
Like ivory and golden marble: two black crows hold
Sentry upon the dead oak, while another below
Flaps up from the playground as a great train steams south
With her silken steam like a banner behind her aflow.

The men uplifted on the new white woodstack stand
Still in the sun to watch, and I can see
Dark waving of their arms against the bland
Blue silken sky, before they bend anew
To hoist the next white plank: their movement seems
Like a glittering of shadows within the morning air,
Dark glitter of life amid a sky that teems
With light and luxurious blueness:
                              But the noise of life
The surge and tide of life in the turbulent class
Comes over the softness and silence of morning: I pass
                              Reluctantly,
To the reckless extravagant turmoil of living, the strife
                              Of the boys with me.

I I

Afternoon

The Last Lesson
When will the bell ring, and end this weariness?
How long have they tugged the leash, and strained apart
My pack of unruly hounds: I cannot start
Them again on a quarry of knowledge they hate to hunt,
I can haul them and urge them no more.
No more can I endure to bear the brunt
Of the books that lie out on the desks: a full three score
Of several insults of blotted pages and scrawl
Of slovenly work that they have offered me.
I am sick, and tired more than any thrall
Upon the woodstacks working weariedly.
                              And shall I take
The last dear fuel and heap it on my soul
Till I rouse my will like a fire to consume
Their dross of indifference, and burn the scroll
Of their insults in punishment?—I will not!
I will not waste myself to embers for them,
Not all for them shall the fires of my life be hot,

For myself a heap of ashes of weariness, till sleep
Shall have raked the embers clear: I will keep
Some of my strength for myself, for if I should sell
It all for them, I should hate them—
      —I will sit and wait for the bell.

III

Evening

The hours have tumbled their lustreless, tarnished sands:
There lies the dull red heap of their sand in the west.
I carry my anger sullenly 'cross these waste lands,
For tomorrow will pour them all back, the school hours I detest.

I pick my way over threadbare grass, which is pressed
Into mud—the space fast shrinks in the builder's hands,
As my wild soul shrinks, and the songs are driven from my breast.
The hours have tumbled their lustreless, tarnished sands.

One broken thorn-tree still in the twilight stands
Defending the memory of birds that used to nest
And sing in this space that the builder now demands:
There lies a dull red heap of his sand in the west.

All day the clink of the hammers has oppressed
The poor shut dandelions whom small warmth expands
Into rollicking suns: and their lost gold rots—compressed.
—I carry my anger sullenly 'cross these waste lands.

The hours have ceased to fall, and a star commands
Darkness to raise the stricken dignity, and Rest
To open my blossom-full breast from its dreary bands—
   To-morrow will pour them all back, the dull hours I detest.

IV

The Punisher

I have fetched the tears up out of the little wells,
Scooped them up with small iron words
    Dripping over the runnels.

The harsh cold wrath of my words drove on, and still
I watched the tears on the fruited cheeks of the boys
    Glitter and spill.

Cringing Pity, and my Self, white-handed, came
Hovering to pluck at the Judgment which stood in my eyes
    Whirling a flame.

The tears are dry, the cheeks' young fruits are fresh
For laughter, and glad the exonerated eyes, for I
    Am caught in the mesh.

The Cherubim of Judgment have departed from me,
Desolate and despoiled am I, for their flaming storm
    Wrecked chiefly me.

The fire rose up and the bush blazed forth God's grace,
The thorn-leaves crackled and twisted and sweated in anguish.
    Then God left the place.

Like a flower that the frost has hugged and let go, my heart
Is heavy, is clogged and heavy with wasted ash;
    For it gave the smart;
My hand is heavy and helpless, since wielding the lash.

V

A Snowy Day in School

All the slow school hours, round the irregular hum of the class,
Have pressed the immeasurable spaces of hoarse silence,
Muffling my mind, as snow muffles the sounds that pass
Down the soiled street. We have pattered the lessons ceaselessly—

But the faces of the boys, in the brooding, yellow light
Have shone for me like a crowded constellation of stars,
Like full-blown flowers dimly shaking at the night,
Like floating froth on an ebbing shore in the moon.

Out of each star, dark, strange beams that disquiet:
In the open depths of each flower, dark restless drops:
Twin bubbles, shadow-full of mystery and challenge in the foam's
    whispering riot:
—How can I answer the challenge of so many eyes!

The thick snow is crumpled on the roof, it plunges down
Awfully. Must I call back those hundred eyes?—A voice
Wakes from the hum, faltering about a noun—
My question! My God, I must break from this hoarse silence,

That rustles beyond the stars to me.—There,
I have startled a hundred eyes, and I must look
Them an answer back. It is more than I can bear.

The snow descends as if the dull sky shook
In flakes of shadow down; and through the gap
Between the ruddy schools sweeps one black rook.

The rough snowball in the playground stands huge and still
With fair flakes settling down on it.—Beyond, the town
Is lost in the shadowed silence the skies distil.

And all things are possessed by silence, and they can brood
Wrapped up in the sky's dim space of hoarse silence
Earnestly—and oh for me this class is a bitter rood.

VI

The Best of School

The blinds are drawn because of the sun,
And the boys and the room in a colourless gloom
Of under-water float: bright ripples run
Across the walls as the blinds are blown
To let the sunlight in; and I,
As I sit on the beach of the class alone,
Watch the boys in their summer blouses,
As they write, their round heads busily bowed:
And one after another rouses
And lifts his face and looks at me,
And my eyes meet his very quietly,
Then he turns again to his work, with glee.

With glee he turns, with a little glad
Ecstasy of work he turns from me,
An ecstasy surely sweet to be had.

And very sweet while the sunlight waves
In the fresh of the morning, it is to be
A teacher of these young boys, my slaves
Only as swallows are slaves to the eaves
They build upon, as mice are slaves
To the man who threshes and sows the sheaves.

Oh, sweet it is
To feel the lads' looks light on me,
Then back in a swift, bright flutter to work,
As birds who are stealing turn and flee.

Touch after touch I feel on me
As their eyes glance at me for the grain
Of rigour they taste delightedly.

And all the class,
As tendrils reached out yearningly
Slowly rotate till they touch the tree
That they cleave unto, that they leap along
Up to their lives—so they to me.

So do they cleave and cling to me,
So I lead them up, so do they twine
Me up, caress and clothe with free
Fine foliage of lives this life of mine;
The lowest stem of this life of mine,
The old hard stem of my life
That bears aloft toward rarer skies
My top of life, that buds on high
Amid the high wind's enterprise.

They all do clothe my ungrowing life
With a rich, a thrilled young clasp of life:
A clutch of attachment, like parenthood,
Mounts up to my heart, and I find it good.

And I lift my head upon the troubled tangled world, and though the
    pain
Of living my life were doubled, I still have this to comfort and
    sustain,
I have such swarming sense of lives at the base of me, such sense of
    lives
Clustering upon me, reaching up, as each after the other strives
To follow my life aloft to the fine wild air of life and the storm of
    thought,
And though I scarcely see the boys, or know that they are there,
    distraught
As I am with living my life in earnestness, still progressively and
    alone,
Though they cling, forgotten the most part, not companions, scarcely
    known
To me—yet still because of the sense of their closeness clinging
    densely to me,
And slowly fingering up my stem and following all tinily
The way that I have gone and now am leading, they are dear to me.

They keep me assured, and when my soul feels lonely,
All mistrustful of thrusting its shoots where only
I alone am living, then it keeps
Me comforted to feel the warmth that creeps
Up dimly from their striving; it heartens my strife:
And when my heart is chill with loneliness,
Then comforts it the creeping tenderness
Of all the strays of life that climb my life.

THE SCHOOLMASTER [B]

I

A Snowy Day in School

All the slow school hours, round the irregular hum of the class,
Have pressed immeasurable spaces of hoarse silence
Muffling my mind, as snow muffles the sounds that pass
Down the soiled street. We have pattered the lessons
ceaselessly—

But the faces of the boys, in the brooding, yellow light
Have shone for me like a crowded constellation of stars,
Like full-blown flowers dimly shaking at the night,
Like floating froth on an ebbing shore in the moon.

Out of each star, dark, strange beams that disquiet:
In the open depths of each flower, dark restless drops:
Twin bubbles, shadow-full of mystery and challenge in the foam's
    whispering riot:
—How can I answer the challenge of so many eyes!

The thick snow is crumpled on the roof, it plunges down
Awfully. Must I call back those hundred eyes?—A voice
Wakes from the hum, faltering about a noun—
My question! My God, I must break from this hoarse silence

That rustles beyond the stars to me.—There,
I have startled a hundred eyes, and I must look
Them an answer back. It is more than I can bear.

The snow descends as if the dull sky shook
In flakes of shadow down; and through the gap
Between the ruddy schools sweeps one black rook.

The rough snowball in the playground stands huge and still
With fair flakes settling down on it.—Beyond, the town
Is lost in the shadowed silence the skies distil.

And all things are possessed by silence, and they can brood
Wrapped up in the sky's dim space of hoarse silence
Earnestly—and oh for me this class is a bitter rood.

The Best of School

The blinds are drawn because of the sun,
And the boys and the room in a colourless gloom
Of under-water float: bright ripples run
Across the walls as the blinds are blown
To let the sunlight in; and I,
As I sit on the beach of the class alone,
Watch the boys in their summer blouses,
As they write, their round heads busily bowed:
And one after another rouses
And lifts his face and looks at me,
And my eyes meet his very quietly,
Then he turns again to his work, with glee.

With glee he turns, with a little glad
Ecstasy of work he turns from me,
An ecstasy surely sweet to be had.
And very sweet while the sunlight waves
In the fresh of the morning, it is to be
A teacher of these young boys, my slaves
Only as swallows are slaves to the eaves
They build upon, as mice are slaves
To the man who threshes and sows the sheaves.

Oh, sweet it is
To feel the lads' looks light on me,
Then back in a swift, bright flutter to work,
As birds who are stealing turn and flee.

Touch after touch I feel on me
As their eyes glance at me for the grain
Of rigour they taste delightedly.

And all the class,
As tendrils reached out yearningly
Slowly rotate till they touch the tree
That they cleave unto, that they leap along
Up to their lives—so they to me.

So do they cleave and cling to me,
So I lead them up, so do they twine
Me up, caress and clothe with free
Fine foliage of lives this life of mine;
The lowest stem of this life of mine,
The old hard stem of my life
That bears aloft towards rarer skies
My top of life, that buds on high
Amid the high wind's enterprise.

They all do clothe my ungrowing life
With a rich, a thrilled young clasp of life;
A clutch of attachment, like parenthood,
Mounts up to my heart, and I find it good.

And I lift my head upon the troubled tangled world, and though the
  pain
Of living my life were doubled, I still have this to comfort and sustain,
I have such swarming sense of lives at the base of me, such sense of
  lives
Clustering upon me, reaching up, as each after the other strives
To follow my life aloft to the fine wild air of life and the storm of
  thought,
And though I scarcely see the boys, or know that they are there,
  distraught
As I am with living my life in earnestness, still progressively and
  alone,
Though they cling, forgotten the most part, not companions,
  scarcely known
To me—yet still because of the sense of their closeness clinging
  densely to me,
And slowly fingering up my stem and following all tinily
The way that I have gone and now am leading, they are dear to me.

They keep me assured, and when my soul feels lonely,
All mistrustful of thrusting its shoots where only
I alone am living, then it keeps
Me comforted to feel the warmth that creeps
Up dimly from their striving; it heartens my strife:

And when my heart is chill with loneliness,
Then comforts it the creeping tenderness
Of all the strays of life that climb my life.

III

Afternoon in School

The Last Lesson
When will the bell ring, and end this weariness?
How long have they tugged the leash, and strained apart
My pack of unruly hounds: I cannot start
Them again on a quarry of knowledge they hate to hunt,
I can haul them and urge them no more.
No more can I endure to bear the brunt
Of the books that lie out on the desks: a full three score
Of several insults of blotted pages and scrawl
Of slovenly work that they have offered me.
I am sick, and tired more than any thrall
Upon the woodstacks working weariedly.

              And shall I take
The last dear fuel and heap it on my soul
Till I rouse my will like a fire to consume
Their dross of indifference, and burn the scroll
Of their insults in punishment?—I will not!
I will not waste myself to embers for them,
Not all for them shall the fires of my life be hot,
For myself a heap of ashes of weariness, till sleep
Shall have raked the embers clear: I will keep
Some of my strength for myself, for if I should sell
It all for them, I should hate them—
        —I will sit and wait for the bell.

DREAMS OLD AND NASCENT

OLD

I

I have opened the window to warm my hands on the sill
Where the sunlight soaks in the stone: the afternoon
Is full of dreams, my love; the boys are all still
In a wishful dream of Lorna Doone.

The clink of the shunting engines is sharp and fine
Like savage music striking far off; and away
On the uplifted blue Palace, light pools stir and shine
Where the glass is domed up the blue, soft day.

II

There lies the world, my Darling, full of wonder, and wistfulness,
    and strange
Recognitions and greetings of half-acquaint things, as I greet the
    cloud
Of blue Palace aloft there, among the misty indefinite dreams that
    range
At the back of my life's horizon, where the dreams from the past
    lives crowd.

Over the nearness of Norwood Hill, through the mellow veil
Of the afternoon, glows only the old romance of David and Dora,
With the old, sweet, soothing tears, and laughter that shakes the sail
Of the ship of the soul over seas where dreamed dreams lure the
    unoceaned explorer.

III

Over the bygone, hushèd years
Streaming back where the mist distils
Into forgetfulness: soft sailing waters, where fears
No longer shake: where the silk sail fills
With the unfelt breeze that ebbs over the seas, when the storm
Of living has passed, on and on
Through the coloured iridescence that swims in the warm
Wake of the hushèd tumult now spent and gone
Drifts my boat, wistfully lapsing after
The mists of receding tears, and the echo of laughter.

IV

My world is a painted fresco, where coloured shapes
Of old ineffectual lives linger blurred and warm:
An endless tapestry the past has woven, drapes
The halls of my life, and compels my soul to conform.

NASCENT

V

Through the wakened afternoon, riding down my dreams
Fluent active figures of men pass along the railway.
There is something stirs in me from the flow of their limbs as they
    move
Out of the distance, nearer.
Here in the subtle, rounded flesh
Beats the active ecstasy, suddenly lifting my eyes
Into quick response.
The fascination of the restless Creator, through the mesh of men
Moving, vibrating endlessly in the rounded flesh
Challenges me, and is answered.

V I

Oh my boys, bending over your books
In you is trembling and fusing
The creation of a new-patterned dream, dream of a generation.

V I I

The old dreams are beloved, beautiful, soft-toned, and sure
But the dream-stuff is molten and moving mysteriously.
This is no wistful allure
For am I not also dream-stuff, diffusing myself in the pattern,
Flowing I know not how, yet seriously
Going into my place.

V I I I

Here have I found an answer for my hollow yearning:
Eyes where I can watch the swim of old dreams reflected on the
    molten metal of dreams,
Watch the stir whose rhythm is secret, whose secret is sure and safe:
The great activity swelling, through the round flesh pulsing,
Impelling, shaping the coming dream;
Visible under the changing eyes,
Under the mobile features.

I X

The flush of the great mystery,
The radiance of the Unseen Shaper,
Is in me a trembling gladness.
As the subtle heat
Quickens the hastening, white-hot metal,
The power of the melting, fusing force,
The great, mysterious One, is swelling and shaping the dreams in
    the flesh,
Is swelling and shaping a bud into blossom,
The whole teeming flesh of mankind.

The gigantic flesh of the world
Is swelling with widespread, labouring concentration
Into one bud on the stalk of eternity,
Rounded and swelling towards the fruit of a dream.

DREAMS OLD AND NASCENT

NASCENT

My world is a painted fresco, where coloured shapes
Of old, ineffectual lives linger blurred and warm;
An endless tapestry the past has woven drapes
The halls of my life, compelling my soul to conform.

The surface of dreams is broken,
The picture of the past is shaken and scattered.
Fluent, active figures of men pass along the railway, and I am woken
From the dreams that the distance flattered.

Along the railway, active figures of men.
They have a secret that stirs in their limbs as they move
Out of the distance, nearer, commanding my dreamy world.

Here in the subtle, rounded flesh
Beats the active ecstasy.
In the sudden lifting my eyes, it is clearer,
The fascination of the quick, restless Creator moving through the
        mesh
Of men, vibrating in ecstasy through the rounded flesh.

Oh my boys, bending over your books,
In you is trembling and fusing
The creation of a new-patterned dream, dream of a generation:
And I watch to see the Creator, the power that patterns the dream.

The old dreams are beautiful, beloved, soft-toned, and sure,
But the dream-stuff is molten and moving mysteriously,
Alluring my eyes; for I, am I not also dream-stuff,
Am I not quickening, diffusing myself in the pattern, shaping and
    shapen?

Here in my class is the answer for the great yearning:
Eyes where I can watch the swim of old dreams reflected on the
    molten metal of dreams,
Watch the stir which is rhythmic and moves them all as a heart-beat
    moves the blood,
Here in the swelling flesh the great activity working,
Visible there in the change of eyes and the mobile features.

Oh the great mystery and fascination of the unseen Shaper,
The power of the melting, fusing Force—heat, light, all in one,
Everything great and mysterious in one, swelling and shaping the
    dream in the flesh,
As it swells and shapes a bud into blossom.

Oh the terrible ecstasy of the consciousness that I am life!
Oh the miracle of the whole, the widespread, labouring concentration
Swelling mankind like one bud to bring forth the fruit of a dream,
Oh the terror of lifting the innermost I out of the sweep of the
    impulse of life,
And watching the great Thing labouring through the whole round
    flesh of the world;
And striving to catch a glimpse of the shape of the coming dream,
As it quickens within the labouring, white-hot metal,
Catch the scent and the colour of the coming dream,
Then to fall back exhausted into the unconscious, molten life!

VIOLETS FOR THE DEAD

"Did ter notice that lass, sister, as stood away back
By a head-stone?"—
"Nay, I saw nöwt but th' coffin, an' th' yeller clay, an' 'ow th' black
Was blown"—

"While th' parson was prayin', I watches 'er, an' she wor fair shaken
To bits"—
"I could think o' nöwt but our Ted, an' 'im taken
In his wild fits."—

"When you'd gone, I slipped back, ter see who she might be—
Poor thing"—
"No good, I warrant; this trouble is such as she
Helped to bring."

"You should 'a seen her slive up when we'd gone
You should 'a seen her kneel an' look down.
I couldna' see her face, but her little neck shone
White, when the wind shifted her hair; that was soft an' brown,

"An' 'er body fair shook again
Wi' little sobs as you scarce could hear
An' she undid 'er jacket neck, an' then
A lot o' violets fell out of 'er bosom on 'im down theer.

"They was wild ones, white and blue;—I could tell
Because they was warm, an' the wind blew
Me a little wift, an' I knew the smell
Then she rummaged her hand in 'er bosom, an' kissed the last little
    few.

"I come away, for fear she should see
Me watchin'. Dost think there was öwt between 'em?
Tha knows 'e 'd a winsome way wi 'im, an' she
Was th' little, lovin' sort, as 'as nöwt ter screen 'em."

VIOLETS

Sister, tha knows while we was on the planks
    Aside o' th' grave, while th' coffin wor lyin' yet
On th' yaller clay, an' th' white flowers top of it
    Tryin' to keep off 'n him a bit o' th' wet,

An' parson makin' haste, an' a' the black
   Huddlin' close together a cause o' th' rain,
Did t' 'appen ter notice a bit of a lass away back
   By a head-stun, sobbin' an' sobbin' again?

   —How should I be lookin' round
     An' me standin' on the plank
  Beside the open ground,
     Where our Ted 'ud soon be sank?

  Yi, an' 'im that young,
     Snapped sudden out of all
  His wickedness, among
     Pals worse n'r ony name as you could call.

Let be that; there's some o' th' bad as we
   Like better nor all your good, an' 'e was one.
—An' cos I liked him best, yi, bett'r nor thee,
   I canna bide to think where he is gone.

Ah know tha liked 'im bett'r nor me. But let
   Me tell thee about this lass. When you had gone
Ah stopped behind on t' pad i' th' drippin' wet
   An' watched what 'er 'ad on.

Tha should ha' seed her slive up when we'd gone,
   Tha should ha' seed her kneel an' look in
At th' sloppy wet grave—an' 'er little neck shone
   That white, an' 'er shook that much, I'd like to begin

Scraïghtin' my-sen as well. 'En undid her black
   Jacket at th' bosom, an' took from out of it
Over a double 'andful of violets, all in a pack
   Ravelled blue and white—warm, for a bit

O' th' smell come waftin' to me. 'Er put 'er face
   Right intil 'em and scraïghted out again,
Then after a bit 'er dropped 'em down that place,
   An' I come away, because o' the teemin' rain.

LIGHTNING

I felt the lurch and halt of her heart
    Next my breast, where my own heart was beating;
And I laughed to feel it plunge and bound,
And strange in my blood-swept ears was the sound
    Of the words I kept repeating,
Repeating with tightened arms, and the hot blood's blindfold art.

Her breath flew warm against my neck,
    Warm as a flame in the close night air;
And the sense of her clinging flesh was sweet
Where her arms and my neck's blood-surge could meet.
    Holding her thus, did I care
That the black night hid her from me, blotted out every speck?

I leaned me forward to find her lips,
    And claim her utterly in a kiss,
When the lightning flew across her face,
And I saw her for the flaring space
    Of a second, afraid of the clips
Of my arms, inert with dread, wilted in fear of my kiss.

A moment, like a wavering spark,
    Her face lay there before my breast,
Pale love lost in a snow of fear,
And guarded by a glittering tear,
    And lips apart with dumb cries;
A moment, and she was taken again in the merciful dark.

I heard the thunder, and felt the rain,
    And my arms fell loose, and I was dumb.
Almost I hated her, she was so good,
Hated myself, and the place, and my blood,
    Which burned with rage, as I bade her come
Home, away home, ere the lightning floated forth again.

BABY-MOVEMENTS

I

RUNNING BAREFOOT

When the white feet of the baby beat across the grass
White flowers in the wind bob up and down.
And ripples poise and run, lapping across the water.
The sight of their white play among the grass,
Is like a little linnet song, winsome,
Is like when two white butterflies settle in the arms of one
   flower
For a moment, then away with a flutter of wings.
   I wait for the baby to wander hither to me,
Like a wind-shadow wandering over the water,
So she may stand on my knee
With her two bare feet on my hands
Cool as syringa buds
Cool and firm and silken as pink young peony flowers.

II

"TRAILING CLOUDS"

As a drenched, drowned bee
Hangs numb and heavy from the bending flower,
   So clings to me,
My baby, her brown hair brushed with wet tears
   And laid laughterless on her cheek,
Her soft white legs hanging heavily over my arm
   Swinging to my lullaby.
My sleeping baby hangs upon my life
   As a silent bee at the end of a shower
   Draws down the burdened flower.
She who has always seemed so light
   Sways on my arm like sorrowful, storm-heavy boughs,
Even her floating hair sinks like storm-bruised young leaves
Reaching downwards:
   As the wings of a drenched, drowned bee
   Are a heaviness, and a weariness.

A BABY RUNNING BAREFOOT

When the bare feet of the baby beat across the grass
The little white feet nod like white flowers in the wind,
They poise and run like ripples lapping across the water;
And the sight of their white play among the grass
Is like a little robin's song, winsome,
Or as two white butterflies settle in the cup of one flower
For a moment, then away with a flutter of wings.

I long for the baby to wander hither to me
Like a wind-shadow wandering over the water,
So that she can stand on my knee
With her little bare feet in my hands,
Cool like syringa buds,
Firm and silken like pink young peony flowers.

COROT

The music of music is stillness, you birds,
Cease a moment in reverence
And listen, oh Everything, listen, for words
Foil the sense.

The trees rise taller and taller, lifted
On the subtle rush of the cool grey flame
That issuing out of the moon has sifted
The spirit from each leaf's frame.

For the trailing, leisurely rapture of life
Drifts dimly forward easily hidden
By noise of small birds singing: fife
Of noisy birds, be you chidden.

The grey phosphorescent, pellucid advance
Of the luminous Purpose of God shines out
Where the lofty trees athwart stream perchance
Shake flakes of its meaning about.

The subtle, steady rush of the whole
Grey foam-fringe of advancing God
As he silently sweeps to his somewhere, his goal,
Is heard in the grass of the sod.

Is heard in the windless whisper of leaves,
In the far-off labour of men in the field
In the down-ward drooping flimsy sheaves
Of cloud, the morn skies yield.

In the tapping haste of a fallen leaf
In the flapping of red-roof smoke, and the small
Footstepping tap of men beneath
These trees so huge and tall.

For what can all sharp-rimmed substance but catch
In a backward ripple God's progress reveal
For a moment his great direction, scratch
A spark beneath his wheel.

Since God sweeps onward dim and vast
Down every channelled vein of man
Or leaf, and his passing shadow is cast
On each face for us to scan.

Then listen, for silence is not lonely,
Imitate the magnificent trees
That speak no word of their rapture, but only
Breathe largely the Luminous breeze.

MICHAEL-ANGELO

God shook thy roundness in His finger's cup,
He sunk His hands in firmness down thy sides,
And drew the circle of His grasp, O Man,
Along thy limbs delighted, thine, His bride's.

And so thou wert God-shapen: His finger
Curved thy mouth for thee, and His strong shoulder

Planted thee upright: art not proud to see
In the curve of thine exquisite form the joy of the
Moulder?

He took a handful of light and rolled a ball,
Compressed it till its beam grew wondrous dark,
Then gave thee thy dark eyes, O Man, that all
He made had doorway to thee through that spark.

God, lonely, put down His mouth in a kiss of creation,
He kissed thee, O Man, in a passion of love, and left
The vivid life of His love in thy mouth and thy nostrils;
Keep then the kiss from the adultress' theft.

NIGHT SONGS

WORKDAY EVENINGS

I Yesternight

We have shut the doors behind us, and the velvet flowers of night
Lean about us scattering their pollen puffs of golden light:

Now at last we lift our faces, and our faces come aflower
To the hushed, grey-wingèd ministrants the bats of night devour:

Now at last the closèd calyx opens from our tired eyes,
And out of the chambered weariness wanders a perfume abroad on
      its enterprise.

            Still there is left us
         The golden grainèd night aflower across the sky.
            Shall we lament for what is bereft us
         While the street lamp censers swinging high
            Stream golden smoke—?
         And river-lamps like full-blown roses
         Shake down their golden litter, that discloses
            The waters' restless stroke.

Ours even now
The street that is full of the rustling sound of a shell
Hoarsely whispering us how
The waves ran laughing up the shore at the swell

When the tide was high:
—Endless whisper of passing feet
And wash of voices along the street
Where the ebb of life slips by.

The plane-leaves fall through the lamp-light like tired quails sinking
down in the grass,
They sigh just once round our feet and are still, heavy with the dark
narcotic of weariness.

The moon, like a reddening lantern hangs low across the river; we
have eaten the narcotics of night,
We have forgotten the sunny apples of day that we craved to eat;
the moon of sleep is alight.

II Tomorrow Night

When into the night the yellow light is roused like dust above the
towns,
Or like a mist the moon has kissed from off a pool in the midst of
the downs:

Our faces flower for a little hour pale and uncertain along the street,
Daisies that waken all mistaken white-spread in expectancy to meet

The luminous mist which the poor things wist was dawn arriving
across the sky,
When the dawn is far behind the star that the lamp-lit town has
driven so high.

All the birds are folded in a silent ball of sleep,
All the leaves are fallen, and the starlight shines through the tree;

Only the bats are flickering round and round, and keep
The figure of song aflutter in a black-winged revelry.

The small birds that lifted their heads when morning looked in at
    our eyes
Have been caged and covered with darkness all day, and now that
    the doors
Are open for them they are moping, or they break with little cries
Into the night, and are lost, to sadden with jetsam the dawn's pale
    shores.

But the night is full of the flutter of invisible revelry,
And drunk with the death of the soothing, grey-wingèd creatures
    of night. . . .
The bats, depraved, are dropping gaily from off the tree,
Black birds whose songs are unutterable, spinning fantastic flight.

WHETHER OR NOT

I

Dunna thee tell me it's his'n, mother,
    Dunna thee, dunna thee.
—Oh ay! he'll be comin' to tell thee his-sèn
    Wench, wunna he?

Tha doesna mean to say to me, mother,
    He's gone wi that—
—My gel, owt'll do for a man i' the dark,
    Tha's got it flat.

But 'er's old, mother, 'er's twenty year
    Older nor him—
—Ay, an' yaller as a crowflower, an' yet i' the dark
    Er'd do for Tim.

Tha niver believes it, mother, does ter?
    It's somebody's lies.
—Ax him thy-sèn wench—a widder's lodger;
    It's no surprise.

II

A widow of forty-five
With a bitter, swarthy skin,
To ha' 'ticed a lad o' twenty-five
An' 'im to have been took in!

A widow o' forty-five
As has sludged like a horse all her life,
Till 'er's tough as whit-leather, to slive
Atween a lad an' 'is wife!

A widow of forty-five,
A tough old otchel wi' long
Witch teeth, an' 'er black hawk-eyes as I've
Mistrusted all along!

An' me as 'as kep my sèn
Shut like a daisy bud,
Clean an' new an' nice, so's when
He wed he'd ha'e summat good!

An' 'im as nice an' fresh
As any man i' the force,
To ha'e gone an' given his white young flesh
To a woman that coarse!

III

You're stout to brave this snow, Miss Stainwright,
    Are you makin' Brinsley way?
—I'm off up th' line to Underwood
    Wi' a dress as is wanted today.

Oh are you goin' to Underwood?
    'Appen then you've 'eered?
—What's that as 'appen I've 'eered-on, Missis,
    Speak up, you nedna be feared.

Why, your young man an' Widow Naylor,
    Her as he lodges wi',
They say he's got her wi' childt; but there,
    It's nothing to do wi' me.

Though if it's true they'll turn him out
    O' th' p'lice force, without fail;
An' if it's not true, I'd back my life
    They'll listen to *her* tale.

Well, I'm believin' no tale, Missis,
    I'm seein' for my-sèn;
An' when I know for sure, Missis,
    I'll talk *then*.

I V

Nay robin red-breast, tha nedna
    Sit noddin' thy head at me;
My breast's as red as thine, I reckon,
    Flayed red, if tha could but see.

Nay, you blessed pee-whips,
    You nedna screet at me!
I'm screetin' my-sèn, but are-na goin'
    To let iv'rybody see.

Tha *art* smock-ravelled, bunny,
    Larropin' neck an' crop
I' th' snow: but I's warrant thee, bunny,
    I'm further ower th' top.

V

Now sithee theer at th' railroad crossin'
Warmin' his-sèn at the stool o' fire
Under the tank as fills the ingines,
If there isn't my dearly-beloved liar!

My constable wi' 'is buttoned breast
As stout as the truth, my sirs!—An' 'is face
As bold as a robin! It's much he cares
For this nice old shame and disgrace.

Oh but he drops his flag when 'e sees me,
Yes, an' 'is face goes white . . . oh yes
Tha can stare at me wi' thy fierce blue eyes,
But tha doesna stare me out, I guess!

V I

Whativer brings thee out so far
    In a' this depth o' snow?
—I'm takin' 'ome a weddin' dress
    If tha maun know.

Why, is there a weddin' at Underwood,
    As tha ne'd trudge up here?
—It's Widow Naylor's weddin'-dress,
    An' 'er's wantin' it, I hear.

'*Er* doesna want no weddin'-dress . . .
    What—but what dost mean?
—Doesn't ter know what I mean, Tim?—Yi,
    Tha must 'a' been hard to wean!

Tha'rt a good-un at suckin'-in yet, Timmy;
    But tell me, isn't it true
As 'er'll be wantin' *my* weddin' dress
    In a week or two?

Tha's no occasions ter ha'e me on
    Lizzie—what's done is done!
—*Done*, I should think so—Done! But might
    I ask when tha begun?

It's thee as 'as done it as much as me,
    Lizzie, I tell thee that.
—"Me gotten a childt to thy landlady—!"
    Tha's gotten thy answer pat,

As tha allers hast—but let me tell thee
    Hasna ter sent me whoam, when I
Was a'most burstin' mad o' my-sèn
    An' walkin' in agony;

After thy kisses, Lizzie, after
    Tha's lain right up to me Lizzie, an' melted
Into me, melted into me, Lizzie,
    Till I was verily swelted.

An' if my landlady seed me like it,
    An' if 'er clawkin', tiger's eyes
Went through me just as the light went out
    Is it any cause for surprise?

No cause for surprise at all, my lad,
    After lickin' and snuffin' at me, tha could
Turn thy mouth on a woman like her—
    Did ter find her good?

Ay, I did, but afterwards
    I should like to ha' killed her!
—Afterwards!—an' after how long
    Wor it tha'd liked to 'a killed her?

Say no more, Liz, dunna thee,
    I might lose my-sèn.
—I'll only say good-bye to thee, Timothy,
    An' gi'e her thee back again.

I'll ta'e thy word "Good-bye," Liz,
    But I shonna marry her,
shonna for nobody.—It is
    Very nice on you, Sir.

The childt maun ta'e its luck, it maun,
    An' she maun ta'e *her* luck,
For I tell ye I shonna marry her—
    What her's got, her took.

That's spoken like a man, Timmy,
    That's spoken like a man . . .
"He up an' fired off his pistol
    An' then away he ran."

I damn well shanna marry 'er,
    So chew at it no more,
Or I'll chuck the flamin' lot of you—
    —You nedn't have swore.

VII

That's his collar round the candle-stick
An' that's the dark blue tie I bought 'im,
An' these is the woman's kids he's so fond on,
An' 'ere comes the cat that caught 'im.

I dunno where his eyes was—a gret
Round-shouldered hag! My sirs, to think
Of him stoopin' to her! You'd wonder he could
Throw hisself in that sink.

I expect you know who I am, Mrs. Naylor!
    —Who yer are?—yis, you're Lizzie Stainwright.
'An 'appen you might guess what I've come for?
    —'Appen I mightn't, 'appen I might.

You knowed as I was courtin' Tim Merfin.
    —Yis, I knowed 'e wor courtin' thee.
An' yet you've been carryin' on wi' him.
    —Ay, an' 'im wi' me.

Well, now you've got to pay for it,
        —An' if I han, what's that to thee?
For 'e isn't goin' to marry you.
        —Is it a toss-up 'twixt thee an' me?

It's no toss-up 'twixt thee an' me.
        —Then what art colleyfoglin' for?
I'm not havin' your orts an' slarts.
        —Which on us said you wor?

I want you to know 'e's non *marryin'* you.
        —Tha wants 'im thy-sèn too bad.
Though I'll see as 'e pays you, an' comes to the scratch.
        —Tha'rt for doin' a lot wi' th' lad.

VIII

To think I should ha'e to haffle an' caffle
        Wi' a woman, an' pay 'er a price
For lettin' me marry the lad as I thought
        To marry wi' cabs an' rice.

But we'll go unbeknown to the registrar,
        An' give 'er what money there is,
For I won't be beholden to such as her
        For anythink of his.

IX

Take off thy duty stripes, Tim,
        An' come wi' me in here,
Ta'e off thy p'lice-man's helmet
        An' look me clear.

I wish tha hadna done it, Tim,
        I do, an' that I do!
For whenever I look thee i' th' face, I s'll see
        Her face too.

I wish tha could wesh 'er off'n thee,
    For I used to think that thy
Face was the finest thing that iver
    Met my eye. . . .

X

Twenty pound o' thy own tha hast, and fifty pound ha'e I,
Thine shall go to pay the woman, an' wi' my bit we'll buy
All as we shall want for furniture when tha leaves this place,
An' we'll be married at th' registrar—now lift thy face.

Lift thy face an' look at me, man, up an' look at me:
Sorry I am for this business, an' sorry if I ha'e driven thee
To such a thing: but it's a poor tale, that I'm bound to say,
Before I can ta'e thee I've got a widow of forty-five to pay.

Dunnat thee think but what I love thee—I love thee well,
But 'deed an' I wish as this tale o' thine wor niver my tale to tell;
Deed an' I wish as I could stood at the altar wi' thee an' been proud
    o' thee,
That I could ha' been first woman to thee, as thou'rt first man to me.

But we maun ma'e the best on't—I'll rear thy childt if 'er'll yield it
    to me,
An' then wi' that twenty pound we gi'e 'er I s'd think 'er wunna be
So very much worser off than 'er wor before—An' now look up
An' answer me—for I've said my say, an' there's no more sorrow to
    sup.

Yi', tha'rt a man, tha'rt a fine big man, but niver a baby had eyes
As sulky an' ormin' as thine. Hast owt to say otherwise
From what I've arranged wi' thee? Eh man, what a stubborn jackass
    thou art,
Kiss me then—there!—ne'er mind if I scraight—I wor fond o' thee,
    Sweetheart.

DISCIPLINE

It is stormy, and rain-drops cling like silver bees to the pane,
The thin sycamore in the playground is swinging with flattened
    leaves;
The heads of my boys move dimly through the yellow gloom that
    stains
The class: over them all the dark net of my discipline weaves.

It is no good, dear, meekness and forbearance—I endured too long.
I have pushed my hands in the dark loam under the flowers of my
    soul,
Under the caressing leaves, and felt where the roots were strong
Fixed in the darkness, grappling for the deep soil's little control.

Far and wide run the easy roots that bear the leaves of pity.
I'd have torn them up had they borne away the patient bulbs of my
    hopes:
Oh I tore them up, though the wistful leaves were fragrant, and soft,
    and pretty,
And I twisted them over the broken leaves into unbreakable ropes.

Ah, my Darling, when over the purple horizon shall loom
The shrouded Mother of a new idea, men hide their faces,
Cry out, and fend her off, as she seeks her procreant groom,
Wounding themselves against her, denying her great embraces.

And do I not seek to mate my grown, desirous soul
With the lusty souls of my boys?—yet they hide their faces,
And strike with a blindness of fury against me; can I cajole
The hate of terror?—or deny the fecund soul her embraces?

The flower of forgiveness is plucked from off the offender's plot
To wither on the bosom of the merciful:—so many seeds the less,
So much more room for riot! The great God spareth not,
He waters our face with tears, our young fruits fills with bitterness.

LAST WORDS TO MURIEL

It is You have borne the shame and sorrow,
　　But the disgrace is mine;
Your love was innocent and thorough,
Mine was the love of the sun for the flower
　　Loved to life in sunshine.

Yea I was fine enough to explore you,
　　Blossom you stalk by stalk
Till thy full-fed fire of curiosity bore you
Shrivelling down in the final dour
　　Flesh-anguish, then I suffered a balk.

I heard thy cries of pain, and they broke
　　My fine, craftsman's nerve,
Flawed my delicate courage in its stroke,
And I failed in my·cowardice to give thee the last
　　Bright torture thou didst deserve.

Thou art shapely, thou art adorned,
　　But opaque and dull in the flesh,
Who, if but I had piercèd with the thorned
Fire-threshing anguish, had been fused and cast
　　In a lovely illumined mesh.

Like a painted window: that last suffering
　　Would have withered through thy flesh
Undrossed it and blessed it with a quivering
Sweet wisdom of grace. Now who will free
　　Thy body from its terrors awkward leash?

And who will remove from me the disgrace
　　Of a live sad work unfinished;
A mute, nearly beautiful thing is thy face
That fills with grief all those that see
　　Thee a God-joy diminished
　　It truly a God-thought diminished.

LAST WORDS TO MIRIAM

Yours is the shame and sorrow,
    But the disgrace is mine;
Your love was dark and thorough,
Mine was the love of the sun for a flower
    He creates with his shine.

I was diligent to explore you,
    Blossom you stalk by stalk,
Till my fire of creation bore you
Shrivelling down in the final dour
    Anguish—then I suffered a balk.

I knew your pain, and it broke
    My fine, craftsman's nerve;
Your body quailed at my stroke,
And my courage failed to give you the last
    Fine torture you did deserve.

You are shapely, you are adorned,
    But opaque and dull in the flesh,
Who, had I but pierced with the thorned
Fire-threshing anguish, were fused and cast
    In a lovely illumined mesh.

Like a painted window: the best
    Suffering burnt through your flesh,
Undrossed it and left it blest
With a quivering sweet wisdom of grace: but now
    Who shall take you afresh?

Now who will burn you free
    From your body's terrors and dross,
Since the fire has failed in me?
What man will stoop in your flesh to plough
    The shrieking cross?

A mute, nearly beautiful thing
    Is your face, that fills me with shame
As I see it hardening,
    Warping the perfect image of God,
        And darkening my eternal fame.

LIAISON

A big bud of moon hangs out of the twilight,
    Star-spiders, spinning their thread,
Hang high suspended, withouten respite
    Watching us overhead.

Come then under the trees, where the leaf-cloths
    Curtain us in so dark
That here we're safe from even the ermine-moth's
    Suspicious remark.

Here in this swarthy, secret tent,
    Where black boughs flap the ground,
You shall draw the thorn from my discontent,
    Surgeon me sound.

This rare, rich night! For in here
    Under the yew-tree tent
The darkness is loveliest, where I could sear
    You like frankincense into scent.

Here not even the stars can spy us,
    Not even the white moths write
With their little pale signs on the wall, to try us
    And set us affright.

Kiss but then the dust from off my lips,
    But draw the turgid pain
From my breast to your bosom, eclipse
    My soul again.

Waste me not, I beg you, waste
　　Not the inner night:
Taste, oh taste and let me taste
　　Of joy in the fight.

DISSOLUTE

Many years have I still to burn, detained
Like a candle flame on this body; but I enshrine
A darkness within me, a presence which sleeps contained
In my flame of living, a shadow within the shine.

And through these years, while I burn on the fuel of life,
What matter the stuff I lick up in my living flame,
Seeing I keep in the fire-core, inviolate,
A darkness that dreams my dreams for me, ever the same.

HONEYMOON

　　I wonder, can the night go by,
　　Can this shot arrow of travel fly
　　Shaft-golden with light, at the joint of the sky
　　　　And out into morning,
　　Without delivering once my eye
　　From sight of me, without once your turning
　　　　Your face toward my agony?

　　What is it then that you can see,
　　As at the window endlessly
　　You watch the fire sparks swirl and flee
　　　　And the night look through?
　　The sight of you peering lonely there
　　Oppresses me, I can scarcely bear
　　　　To share the train with you.

Still I must sit in agony
As you crouch and turn away from me,
In torture of your proximity—
    Oh, I would not love you—
How I have longed for this night in the train,
Yet every fibre of me cries in pain
    Now to God to remove you.

But surely, surely I know that still
Come on us another night, you will
Lift up your measure to me to fill—
    Touch cups and drink.
It is only I find it hard to bear,
To have you sitting averted there
    With all your senses ashrink.

But my dear love, when another night
Comes on us, you'll lift your fingers white
And strip me naked, touch me alight,
    Light, light all over?
For I ache most earnestly for your touch,
I am ashamed that I ache so much
    For you, my lover.

For night after night with a blemish of day
Unblown and unblossomed has withered away:
Come another night, come tomorrow, say
    Will you pluck it apart?
Will you loose the heavy, weary bud
To the fire and rain, will you take the flood
    Of me to heart,
    To the very heart?

A SPIRITUAL WOMAN

Close your eyes, my love, let me make you blind;
    They have taught you to see
Only a mean arithmetic on the face of things,

A cunning algebra in the faces of men,
     And God like geometry
Completing his circles, and working cleverly.

I'll kiss you over the eyes till I kiss you blind;
     If I can—if any one could.
Then perhaps in the dark you'll have got what you want to find.
You've discovered so many bits, with your clever eyes,
     And I'm a kaleidoscope
That you shake and shake, and yet it won't come to your mind.

Now stop carping at me.—But God, how I hate you!
     Do you fear I shall swindle you?
Do you think if you take me, that that will abate you
Somehow?—so sad, so intrinsic, so spiritual, yet so cautious, you
Must have me all in your will and your knowledge, and I
     In knowledge must mate you.

ANOTHER OPHELIA

Oh the green glimmer of apples in the orchard,
     Lamps in a wash of rain!
Oh the wet walk of my brown hen through the stackyard,
     Oh tears on the window pain. [*sic*]

Nothing now will ripen the bright green apples
     Full of disappointment and of rain,
Brackish they will taste of tears when the yellow dapples
     Of leaves like yellow fruits show plain.

All round the yard it is cluck! my brown hen,
     Cluck and the rain-wet wings!
Cluck! my marigold bird and again
     Cluck to your yellow darlings.

For the grey rat found the gold thirteen
     Huddled away in the dark.
Then flutter for a moment, and the rat's long teeth are keen,
     Extinct one yellow bloody spark.

935

Thirteen times the teeth flashed in a fire of blood,
 Thirteen were the slithering, silent journeys,
Thirteen lay the yellow chicks beneath the joist of wood,
 And restless were the whimpering rat-bairnies.

So we found the dead clatch side by side
 Plenishing the grey rat's nest:
The white dog nipped the mother rat, the father rat beside,
 And the brown dog settled the rest.

Rattle the rain-drops, ruin the apples,
 But bonnie and bright were the chickens:
Then up comes a grey rat, a floss-gold chicken grapples,
 Then up with wrath the red-eyed morning quickens.

Once I had a lover bright like running water,
 Once I knew a summer that sparkled
With golden chicks of cloud and a sky of running laughter,
 And now the sky with dreary dirt is barkled.

Then the days ran round me in a golden brood,
 Then, like chickens mounted in my hand;
The hours pecked pleasure from me, and the sun delighted stood:
 Where is the sun, I cannot understand?

Oh where-out now has wandered the golden hen of sunshine?
 Is it only that the great, wet haystacks mars
My sight! But then who has stole the bright, white hen of moon-
shine,
 And what has become of the fluffy yellow stars?

But I was rosy, for him I did flush mellow,
 Ripeness welled through me at his kiss,
Ah where his mouth's red summer, and where is now the yellow
 Sunshine of his hair I used to kiss!

All the trees are hanging with dishonoured flags' disgrace,
 All the fruits are sulking in the wet;
Ah, and my hair is hanging wet and bitter on my face,
 And Ah my bitter breasts, that sulk and fret!

SNAP-DRAGON

She bade me follow to her garden where
The mellow sunlight stood as in a cup
Between the old red walls! I did not dare
To raise my face, I did not dare look up,
Lest her bright eyes like sparrows should fly in
My windows of discovery, and shrill "Sin!"

So with a downcast mien and laughing voice
I followed, followed the swing of her white dress
That rocked in a lilt along: I watched the poise
Of her feet as they lept for a space, then pause to press
The grass deep down with her royal burden; and I
Would gladly have offered my breast for her tread to try.

"I like to see," she said, and she crouched her down,
She sunk into my sight like a settling bird,
And I saw her bosom couch in the nest of her gown
Like a heavy bird disturbed, and her shoulders stirred
Strong and slow: "I like to see," said she,
"The snapdragon put out his tongue at me."
She laughed, she reached her hand out down to the flower
Closing its crimson throat: my own throat in her power
Strangled, my heart swelled up so full
As if it would burst its wineskin in my throat,
And choke me in my own crimson: I watched her pull
The gorge of the gaping flower till the blood did float
      Over my eyes and I was blind:
          Her large, brown hand loomed over
          The windows of my mind,
          And in the dark I did discover
          Things I was out to find!
          My grail whose bowl was twined
          With swollen veins that met in the wrist,
          Under whose brown the amethyst
          Pulsed thickly; and I longed to pour
          My heart's red measure in the cup,

I longed to pour the burning store
Of my blood in her darkened cup.

Then suddenly she looked up,
And dazed with a tawny-gold display
Was I, till she took her eyes away.
It seemed that I and the woven world
Were pressed cup-shape to take this reiver
Bird who was weary to have furled
Her wings, As we were weary to receive her:
     This bird, this rich
     Sumptuous central grain,
     This mutable witch,
     This found refrain,
     This laugh in the fight,
     This clot of light,
     This brown core of night,
     This sum of delight.

She spoke, and I closed my eyes
To shut hallucinations out,
My heart re-echoed in surprise,
Hearing my mere lips shout
The answer they did devise.

She turned her flushed face towards me for the glint
Of a moment: "See", she laughed, "if you also
Can make them yawn." I stretched my hand to the dint
In the flower's throat, and the flower gaped wide with woe
—She watched, she went of a sudden intensely still,
She watched my hand, and the skies began to thrill!

     And then I saw a brown bird hover
     Over the flowers at my feet;
     Again, and I felt a brown bird hover
     Over my heart; like heat
     Its shadow lay on my heart . . .

     I thought I saw on the clover
     A brown bee pull apart
     The closed flesh of the clover
     And dip in the heart.

She swooped her hand, and the rover
Bird above my heart,
Came down on my breast, shoving over
The cares and the restless smart
Of responsibility:
Like a reiving cuckoo she settled down
On my breast, with her wings and her feathers to drown
My anxiety in a heat of love;
And ah, I held my heart aloft
To the cuckoo bird as she fluttered above,
So she settled soft.

l pressed the wretched, throttled flower between
My fingers, till its head gaped back, its fangs
Poisèd at her: like a weapon my hand was white and keen,
And I kept the choked, snake flower in its pangs
Of anguish till she ceased to laugh, till down
Her soul's flag sank, and her pride put off its crown.

She hid her face, she murmured between her lips
The low word "Don't!" I let the flower fall
But held my hand afloat still towards the slips
Of blossom she fingered: and my poised fingers all
Put forth toward her: She did not move, nor I,
And my hand like a snake watched hers that could not fly.

Then I laughed in the dark of my heart, I did exult
Like a sudden chuckling of music: I bade her eyes
To mine, I opened her helpless eyes to consult
Their fear, their shame, their joy that underlies
Defeat in such a battle: in the dark of her eyes
My heart was fierce to make her homage rise.

Till her dark deeps shook with convulsive thrills, and the dark
Of her spirit wavered like water threaded with light,
And my heart leaped up in longing to plunge its stark
Dry fever in her pool of full twilight,
Within the spacious gloom of mystery
In her barbarous soul to grope with ecstasy.

And I do not care though the large hands of revenge
Shall get my throat at last—shall get it soon,
If the joy which they are lifted to avenge
Shall have risen red on my night as a harvest moon;
Which even death can not put out from me,
But leaves alight and lovely eternally . . .

> For I have seen the vein
> Swell down her rich, hot wrist,
> Branch and enchain
> Her fingers as if it would twist
> Through the whole blue sky, and the noon
> Of flowers and the sweltering earth:
> And I, in a swoon
> Have felt the day darken and shudder,
> As her hand groped over its nakedness,
> Sending into its slumbering flesh
> Her fire, infusing its lifelessness
> With life, till the earth and the sky have tumbled
> entire
> Into darkness, open and eager for the thrust of the
> torches' fire.

TO LETTICE, MY SISTER

The shorn moon trembling indistinct on her path,
Frail as a scar upon the pale blue sky
Draws towards the downward slope: some sickness hath
Worn her away to the quick, so she faintly faces
Along her foot-searched way, her sorrow-closed eye
Down the sky's steep stairs charting no track for her.

Some say they see, though I have never seen
The dead moon heaped within the young moon's arms
For surely the fragile fine young thing had been
Too heavily burdened to mount the heavens so.
My heart, disturbed in its dream slow-stepping, alarms
Me lest you, my sister, should go heaped with such shadow of woe.

Since Death from the mother moon has pared close to the quick
And cast us forth like shorn thin moons to travel
Our chartered way among the myriad thick
Strewn stars of pallid people, and through luminous litter
Of lives that sorrows like mischievous, strange mice chavel
To strew round our way, to diminish each full star's glitter.

Since Death has delivered naked and thin and white,
Since the month of childhood is over, and we start afresh,
Since the beloved, faded moon that set us alight
Is delivered from us, herself born again amid the moan
Of all us flesh, and we stand in our nakedness, nesh
And fearful to file forth now for the first time alone.

Let us seek to win her back unto us. The moon
That is dead, the mother-love like light that flowed
To stead her womb around us, beyond the swoon
Of death, commingles in God's mighty gloom
Whence issue unblemished the atoms which, soft bestowed
Settle upon us magnetic, so we wax and bloom.

For out in the waste, wild soul space that shall
Sing like a chorus some day
Still plies the love of our mother for us, straining our way
Wise, wonderful strands of winds that are laden with rare
Effluence from suffering folk-stuff which death has laid bare
On the air for our nourishment, who from these weave fair on fair.

GRIEF

The darkness steals the forms of all the queens.
But oh, the palms of her two black hands are red!
—It is Death I fear so much, it is not the dead—
Not this gray book, but the red and bloody scenes.

The lamps are white like snowdrops in the grass;
The town is like a churchyard, all so still
And gray, now night is here: nor will
Another torn red sunset come to pass.

And so I sit and turn the book of gray,
Feeling the shadows like a blind man reading,
All fearful lest I find some next word bleeding.
—Nay, take my painted missal book away.

TWILIGHT

Under the blue-grey twilight, heaped
Beyond the withering snow of the shorn fields,
A rubble of stunted houses stands unreaped
Of the long scythe the stooping mower wields.

And lamps like venturous glow-worms steal among
The shadowy stubble of the under-dusk,
And silence issues slowly from the husk
As further off the scythe of night is swung.

And all the town is gone into a dust
Of blueness mingled with a fume of gold,
And pale, hot skies have darkened and gone cold,
And all the flowers are fallen in disgust.

But I remember still the sunny hours
Of queens in hyacinth 'neath skies of gold,
And morning singing where the woods were scrolled
And diapered above the chaunting flowers.

The darkness steals the forms of all the queens,
But oh, the palms of his black hands are red
Inflamed with binding up the sheaves of dead
Hours that were once all glory and all queens.

THE PIANO

Somewhere beneath that piano's superb sleek black
Must hide my mother's piano, little and brown, with the back
That stood close to the wall, and the front's faded silk, both torn,
And the keys with little hollows, that my mother's fingers had worn.

Softly, in the shadows, a woman is singing to me
Quietly, through the years I have crept back to see
A child sitting under the piano, in the boom of the shaking strings
Pressing the little poised feet of the mother who smiles as she sings.

The full throated woman has chosen a winning, living song
And surely the heart that is in me must belong
To the old Sunday evenings, when darkness wandered outside
And hymns gleamed on our warm lips, as we watched mother's
     fingers glide.

Or this is my sister at home in the old front room
Singing love's first surprised gladness, alone in the gloom.
She will start when she sees me, and blushing, spread out her hands
To cover my mouth's raillery, till I'm bound in her shame's heart-
     spun bands.

A woman is singing me a wild Hungarian air
And her arms, and her bosom, and the whole of her soul is bare,
And the great black piano is clamouring as my mother's never could
     clamour
And my mother's tunes are devoured of this music's ravaging
     glamour.

BIRTHDAY

If I were well-to-do
I would put roses on roses, and cover your grave
With multitude of white roses, and just a few
Red ones, a bloody-white flag over you.

So people passing under
The ash-trees of the valley road, should raise
Their eyes to your bright place, and then in wonder
    Should climb the hill, and put the flowers asunder.

And seeing it is your birthday,
They would say, seeing each mouth of white rose praise
You highly, every blood-red rose display
    Your triumph of anguish above you, they would say:

" 'Tis strange, we never knew
While she was here and walking in our ways
That she was as the wine-jar whence we drew
    Our draught of faith that sent us on anew."

And so I'd raise
A rose-bush unto you in all their hearts
A rose of memory with a scent of praise
    Wafting like solace down their length of days.

EARLY SPRING

The sun sets wide the yellow crocuses
To fill them up their brimming measures,
And deep in the golden wine of their chalices
Sway the live pearls their flowering pledges.

The breeze wakes up a music in the sallow,
About it golden-stoppèd notes,
Then down the breeze, light wafting o'er the fallow,
Pass like a tune the sallow's golden notes.

When softly I call at her door, and enter the room,
Gold, gold, deep gold her glowing eyes unfold,
While trembling somewhere in their wondrous gloom
A little wild bubble is loosing hold.

So she closes her eyes; but the aimless breeze of the woods
Comes over to me with a covert music that stirs
My quivering answer, and kisses like fragrance of flowers
Pass unseen from my lips to hers.

ALL OF ROSES

I

By the Isar, in the twilight
We were wandering and singing;
By the Isar, in the evening
We climbed the huntsman's ladder and sat swinging
In the fir-tree overlooking the marshes;
While river met with river, and the ringing
Of their pale-green glacier-water filled the evening.

By the Isar, in the twilight
We found our warm wild roses
Hanging red at the river; and simmering
Frogs were singing, and over the river closes
Was scent of roses, and glimmering
In the twilight, our kisses across the roses
Met, and her face, and my face, were roses.

II

When she rises in the morning
I linger to watch her.
She stands in silhouette against the window,
And the sunbeams catch her
Glistening white on the shoulders;
　　While down her sides, the mellow
　　Golden shadow glows, and her breasts
　　Swing like full-blown yellow
　　Gloire de Dijon roses.

She drips herself with water,
And her shoulders
Glisten as silver, they crumple up
Like wet and shaken roses, and I listen
For the rustling of their white, unfolding petals.
In the window full of sunlight
She stirs her golden shadow,
And flashes all herself as sun-bright
As if roses fought with roses.

III

Just a few of the roses we gathered from the Isar
Are fallen, and their mauve-red petals on the cloth
Float like boats on a river, waiting
For a fairy-wind to wake them from their sloth.

She laughs at me across the table, saying
She loves me; and I blow a little boat
Rocking down the shoals between the tea-cups
And so kiss-beladen that it scarce can float.

IV

Now like a rose come tip-toe out of bud
I see the woman's soul steal in her eyes,
And wide in ecstasy I sit and watch
The unknown flower issued magic-wise.

And day by day out of the envious bud
My treasure softly slips uncurled,
And day by day my happiness vibrates
In wide and wider circles round the world.

THE MOWERS

There's four men mowing down by the river;
    I can hear the sound of the scythe strokes, four
Sharp breaths swishing:—yea, but I
    Am sorry for what's i' store.

The first man out o' the four that's mowin'
    Is mine: I mun claim him once for all;
—But I'm sorry for him, on his young feet, knowin'
    None o' the trouble he's led to stall.

As he sees me bringin' the dinner, he lifts
    His head as proud as a deer that looks
Shoulder-deep out o' th' corn: and wipes
    His scythe blade bright, unhooks

His scythe stone, an' over the grass to me!
    —Lad, tha's gotten a childt in me,
An' a man an' a father tha'lt ha'e to be,
    My young slim lad, an' I'm sorry for thee.

FIREFLIES IN THE CORN

A woman taunts her lover.
    Look at the little darlings in the corn!
    The rye is taller than you, who think yourself
    So high and mighty: look how its heads are borne
    Dark and proud on the sky, like a number of knights
    Passing with spears and pennants and manly scorn.

    And always likely!—Oh, if I could ride
    With my head held high-serene against the sky
    Do you think I'd have a creature like you at my side
    With your gloom and your doubt that you love me?
        O darling rye,
    How I adore you for your simple pride!

And those bright fireflies wafting in between
And over the swaying cornstalks, just above
All their dark-feathered helmets, like little green
Stars come low and wandering here for love
Of this dark earth, and wandering all serene—!

How I adore you, you happy things, you dears
Riding the air and carrying all the time
Your little lanterns behind you: it cheers
My heart to see you settling and trying to climb
The corn-stalks, tipping with fire their spears.

All over the corn's dim motion, against the blue
Dark sky of night, the wandering glitter, the swarm
Of questing brilliant things:—you joy, you true
Spirit of careless joy: ah, how I warm
My poor and perished soul at the joy of you!

The man answers and she mocks.
   You're a fool, woman. I love you, and you know I do!
     —Lord, take his love away, it makes him whine.
   And I give you everything that you want me to.
     —Lord, dear Lord, do you think he ever *can* shine?

SONG OF A MAN WHO IS LOVED

Between her breasts is my home, between her breasts.
Three sides set on me space and fear, but the fourth side rests,
Warm in a city of strength, between her breasts.

All day long I am busy and happy at my work
I need not glance over my shoulder in fear of the terrors that lurk
Behind. I am fortified, I am glad at my work.

I need not look after my soul; beguile my fear
With prayer, I need only come home each night to find the dear
Door on the latch, and shut myself in, shut out fear.

I need only come home each night and lay
My face between her breasts;
And what of good I have given the day, my peace attests.

And what I have failed in, what I have wronged
Comes up unnamed from her body and surely
Silent tongued I am ashamed.

And I hope to spend eternity
With my face down-buried between her breasts
And my still heart full of security
And my still hands full of her breasts.

RELIGION

Life is nothing without religion
and religion nothing without the father of all things
stooping over his bride.

And the father was once grey-bearded and fulminative
and once he was a young man pale and refusing fatherhood
leaving all to the woman. Madonna mia! poor virgin!
And once he was gay and hearty with his eye on the immortal tarts
and once again a suave young god
wooing boys and beauty.

But farther off, much farther
a great bull bellowed through space, calling to the milky cows, ah
    fatherhood
and beyond, the eagle rose, and the phoenix, parent, soaring golden
    over the great egg
and further still, before the curled horns of the ram stepped forth
before the stout swart beetle had a ball of dung to roll and hatch
before the golden fatherly serpent lifted his head off the earth, in
    the first effort to think.

Upon the waters that ended in marshes
swam the still swan, swept the wide goose above the mists,
honked in the gloom the honk of procreation from such throats.

But now
only the electron behaves and misbehaves incomprehensibly
and forces tie themselves up into knots of atoms, then come untied:
and nothing else but this
that everything ties itself up into complicated little knots, that barge
    about
and bump on one another, and come untied.
and either release energy, or swallow it up
and make the considerable mess that isn't even worth the name of
    universe any more.

For me, it's not good enough
I'm a religious soul.
For me, at the moment
the Father of all things swims in the vast dusk of all the atoms
like a wild swan, or a goose, whose honk goes through my bladder.

And in the dark I feel his cold webbed feet, mud black
brush over my face as he goes to tread our weird women
with dreams and thrusts that make them cry in their sleep.

And wait, wait awhile.
Don't you think, little man, you'll be father of human babies.
There'll be babies born that are young wild swans, O my soul,
and wild geese, O my heart;
and the geese that saved Rome will lose London.

[I KNOW A NOBLE ENGLISHMAN]

    I know a noble Englishman,
    One of nature's gentlemen
    Don't you know!
    Eked out by his tailor and his hatter
    And the Rock of Ages of his public school.

This noble gentleman
Is nothing if not normal
A great coureur de femmes.
Speaking of "perverts", he takes on an amused but icy
    contempt,
Himself so superior.

However
One of his beloveds, looking rather a wreck
After an affair with this noble Englishman,
Said: Ronald, you see, is quite a clever sadist:
He's most frightfully skilful in his love-making
And makes a point of being very gentle, very tender
Don't you know?
And he *is* very gentle and tender—

Till he's got a woman a bit soft and trustful
Then he turns away and wipes her from his consciousness
As if she were a worm, or a hired whore who bored him,
An absolute nothing.

So the poor thing is left feeling an utter worm.
Not good enough to be loved by this expert.

But it's all a trick.
I've realised it is all a trick on his part.
He never wants a woman, he doesn't like women,
They are really repugnant to him.
So he cleverly plays the normal, the Don Juan
To make them feel absolute worms
Under his noble boot-sole.

As a matter of fact,
If the mean devil has any sex-feeling at all,
It is for men: he's an instinctive homosexual,
Like almost all Englishmen.
But he's far too great a coward ever to admit his instincts.

Too great a boor to realise his true feelings,
Too great a skunk to abide by his own self,
Too dirty a hypocrite to admit his own nature.
He shows an amused superior contempt at the prevalence of
     sodomy
And is himself normal, a lover of women.

But ask the women!
Ask all the women he's ever had
What about him.

The dirty little Don Juan
Balking his own nature
And taking it out on women,
Leaving them crushed worms
And going blandly on to his next spite.

Every single erection of his is an erection of mean spite.

Don Juan! If you ask me,
Don Juan was never anything but a self-thwarted sodomist,
Taking it out, in spite, on women.

WORK

There is no point in work
unless it pre-occupies you as well as occupies you.
When you are only occupied, you are an empty shell.
A man needs to be independent at his work, so that he can put his
     own self into it.

When a man puts his own self into his work
he is living, not merely working.
When men wove with their hands and their soul's attention the
     cloth they wore,
they lived themselves forth, like a tree putting out woven leaves
and it made them happy, and the woven cloth of their hands
came from them living like leaves from the tree of their life
and clothed them with living leaves.

And as with cloth, so with all things, houses, shoes, wagons or cups,
men used to put them forth sensitively like boughs, leaves, fruits,
flowers
from their tree of life, and villages, whole cities lived, lived as true
bowers of men.

—It will be so again, for man will smash all his machines again
at last, and for the sake of clothing himself in his own leaf-like cloth,
tissued from his life
and dwelling in his own bowery house, like a bird in a bush
and drinking from the cups that have flowered from his own fingers
he will cancel again these machines we have got.

IN NOTTINGHAM

In Nottingham, where I went to school and college,
they have built a new and cakey university
very sumptuous, with the money of Sir Jesse Boot, of Cash Chemist
fame,
now first citizen of Nottingham.

The whole thing has risen out of this Cash-Chemist money
and looks it. And I put it to you
in such a Cash-Chemist university, what can they teach
but cash-chemistry, cash-physics, cash-classics, and cash-culture
altogether?

And when this cash-chemist university grants degrees, like Birming-
ham,
it will be Bachelor of Cash Arts, Master of Cash Science,
Professor of Quintessential Cash.

MORALITY

What a pity, when a man looks at himself in the glass,
He doesn't bark at it, like a dog does,
Or fluff up in indignant fury, like a cat!
What a pity he takes himself seriously, and draws a
moral lesson.

DEEPER THAN LOVE

O love is a deep thing
but there are deeper things than love.

First and last, man is alone:
born alone, dies alone
lives while he lives most of his time alone
and in his deepest self, never ceases to be alone.

It would be a naked life without love
which clothes our nakedness like grass the plains and trees the hills
and makes our bare manyness into a oneness.

But underneath, man is alone, each one a rock to himself.

Under the green grassy unison of all our friendliness,
under the summery flowering of the roses of love
and the roots of the great tree of family and the forest of nation,
under it all, underneath
is rock
and each man a rock unto himself
bed-rocked in his own primordial pride
pride pristine and deeper than consciousness, the native pride of a
      man.

And the rock goes down, down deeper, from cold into heat
and greater heat, into fire more heavy and hotter than anything
      known,
and this is the core of a man.

Central primordial fire of the soul, heavier than iron
so ponderously central, heavier and hotter than anything known;
and also alone
and yet
reeling with connection,
heavy with the heaviness of balance
balance with the other, the vast unknowable fire
that centres and balances all things.

Central primordial fire of the soul, heavier than iron,
so ponderously central, yet leaning its weight towards
the vaster fire,
leaning in the massive, unconscious inclination we call religion
as earth leans on the sun.

Central primordial fire of the soul that leans and yearns,
that convulses and trembles again with the sympathy of utter life
coils and recoils sensitive to life, and conscious of truth,
and poised with a sense of justice, as worlds are poised.

O underneath all struggling love lies the silent rock of pride
which so often we see denuded;
and under the rock, as we deeper go, we feel the dark fire of the soul
heavy and sunk below knowing, deepening massive in fieriness
and giving another answer,
answering not us, nor anything known of us, yet answering
from the depth to the greater depth in the dark call of religion.

The fiery dark calling of the soul into the darkness away from us
away from us
towards we know not what of dark life massive in the unknowable,
this is our helpless religiousness that ultimately sways us altogether.

And in the clenched fire that calls and is answered out of the dark
run tremors of sense, sense quivering for the first time awake
in a sense of the coming of life, of the going of life
the soul's first awareness:
and immediately the distinction between the two, which is the sense
    of truth.

Oh long before love is possible
passion has roused in the soul
the primordial passion of truth
is awake, the passion for life, and the passion to be aware of life.
For truth, oldest mystery of the consciousness, is passionate aware-
    ness of life.

And the twin passion, long, long before possibility of love
is the passion of balance between the fiery self and the huger fire
the passion of balanced truth
the passion of justice
which is in the soul what the earth's great poise is in the universe.

At the depth of the human soul
the fiery yearning is towards the huger fire pre-human,
and the first fiery passions stir the living, molten soul
in passionate awareness of incoming, outgoing life, which is truth,
in passionate effort to balance between the coming and going
which is justice taking place in our very origins.

We are older than love.
We are as old as truth
as old as justice
as old as life and response to life.

Even in the coal age, there was no love.
Who would connect the ichthyosaurus with love[?]
Yet the ichthyosaurus is not devoid of truth
in his own justice he balanced himself
and he was aware of life, he called out in the dark of darks.

WHAT'S SANE AND WHAT ISN'T——

Bawdy can be sane and wholesome,
in fact a little bawdy is necessary in every life
to keep it sane and healthy.

And a little whoring can be sane and healthy,
in fact a little whoring is necessary in every life
to keep it sane and wholesome.

Even, at the right times, sodomy can be sane and wholesome,
granted there is a proper give and take.
In fact, it may be that a little sodomy is necessary to human life.

But bawdy on the brain is lewd and nauseous, a sort of idiocy.
And whoring on the brain as bad as syphilis, incipient insanity.
And sodomy on the brain is a sort of mission, and what is more
    crazy!

Chastity in its hour is sweet and wholesome,
in fact quite a lot of chastity is necessary in life, to keep it sane and
    wholesome.
But chastity on the brain is another vice, it ends in lunacy.
Purity, however, is never sane and never wholesome.
It should always be tacitly understood between all of us
that we have blood and bowels and lively genitals,
whereas puritanism is bent on suppressing the fact.
And suppression of such fact leads, as we know, direct to raving
    insanity.
The fifth generation of puritans, when it isn't debauched,
is idiot.

Life is a thing you've got to be flexible and intelligent about,
and steer according to the currents and winds and tides, and the
    vessel itself.

THE TRIUMPH OF THE MACHINE

They talk of the triumph of the machine,
but the machine will never triumph.

Out of the thousands and thousands of centuries of man
the unrolling of ferns, while tongues of acanthus lapping at the sun
for one sad century
machines have triumphed, rolled us hither and thither,
hardened the earth, shaking the lark's nest till the eggs have broken.

Shaken the marshes, till the geese have gone
and the wild swans flown away, singing the swan-song of us.

Hard, hard on the earth the machines are rolling,
but through some hearts they will never roll.

Ah no, in the hearts of some men there still is sanctuary
where the lark nests safely.

The lark nests in his heart,
and through the reeds of his marshy loins
swims the mallard duck at dawn, in that quick joy;
deer crash their horns in the mountains of his breast,
there are foxes in the cover of his beard.

Ah no, the machine will never triumph;
in some hearts still the sanctuaries of wild life
are quite untouched.

And at last
all the creatures that cannot die while one heart harbours them
they will hear a silence fall
as the machines fail and finish;
they will hear the faint rending of the asphalt roads
as the hornbeam pushes up his sprouts;
they will hear far, far away the last factory hooter
send up the last wild cry of despair
as the machine breaks finally down.

And then at last
all the creatures that were driven back into the uttermost corners of
     the soul
they will peep forth.

GLORY OF DARKNESS

[Ink version:]

Blue and dark
Oh Bavarian gentians, tall ones
make a dark-blue gloom
in the sunny room.

They have added blueness to blueness, until
it is dark: beauty
blue joy of my soul
Bavarian gentians
your dark blue gloom is so noble!

How deep I have gone
dark gentians
since I embarked on your dark blue fringes
how deep, how deep, how happy!
What a journey for my soul
in the blue dark gloom
of gentians here in the sunny room!

[Pencil version:]

. . . .
it is dark
and the door is open
to the depths.

It is so blue, it is so dark
in the dark doorway
and the way is open
to Hades.

Oh, I know—
Persephone has just gone back
down the thickening thickening gloom
of dark-blue gentians to Pluto
to her bridegroom in the dark
and all the dead
and all the dark great ones of the underworld
down there, down there
down the blue depths of mountain gentian flowers
cold, cold
are gathering to a wedding in the [winter] dark
down the dark blue path

What a dark-blue gloom
of gentians here in the sunny room!

BAVARIAN GENTIANS

Not every man has gentians in his house
In soft September, at slow, sad Michaelmas.
Bavarian gentians, tall and dark, but dark
darkening the daytime torch-like with the smoking blueness of
    Pluto's gloom,
ribbed hellish flowers erect, with their blaze of darkness spread blue,
blown flat into points, by the heavy white draught of the day.

Torch-flowers of the blue-smoking darkness, Pluto's dark-blue blaze
black lamps from the halls of Dis, smoking dark blue
giving off darkness, blue darkness, upon Demeter's yellow-pale day
whom have you come for, here in the white-cast day?

Reach me a gentian, give me a torch!
let me guide myself with the blue, forked torch of a flower
down the darker and darker stairs, where blue is darkened on blue-
    ness
down the way Persephone goes, just now, in first-frosted September,
to the sightless realm where darkness is married to dark
and Persephone herself is but a voice, as a bride,
a gloom invisible enfolded in the deeper dark
of the arms of Pluto as he ravishes her once again
and pierces her once more with his passion of the utter dark
among the splendour of black-blue torches, shedding fathomless dark-
    ness on the nuptials.

Give me a flower on a tall stem, and three dark flames,
for I will go to the wedding, and be wedding-guest
at the marriage of the living dark.

SHIP OF DEATH

I sing of autumn and the falling fruit
and the long journey towards oblivion.

The apples falling like great drops of dew
to bruise themselves an exit from themselves.

Have you built your ship of death, oh, have you?
Build then your ship of death, for you will need it!
Can man his own quietus make
with a bare bodkin?

With daggers, bodkins, bullets, man can make
a bruise or break of exit for his life
but is that a quietus, oh tell me, is it quietus?

Quietus is the goal of the long journey,
the longest journey towards oblivion.

Slips out the soul, invisible one, wrapped still
in the white shirt of the mind's experiences
and folded in the dark-red, unseen
mantle of the body's still mortal memories.

Frightened and alone, the soul slips out of the house
or is pushed out
to find himself on the crowded, arid margins of existence,

The margins, the grey beaches of shadow
strewn with dim wreckage, and crowded with crying souls
that lie outside the silvery walls of our body's builded city.

Oh, it is not so easy, I tell you it is not so easy
to set softly forth on the longest journey, the longest journey.

It is easy to be pushed out of the silvery city of the body
through any breach in the wall,
thrust out onto the grey grey beaches of shadow,
the long marginal stretches of existence, crowded with lost souls
that intervene between our tower and the slinking sea of the beyond.

Oh build your ship of death, oh build it in time
and build it lovingly, and put it between the hands of your soul.

Once outside the gate of this walled silvery life of days,
once outside, upon the grey marsh beaches, where lost souls moan
in millions, unable to depart,
having no boat to launch upon the shaken, soundless,
deepest and longest of seas,
once outside the gate,
what will you do, if you have no ship of the soul?

Oh pity the dead that are dead, but cannot take
the journey, still they moan and beat
against the silvery adamant walls of this our exclusive existence.
They moan and beat, they gnash, they rage
they fall upon the new outcoming souls with rage
and they send arrows of anger, bullets and bombs of frustration
over the adamant walls of this, our by-no-means impregnable exist-
ence.

Pity, oh pity the poor dead that are only ousted from life
and crowd there on the grey mud beaches of the margins,
gaunt and horrible,
waiting, waiting till at last the ancient boatman with the common
barge
shall take them aboard, towards the great goal of oblivion.

Pity the poor gaunt dead that cannot die
into the distance with receding oars
but must roam like outcast dogs on the margins of life,
and think of them, and with the soul's deep sigh
waft nearer to them the bark of delivery.

But for myself, but for my soul, dear soul,
let me build a little ship with oars and food
and little dishes, and all accoutrements
dainty and ready for the departing soul.

And put it between the hands of the trembling soul.
So that when the hour comes, and the last door closes behind him
he shall slip down the shores invisible
between the half-visible hordes
to where the furthest and the longest sea
touches the margins of our life's existence
with wincing unwilling waves.

And launching there his little ship,
wrapped in the dark-red mantle of the body's memories,
the little, slender soul sits swiftly down, and takes the oars
and draws away, away, away, towards the dark depths,
fathomless deep ahead, far, far from the grey shores
that fringe with shadow all this world's existence.

Over the sea, over the farthest sea,
on the longest journey,
past the jutting rocks of shadow,
past the lurking, octopus arms of agonised memory,
past the strange whirlpools of remembered greed,
through the dead weed of a life-time's falsity,
slow, slow my soul, in his little ship
on the most soundless of all seas
taking the longest journey.

Pulling the long oars of a life-time's courage,
drinking the confident water from the little jug
and eating the brave bread of a wholesome knowledge,
row, little soul, row on,
on the longest journey, towards the greatest goal.

Neither straight nor crooked, neither here nor there
but shadows folded on deeper shadows   ′
and deeper, to a core of sheer oblivion
like the convolutions of shadow-shell
or deeper, like the foldings and involvings of a womb.

Drift on, drift on, my soul, towards the most pure
most dark oblivion.

And at the penultimate porches, the dark-red mantle
of the body's memories slips and is absorbed
into the shell-like, womb-like convoluted shadow.

And round the great final bend of unbroken dark
the skirt of the spirit's experience has melted away,
the oars have gone from the boat, and the little dishes
gone, gone, and the boat dissolves like pearl
as the soul at last slips perfect into the goal, the core
of sheer oblivion and of utter peace,
the womb of silence in the living night.
Ah peace, ah lovely peace, most lovely lapsing
of this my soul into the plasm of peace.

Oh lovely last, last lapse of death, into pure oblivion
at the end of the longest journey,
peace, complete peace—!
But can it be that also it is procreation?

Oh build your ship of death
oh build it!
Oh, nothing matters but the longest journey.

THE SHIP OF DEATH

Have you built your ship of death, oh have you?
Oh build your ship of death, for you will need it.

Now in the twilight, sit by the invisible sea
Of peace, and build your little ship
Of death, that will carry the soul
On its last journey, on and on, so still
So beautiful, over the last of seas.

When the day comes, that will come.
Oh think of it in the twilight peacefully!
The last day, and the setting forth
On the longest journey, over the hidden sea
To the last wonder of oblivion.

Oblivion, the last wonder!
When we have trusted ourselves entirely
To the unknown, and are taken up
Out of our little ships of death
Into pure oblivion.

Oh build your ship of death, be building it now
With dim, calm thoughts and quiet hands
Putting its timbers together in the dusk,

Rigging its mast with the silent, invisible sail
That will spread in death to the breeze
Of the kindness of the cosmos, that will waft
The little ship with its soul to the wonder-goal.

Ah, if you want to live in peace on the face of the earth
Then build your ship of death, in readiness
For the longest journey, over the last of seas.

SONG OF DEATH

Sing the song of death, oh sing it!
For without the song of death, the song of life
becomes pointless and silly.

Sing then the song of death, and the longest journey
and what the soul carries with him, and what he leaves behind
and how he finds the darkness that enfolds him into utter peace
at last, at last, beyond innumerable seas.

NOTES

Abbreviations used in Notes:

A	*AMORES*. London: Duckworth 1916. (Roberts, A9)
ALP	*LAST POEMS*. Ed. Richard Aldington and Giuseppe Orioli with an Introduction. Florence: Orioli 1932. (Roberts, A62)
A.P.	*D. H. Lawrence*. The Augustan Books of Poetry, Second Series (Number Twenty-Two). London: Ernest Benn 1928. (Roberts, A38)
BAY	*BAY: A BOOK OF POEMS*. London: Cyril Beaumont 1919. (Roberts, A12)
BBF	*BIRDS, BEASTS AND FLOWERS*. London: Martin Secker 1923. (Roberts, A27b)
Brewster	Brewster, Earl and Achsah. *D. H. Lawrence: Reminiscences and Correspondence*. London: Martin Secker 1934. (Roberts, B39)
Carswell	Carswell, Catherine. *The Savage Pilgrimage. A Narrative of D. H. Lawrence*. London: Martin Secker 1932. (Roberts, B37)
CP	*THE COLLECTED POEMS*. 2 vols. London: Martin Secker 1928. (Roberts, A43)
E.T.	"E.T." [Jessie Chambers]. *D. H. Lawrence: A Personal Record*. London: Cape 1935. (Roberts, B43)
FIRE	*FIRE AND OTHER POEMS*. Foreword by Robinson Jeffers. San Francisco: Book Club of California 1940. (Roberts, A80)
Letters	*The Collected Letters*. Ed. with an Introd. by Harry T. Moore. 2 vols. London: Heinemann 1962; New York: Viking 1962.
Letters—H	*The Letters*. Ed. with an Introd. by Aldous Huxley. London: Heinemann 1932. (Roberts, A61)

LP	*LOVE POEMS AND OTHERS*. London: Duckworth 1913. (Roberts, A3)
LWH	*LOOK! WE HAVE COME THROUGH!* London: Chatto and Windus 1917. (Roberts, A10a)
LWH–WR	*LOOK! WE HAVE COME THROUGH! / A cycle of Love Poems.* Cornwall: The Ark Press 1959. (Roberts, A10c)
Moore	Moore, Harry T. *The Intelligent Heart: The Story of D. H. Lawrence.* London: Heinemann 1955; New York: Farrar, Straus 1955.
MS. 1479	Notebook containing MS. drafts of early poems by DHL, formerly belonging to Mrs King, now MS. 1479 in the Library of the University of Nottingham.
Nardi	*D. H. Lawrence: Tutte le Poesie.* Traduzione, introduzione, e note di Piero Nardi. 2 vols Milan: Mondadori 1959.
Nehls	*D. H. Lawrence: A Composite Biography.* Gathered, arranged and edited by Edward Nehls. 3 vols. Madison, Wisc.: University of Wisconsin Press 1957–59. (Roberts, B60)
NETTLES	*NETTLES*. London: Faber and Faber 1930. (Roberts, A52)
N.I.B.	Lawrence, Frieda, geb. Freiin von Richthofen. *"Not I But the Wind".* London: Heinemann 1935. (Roberts, B40)
NP	*NEW POEMS*. London: Martin Secker 1918. (Roberts, A11)
PANSIES—1	*PANSIES*. June 1929 (the "definitive", unexpurgated edition). (Roberts, A47c)
PANSIES—2	*PANSIES / Poems by D. H. Lawrence.* London: Martin Secker 1929. (the expurgated, "trade" edition; Roberts, A47b)
PANSIES—L	Revised typescript of *PANSIES* in the George Lazarus Collection.

PE   *The Complete Poems.* Phoenix edition. 3 vols.
             London: Heinemann 1957. (Roberts, A98)

P.G.B.   Aldington, Richard. *Portrait of a Genius, But . . .:*
             The Life of D. H. Lawrence. London: Heinemann
             1950. (Roberts, F52). New York: Duell, Sloan and
             Pearce—Little, Brown 1950

Phoenix   *Phoenix / The Posthumous Papers of D. H. Lawrence.*
             Ed. with an Introd. by Edward McDonald.
             London: Heinemann 1936. (Roberts, A76)

Roberts   Roberts, Warren. *A Bibliography of D. H. Lawrence.*
             Soho Bibliographies No. XII. London: Rupert Hart-
             Davis 1963.

TLS   *Times Literary Supplement*

V.R.M.   Pinto, Vivian de Sola. "D. H. Lawrence, Letter-writer
             and Craftsman in Verse", *Renaissance and
             Modern Studies.* vol. I (1957), pp. 1–34. (Roberts,
             C239)

Y.L.   Lawrence, Ada, and Gelder, G. Stuart. *Young
             Lorenzo / Early Life of D. H. Lawrence.* Florence:
             Orioli 1932. (Roberts, B34)

NOTES TO INTRODUCTION

1. R. P. Blackmur, *Language as Gesture: Essays in Poetry* (London: Allen and Unwin 1954; New York: Harcourt, Brace 1954) p. 288

2. D. H. Lawrence, *Fantasia of the Unconscious* (Phoenix Edition, London: Heinemann 1961; New York: Viking 1960) p. 9

3. Blackmur, op. cit., p. 289

4. Yone Noguchi: Japanese poet (1875-1947) who wrote English verse under the name of "Miss Morning Glory"

5. Letters, p. 221

6. J. W. Mackail (ed.), *Coleridge's Literary Criticism* (London: Oxford University Press 1918), p. 186

7. Blackmur, op. cit., p. 297

8. See Appendix III, p. 946

9. E. T., p. 122

10. *I Poeti Futuristi . . . con un proclama di F. T. Marinetti e un studio sul verso libero di P. Buzzi* (Milano: Edizioni Futuriste 1912)

11. ibid., p. 11

12. Letters, p. 280

13. See Roberts, B2, B4, B27

14. Anthony Beal (ed.), *D. H. Lawrence: Selected Literary Criticism.* (London: Heinemann 1955; New York: Viking 1956), pp. 495, 500

15. See below, p. 184

16. Sir Herbert Read, *The True Voice of Feeling.* (London: Faber 1953; New York: Pantheon 1953), p. 100

17. E.T., p. 223

18. Blackmur, op. cit., p. 299

19. Phoenix, p. 285; cf. John vi, 33

20. Blackmur, loc. cit.

21. Blackmur, op. cit., pp. 295, 296, 300

22. ibid., pp. 295, 296

23. Alfred Alvarez, *The Shaping Spirit*. (London: Chatto and Windus 1958; in the United States, *Stewards of Excellence*, New York: Scribner, 1958), p. 157

24. Richard Hoggart, "Poems of D. H. Lawrence, chosen and introduced by . . .". Originally broadcast in the B.B.C.'s Third Programme, 14 January 1961, and repeated several times since. I quote from Professor Hoggart's typescript, which he kindly lent me, by his permission and that of the B.B.C.

25. Christopher Hassall, "D. H. Lawrence and the Etruscans", Giff Edmonds Memorial Lecture, *Essays by Divers Hands, Being the Transactions of the Royal Society of Literature*, Vol. XXXI, pp. 61–78

26. Brewster, p. 123

27. Hassall, op. cit., p. 77

28. I owe this phrase as well as other things in this Introduction to Dr F. R. Leavis.

29. *Etruscan Places*, Phoenix ed. p. 10

30. Blackmur, op. cit., p. 300

NOTES TO POEMS

NOTE

"To Guelder Roses" . . . "To Campions":
For texts of these poems, see Appendix II, p. 854.

RHYMING POEMS

THE WILD COMMON

For early version printed in *A*, see below, Appendix III, p. 897 and note.

DOG-TIRED

First published in *LP*; reprinted with changes in *CP*. A slightly different early draft appears in MS. 1479, No. 32.

FROM A COLLEGE WINDOW

First published in *NP*; reprinted unchanged in *CP*. A different and more diffuse early draft appears in MS. 1479, No. 8. The College is the old University College in Shakespeare Street, Nottingham, built in 1881. Lawrence was a student there from 1906 till 1908. He describes it in *The Rainbow* (Ch. XV) as "the big college built of stone, standing in the quiet street, with a rim of grass and lime-trees all so peaceful".

DISCORD IN CHILDHOOD

First printed in *A*; reprinted with slight alterations in *CP*. According to Lawrence, this was originally part of a longer poem. See p. 850.

CHERRY ROBBERS

First published in *LP*; reprinted with changes in *CP*. A slightly different early draft appears in MS. 1479, No. 25. This poem is closely paralleled by a prose passage obviously describing the same incident in *Sons and Lovers*, Part II, Chapter 11.

DREAM-CONFUSED

First published in *LP*; reprinted with changes in *CP*. An earlier version of this poem entitled "Wakened" appeared in *The English Review*, April 1910. Two earlier drafts, both entitled "Dream", appear in MS. 1479, Nos. 68, 69.

RENASCENCE

First published in *LP*; reprinted with changes in *CP*. For early draft entitled RENAISSANCE (MS. 1479, No. 28) see Appendix III, p. 898.

VIRGIN YOUTH

For version of this poem printed in *A*, see below, Appendix III, p. 899. An earlier draft appears in MS. 1479, No. 51 under the title "The Body Awake".

STUDY

First published in *A*; reprinted with slight alterations in *CP*. An earlier draft appears in MS. 1479, No. 9. l.6: *"Biuret"* – a chemical term for "a substance formed from urea at 150°–170°C. with liberation of NH_2" (*Chambers's Technical Dictionary*). The speaker is obviously a student of chemistry. This was the first poem that Lawrence tried to have published. He submitted it to *The Gong*, the students' magazine of University College, Nottingham, and it was rejected. See below, Appendix I, p. 851.

TWILIGHT

First published in *NP* under the title "Palimpsest of Twilight", reprinted unchanged, except for title, in *CP*.

LOVE ON THE FARM

First published in *LP* under the title "Cruelty and Love"; reprinted under this title in *Georgian Poetry 1913–1915*, reprinted with slight alterations and with present title in *CP*.

GIPSY

First published in *NP*; reprinted unchanged in *CP*. In a letter to Louie Burrows dated 6 Dec., 1910 Lawrence writes as follows: "I have been translating some of these fellah songs which are done into German. Here is one, called

SELF-CONTEMPT

A laborer speaks
I, the man with the red scarf, I
Will give thee what I have left of my week's wages
So thou wilt take it and be mine; it will buy
Thee a silver ring to prove thyself by.

More I have nothing, yea I will wear
A cap of sweat day-in, day-out, and thou
Shalt see me come home with steaming hair,
Shalt know thou the worth of that money there.

NEAR THE MARK

Come hither, cousin, cousin my dear!
I think my cousin cannot hear,
So I'll wave my sleeve for a sign "Come here!"
Come here, my cousin, cousin, my dear,
I am here, and God is near
The gladsome God is very near
I am smiling towards thee for good cheer.
Oh cousin, my cousin, oh very dear
Kiss me for God is standing near.

They are ingenuous and touching, I think. But I am a bad translator." Lawrence is obviously referring to the German translations of Arabic poems made by Fritz Krenkow (see p. 1039). "Gipsy" appears to be founded on the first of the translations quoted in Lawrence's letter.

THE COLLIER'S WIFE

First published in *LP* under the title "A Collier's Wife"; reprinted in *CP* with changes.

FLAPPER

First published in *The Egoist*, 1 April 1914, under the title "Song"; reprinted under the same title in *Poetry*, December 1914; reprinted with changes under the title "Flapper" in *NP* and *CP*.

THIEF IN THE NIGHT

First published in *NP*; reprinted unchanged in *CP*.

MONOLOGUE OF A MOTHER

First published in *Poetry*, January 1914, in a slightly different version under the title "A Mother of Sons". A revised version under the present title appeared in *A* and was reprinted with a few slight alterations in *CP*.

THE LITTLE TOWN AT EVENING

First published in *The Monthly Chapbook*, July 1919; reprinted with changes in *BAY* and *CP*. An early draft entitled "Eastwood Evening" appears in MS. 1479, No. 13.

IN A BOAT

First published in *The English Review*, October 1910 as "Tired of the Boat"; reprinted with slight alterations in *CP*. An early draft appears in MS. 1479, No. 26. Another version entitled "Tired in a Boat" appeared in *The English Review*, October 1910.

LAST HOURS

First published in *BAY*, reprinted unchanged in *CP*. Early draft in MS. 1479, No. 10. Written when Lawrence was a schoolmaster at Croydon (1909–12) and on holiday at Eastwood. The "townward train" is the train that would take him "southwards, alas!" to Croydon.

FLAT SUBURBS, S.W., IN THE MORNING

First published in *NP*, reprinted unchanged in *CP*. The suburbs are S.W. London where Lawrence lived when he taught at Croydon.

THE BEST OF SCHOOL

Originally part of the sequence called THE SCHOOLMASTER first published in *The Saturday Westminster Gazette*, May–June 1912; reprinted in an altered form in *LP*. For these versions see Appendix III, pp. 900–910. The text printed here is the considerably shortened version published by Lawrence in *CP*.

DREAMS OLD AND NASCENT: OLD

The original version of this poem was the first part of a sequence published in *The English Review*, November 1909, the first poem by Lawrence to be accepted for publication by the editor, Ford Madox Hueffer (Ford). The sequence was part of a group of his poems sent to Hueffer by Jessie Chambers to whom DREAMS OLD AND NASCENT is addressed. The text published in *The English Review* will be found in Appendix III, pp. 911–914.

Another version of the sequence was printed in *A* (see Appendix III, pp. 914–915). The two parts of the sequence were printed separately in a considerably altered form in *CP* (cf. Appendix I, p. 852).

There is an early draft called "A Still Afternoon in School" in MS. 1479, No. 46. For the other part of the sequence, NASCENT, see below, p. 173.

l. 4: "Lorna Doone" – the famous romance by R. D. Blackmore published in 1869.

l. 7: "The great blue palace at Sydenham" – the Crystal Palace, destroyed by fire in 1936.

l. 14: "The old romance of David and Dora" – This is, of course, a reference to *David Copperfield*. Dora's parents in that novel live at Norwood. See *David Copperfield*, Ch. xxvi.

SUBURBS ON A HAZY DAY

First published in *NP*; reprinted unchanged in *CP*.

WEEKNIGHT SERVICE

First published in *A*; reprinted with alterations in *CP*. Early draft in MS. 1479, No. 66.

CP and *PE* have no punctuation at the ends of stanzas 1 and 3. The version in *A*, however, has full stops in these places, and we have, therefore, felt justified in inserting them here.

A MAN WHO DIED

An early version of this poem was published in *Poetry*, January 1914, under the title "A Woman and her Dead Husband". A version with the same title appeared in *Some Imagist Poets* (1915) (Roberts, B2). The same text appeared in *NP* under the title "Bitterness of Death" and was reprinted in *CP* under the present title. There are manuscript versions in the University of New Mexico library ("The Man who Died"), in Columbia University library ("A Woman to her Dead Husband"), in the Berg Collection in the New York Public Library ("Nils Lykke Dead"), and among the Louie Burrows papers in the Library of the University of Nottingham.

LETTER FROM TOWN:
ON A GREY MORNING IN MARCH

First published in *NP* as "Letter From Town on a Grey Evening in March". Reprinted with changes in *CP*. Early draft in MS. 1479, No. 44.

LETTER FROM TOWN: THE ALMOND-TREE

First published in *NP*; reprinted with changes in *CP*. Early draft in MS. 1479, No. 44.

WEDDING MORN

First published in *LP*; reprinted with changes in *CP*. Manuscript copy in Nottingham University library.

VIOLETS

For early draft in MS. 1479, No. 34 ("Violets for the Dead") and early printed version in *LP*, see Appendix III, pp. 915–916.

LIGHTNING

First published in the *Nation*, 4 November 1911, and reprinted in *LP*. For this version, see Appendix, p. 918.

END OF ANOTHER HOME HOLIDAY

First published in *LP*. Reprinted with alterations in *CP*.

BABY RUNNING BAREFOOT

This is one of a group of poems inspired apparently by Hilda Mary, the baby daughter of Mr and Mrs J. W. Jones, at whose house Lawrence lodged when he was teaching at Croydon. For early version in sequence called "Baby Movements" printed in *The English Review* and another version printed in *A*, see below, Appendix III, p. 918.

In a letter to May Chambers Holbrook dated 2 December 1908, Lawrence describes Hilda Mary as follows: ". . . We have the jolliest fat baby, eight months old. You cannot tell how fond I am of her; her fine hazel eyes laugh at me so brightly, and her soft fingers wandering over my face and grasping at my cheeks speak to me so cunningly. . . ." (Letters, p. 39)

SIGH NO MORE

First published in *The English Review*, October 1910; reprinted with changes in *NP* and *CP*.

GUARDS

First published in *BAY* under title "Guards, A Review in Hyde Park", 1913. Early draft in MS. 1479, No. 53 has title "A Review of the Scots Guards". Revised version with present title in *CP*. This poem seems to have been part of a sequence called "Movements" in MS. 1479.

AWARE

First published in *LP*; reprinted with changes in A.P. and *CP*.

A PANG OF REMINISCENCE

First published in *LP*; reprinted with changes in *CP*.

A WHITE BLOSSOM

First published in *LP*; reprinted with changes in *CP*.

COROT

First published in *LP*; reprinted with alterations in *CP*. For early version printed in Y.L., see Appendix III, p. 920. Helen Corke in her article "D. H. Lawrence as I saw him" (*Renaissance and Modern Studies*, IV, 1960, p. 12), states that this and the following poem were written after a visit paid by her with Lawrence to a London art gallery, when he was teaching at Croydon. Ada Lawrence, however, writes that the original version of COROT consists of "thoughts which probably came to him [D. H. Lawrence] when he was copying the artist's work at Lynn Croft." (Y.L., p. 67)

MICHAEL ANGELO

For early version published in *LP*, see below, Appendix III, p. 921. In spite of Miss Corke's statement (see preceding note), this poem seems to be inspired by a reproduction of Michelangelo's "The Creation of Adam" in the Sistine Chapel, with some reminiscences of Blake's "The Tyger" in *Songs of Experience*.

HYDE PARK AT NIGHT, BEFORE THE WAR / CLERKS

First published in *The English Review*, April 1910, under the title "Yesternight" as part of a sequence called "Workday Evenings". For this version see Appendix III, p. 922. Reprinted with changes in *NP* and *CP*.

There is an early draft in MS. 1479, No. 61, as part of a sequence called "The Songless".

PICCADILLY CIRCUS AT NIGHT / STREET-WALKERS

For early version in sequence called "Workday Evenings" see Appendix III, p. 923. The present version appeared in *NP* and was reprinted unchanged in *CP*. Early draft in MS. 1479, No. 62.

AFTER THE OPERA

First published in *The English Review*, June 1918. Reprinted in *BAY* and with alterations in *CP*.

There is a manuscript version in the University of Chicago library. Miss Helen Corke (op. cit.) recalls going to the opera with Lawrence when he was at Croydon: "Once we attended a performance of Strauss' *Electra* at the Opera House, climbing endless stairs and sitting on the stone parapet of the gallery steps."

MORNING WORK

First published in *LP*; reprinted with alterations in *CP*.

TRANSFORMATIONS

First published in *LP*; reprinted with changes in *CP*.

A BABY ASLEEP AFTER PAIN

First published in *The English Review*, November 1909, under the title "Trailing Clouds" in sequence called "Baby Movements". See above, note to BABY RUNNING BAREFOOT. Reprinted with changes in *A* and with further alterations in *CP*.
l. 8: *CP* and *PE* have no punctuation at the end of this line; *A* has a comma, which we have inserted in the present text.

LAST LESSON OF THE AFTERNOON

This poem and A SNOWY DAY IN SCHOOL were first published as part of a sequence called "The Schoolmaster"; see Appendix III, pp. 906–910 and note. They were reprinted with alterations in *LP* and additional changes in *CP*.

SCHOOL ON THE OUTSKIRTS

First published in *NP*; reprinted unchanged in *CP*. The school is the Davidson Road School, Croydon, where Lawrence taught from 1909 till 1912. It was quite new when Lawrence joined the staff, having been opened in 1907.

A SNOWY DAY IN SCHOOL

See note to LAST LESSON OF THE AFTERNOON above.

WHETHER OR NOT

For earlier version published in *LP*, see Appendix III, p. 924. Edward Garnett apparently objected to the "happy ending" of the original version and the version in *CP* was due to his criticism. See above, p. 852.

A WINTER'S TALE

First published in *The Egoist*, 1 April 1914; reprinted with changes in *A* and *CP*.

RETURN

First published in *LP*; reprinted with changes in *CP*.

THE APPEAL

First published in *LP* and reprinted with changes in *CP*.

LILIES IN THE FIRE

First published in *LP* and reprinted with changes in *CP*.

RED MOON-RISE

First published in *LP* and reprinted with alterations in *CP*.

SCENT OF IRISES

First published in *Some Imagist Poets* (1915), collected in *A* and reprinted with alterations in *CP*.

I. 31 : The comma at the end of the line is restored from *A*. *CP* has no punctuation here.

FORECAST

First published in *A* with title "Epilogue". Considerably altered version in *CP*.

PROPHET

First published in *The English Review*, November 1909, as part of DISCIPLINE (see Appendix III, p. 932); reprinted separately in slightly altered form in *A* and *CP*.

DISCIPLINE

For early version first published in *The English Review*, November 1909, see Appendix III, p. 932. Revised version printed in *A* and. again with further revision in *CP*.

THE PUNISHER

For early version as part of the "Schoolmaster" sequence, see Appendix III, pp. 902–903. Revised version appeared in *A* and was reprinted with changes in *CP*.

TEASE

First published under the title "Teasing" in *Poetry and Drama* December 1914. Reprinted in *A*, and with changes in *CP*.

l. 14. The comma at the end of this line is restored from *A*. *CP* has no punctuation here.

MYSTERY

First published in *A*; reprinted in *CP* with changes.

REPULSED; COLDNESS IN LOVE

First published in *LP*; reprinted with changes in *CP*.

SUSPENSE

First published in *A* under title "Patience" and reprinted with changes in *CP*. This and the following four poems all refer to the last illness and death of Lawrence's mother in the winter of 1910.

ENDLESS ANXIETY

First published in *A* as "Anxiety". Reprinted with changes in *CP*.

THE END

First published as "Memories" in *Poetry* (December 1914), collected in *A* as "The End" and reprinted with slight changes in *CP*.

THE BRIDE

First published in *A*. A different version entitled "The Dead Mother" is printed on p. 161 of the English edition of Y. L. (Roberts, B 346). It is reprinted in *TLS*, 2 September 1965, p. 755.

THE VIRGIN MOTHER

First published in *A*; reprinted with some alterations in *CP*.

AT THE WINDOW

First published in *The English Review*, April 1910; reprinted with alterations in *A* and again with further revision in *CP*.

REMINDER

First published in *LP*; reprinted with changes in *CP*.

DRUNK

First published in *A*; reprinted with some alterations in *CP*.

SORROW

First published in *Poetry* (December 1914) as "Weariness" and collected in *A* as "Sorrow"; reprinted with some alterations in *CP*. There is an early draft in MS. 1479, No. 73.

DOLOUR OF AUTUMN

First published in *A* under the title "Dolor of Autumn"; reprinted with changes, except for title, in *CP*.

THE INHERITANCE

First published in *A*; reprinted in *CP* with changes.

SILENCE

First published in *A*; reprinted in *CP* with changes.

LISTENING

First published in *A*; reprinted in *CP* with changes.
First published in *A*; reprinted with changes in *CP*.

BROODING GRIEF

First published in *Some Imagist Poets* (1916) (Roberts, B4). Reprinted in *A* and, with slight change in the last line, in *CP*. There is an early draft in MS. 1479, No. 71.

LAST WORDS TO MIRIAM

For early draft of this poem in MS. 1479, No. 5 and early printed version in *A*, see Appendix III, pp. 934–935. For critical comment on the genesis of the poem, see V.R.M., pp. 23–26.

MALADE

First published in *A*; reprinted in *CP* with changes.

LOTUS AND FROST

First published in *A* under the title "Lotus Hurt by the Cold"; reprinted under present title with slight alterations in *CP*.

THE YEW-TREE ON THE DOWNS

For early version of this poem, entitled L I A I S O N, printed in *A*, see Appendix III, p. 935.

TROTH WITH THE DEAD

First published in A; reprinted with considerable alterations in *CP*.

AT A LOOSE END

For early version published in *A* under title DISSOLUTE, see Appendix III, p. 936.

SUBMERGENCE

This and the following poem in the text were both first published in *A* and reprinted with slight alterations in *CP*.

EXCURSION TRAIN

For early version published in *The Egoist*, 1 April 1914, under title HONEYMOON, see Appendix III, p. 936. An early draft of HONEYMOON appears in MS. 1479, No. 3. A revised version, called "Excursion", was published in *A* and reprinted with slight alterations in *CP*.

RELEASE

First published in *A* under title "Reproach"; reprinted with alterations in *CP*. See ALOOF IN GAIETY, Appendix II, 878 and note.

THESE CLEVER WOMEN

For early version published in *A* under title A SPIRITUAL WOMAN see Appendix III, p. 937.

BALLAD OF ANOTHER OPHELIA

First printed in *Some Imagist Poets* (1915) (Roberts, B2). Reprinted in *A* and with slight alterations in *CP*. Lawrence sent this poem with six others to Harriet Monroe on 31 July 1914; in a letter accompanying the poems he wrote, "Why, oh why, do you want to cut off the tail of poor 'Ophelia's' ballad? Don't you see the poor thing is cracked, and she used all those verses—apples and chickens and rat—according to true instinctive or *dream* symbolism? This poem—I am very proud of it—has got the quality of a troublesome dream that seems incoherent but is selected by another sort of consciousness. The latter part is the waking up part, yet never really awake, because she is mad. No, you mustn't cut it in two. It is a good poem: I couldn't do it again to save my life. Use it whole or not at all . . ." (Letters, p. 288). For early version entitled ANOTHER OPHELIA, see Appendix III, p. 938.

KISSES IN THE TRAIN

First published in *LP*; reprinted with alterations in *CP*.

TURNED DOWN

First published under the title "Fooled" in *The Egoist*, 1 April 1914; reprinted as "Perfidy" in *Some Imagist Poets* (1916), and in *A*, and with alterations under the present title in *CP*. Early draft entitled "Lost" in MS. 1479, No. 56.

AFTER MANY DAYS

First published in *A*, reprinted with slight changes in *CP*.

SNAP-DRAGON

First published in *The English Review*, June 1912. Reprinted in *Georgian Poetry 1911–1912*; reprinted with alterations in *A*. The version in *A* was reprinted with slight changes in *CP*. For early manuscript version see Appendix III, p. 940.

COME SPRING, COME SORROW

First published in *A* under title "Mating"; reprinted with alterations in *CP*.

THE HANDS OF THE BETROTHED

First published in *A*; reprinted with alterations in *CP*.

A LOVE SONG

First published in *A*; reprinted in *CP* with changes.

TWOFOLD

This and the following poem were first published in *NP* and reprinted unchanged in *CP*.

UNDER THE OAK

First published in *NP* and reprinted with changes in *CP*.

TARANTELLA

Early draft entitled "A Tarantella", in MS. 1479, No. 23.

BROTHER AND SISTER

First published in *A*; reprinted with changes in *CP*. For early version entitled TO LETTICE, MY SISTER, see Appendix III, p. 943.

THE SHADOW OF DEATH

First published in *A* in a much longer version under title "Blue"; reprinted (shortened, revised version) in *CP*.

BIRDCAGE WALK

First published in *NP*; reprinted unchanged in *CP*. There is an early draft in MS. 1479, No. 37, entitled "Triolet", followed by drafts of two other triolets, both crossed out and the third partly illegible.

The second triolet reads as follows:

> I knew you'd come back
>   And I said I'd not kiss you
> For you were horrid, Jack.
> I knew you'd come back
> 'Cause the night's wet and black
>   And—Oh, I should miss you.
> I knew you'd come back
>   And I said I'd not kiss you.

The third triolet begins.

> You may well laugh
>   You bold little hussy . . .

The triolets are followed by a draft of a poem called "Rondeau Redoublé" (see note to RONDEAU OF A CONSCIENTIOUS OBJECTOR below, p. 993). These poems seem to belong to a period when Lawrence was experimenting with the old French verse forms made fashionable by Andrew Lang and Austin Dobson.

CALL INTO DEATH

First published in *A* under title "Elegy"; reprinted with changes in *CP*.

GREY EVENING

First published in *A*; reprinted with changes in *CP*.

FIRELIGHT AND NIGHTFALL

For the poem called GRIEF, which combines elements from this and the preceding poem, sent by Lawrence to Edward Marsh in

December 1913 and printed in *Poetry*, December 1914, see Appendix III, p. 944.
Another version called TWILIGHT, printed in *The English Review*, February 1914, will be found in Appendix III, p. 945. The present text was first published in *A* and was reprinted with changes in *CP*.

BLUENESS

First published in *A* under title "The Mystic Blue"; reprinted under present title with some alterations in *CP*.

A PASSING-BELL

First published in *A*; reprinted with changes in *CP*. There is an early draft in MS. 1479.

THE DRAINED CUP

First published in *LP*; reprinted with numerous alterations in *CP*.

LATE AT NIGHT

First published in *NP* under title "Phantasmagoria"; reprinted with changes in *CP*.

NEXT MORNING

This and the following six poems were all first published in *NP* and reprinted in *CP*.

PIANO

For early version in MS. 1479, entitled THE PIANO, see Appendix III, p. 946. The present text first appeared in *NP* and was reprinted unchanged in *CP*. For comment see V.R.M., pp. 26-8.

THE NORTH COUNTRY

First published in *NP* and reprinted unchanged in *CP*.

PASSING VISIT TO HELEN

First published in *NP* as "Intime", reprinted in *CP* with changes.

READING A LETTER

The draft of a poem called "Reading in the Evening", MS. 1479, No. 48, bears some resemblance to this poem.

TWO WIVES

The first five sections of this poem were published in *NP* under the present title. The poem was reprinted in *CP* with the addition of the two last sections.

NOISE OF BATTLE

First published in *NP* under title "Apprehension"; reprinted unchanged, except for title, in *CP*.

AT THE FRONT

First published under title "Heimweh" in *NP*; reprinted unchanged, except for title, in *CP*. A draft (without title) bearing some resemblance to this poem appears in MS. 1479, No. 2.

REALITY OF PEACE, 1916

First published under title "Débâcle" in *NP*; reprinted with changes in *CP*.

NARCISSUS

First published in *NP*; reprinted with minor changes in *CP*. An early draft entitled "Dim Recollections" appears in MS. 1479, No. 27.

TOMMIES IN THE TRAIN

First published in *Poetry*, February 1919; reprinted with changes in *BAY* and *CP*.

ON THE MARCH

This and the following five poems were first printed in *BAY* and reprinted in *CP*.

RONDEAU OF A CONSCIENTIOUS OBJECTOR

There is an early draft of this poem in MS. 1479, No. 38, with title "Workdays Coming Home from School: Rondeau Redoublé"; see note to BIRDCAGE WALK, above, p. 991.

OBSEQUIAL ODE

First published in *Poetry*, February 1919, under title "Obsequial Chant"; reprinted with changes in *BAY* and *CP*.

GOING BACK

First published in *BAY*; reprinted with minor changes in *CP*.

SHADES

First published in *Poetry*, February 1919, under title "Pentecostal"; reprinted with changes in *BAY* and *CP*.

TOWN IN 1917

First published in *The English Review*, June 1918, under title "Town"; reprinted unchanged, except for title, in *BAY* and *CP*.

BREAD UPON THE WATERS

First published in *Poetry*, February 1919; reprinted with changes in *BAY* and *CP*.

WAR-BABY

First published in *The English Review*, June 1918; reprinted with changes in *BAY* and *CP*.

NOSTALGIA

First published in *Poetry*, February 1919; reprinted with changes in *BAY*, *Palms*, Midsummer 1923, and *CP*.

DREAMS OLD AND NASCENT: NASCENT

See note to DREAMS OLD AND NASCENT: OLD, above, p. 981, and Appendix III, p. 911.

ON THAT DAY

For early version entitled BIRTHDAY, see Appendix III, p. 942. The present version was published in *NP* and reprinted with minor changes in *CP*. The poem clearly refers to the birthday of Lawrence's mother (born 19 July 1852).

AUTUMN SUNSHINE

For early version entitled EARLY SPRING, published in *The Egoist*, 1 April 1914, see Appendix III, p. 947. The present version was first printed in *NP* and reprinted with minor changes in *CP*.

SONG-DAY IN AUTUMN

This and the following two poems were not included in *CP* but were reprinted in *PE*, vol. 1, and Nardi, Appendix II. SONG-DAY IN AUTUMN was first published in *LP* and the other two both in *A*.

POETRY OF THE PRESENT

Text from *The Playboy*, Nos. 4 and 5, 1919 (Roberts, C 69, 70). This essay was reprinted by Lawrence as the Preface to the American edition of *NP*, see above, p. 23.

UNRHYMING POEMS

LOOK! WE HAVE COME THROUGH!

According to Catherine Carswell the original title of this collection was "Man and Woman". This was changed to "Poems of a Married Man" and then again to *LOOK! WE HAVE COME THROUGH!* (see Carswell, p. 91). All the poems in this section, except where otherwise indicated, were first printed in *LWH* and reprinted unchanged in *CP*.

In the summer of 1962 Mr George Lazarus acquired from Bertram Rota Ltd a set of page-proofs of *LWH* containing Lawrence's manuscript corrections. V. de S. P. was enabled by the kindness of Mr Lazarus and Mr Rota to examine these proofs. Some of the more interesting corrections are recorded in the following notes. The words "in proof" in the notes on poems in this collection refer to this set of proofs.

FOREWORD

Printed in *LWH*; omitted from *CP*.

ARGUMENT

This is the version as printed in *LWH*. In version printed in *CP*, the last seven words are omitted.

DON JUAN

First printed in *Poetry*, December 1914. Reprinted with changes in *LWH* and *CP*.

THE SEA

First published in *The English Review*, September 1917; reprinted unchanged in *LWH* and *CP*.

l. 16: "sophisticated" – substituted in proof for "you alone subjected".

l. 29: "shadow" – substituted in proof for "Twilight".

HYMN TO PRIAPUS

First published in *The English Review*, September 1917, under title "Constancy of a Sort"; reprinted under present title in *LWH* and *CP*.

BALLAD OF A WILFUL WOMAN

Second Part, l. 6: "white" – substituted in proof for "sea".

BEI HENNEF

First published in *LP*; not included in *LWH*, but placed by Lawrence in the *LOOK! WE HAVE COME THROUGH!* cycle in *CP*. Written at Hennef in the Rheinprovinz in May 1912, when Lawrence was on his way from Trier to Waldbrol, where he went to visit his relatives, Professor and Mrs Krenkow. See Moore, pp. 122-3.

SHE LOOKS BACK

l. 26: "under-dusk" – substituted in proof for "wonderful dusk".

l. 32: "quaint" – deleted in proof before "extravagance".

l. 55: cf. Genesis xix, 26.

l. 69: "rain" – substituted in proof for "wind".

l. 79: "vision" – substituted in proof for "soul".

ON THE BALCONY

First published under title "Illicit", in *Poetry*, January 1914; reprinted under that title in *Some Imagist Poets* (1915) (Roberts, B2), and under present title in *LWH* and *CP*.

FROHNLEICHNAM

l. 15: "morning" – substituted in proof for "daylight".

l. 37: "sheer" – substituted in proof for "clean".

MUTILATION

l. 37: "Tuatha De Danaan" – These are the gods of ancient Ireland. Lawrence probably knew of them from the poems of W. B. Yeats.

GREEN

First published in *Poetry*, January 1914; reprinted in *Some Imagist Poets* (1915), *LWH* and *CP*.

RIVER ROSES

For early version of this and the following four poems published in N.I.B. under title ALL OF ROSES, see Appendix III, p. 948.

GLOIRE DE DIJON

l. 14: "sluicing" – substituted in proof for the much less vivid "showering".

ROSES ON THE BREAKFAST TABLE

l. 4: "reluctant" – substituted in proof for "though lingering".

ROSE OF ALL THE WORLD

l. 23: "perfect" – substituted in proof for "august".

A YOUTH MOWING

For early version of this poem published in *The Smart Set*, under title "The Mowers", see Appendix III, p. 950.

FIREFLIES IN THE CORN

For early version of this poem published in *Poetry*, see Appendix III, p. 955.

MISERY

The experience which produced this poem is described by Lawrence in a letter to A. W. McLeod from Sterzing am Brenner (Austrian Tyrol) dated 2 September 1912: ". . . I have walked here from Mayrhofen – quite an exciting scramble. And last night again we slept in a hut 2000 – some odd hundred metres high. It was damnably cold. The water was simply freezing. And I nearly got lost. Don't be surprised if I do vanish some day in some oubliette or other among these mountains. . . ." (Letters, p. 141.)

MEETING AMONG THE MOUNTAINS

This fine poem was omitted by Lawrence from the 1917 edition of *LWH* at the request of the publishers (see Letters, p. 521). He did not include it in *CP*. It was originally printed in *The English Review*, February 1914, and again in *Georgian Poetry, 1913–1915* (Roberts, B3). A version of it was printed by Frieda Lawrence in N.I.B. and reprinted by Warren Roberts in *LWH–WR*. The text printed here is that which appeared in *Georgian Poetry 1913–1915*, pp. 154–5. According to Frieda, there was some connection between the peasant with "brown eyes black with misery and hate" in the poem and Professor Ernest Weekley, Frieda's first husband, for whom, Frieda said, Lawrence "felt strongly" (Moore, p. 128). It was probably because of the painful memories associated with this poem that Lawrence decided not to reprint it in *CP*. The text printed in *The English Review* is reprinted in Nardi, Appendix II.

EVERLASTING FLOWERS

First published in *NP*, not included in *LWH*, but placed by Lawrence in this position in the *Look! We Have Come Through!* cycle in *CP*.

GIORNO DEI MORTI

First published in the *New Statesman*, 15 November 1913, under title "Service of All the Dead"; reprinted under that title in *Georgian Poetry 1913–1915* and under the present title in *LWH* and *CP*.

LADY WIFE

l. 5: "The angels came to Abraham" – see Genesis xviii, 2-15.
l. 7: "happily" – substituted in proof for "willingly".
l. 23: "sweetness" – substituted in proof for "manna".
l. 31: "imminent" – substituted in proof for "awful".

RABBIT SNARED IN THE NIGHT

l. 2: "like that" – these words were inserted in proof.
l. 21: "bale-fire" – substituted in proof for "blood-fire".
ll. 34-6, ll. 40-2: these lines were inserted in proof.

SONG OF A MAN WHO IS LOVED

This poem was excluded from *LWH* at the request of the publishers, who objected to it strongly, in spite of the fact that Lawrence protested that it was "beautiful, necessary and innocuous as a sprig of mignonette" (Letters, p. 521). He restored it to its original place in the sequence in *CP*, from which the present text is taken. For an early version printed by Frieda Lawrence in N.I.B. see Appendix III, p. 951.

THE SONG OF A MAN WHO HAS COME THROUGH

l. 11: "wonder" – substituted in proof for "word".
l. 17: ". . . the three strange angels" – probably the three angels who appeared to Abraham in Genesis xviii; see note to LADY WIFE, above.

ONE WOMAN TO ALL WOMEN

l. 20: "straggling" – substituted in proof for "meagre".

PEOPLE

This poem was reprinted in *Poetry*, July 1918.

NEW HEAVEN AND NEW EARTH

First printed under title "Terra Nuova" in *Some Imagist Poets* (1917) (Roberts, B7); reprinted under present title in *LWH* and *CP*.
VI, l. 24: After this line "Eureka!" is deleted in proof.

MANIFESTO

VII, l. 26: This line, apparently an afterthought, was inserted in proof.

AUTUMN RAIN

First published in *The Egoist*, February 1917; reprinted in *LWH* and *CP*.

FROST FLOWERS

First published in *The English Review*, September 1917.
l. 35: "dissolution" – substituted for "corruption".

CRAVING FOR SPRING

l. 79: "death-edged" – substituted in proof for "saw-edged".
l. 88: "that are out" – these words are inserted in proof.
l. 96: "of the living" – substituted in proof for "of men".

l. 98: This is reading of *CP* and *PE*. *LWH* reads "stirring of new heaven and new earth", substituted in proof for "happiness of mankind".

l. 99: "such anticipation" – substituted in proof for "so much hope!".

BIRDS, BEASTS AND FLOWERS

In a letter dated 10 February 1923, Lawrence wrote that he considered this collection to be his "best book of poems" (Letters, p. 737). He seems to have taken the title from S. Baring-Gould's "Evening Hymn" (Hymns A. and M., No. 346), the second stanza of which reads as follows:

> Now the darkness gathers,
> Stars begin to peep,
> Birds and beasts and flowers
> Soon will be asleep.

All the poems in this section, unless the contrary is stated in the notes, were first printed in *BBF* and reprinted in *CP* and *PE*.

The little prose prefaces to the various sections of the collection were first printed in the illustrated edition of *BBF* published by the Cresset Press in June 1930 (Roberts, A27C), and reprinted in Phoenix, pp. 65–8. These prefaces contain a number of quotations, chiefly from John Burnet's *Early Greek Philosophy* (3rd Edition, 1920). Lawrence seems to have first read Burnet's book (which was given to him by Bertrand Russell) when he was in Cornwall in 1916. According to Richard Aldington, he "delighted in this work [Burnet's book], and was influenced by it considerably" (P.G.B., p. 168). Russell must have given him the 1st Edition (1892) or the 2nd (1908). The quotations in *BBF*, however, seem to come from the 3rd Edition, as they refer to a passage that does not occur in the two earlier ones. The Cresset Press text places every paragraph of the prefaces in inverted commas. Where Lawrence is evidently speaking in his own person, these quotation marks have been deleted in the present text, but they have been retained where it seems to be clear that the passage is a quotation.

FRUITS

The last sentence of this preface seems to be a quotation, but we have been unable to trace its origin.

MEDLARS AND SORB-APPLES

First published in *New Republic*, 5 January 1921; reprinted in *The English Review*, August 1921, and in *BBF* and *CP*. This was the first of *BIRDS, BEASTS AND FLOWERS* to be published. It was written when Lawrence was staying with his friend, Mrs Popham, at San Gervasio, near Florence, in the autumn of 1920 (Moore, p. 273).

THE REVOLUTIONARY

First published in *New Republic*, 19 January 1921; reprinted in *The English Review*, September 1921, *The Literary Digest*, 29 October 1921, *BBF* and *CP*.

THE EVENING LAND

First printed in *Poetry*, November 1922; reprinted in *BBF* and *CP*. Penultimate line: "'These States!'" – a favourite phrase of Whitman, occurring in a number of his poems.

TREES

"'Empedokles says . . . fire in plants'" – This passage is from Burnet, op. cit., p. 241. It is translated by Burnet from the Greek account of Empedokles by Aetius.

CYPRESSES

First published in *The Adelphi*, October 1923, reprinted in *BBF* and *CP*. This poem contains the first allusion in Lawrence's writings to the Etruscans. His interest in them was apparently first aroused by the fragmentary Etruscan walls near Fiesole, when he was staying there with Mrs Popham in September 1920. Cp. Hassall, op. cit., pp. 64–80.

FLOWERS

"'Oh Persephone, Persephone . . . dead man.'" – This seems to be a quotation, but we have been unable to trace its origin.

" 'Wretches, utter wretches, keep your hands from beans!' ":
Empedokles, fragment 141. See Burnet, op. cit., p. 226.

ALMOND BLOSSOM

First published in *The English Review*, February 1922; reprinted in
BBF and *CP*.

ST MATTHEW

Published in *Poetry*, April 1923; reprinted in *BBF* and *CP* with the
following three poems under the general title "Evangelistic Beasts".

l. 52:" ΙΧΘΥΣ – an early Christian symbol for Christ was a fish, the
Greek word for which (ἰχθύς) is spelled with the initial letters of
some of Christ's attributes: Ἰ[ησοῦς] Χ[ριστός], Θ[εοῦ] Ὺ[ιος]
Σ[ωτήρ] – Jesus Christ, Son of God, Saviour.

ST MARK

l. 6: "Daniele Manin" – Venetian patriot, 1804–57, of Jewish descent,
president of the revived Venetian Republic in 1848. He defended
Venice in a siege of five months against the Austrian Army in 1849.
Professor Nardi has suggested that Lawrence may have been think-
ing of the fine statue of Manin in the Campo Manin at Venice, in
which the hero is represented with the lion of St Mark at his feet.
l. 36: "Carpaccio" – Venetian painter, d. 1526. The allusion, as Nardi
notes in his edition (Nardi, II, 2225), is to Carpaccio's picture of the
Lion of St Mark, now in the Palazzo Ducale in Venice.

CREATURES

" 'But fishes . . . cool themselves.' " – This opinion is attributed to
Empedokles by Aristotle; see Burnet, op. cit., p. 245.
"To those things that love darkness . . . fires, that die." – Though not
apparently a quotation, this passage seems to owe something to the
account of Empedokles's theory of perception translated by Burnet
from Theophrastus, Burnet, op. cit., pp. 246–7.

FISH

First published in *The English Review*, June 1922; reprinted in *BBF*
and *CP*. Lawrence sent this and the following two poems with a

letter to Curtis Brown dated 17 September 1921 from Florence with instructions to place them among the "beasts" in *BBF* (Letters, p. 663). Penultimate line: "Jesus was called The Fish. . . ." – c.f. note to ST MATTHEW, l. 51, above.

BAT

First published in *The English Review*, November 1922; reprinted in *BBF* and *CP*.

REPTILES

" 'Homer was wrong . . . would pass away" ' – this passage is Burnet's translation from the Greek of Herakleitos (Fragment 43, Burnet, op. cit., p. 136).

SNAKE

First published in *The Dial*, July 1921; reprinted in *The London Mercury*, October 1921, in *Georgian Poetry 1920–22*, *BBF* and *CP*. This famous poem certainly grew out of Lawrence's actual encounter with a snake which he saw drinking from his water-trough when he was living at Fontana Vecchia, Taormina in 1920–21, but there is a curious anticipation of it in his prose essay "The Reality of Peace" published in May 1917. (See Phoenix, p. 678 and Moore, p. 265.)

BABY TORTOISE

This and the following five poems (the TORTOISE sequence) were first published in a volume called *Tortoises* by Thomas Seltzer at New York in 1921 (Roberts, A19). Seltzer published the first edition of *BBF* (Roberts, A27a). He did not include in it the TORTOISE poems, but they were included in the first English edition published by Secker (Roberts, A27b) and were reprinted in *CP*. BABY TORTOISE was printed also in *The English Review*, November 1922.

TURKEY-COCK

First published in *Poetry*, November 1922; reprinted in *BBF* and *CP*. In a letter to Harriet Monroe from Taos, dated 23 September 1922, Lawrence wrote that this poem was one of his favourites (Letters, p. 719).
l. 89: "Dross-jabot" – This word seems to be compounded by Lawrence from dross + jabot = "a frill formerly worn by men on the front or bosom of the shirt edging the opening" (O.E.D.).

l. 61: "Huichilobos" – probably = Huitzilopochtli, the ancient Mexican wargod, see below, p. 1031.

HUMMING-BIRD

First published in *New Republic*, 11 May 1921; reprinted in *Nation* (New York) 10 October 1923, *The Bookman* (New York) January 1924, *BBF* and *CP*.

EAGLE IN NEW MEXICO

For different version of this poem published in *FIRE*, see p. 780.

ANIMALS

" 'Yes and if oxen or lions . . . image of their several kinds,' " – this is a famous fragment of Xenophanes (No. 15). See Burnet, op. cit., p.119.

" 'Once they say . . . heard its voice' " – this is a story told of Pythagoras by Xenophanes quoted by Burnet, op. cit., p. 84.

" 'Swine wash in mire . . . fowls in dust.' " – This is Burnet's translation of fragment 53 of Herakleitos, see Burnet, op. cit., p. 137.

THE ASS

l. 32: ". . . *noli me tangere*" – see John xx, 17.

l. 49: ". . . Jesus rode him . . ." – see Matthew xxi, 7 and John xii, 14.

SHE-GOAT

l. 13: "*Tace, tu, crapa, bestia!*" – Sicilian dialect for "Taci, tu, capra, bestia" = "Shut up, you she-goat, animal". *Crapa* is Sicilian dialect for *capra* by metathesis. We are indebted to Professor E. R. Vincent for this note.

i. 35: ". . . hairy horrid God the Father in a William Blake imagination." – Lawrence is almost certainly thinking of Blake's famous picture "The Ancient of Days" representing God the Father (Urizen-Jehovah), with streaming hair and beard, creating the world.

ELEPHANT

First published in *The English Review*, April 1923; reprinted in *BBF* and *CP*. This was apparently the only poem written by Lawrence when he was in Ceylon in the spring of 1922. It describes the Perahera, or Ceylonese festival, in which Lawrence saw the Prince of Wales (afterwards Edward VIII) riding on an elephant. Lawrence sent a vivid prose description of the scene at the Perahera to his sister, Emily (Mrs King), in a letter dated 24 March 1922: "Yesterday the Prince of Wales was here—great doings. We were down at the Perahera at night—were just opposite the Prince. Poor devil, he is so thin and nervy: all twitchy: and seems worn out and disheartened. No wonder, badgered about like a doll among a mob of children. . . . "But the Perahera was wonderful: it was night & flaming torches of cocoanut blazing, & the great elephants in their trappings, about a hundred, & the dancers with tomtoms & bagpipes, & half naked & jewelled, then the Kandyan chiefs in their costumes, & more dancers, & more elephants, & more chiefs, & more dancers, so wild and strange & perfectly fascinating, heaving along by the flame of torches in hot, still, starry night. Afterwards fireworks over the lake, and thousands & thousands of natives, so that it looked like some queer dream when the fire flared up & showed their thousands of dark faces & white wraps packed on the banks." See V.R.M., p. 8, and Letters, 696-7.

BIBBLES

See Moore, p. 383.
l. 11: "Adolph, and Rex . . ." – see the essays on these two animals in Phoenix, pp. 7 and 14.
l. 31: "*miserere*" – for *miserere mei* = pity me.
l. 110: "*Reject nothing,*" – Lawrence is probably referring to the line from Whitman's poem "With Antecedents": "I believe materialism is true and spiritualism is true, I reject no part" (*Complete Verse and Selected Prose and Letters*, ed. E. Holloway, London: Nonesuch Press 1932, p.223).

GHOSTS

" 'the dog with its nostrils . . . the soft grass' ": this is Burnet's translation of fragment 101 of Empedokles (op. cit., p. 220).

AUTUMN AT TAOS

Published in *Palms*, Autumn 1923, as "Autumn in New Mexico" in *BBF* and *CP* under present title.

SPIRITS SUMMONED WEST

First published in *The Adelphi*, October 1923; reprinted in *BBF* and *CP*.

PANSIES

This section consists of the poems published in *PANSIES—1*. The notes indicate those which were omitted from *PANSIES—2* and *PE*, vol. II, where the text of *PANSIES—2* is reprinted.

The following poems in this section appeared in *The Dial*, July 1929: TO LET GO OR TO HOLD ON——?, THINGS MEN HAVE MADE——, WHATEVER MAN MAKES——, WORK, WHAT WOULD YOU FIGHT FOR?, ATTILA, SEA-WEED, LIZARD, CENSORS, NOVEMBER BY THE SEA——.

INTRODUCTION

Text from *PANSIES—1*; reprinted in Phoenix, p. 279.

p. 419: "the Voltaire story" – See *Candide*, ch. xii.

"poem of Swift's" – This is "The Lady's Dressing Room, 1730":

> Thus finishing his grand survey.
> Disgusted Strephon slunk away;
> Repeating in his amorous fits,
> "O Celia, Celia, Celia shits!"

FOREWORD

Text from *PANSIES—2*, pp. 5, 6; reprinted as "Note" in *PE*, II, xxxv, xxxvi.

p. 423. " 'He who hath wife . . . to fortune" – See Bacon, *Essays*, "Of Marriage and Single Life".

"Some of the poems are perforce omitted – about a dozen" – This refers to the fourteen Pansies which were omitted from Secker's "trade" edition.

"Scotland Yard seized the MS. in the post" – See Moore, p. 396–9, and Nehls, III, 304–12.

"Mrs Caudle's curtain lecture" – The reference is to Douglas Jerrold's humorous dialogues, *Mrs Caudle's Curtain Lectures* (1845).

GIVE US GODS

For early draft of this poem entitled RELIGION, see below, Appendix III, p. 952.

SPIRAL FLAME

l. 8: "Sum ergo non cogito" = I am, therefore I do not think: reversal of Descartes' famous aphorism, "Cogito ergo sum" = I think, therefore I am.

THE NOBLE ENGLISHMAN

Omitted from *PANSIES*—2, reprinted in Nardi, Appendix II. For variant version see below Appendix III, p. 953.

LET US BE MEN——

This poem, under the title "For God's Sake——", together with O! START A REVOLUTION—— and IT'S EITHER YOU FIGHT OR YOU DIE—— (see below) were sent by Lawrence in a letter to Charles Wilson from Hotel Beau Rivage, Bandol Var, dated 28 December 1928. We are indebted to Mr Laurence Pollinger and Mr Wearing King for drawing our attention to this letter and the accompanying poems. They kindly supplied us with a photostat of a typed copy of the letter and poems made by Mr W. A. Wilson, who sent it to Mr Wearing King, Chief Education Officer for the County of Surrey. The original is now in the possession of Mr G. L. Lazarus, who has kindly made it available to the editors. Lawrence's letter, but not the text of the poems, is printed on p. 1110 of Letters.

According to information supplied by Mr W. A. Wilson to Mr Wearing King, at the time when Lawrence's letter was written Charles Wilson was a freelance journalist taking an active part in the Labour Movement and living at the mining village of Willington, Co. Durham. It would appear that he had asked Lawrence for a New Year's message for the men of the Willington Colliery. In his letter to Wilson Lawrence writes: "Here are three scraps of a sort of poetry which will perhaps do as 'message'. I've done a book of such poems—really they are *pensées*—which I shall publish later—but you may as well start in with these three bits. . . . I wonder when we shall come to England. I read with shame of the miners' 'hampers' and the 'fund'. It's a nice thing to make them live on charity and crumbs of cake, when what they want is manly independence. The whole scheme of things is unjust and rotten, and money is just a disease upon humanity. It's time there was an *enormous* revolution—not to instal soviets but to give life itself a chance. What's the good of an industrial system piling up rubbish, while nobody lives. We want a revolution not in the name of money or work or any of that, but of life—and let money and work be as casual in human life as they are in a bird's life, damn it all. Oh it's time the whole thing was changed absolutely. And the men will have to do it—you've got to smash money and this beastly *possessive* spirit. I get more revolutionary every minute, but for *life's* sake. The dead materialism of Marx Socialism and Soviets seems to me no better than what we've got. What we want is life and *trust*: men trusting men, and making living a free thing, not a thing to be *earned*. But if men trusted men, we could soon have a new world, and send this one to the devil.

"There's more message—perhaps too strong for you. But the beastliness of the show, the *injustice*—just see the rich English down here on the Riviera, *thousands* of them—nauseates me. Men can't stand injustice."

The three poems accompanying the letter are headed "New Year's Greeting to the Willington Men for 1929." They show the following variants from the printed texts in *PANSIES—1* and *—2* and *PE* (apart from the title of LET US BE MEN and heavier punctuation probably inserted by Huxley). In the versions printed by Huxley all lines of all three poems begin with capitals. In FOR GOD'S SAKE (LET US BE MEN—), l. 4: "the" is omitted before "radio"; dash is placed after "gramophone" instead of at the end of the poem. In O START A REVOLUTION, title ends with exclamation mark not full stop; l. 5 has "instal" instead of "install". In IT'S EITHER YOU FIGHT OR YOU DIE—, l. 10: "nice" instead of "great"; l. 11: "Blousy" instead of "blowsy".

WORK

For early draft of this poem, see below, Appendix III, p. 955.

WOMEN WANT FIGHTERS FOR THEIR LOVERS

Omitted from *PANSIES—2* and *PE*. Reprinted in Nardi, Appendix II.

NOLI ME TANGERE

see John xx, 17.

CLIMB DOWN, O LORDLY MIND——

ll. 38, 40: see above, note to SPIRAL FLAME, p. 1007.

EGO-BOUND WOMEN——

Omitted from *PANSIES*—2, reprinted in Nardi, Appendix II.

FIDELITY

l. 21: "All flows——" – Possibly a reminiscence of the famous Greek saying πάντα ῥεῖ, wrongly attributed to Herakleitos, which Lawrence would have found in Burnet, op. cit., p. 146.

l. 30: "foraminiferæ" – foraminifera = "a type of rhizopod, one of the most primitive kinds of organism, having a minute shell" (O.E.D.).

THE UNIVERSE FLOWS——

The title of this poem is probably suggested by Herakleitos's doctrine of perpetual flux. See Burnet, op. cit., pp. 145–6.

NOTTINGHAM'S NEW UNIVERSITY

This poem refers to the erection at Highfield, Nottingham, of the building designed by Morley Horder, presented by Sir Jesse Boot, afterwards first Lord Trent, to house University College, Nottingham. It was opened by King George V on 10 July 1928, and is now the Trent Building of the University of Nottingham. Mr Rolf Gardiner, who was intimate with Lawrence at that time, gives the following account of the origin of this poem. He was at Nottingham in October 1928 with a choir of German singers, who performed in the great hall of the new building at Highfield. "On 13th," writes Mr Gardiner, "the company was entertained at lunch in the refectory of the new buildings. . . . Professor Weekley was among those who acted as hosts. It was then that I remarked on the new buildings built by Morley Horder, and on the tower 'in grand and cakey style' insisted on by the good Sir Jesse Boot. I thereupon wrote to Lawrence, who had followed the activity of the music hour, . . . and described the occasion and the setting. Lawrence replied by writing his pansy beginning:

In Nottingham, that dismal town
where I went to school and college, . . ."

In a letter to Edward Garnett dated 13 January 1915, Lawrence wrote, ". . . You know that my mother's father and this grand-duke of drugs [Jesse Boot] quarrelled and had a long war as to which of them should govern a chapel in Sneinton, in Nottingham. My grandfather won. So now, *Weh'mir, dass ich ein Enkel bin* – woe is me that I am a grandchild, for I am booted out of my place as a popular novelist." (Letters—H, p. 214) This poem may, perhaps, be regarded as the final episode in the "long war". For variant version entitled IN NOTTINGHAM, see Appendix III, p. 956.

I AM IN A NOVEL——

The novel is Aldous Huxley's *Point Counter Point*, published in 1928. The character of Mark Rampion in this novel is modelled on Huxley's impressions of Lawrence. According to Richard Aldington, Lawrence "took serious exception" to Rampion (P.G.B., p. 317). He wrote to William Gerhardi on 14 November 1928: "I refuse to be Rampioned. Aldous' admiration for me is only skin-deep, and out of a Mary Mary quite contrary impulse" (Moore, p. 393).

MY NAUGHTY BOOK; THE LITTLE WOWSER; THE YOUNG MEN AND THEIR MORAL GUARDIANS

These three poems were omitted from *PANSIES*—2 and *PE*. They are reprinted in Nardi, Appendix II.

MY NAUGHTY BOOK

This is, of course, *Lady Chatterley's Lover*, the first (privately printed) edition of which appeared in July 1928.

THE LITTLE WOWSER

"Wowser" is Australian slang, probably heard by Lawrence when he was in Australia in 1922. For meaning, see Glossary. In *PANSIES*—*L* and in a manuscript version in the Library of the University of Texas this poem is entitled "An Old Acquaintance".

ATTILA

In his *Movements in European History* (1912) p. 83, Lawrence describes Attila as "the greatest of the Huns . . . a squat broad-backed man with a large head and a flat face. . . . A haughty little creature, he had a prancing way of walking, and he rolled his eyes fiercely, filling the onlookers with terror, and enjoying the terror he inspired".

WELLSIAN FUTURES

Lawrence is, doubtless, thinking here of such books of H. G. Wells as *Anticipations* (1901), *Mankind in the Making* (1903), *A Modern Utopia* (1905), *The World Set Free* (1914) and *Men like Gods* (1923). Lawrence's "men made in bottles", in this poem, curiously anticipates the "Wellsian future" of Aldous Huxley's *Brave New World* of 1932.

GRASSHOPPER IS A BURDEN——

See Ecclesiastes xii, 5.

DIES IRAE; DIES ILLA

These poems refer to the opening lines of the famous mediaeval hymn, *Dies Irae*, attributed to Thomas of Celano (*c.* 1250). The following is the seventeenth-century translation of the lines by the Earl of Roscommon:

> The Day of Wrath, that dreadful Day,
> Shall the whole World in Ashes lay,
> As David and the Sybils say.

WAGES

A version of this poem which appears on p. 68 of *PANSIES—L* ends with the following lines in place of the last line of the present text:

> . . . Of course living should be free,
>   and work should be each man's choice of fun.

MAN'S IMAGE

For early draft of this poem entitled MORALITY, see Appendix III, p. 956.

THINK—!

l. 4: "alumina" – "one of the earths, a white insoluble, tasteless amorphous substance; the only oxide (Al_2O_3) of the metal Aluminium, the basis of alum, the chief constituent of all clays, and found crystallized in the sapphire" (O.E.D.).

WHAT MATTERS

Omitted from *PANSIES*—2 and *PE*; reprinted in Nardi, Appendix II.

FATE AND THE YOUNGER GENERATION

i. 1: "Annas . . . Vronskys" – see Tolstoy's *Anna Karenina;* "Pierres" – see Tolstoy's *War and Peace.*
l. 3: "Alyoshas . . . Dmitris" – see Dostoevski's *The Brothers Karamazov;* "Myshkins" – see Dostoevski's *The Idiot;* Stravrogins" – see Dostoevski's *The Possessed.*

FILM PASSION

l. 2: "Rudolf Valentino" – American film-star popular in the nineteen-twenties. His great success was in *The Four Horsemen of the Apocalypse* (1921).

VOLCANIC VENUS

l. 6: "Ixtaccihuatl" – This is Ixtaccihuatl, a volcano in Mexico, ten miles north of Popocatapetl and about forty miles SSE of Mexico City.

WHAT DOES SHE WANT?

Omitted from *PANSIES*—2 and *PE*; reprinted in Nardi, Appendix II.

DON'T LOOK AT ME

Omitted from *PANSIES*—2 and *PE*; reprinted in Nardi, Appendix II.

WHAT IS MAN WITHOUT AN INCOME?—

ll. 24, 25: See *Hamlet*, V, 1, 235-6.

TO CLARINDA

Omitted from *PANSIES*—2 and *PE*; reprinted in Nardi, Appendix II. Clarinda is Mrs Aldous (Maria) Huxley (d. 1955). The following passage from a letter of Lawrence to Aldous Huxley, dated 30 December 1928, throws light on this poem: "I have done my *Pansies*, nice and peppery. I altered Maria's a bit—she must say if she doesn't want it in. I don't know if she had it even. But I changed it to Dear Clarinda. There, Maria! get a new nickname, be a new maid. Now you're Clarinda, my dear!" (Letters, p. 1113).

THE SADDEST DAY

The opening quatrain of this poem is a parody of the following stanza from Reginald Heber's hymn, "The Son of God goes forth to war":

> They climb'd the steep ascent of Heav'n
> Through peril, toil, and pain;
> O God, to us may grace be given
> To follow in their train.
> (*Hymns Ancient and Modern*, No. 439)

HENRIETTE

This name seems to stand for Juliette, Aldous Huxley's sister-in-law, wife of Julian Huxley. She was one of the party at Les Diablerets in February 1928 when Mrs Aldous Huxley was typing the "worst bits" of *Lady Chatterley's Lover*. Mrs Julian Huxley " 'was *very* cross, morally so' over the book and 'suggested rather savagely' that Lawrence call it *John Thomas and Lady Jane*, which for a while he did" (Moore, pp. 375–6).

STAND UP!——

The first line of this poem parodies the first line of the hymn "Soldiers of the Cross", by Dr George Duffield of Philadelphia: "Stand up, stand up for Jesus". This was one of the hymns learned by Lawrence at the Congregational Sunday School at Eastwood in his boyhood. He quotes it in his essay "Hymns in a Man's Life" (*Assorted Articles*, 1932, p. 155).

DEMON JUSTICE; BE A DEMON!; THE JEUNE FILLE

These three poems were omited from *PANSIES*—2 and *PE*. They are reprinted in Nardi, Appendix II.

NETTLES

CHANGE OF GOVERNMENT

This poem refers to the general election of May 1929, when the second Labour government of J. Ramsay MacDonald came into power. "Aunt Maud" = the Labour party; "Aunt Gwendoline" = the Conservatives; "Aunt Libby" = the Liberals; "Aunt Lou" = the Communists.

CLYDESIDER

The "Clydesiders" were the left-wing Labour group of Glasgow members in the House of Commons in the late nineteen-twenties, including James Maxton, John Wheatley and David Kirkwood.

FLAPPER VOTE

The reference is to the Act of Parliament of 1928 which lowered the age when women could vote from thirty to twenty-one.

THE BRITISH BOY

This and the three following poems refer to the exhibition of Lawrence's pictures at the Warren Gallery and the raid on the exhibition by the police on 5 July 1929. See Moore, p. 394; Nehls, III, 326 seq.

INNOCENT ENGLAND

l. 7: The "virginal, pure policemen" are the six policemen who carried off Lawrence's pictures from the Warren Gallery, see preceding note.

l. 11: "Mr Mead" – This is Frederick Mead, the eighty-two-year-old stipendiary magistrate, before whom the case of Lawrence's pictures was brought at the Marlborough Street Police Court on 8 August 1929. See Nehls, III, 381-7; Moore, 413-14.

LONDON MERCURY

Literary journal edited by Sir J. C. Squire from 1919 till 1934.

DADDY-DO-NOTHING

l. 1: "Mr Gladstone" – The reference is to Gladstone's well-meaning attempts to befriend and reclaim London prostitutes. See *Gladstone* by Sir P. Magnus (1954), pp. 105-10. Lawrence probably read Osbert Burdett's *W. E. Gladstone*, published in 1927. The story that the street-walkers called Gladstone "Daddy-do-Nothing" occurs on p. 103 of Burdett's book.

This poem and QUESTION were omitted from the Faber edition of *NETTLES*. They are included in the typescript of the collection now in the Columbia University library, from which the present texts are taken.

MORE PANSIES and *LAST POEMS*

These two collections were printed by Aldington and Orioli in *ALP* from two notebooks containing manuscript poems written by Lawrence in the last months of his life. Aldington, in his Introduction to *ALP*, calls them MS. "A" and MS. "B". For description of the notebooks are Aldington's Introduction, above, p. 591. The present texts have been corrected from photostats of the notebooks, now in the library of the University of Texas. See above, "Editors' Note on the Text", p. 24. At the end of *ALP* Aldington and Orioli printed an Appendix containing variant texts of THE SHIP OF DEATH, SONG OF DEATH and BAVARIAN GENTIANS. These have been transferred in the present edition to the end of Appendix III; see pp. 963-968.

INTRODUCTION TO *LAST POEMS* AND *MORE PANSIES*

This Introduction by Richard Aldington was first printed in *ALP* and was reprinted in *PE*, III, xxxv-xliv.

IMAGE-MAKING LOVE

l. 11: "From hot, digging-in fingers of love." – This fine line, though not crossed out in the manuscript, is omitted in *ALP* and *PE*.

l. 19: "like a gibe at me" – This phrase is repeated in the manuscript and the repetition is not crossed out. It is just possible that Lawrence intended the repetition, but more probably it is an example of unconscious "dittography".

ULTIMATE REALITY

l. 4: The word "again" was omitted in *ALP* and *PE*, though it appears clearly in the manuscript, written above the line.

TRUE LOVE AT LAST

l. 3: This line was omitted in *ALP* and *PE*, though it appears in the manuscript, and a full stop (not in the manuscript) was inserted after "girl" in the previous line.

ll. 15-18: The last stanza of the poem in the manuscript reads as follows:

>   they simply adored one another
> So it was a case of true love,
>   and in the end
> And in the end they were both nervous wrecks,
>   they were both nervous wrecks, because
> because in self-love and self-absorption they were equally matched
>   in self-absorption and self-interest they were equally matched.

ALP edited this draft as follows:

> So they simply adored one another
> and in the end they were both nervous wrecks, because
> in self-obsorption and self-interest they were equally matched.

The text here is from *Imagist Anthology 1930*.

ANDRAITX—POMEGRANATE FLOWERS

Andraitx is in Majorca, and the poem must have been written when Lawrence was there in June 1929.

I DARE DO ALL

See *Macbeth* I, vii, 46.

LUCIFER

l. 1: See *Macbeth* IV, iii, 22.

FALLEN LEAVES

l. 2: ". . . upon the earth." – *ALP* and *PE* print incorrectly "to the earth".

THE BREATH OF LIFE

l. 4: This line is omitted in *ALP* and *PE*.

IN A SPANISH TRAM-CAR

This and the following three poems reflect Lawrence's impressions of Spain during his brief visit to the country in the spring of 1929. (Moore, p. 403; Letters, pp. 1141–62)

MODERN PROBLEMS

l. 3: "ecstasised" – *ALP* and *PE* read incorrectly "ecstatised"

BELLS

l. 21: "on and on" – *ALP* and *PE* omit "and on".
l. 24: "who" – *ALP* and *PE* read incorrectly "they".

THE TRIUMPH OF THE MACHINE

For version of this poem printed in *The London Mercury*, June 1930, see Appendix III, p. 960.
l. 20: "arrows" – This word is omitted in *ALP* and *PE*.
l. 37: *ALP* prints "a" before "new day" but this word is crossed out in the manuscript.
l. 39: "very friskiness" – *ALP* omits "very".

FORTE DEI MARMI

A holiday resort on the Ligurian coast. The Huxleys took Lawrence there at the end of June 1929. He disliked it very much: "beastly as a place; flat, dead sea, jellyfishy, and millions of villas". See Moore, p. 406.

SEA-BATHERS

l. 3: "robinetto": This is reading of the MS. "Rubinetto" is the usual Italian spelling, but Lawrence wrote "robinetto". See Glossary.

WHAT ARE THE WILD WAVES SAYING?

See Dickens, *Dombey and Son*, Ch. viii. According to Jessie Chambers, *"Bleak House* and *Dombey and Son* were great favourites" of Lawrence (E.T., p. 96).

DARK SATANIC MILLS

The reference is, of course, to Blake's famous lyric in the Preface to *Milton*:

> . . . And was Jerusalem builded here,
> Among these dark Satanic mills?

l. 15: "Retro me, Satanas!" – "Get thee behind me, Satan!" See Matthew xvi, 23. The reading of the Vulgate is "Vade retro me Satana".

l. 21: "jerk" – *ALP* reads incorrectly "just".

l. 22: "What is man that thou art no longer mindful of him!" – See Psalms viii, 4.

WHAT HAVE THEY DONE TO YOU?

ALP appends the following footnote to this poem: "Another version of the opening lines appears in *NETTLES*; see above, WHAT HAVE THEY DONE TO YOU——?, p. 585.

l. 8: "the cinema" – *ALP* and *PE* omit "the".

CITY-LIFE

"When I see the great cities— . . ." – These words are omitted in *ALP*. Lawrence is possibly remembering inaccurately the following line in Whitman's poem "Salut au Monde": "I see . . . the cities of the earth and make myself at random a part of them." (Whitman, op. cit., p. 132)

13 PICTURES

Manuscript reads "13"; *ALP* and *PE* print "thirteen".

The poem refers to the police raid on Lawrence's exhibition of pictures at the Warren Gallery on 5 July 1929, when thirteen of the pictures were taken to Marlborough Street Police Station. The proper names in the second stanza are those of pictures that were seized on that occasion. "my Boccaccio" is the picture called "The Boccaccio Story" (one of the best in the collection) based on the first story of the Third Day in *The Decameron*.

l. 10: "a magistrate" – This is Frederick Mead. See above, note to INNOCENT ENGLAND, l. 11, p. 1014.

ROSE AND CABBAGE

ALP has the following footnote: "The first part of this poem appeared in *NETTLES*." See A ROSE IS NOT A CABBAGE, above, p. 569.

MEN LIKE GODS

The title of H. G. Wells's utopian romance; see above, note to WELLSIAN FUTURES, p. 1011.

MASSES AND CLASSES

l. 8: "God cannot do without me" – Variants of this saying, as several correspondents have pointed out, occur in the works of the German mystics, Meister Eckhart (*c.* 1260–1327) and Angelus Silesius [J. Scheffler] (1624–77). In a footnote on p. 225 of *The Essence of Christianity* by L. Feuerbach, tr. M. Evans [George Eliot], 1854, the following version occurs: "God can as little do without us as we without him." Feuerbach gives *Predigten etzlicher Lehrer*, a book of German medieval sermons published in 1621, as the origin of this text, and also refers to Strauss and Pierre Bayle, the French sceptic and encyclopaedist (1647–1706), who may be the "old Frenchman" of l. 7 of Lawrence's poem. Professor D. B. Dickens of Washington and Lee University has drawn our attention to the following interesting parallel in the *Stundenbuch* of Rainer Maria Rilke:

> Was wirst Du tun, Gott, wenn ich sterbe?
> Ich bin dein Krug (wenn ich zerscherbe?)
> Ich bin dein Trank (wenn ich verderbe?)
> Bin dein gewand und dein Gewerbe. . . .

TREES IN THE GARDEN

"Lichtental": Lawrence was staying at the Hotel Goldner Löwen at Lichtental, Baden-Baden in July 1929. On 20 July he wrote to L. E. Pollinger: "This is a nice old *Gasthaus*, quiet rooms on the garden. . . . Just now the trees are very green, the roses very pink and very numerous, the fountains very white. . . ." (Letters, pp. 1166–7)

STORM IN THE BLACK FOREST

l. 5: "bent" – *ALP* reads incorrectly "beat".

ROBOT-DEMOCRACY; REAL DEMOCRACY

These poems are printed here in the order in which they are found in the manuscript. The order is reversed in *ALP* and *PE*.

THERE ARE NO GODS

l. 13: "where" – *ALP* incorrectly prints "when".

EMASCULATION

This poem was omitted from *ALP* and *PE* and is now printed for the first time from the manuscript, where it is not crossed out.
l. 3: "Mr Watts" – This is G. F. Watts, the famous Victorian painter. One of his best-known paintings was "Love and Death" (1874). "Physical Energy" was the title of his most considerable work in sculpture.
l. 6: "Daddy-do-nothings" – See note to DADDY-DO-NOTHING above, p. 1015.

BRITISH SINCERITY

l. 2: "Jixery" – a word compounded by Lawrence from "Jix" the nickname of Sir W. Joynson-Hicks, Home Secretary in the Baldwin government of 1924–29, responsible for seizure of copies of *Lady Chatterley's Lover*.

THE HILLS

l. 1: see Psalm cxxi.

LORD TENNYSON AND LORD MELCHETT

ll. 1, 2: Lawrence is quoting not quite accurately the first two lines of Tennyson's "The Northern Farmer: New Style":

> Dosn't thou 'ear my 'erses' legs, as they canters awaäy?————
> Proputty, proputty, proputty—that's, that's what I 'ears 'em
> saäy.

Lord Melchett is Alfred Mond, financier and Conservative politician, created Viscount Melchett in 1928.

TO PINO

l. 1: "Pino" is Giuseppe Orioli, the Florentine bookseller who published the original edition of *Lady Chatterley's Lover*.
l. 4: "Giuntina" is the printing firm at Florence, "Tipographia Giuntina", which printed *Lady Chatterley's Lover*. For the story of the comment of the Italian printer on the book, see letter from Frieda Lawrence to Dorothy Warren printed in Nehls, III, 378–9.

LUCKY LITTLE BRITISHER

These three lines are followed by seventeen which are almost identical with ll. 11–25 of BRITANNIA'S BABY in *NETTLES*, see above, p. 570. Neither this nor the following poem was printed in *ALP* or *PE*.

THE WORKING MAN

This is a different version of the poem entitled CLYDESIDER in *NETTLES*, see above, p. 573. The differences seem to be sufficient to justify the printing of the poem in its place in this section. Neither this nor the preceding poem is crossed out in the manuscrpt.

ALL SORTS OF GODS

l. 3: "Scandinavian" – Printed incorrectly in *ALP* and *PE* as "Scandinavians".

MEN LIKE GODS

See note to poem with same title above, p. 1019.

[THE GODS]

These two lines were not printed in *ALP* or *PE*. They are not crossed out in the manuscript.

BE IT SO

l. 2: ". . . you flicker . . ." – "you" is omitted in *ALP* and *PE*, and "flicker" incorrectly printed as "flickers".

TWO WAYS OF LIVING AND DYING

l. 13: This line is omitted in *ALP* and *PE*.

l. 31: "hands" – incorrectly printed as "hand" in *ALP*.

SHEDDING OF BLOOD

l. 1: Quotation from Hebrews ix, 22.

[THOMAS EARP]

T. W. Earp (1892–1958), art critic and author, criticised adversely in the *New Statesman*, 17 August 1929, Lawrence's Introduction to the Catalogue of his Paintings exhibited at the Warren Gallery as well as the paintings themselves. See Nehls, III, 331, 335, 342, 715. V. de S. P. had some acquaintance with Earp in the early nineteen-twenties, and remembers that he was an enthusiastic admirer of Lawrence's writings. Earp had a curious, high-pitched voice, of which Lawrence's word "chirp" is a good description. This makes one suspect that he may have met Earp, though he might, of course, have heard about the voice from somebody else. Earp was a Nottinghamshire man and it is possible that behind this squib lies some family feud like that between the Beardsalls and the Boots, which probably colours NOTTINGHAM'S NEW UNIVERSITY. See note to that poem, above, p. 1009.

''GROSS, COARSE, HIDEOUS''

See notes to THE BRITISH BOY and INNOCENT ENGLAND above, p. 1014.

[MR SQUIRE]

This is Sir J. C. Squire (1884–1958), poet, critic and editor of *The London Mercury*, to which Lawrence contributed some poems. For his opinion of Squire, see Letters, pp. 801, 1169.

l. 14: ". . . once and forever . . ." – *ALP* and *PE* print incorrectly "once forever".

GOD IS BORN

l. 14: "wreathe" – incorrectly printed as "wreath" in *ALP* and *PE*.

FLOWERS AND MEN

l. 10: "I want you to be as savage . . ." – These words are crossed out in the manuscript and, therefore, have been placed in square brackets. They are omitted in *ALP* and *PE*. The last stanza of the poem reads as follows in the manuscript (deleted words are placed in square brackets):

> Oh leave off saying I want you to be savages.
> Tell me, is the gentian savage, at the top of its coarse stem?
>   [is the daffodil, is the Scent poppy?]
> Oh what in you can answer to this blueness?
> [I want you to be as savage] as the gentian and the daffodil
> Tell me! tell me! is there in you a beauty to compare
> or to the honeysuckle at evening now
> pouring out [his] breath. [of his godhead.]
>   [the]

LAST POEMS

THE GREEKS ARE COMING!

l. 5: ". . . end of . . ." – *ALP* and *PE* incorrectly print "and".

MAXIMUS

Lawrence was probably thinking of Maximus of Smyrna ("the Mystic"), tutor to the Emperor Julian, a champion of Greek paganism in the fourth century A.D., of whom he would have read in Ibsen's *Emperor and Galilean*.

THE MAN OF TYRE

Lawrence had a poor opinion of James Joyce's writings (Letters, p. 1076), but it is difficult to believe that the third stanza of this fine poem does not echo, consciously or unconsciously, the famous description of Stephen Dedalus's vision of the girl wading in the sea near Dublin near the end of Chapter IV of *Portrait of the Artist as a Young Man*.

WHALES WEEP NOT!

This poem is almost certainly based on memories of Herman Melville's *Moby Dick*, a book for which Lawrence had an unbounded admiration. Cf. the following passage in his *Studies in Classic American Literature* (1924), where he quotes from Ch. LXXXVII of *Moby Dick*:

> "There the females swam in peace, and the young whales came snuffing tamely at the boat, like dogs. And there the astonished seamen watched the love-making of these amazing monsters, mammals, now in rut far down in the sea—'But far beneath this wondrous world upon the surface, another and still stranger world met our eyes, as we gazed over the side. . . . Some of the subtlest secrets of the seas seemed divulged to us in this enchanted pond. We saw young Leviathan amours in the deep. And thus, though surrounded by circle upon circle of consternation and affrights, did these inscrutable creatures at the centre freely and fearlessly indulge in all peaceful concernments; yea, serenely revelled in dalliance and delight—' " (Beal, op. cit., pp. 386–7).

BAVARIAN GENTIANS

Another version of this poem, perhaps not inferior to the present text, immediately follows this version in MS. "A". In MS. "B" there appear two drafts of a poem entitled "Glory of Darkness", which also seem to be versions of BAVARIAN GENTIANS. For these variants see Appendix III, pp. 961–963.

l. 8: "Dis" – *ALP* and *PE* print incorrectly "Dio". The reading of the manuscript is clearly "Dis".

l. 11: *ALP* and *PE* omit the exclamation mark.

SILENCE

"Invocation to Silence" by the seventeenth-century poet Richard Flecknoe (d. 1678?) begins with two fine lines that Lawrence may have remembered:

> Still-born *Silence*, thou that art
> Floud-gate of the deeper heart . . .

Lamb quotes Flecknoe's poem at the head of his essay on "Quaker Meetings" in *Essays of Elia*, where Lawrence may have seen it.

THE HANDS OF GOD

l. 1: See Hebrews x, 31.

LORD'S PRAYER

l. 16: "honking" – *ALP* and *PE* read, incorrectly, "hawking".

ANAXAGORAS

l. 1: "... Even the snow is black!" – This saying of Anaxagoras is quoted in Burnet, op. cit., p. 264.

KISSING AND HORRID STRIFE

l. 20: "black" – *ALP* and *PE* read, incorrectly, "bleak".

THE EVIL WORLD-SOUL

l. 12: "robot" – Lawrence had probably read Selver's translation of Karel Čapek's *R.U.R.*, which appeared in 1923, and introduced the word "robot" into the English language.

DEATH IS NOT EVIL, EVIL IS MECHANICAL

l. 18: This fine line and the word "and" at the beginning of the next line are omitted in *ALP* and *PE*.

THE SHIP OF DEATH

For different versions of this poem in MS. "B", see Appendix III, pp. 964–968.
VIII. l. 6: This line is omitted in *ALP* and *PE*.
X. l. 5: "her" – *ALP* and *PE* incorrectly read "the".

THE HOUSELESS DEAD

ll. 12, 13:
". . . and with the soul's deep sigh
set food for them, . . ." – This passage is omitted in *ALP* and *PE*, which read incorrectly:
"Oh think of them, and encourage them to build . . ."

SONG OF DEATH

For different version of this poem in MS. "B", see Appendix III, p. 968.

SHADOWS

l. 30: ". . . hands [of] the unknown God . . ." – The manuscript reads "hands the unknown God".
ALP inserts "of". Lawrence obviously intended to write this word, but, as he did not, it is inserted in square brackets.

UNCOLLECTED POEMS

REBUKED

This poem was published in *The English Review*, April 1910, from which it is reprinted in the present edition. It was not included in any of Lawrence's collections of verse but is reprinted in Nardi, Appendix II. There is an early draft of it in MS. 1479, No. 67, entitled "Fooled".

THE WIND, THE RASCAL

This poem was published in *Poetry*, January 1914, from which the present text is reprinted. It was not included in any of Lawrence's books of verse but was printed separately by Catherine Carswell as an *Original Poem by D. H. Lawrence* in 1934 (see Roberts, A70), from a manuscript in a little autograph book left in her house by Enid Hilton (Mrs Hopkin). There is a typescript of it in the Berg Collection, New York Public Library, where it is included in a sequence of poems written by Lawrence when he was in Bavaria in the spring of 1912, published in an amended form, without this poem, in *LWH*. The following verse translations, obviously from Krenkow's versions of Arabic poems (see p. 979) are appended to a letter from Lawrence to Louie Burrows, dated 15 Dec., 1910. "The Wind, the Rascal" is clearly based on the first of them.

THE WIND, THE RASCAL

The wind knocked at the door, and I said
"It is my coy love come to me!"
But oh wind, thou knave that thou art
To make merry over my sorrowful heart.
          a pure translation

and another [Lawrence's note]

THE PHYSICIAN

I am hurt, I am very much hurt
Oh bring me my physician!
I am hurt in my heart, in my heart!
Sir, fetch my full-bosomed magician.

and again [Lawrence's note]

    Dusk-flower, look hither
Thou dusk, thou voluptuous dusk flower, look hither
    Over the land at me.
Then looked she out from her dusk-gold eyes
    Shining so wondrously
Like the humming of two dusk-gold bees
    —and longing tortures ne.
"Have pity, look hither at my miseries!"

THE YOUNG SOLDIER WITH BLOODY SPURS

This poem was sent by Lawrence to Edward Garnett with a letter dated 22 August 1912 from Mayrhofen in the Austrian Tyrol. It was printed by Aldous Huxley in Letters—H, p. 51, from which the present text is taken. It is reprinted in Nardi, Appendix II.

AH, MURIEL!

This poem was published in *The English Review*, October 1914, from which the present text is reprinted. It was not included in any of Lawrence's collections of verse but was printed in Moore, p. 97 and reprinted in Nardi, Appendix II. The original manuscript is in the Library of the University of Texas. "Muriel" is Jessie Chambers.

WE HAVE GONE TOO FAR

This poem was sent by Lawrence with a letter to Lady Cynthia Asquith from Hampstead, dated 2 November 1915. It was printed by Aldous Huxley in Letters—H, pp. 267–8, from which the present text is reprinted. It is reprinted in Nardi, Appendix II.

RESURRECTION OF THE FLESH

This poem, said to be "written *c.* 1915", was published in *Wake*, No. 7, 1948 (Roberts, C229), from which the present text is reprinted.

ERINNYES

This poem was published in *Some Imagist Poets* (1916) (Roberts, B4), from which the present text is reprinted. It is reprinted in Nardi, Appendix II.

ELOI, ELOI, LAMA SABACHTHANI?

This poem was published in *The Egoist*, 1 May 1915 (Roberts, C37), from which the present text is reprinted.

RESURRECTION

This poem was published in *Poetry*, June 1917, from which the present text is reprinted. It was reprinted in *New Poetry, An Anthology of Twentieth Century Verse in English* (New York, 1923) and in Nardi, Appendix II. See Roberts, B12, C47, E346.

LABOUR BATTALION; NO NEWS

Both these poems were published in *New Paths*, 1918, from which the present text is reprinted. They are reprinted in Nardi, Appendix II.

BITS

These thirty short poems are printed from a holograph manuscript of 6 pp. now in Chicago University library (Roberts, E49). The numbering has been inserted by the editors.

Nos. IV, V, VIII, IX, X, XII, XIV, XVII, XVIII, XXI, XXV, and XXX were published in *Poetry*, July 1919, under the title "War Films" (Roberts, C67) and are reprinted in Nardi, Appendix II under that title. No. XXIII, TALES, was included by Lawrence in *PANSIES* under the title THE GAZELLE CALF, see above, p. 466.

APOSTROPHE TO A BUDDHIST MONK

This poem is printed in Brewster, p. 50, from which the present text is taken. There is a holograph MS. in the Texas University library (Roberts, E19).

Earl and Achsah Brewster, Lawrence's American friends, were Buddhists. Lawrence stayed with them in Ceylon in the spring of 1922, when this poem was written. Earl Brewster was thinking of going to Burma and asked Lawrence's advice. "It is best to do what you very much want to do, and so maybe get it out of your system," advised Lawrence. Then, according to Brewster, "in a teasing humour, picturing me [Brewster] as a Buddhist monk in Burma, he wrote the following [i.e., this poem]."

For Lawrence's opinion of Buddhism, see his letter to the Brewsters dated 16 November 1921 (Letters, pp. 677–8).

HIM WITH HIS TAIL IN HIS MOUTH

This little parable of creative evolution is reprinted from p. 136 of *Reflections on the Death of a Porcupine* (1932; Roberts, A32).

It has been thought appropriate to print this and the following poem in their prose settings.

[FLAT-FOOT'S SONG]

Reprinted from p. 136 of *Reflections on the Death of a Porcupine*. See preceding note.

TRAITORS; REACH OVER; SOFTLY, THEN,
    SOFTLY; CHANGE OF LIFE; WHAT DO I
    CARE?; ARE YOU PINING?; O! AMERI-
    CANS; EAGLE IN NEW MEXICO; FIRE

These nine poems were published in *FIRE* (Roberts, A80), from which the present texts are reprinted. EAGLE IN NEW MEXICO had already appeared in *The New Mexico Quarterly*, November 1938; it is a different version of the poem with the same title in *BBF* (see above, p. 372).

O! AMERICANS had been published in *The New Mexico Quarterly*,

May 1938. The other poems all seem to have been published in *FIRE* for the first time.

POEMS FROM The Plumed Serpent

The texts of these poems are taken from the first edition of *The Plumed Serpent* (1926) and they are arranged in the order in which they occur in the novel. Quetzalcoatl, Huitzilopochtli and Malentzi are ancient Aztec gods whose worship is supposed in the novel to be re-introduced into Mexico as part of a politico-religious revolution carried out by the two leaders Don Ramón and Don Cipriano. The poems are probably indebted to the versions of ancient Aztec hymns in Lewis Spence's *The Gods of Mexico* (1923) and also the hymns which Lawrence sang in the Congregational Church at Eastwood in his youth. See Moore, pp. 392–3.

VII

Song sung by the boys in mockery of Don Ramón, which he makes his younger son repeat to him in Chapter XVIII of *The Plumed Serpent*.

VIII: JESUS' FAREWELL

Song sung outside the Sayula church by one of Ramón's followers, as they stand outside the closed doors of the church in Chapter XVIII of *The Plumed Serpent*. After the eighth stanza, Ramón opens the church-doors and the "young slim priest" sings the last stanza.

IX-XII

These poems are sung in Chapter XXI, "The Opening of the Church". They celebrate the instalment in the church of the cult of Quetzalcoatl.

XVII, XVIII

Songs sung in Chapter XVIII, "Huitzilopochtli's Night", at the inauguration of the cult of Huitzilopochtli, the ancient Mexican war-god impersonated by Don Cipriano.
XVII is sung by a man "in a clear, defiant voice".
These poems were probably suggested by the ancient Mexican "Song of Uitzilopochtli" quoted by Lewis Spence (op. cit., p. 80). The follow-

ing are the opening lines of the ancient Mexican poem as translated by Spence:

> Uitzilopochtli the warrior, no one is my equal,
> Not in vain have I put on the vestment of yellow feathers,
> For through me the sun has risen
> [i.e. the time of sacrifice appears]. . .

Spence notes that "this song was probably a chant sung before sacrifice to the god".

XVIII

Song sung by "the men of Huitzilopochtli" who take up the song "changing the 'I' into 'he'".

XIX

This poem is said to be spoken by Cipriano "in his short, martial sentences".

XX – XXV

These poems are sung at the execution of the peons who conspired to kill Don Ramón in Chapter XXIII.

MEDITERRANEAN IN JANUARY; BEYOND THE ROCKIES

These two poems were published in *The Laughing Horse*, April 1926, from which the present texts are reprinted. They are reprinted in Nardi, Appendix II. MEDITERRANEAN IN JANUARY also appeared in *Life and Letters*, March 1932. According to a diary of Lawrence's preserved in the Frieda Lawrence Collection, these poems were written at the Villa Bernarda, Spotorno, in February 1926. See Roberts, p. 271, C139 and also E233.

THE OLD ORCHARD; RAINBOW

These two poems were published in *The Calendar of Modern Letters*, April 1927, from which the present text is reprinted. They are reprinted in Nardi, Appendix II. See Roberts, C153, E287.

ADDITIONAL PANSIES

The following thirty-two poems are printed from a collection of holograph manuscripts by Lawrence now in the Library of the University of Texas: HYMN TO NOTHINGNESS, AUGUST HOLIDAYS, BATHING RESORT and the limerick THERE WAS A GAY BIRD NAMED CHRISTINE are on separate sheets. The other poems are in a notebook containing what is obviously a draft for the collection which Lawrence published under the title *PANSIES*. The texts of a number of the poems in the notebook are either identical with or very similar to those of poems published in *PANSIES*. The poems printed here are those which Lawrence did not print. They are crossed out in the manuscript but this does not necessarily mean that they were rejected by the author as a number of the poems which he printed are also crossed out.

There is another early draft of *PANSIES* in the form of a typescript collection sent by Lawrence to St John Hutchinson asking him to give it to his friend, S. S. Koteliansky. It is now in the George Lazarus Collection and is headed "Author's Revised Typescript".

It contains a number of variations from the printed text and also variant versions of the poems in the Texas University collection not included in *PANSIES—1*. It is referred to in the following notes as *PANSIES—L*.

HYMN TO NOTHINGNESS

Two alternative titles, "Red Evening" and "The Winner", are crossed out in the manuscript. There are curious parallels between this poem and "Upon Nothing" by the Restoration poet John Wilmot, Earl of Rochester, (1647–80), and "God's Funeral" by Thomas Hardy.

ROSES

This poem occurs on p. 77 of *PANSIES—L*. The only variant in the text is that the last word is "rosy" instead of "splendid".

SO THERE!

l. 32: ". . . Lord Ribblesdale . . ." – Lawrence may be thinking of Sargent's well-known portrait of the elegant Lord Redesdale, whose title he remembered imperfectly. The reference, however, may be to the fourth Baron Ribblesdale, who died in October 1925.

MORALITY; IMMORALITY

Cf. the two poems in *PANSIES* entitled IMMORALITY and MAN'S IMAGE; see above, p. 528.

CENSORS

Cf. the entirely different poem with the same title in *PANSIES*, see above, p. 528.
l. 10: capsicum – "genus of tropical plants or shrubs . . . the fruit of the capsicum . . . an active stimulant" (O.E.D.).

RALLYING-POINT

The following version of this poem occurs on p. 65 of *PANSIES—L*:

> If we rally at all today, instead of keeping stark asunder
> let us rally for a bit of common sanity.
> It is so shameful to be insane,
> and so hideously humiliating and dangerous
> to be at the mercy of a collective insanity,
> as we were during the war, and are now, though less obviously.
>
> If we can but contain ourselves
> we can then rally together
> to keep a sane core to life.

GODS

This poem is obviously related to the poem in *PANSIES*, GIVE US GODS (see above, p. 436). It differs sufficiently, however, to be considered, perhaps, as an independent work rather than a mere variant.

SEX WON'T WORK

Cf. the poem WILD THINGS IN CAPTIVITY in *PANSIES*, above, p. 484.

DEEPER THAN LOVE

For variant version of this poem, see Appendix III, p. 957.

[BAWDY CAN BE SANE]

For variant version of this poem, see Appendix III, p. 959.

[THERE WAS A GAY BIRD NAMED CHRISTINE]

This is, perhaps, the only extant limerick by Lawrence. The holograph manuscript is written on a small slip of paper now in the Library of the University of Texas (PA 18612A). "Christine" is probably Christine Hughes or her daughter, Mary Christine Hughes. These were two American women whom Lawrence met in New Mexico in 1924. They turned up at the Villa Scandicci (where Lawrence was living at the time) in June 1926, and Lawrence had to show them round Florence. Mary Christine is said to be the original of "Laura Philippine" of the amusing sketch by Lawrence with that title published in *Assorted Articles* (1930). See Moore, p. 366, and Letters, pp. 976, 983–4.

À LA MANIÈRE DE D. H. LAWRENCE

The holograph manuscript of this curious little self-parody is now in Princeton University library (AM. 13568). A note at the bottom of the quarto sheet on which it is written reads: "An Unpublished Poem by D. H. Lawrence satirising his own style of poetry written on the verso of a letterhead of his Publisher, Orioli".
The curious spellings "Lilly" and "cabage" may be part of the joke, but it is difficult to see why, because Lawrence's spelling is generally impeccable.

APPENDICES

APPENDIX I: Foreword to COLLECTED POEMS

This Foreword is printed from the holograph manuscript now in the Library of the University of California at Los Angeles. It was first published in *PHOENIX*, pp. 251–4.
The following note in Frieda Lawrence's handwriting appears at the end of the manuscript: "This fresh looking MSS belongs to Lawrence Powell who helps to keep Lawrence's spirit fresh—Frieda Lawrence."
* *"Sapientiae Urbs Conditur"* – Lawrence is misquoting the motto of University College, Nottingham (now the University of Nottingham), which appeared on the coat of arms stamped on the college exercise-books. The motto is actually "Sapientia Urbs Conditur (The city is built by wisdom)".

APPENDIX II: JUVENILIA: 1904–1912

The first twenty-one poems in this section (up to and including GRIEF) are taken from the notebook bearing the arms of University College, Nottingham, referred to by Lawrence in his draft "Foreword to *Collected Poems*" as "the foundation of the poetic me" (see above, p. 849). The notebook is now MS. 1479, in the Library of the University of Nottingham. It was acquired by the university from Lawrence's sister, Mrs Emily King, in 1956. Its contents are described and classified in V.R.M. The poems are referred to in the following notes by the numbers given to them in the list appended to that article. Mrs King told V. de S. P. that, during the many days that Lawrence spent by his mother's bedside when she was dying in the winter of 1910–11, he had this notebook with him and constantly wrote in it. Of the seventy-five poems in the notebook, twenty-one were not published by Lawrence. The others are drafts of poems printed later. Some of these are reprinted in Appendix III of the present edition.

CAMPIONS

MS. 1479, No. 6. Printed in V.R.M., pp. 14, 15. According to Lawrence (see above, p. 849), this and the following poem were the first verses that he wrote. As he states that he was nineteen when they were "composed", they must have been written in 1904, when he was still at the Pupil-Teacher Centre at Ilkeston preparing for the London Matriculation Examination.
l. 1: "green clouded" is written above "unclouded" in the manuscript.

GUELDER ROSES

MS. 1479, No. 7. Printed in V.R.M., pp. 13, 14. The fourth and fifth stanzas, enclosed here in square brackets, are crossed out in the manuscript.

THE FALL OF DAY

MS. 1479, No. 11. Possibly suggested by D. G. Rossetti's poem "Sunset Wings" (*The Works of D. G. Rossetti*, 1911, p. 220).

MARRIED IN JUNE

MS. 1479, No. 16. Printed in V.R.M., p. 17.

THE WORM TURNS

MS. 1479, No. 18. This poem is heavily scored out in the manuscript.
l. 8: Substituted for "Saprophyte mould". This piece of scientific

jargon reminds us that Lawrence studied botany at the University
College.

ON THE ROAD

MS. 1479, No. 19.

THE DEATH OF THE BARON

MS. 1479, No. 20. Printed in V.R.M., pp. 15; 16.
The "Baron" in this poem is Baron von Huben, Vicar of Greasley,
near Eastwood, Notts. This strange figure claimed to be a Polish
refugee. He appears in Lawrence's novel *The Rainbow* as Rudolf
Skrebensky, Vicar of Brinsley. The poem is a monologue placed in
the mouth of a labourer who hears the bells ringing for the funeral
of the baron-vicar, as he is working in the fields near Greasley church
with his mare, Jeannette. Lawrence used to work sometimes for Mr
Chambers, owner of the Haggs Farm (the "Mr Leivers" of *Sons and
Lovers*), in two of the fields opposite Greasley church, and he may
well have heard the bells ringing for Von Huben's funeral. Ada
Lawrence and Stuart Gelder write: "Mr Chambers rented two fine
mowing meadows opposite Greasley church and each year Bert
[D. H. Lawrence] helped with the haymaking, going early in the
morning and working till after sundown" (Nehls, I, 53).

LOVE COMES LATE

MS. 1479, No. 22.

SONG

MS. 1479, No. 24.
ii. 7, 8: These lines are written above the following version which is
not crossed out:

> Cool red fruits glitter
> Against my mouth

l. 13: "cherry" – written above "burning".
l. 19: The word "gold" appears ringed in the manuscript after "Red".
l. 23: "Now see her . . ." written above "See her now".

A FAILURE

MS. 1479, No. 29. This fragment is heavily scored out in the manu-
script.

A DECISION

MS. 1479, No. 31.

A TRAIN AT NIGHT

MS. 1479, No. 33.

BABY SONGS / TEN MONTHS OLD

MS. 1479, No. 35. Lawrence seems tó have planned a sequence of "Baby Songs" inspired by Hilda Mary, the baby daughter of his landlady at Croydon, Mrs Jones. See note to BABY RUNNING BAREFOOT above, p. 983.
A FAILURE (No. 29 above) may also have belonged to this series.
l. 9: " 'Sweet Joy' " – a quotation from Blake's poem "Infant Joy" in *Songs of Innocence*.

EVE

MS. 1479, No. 39.
l. 18: "endeaver" – *sic* in MS.

AFTER SCHOOL

MS. 1479, No. 40. This and the following two poems were obviously written when Lawrence was teaching at the Davidson Road School in 1908–11.

A SNOWY DAY AT SCHOOL

MS. 1479, No. 42. This vivid sketch can be compared with the entirely different poem with the same title printed in *LP* and *CP*, see above, p. 75.
l. 8: "Thaulow" – This is Fritz Thaulow (1846–1906), Norwegian impressionist landscape-painter, who painted many snow scenes.

READING IN THE EVENING

MS. 1479, No. 48.

A MAN AT PLAY ON THE RIVER

MS. 1479, No. 52.

AMOUR

MS. 1479, No. 64. This poem bears some resemblance to AUTUMN SUNSHINE, see p. 177.

BEREAVEMENT

MS. 1479, No. 70. This and the following two poems clearly refers to the death of Lawrence's mother in December 1910.

LOSS

MS. 1479, No. 72.

GRIEF

MS. 1479, No. 75. The first two lines of this poem are heavily scored through in the manuscript and the next five scribbled over.

TWO FRAGMENTS ON SLEEP

These and the following thirteen poems (up to and including TWO-FOLD) are here printed for the first time from Lawrence's holograph manuscripts among the Louie Burrows papers, now in the Library of the University of Nottingham. Lawrence was intimate with Louie [Louise] Burrows (afterwards Mrs Louise Burrows Heath) from about 1905 till 1912, and, for a time, was engaged to be married to her. She is said to have been in some degree the "original" of Ursula Brangwen in *The Rainbow* and *Women in Love* (see Moore *passim*). The valuable collection of her papers, now in the Library of the University of Nottingham, includes many letters of Lawrence to her and these poems, which he sent to her, probably between 1908 and 1911.

[FRAGMENT ON SLEEP I]

l. 2: The word "struggling" is deleted in the MS.
l. 26: Lawrence seems to have originally begun this line with the word "Falls", which is deleted. Another word is written over it which it is difficult to decipher. To V. de S. P. it appears to be "Drops". Professor J. T. Boulton suggests "Trips".
l. 35: This line is hard to decipher. A word follows "pain" at the end of the line, but it is illegible.
At the end of the fragment, after a space, the words "Is not the wonder of being flung" occur. They are probably the first draft of the opening line of the second fragment.

THE WITCH II

l. 6: "ramel" or "rammel": a Midland dialect word = rubbish (O.E.D.).

ELIXIR

This poem is followed by this note in Lawrence's hand apparently addressed to Louie Burrows:

> Aint it funny how a little love in oneself
> makes a lot of stuff you'd have called
> daft, very pertinent & particular.
> You'll have to burn all these papers—
> & I keep no copies. Joke!
> > Baiser
> > > DHL

SYMPATHY

l. 6: "Encyster", apparently from "encyst" = "to enclose in a cyst" (O.E.D.). Lawrence's use of this pedantic word is possibly due to his biological studies.

THE TRAIN

The sheet on which this poem is written is torn and only a fragment of the third stanza remains. The biblical reference in ll. 9–12 is obviously Daniel, III, 12–27.

AT MIDNIGHT

Louie Burrows transcribed this and the following five poems. She heads her transcription: "By DHL from translations from the Arabic by his uncle Dr Fritz Krenkow". Fritz Krenkow, a learned German orientalist, was the husband of Ada Rose Beardsall, sister of Lawrence's mother. A letter of Lawrence to him will be found in Letters, p. 623. It is interesting to compare these poems with the collection entitled "Bits", see pp. 749–59 of the present edition.
l. 3: "Divan = tent" [Note by D.H.L.].

A LOVE-PASSAGE

This poem and those following, up to the end of Appendix II, are taken from a collection of holograph manuscript poems now in the Henry A. and Walter W. Berg Collection in the New York Public Library. They have been selected as the poems in that collection which have never hitherto been published. The manuscripts seem to be fair copies written in a neat hand and somebody has inserted approximate dates at the head of all the poems except two. These dates show that they were written between 1909 and 1912; it has, therefore, seemed appropriate to include them among the juvenilia. The dated poems come first, followed by those to which no dates are assigned. Dates given in the manuscripts are indicated in the notes. A LOVE-PASSAGE and RED (see below, p. 1041) are clearly related to the story on which Lawrence's novel *The Trespasser* (1912) was based. He heard the story from Miss Helen Corke, who used it in her own novel *Neutral Ground* (1934). Miss Corke, to whom photostats of the manuscripts of the two poems in the Berg Collection were sent, writes as follows in a letter dated 19 May 1962:

My impression is that the photostats represent, not the original writing, but a revision which L. possibly made in the spring of 1912, when he was finally revising *The Trespasser*. This impression is based upon two considerations. Under the title 'A Rift in the Lute' one poem [i.e. A LOVE-PASSAGE] comes wholly back to memory. It is all familiar except line 10 and lines 16–18 which would seem to be later interpolations. It was written, and shown to me, in the spring of 1910 [the poem is dated '*c*. 1909–10' in the manuscript]. I don't recognise 'Red' as the title of the second poem. It may have been originally 'Red Sunset'. But I remember only the three opening lines and the first five lines of the second section. The many corrections on the second page suggest that this final section was composed at the time of the revision. But the rest belongs to the same period as 'A Rift in the Lute'. The impression of sunset glow over fields of marguerite daisies shot with sorrel is D.H.L.'s reflection of an evening walk in Surrey country. . . . Both 'Red' and 'A Love Passage' were the outcome of D.H.L.'s effort to interpret in his own terms the mind of 'Siegmund', whom he saw only in the mirror I held up to him—a cracked mirror at that. The two men never met."

[AH, WITH HIS BLESSING BRIGHT ON THY MOUTH AND THY BROW]

This poem has no title in the manuscript. It is dated *c.* 1909–10.

ALOOF IN GAIETY

Dated in manuscript *c.* 1910. A rejected title, "Reproach", is scored out. Cf. RELEASE, p. 117 and note.

AND JUDE THE OBSCURE AND HIS BELOVED

Dated in manuscript *c.* 1910. This poem appears to be a dialogue between Jude Fawley and Sue Bridehead in Hardy's *Jude the Obscure*. Lawrence may have been identifying himself with Jude and Sue Bridehead with Jessie Chambers.

A DRAMA

Dated in manuscript *c.* 1910. This impressive if immature poem is a curiosity as Lawrence's most sustained work in conventional blank verse.

SEPARATED

Dated in manuscript *c.* 1910.

ASSUMING THE BURDEN

Dated in manuscript *c.* 1911.

THE CHIEF MYSTERY

Dated in manuscript *c.* 1911.

EROTIC

Dated in manuscript *c.* 1911.

MOON NEW-RISEN

Dated in manuscript *c.* 1911.

RED

Dated in manuscript *c.* 1911.
See note to A LOVE-PASSAGE above, p. 1040.

SHE WAS A GOOD LITTLE WIFE

Dated in manuscript c. 1912.

PEAR-BLOSSOM

Dated in manuscript c. 1912.

AT THE CEARNE

Dated in manuscript April 1912. The Cearne was the house of Edward Garnett near Edenbridge, Kent. Lawrence was there with Frieda in April 1912, and this poem was almost certainly written during that visit. In a letter to Garnett dated 29 April, just after his visit to the Cearne, Lawrence mentions the apple blossom there. See Letters, p. 110.

A KISS

Undated in manuscript. Lawrence has written in the margin: "This is rotten."

[OTHER WOMEN HAVE REARED IN ME]

Undated and without title in manuscript.

APPENDIX III: *VARIANTS AND EARLY DRAFTS*

THE WILD COMMON

Text from *A*. In his Note, Lawrence mentions that this poem was much "rewritten". See above, p. 28. For version printed in *CP*, see above, p. 33. A still earlier version of three stanzas of the poem is found in MS. 1479, No. 17.

RENAISSANCE

Text from MS. 1479, No. 28, printed in V.R.M., pp. 20–1. For version published in *CP* under title RENASCENCE, see above, p. 37, and note.

VIRGIN YOUTH

Text from *A*. For version publish in *CP*, see above, p. 38, and note. There is a still earlier draft in MS. 1479 entitled "The Body Awake".

THE SCHOOLMASTER [A]

This is the first published version of the *SCHOOLMASTER* sequence. Text from *The Westminster Gazette*, 11, 18, 25 May and 1 June 1912. See notes to THE BEST OF SCHOOL, LAST LESSON OF THE AFTERNOON and SCHOOL ON THE OUTSKIRTS, above, pp. 980, 985.

THE SCHOOLMASTER [B]

This version of the sequence appeared in *LP*.

DREAMS OLD AND NASCENT: OLD

Text from *The English Review*, November 1909. See note to DREAMS OLD AND NASCENT: OLD, above, p. 981.

DREAMS OLD AND NASCENT: NASCENT

Text from *A*.

VIOLETS FOR THE DEAD

Text from MS. 1479, No. 34. For this and the following poem, see note to VIOLETS, above, p. 982.

VIOLETS

Text from *LP*. For version published in *CP*, see above, p. 60.

LIGHTNING

Text from *LP*. For version published in *CP*, see above, p. 61.

BABY-MOVEMENTS

Text from *The English Review*, November 1909. See notes to BABY RUNNING BAREFOOT and to BABY SONGS: TEN MONTHS OLD, pp. 983, 1037 above.

COROT

Text from Y.L., pp. 67–9. For version published in *CP*, see above, p. 68, and note.

MICHAEL-ANGELO

Text from *LP*. For version published in *CP*, see above, p. 69, and note.

NIGHT SONGS

Text from *The English Review*, April 1910. See HYDE PARK AT NIGHT, BEFORE THE WAR / *CLERKS* and PICCADILLY AT NIGHT / *STREET-WALKERS*, p. 70 and notes.

WHETHER OR NOT

Text from *LP*. For version published in *CP*, see above, p. 76, and note.

DISCIPLINE

Text from *The English Review*, November 1909. For version published in *CP*, see above, p. 92.

LAST WORDS TO MURIEL

Text from MS. 1479, No. 5. Printed in V.R.M., p. 24. This and the following poem are early versions of LAST WORDS TO MIRIAM, published in *CP*, see p. 111, and note. Muriel seems to have been the first name given by Lawrence to Jessie Chambers. For comment, see V.R.M., pp. 24–6.

LAST WORDS TO MIRIAM

Text from *A*.

LIAISON

Text from *A*. This is an early version of the poem published in *CP* as THE YEW-TREE ON THE DOWNS, see above, p. 113.

DISSOLUTE

Text from *A*. This is an early version of the poem published in *CP* as AT A LOOSE END, see above, p. 115.

HONEYMOON

Text from *The Egoist*, 1 April 1914. For version printed in *CP* under title EXCURSION TRAIN, see above, p. 116.

A SPIRITUAL WOMAN

Text from *A*. For version published in *CP* as THESE CLEVER WOMEN, see above, p. 118, and note.

ANOTHER OPHELIA

The text of this version of the poem published under the title BALLAD OF ANOTHER OPHELIA (see above, p. 119, and note) is from a holograph manuscript in the Berg Collection, New York Public Library (see p. 1040).
l. 4: "pain" – *sic* in MS.

SNAP-DRAGON

Text from manuscript in the Berg Collection, New York Public Library; see preceding note. For published version, see above, p. 122.

TO LETTICE, MY SISTER

Text from Y.L., pp. 209–10. For published version entitled BROTHER AND SISTER, see above, p. 131.
"Lettice" is Lawrence's sister, Ada (Mrs W. E. Clarke).

GRIEF

Text from *Poetry*, December 1914. This poem was sent by Lawrence to Edward Marsh as a Christmas card dated 16 December 1916. See Letters—H, p. 167. This and the following poem seem to be early versions of the poem published as FIRELIGHT AND NIGHTFALL, see above, p. 135, and note.

TWILIGHT

Text from *The English Review*, February 1914.

THE PIANO

Text from MS. 1479, No. 14. Printed in V.R.M., p. 26. This is an early version of the poem published as PIANO, see above, p. 148. For comment, see V.R.M., pp. 27–8.

BIRTHDAY

Text from *Poetry*, January 1914. Early version of ON THAT DAY, see above, p. 176.

EARLY SPRING

Text from *The Egoist*, 1 April 1914. For early version called AMOUR, see above, p. 868, and later version entitled AUTUMN SUNSHINE, see above, p. 177, and note.

ALL OF ROSES

Text from *Poetry*, January 1914. For versions of these poems published in *LWH*, see above, pp. 216–18.

THE MOWERS

Text from *The Smart Set*, November 1913. For version published in *LWH* as A YOUTH MOWING, see above, p. 219.

FIREFLIES IN THE CORN

Text from *Poetry*, January 1914. For version published in *LWH*, see above, p. 221.

SONG OF A MAN THAT IS LOVED

Text from N.I.B., p. 41, reprinted in *LWH—WR*, p. 79. For version published in *CP*, see above, p. 249 and note. Frieda Lawrence states that "This poem was written in the Isartal" (N.I.B., p. 42). A slightly different version is found in a holograph manuscript now in the Berg Collection in New York Public Library.

RELIGION

This and the following four poems are all drafts of "pansies" from holograph manuscripts in the Library of the University of Texas; see above, p. 1022. RELIGION seems to be an early draft of GIVE US GODS, see above, p. 436.

I KNOW A NOBLE ENGLISHMAN

See THE NOBLE ENGLISHMAN, above, p. 446.

WORK

See poem published in *PANSIES—1* under this title, above, p. 450.

IN NOTTINGHAM

This seems to be an early draft of NOTTINGHAM'S NEW UNIVERSITY; see above, p. 488.

MORALITY

See MAN'S IMAGE, above, p. 528.

DEEPER THAN LOVE——

Text from *PANSIES—L.* See KNOW DEEPLY, KNOW THYSELF MORE DEEPLY——, above, p. 477.

WHAT'S SANE AND WHAT ISN'T——

Text from *PANSIES—L.* See [BAWDY CAN BE SANE], above, p. 844.

THE TRIUMPH OF THE MACHINE

Text from *The London Mercury*, June 1930. For version of this poem published in *ALP*, see above, p. 623.

GLORY OF DARKNESS

This and the following poems to the end of the section were printed as an Appendix in *ALP*. The order in which they appeared there has, however, been changed in the present text. In *ALP* the order was as follows: SHIP OF DEATH, THE SHIP OF DEATH, SONG OF DEATH, GLORY OF DARKNESS, BAVARIAN GENTIANS. In the present text GLORY OF DARKNESS and BAVARIAN GENTIANS have been moved to the beginning of the sequence to correspond with the order in which the versions of the poems appear in *LAST POEMS*. SHIP OF DEATH, SONG OF DEATH and the two versions of GLORY OF DARKNESS (apparently alternative versions of BAVARIAN GENTIANS) all come from MS. "B" and BAVARIAN GENTIANS is a version of the poem from MS. "A" immediately following the version printed on p. 697. These texts have been taken from photostats of the original holograph MSS. in the Library of the University of Texas, see above, note to *MORE PANSIES* and *LAST POEMS*, p. 591. The text of THE SHIP OF DEATH on p. 967 is taken from the Appendix to *ALP*, pp. 177–8, where it is said to be printed from Lawrence's typescript. This typescript does not appear to have survived.

The punctuation of Lawrence's manuscript has been retained in the two versions of GLORY OF DARKNESS. The word "Oh" at the beginning of l. 2 of the ink version is added in pencil in the MS.; it was omitted in *ALP*.

SHIP OF DEATH

ll. 21–23: these lines are omitted in *ALP* and *PE*.
l. 23: "that". MS. reads "the", an obvious slip.

GLOSSARY

O.E.D. = *The Oxford English Dictionary*
D.D. = *The English Dialect Dictionary*, ed. J. Wright (1902)
G.L.T. = "A List of Words Illustrating Nottingham Dialect" by
E. L. Guilford, *Transactions of the Thoroton Society*,
Nottingham, Vols. 32–50 (1932–50)
Austral. = Australian
Fr. = French
Ital. = Italian
Span. = Spanish
Germ. = German

A.

'affle—see haffle and caffle.
'appen—see happen.
asinello—little donkey (Ital.).

B.

barkle—"of dirt; to cake, encrust, adhere" (D.D.).
basta—enough (Ital.).
battle-twig—"earwig" (D.D.).
bract—"a small modified leaf or scale growing immediately below
the calyx of a plant, or upon the peduncle of a flower" (O.E.D.).

C.

caffle—"to cavil, quarrel, wrangle" (G.L.T.). See also haffle and caffle.
chavel—"to chew slowly and imperfectly; to mumble, to gnaw,
nibble; to tear with the teeth" (D.D.).
ciuco—donkey (Ital.).
clatch—dialect form of "clutch" = a brood of chickens.
clawk—"to tear or snatch with nails or claws" (D.D.).

collyfog—"to deceive, cheat, scheme, wheadle" (D.D.).
compari—pl. of *compare* = godfather, gossip (Ital.).
crapa—Sicilian dialect form of *capra* = she-goat.
crowflower—"the common buttercup" (D.D.).

D.

dool-owl—Not in O.E.D., D.D. or G.L.T. Probably ≠ a miserable,
    dreary creature from "dool", variant of dole" = "grief or
    mourning" (O.E.D.).
dree—"long, slow, tedious" (G.L.T.).

F.

flig—"full-fledged, able to fly" (D.D.), hence quick, lively.
frit—probably = "fritted, frightened" (G.L.T.).
Frohnleichnam—Corpus Christi (Germ.).

G.

gen—given, gave.

H.

haffle and caffle—"to shilly-shally" (D.D.).
happen ('appen)—perhaps.
hermoso es—He is beautiful (Span.).

I.

is-sèn—himself.
Ist dir weh?—Art thou sad? (Germ.).

L.

larropin'—"slouching, shambling" (D.D.).
Le bestie non parlano, poverine—The animals do not talk, poor
    things. (Ital.).
león—lion (Span.).
linty—"idle, lazy" (G.L.T.).

M.

maquillage—painting of the face, "make-up" (Fr.).
mard-arsed—from mard = "spoilt, petted" (D.D.).
maun—must.
may-blobs—"marsh marigolds" (D.D.).
mowie—apparently = mown grass. Not in O.E.D., D.D. or G.L.T.
my-sèn—myself.

N.

nesh—"soft to the touch" (D.D.).

O.

orts—"leavings, scraps, fragments" (D.D.).
otchel—perhaps a form of "urchin" = "a humped backed person"
    (D.D.).

P.

pappus—"the downy or feathery appendage on certain fruits, esp.
    on the achenes or 'seeds' of many *Compositae*, as thistles,
    dandelions, etc." (O.E.D.).
pee-whip—"peewit, lapwing" (G.L.T.).
piñón—pine-kernel (Span.).
pipistrello—bat (Ital.).

Q.

Qué tiene, amigo?—What have you got, my friend? (Span.).

R.

ricotta—buttermilk curd (Ital.).
robinetto = *rubinetto*—tap (Ital.).
rusties—apparently = buttocks. D.D. gives "rusty-bum, a rough
    game played by boys".

S.

scraight—scream, cry, weep. Not in O.E.D., D.D. or G.L.T., but probably = "scraigh, to shriek, scream" (D.D.).

sghembo—crooked, oblique (Ital.).

slart—"splash, of rain or mud" (D.D.).

slive—"sneak about, creep in a stealthy way" (D.D.).

sludge—"work or walk in a slovenly way so as to bemire oneself with mud" (DD.).

somaro—ass, donkey (Ital.).

sono io—I am (Ital.).

sprottle—"to sprawl, kick about helplessly" (D.D.).

swaling—burning, from swale = "burn, blaze" (D.D.).

swelted—from swelt = "faint, swoon, suffocate" (D.D.).

T.

traipse—"to tramp, trudge, go on foot, plod along" (D.D.).

W.

water blob—"yellow water-lily" (D.D.).

Wehmut—sadness (Germ.).

whit-leather—"horse-skin cured white and not tanned, used for whip-thongs, hedge-mittens, etc." (D.D.).

wift—dialect form of "whift" = "whiff" (O.E.D.).

winrow—dial. form of windrow = "a row in which mown grass or hay is laid before being made up into heaps or cocks, in which sods, peats or sheaves of corn are set up to be dried by exposure to the wind" (O.E.D.).

wowser—(Austral.) "Puritanical enthusiast or fanatic" (O.E.D.). According to *The Nation*, 11 May 1912 (quoted in O.E.D.) "a wowser is one who wants to compel everybody else . . . to do whatever he thinks right, and abstain from everything he thinks wrong".

INDEX OF FIRST LINES

INDEX OF TITLES

(Titles of Variants and Early Drafts in Appendix III Are Marked
with an Asterisk.)